BETWEEN FILM AND SCREEN

1

P R E T I T L E
S E Q U E N C E

IT MUST BE ONE OF THE LEAST CATCHY TITLES IN THE ANNALS OF popular film: *The Asphyx*. Anyone who could spell it should have been admitted free back in 1973. Yet it is just the film to bring forward here as prelude to an unrolling look at the intersection of photography and film: or more exactly, at the instantaneous cross sections of the former on the swift strip of the latter.

Sensing this intersection is as foreign to most criticism as it is to most moviegoing. Yet the bond of the two media, not only genetic but operational, has its own history—both within their linked evolution and within the theoretical discourses about them. *The Asphyx* tells its own unlicensed version of this history in a way that presses a familiar line of inquiry further into a single film's own specular process. In comparing photography with cinema, media theory long ago began worrying about the relation of the preserved image to the death whose fixity it mocks in one case, artificially overcomes in the other. The plot of this gothic potboiler both tropes and negotiates just that difference between deathlike stasis and its overflow in motion.

Like this book, *The Asphyx* too gets under way before its title and credits set in. After an auto accident in modern-day London where two cars converge upon an aged pedestrian, we cut to a bobby's astonishment over the surviving decrepit body of an unspeakably old man. The adverbial double take of "This man's still alive!"—after the crash, after all these years—precipitates the second stage of the prologue, overlapping eventually with the emerging titles. A Victorian laboratory has long ago gone to seed, with cobwebs strangling the four family photographs still arrayed on the decaying mantelpiece as the camera roves past each image: the photographic mausoleum as matrix of the entire narrative. Seen repeatedly in the background of subsequent retrospective action in this very room (fig. 1), these fixed images from a time long gone identify the four subsidiary characters—and chief victims—in a plot that will concern the protagonist's demonic efforts at immortality.

Peter Newbrook's *The Asphyx* (unknown to buffs and scholars alike in my acquaintance) is a film that cannot be overread, since it is all media allegory to begin with, Frankenstein in the age of mechanical reproduction. What the Victorian lord Sir Hugo Cunningham has secretly connived, in his excessive cunning, is not just an experimental procedure like Victor Frankenstein's but a full-fledged apparatus. It will turn out to be a contrivance of death in perpetual arrest. Cinema itself becomes the overweening scientist's monstrous progeny, with its own access to mechanical immortality emerging—across the baroque details of the fable—as the ultimate revenge against its Promethean creator. If to make a man is to steal God's thunder, to capture eternity in a projected beam of light is to steal the supernal fire of a demiurge.

For this book *The Asphyx* should do three things at the outset. First, it should help sketch a difference in the figuration of visual technology that will necessarily pervade these chapters: between the relation of death to photography on the one hand and to film on the other. Second, it should serve up another distinction: between the vexing temporality of filmed photographs (even full screen) and film's own photograms (separate celluloid imprints on the strip) when these single images are prolonged (reduplicated) in the screen stasis of the so-called freeze-frame. And third, it should begin contextualizing these issues in Victorian photographic experiments and their impact (among other ocular influences) on the fin-de-siècle invention of motion pictures, a transitional moment to which the last two chapters will, in different ways, return at length.

The technological fable devised by *The Asphyx* rests on a satire of aristocratic privilege and its desperate attempts at an inbred familial longevity. In his explicit desire that his own Cunningham spawn should oversee all future historical development, the aging Sir Hugo has at first a fairly modest and mainstream plan. As he explains to his son during a chat in the family burial vault, he has decided on a young second wife eager to bear him more heirs. Alas, the fiancée and Sir Hugo's son are killed in a boating accident in the very next scene. It is an accident caused by Sir Hugo's insistence on having them row on the family lake so he can preserve their images with his newest invention, matter-of-factly announced as "a device whereby I can record moving objects." Cut to the laboratory, where he screens the results. These are the world's first home movies, memorializing the dead in a second ancestral tomb. The Victorian craze for spirit photography has been upgraded to produce a kinetic revenant: the ghostly image of ghosts in the making, of death in process. With Lumière and Edison turning over in their graves, Sir Hugo is imagined by this plot to have beaten them to the punch in order, finally, to avoid his own grave—not, as we might so far expect, by preserving life in motion but by entombing the very agency of death.

The allegory needs now to secure its missing link between photography and moving pictures. It does so by evoking (again prematurely) certain refinements in the former technology, to be discussed later in this book, that allowed for the proliferation of instantaneous imaging among amateur photographers in the decade just before the cinematograph. In the course of his charity work with the dying, as he himself admits, Sir Hugo ended up taking more interest in recording death than in easing it. In photographing the

2

sufferers he was repeatedly able to capture a certain smear on the picture near
the head of the dying, as he demonstrates in one scene to a society of gentleman amateurs (fig. 2). Was it the soul
leaving the body? Good guess, but Sir
Hugo comes to suspect that what he
has photographed is, instead, the instantaneous descent rather than the
spiritual upshot of death: something
like the literalized form of the proverbial shadow of death. To be certain
which way that shadow is moving, he
therefore needs to invent the moving-
picture camera, years ahead of its time,
an ad hoc contraption to which he neg-
lects to give a name. Think of it, in one
of the terms for early cinema, as a "biograph"—at least until the ghoulish
metaplot thickens around it.

We know already of the machine's
ill-fated debut. And even there the results were inconclusive, since filming
was suspended in panic after the accident before it could be decided whether
the shadow was coming or going. Certainly Sir Hugo's unexplained ability to
still the frame in replaying this fatal
footage (fig. 3) doesn't settle the issue of
directionality. Where better to try again
than at a public execution, a hanging?
Says the surviving adopted son, "This
can prove nothing—but harmful."
Nonsense. Off to the execution, with a
newly sophisticated two-part apparatus.
Sir Hugo's own moving-image camera
is now accompanied by a high-pow-
ered—and of all things chemically fu-

eled—lamp, set up right behind the mob at the hanging (fig. 4). Just as the body
drops through the trap, what Sir Hugo discovers in action is that the puzzling
smudge he has been studying is in fact an ectoplasmic phantom captured—yes, as
it *arrives* on the scene—in the ancillary beam of light (fig. 5). This is our long-
awaited title figure, the Greek spirit of death, the asphyx itself (associated first with
the asphyxiation of drowning, now with the strangulation of hanging).

Among the questions that remain (to prolong the narrative) is whether this figure of fate is subjectively present to its victim, seen from within as well as objectively visible to an onlooker. This is to wonder whether the asphyx arrives as a revelation about the event of dying or just an external sign of death's advent. The whole pursuit of this question seems in retrospect a diversion—yet a pointed one—from the main business of the plot. In deciding the question of the death spirit's subjective apprehension among its victims, even still photography, apart from the new moving-image apparatus, might be of further use. "There is a widely held belief," Sir Hugo soon recalls, "that a dead man retains the indelible image of death" (alluding, no doubt, to human eye tissue as offering a fleeting *optogramme* of the death moment, a proposal of nineteenth-century ophthalmic science that earlier makes its way, we will find, into the history of science fiction film). If the seeing body, as storage mechanism, is already an instantaneous photograph of its own fate, what might it yield up to a secondary photographic probe? One must find out. Having exhumed his dead son after two weeks of burial, Sir Hugo takes a posthumous image of the potentially telltale body (fig. 6), to be studied later in

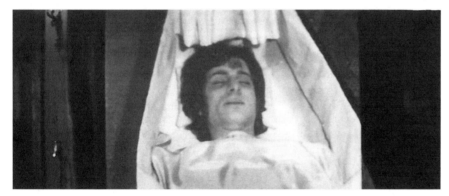

6

the laboratory (to no avail). Same with the executed man still hanging from the rope in the city square, whose close-up image, when illuminated by Sir Hugo's magnesium flare, cuts from a color shot to a black-and-white freeze-frame that doubles (across the scene change) for a projected laboratory slide (fig. 7). But the hanged man's swollen visage does nothing but repeat his deadness; it does not show the coming of his death. To rephotograph the moment itself as captured on the body's own film, Sir Hugo suspects, you had to have been there sooner.

Yet there may be a better explanation altogether. Thinking back to the execution, Sir Hugo guesses out loud that the resistant will of the hanged man, some residual life force inwardly generated, may have been less instrumental in stalling death's lethal moment than was the objective illumination of the experiment's own chemically generated beam of light, which seemed momentarily able to

7

edge the death phantom away from its victim. The speculation solidifies on the spot to the narrative's own axiom. Detached from recording itself in this schematic setup, and anticipating instead film's destiny in projection, the supplemental beam—the so-called booster light—is of course necessary not only to secure and *convey*, as it were, the moving image but, in this exacerbated case, to trap and transport its deathly essence.

So back to the laboratory once more, for an experiment on Sir Hugo himself. We learn there how the beam that pinions the asphyx in a tubular prison of light must be sustained by the continuous dripping of water on phosphite crystals, a chemistry associated with Sir Hugo's previous cutting-edge laboratory work in the enhanced development of photos. He now nearly electrocutes himself in order to secure the gothic equivalent of cinema's electrical afterlife, halting the current just in time. At the first sign of galvanic spasms and the encroachment of the asphyx, the stepson is ordered to edge the ghoul-laden beam into a coffin-shaped box, screen right (fig. 8), with a small rectangular window to disclose its contents to perpetual view. The father's death spirit is then carried into the family crypt, hence laying to rest the specter of death itself. The encrypted cinematic reference is hardly contained there, however, even though death, lit from within the apparatus, has been turned into a continuous framed spectacle in a wide-screen field of view (fig. 9).

8

Let me interrupt my capsule rebroadcast of this late-night TV rerun (just reissued as a "cult classic" in DVD) to examine the spectatorial genealogy written across the mounting violence

9

of the narrative. We've noted the scientist's inspirational leap from gallows to lethal electric jolts, and that's only the half of it. Two modes of execution down, two to go. It is from the tombstone of his subsequently slain daughter that we know precisely that Sir Hugo Cunningham's invention of the motion-picture camera and projector took place in 1875, twenty years before the historical fact. As it happens, the daughter met her death when a laboratory accident prevented Sir Hugo, after briefly seizing her asphyx, from arresting her guillotine in the nick of time. In the wake of the father's own near death in a makeshift electric chair, this Continental violence à la mode is followed by the adopted son's successful suicide in a glassed-in gas chamber, completing a series begun with the urban spectacle of the hanging. Four times over, the techniques of ritualized public violence have been turned to private account. Figuratively speaking—and such figuration is the film's true discourse—the cinematic projector (disguised finally as a perpetually lit coffin) emerges from these commandeered mechanisms of formalized state slaughter not only as an immortality machine but as a new form of mass-cultural exhibition.

While cinema's private manipulation by the mad scientist is being extrapolated to the level of its eventual public consumption, its photochemical essence is also being slyly redoubled at the level of the thrown image itself. The lone "special" effect that precedes this boxing in of the fantastic lays bare a double trick of cinematic specificity. The logic is as simple as it is circular. Turn on a projector with prepared footage of a slithering monster, probably a rubber hand puppet, direct the beam against a backdrop that will permit the imaged creature's hazy materialization (in the case of fig. 8 again, an almost theatrical curtain), and then call the optical labor ensnaring rather than relinquishing, capture rather than projection. Such is the mumbo jumbo of cinema as demonic effect to its own technological cause.

So too with the subsequent explosion of the laboratory. At the moment the gas chamber ignites, the whole image field goes gaseous, layered, disintegrated. It does so through that oldest (and literally cheapest) trick in the book: superimposition. You needn't trouble to fill a set with smoke, or even dry ice fumes. You can simply cloud the image, rather than the space, with another semiopaque image. The almost palpable dissolution of these so-called lap dissolves works to image—to figure as well as represent—the meltdown of Sir Hugo's whole scheme. Dynastic catastrophe penetrates to the very lab work of montage, with the film itself vaporized before our gaze. Not accidentally, in other words, the scientist's lair is disintegrated by evoking the material basis—filmy, flimsy, diaphanous, ultimately photographic rather than three-dimensional—of the very technology that sponsors plot's attempted fusion of deathly absentation and immortal maintenance. Paired with the earlier effect of infernal manifestation—where the ontology of the monstrous was reduced to a luminous monstration, with the asphyx manufactured by the very beam designed to jail it—the privileged "special effect" within plot has finally met its match at the level of the medium's own "specified" textuality.

Cut back from the blasted apparatus of the laboratory, crumbling in filmic palimpsest, to the present-day London street scene we began with. Once Sir Hugo's remaining family has been done in by his experiments and his demonic lair exploded, the only machine left that can tamper with mortality is the cinema's own. And so another metalepsis, by any other name: another implosion of form upon content. We return to the car crash—and this time for a freeze-frame (stop-action on the brink of impaction) just a split second before the withered Sir Hugo meets his yet again forestalled death: the new Victorian Tithonus as a photomechanical image of his own photochemical longevity. Echoing the early freeze-frame on the son's death moment when rescreened for inspection, with its exaggerated foreclosure of patrilinear continuance, this later suspension of time's inexorable force is accompanied by the ongoing noise of the crash on the sound track. The implacable momentum of death seems still at work in the world. Only the tampered-with image dissevers itself from such fateful duration.

It is by no means merely the subsequent preoccupations of this book's first chapter, concerning the relation of reframed photographs on-screen to the photolike arrest of the screen image per se, that has recommended *The Asphyx* as a conceptual preamble. More deeply embedded in its fable, and more thoroughly dispersed across the discussions to come—as across the theoretical positions adduced to orient them—is the triangular relation of death (rather than mere fixity) to photography and cinema. I keep saying fable (or allegory), and by the end of *The Asphyx* it should be clear just what its gothic fabulation has proposed, under the thinnest of generic wraps, about the medium of film.

It would go like this, sprung from the overheated interrogations of the film's own dialogue. On the inherent shadow play of the photographic plate, what is that further intrusive shadow associated with death? Intrinsic or contingent? The speculative scientist cannot be sure, in short, whether photography suspends death or in its own right instantiates it (also a problem for the theorists of the medium from the 1840s through André Bazin to Roland Barthes and beyond). So the amateur photographer sets about inventing cinema to find out. Not just a moving-picture machine, but the whole manifold cinematic apparatus: from recording to projection and screening. Sir Hugo's secret device, the prosthetic extension of his will to undying presence, implements perpetuity in the intervals of a radical transience, a transience subject in turn to further disembodiment in the very mode of its projected materialization. Although at the stage of initial imprint the machinated sequence of frame upon frame does seem to capture death in action (the arriving asphyx, as at another level the single arresting and remobilized photogram), it is really the beam of delivered rather than received light, at the other pole of the apparatus, that catches (and detains) death in its true cinematic aspect. This is the death that is always on the way but always postponed, on hold in the same chamber of channeled light that allows for the materialized timeless continuance of a moving human figure—one whose natural aging is in this way photochemically forestalled. Thus does the mad scientist's variant of cinematic technology deflect the visitation of death by rendering its virtual spirit visible within a rectangular viewing frame. The bulky wooden repository is death's prepared coffin, not life's. And balancing it (screen left) in its first appearance (fig. 8) is the large wooden clock whose marked rotational calibrations may remind us of everything cinema's different work with spatiotemporal intervals operates to transfigure and preserve.

Much that is to come in the investigations of this book gets sketched by the logic of this tortuous plot. In the invented material transformations of photography into cinema, the human body becomes the switch point between a discredited metaphysics of presence and an installed psychology of reception. This last emphasis on subjective response has been routed through Sir Hugo's distracting interest in the psychology of the dying, in the apparition rather than the biology of death. To quarantine the asphyx is to isolate and contain the terror of death, not to dispel but temporarily to quell it by the mere visualization of its curtailed force. The plot's early false lead has been the true clue. Photochemistry does not capture the soul, some immaterial essence of the living, and hence does not transcend death. Once multiplied into animation, sequential photography wards off only the horrific specter of death, mitigating primarily the fear, not the fact, of mortal closure.

This is why Sir Hugo was half on the right track, the film's own, in wishing to ascertain the subjective visibility of the death spirit. *The Asphyx* itself is specular screen experience rather than specter, and hence like all film it plays between subjective and objective manifestation in its own plotlong arrival (one upon the other) of photograms, flashed past us in their transient fixity. We in the audience (sometimes through the eyes of the victim) watch the spirit of death in action, both as a realized phantom and as a fact of film. Death temporarily neutered by the serial erasure of its founding stasis, its inherent finality: this, then, is what we further see, and are reminded that we always see, through the cinematic coffin's lit frame. There the image of life's ultimate anxiety is held in check, but only to the extent that associated aspects of the new moving-picture machine also keep available the materialized human body rather than the soul, the body in the comforting image of its ongoing life and motion. By being an art of motorized photographs, cinema, even from within its own quantified transience and disguised stasis, is the art of the provisionally overridden—rather than overcome—fear not only of a finalized inscription but of an absolute passing.

This again, then, is where Sir Hugo's digressive investigation into what the body sees when it dies, rather than what it looks like, does in the long run strike home. This is also where the plot's strenuous supernaturalism collapses under its own squirming weight and falls through to a level of existential common sense. The blatantly implausible operates as a metaphor for the therapeutic; carnal eternity stands for allayed moral anxiety. Movies are where we ordinarily go to see death outfaced by the human image returning forever in its experiential time. Movies are where we go to look death in the (thereby averted) face. Filmic mechanism in this sense takes the sting out of the transience it must maximize. As montage rather than narrative, movies show us the mortal in the act of surviving itself, invincible in its continuities. Photographs on the fly, that is, work to manufacture the persistent under the sponsorship of the repeatable. And just as fixity is cheated by speed, finality is outplayed by recurrence.

Doing research a while back at the National Film Institute in Stockholm, I contributed to its mission by buying a souvenir T-shirt printed, in tiny Swedish script, with the following quotation, dated 30 December 1895, from the French journal *La Poste:* "On that day when the public can partake of such apparatuses as these and everybody can photograph their near and dear not just as still pictures but even in movement, with their familiar gestures and lips formed to words, death will no longer be terminal." Real enough, but no longer *terminal;* no longer *quite* over. In its own gothic code, this is roughly what *The Asphyx,* too, has to say—as well as show—for itself on the matter of photography, cinema, and the alternative valences of death that drive them: the mortal versus the endless, each equally of a piece, as it were, with lifelessness. So has a single mixed exercise in popular narrative genres, fictional science crossed with the supernatural, served to depopulate the entrenched humanist dimension of a whole school of film theory. If cinema intercedes in the deathwork of photography to do no more than defer its fixity indefinitely rather than to transcend it, so much for phenomenology's sense of cinema as lived duration under the sign of becoming. So much for animation as more than an effect of stasis and its motorized traces. Encapsulated and encoded in this one frail film artifact, the metaplot of cinematic history has come to the corrective rescue of the apparatus's own mystification. If not exactly a good movie, it's not a bad ghost story, after all.

To come to momentary rest with a B movie and a T-shirt is only to suggest that any popular filmmaker who recovers the preternatural filiations between photography and early cinema so dear to the nineteenth century has taken a stand of sorts in the contemporary debates of media theory, resisting the overly schematic dichotomy between photography's death mask and film's "animated" field. Keeping in mind both the vanishing trace of the photogram and Sir Hugo's weird science, each seizing the onset of an absentation, we may leave it for now as follows: Photography is death in replica; cinema is a dying away in progress, hence death in serial abeyance. Lined up in rows, pieced out, flicked past, then thrown forward toward the lit screen, the elementing photographs on the film track vibrate before us as the death throes of presence succumbing to a temporality not its own, world time transposed to screen time. This is to say that cinema exists in the interval between two absences, the one whose loss is marked by any and all photographic images and the one brought on by tossing away each image in instantaneous turn. The effects are different enough to make for two separate media, two distinct powers of mortal mediation. Whereas photography engraves the death it resembles, cinema defers the death whose escape it simulates. The isolated photo or photogram is the still work of death; cinema is death always still at work. That should certainly be enough to get us going.

BETWEEN FILM

MODERNISM'S

PHOTO SYNTHESIS

AND SCREEN

GARRETT STEWART

THE UNIVERSITY OF CHICAGO PRESS
CHICAGO AND LONDON

Garrett Stewart is the
James O. Freedman Professor of
Letters at the University of Iowa and
the author of five books, most recently *Dear Reader: The Conscripted Audience in Nineteenth-
Century British Fiction.*

The University of Chicago Press, Chicago 60637
The University of Chicago Press, Ltd., London
© 1999 by Garrett Stewart
All rights reserved. Published 1999
08 07 06 05 04 03 02 01 00 99 1 2 3 4 5

ISBN: 0-226-77411-2 (cloth)
ISBN: 0-226-77412-0 (paper)

Library of Congress Cataloging-in-Publication Data

Stewart, Garrett.
    Between film and screen : modernism's photo
    synthesis / Garrett Stewart
p.   cm.
    Includes bibliographical references and index.
    ISBN 0-226-77411-2 (cloth : alk. paper). — ISBN
0-226-77412-0 (paper : alk. paper)
    1. Motion pictures—Aesthetics. 2. Cinematogra-
phy. I. Title. PN1995.S726 1999
99-32792
791.43′01—dc21   CIP

CONTENTS

Narrative Cinema as Film

Photographs are taken, taken down. Movies take us up, carry us along, if not away. Photographs are taken from time. Movies take time, take it in their automated stride. But it takes photographs to make a movie, two dozen of them every second, to be exact (and they must be). They add up, but only by being mechanically subtracted from any separate notice. In this way movies take the photograph for granted, their difference from it. But more to the point, movies *are* their difference from photographs one after the other, a difference on the run. This is as obvious as it is invisible. So how might it be possible, in response, to take movies photographically, to reclaim their forgone piecemeal essence in the act of reception? Only movies that themselves take up this question—in their own inferred materiality—can show us to the threshold of an answer.

The chapters to follow converge from distinctly different angles, pursuing various slants along separate facets of the same conceptual (not always perceptual) problem. Many began as considered opinions on the release or reissue of a given film. What remain are the abiding considerations: the more or less direct (and reversible) interchange of analysis and theory. The nature of these considerations is already before us. My governing question has been how to conceive of a photographic relation to cinema even when the single photographic imprint (known in film analysis as the photogram) goes unperceived as such on-screen. This is not so much a question of how to "think the photograph" from within the moving image as of how to read its suppressions, how to know it as the pertinent underside—what I will come to term the specular unconscious—of image reception. Because this same problem is tackled from different perspectives in each essay, there is an inevitable overlap from one to the next—but also an unexpected destination not foreseen in their separate composition. The end result is that individual essays on

1

film narrative have now mutated into a study of modernist textuality at large—
and at base.

The previously published material that makes up about half this book was
often written to address a persistent crux in image studies, sometimes prominent,
sometimes backgrounded in discussion: namely, the association of photographic
temporality with a fixity and deathliness all too easily (and facilely) distinguished
from screen "being." Addressed to various narrative stress points in American and
European cinema, these essays were meant to follow cinematic practice itself—in
certain of its more ambitious instances—in dismantling such a phenomenological
given. Collected and amplified with new investigations, however, these position
papers ended up requiring something further: a more historicized (and a more
fully theorized) view of cinema's emergence with and within the dawn of an international modernism characterized in part by a new textual leeway in the vibratory equivocations of the verbal interval from Conrad through Forster to Joyce
and beyond. Hence the last chapter, where a politics of form in Fredric Jameson's
work on the modernist turn in literary "style" (and antistyle) is asked to enter a
conflicted field of historical research and speculation on the genealogy of the dynamized screen image (sometimes narrowing and specifying the photographic
debt, sometimes minimizing it). It is this contest of historical masterplots that
ends up inviting a suggestive comparison between the photogram's pressure on
screen "presence" and the undoing of lexical integrity by what I am now led to
term the "phonogram" of literary language.

There have been many books on literature into film as well as several on the
shared place of their respective aesthetics in the transitional culture of modernism
(the poetics of montage). But there has been no study of the textual basis of the
two forms—the two formative systems—in the articulation of a modernist inscriptive practice. This is that book. So why doesn't it say so up front, announcing
by title its programmatic crossover between media? In its own way it does. For at
considerable cost to representation if not to pleasure, conceiving the photofusions
of the filmic beneath the cinematic is, at least feasibly, a way of opening comparable attention to the phonographemic byplay in literature's different but equally
differential mode of representation. What happens, in short, between film and
screen, what takes place by serial displacement there, is a close model for the slippages in transit between an alphabetically marked page and the mental shapes it
generates. Still, the burden of proof must rest with motion pictures, in particular
with traditional narrative film, whose resistance to anything we might want to call
deconstruction is far more entrenched by illusionism than any of literature's so-
called reality effects. If this resistance can be seen weakened by a sufficient number of refractory moments in films from several traditions, then such a hard-won
understanding of the photographic stratum in cinematic mimesis may be more
readily brought alongside a view of the oscillating literary signifier: the continual
churning of wording beneath words themselves. Such, at least, are the stakes of
the present analytic gamble.

Filmic frames flickeringly disappear into cinematic image rather as the fluctuations of alphabetic language congeal into units of meaning on the page, in each

case awaiting normative reception at a level other that the medium's material base. Such are the operative effects spun out from the more rudimentary fusions, beneath the pictured and the phrased, of formative picturation and a never settled phrasing, of animation and enunciation respectively—or in a single word, of articulation, with all its interstitial risks. It is precisely this comparable distance of each fluctuant medium from its more smoothly manifested effects that offers the very definition of their shared textuality. The comparison, though rough, should prove revealing. What I am calling photo synthesis is to screen motion as phonemic transfusion is to inscribed meaning.[1]

Much depends, of course, on the terms of debate. The conceptual burden of this introduction's title and premise, "cinema as film," happens by accident to pose an inversion of that tired cliché about the difference between those who like films (or moviegoing), the casual buffs, and those who dote on the Cinema with a capital C. My reversal is meant, instead, to expose at one level the misnomer within the former characterization itself. Idiom notwithstanding, film cannot properly be pluralized; only a movie can. Film is the underlying stuff of the apparition, a movie or movies the effect in process. To mention (without insisting on) this is neither to mince words nor, oddly enough, to make the mistake excoriated in certain attacks on medium-specificity theory encountered below. But it does raise a further problem of nomenclature whose potential difficulties can be faced down only by a few words more at the start.

In working back to an often forgotten and almost always ignored distinction in the experience of cinema—between the material base that must be dematerialized in projection and the screen effect that results—I am working uphill against a different tendency in media studies. This trend results from the terminological divide between film and cinema when the latter is understood to concern the institution and social emplacements of the former. What ends up happening in this second branch of inquiry is that production, distribution, and reception are put forward as a field (no longer an object) of study more urgent, for instance, than aesthetics, poetics, narratology, or cognitive theory.[2] But my point is that even film studies, so designated, does not have a material object in the strict sense until the attention of such study is drawn back to the track. So that the breakpoint in these pages between cinema and film locates the "cinematic" experience at the site of its manifestation and dissemination on-screen (however it got there and to whatever ends "cinema studies" might properly trace out), while seeking the "filmic" cause on the material strip: the film *object* awaiting in every sense the *project* of cinema.

This book will dwell, that is, on the material divulgences within screen materialization. But only because they can be understood in the long run as part of cinema studies as well, part of a psychodynamics of reception and even a sociology of response. But this is the long run. Short term, our terms are held to the beamed span between frames on the strip and the framed screen image. From a seat in the audience, to attend to the genuinely filmic within the so-called film is not necessarily to elevate footage over image, let alone to watch for this raw filmic matter where it cannot be seen. Rather, to attend to cinema (public institution) in view of its aspect as film (plastic constitution) is to appreciate the underlying difference—

not just as a distinction but as an *operation*—between the photochemical trace and
the moving illusion. Far from making a fetish of footage, such attention is meant
to credit the *inching* into view of motion's own components, the elementing ce-
ment of a fragile continuity rooted in the photographic increment.

Nor does this approach sign on to a monorail-like teleology of cinema's
emergence from an overspecified media forebear, a tendency widely discredited
by the newer historicisms of cinematic spectation. Rather than demarcating the
streamlined historical *passage* from photography to cinema, this book about cinema as film and about film as text is ultimately about the marked *slippage*—in
action—from photographic to filmic frame. So when photographic history comes
into conversation with film theory in these chapters, it does so in deference to the
frictive tension in film's own *ongoing* relation to a parent (if no longer apparent)
medium, which survives within it by way of the descendant medium's new combinatory makeup. To remind oneself that parentage does not exhaust the formative influences on an offspring, that other conditioning features precede and contextualize the new arrival, is only to abide by the obvious. In glancing at the
prehistory of the cinema as a medium of collective exhibition, Walter Benjamin
(in a seldom-explored footnote to his famous Artwork essay) looks back, like
Jonathan Crary with comparable evidence, not only to the enforced privacy of the
individual stereoscopes mounted before the relay of separate images in the
Kaiserpanorama, but further back yet to the hand-held intimacy of those "photo
booklets with pictures which flitted by the onlooker under pressure of the
thumb."[3] Each flitting imprint, Benjamin might have added, was a predecessor of
the celluloid photogram in a privately regulated motion-picture device not yet
readied for mass public consumption.

This book, then, is concerned with a mere technicality. Its topic is a simple material fact beaten into retreat by film commentary, even by much film theory, so
often that the resolute mention of it becomes polemical. The resulting claim advanced by these cumulative essays is a correspondingly simple one—and would
be mostly unnecessary were it not for the (often outright) denial of such considerations in much classic and contemporary thinking about the cinema. The point
is this: that the film medium owes a more *immediate*—rather than just historical
and mechanical—debt to the photograph than we can ever (quite) see on-screen.
It is a debt compounded and reinvested (or "rolled over" with interest) by the
technics of projection and the psychodynamics of viewing. And it is within this
contractual economy that we can eventually speak, in textual terms, about a specular unconscious in relation to the received cinematic apparition.

If this is the argument, what is the nature of its intended proof? Its name,
again, is the photogram, the image track's smallest sequenced unit of eventual
screen manifestation. Photos are taken and then developed in the form of photograms on the strip. On the activated track, they are given out to the screen as
motion, the filmic realizing—and realized in—the cinematic, but only because, as
Sergei Eisenstein will help us to see, the glimpse of each frame passes so quickly
that its so-called successor actually overlaps rather than follows it (as highlighted,

for instance, by those photo flip-books Benjamin alludes to as direct predecessors of the cinema). This amounts to saying that motion depends in part on a mental afterimage of the photographic trace and its continually—hence continuously—masked stasis. In regard to this stasis, definition comes easy; application comes later. Once again: The photogram is the individuated photographic unit on the transparent strip that conduces in motion to screen movement.[4] Shot past the projector's gate, the photogram propagates itself as film only in order to vanish on-screen. By definition, then, the photogram has no ordinary place in the movies, no prevalent role in the cinematic institution. It is mostly on film alone—though with exceptions that test and prove the rule of its suppression. Its function in the apparatus of cinema, however, is so widely overlooked in commentary that to reclaim its sometimes demonstrable (and always necessary) contribution counts as a theoretical proposal in its own right. A proposal that would now sound like this on a first consolidated rephrasing: The photogram is the cellular unit pressed into the service of movement by ocular suppression in the apparatus—and then at times returned to(ward) view as if by the textual condensations and displacements (however mechanized) of the viewer's specular unconscious.

There is of course a rudimentary process before any rotary procession, in camera or projector. It all starts with the material body of an object or human subject submitted to photomechanical record. Light glances off the body. The mechanically glanced body stamps itself in light, one instantaneous pose after another on that oldest form of portable inscription: the scroll. Motion pictures provide the continuous excavation of this fossilized light, one traced image racing over the last. At base is an inscription that cuts no groove, layers no mass, leaves no sign of textured imprint—unlike pigment, carving, coinage, even inked letters.[5] No surface residue: merely the residual image of something seeming to recede into its own space from the (transparent) surface of the print. The distinction from the so-called graphic arts is suggested, for instance, by the way the term "painting" as substantive (unlike "filming") is a gerund that dries on canvas into a noun, compact of pigment and its distribution. In *a* painting, the medium is always with us, tugging at the representation, threatening to depresent it, doubling our vision. In cinema, as in the photography that constitutes it, the illusion is much more complete. Or let us say that the double vision is now temporal (conceptual) rather than spatial (textural). The filmic medium is the *once having been there* of the represented spaces themselves, absented by necessity to make possible the materiality of their moving image on the track.

FILM'S TRIP

We need to be as precise as possible about the filmic substrate's elusive reconstitution as cinematic image, since the facts will then speak for themselves in more ways than one. Here and there in these pages at their most technical, at intervals and in the very disturbance of prose intervals, alphabetic writing evokes the photogram's racing aggregation into motion pictures by unleashing—through chance collisions—the flawed and phantom letter of the law of language from the words into which it usually vanishes. Prose submits, once again, to that never fully constrained work of wording beneath words. In the most painstaking verbal account of cinema's differential oscillations, the accidental dissolves of syllabification may themselves serve to analyze as well as to capture the medium's modernist filiations in an exploratory flutter of utterance. If this seems at least plausible, then any ripples and splits of signification en route may usefully anticipate the theory of modernism—as a textual flicker effect—to be broached in the concluding chapter along with a fuller comparison between the photogrammatic and sublexical rudiments of the respective media. More than chance wordplay—a deeper-going principle—is actually on the line in each medium: a lineation, that is, of script and strip that in each case is both continuous and laminated. When, for example, lexemes encroach upon each other in what follows to evoke the workings of the cinematic apparatus, these abutting and undone word units are attuned to a layered nature other than their own: to cinema's basis in a film strip based in turn in a fluctuant run of photograms, however much this flickering basis is masked in practice by the cinematic shimmer. But a crucial clarification is in order. Just as this book's largest argument is in no way meant to single out the photograph as the sole historical precursor of cinema (apart from the wider ocular episteme of the nineteenth century), so its verbal analogues for the film track's fused breaks in no way represent a nostalgia for the "linguistic turn" in film analysis, the taxonomy of syntactic operations. Textuality is, in brief, a word for something more material than the abstract linguistic order, something to be found in each medium separately—even if best apprehended in tandem.

What I am saying is that, quite apart from linguistic paradigms, words recruited to describe the infinitesimals of cinematic process on its way from strip through moving track to screen may often catch at effects beyond or beneath their usual reach. Ekphrasis (verbally portrayed visuality) can easily veer into parapraxis (slips or skids of the lettered tongue), description succumbing to the contingent spin of vagrant inscription. This has nothing to do with wordplay onscreen—jokes, rebuses, punning intertitles—and everything to do with the play of imprint that brings any image to that screen. Attempting to account for this filmic undertext at the motion picture's plastic basis, in its homology with an often overlooked aspect of modernist verbal textuality, I started noticing early on that my own prose about this matter, this vanishing materiality, tended to unfurl in a curious fit with the race and perceptual overlap, the slamming together and hence lamination, of adjacent film frames. I came eventually to think that what I had once posited as the "phonotext" of an anything but period-bound modernism could now be further specified—because better understood comparatively—as the work of the lexical *phonogram*, rough morphophonemic equivalent of the photomechanical imprint on the strip.[6] Equivalent how? Let's say, for starters, as the contributory increment that disappears in process into the net effect of the representational function. For one thing is clear. Filmic seriality replays on the track the phylogeny of its representational kind or species, the immediate genesis (however historically contextualized) of the motion picture out of late nineteenth-century advances made in instantaneous photography.[7] It does so by speeding together the incremental photographs of an analytically dissevered motion: a reversal of the biomotor studies of Etienne-Jules Marey or Eadweard Muybridge, with their photo strips of galloping horses and hurdling men.[8] Put it this way about all that constitutively cannot stay put in the photomechanics of the motion picture: like movement of any sort in cinema, all sprints derive by serial collision, on a different racetrack, from the enchainment of the film's prints.

Verbal form has an unruly way of redoubling its referent in even the flattest definitional formulation of the filmic process. The film's strip—already elided in common parlance to film strip—is activated as a differential screen text only by its trip through the projector. Once still, now flashing by, one still lingers till the next one in line, flicking past our gaze as if at the same time licking up its forerunner in the flame of the apparatus. The margin of discrepancy makes all the difference in the world. For as regards screen movement in projected space, it makes all the world in a difference: one from the other in the flurry of photograms.

On the way to screen action, however, there is always the rescinded gap between photograms, marked by a thin black bar of requisite but invisible (on-screen) width. This is the bridgework of disjunction itself by which the photogram's linked sequence slinks at high velocity past the forced intermittence of channeled light, each increment a chink between blanks that lets the beam through. Something like the original activity on the set is later miniaturized in this way by the work of the apparatus. Lights. Cameraction. Cut. Our ultimate concern is with the systematic (the mechanical) internalizing of that cut, its implanting in cinematographic process as the seed of all screened motion: a break between caught frames, a suspended registration, an edge that becomes (in the event of projection) a verge. Well before that event, one can almost overhear the camera's own mechanics with an ear to theory. Click, clack, lack—in that double absentation of the forgone and the just gone past. Again and again, gaining on movement, getting it down by degrees, one frame vanishes on the clicked heels of the other. In the projector later, skating past its gate and lamp, those frames are seen rolling over each other, re(e)merging into motion. Having taken light in and on, the apparatus must also give it off—that is, let the beam through by slits and starts. The analysis of movement passes to its fabrication. The vivisection of motion yields to its spectral rebirth and rearticulation. Like a palindrome, a perfect reversal: the spool of stock becoming the loops of the strip in projection. The contraption that entrapped light, digesting it as tinctured imprint, has met its allotted, its slotted, fate in the gadget burning to emit a reciprocal light.

This is possible only because the camera's original discontinuity of taken frames finds its equivalent in the projector's shutter action, which closes our eyes to the thin width of nonvision (and hence to the static nature of its units of supposed motion), barring the bar between separate shot cells. In so doing, the shutter (originally in the form of a rotating Maltese cross) simply underscores the basic process of photogrammatic animation, which brings the partially self-expunged image field (like a self-razed verbal phrasing on the run) to light only under erasure. Offscreen, on again, off/on, more often than perception can discern.

In the end, an intermittent projectile of machine-gunned light. Now you see it, now (infinitesimally) you don't.

This is what students don't know they mean when inadvertently writing, for instance, about cinema's overtaking photographic science through a more "advance technology." In solecism begins analysis. The vernacular elision of the *d* in their own (phonetically prompted) misspelling (in technical terminology, its "assimilation" to the approximately equivalent dental phoneme *t*) hits an accidental nail on the head: the "advance" technique of photogrammatic succession itself, the so-called frame advance. Here is where our vision unconsciously fills in the subliminal blank, forgiving the shutter, the masked bar of the flicker effect, precisely because it occludes a border, heals a gash. The more interruptions, the more surreptitious they become. Flick or fusion? "Critical flicker fusion" is the professional term for the threshold at which the difference disappears into a steadied apparition.[9]

I linger over what may be to some readers all too familiar as technological background (and optic underlay) largely to defamiliarize its very mechanics—to highlight, that is, the entirely strange way that jagged seriality conduces to the unruffled flow of movement in screen action. Film's relay race of movement is taken down upon numberless disjunct rectangles, the construction blocks of continuity, each punctually cut off from its predecessor and successor on the track. The hazard of the chasm is in fact a structuring chiasm, an ocular pivot. Blink, blank, gap, link. One plus two plus three, twenty-four increments per second, over 150,000 in the average length (apt measure of time in this case) of a narrative film. One / plus / two / plus / three / plus. What we see, really, is the plus or pulse between (the additive difference)—in other words, the supplement, awaiting the supple mentation of cognitive receipt. The shutter's bridgework is thus engineered so as to be displaced entirely onto a faintly stroboscopic—and, in the history of cinema, increasingly imperceptible—flutter in the screened frame. All materialized screen space is thereby a function of image pace, all specular extension a material tension of elementing photograms, all visible transition derived from what cinema in transit shuns: namely, the intermittence it masks in action.

All because you can't pick out the separate pictures from the picturing. This bears stressing one more time for the internal conflict (Eisenstein) it transcends. Cinematic continuity synthesizes difference by distending the optical trace, holding on (to) the gone, giving way to the waiting. In the hairbreadth space between images, between staccato data, there flickers a gap, a join, a seam. Here is the deepest logic of film in its geared and meshed procession. As *The Asphyx* was staged to "anticipate," the photo as tomb of original movement—sliced from time, iced to gesture—gets rescanned in lockstep sequence as the photo synthesis of a motion revived (even while reinterred) on-screen out of its partitioned constituents. In the elided divide between images, in their nondi*visibility* if you will, lurks that equivocated leaving behind of one image for another that has already invaded it: the definitive photogrammatic cleaving.

But why indulge rather than police the tendency of critical prose to reduplicate in lexical progress the inherent slippages of cinematic animation? What inclined me to think of this distraction as exerting a certain analytic traction after all? It was this. The seepages of wording, the duplicities of lexical juncture, came to seem uniquely good at keeping in play the elusiveness and elision shared by the speeding photogram beneath the cinematographic trace. Collectively, such fugitive phonemic overlays make a deep-seated point even (or especially) when they go typographically unenforced and mostly unnoticed, retained only as the flickering afterimage—phonic rather than retinal—of some subsemantic overload, an excess subsumed to signifying continuity. Forget all about them and they have carried the day. For these junctural breaks end up epitomizing a system in their very dismissibility, a system cinematic as well as verbal—or let us say again, to get beneath rather than beyond the distinction, textual. Ruptures overlooked: that's film for you.

PHOTOTROPIC POLES

But where, if at all, does the photogram make a tacit appearance in the ordinary experience of narrative film? Or reverse the question. As the vanishing slice of aggregated screen action, how does the photogram make its absence felt on the fly? How in a given film narrative does it mark its own makeup of the screen scene? By one of two means, usually. The photogrammatic undertext of screen narrative may be (more or less implicitly) alluded to on-screen by "quoted" photos. Alternatively, this undertext may be obtruded in multiple duplicates on the strip in the form of the so-called stop-action image. This is the rapid fabrication of stasis that isolates a single visual moment, artificially lifted from narrative pace, and sets it apart from the real motion that invisibly spins it past in the form of separate (and now anomalously redoubled) imprints. To clarify these poles, I will begin by sampling the most cinematically inflected of the former type. This is not just the reshot photo on-screen but what we might call the photopan. The term may be taken to name all those lateral movements of ongoing cinematic record that cling to, linger over, and then disengage from serial photographic images in cinema's own procedural difference from them. The effect is sometimes to rehearse the retention and release of single images on cinema's own wheeling track. It is against this play between moving camera and still photographic image that the alternative case of photogrammatic disclosure, the freeze-frame, will then come into sharper relief, arresting camerawork and narrative agency at once, canceling the cinematic in deference to the sheerly filmic. To point up the contrast, I will be bringing into comparison the divergent effects of two famous examples in particular: a photopan from the postmodernist classic *Blade Runner* over against a freeze-frame from the classic Hollywood cinema of *It's a Wonderful Life*. Each image waxes metaphysical in its ironic wrench of cinema—through photographic evocation—toward its own filmic basis. Each in another sense inscribes the untoward imposition of a mortal and finalizing perspective upon the horizontal progress of plot.

What, one must wonder in general, explains the frequent melancholy eloquence of the slow pan across photographs glazed or otherwise—but always in a sense glassy-eyed in their intangible afterlife—as, for example, in those sealed-up family portraits ranged like cenotaphic icons on a Victorian mantel in the credit sequence to *The Asphyx?* Space is being swallowed up to your left or right, you there at the cutting edge of the camera's movement. Within this traveling field of view, another space is opened up, photochemical rather than narrative space—absent, past, flat (or flatter)—an optic plane giving upon an illusory scopic field that is held at an untraversable remove from the scanning eye. But what else is new? Isn't this how the whole film world stands to us, an audience one step back in the seated zone of spectation? Static, then: that must be the definitive difference between those passing photographic rectangles and our larger screen frame. It is because of such fixity that the inset photos are so obviously filed away in a past yet farther removed from us than the screen's constructed rectangular present. In roving past or fixating upon photographs, cinema undergoes—which is only to say stages—a pregnant suspension. The motion picture stalls upon a glimpse into its own origin and negation at once. Such an instant is given over to that latent plangency generated in the screen's contrast between an immobile past and the passing movement that sweeps it into—and from—view. Everything stirring, elusive, and uncanny about the form of photography itself, even before the superaddition of the content—the unsettling imprint of time past apart from the specific drama of the dead parent, of the wedding before the marriage went sour, of the unreturned sol-

dier, or simply of the younger self that was—everything about the photochemistry of indexed presence is not simply redoubled by the submission to cinematic camerawork of such former works of a still camera. Such photochemistry is squared, raised to the power of its own twice-bracketed preservation.

A particularly elegiac example, complete with mandatory musical overlay, turns up in the unlikeliest of places: Ridley Scott's techno-noir thriller *Blade Runner* (1982). It enters there upon a postmodern disquisition (anticipating my fifth chapter) into the operative differences among photographic technology, its kindred cinematic sophistications, and its digital extension (and potential nemesis) in electronic circuitry, optical as well as biogenetic. Deckard (Harrison Ford) has just failed to be convinced by weak photographic testimony offered by the heroine (Sean Young) in support of her claim to human rather than android status. Her would-be retroactive passport to normal "identity" is an ID photograph, she thinks, of herself as a child on her mother's lap (fig. 10).[10] Says Deckard out loud to himself after she has left his apartment, leaving the photo behind, this cannot prove anything. It is merely a picture of a mother she never had and a girl she never was. In a single dismissal, Deckard invalidates for her the optical trace of her own recapitulated mirror stage. She has, it seems, entered into the digital (or cyborg) symbolic without the unconscious of an authentic imaginary.

That's just the beginning. The hero's skepticism about her photograph seems to remind him, at once, of other photographs in his keeping, an assortment found in the apartment of another replicant now hunted for murder. Maybe, Deckard speculates, "they"—all of the replicants—need pictures in lieu of real memories. We are about to begin the extended and unforgettable sequence in which the ordinary snapshot of a cluttered room is submitted to computer scanning and magnification on Deckard's desktop optical printer—until the picture plane is geometrically transformed into a scenographic design recalling the heyday of flamboyant perspectivism in the northern High Re-

naissance, more Dutch school than Kodak. Inch by inch, the surface is electronically blocked out, reframed, enlarged (fig. 11), until the Van Eyck-like convex mirror glimpsed through an open door on the far wall of a second room doubles the space of the print and permits a virtual reverse shot of the facing (otherwise invisible) wall. Or think of it this way: the photo is, in short, cinematized—edited, cut, motorized, even lent the illusion of three-dimensional-

11

ity resulting from shifts of perspective as the camera roams the already fixed image plane. Except that the cinematic effect of motion and variable sight lines is here entirely displaced (denaturalized one degree further) by the dynamics of digitization.

What has happened just before, in the lingering moment I am about to recall, is the structural opposite of this scopic tour de force: instead of the surrender to electronics, the recursion of the cinematic track toward the photographic segment. Neither half of the episode occurs in the novel the film is based on.[11] Each offers an instance, above and beyond plot imperatives, of cinema's empaneling an inquiry into its own affective and cognitive disposition. Where the digital transformation of photograph into *mise en scène* is achieved by rehearsing the history of perspectival representation—as it now gains its most instrumental ramification in computer technology—another technological rehearsal has laid the groundwork. For the previous phase of this sequence has more specifically replayed the transition (in the form of the difference) between Victorian photography and motion pictures (thus anticipating my sixth chapter as well). It has done so, moreover, not just within the perspectival codes of visual representation but within the ontological codes of culture's discourse of the self.

Just before Deckard staggers to his computer screen, he is seen slumped drunk at his piano, fingering a bar or two of a jazz melody to anchor the nondiegetic Vangelis score—while the panning camera moodily drifts over his head across an

12, 13

array of photographs on the piano's music stand, some Victorian, most of them pre–World War II, only one of them easily recognized from the confiscated mixed stash of the murderous replicant that Deckard has thumbed through earlier. All that can be illustrated here of this languorous panning shot is the first and last stage—hence the poles of the spectrum without the glide of the camera's lateral sweep (figs. 12-13). Lost to view by such isolated frame enlargement is the counterpoint between motion and stasis that deepens the scene by further flattening the time-space of the reshot photos. There would be more to regret in this deficit if it did not testify precisely to my point about the irreplaceable cinematic effect on display—and at issue—in the scene. For it is a scene in which the individual image must, as it were, be orchestrated into action. This may well be why we now move from the piano to the computer screen across a shot in which the evidentiary photograph from the trove of the replicant is situated to displace some of the sheet-music score on the piano (fig. 14). This is the score *as text*, before the photo itself, as text, is submitted not so much to analysis as to *performance* on another nearby console.

But whose were those other photos, anyway? Deckard's private collection? Thus casting into doubt his own humanity, which like a cyborg's stands in need of photochemical prosthesis? In the year 2129, when the film is set, these photographs cannot even be fantasized family portraits of the hero's own near relatives. If Deckard is right, that photographs are what an artificial intelligence has instead

14

of felt memories, then they are, when collected at random from pasts other than the replicant's own, the displaced collective memory of another species— and of a medium that first of all, and before film, vouched for the bodily manifestation (even before movement) of the human self. In another sense, therefore, these photos represent one implied strain in the Victorian prehistory of cinema not only as a medium of visual record but in its lineal descent from the photochemical imprint. Moreover, in the lateral pan itself, as camera movement, postmodern pastiche (the hodgepodge of recycled arbitrary images) is offered up both as the narrated form of a memory substitute and as the present narrational mode in which a long-standing formulaic gesture—the camera's dwelling en route over a photo array—lodges its borrowed charge. We may well perceive the familiar "gallery of the past shot" evoked here as a knowingly bracketed intertext from the arsenal of classic film rhetoric. And we may extrapolate its rhetorical conceit, in situ, in terms something like this: without cinema, just as without albums and trunks of old snapshots, we all might be less sure we are human. But in *Blade Runner* this reassurance isn't quite enough.

Now for the alternative form of filmic disclosure on-screen, the so-called freeze: a kind of simulated photogrammatic immanence where dozens or hundreds of rushing identical frames are needed to picture the fixity of any one (or anyone) in particular. Whereas the panning across or tracking in upon an internally demarcated photographic space may appeal to the viewer as a summons into a world beyond and behind the screen world, the freeze-frame snags and cancels the world in passing, plasters it over with the implacable image of itself in arrest. Trademark index of post–New Wave "artiness," the sporadic accentuation of the freeze-frame (in its immediate descent from the influential closing shot of Truffaut's *The 400 Blows* in 1959) has a far longer, if intermittent, history. Like so much of film innovation, it began as vaguely funny—and passed, reversing the dictum about historical recurrence, from its farcical to its tragic (or at least melodramatic) phase. Appearing as early as 1929 in the Berlin city film *People on Sunday* (Robert Siodmak, Fred Zinnemann, et al.) to italicize the work of a commercial photographer as he snaps the mugging of Sunday beachgoers, the freeze-frame both alludes to and outgrows the roots it shares with cinema in the optical gadgetry and commercial distractions of boardwalk, fairway, and carnival as it takes up its marginal but potent role in film history. In a passage later elaborated upon by Siegfried Kracauer, however, Rudolph Arnheim accounts for the filmic treatment of this photographic sequence in a vocabulary that falls oddly outside the immediate cinematic apparatus, writing as if the "uncannily petrified" figures result from a "photographic" interpolation into the film track (rather than a reprinting of its own cellular constituents). He is responding to the fact that the caught poses of the bathers are fractionally advanced on the track from the deferred moment of photographic capture. Hence he can say of this sequence that "a still photograph cut into a film acts like the curse on Lot's wife."[12] To subsume the arrested and reedited frame to a photographic insert is a symptomatic moment—locally misleading, perhaps, but broadly enlightening. It puts us on the alert for the more insistent distinctions, but also for the claimed complementarity, of this book's two chief categories of resisted photo synthesis: the inset photo and the seized frame.

The locus classicus of their convergence is the editing work that interrupts the cinematographer's own on-site labor with camera and tripod in *Man with a Movie Camera* (1929), an interruption that brings the photogram per se into stilled view. Between the extended sequence of his photographing Soviet life from a moving

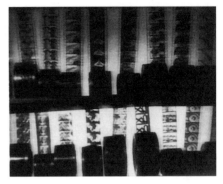

15

16

17

auto and his subsequent lugging the camera along a city street, half a dozen freeze-frames—of a carriage horse (fig. 15), its speeding passengers (fig. 16), and so on—halt his POV in progress and catapult us back to the editing table, where the jump-cut aesthetic of Vertov's screened text is segmentally fabricated. It is as if the specific deviance of the freeze-frame has precipitated a representational hiatus that returns us to the laboratory of filmic process itself. As functional antithesis to this one film's hectic manufacture of the disjunct but moving image, the filmic freeze has interceded as a cut on action that merely recapitulates the same pose in its truncated temporality, what Vertov called a "paralyzed time sequence," as cited by Yuri Tsivian in his audio essay on the 1996 laserdisc reissue ("Classics of Soviet Cinema," Blackhawk Films). The stop-action exception must now give way to a visible proof of the filmic (before cinematic) rule. Once in the lab, we cut from a selection of partly unspooled film strips (fig. 17) to the passage of one selected roll, sideways, through the editing machine (fig. 18). After this same stretch of strip speeds past in a blur that recalls an earlier shot of tram windows on the run (fig. 19), it gets slowed for cutting and splicing (fig. 20), clipped as a vertical run of differential photograms, and then displaced to a full-screen moving image of the same child's energized wonderment (at what we later find to be a magic show), followed in turn by two further and more exact splices from strip to reactivated screen movement for other children in the audience (e.g., figs. 21-22). After a couple more inset freeze-frames and a last look by the editor at the transparent strip, the city film resumes its mo-

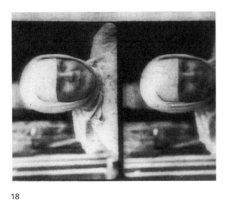

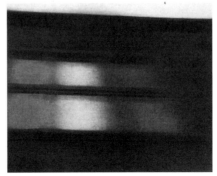

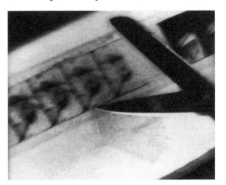

18

19

20

mentum with the cameraman's new venue. The labor of production is now visible again back on the street rather than behind the scenes.

In Hollywood cinema Stanley Cavell gets much justified mileage out of a deliberate cinematic stoppage in his discussion of the closing freeze-frames in *The Philadelphia Story* (George Cukor, 1940), frames transformed on the instant to unauthorized journalistic snapshots.[13] There we see the use of the immediate (rather than deferred) image in arrest—induced on the strip, again, by the invisibly reprinted photogram—to mark the journalistic "abstraction" of reality (as it will be seen extensively to do in the coming chapter). Seizure achieves a theft of the very texture of dailiness for further if ephemeral circulation. (As such, this conversion of mimetic screen presence to tabloid absence is already so well established an intertext from city films and newspaper plots of the 1930s, both documentary and fiction, that its use by Orson Welles for the "Kane Caught in Love-Nest with 'Singer'" transition the next year is less an ingenuity than an in-joke.)[14]

21, 22

Beyond this stealing of the quotidian for mass imprint, elsewhere the freeze-frame can readily wax extratemporal as well—and be held, not just for a transitional instant but for what seems like an eternity in little. Five years after Cukor's comic stunt of disruption, that is, an early shot in a comedy by Frank Capra more explicitly mocks cinema's own dynamism: the arrested present as seen from the vantage of Last Things and their heavenly minions. In *It's a Wonderful Life* (1945), divine intervention is necessary to halt the hero's decline into suicide, to still time in its deadly tracks on the brink of his leap from the bridge, to give (back) time to think. Once that power is granted to the plot as a fantastic premise—in the form of the proverbial guardian angel, named Clarence—it soon enters the representation as a device: the providential machine at work. Time is now halted for the viewer, not for the hero, in the midstream review of his life. Here, then, is one freeze-frame whose most striking effect is caught rather than squandered by an illustration (fig. 23). The image is held for so long on-screen, held up there in both senses, that to examine it at leisure on a page hardly violates the nature of its narrative disruption. In the angel's swift replay of George Bailey's life,

23

an adult Jimmy Stewart is describing the size of the suitcase he needs for his planned adventures, and as he opens his arms and eyes wide, the film goes dead as motion picture. In the voice-over dialogue from our continuing cosmic oversight, Clarence asks, "Hey, what did you stop it for?" To what antecedent spectacle does the otherworldly purview refer? The event? The film? The latter (from the point of view of an angelic naïf) understood as the best metaphor for the former? From a supernal elevation, history is certainly as manipulable as the earthly media meant to capture or simulate it. In any case, the reason for the stoppage—for putting the brakes on human time—is given by the executive angel in charge: "I want you to take a good look at that face." For over thirty seconds, the frame is held as his voice-over narration sketches in some missing details about the

young man's aspiration—all while the subject remains stretched in an open-armed embrace of his own unmaterialized dreams. Clarence asks just before the end of the freeze: "Did he ever marry that girl? Did he ever go traveling?" The answer, as the film starts up again: "Well, wait and see." This fitting idiom for exercising patience dispels the long wait—the magic spell of hiatus in dramatic seeing itself—which has by this point brought us up to the speed of biographical narration, now resumed in seen (cinematic) form.

What is the moral of this mode of story? We won't be able to answer such a question fully, perhaps, until chapter 3, where the vacancy of the freeze can be understood as a form of emptied and displaced (rather than merely suspended) duration. For now, what should be clear is that the freeze stands revealed here, in this case and in general, as the marked convergence of two time schemes, those of presentation (the plotted actions of characters) and narration (the discursive activity sheared off from narrative). The freeze is the abrupt subordination of the former to the latter, whether or not (as anomalously in Capra's scene) the sound track bears further story information (as in a different sense it does with the crash at the end of *The Asphyx*). The held image is a narrational rather than a diegetic act of stoppage ("diegesis" as the represented world on film), a haltedness credited to the realm of the telling rather than the perceived scene, hence a metatextual (even when not metaphysical) intervention. It is, in fact, a contravention of sequence under the aberrant sway of the single image.

Because my concern in this book is primarily with narrative film, and hence with a motoring drive of image continuity that invisibly subtends screen narrative but upon which it *manifestly* depends, it behooves this introduction to revisit the most lucid and influential definition of film narration. Adopting an abiding Russian formalist distinction between the *fabula* (the cause-and-effect chain of story events) and the *syuzhet* (the structuring plot elements), and overturning the mistaken assumption that the former has to do with a profilmic world, David Bordwell decisively reconstrues the priority of the given and the made: "In the fiction film, narration is *the process whereby the film's syuzhet and style interact in the course of cueing and channeling the spectator's construction of the fabula.*"[15] Only through structure and the superadded inflections of technique does one arrive at that least immanent of forms: the story world of the narrative. Bordwell no doubt could—and would—subordinate most of what I am calling the photogrammatic moment in film textuality, the regress from cinematic narration to its animating track (though such effects go mostly underdiscussed by him), to the broad notion of "style." This is a term he uses to name "simply" the "systematic use of cinematic devices" which, though in excess of plot, remain "wholly ingredient to the medium" (50). But the coming chapters are preoccupied with the *reductio* rather than the surplus of narrative structure: a reversion to the synthetic nature of the image itself.

Since we are on alert for those exceedings of narration that plunge the viewer from stylistic inflection back to mechanical process, from hypertrophic screen effect to the normative action of the track, we need a codicil to Bordwell's definition. I thus reactivate his formulation in midstream, with appended italics of my own.

In fundamental narrative procedure, all devices collaborate "in the course of cueing and channeling the spectator's construction of the fabula, *whose mimesis may
at any time be breached by a stylistic extremity clueing the viewer in to the constructedness not just of the story but of the image itself.*" I say "stylistic" not just
in reference to Bordwell's catchall term but also in anticipation of a new account
of the modernist styleme, linked in revealing ways to cinematic process, hinted at
by Fredric Jameson and awaiting further ramifications in my last chapter.

Present and future definitions of "style" aside for now, we may return to the
examples already under consideration of that mimetic "breach" mentioned above,
whether tacit and in passing or exacerbated by arrest. This is a return, in effect, to
the textuality beneath style. In isolation, we already have before us two definitive
scopic formations as they burrow—either by internal allusion (the photograph) or
by contusion (the impacted single frame)—to the formative nature of the filmic
photogram. Bounding terms are therefore in place, with our guiding distinctions
ready to take their lead. Freeze-frame versus reshot photo are the tropic poles, in
two senses, of screen movement. They are tropes (synecdochic figures) of the
whole cinematic process in its relation to photography. This on the one hand. On
the other, from the very momentum of narrative, they are drawn by a kind of recursive tropism (or turning, like a heliotropic organism) back from the cinematic
projection to the lit filmic track. Whereas in the photopan film may look back to
its own origin (and potential cancellation) in the discrete image, working (as in another sense it always does) to contain the image in frame, in the freeze shot the
photogrammatic undertext is cast up (cast forward) as the whole screen picture. In
between these poles, the camera moves across a space furnished with other than
secondary photochemical representation—and keeps moving, without lapsing to
a photomechanical stasis of its own. When cinema projects in this way, and without self-allusion, the illusion of an embodied space, it of course performs its ordinary function as representational (and narrative) medium. But at the extremity of
the poles appear, by defining contrast, those complementary figures of mediation
(concentrated emblems rather than pervasive modes): the on-screen photo versus
the radically photogrammatic screen freeze.

In practice, it will be the job of chapter 1 to examine more particularly the way
the stylistic "cues" of film narrative work to structure our access to screen action's
photogrammatic basis. What should soon grow clear is that the reframed photograph and the consecutively rephotographed film frame can operate as systemic
alternatives to each other within the same metatextual field. This is crucial. If in
the long run, via Eisenstein, these chapters wish to emerge as a full-fledged dialectics of the filmic within the cinematic, they must right from the start clarify
their emphasis on screen spectation's definitive third (or synthetic) term. Between
photographic input and cinematic output, spectation's middle term is the cognitive
photo synthesis of subliminally determined movement. Much that attaches to this
notion can be specified in four related ways: Between optic signal and cinema's
viewed world, the event of filmic manifestation. Between photographic still and
motion picture, the photogram in motion. Between strip and screen, the track in
action. Between footage and image, the text in process.

To be *read* in process. When I refer to narrative cinema "as film," that mix of tautology and vaunt has an intended parallel at the level of analytic practice. In these chapters, narrative cinema is to the filmic stratum that comprises and composes it as reading is to theory, locked in a relationship intimate and nonhierarchical. With certain films, you cannot help but get from one to the other under the pressure of close attention. Often in these chapters we will detect a reversible commutation between narrative and its material ingredients. This is not a narrow path to theory but a two-way street that constitutes theory.[16] The analytic attention proposed here operates by a concerted shift in generative levels *and a transaction between them.* Or spelled out more fully, it operates by manifesting (that is, monitoring as manifested) the implications of one level in another, strip in track, track in moving image.[17]

This is the productive space between film and screen that even film theory, like the cinematic institution, tends to downplay. What seems to make photogrammatic consideration something less than theoretically urgent? What *could* it be? The absence of the photogram from the screen view? Its merely technical function? Its narrative negligibility? Its micro nature in the optic chain? The cell's operative invisibility as a separate element? Its ephemerality? Its elided phenomenality? Its masked de/cisiveness in the scissored flow? Its strictly superimpositional site? Its only rarely disjunctive potential within an ordinarily forgettable function? Its relegation to the unconscious premise of our rapt (and narratively apter) visual attention? Guilty on each count—but exonerated on all from the charge of marginality. For it is exactly what makes the photogram a mere *abstraction* in screen experience ("steals" it from view by the stealthy speed of its simultaneous manifestation and suppression as optic unit) that lends it an almost exclusively "theoretical" weight. So if the photogram cannot rightly be discounted, one good question is, again, how—and to what immediate effect—certain films can be found to factor it in: in other words, to theorize it for themselves.[18]

CURRENT PROGRAM INFORMATION

So what kinds of films do we have in store for consideration? And in what light but their own? It is time to admit that I fancy salvaging some advantage from the twilight mood of this project. Glanced back upon from its fading ascendancy, the cinematic artifact becomes more than ever a historical object. Which means in this case both a modern and twice over a modernist object—as regards first the timing of cinema's fin-de-siècle advent and then, after its early avant-garde phase in the 1920s, its midcentury narrative transformations under the international influence of postwar neorealism and the French New Wave.[19] In a manner intrinsic to the medium but maximized in its later modernist phase, narrative cinema is unavoidably an optic text of synthetic means, an artifact of technology and an object of reading. What about it? What about it, I mean, will we be reading in these pages?

Photography, Film, and . . . Typically, the triadic field of investigation links the two photomechanical processes in relation to a third object or consideration independent of their conjuncture. The genetically related media touchstones thus attach themselves to each other as coordinated vantage points on a period they each inhabit, a topic they take up in common, or a third technology or art they derive from or propagate. Photography, Film, and Victorian Culture. Photography, Film, and the Colonial Landscape. Photography, Film, and Painting. So it usually goes. In the pages to come, the third term ultimately drops out, subsumed to the procedure by which photograph becomes film: designated for now, and soon to be called out for analysis from several perspectives, the serial photo's synthesis in filmic photo synthesis. In this book the separate but kindred media are therefore meant to triangulate their own interrelation. But this is not to say that each chapter does not proceed by a comparable logic of its own: Photography, Film, and the Stilled Image. Photography, Film, and the Apocalyptic Moment of Negated Motion. Photography, Film, and the Freeze-Frame. Photography, Film, and Death. Photography, Film, and the Ontology of the Science Fiction Body. Photography, Film, and Victorian Imaging. Photography, Film, and Modernism. This is the ground plan of the chapters in the recurrent three-way fix they seek to articulate.

As should already be clear, I am concerned from here on out with the photographic or photogrammatic moment on—because in and of—film: the nodalized scopic materiality of still image (filmed photograph) or stalled imaging (photolike halt of film). Indeed, the former (photo) may implicate the latter (seized frame) by bringing to mind the fixed imprint within the chain of represented action. Whether rippling or rupturing the cinematic continuum with such traces of its own propellant frames, both the reset photo and the arrested (and so asserted) track depend upon a spatial disjunction between filmic record and cinematic apparition. Yet this discrepancy registers, in turn, as a more fundamental disjuncture within time itself between the fixed and the successive. When ontological worries impinge on this distinction between the portrayed time of imprint and the time of projection, they arrive, as one might suspect, from the immediate narrative vicinity: from the plot that dictates—or precipitates—the filmic extrusion to begin with. They often arrive as well, as the next chapter will set out by surveying, from practices of avant-garde film that, whether more or less narrative in their own right, tend to explore the dynamic between strip and track with more determination than in mainstream cinema.

Absence, loss, objectification, self-division, death—dislocations of all sorts, sudden overviews from an untoward vantage, the violence effected by temporal severance in a certain mode of preservation—all such narrative issues hit the screen with a frequent recoil upon the track. By inference from either photographic citation or photogrammatic buckle, the filmic increment may well get pitched in sudden resistance to the cinematic drift. As discussion fans out in later chapters to entertain that unresolved cultural disquiet routinely harmonized by the formulas of genre plotting (in the case of Victorian period dramas as well as futurist science fiction), aspects of loss and death gather as modes of mechanical absentation—as well as modes of temporal rupture—within an inferred arc of historical transformation. They develop, that is, according to the noncontinuities at stake between us and the virtual future on the one hand, us and the image culture of the Victorian past on the other. Photography (and its primal allegiance to the body) retains its pivotal place between the precinematic past we know in part through its mediation and the postcinematic future that is foreseen to invalidate the human(ist) basis of photograph's own evidentiary weight.

Before the counterpull of such contemporary genres as costume melodrama and sci fi adventure can be compared at this level, however, film's generative undertext must be, in a word, more closely tracked. Signposts are at their most frequent in films from that period of late modernist ferment in commercial cinema stretching from the late 1950s through the mid-1970s, a period influenced in any number of ways by avant-garde practice. The first chapter will shortly close in upon two screen narratives (*Badlands* and *Under Fire*) that emerge from—or just after—the latter phase of this period. These are films that participate in the inquisition of their own time-laden and mortally fraught medium from opposite and complementary perspectives already laid out, the photograph refilmed and the film arrested in its own frozen (because statically proliferated) photogram. The next question would therefore be: Not only in what other ways but in what other respects might the photogram refuse simply to fuse into movement and be forgotten? Such a phrasing of the question starts us on the further path to its own answer. If the photogram is to be in certain cases remembered, then it must recall itself to the mind of an audience. An account of representation must thus be broadened to include a logic of reception, but with each, nonetheless, to be understood as forms of textual productivity—each, in a word, readable. The seductions of cinematic reception to be investigated here are more transferential than Oedipal; that is, they are concerned more with a deliberately blinkered narrative investment than with an accession to some eroticized symbolic order of desire and displacement. What chapter 2 on the return of a specular unconscious through photogrammatic disruption needs to demonstrate is less how an artificial imaginary contrives wholesale to erase the symbolic by fetishistic disavowal (Metz's gist) than how the screen spectacle locally suppresses—or strategically fails to suppress—its own specific materiality, thereby renegotiating the fundamental relations between image and scene. In all its inevitably disguised forms, the filmic moment within cinematic momentum is what brokers that negotiation.

First appearing in a special journal issue devoted to a wide-ranging consideration of "Photography and Apocalypse," this second chapter records my attempt to enter the topic from another medium altogether, working back to the photograph (and photogram) from the cinematic spectacle. As in chapter 1, death is once more a triadic point of reference. (It will, as suggested, never fade far from consideration in the chapters that remain—for reasons having not least to do with the currency of death as both trope and topos in photographic theory.) What the evidence of this second chapter brings out is the frequency with which textual or material revelation (in the place of mortal arrest, often exactly the place) ends up refiguring death in the receptive disturbances of the filmic metaplot. Here debate is joined with a wider range of criticism taking screen movement at face value, especially the phenomenological (or phenomenalist) camp—as represented primarily at this stage in its highly modified semiotic form by the writing of Gilles Deleuze (in later discussion, by that of Stanley Cavell and Vivian Sobchack). This second chapter's effort is to adjust the immanent or manifestational bias of all such approaches to the moving image with a textual model involving levels of screen engagement beneath spectatorial consciousness. This last is an emphasis I derive, revised, from Walter Benjamin—and in distinction from the use made of his concept in the titular homage of Rosalind Krauss's *The Optical Unconscious*.[20]

One thing leads to another. This discussion of textual self-apocalypse next required, I found, a fuller position paper on the relation of the freeze-frame to the inset photograph—and of each to the manufactured presence of the screen world. Hence the third and most exclusively theoretical chapter. The racing generation of stasis, erasing the very motion that sustains its still picture, becomes at this level the frame of reference for all screen movement. The freeze ends up situated in a curious interspace—or phenomenal hinterland—between Deleuze's influential categories of movement and time. After a close account of such photogrammatic intercession on-screen, in its purest mimetic anomaly of the freeze-frame, we will be primed to reconsider in chapter 4 the textual determinations discharged around the lightning rod of the freeze as they inflect a fuller reading yet, more detailed and optically materialist, of two films (*Citizen Kane* and *The Shining*) whose deliberate and marked avoidance of the freeze is merely the sign of their engagement with its larger questions. In this fourth chapter, to note the way photography rushes in to fill the gap of an elided freeze-frame is to notice further how photogrammatic slippage—as the motoring vitality of cinematic animation—is drawn directly into death's thematic vacuum.

And in the fifth chapter as well, where death is transformed from the existential testing ground of cinematic manifestation to another name, within science fiction cinema, for a posthumanist crisis in the technology of simulation. This is the point at which the purview of the book widens to the cultural parameters of genre study. The effort is to rethink earlier claims of mine, published elsewhere, about futuristic film and its rendered internal viewing screens. I now relate this mode of autoenclosure to the photographic inset or regress of such science fiction narratives. Further, this chapter retains from the one before it an emphasis on the body itself, the carnal surface or envelope of the human subject, as the common term of death and photography: the body that was once there intact and whose absentation, in epochal transit to simulation, may be caught in passing by photographic (even photogrammatic) intervention in one (often ironic) form or another.

Photography's manufactured trace of bodily presence also offers connection between a genre study of futuristic technological fantasy and the sixth chapter's investigation into the uses of photography and (less often) cinematography in a proliferating fin-de-siècle subgenre of Victorian nostalgia film. Each discussion offers up the material of a broad-gauge cultural study sieved through a closely webbed network of formal determinants and loopholes. Pitting the cinematograph and its precursors against the simulacrum, one chapter concerns the mortal body newly preserved by technology, one the mortal body gradually usurped thereby. The photomechanical moment of the so-called heritage film is a synecdoche for the coming procedures of its own mimesis as cinematic retrospect. The synecdoche is therefore proleptic, the embedded seed of a cinematic presencing not yet available to the cultural subjects (sometimes photographic objects) of such recounted history. In science fiction cinema, by contrast, or what we might call the legacy film, the photographic synecdoche is instead nostalgic. It arrives as an elegy for the former indexical and ontological grounding of a moving-image medium (now narratively—and even textually—caught up in prognosticated electronic imaging of all sorts), a medium whose present instance stalls briefly over such a photographic incursion as an idyllic or ironic reversion.

From either end of the historical gulf between the media anxieties of Victorian and postmodern technology, in the final chapter I close in on the assaulting discontinuities that modernist representational practice so often theorizes by inference in its own fractured materiality. To do so requires further engagement with perhaps the most active contemporary debates in mainstream cinema studies, debates about the nineteenth-century genealogy of the apparatus and its ocular disposition in modernity. Two reconceptions seem necessary, and each finds a tentative ally in recently published scholarship. First, in adjudicating between the broad history-of-invention approach to the motorizing of the still image and the equally sweeping Foucauldian archaeologies of the gaze, there is important new evidence. A closely attended prehistory of the Lumière cinematograph within the popular diffusion of "instantaneous photography" (in the work of Tom Gunning) should help make conceptual place for the photogrammatic quotient of the screen image—in early cinema and beyond. Second, and with this in view, the long *durées* of theoretical science and its artistic mutations (adduced by writers from Baudry to Deleuze) and the comparably epochal view of the modernist literary signifier delinked from the whole rhetorical tradition of expressive subjectivity and virtually automatized (in Fredric Jameson's recent work) make space for a comparative account of intervallic inscription between two forms of modernist print, cinema and literature.

Under the same magnifying glass in the final chapter, then, are placed the photogrammatic minim of screen projection and the sliding signifier of literary *écriture*, each as a testing of material (ultimately ontological) self-presence. Aligned with the filmic strip in sped manifestation is a modernist literary agenda smitten with the differential signifier (in this case the sliding phonogram of subvocal articulation) in any number of historicizable ways—charged with the intervallic play of the infinitesimal as both increment and supplement at once. Part of this final chapter's assignment is to cross-examine rival yet dovetailing accounts of modernism's gradual dawn for ways the flack and static of an increasingly "technologized" literary technique run parallel to the film track's flitting litter of images. In aligning the synthesis of filmic fragments with the aggregate but riven lexicality that typifies many a modernist literary text, we will move, for instance, from a microanalysis of Chris Marker's title *La jetée* to a metanarrative analysis of the vanishing photographs in Antonioni's *Blow-Up.* As with the culminating discussion of photogrammatic space/time ratios in Chaplin's *Modern Times,* we will again be keeping our *reading* eyes on the filmic frame's constitutive vanishing act in screen manifestation.

I say reading, here and everywhere, rather than interpretation. I do so in subscription to the principle that interpretation settles for the rhetoric of effect rather than probing its structural logic. In the encounter with screen narrative, for instance, interpretation takes narrative on its own communicative terms, whereas reading would take up narrative production at the level of its communicating means. We interpret screen narratives; we read their textuality. What many of the readings to come will track, at moments of impacted screen imagery, is the track itself. Make no mistake about it. The position I wish to advance in these readings is to some extent counterintuitive to most moviegoing practice. To insist on the photogram at the basis of film is a labor of attention that hovers between the obvious and the obviated, self-evident on the one hand, irrelevant on the other, true enough in the canister or the projector, swept under and away on-screen.

But not wholly abrogated. And my sense is that we are neither mystified by such a process (what one could dub the efflor*essence* of the cinematic effect) nor quite familiar with it either. It stays just a touch strange in the way our own language, our own tongue, remains marginally foreign to us, not just when defacilitated as utterance by the excess of literary signification but even in our own workaday twisters, slips, and mishearings. This tolerated estrangement makes for a comfortable wariness that seldom threatens to spoil either transparency or pleasure, even when it may enhance the latter at the expense of the former. I keep coming back to this (and will again in chapter 7): the internal return of wording upon words as the deepest, if not the best or the only, analogy for the operation of the filmic track in its cinematic effect. And the analogy applies not just in textual theory but, I hope we can finally agree, in regular cognitive engagement. Think about it. Think about it (as you don't usually do), and the case begins to be made.

I must be quick to add that all due distinctions between the two media— film's photo synthesis as cinema, writing's phonemic accretion as utterance—will attend this book in good time. But these would hold little interest here if they were not meant to clarify a common bond across these separate inscriptive systems in the operative bondings of their own minimal elements: namely, the overriding of the fixed mark that makes for the fusions of reference in each mode of presentation. In projection generally, one image doesn't make place for the next but is, so to speak, internally displaced by it. No matter how fleeting, one view is always of a few at once. In reading, silently as much as otherwise, one word doesn't give way to the next but momentarily takes hold of it before being sold off to succession in the lexical economy. Strip is to track is to screen, then, as script is to subvocal phonemic activation is to significance. Approximately. Indeed, I would hope that the obvious failure of any exact parallel between the two media as distinct inscriptive systems in motion would eventually help clarify the principle at issue for each alone as well as for the one in sight of the other. That principle is this: that we are no more certain where the smallest image of the screen view begins and ends than we are certain in the event of reading precisely where one phonetic block cleaves off and the next starts up. It follows that there are important nonnormative cinematic as well as literary texts that may and do seek to maximize this uncertainty. What they lift to recognition is the fact that, along the slippery slope of aggregate language, as well as along the vertical plummet of the precipitous strip in projection, all is overlapping flow.

This is why we will be encouraged to conclude, in the last chapter, that the newly christened phonogram of verbal production offers a decidedly approximate (but all the more telling) lexical match for the photogram of projected motion. By then it should be clear why the optic equivalent for the two-ply slice of lexical textuality, a continual splicing on the run, is all the more pertinent when it lies in hiding, veiled by the very availability of the moving image. Such is the way the discrete filmic frame is finessed into its own kind of assimilation, shuffled under in the lightning-fast deal of the lit image released from the projector's slit aperture. Just where this happens, even as it goes unseen, is important to isolate and define. Between (sub)perceptual integer and the released image, then, the technical impulsion requires in fact a conceptual (as well as a cognitive) transumption. Here we find the new transitive use of the verb *disappear* invited to deliver one more version of our basic axiom: The filmic apparatus disappears the photogram in the former's apparition as cinema.

Such, of course, is the premise of this book even before it leads to any particular thesis: that film is first and before all, if not foremost, a synthesis of photograms. What will slowly grow obvious across their terracing of arguments, however, is that these chapters, in working out a number of specific claims about the photofusion of the moving image on-screen, are after another level of amalgam—or synthesis—whose net is cast more broadly than the material substrate of cinematic narrative. I had best underscore this aspect of the prospectus up front. *The methodological synthesis envisaged by these pages is between the formal and the cultural under the intermediate and overdetermined sign of the textual.* In the resultant reading rather than merely interpretation of the screen text, under pressure of one question after another generated en route, such a theoretical synthesis will need to equilibrate various presuppositions of media study in a new contiguous mix—like perspectival frames succeeding or outgrowing each other on the track of some tentative answers. This critical synthesis will need to make common cause, that is, among an ontology of imprint, a grammatology of difference, a philosophy of movement/time ratios, a narratology of the look and its relays, a cognitive account of the filmic beneath the cinematic, a psychoanalytics of spectation, and a sociology of distraction (via Kracauer and Benjamin) within a critique of reality's naturalized construct(s).

At issue throughout is that tissue of cellular illusion known as motion pictures, a disclosed photogrammatic chain motivated at times by a narrative investment that only reading can bring out. At such moments, theme is drawn back into process, hermeneutics into materialist theory, ideology into the tactics of illusionism. Reading, I am ready to say before doing a good deal more of it, responds in this way to the materiality of the track at the very moment when, under narrative prompting, the action of the track becomes *thematerialized*—and demonstrably so. As we go, the prevailing feel of such demonstration, its grain, its scale, will already be familiar from passing examples in these introductory remarks. What remains is the test of its reach.

ONE

Photo-gravure

CINEMA CAN ENGRAVE ITS OWN RELATION
TO THE STILL IMAGE FROM WITHIN
THE FLOW OF MOTION

My early paper titled "Photo-gravure" set out to imagine the potential intersection of Roland Barthes's emphasis on the deathlike stasis of photography with a materialist approach to cinema's filmic increments, their fixity in continuous eclipse.[1] The diverse texts held up for inspection included two period films of vastly different quality involving nineteenth-century photographic technology, films from cinema's classic era and from the cinematographically self-trumpeting late 1960s, respectively (*Letter from an Unknown Woman, Butch Cassidy and the Sundance Kid*); a meticulously conceived narrative from the 1970s harking back to old-fashioned stereographic device (*Badlands*); and a fourth, smartly executed text from the 1980s saturated by the high-tech photojournalism (and photomechanics) of its Third World detection and conspiracy plot (*Under Fire*). They remain, amplified now by a further look at evidence both before and after them in the course of American film history that extends their deployment of technique as critique (whether social, cultural, or geopolitical). New remarks on a primal coalition of rephotographed photo and freeze-frame in Fritz Lang's *Fury*, from the mid-1930s, will be followed by consideration of the allusive retread of photomechanical devices in the postmodern feminist road western *Thelma and Louise* and in the photojournalistic subtext—and specular undertext—of *Apocalypse Now*.

Even the original conference exhibits were and are not so much arbitrary in their assortment as extreme, their end points the bracket of a media-historical spectrum. Between the depicted nineteenth-century force of photography (*Letter*) and the post-Vietnam ethos of Third World photojournalism and frontline TV reportage (*Under Fire*) falls the intermediate history of an entire medium: cinema. Here is a history that, when evoked in quite divergent ways by these films, is already shot through with allusions to its own roots and rudiments. This is never more apparent than with the foursquare imaging on-screen of an image in photo-chemical recession: an inset still photo. At such moments, death shadows the picture from more than one direction. It infiltrates the image either as figure in the plot or as metaphor for cinema's intrinsic dismemberment. And by the latter I mean the strip's deconstruction from figments of light to fixtures of imprint, its imaged doings and agents s/lain along the modular file of the photogrammatic strip.

Along with a stress on both the narrativity of the screen image and its occasional discomfiture by this recursion of the strip, the introduction spoke of an "undertext" to cinema's scopic field. On-screen, a world in action; behind and beneath it all (and behind all of us, in the projection booth), an activated spool of separately framed imprints. A definitive stratification is thereby proposed—one related, as we will eventually find, to the topographic model of psychoanalysis. Surface and depth; seen and unthought; mirage of motion and moving image strip. Such a stratification for the most part limits consideration in these chapters to a traditional narrative cinema in which mimesis and materiality not only are distinctly at odds but make their tensions evident in a shearing force at the surface of the text. This emphasis is certainly not meant to *favor* narrative over abstract cinema or (more broadly) industrial and commercial over experimental practice. It is meant only to highlight the exposed photosynthetic effect where it does the most immediate and visible damage to realist cinema's illusionist system—and where that system is pressed into its most revealing maneuvers to recoup such losses, to alleviate their drag on transparency.

CINEMATIC MIMESIS, FILMIC POESIS

In commercial cinema, surface covers for depth, moving image for the discrete images that move past to induce it. Traditional narrative invites as much. Whereas avant-garde film is full of narrative momentum that does not depend on the seductions of the real, in general mainstream cinema attempts to naturalize its storytelling according to the tenets of that realist code. Failing this at odd moments, certain conflicting demands of prosecuted story and seen world may be forced into the open by the obtruded sheer image. But this entails a new story in its own right, of source and machination. Beneath the blandishments of even the most accomplished naturalistic illusion, in other words, there may sometimes run a paranarrative counterplot. This is a plot whose double agent is the photogram itself, playing the overall game of representational containment even while sowing occasional mimetic distress. It is from this counterplot that the event of stasis is usually folded back into the current of mainstream plotting as a virtual metaphor for death, death as arrest rather than annihilation.

Elsewhere, of course, a whole aesthetic is founded on the refusal to subsume the single print. Such film work insists throughout—rather than just in moments of deviant visual impedance—on the optically engraved or imprinted constituents of all screen seeing. Like many of the commercial directors taken up in them, these chapters necessarily went to school in part with the work of this minimalist avant-garde—or with its predecessors in earlier decades of international film experiment. The chief concern of this book, however, is with the unexpected yield of those lessons in more normative screen practice: a yield taking the form of a material (well before a political) *resistance* typical of materialist—or filmic—experimentation, where the ethical mandate to see more clearly is not yet entirely a metaphor. These pages are concerned, that is, with the clarifying *occasion* of structure in eruption, with materiality materialized. To the so-called structuralist/materialist practice of the avant-garde cinema in particular they therefore owe a debt that cannot be fully repaid in their chosen emphasis, where what I would call the medium's photographic self-exposure is permitted only circumscribed license—and covered by limited liability—within realistic narrative.[2]

So a more explicit word is in order at the start about the reduced, minimalized, and purified form of the very effects whose diluted appearance, from beneath the naturalistic apparition of commercial cinema, will catch the eye in coming discussions. Structural/materialist filmmaking enacts the theory of a practice that turns fitful but is still illuminating in its commercial dissemination. As suggested, this practice includes the uprush of the track from undertext to screen immanence, a disturbance in the naturalized course of rendered event that occurs at certain "modernist" stress points in narratives generated even by industrial norms. Such is a *pedagogy* of the track inherited from its artisans in the experimental ranks. Such is the tutelage of the taut spool within an institution of the screen scene. Frame by frame on the speeding reel, the sprockets' training round—past the aperture—of the differential strip becomes the training ground, however intermittent, of a more precise and resistant encounter with film: what we may want to call a seeing rather than a viewing.

Experimental works that enforce our notice of the photogram by rubbing or abrading its surface on the strip, puncturing or scarring it, eccentrically reframing it to expose its sprocket holes, layering it in the lab with multiple superimpositions, or alternating it discordantly with other imprints timed to dislocate perception into random and irreconcilable animation effects: such works educate the eye by jostling the relative passivity of standard reception. In the process, such consciousness raising about film's perceptual ingredients often raises the question of consciousness itself. That is why materialist film experiments do not always quite feel like "pure" film after all.[3] Their ocular strategies grow contaminating. They infiltrate not only the screen's mirage of movement (with the eruption of its ingredient bits) but the whole way we view our own perceptual mechanisms and inclinations. Even within mainstream cinema, the implications of this cognitive reflex of the filmic within the cinematic—its implications for a transferential dynamic of screen experience, as well as for its heightened sensual presencing—await several stages of investigation en route to their summary in the book's coda, "End Title/Exeunt."

The materialist avant-garde points the way in more than one respect. If *The Flicker* (Tony Conrad, 1966), for instance, drives cinema back into the crevices of film, and even beyond to the *pre*photographic alternation of frames (with the film's instantaneous toggling between lit and black rectangles as its exclusive—and exclusionary—visual matter), it may also seem to figure the latent noncontinuity of other image systems, including human cognition. Placing photographic images rather than just graphic celluloid patterns of black and white in such an alternating framework and then foregrounding the equal artifice of its reception as continuous image is only the logical extension—in other so-called flicker films—of Conrad's "stripped down" effect.

Other angles of attack on the constructed nature of the moving image and its differential printing fill the roster of minimalist experiment, none spookier and more elusive that Ernie Gehr's 1970 *Serene Velocity*. We cannot at a glance be quite sure what we are seeing or how we are seeing it: a motion going nowhere, running in place by the mere alternation—it begins to appear—of focal lengths. It may at first look as if the camera is lurching forward (or is it back?) down a long institutional hallway, the only real color in the shot being the red (and readable) EXIT sign overhead about halfway down. But the mechanically induced lurch registers soon enough not as a choked dolly shot but as the internal work of a zoom lens—farther removed, as such, from the space it seems to penetrate. Hallucinated thereby is a velocity or vector of motion so serene and at peace with itself, so happily trapped within its closed-circuit loop of discrepant focal lengths, that it slowly comes clean as no motion at all, just the shunting of positional alternatives—carried, of course, by discontinuous batches of photogrammatic frames in rapid exchange and superimposition on the strip. Yet these images carry in turn, at degree zero, a kind of narrative residue or tease. In the spatial fable they generate, any *passage* in film, whether EXIT, entrance, or otherwise, is brought forward as in part the work of the camera and the strip's material base. Such is the reductive but still tantalizing narrativity of this fixed-frame loop. Put it like this. So strong is the closural imperative in any film event that, once smitten with the image, we are always looking for a visually articulated way out. Beyond this, in the oscillating relativity of perspective, the very walls and ceiling of the film's optic corridor seem racing by as well, almost indescribably, in the weird approach/avoidance of our fluctuant ocular fixation. And from within this illusion of architectural motion, a further visual metaphor. Unmistakable over the prolonged time of viewing, the row of inset rectangular light fixtures above, along with the panels and doorways on either side of the passageway, seem to shunt past with the clockwork regularity of photograms doled out on three receding—or advancing—strips of flicker film.

Two bases have been covered by my first two examples: sheer difference (without photographic imaging) and sheer photo-synthetic illusion (without standard cinematic motion). But no sooner is everything but the apparatus peeled away from such filmic reduction than it seems to be no longer just the filmic apparatus that submits to investigation, but the whole technique of perception. With a shared premium placed on the quasi-hypnotic effects of sheer optic alternation, the "transcendental" or meditative line of experimental practice (so-called visionary filmmaking) as well as the more implacable materialist school (strictly visualistic) are close cousins.[4] Such minimalist exploration frequently brings the most ascetic concerns about material constituents up against the most speculative investigations of "consciousness" per se, a consciousness anatomized in its cognitive apparatus or released at times into mystic pulsations from the sheer impulse to perceive.

The most fascinating examples continue to move between isolated filmic speculations—and indeed potential tantric meditations—on the fleeting strip per se, photochemically imprinted or not, and comparable bracketings of its discrete photogrammatic modules. Like Conrad with *The Flicker*, Stan Brakhage can adduce the contribution of the photogram precisely by avoiding its inclusion in a *non*filmic metacinema. His *Mothlight* (1963) substitutes for photographic record and filmic emulsion an adhesive editing tape to which bits of moth wings, seeds, and petals are affixed. Borrowed rather than imprinted from the real, they are nevertheless, in the lurking second sense of the title, all but as weightless as filmic record in their transference to the strip. Once the tape is projected (in the form of a processed print taken from it), the result is that nature, as it were, shines through unadulterated, unmediated, without the fabrication of photography but with a fluttering animation effect nonetheless. Yet in another sense (and not unlike single photograms in this respect) the traces of organic reality are pinioned and dead—as in some entomology of the real rather than its re-creation. Even without camerawork and frame advance, the impasted strip, though all the more an index of the world in the semiotic sense, is in no way its revivification.

In the realm of photographically composed filmic reflection there is the work of, among other influential minimalists, Paul Sharits. He has a much-discussed 1970 film that seems an extended visual conceit on the very flux of consciousness, a conceit that is even typographically performed up front by the title. As the film unfurls, many layers of overlapped images show streaming water channeled past the screen's rectangular field of view. As the flip side of the unavoidable pun on a modernist stream of consciousness seems to insist, here is the real guilty secret of even "mainstream" film, its sheer (because plastic) materiality and its layered optic rush. It is in this light that Sharits's title—for this film about all filmic flow—brazenly taps the scriptive junctures and ambiguous phonemic overlap that I will be advancing in the last chapter as a constitutive fluxion of the undertextual *phonogram* in impacted literary inscription. At the same time, Sharits's title smuggles in, as part of this same telling irregularity, a typographic play on the sprocket holes of filmic progression in an overload of two-pronged subgrammatical colons. The film is named, if named is the word for it, *S:TREAM:S:S:EC-TION:S:ECTION:S:S:ECTIONED*—or in other words, other more decipherable wording, *Streams Section Sections Sectioned*. The sequential in(de)cisions of this alphabetic ribbon are thus modeled on the very first move of its cross-lexical nexus. *S:TREAM:S*—singular or plural, it comes to the same thing, each photogrammatic image span of streaming water a synecdoche for the flow of the whole strip. The film's title thereby releases, by a stroboscopic elision of its own sibilants, the very root—etymological and material—of its rippling superimpositions. This is only to say, anticipating the Bergsonian critique of cinema's sectioned duration to be explored in the next two chapters, that Sharits's film puts s/ections (photograms) back in any and all projections. It is in this manner that the film not only participates in but inculcates what he elsewhere terms a "cinematics" of the medium.[5]

In a similar spirit, the title of Morgan Fisher's *Production Stills* (1970) seems a sentence as well as a phrase. All cinema stills the world in production, from microsecond to microsecond. Fisher's "stagy" exception sardonically distorts the norm, even while taming and clarifying it. The film is wholly composed of shots from the set of the film being made, this film right here and now. These are still shots printed and pinned to a white background recording various stages in camera placement, blocking, and lighting. One affixation of the profilmic space after another, of course, is all a movie ever is, only more so (and less) here—where one means of fixing the image alludes to another. This happens when the black-shadowed pushpins that hold each of the sequential stills tight to its nonprojected wall end up, the longer we look, resembling the sprocket holes that would flank the same image if it had become a photogram on the celluloid strip—or, as Sharits might say, on the sectioned s:t:rip.

Where *The Flicker* and *Mothlight* trump the photogram with modes of filmic marking more rudimentary yet, and *S:TREAM:S* evokes by full title the essentially photogrammatic discontinuities its lyric eddy of images washes away onscreen, two of Hollis Frampton's most renowned films, like Fisher's *Production Stills,* encounter the renegade photogram only through the metonymy of the single opaque print. Frampton's stringent, witty variations on what we will later find him insisting on in his prose texts as the screen's absolute "rectangle" do not so much expose the single photogram as exposit its operations in regard to a whole range of photographic associations, from emotive to ontological. Two of his titles again give direct guidance. Together *(nostalgia)* (1971), with a small *n* for immediately bracketed photogrammatic losses rather than a melodramatic uppercase for the past mourned in general by cinematography, and *Poetic Justice* (1972), with its own metapoetic revenge on the scripted image of cinema, theorize the very basis of cinematic referentiality in synchronous mechanization.

One of the most celebrated avant-garde films about photography, Frampton's *(nostalgia)* is therefore, in structural force, as much about the photogram as about the photograph: an encoded fable of filmic succession. In this respect, and more than the self-referential closed circuit of *Production Stills,* it delves into the always syncopated elisions of the projective mechanism. *(nostalgia)* is a first-person film essay constructed around (and upon) a dozen separate photographs (of Frampton's own earlier making) burned away in slow sequence over a hot plate, each new image come and gone while the next in line (still unseen) is being verbally described on the vocal track. In a tempting synecdoche for the film's whole procedure, a piece of Frampton's wry voice-over concerning his self-portrait—"My entire physical body has been replaced more than once since it made this portrait of its face" (47)—has a way of putting us in mind of the underlying file of photograms themselves.[6] Any image on film (including any index of the filmmaker's person) is, like the molecular body itself, replaced from microsecond to microsecond by a structure much like it—but not self-identical with it. Then, too, every single screen image is always out of sync with the narrativity that consumes it in passing, the discrete image frame unseen as such within the enunciation that motivates and outruns it—unseen except in (ordinarily instantaneous and here protracted) vanishing. Even the animation effect of the disappearing photogram is evoked by the wriggling dance of ashen fragments as they writhe and buckle in disintegration on the hot plate, long after the image itself has passed from visibility. And Frampton goes further yet in laying bare his own material base as filmmaker. To halt what looks to the naked eye like the rudimentary single image (the photograph, portrait or otherwise), only to find that it burns up in its arrest as if it were a photogram fatally detained not over a kitchen appliance but before the lamp of the apparatus, is surely to thicken the film's photogrammatic allegory.[7]

The same may be happening with the mounting, hyperbolic "horror" of the last verbally depicted but never seen photo, involving (we are told) a mysterious double reflection from a truck's rearview mirror and a facing warehouse window. If we yearn for an actual photograph, just one more, to be brought into belated fit with this last portentous account, we have only one choice at (distant) hand: the imprint that began the whole sequence, a photograph never mentioned on the voice track—and thus still begging for some frail delayed ties to verbal explication. First of the twelve, this is the shot of a photographic laboratory where, though unseen on-screen, any and all film begins—and whose revelation at any point would indeed come as a shock to the projective system, a horror of horrors for the cause of transparent mimesis.

Like *(nostalgia)*, where the expendable photograph may stand in for the photogram, *Poetic Justice* seems denuded of photogrammatic evidence or reference until editing alone comes to infer its rapid passing. Here is the setup—a single one at that. The camera holds on a tabletop where loose-leaf pages accrue (by quickcut editing alone) in a mounting stack, each describing a single camera shot or movement. Page by page, frame by frame, we get only the transcribed shot plan that scripts in advance a sequence of still or dissolving images—never the images themselves.[8] The last of the pages in *Poetic Justice*, accreting as they do only toward a film about themselves in series, is number 240. Arbitrary multiple, perhaps, of cinema's twenty-four frames per second, the descriptor reads ambiguously: "(Close-Up) Your hand covers a still photo of my own face." Is this a still shot or a moving image? Is the hand seen already covering the face or filmed in the act of covering it? There is no telling from not showing. With film's very animation effect in suspension, what follows (from this) is the next and last jump cut across the duration (as always) of a single photogram—precipitating what we might call the title scene of the whole unrealized visual narrative: a scene of poetic (that is, filmic) justice in an ironic reversal of cinematic expectation. Throughout Frampton's film, thirsting for the true photographic index as we are prodded to do, we get mere verbal symbols instead—until the sudden appearance of a latex glove instantaneously blocking out the last page of script with its final slap in the face to the very idea of a photographed live body. The glove is merely the veneer and prosthesis of an organic real: a parodic plastic index. Still perhaps warm from the retained form of fingers, it offers a reductive version of that sculptural mold—displaced vesture rather than residue—of the lived body from which André Bazin famously sees all photographic art deriving, a kind of "decal" or "transfer" of the real.[9] Like a photograph, and unlike the signifier "photograph," this index would (naturally enough) arrive like the removed superfice of visual reality, the virtual shed skin of its now inorganic basis.

I have spoken twice in connection with Frampton, and implicitly before, of filmic fable or allegory. What I mean by this needs to be distinguished from a different but symmetrical argument advanced by a recent scholar of the avant-garde. David James makes a symptomatic claim in this regard about *(nostalgia)*, and implicitly about much subcultural or avant-garde film. For him too Frampton's automatic burning up of photographs over the hot plate is figurative, yet not of the fragility of film's plastic matter but rather of the social context that inevitably embeds both portraiture and other naturalistic photography. In this particular film, with its long good-bye to the auteurist freight of autobiography, Frampton is found "burning his social bridges behind him, as if he were allegorizing his passage into an aesthetic and institutional system that demanded the cancellation of personal history"[10]—canceled, that is, to make room for the rigorous scrutiny, elsewhere and to come, of what James calls "pure film." My own reading suggests that the figuration of Frampton's experiment, by contrast, has at present embarked upon the inquisition of film's autonomous incrementality. In the mechanically desynchronized lag time of their sequential incineration, the burned traces of the social real have *already* given way—and just before their realization as plausible documents—given way formally or structurally, that is, to the narratively disabled disappearing act of "pure" filmic seriality.

What is really at stake in my difference from James on this point? The answer comes clear only by thinking of the photogram as merely the thinnest driven wedge of a heightened perceptual attention. Rightly for James, films of the 1960s subculture explicitly engage, in both intent and effect, the very operations of perception and reception. Moreover, such cinema offers "privileged occasions" for understanding the workings of the mind (260)—in other words, the working over of world by mind. For commercial narrative cinema, of course, this disruptive assumption about the radical mindscape of screen space must go mostly undeclared in the screen's relatively transparent world view. It remains part of the camera's naturalized adequation to perceptual life. Otherwise reception ends up questioning its own operative mechanisms through screen perturbance. The photogram in its rare mainstream obtrusion thus seems to be probing at an unsettling level the mind's processing of submerged signals. Again the undertext: a concept readily assimilated to a vertical model of the psyche, with its surface resilience and its unruly depth charges. To this psychodynamic layering of familiar narrative cinema as filmic matter—indebted, as it is, more to the clinical abstractions of avant-garde materialism than to any attempted evocation of unconscious or dream states in a surrealist screen rhetoric—we will be returning at the end of the second chapter. In anticipation I would suggest that whereas photogrammatic upheaval in experimental cinema may seem to figure rather directly the vagaries of consciousness, the effect is more oblique, to say nothing of less frequent, in commercial production. There the prototype from human consciousness (and nonconsciousness) functions via a generally suppressed level of machination whose very suppression, and by the automatism itself, serves the purpose of a realized—and realistically invested—subjectivity in the act of reception.

Which brings us round again to the more than terminological difference between James's "allegories of cinema" (the commercial institution refigured in its very exile through purified device) and my reciprocal stress on the "filmic" moment within cinema. In the subcultural avant-garde, according to James, film encodes its own properties and operations in such a way as to evoke (often ironically) all that it exempts from attention, all the commerce and cultural emplacement it temporarily suspends. In industrial narrative filmmaking, by contrast, the allegorical tendency would have to go in the other direction, from commodity circulation within a mass audience's naturalistic expectations of the medium to a resurgent stress on the textuality of the image. Viewed under contextual pressure, according to James, experimental film factors in the austere constraints of its making and reception—and all they exclude. Under another pressure, realist cinema narrates, far more sporadically, the masked ingredients of its mediation. For James, all the rigorous delimitations of avant-garde practice, in their structural "purity," are in fact a forced (but always incomplete) purge, vulnerable at every turn to "the return of its repressed milieu" (275). Everything these films banish from view, not only about the assembly-line cinema they repudiate but about the social sphere from which its commercialism derives, becomes the structuring absence, so to speak, of their structuration. This is the allegory James finds them performing over and over again: the encrypted cognizance of all they seem to have evaded. Even if one is not everywhere ready to grant this argument about particular experimental texts, it should be possible to entertain its obverse in the coming chapters. Whether or not minimalist cinema may be able at some points to keep relatively free of, rather than just to hold at bay, the conditions of cultural production from which it departs, it is certainly the case that narrative cinema in its traditional commercial form need not naturalize into total oblivion the artifice it lives on, photograms and all. On the contrary, their return to cinematic attention as a filmic engravement within narrative engagement is the very subject this chapter has set out to explore. We should be prepared to think of it by this point, reversing James, as the "allegory of film" from within the naturalistic apparition of industrial cinema.

THE MUMMY'S RETURN

Building on the "phototropic" polarity sketched in the introduction, this chapter will now move between the scene of inlaid photographs and that site of cinematographic registration per se where film offers a more forthright manifesto of its own photomechanical manifestation. Discussion will focus on the filmed photo in correlation with the film-as-photograms—a difference, let us say, between the photopan of *Blade Runner* and the famous freeze at the end of François Truffaut's *The 400 Blows* (whose detailed discussion is postponed until chapter 3). Surfaced by this correlation is the generative systemic connection between the photographs you see at times within a screened space and those that, by seeing the space as such, you don't. Questions of presence that surround (virtually frame) the former may accrue to the latter as well. Is it photography or death one associates with an absolute halt to human time, a conversion of subject to object, a displacement of the perceived from the world's space into an "otherworld" of disembodiment, a visible limit to the capacity for ever returning a look? Such conditions apply, in fact, to both death *and* photography at once—or to the one in terms of the other, interchangeably—in the implicit interchange they sometimes establish not only within the course of a film narrative but at the material basis of its cellular advance.

Fifteen years before Bazin published his influential remarks on the relation of plastic arts to the "mummy complex," the original film version of *The Mummy* (Carl Freund, 1932) showed Boris Karloff, having escaped from the cerements of a millennial coffin in the opening scene, being handed a photograph that must have been taken just after exhumation and made to stare at a preserved image of himself as preserved mummy: in every sense an *arresting* redundancy.[11] One then asks to what extent the film itself—as in some sense the reanimated "mummy" its name denotes, and yet standing in this way for all film—might partake in the status of its own protagonist: an instance of death in motion, a chemical burial and its fleeting resuscitation, frame upon (rather than after) frame. If so, prevailing views would have to be revised. Certainly the predominant trend of recent image theory, much of it taking its cues from Bazin, is disposed, in contrasting film to photography, to align only the latter with death—and this despite Bazin's own extension of the "mummy complex" to include time's sequential animation as a paradoxically embalmed duration (see chapter 3). In "What Photography Calls Thinking," Stanley Cavell notes in retrospect, concerning his intermittent speculation in *The World Viewed* on the question of "photography's participation in death," that he was "prompted to it by what I had read of André Bazin, with his recurrent sense of the photograph as a kind of life mask of the world, the twin of a death mask."[12] Further along, Cavell hints at an overarching distinction between photography in this regard and film, pointing out that "stillness emphasizes the death in mortal existence while motion emphasizes the life of it" (12). Though he quickly (if cryptically) adds that "both speak of both, in their particular ways," Cavell's abiding figure of stasis as deathlike is comparable to that of Barthes, whose *Camera Lucida* has set the tone, and offered the metaphors, for the most influential recent approaches to photography. The deathliness of the photograph is in fact, in its visual candor, what recommends the medium to Barthes in preference to cinema.[13]

For Barthes the photograph is the epitome of the transgression of antithesis that preoccupied him in his major work on narrative theory, *S/Z*. In photography, what Barthes calls the "paradigm" of "Life/Death" is "reduced to a simple click, the one separating the initial pose from the final print."[14] He considers this breach a species of murder that also results in a sort of memorial preservation, since the stilled image can be read at the same time, in its stopped time, as both a "fatality" (6) and a "return of the dead" (9), a kind of slaughter and a kind of haunting. Christian Metz cites the work of Philippe Dubois as developing further a notion of photography as "thanatography."[15] Metz agrees with Dubois and Barthes that this is a conceptualization to be reserved for photography rather than cinematography. Since for Metz "immobility and silence" are not only "objective aspects" of death but its chief *figurations* in our culture (83), photography falls into place as a comparable instance of such silent arrest. Metz insists, like Barthes, on "the selective kinship of photography (not film) with death," since film "gives back to the dead a semblance of life" (84), at least of that motion associated with life. Yet what is this "semblance of life" but a form of nonlife, another mode of death, a phantasmal perpetuation, wrested from and spun out of its own time into another?

Cavell is of course quite right about the general relation of stillness to death, by contrast to the motion that conveys life. This is, however, a distinction within what seems a deeper common denominator. For the interrelation of film and photography emphasizes, before all, the *absence* at the back of each, with moving images as much as stilled ones an "abduction" (Metz's term for photography alone [84]) from one world into another. What is dead about a corpse is not only its stasis but the sense of subtracted life it conveys, the sense of what has been evacuated from behind its eyes. Moving pictures no less than static ones are a visible function of nonpresence, a trace of the passed away. Such photographically based representation results in either a disembodied imprint on paper or a spectral emanation from the imprinted celluloid in the projector. The immediate difference of stillness from motion in these two media may therefore serve in the end merely to specify death's relation to both. The difference, one might say, is between the cadaverous and the ghostly. (Or in the terms offered to us by *The Asphyx* at the start, between an encorpsed death and death's perpetual encroachment, between the dead as absent and the mediate presence of death-at-work.)

To observe all this, however, is still to leave undetailed the deepest (because smallest) relation of cinema to photography—hence of cinema to the ephemera of the single image. This is the relation that the rest of the book will build on the present essay to investigate: the *passing away* that precedes all *coming to be* in cinema's spectral presence, each instant of imaging the ghost of its own foremath. Short of disclosing this fact by breaking the flow of motion entirely, there is much that narrative film's attraction to photographic moments can bring up as topic— and bring out as optic trope—concerning the life-denying photographicity at the plastic basis of the moving image. I take this to be at least part of what is going on, going forward, in the single forty-five-minute zoom shot of a New York loft in that most influential of all minimalist films, Michael Snow's *Wavelength* (1967). Long before the shot has closed upon the photograph of ocean waves pinned between windows on the opposite wall, it has floated forward over the fallen body (corpse?) of a man who has entered the filmic space from our side of the camera, entered it only to drop to the floor and eventually drop from advancing sight. Aside from what David James might call this "allegory" of excluded melodramatic narrative, what is the underlying *filmic* point? It might well be this: The camera's telos is always photographic, the only true alternative it has to those flanking windows that offer a different ocular access to the outside world. Further, for film to keep going, it must always ignore those otherwise distracting stop-actions (the

small passing deaths of the moving real) that in this case, with the asymptotic photograph on the far wall, it must for once eventually confront.

   Given the prominence of death and dying both represented and figured by
the still image across my chapters, this first of them is perhaps overdue for a disclaimer. This book does not set itself the task of broadly aligning photographic theory with film theory. It proposes no definitive conceptual intersection of the two
media. It is, in short, not about cinema and photography but about cinema *as* photography. That is why it must necessarily remain unconcerned in any detail with
all the things that may properly be noted about photographic ways of seeing apart
from their instituted arrest. Set aside for the most part are the social, economic,
and psychosexual uses and abuses of the photochemically indexed world, except
when certain screen narratives take them up. This book is preoccupied instead with
the mechanical fixation of the photograph and with the incursions of its discreteness into the projected filmic track.

   That is why, in turn, it is drawn primarily to the Bazin-Barthes line among
commentators on the photographic medium—and drawn, further, to entertain the
likely reasons behind Barthes's own singular emphasis on violated temporality in
the photographic object. It appears that his interest in photography derives less
from his free-form semiotics than from his career-long emphasis on denaturalization. He thus parts company with a whole tradition of historicized photographic
theory, which sees the mid-nineteenth century's breakthrough medium as the
evolutionary fulfillment of the mimetic impulse in a new immediacy and vividness of mechanized representation. For Barthes, the medium's automatic quality
does not guarantee the unprecedentedly lifelike. This is the mythology he sets out
to detonate. By insisting on the way photographic capture makes for an amputa-
tion of lived time, he denaturalizes its tacit claims for the lifelike preservation of
the moment. In any case, Barthes's tendentious stress on mechanized death need
not be true, crucial, or paramount about photography as a cultural or aesthetic object in order for arrest to be the most apposite and determining aspect of photography in the normal *overcoming* of its medium by film. That's all we need to agree
on in order to proceed. Here too a distinction between commercial and experimental practice grows apparent. With a notable exception like *Wavelength* (but
only because it has established a diegetic space and its traverse), the recursive photographicity of the filmic projection is not repeatedly thematized as death in
avant-garde cinema because such abstract or mimimalist images are not usually
vested with lifelike transparency in the first place. When experimental cinema re-
constitutes the spectatorial gaze, its medium-specificity does not need to figure
what it reforms. That is a large part of its point. Narrative cinema, on the other
hand, reaches for an idea, often the stark notion of mortal fixity, in order to placate thematically the textual gaps it sometimes brings to the surface.

   In such narrative, a moment of photographic stasis associated with death, loss,
memory—a moment psychologically fixed upon or technologically held fixed, as
for instance in a photopan and freeze-frame, respectively—may nevertheless give
time for an indirect confession of a film's own founding upon both absence and
stasis. This might happen despite the way death within plot often tends to thema-

tize—and so to absorb—the disruptive potential that could otherwise sabotage the photochemical illusions of the whole cinematic continuum. For the most part stasis is deployed as a strategy of enunciation, so that in turn it can be comfortably *interpreted* by the viewer: the freeze-frame, say, as a figuration for death's violent arrest of time. Interpreting a film as narrative, however, need not exhaust our reading of it as text. Between a film narrative's sustained enunciation and a film text's momentarily displayed constitution by photograms, between ocular effect and material basis, there opens, as suggested, the space for a theoretical interception of the text. It is at this level that the photogrammatic moment, even against the grain of narrative recuperation, may sometimes dynamite and anatomize a film's illusion of movement. For doesn't the held image occasionally remind us that the stillness of photography, its halt and hush, is never entirely shaken loose by sequential movement in and as film but is merely lost to notice? And if and when this founding stillness is "recalled" to view, may it not be understood as a sign of a death-dealing discreteness? At the very least we may assume that before film can whisk away such stasis into reactivated continuity, the questions induced by a freeze-frame may swell to the conceptual breaking point. Is the photographic arrest of film a temporary rejection of cinematic kinesis or the smallest measurable unit of its projection, a fleeting default of the moving image or its vivisection? In other words, film's absolute contradiction or its basic component? The immediate discursive *effect* is usually a controlled rupture (interpretable, say, as metaphor) rather than a disclosed rudiment. Especially if such a moment is quickly covered over, covered for, by the return to moving images, the film system may serve to fend off—by defining itself against—the intrusion of stillness. Nevertheless, the foregrounding of the photographic element, precisely *because* it can provide a node of contrast with cinema, recovers in the process a cinematic precondition. The confident differentiation of film *from* mere photography cannot, in short, be secured without the reciprocal implication of those differences *between* successive photograms upon which all film is fashioned.

IN PLANE SIGHT: CINEMA'S OPTIC RECESS

I want therefore to look at the way certain mainstream films look at photographs and, in so doing, at themselves implicitly as photographs. A classic instance recommends itself as a point of departure, partly because it has not escaped previous notice in just the terms we need. The instance is Max Ophuls's *Letter from an Unknown Woman* (1948), the brief suggestive commentary an article by Raymond Bellour.[16] Ophuls's main narrative is a flashback bracketed by the protagonist (Louis Jourdan) reading a letter from a former mistress (Joan Fontaine) left unsigned at her death and posted by hospital authorities. In a scene interrupting the flashback about midway through its reconstruction of her story, the hero examines a set of photos, enclosed in the letter, of the dead woman he barely remembers and the dead son he never saw (figs. 24-26). To study the reframing of these postmortem photographic documents within cinematic space, Bellour draws on Barthes's distinction between cinematic temporality as that which "doubles life"

24

25

26

and photographic temporality as that which "is brushed by death" (6). Though Bellour doesn't mention the thematic parallel, the posthumously delivered image of a woman already in the grave, whose enunciated letter inaugurates the film in voice-over with the words "By the time you read this I may be dead," serves to recall in particular Barthes's favored example of a young man photographed on death row. The doomed man's image—and in this it digests all photography for Barthes—seems to announce its referent, through a demonstrative rather than a personal or impersonal pronoun, with the tacit admission: "*that* is dead and *that* is going to die."[17] The paradoxical reverse order of this admission, death before dying, is exactly Barthes's point: image executed before body, the given finality anticipating the eventual. In other words, every photograph in a sense announces that "by the time you see me I'll be dead"—dead in at least one sense, gone from my time into yours.

A Barthesian double take on the nature of photography—life canceled by being captured—sends provocative shock waves through the scene of contemplated photographs in the middle of Ophuls's film. According to Bellour our view of them, along the hero's line of sight, retards narrative just long enough to induce a meditation on filmic images (photograms in motion) in precisely their difference from photography. We might add that the funerary overtone of this effect is enhanced by the sequential shots (figs. 24 and 26) of the son growing from infancy through a dead-ended boyhood in two discrete stages of ultimately truncated aging.[18] In any case, Bellour says, what results from such contemplated photos is a "recoil" (6) in the system that is also, it seems, conveyed to the ironies of plot. It is not simply that the hero receives photographs that one might call obituary images because of their subjects' previous deaths within the plot. The time he has killed in examining these images, and the letter that contained them, has delayed him too long to flee, as he had initially planned, from an impending duel. (By the time you read this, *you* may be as good as dead.) Dramatized here is something of what Barthes means when, about three-quarters of the way through *Camera Lucida*, he shifts his previous axis of comparison between photography and death. From that point on he sees not only the execution of a photograph but also its reception as participating in such dying. He thereby personalizes, internalizes, the "that has been" of a photograph as "this imperious sign of my future death" (97).

One particular photograph of the past, the image of mother and son together (fig. 25), carries a further ironic charge. They are photographed in a carnival attraction that inserts their living bodies within a painted artifice of flight, inevitably recalling the famous scene earlier in the film when Lisa and Stefan, on their first night together, visit a fairground. It is there that they "ride" in a simulated train car while pay-by-the-mile vistas on a painted protofilmic scroll sweep past their curtain-framed window. Taken years after this moment, the balloon photo seems to hint that the mother has returned with the son, issue of her deluded passion, to a sideshow comparable to the site of an original romantic illusion(ism). She locates herself once more against a pictured sham of motion, though a motion caught this time in stasis. The carnival backdrop thus puts the effect of stasis even before its supplemental photographic cause. But there is still more. When the images are enlarged through a magnifying glass held by the hero, and for us by a cinematic close-up, what results is the ironic telescoping of a fatally elapsed history. For the enlarged photo recovers a glimpse of the image as it was originally received through the camera lens: the image, that is, as available to focus and registration when still in the reciprocal presence of the living subject and the photographer. In this illusionistic tunnel vision into the past, a ghostly parody of the aura of origin is no sooner conveyed by the curved glass, however, than it is ruled out as a mere ocular association, putting the final seal on the over and gone.[19]

In *Letter from an Unknown Woman,* the images of the dead lover and son, by never fitting flush with the cinematic frame—never filling up the entire plane of vision—do not entirely close the gap between the cinematic rudiment and the funereal status of their own images as separable photographs. If, on consideration, these static images briefly disturb our acceptance of the film's continuous image track, they do so only up to a point. For a more decisive irruption of the illusionistic system, cinematic narrative requires the encompassing (often elegiac) stasis of either a full-screen photograph or a multiplied single photogram. In either case, what remains to be explored in this chapter is the way narrative can move to contain even the very potential for such disruption. It does so either by plotting the photomechanical incursion as the scene's own inclusion of a photographic object or else by absorbing such stasis to the system of enunciation as the punctuating rhetoric of a freeze-frame.

The difference in question is between imaged motionlessness and the "motionless" image. Whereas the cinematic inset of the refilmed still print is often visibly "recessed" from the screen plane, the displacement occasioned by the freeze-frame is conceptual instead, dropping back in recognition from projected scene to projecting track. In each recursive case, however, cinema prosecutes its on-screen image by allusive recourse to its photographic basis. Cinema in this sense recurs to the filmic either by embedding photography's kindred imprint— both precursor and contributor to the cinematic apparatus—or by installing in suspension not only film's frame-based stasis but the discreteness of its accretions in and as cinema. Instead of a recursion built upon sheer recurrence, that is, in the case of internal recess cinema seems rather to *incur* the photographic object as part of its recording obligation. Not so with the freeze-frame, which jams the system by thrusting its constitutive elements into the forefront. What we will come to see is that in either case, such a holding action of photographic stasis against the normal progression of cinematic picture(s)—this affront to the movie by the still—highlights the death that frequently motivates it within plot as a profound correlative of cinematic (not just photographic) imaging. Any such full-screen, hermetically sealed fit between visual continuity and the units of its succession, whether secured by a photograph in close-up or by the closing down of narrative upon a freeze-frame, becomes a temporal crisis for narrative discourse itself, around which the temporal violence of plotted death tends to gather implications.[20]

These implications have to do with a constitutive difference between the photographic frame and the cinematic edge. A photograph appears to contain its image, we might say, whereas a film seems to constrain what it places on view, to keep back all that might from moment to moment crowd upon its moving visual field. One effect of a photograph filling the cinematic frame is to deny to this cinematic "constraint"—in its sudden coincidence with the borders of the photographic "enclosure"—any sense of a world impinging upon it from offscreen, any latent indexing of the contiguous. This is to say that the film camera may seem almost to trespass upon the photograph's space without at all broadening the perimeters of that scopic field. (An exception like the digital scan of the replicant's photo in *Blade Runner,* where we seem to peer around the edges of recorded space, only teases us into certifying the norm.) The difference between any such inlaid photograph and the freeze-frame serves in turn to divide up the general aspects of narrative between the diegetic activity of rendered story and the optic activity of projected narration.[21] Photographic stillness—glimpsed momentarily in either the isolable framed images of a photopan, say, or the negated action of full-screen fixity—is the death-in-life of the cinematic continuum, what the next chapter will call the negative imprint of its own momentum.

In the latter case, when the image track reprints a differential unit of its own duration, renewing itself through a second-generation image, such cinematic reflexivity, though arrested, has become curiously exact. The film has become almost transparent to itself, but only at the moment, and at the price, of its canceled succession, its negation as moving picture. The freeze-frame thus is not in the ordinary sense self-referential, for its point of reference is not the continuous representational illusion that is film. Such a held frame does not really so much reduplicate the nature or effect of cinema as repudiate it, by stalling upon the cinema's smallest unit. If in a scene involving a framed still image (a photograph in close-up, say) the density of representation inevitably seems thickened, compounded, then in the case of a stop-action image this density appears raised to the power of itself.

Motion is not a deceit in cinema; images are in fact speeding past all the time. But there are no bodies moving, no faces changing expression, only the pictures of bodies and faces being constantly replaced by others somewhat like them. The freeze "frame," involving no fewer actual "frames" per second than any of those shots that seem to contain action, can therefore be seen as that paradoxical case of real motion without real movements that takes the condition of cinema to its extinguishing limit. By contrast, the refilmed photograph is inevitably a more conservative gesture toward the image track that permits it. Even when, framed and glassed or not, it is widened to the edges of the screen frame, it is still not identical, only coextensive, with the other sense of the cinematographic frame, the photogram in iteration. Such an image remains an object of the camera, profilmic, even as—like a painting on film, though in very different ways—it can generate metafilmic ramifications.[22]

It is time again to answer the call of examples. After considering the bond between visual arrest and fatality induced by stop-action frames in Roger Spottiswoode's 1983 film *Under Fire,* I will turn to the more elusive overtones of mortality in the calculated fusion of cinematographic photograms and diegetic photographs in a pivotal scene of inset imaging from Terrence Malick's 1973 *Badlands*. In neither film is that "participation in death" (Cavell's term again) finally contained within the story as exclusively an aspect of the single photographic image. Rather, such an association with death contaminates the materiality of cinematic discourse itself as another name for those disavowed fundaments of absence and stasis that are continuously masked by illusory moving presences on the screen.

TAKEN FROM LIFE

In medias res: a shooting spree. From moment to moment in the title sequence of *Under Fire*, the instantaneous absentation of body from its image. Life ambushed by trigger-happy craft. From gun barrel to the camera's telescopic sight, one never knows where the next shot is coming from. Spottiswoode's film opens by interrupting the continuous-action color footage of Chad guerrilla fighters with black-and-white freeze-frames that halt them in their tracks, one after the other brought up short in the serial line of fire. The last of these stopped frames comes before us as the black-masked rectangle of a cropped image—warrior on elephant in combat with helicopter (fig. 27)—that eventually becomes, by quick transition, the photographer-hero's *Time* cover story on commercial display in another international "hot spot" (fig. 28). Its doctored color offers merely a more salable representation of the violence it feeds on, stolen from one time and sold to another. With the prologue over, the plot is now upon us. In a different Third World "market" (Nicaragua now), the original agent of this journalistic sale is about to pay, rather than receive, a very different price for the enforced exercise of his craft. At risk of his own life, he must turn death's fixity back into a simulation of mere technological arrest.

The ironic reversal comes about in no uncertain terms. When the photographer (Nick Nolte) shifts assignments to Central America, he is soon kidnapped and ordered by Nicaraguan guerrillas to simulate a "live" photograph of their recently gunned down leader, Rafael, to keep the revolution itself alive. So far the rebel leader "has never been photographed," his fame broadcast instead—or desecrated

27   28

29

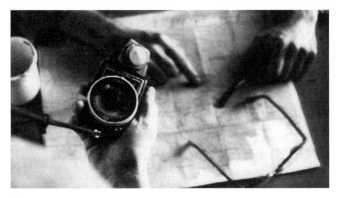

32

30

(fig. 29)—in the form of painted placards. The idea of the rephotographed corpse is a stunning one, on the part of the rebels and the film as well. Nolte hears of this bizarre demand when encountering the dead man in the dark barn of a makeshift mausoleum. As light pierces the chinks of shutters (fig. 30) and falls upon the bloodless corpse already beginning to turn "monochromatic," like a photograph (fig. 31), this secret funereal chamber (in Spanish, this *camera oscura*) stages in advance a combined process of arrested time and photosynthetic restitution similar to what takes place behind the lens the next morning, from a point of view we now share with Nolte. Amid various props of the campaign, including a map of the territory he would reclaim and glasses removed from his (forever sightless) eyes, the stiffened hands of Rafael are posed in a dissimulated temporary repose (fig. 32) while a henchman next to the momentarily vertical cadaver (his head held up by the hair by an invisible hand behind) defiantly brandishes a newspaper headline supposedly misrepresenting the hero's death (fig. 33). The scene is thus readied for the second most important shot of Rafael's career after the one that took his life: this time, a shot that will seem merely to take him in his life.

An inert body braced from behind for its tautological arrest by the camera seems almost to parody the nineteenth-century prosthetic devices, mentioned by Barthes (13), whereby the first photographic subjects were trussed into stasis long enough for registration. It was originally as if the body had to become a sarcophagus of itself before being taken over as photographic effigy. Here, by contrast, speed is everything. Timed to the photographer's flash, the head must be yanked into position for an apparent stare into the camera, at which point the color tableau at the moment of

31

registration cuts—without freezing for once—into the black and white of newsprint reproduction (fig. 34), visible in immediate transition as a perused international headline (fig. 35) and immediately thereafter as a new placard held aloft by the vanguard of the revolution's second wind (fig. 36).[23]

The world press is so galvanized by this miraculous revival that a former reporter promoted to television anchorman (Gene Hackman) is sent back into action to cover the story. When, in the film's climactic sequence, Hackman is shot to death in the street at point-blank range, we once again, as in the opening sequence, see the action footage of his fall broken down as staccato freeze-frames. Again each image appears in the form of black-and-white point-of-view (POV) shots through the lens of Nolte's power-drive camera (fig. 37), its operator immobilized at a distance and unable to help his friend. These pictures, too, are awaited by the media, to be processed in ways that reflect back on the routine mode of their capture so far.

This asks for a moment's additional reflection. Whenever the film has previously blocked out a unit of its own duration, the pictorial and the narrational have seemed to coincide in an evocation of the photographer's eventual printed record, present on the screen almost by metonymy. Seen through the lens of the camera before the shutter closes again, the world would of course be channeled through in color. As chemically processed, however, perhaps even as imagined on the spot in the expert eye of the photographer behind the lens, the 35 mm status of the framed image is already translated to that of black-and-white print. In other words, what we might for once call a literal subjective-camera shot (in a photographer's eye line but as yet

33, 34, 35

36

37

38   39

prospective view of the image as finished print) is transferred on the spot to a
processed and developed registration of the visual field, the world already flattened to newsprint-ready image. Then, too, the connection between this canni-
balizing of the world for documents and the murder of its autonomous vitality
is directly thematized by the plot.

    This ironic development of the narrative reverses yet again, in effect, the ear-
lier animation of the heroic corpse. It turns out that many of the photos of guerrillas taken in idle fascination by Nolte, having fallen into the hands of the government forces, are used as a kind of visual hit list that the hero, the unwitting
culprit of imprint, discovers late in the game in a spy's secret chamber (fig. 38). No
sooner are they brought to light than the revolutionary subjects are expunged. As
if making good on an atavistic fear, modern technology and its media circuits have
indeed stolen the soul (at least the life) of the Third World combatants whose
image they have made over to spectacle. At the same time, as if to rescue the evidentiary status of photography, it is the photo of the hero and friends with his
Time cover, held up in celebration at a nightclub early on, that the heroine will
later use to track his missing person (fig. 39)—in counterpoint, as it happens, with
the broadcast death of the anchorman and media guru, her former lover, playing
in the background at the hospital where she is searching for Nolte.

    The video dissemination of these images has come about as follows. Just after
Hackman's murder, Nolte has concealed the results of the rapid-fire shooting of
a shooting from the military police, who are attempting to confiscate the negatives. Soon after, these photos appear on international TV in doctored form as
moving (and politically motivating) footage on the evening news—the separate
snapshots, that is, sped together, narrativized, into approximate "live action" (figs.
40-42). What we know we are seeing of the reporter's original photo frames on
television, though, is of course no more and no less than the founding illusion of
all cinema. However disguised in transmission, what we see is not a video image
to begin with, not an image digitalized at the source. Rather, it is generated from
a series of stilled moments stitched together as the represented phases (without
the intervals) of a fatal movement. Whereas the inherent stasis of photography,
in that photo of Rafael, allows the illusion of life in suspension, the inherent sta-

sis-in-motion of cinema permits in this case the illusion of
murder in action. This recalls the technologic of Brian de
Palma's *Blow Out* (1981), where separate photographs of a
mysterious car crash are spliced together by laboratory animation techniques, then matched with a separately
recorded sound track complete with gunshot, to produce an
(artificial?) film document of the incriminating accident.

In the long run, however, *Under Fire* takes its irony beyond cinema into the digital information circuits—where
broadcast transforms artificial montage into authentic reportage—only to return the irony at the end to its source in
photography. After TV's conversion of photographs to putative moving-image narrative in this obituary case, as if by
some compensatory logic *Under Fire* soon closes with the
decinematizing of its own images once again. We revisit certain sites, certain actual shots, that we have seen before, now
in black and white: images of the hero and heroine at various
points of the film's itinerary, in the guerrilla camp, in the
war-ravaged ghetto, crossing deserted streets, taking cover,
and so on, including another image of those lethal if unwitting espionage images in the spy's closet once reshot by the
photographer just before seating himself before them in
mourning (fig. 43). In these freeze-frame truncations of all
further movement, the trajectory of plot, the impulse of narrative itself, returns in fixation to the earlier turning points
that have composed it—to become, in the end-title coda, a
mere dossier of itself in stills. These images no longer register as freeze-frames at all but seem more like a quick-cut
montage of photographs. It is one of the few case I know in
film narrative where virtual production stills are enfolded
into the diegesis—to mark in closing what amounts to the
film's own filing away in the archives.

40, 41, 42

43

These capping images function quite differently both from the locus classicus of the last held shot in *The 400 Blows* (1959) and from the "photo finish" death scenes so frequent in the late 1960s and early 1970s, from *Butch Cassidy and the Sundance Kid* (George Roy Hill, 1969) down through *Gallipoli* (Peter Weir, 1981). Instead of being read as ordinary freeze-frames, the elegiac last stills of *Under Fire* acquire the taint of closure-as-death solely from the ambiguous temporal status of the film's earlier stop-action frames. These have all along provided not only optical arrest but narrative extension: partly a breach in visual continuity, but partly an extrapolation from the immediate scene into its own documentary aftermath (from carnage to cover story, say). Drawing on one of the oldest tropes in documentary cinema and its fictional derivations, the freeze-frames have operated, in other words, as at once the reflexive halt to sequence and the caught moment's eventual consequence in a developed photograph. It is exactly this two-stage process that the final containment by video broadcast, if it were anything but the jerry-built cinematic artifice it is, would inevitably cause to collapse. In the ordinary case, from the moment of video recording to the moment of TV viewing, all is electronic. The material bodies of photograph and photogram alike are long gone. With its late and studied proliferation of the freeze-frame, however, *Under Fire* seems to hold out against this going—this leaving without a photographic taking—as film's own resistance to the new video dispensation. What video has failed on the spot to capture in the anchorman's assassination, the filmic process can successfully manufacture: the revelatory image not just of a corpse but of death in progress. (Something like the political history of this break between cinematic and digital imaging is an issue this chapter will need to come back to in conclusion.)

Looking for funerary prototypes, we might say that cinema is to the mummy's tomb as video is to a crematorium of decomposed light. One method dips the corpsed trace of presence in preserving fluid. One disintegrates it to shimmering bits. But where have we come in our death-troped evidence about the former medium? In the freeze-frame, movement is replaced by sheer visibility; the power of apparition in and of itself takes precedence at such moments over the ordinary power of cinematic illusion, with its shifting forms, moving figures, and in sound film its speaking subjects. In stop-action frames an arrested object or body becomes more a pure image than the fugitive trace of an action invisibly continued elsewhere. This image exhausts, in other words, not only the mirage but the very idea of further movement. With those freeze-finish deaths of *Butch Cassidy* or *Gallipoli*, we don't imagine the heroes, once having been caught by the camera at the moment of their fatal shooting, still running, then finally stumbling and falling, across the Mexican square or the Turkish battlefield. Rather, in the moment of mortal wounding, the contingencies of their narratives are over with those of their lives. Stop-action does just what its name suggests; within the textual system, it stops the narrative action itself, not just the representation of activity. Hence the totalizing force of the freeze-frame in such closing death scenes, its power to subsume narrative entirely to graphic figuration. Into the (metonymic) chain of contiguity, of continuous motion, of sequence, of plot, breaks the radical equation *stasis equals death,* the axis of substitution, the advent of metaphor.

Butch Cassidy and the Sundance Kid takes this process one step further by taking it several steps back in time. As in *Under Fire,* the effect in question hinges on the ambiguous slippage from freeze-frame to evoked photo. But whereas the slippage is always proleptic in *Under Fire,* the uprush of the laboratory from within the moment of registration, in *Butch Cassidy* it is fatally retrospective. As the heroes are held up to view (by the closing freeze-frame) in being shot down, the stop-action image, silencing (only after a while) the thunderous gunfire, then fades to sepia monochrome. The image thus evokes, without being explicitly re-framed as such, the kind of primitive photos taken of the heroes at an amusement arcade earlier in the plot. This allusion within the freeze-frame to its photographic prototype (as well as constituent) has no immediate diegetic force; no one is on hand to photograph the double death in Mexico except the movie crew. The images of inevitable bloodbath attempt to carry, instead, a different conviction. The optic seepage of the last image from color freeze-frame to dun monochrome photograph bears a media-historical charge as well as a dramatic irony. It is an optic transition within temporal arrest toward what we might call the plot's (as well as the medium's) own nostalgia for itself. Its sepia image recapitulates in reverse the history of photography become film. One might say that in this case ontogeny capitulates to phylogeny, with the "photo finish" factoring down the cinematic into a doubly exposed trace of its own basis, material and historical at once. The embryonic (photograph) is there as the cellular (cinematic photogram), the origin implicit in the increment. Death breaks the chain of succession, its totalizing force in such contexts transforming the photographic increment to a mark of cessation.

Even in the petrified image of such closing frames, that is, with their instantaneous shift from the sign of suspended animation to the sign of death, thematic pressure ordinarily serves to rescue such moments from too complete a deconstruction. Stasis as meaning overrides the disclosure of the photogram, a thematic emphasis thereby staving off the full photochemical confession. We encounter here the cinematic system at its most secure and self-regulating. To sense a wholesale breakdown of cinematic motion in a plot's final braking upon a single photogram is to work strenuously against the predominantly thematic continuity often justifying such a frozen shot. Narrative cinema, in other words, when fastening upon a single image, can invoke the deathlike stasis of photography, as I suggested earlier, without necessarily incurring any damage to its own encompassing mobility of representation. (This will often be the case, as well, with the moments of autoapocalypse surveyed in the next chapter, where the scopic field, attaining briefly to the radically filmic, retreats again to the cinematic.) Especially when the relation of photography to cinema is articulated through the explicit theme of death, it is likely that such an emphasis on the temporal violence of dying will manage to naturalize the static disruption, recuperating it as solely a discursive—or enunciative—marker. Hence the particular plausibility, the *legibility,* of the "photo finish." The finality proper to narrative closure is only augmented in such cases by the metaphoric aptness of stasis (thinking of Metz again) as a vehicle for the tenor of death. The immobilization of a freeze-frame death will thus often serve to rescue, motivate, and normalize any assault on continuity otherwise mounted by a frozen image.

But such normalizing can function only up to a point. The image does not always give back to plot everything it momentarily takes from narrativity, is not always decoded exclusively, say, as syntactic (a period) rather than as constituent (a photogram, an increment). Here again, opening beneath interpretation, is that space for theoretical interception, for reading—a space cleared, if not immediately clarified, by the text itself—that I began by suggesting as a methodological ramification of this book. The rhetorical logic that makes stasis figurative for fatality may in turn convert fatality into a tacit figure for the photographic fixity to which film is at times reduced. Even by simply "quoting" a photograph at certain moments, film has all but become one. Or if not, as in our next exhibit, the difference may loom constitutive.

TIME CAPSULES

Given the color freeze-frame drained to sepia keepsake in *Butch Cassidy* or the freeze ambivalently translated to 35 mm photoprint in *Under Fire,* we see that the cinematic module, once locked into place, may in some cases sooner allude to some photographic context outside film narrative than impugn the illusion of movement within the cinematic field. In the face of such examples, too, it must be growing clear that the distinction between inset photos and the material "recession" of the freeze-frame (from screen to track) may well become most interesting when it won't stay put. This is as true of *Badlands* as of *Under Fire.* Also evoking (like *Butch Cassidy*) the nineteenth-century history of photography, the epoch of the daguerreotype and the photogravure, an old-fashioned set of stereographic prints in *Badlands* grows finally to seem—in full-screen cinematic deployment, and despite their divergent technical basis—a textual reflex of the filmic chain. These photographs become, in other words, compressed emblems of the film as a whole in what we might read as the pervasive death drive of its narrative.

What I mean by that is what the film can only mean by its inexorable plot. It chronicles the trail of bloodshed left by the psychopathic Kit (Martin Sheen) and his indifferent girlfriend Holly (Sissy Spacek). To fill up the blank of his life, Kit's obsession is precisely to leave a trace, in police terms a "record." Beyond the corpses he drops in his path, he also records for the authorities a "Voice-o-Graph" 45 rpm disk, with a fake suicide declaration, and later a dictaphone tape with advice to the young, as well as leaving behind a sample of his signature, a buried time capsule, and finally a totemic stone to mark the spot of his capture. His present is sacrificed entirely to a future retrospect that will lend weight, if not any particular meaning, to his having lived. Holly, on the other hand, is still lying in wait for her own life; some confrontation with the fact of the past, of time passing, is needed mainly to situate her own mortality.

 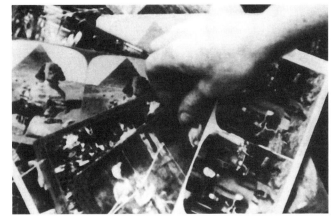

44   45

It is to this end, in a scene midway through the plot, that the film's stake in photography comes forward: right to the edges of the screen frame. For a few moments all moving images are displaced by the moving of still images through a slide viewer. Within a film narrative, this episode asserts the narration of sheer viewing. Holly has been hiding out with Kit in the forest after his murder of her father, and we have last seen her staring through binoculars (fig. 44), as if literalizing the faraway look in her eyes. Her next action is strangely continuous with this, as she reaches at random for a series of double-plate, three-dimensional pictures from her murdered father's stereocard collection (fig. 45) and then studies them in the old-fashioned apparatus (fig. 46). These are images that by their very technology as well as their imaged scenes link the viewer to the past as well as to the faraway. For Holly this past comes into perspective only as it can be drawn on in refocusing her sense of the present. No sentimentality shadows what she calls these "vistas"; no conscious sense of her father's loss haunts them. They are not mementos of the dead, private relics. Instead they constitute, frame after frame, a briefly sustained memento mori for the spectator herself.

"While taking a look at some vistas in Dad's stereopticon, it hit me that I was just this little girl, born in Texas . . . and that I had just so many years to live." Whatever mourning might cling to these photographs is internalized and converted. They become a displaced elegy for the surviving self rather than for the lost father, indeed elegizing that viewing self as if it might never have come into life. The insight Holly listlessly glimpses is an idea no one has put more succinctly than Barthes: "I am the reference of every photograph, and this is what generates my astonishment in addressing myself to the fundamental question: why is it that I am alive *here and now?*"[24]—while these photographs evoke *there and then.* More explicitly than in Ophuls's *Letter from an Unknown Woman,* because underscored directly by dialogue, Holly's premonitory encounter with images of the past demonstrates Barthes's sense, again, of how the "that-has-been" of a photograph is transferred to "this imperious sign of my future death," the point at which I will be only a photograph.

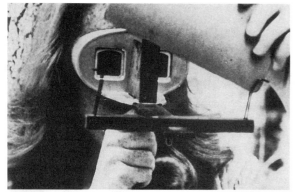

7 Palm-fringed Rua Viscounte de Itauna ... Mangue Canal, Rio de Janeiro, Brasil.

Not only, then, are all photographs in this sense posthumous, they are potentially mortifying; telling of a death that was, they warn of a death coming. In Holly's mind these images inscribe her within the assurance of her own doom.[25] It is a future inevitability that must be softened with fantasies of marriage and family, those events that should proceed and so defer death, those eventualities to which the photos lend vicarious form. As she contemplates the first of them in the viewfinder, the monochromatic reverse shot gives us the first of a half-dozen sepia-toned vistas, a tree-lined canal that provides a facile stunt of stereoptic perspective (fig. 47). Only by adjusting the apparatus (fig. 48), however, does Holly bring the picture, as it were, full screen—in a gradual close-up toward whose always receding vanishing point the film camera inches its way, as if along the grooves of the stereographic apparatus (fig. 49). When Holly begins to riddle her own temporal fate, asking where she'd be if she hadn't met Kit, we see a faded image of that immemorial image of mystery, the Sphinx (fig. 50), followed by a view of a pastoral lake with the smoke plume of a steamboat in the background (fig. 51). As she next wonders about the accident of her parents' meeting, we see the generalized effect of such a cause, a mother with a child (fig. 52). With Holly asking herself what might have happened if her mother had not died, we next see a tinted photo of Victorian ladies (fig. 53) with, apparently, a black-and-white framed photo on the wall behind them: a recessional history of photographic reproduction marking out a doubled vision of the past as irretrievable. A picture of a large family gathering on a front lawn (fig. 54) next overlaps with her thoughts of a past before Kit and a future after him. Yet the succession of these photographs is not exactly timed to the questions that might otherwise be taken to generate them one after the other. Rather, the suggestion that emerges from this syncopation—rather than synchronization—of image and voice-over is that all the photographs *together* trigger her questions about time, mortality, historical accident, and the unknown future. Without a corpse among them, or a scene of violence, or anything of poignancy or of pain, these photos *collectively* raise the question of death. "For days after," Holly closes the sequence by saying, "I lived in dread." The bygone acts to chill the ongoing with a vision of absolute pastness.

Film does not entirely win free from this feeling either. For in that stereopticon scene, Malick's *Badlands* takes under tacit consideration its own process as cinema, its own procession of images—in wry view of their evolved sociocultural effect. By means of the monocular film apparatus that projects Holly's full-screen slides, of course, each vista has been derealized, its tricked fore-

46, 47, 48, 49

shortenings flattened back to ordinary photographic traces. The visual and psychic effect that the imprinted panoramas have on Holly is thus kept private, not accessible to the film camera, regardless of her voice-over's pallid attempt at an explanation. In this respect, a curious point of contrast with Malick's ironically leveling effect has recently come to my attention. It is actually old and undated news. Sometime early in this century, an anonymous stereographer had the idea of highlighting an inset photograph of exaggerated flatness within the plenum of the 3-D image—in a manner that loses all too much in its two-dimensional translation here (fig. 55).[26] Two women, one old, one young, maybe mother and daughter, are seated at a table looking on together at an open volume of a newspaper or journal that we see only from the narrow side, entirely unreadable. This is to say that our own "reading" is to be directed at another, more fully disclosed rectangle poised to arrest attention in mid-ocular field. On the table are two upright photographs, one falling mostly out of frame to the left—and hence every bit as illegible as a third photo on the wall behind. Only the male portrait dead in the center of the table can be made out at all, deadening the whole layered space to an intrusive mere plane. This imaginably patriarchal portrait (for whose original the hugely foreshortened chair in the foreground stands waiting?) is the nodal point of the whole "trick" 3-D shot—and its modal negation. Unyielding in its stark planarity, this ordinary photograph not only centers but seems to puncture the swollen volume of the stereoptic field, a portrait laden with the pathos of abject flatness in the blocked midst of all this depth. Photograph stands to sterograph in this one instance, then, as stereography does to film in *Badlands:* the predecessor measuring both the advance and (in the case of cinema) the deficit of the newer medium.

Another thing bears mention, having to do with stereography's place as a precursor of montage. In film editing per se, the multiple image seeks resolution in a more or less stabilized specularity. The connection with stereography comes about in the following form. Two separate photographs (or photograms) in a contiguous arrangement are made dialectically to collide in order to produce movement in time: in short, film. Two separate photographs in a contiguous arrangement are made dialectically to collide in order to produce space: film too, but also its precursor in the stereopticon—whose received spelling offers us, as it happens, one more instance of a lexical fusion in the form of a transegmental portmanteau (from "stereo-opticon"). Such a mechanism thus takes its place among all the other protocinematic devices (fantascopes, zoetropes, and so forth) where separate images are mechanized into a gestalt—and whose participation in a nineteenth-century

50, 51, 52, 53, 54

55 (Courtesy of Kristianstad Filmmuseum, Sweden)

56, 57

episteme of discontinuous beholding will be explored shortly—and again in the last two chapters. What is signaled by this curiously double evolution in spatial versus temporal contiguity is nothing less, in *Badlands,* than the secret of film's success in photogrammatic succession. But this isn't all.

In Malick's film the spatial field becomes less figural than figurative, less a peopled former scene than a depersonification of the world under the sign of mortality. The optical forms and vectors of the stereopticon prints end up figuring time and not space. Aware that what we see is not what Holly sees, we want to look through the surface of the image to its scopic extrapolation not so much into the third dimension as into the fourth, a Deleuzian time-image in fixed form. Heightened specular perspective is translated to a temporal vanishing point: ultimately, death's point of no return. The cinematic narrative that implants this sequence of diegetic rather than discursive photographs (stereoptically "coupled" in a lateral rather than sequential sense) is thus able to achieve what its visual apparatus alone would be prevented from doing. Beyond the simply optical, *Badlands* investigates the phenomenological impact of images, of "vistas," on the psychology of a viewer, their manifestation of a past that can never come again and that might well have been otherwise.

It does this through a calculated homology between the working of the photographs upon Holly and the working of the film as a whole, including the photographs, upon us. *Badlands* becomes, then, a film within which the stereopticon sequence offers a pointedly circumscribed microcosm. Faced with images passing in rapid sequence to the decidedly loose accompaniment of a voice-over narrative, don't we sense in them the constituent work of this film as a whole? Both editing and camerawork collaborate toward this end. Not only is the relay of stereocards, as Holly shuffles them through the apparatus one after the other, conveyed to us by cuts, but the movement of the camera is geared to convey the escalating intensity of her gaze and concentration. This device is most prominent as the sequence closes (in) upon the last stereograph (fig. 56) via an "enlarged" facial detail (fig. 57) of the soldier and his girl (Holly wondering about the man who might be destined to marry her). As a "close-up," this accentuation could not be achieved by the focal mechanism of the stereopticon, only by a supplemental strategy of cinematic discourse. What begins as a narrated encounter with images thus eases almost imperceptibly into an imaging of the principle of narrativity itself as a flow of images in the cinematic apparatus.

No doubt about it, though, the default of depth in this sequence of photos within the image sets its cinematic reflex at a complicated distance from the apparatus it is situated in part to reprise. We will eventually develop a term for this re-configuring distance. In general, the inset or inlay or regress, the embedded auto-icon, the abyssal duplication, the internal recursion—tag it how you choose—this redoubling from within of a formal feature fits the paradigm to be further explored in the fifth chapter in light of Lucien Dällenbach's structuralist approach to the literary *mise en abyme*. As that chapter will develop it, such is the variously oriented internal "reflection" of a larger governing structure, one whose prominently *obverse* function in science fiction highlights a certain access of cinematic textuality to its own suppressed underside. There the inset photograph regularly approximates film's mechanical increment while setting into relief a whole postcinematic visual culture, often digitally amplified and corporeally eviscerated. In such cases "negative regress" will best name the contrapuntal embedding that cancels the logic of its representational surround, inverting its mimetic priorities. For now we need simply take note of such countering foils to screen motion as effected by a 3-D within a 2-D photomechanical image—without following out the full structuralist logic that determines the semiotic field of their reverberation. Yet I do need to say more about the historical resonance of stereography within cinema (and its history)—especially, in *Badlands,* when flattened to the unrecoverable effect of a superseded apparatus.

As it happens, our sense that the stereographic subtext of Malick's narrative may be linked to its filmic undertext finds support from the dominant current models of historiographic thinking about the origins (or better, preconditions) of cinema, where indeed stereographic perception is one of the missing links between technologies of imprint and projection. On one leading view, that of Jonathan Crary, photography—though no longer, given its circulation and exchange value, participating in the stable monocular rule of classic representation—does not lead directly, by a "technological determinism," to cinema. The motion picture apparatus needs, rather, to be understood as the mechanized fruition of a broader ethos, a whole specular regime characterized by a mobile and heterogeneous gaze unanchored to the object world in the continuous time of cognition.[27] For Jacques Aumont, working within a comparable paradigm of cultural transformation, photography must also be freshly situated with respect to film, no longer the direct seed of its evolution. Aumont stresses, for instance, an overlooked revolution in art history that saw the rise of the *étude* sketch (replacing in popularity the previous *ébauche,* the first study for a more finished easel painting). In its approach toward instantaneity, this fleeting registration of nature prepares the way for photography, yes, but only as one among the many optical precursors of cinema's kinetic dispensation—precursors that include the popularity of mountain vistas (in Friedrich's art, for instance, with the gazing subject built into the scene), painted panoramas, and the new time/space ratios of train travel.[28]

In his parallel archaeology of the observer, Crary's line of descent is equally committed to the strategic demotion of the photograph on the way toward cinema. Having at once fulfilled and overthrown the prototype of the camera obscura, photography gives way to cinema in the latter's role as the mass institutionalization of this decisive eclipse. Fixed perspectivism is dispersed by the shifting foci of a layered and kinetic gaze, as typified well before motion pictures by such devices as the thaumatrope as well as the stereograph. Either account, then, Crary's or Aumont's, minimizes the traditional explanatory axis from photography through sequential motion studies (Marey and Muybridge) to film. According to Crary, what needs emphasis instead is that seismic shifts in the very nature of human observation (or, via his Foucauldian formulation, in the "historical construction" [1] of vision) took place in transition from the ocular model of the camera obscura to the dissociated optics of the stereograph, the latter requiring, like film, the intervention of a mechanism (of alignment and resolution) at the receiving end as well as the producing end. The physiological gaze was no longer tethered to nature but had become a network of various impulses registered by and even generated from the body of the human subject rather than the recorded object. A nervous gulf had therefore widened, one might say, between epistemology and ontology.

Concerning the ocular and cultural cul-de-sac of the stereopticon, we find that Noël Burch has filled in certain missing historical determinants of cinema in advance of Crary's claims. He has done so according to a similar sense that the motion picture institution arrives to fulfill the bourgeois fantasy of lifelike reproduction that had been only roughly approximated, along one route of eventual impasse, by stereography.[29] Classic cinema compensates in Burch's view for the "deficiencies" of the stereograph, mainly stasis, by fulfilling an abiding bourgeois urge for a penetrable and fully dimensioned illusion of the real. But this effect is achieved only after the new medium's first decade and a half of frontal framing and display, whose documentary flatness owes more to the analytic scientism of Marey, among the "ferocious opponents of the synthesis of movement" (13), than it does to the quasi-spiritual duplication of reality dreamed by Edison and his predecessors. This latter dream is what Burch calls, throughout the essay and his book, the "Frankenstein tendency" (13), stressing less (as I did with *The Asphyx*) the piecing together of static images than the wholesale defiance of the grave through immortalization.[30] According to Burch, this Frankenstein complex is the mystification of an apparatus whose false teleological destiny was therefore postponed for over a decade—in prenarrative modes of screen presentation—under the regime of a more or less rationalist analysis of the view rather than a theatricalization of the seen as scene.

Along with other techniques of modernity, cinema arrives as a quintessential division of ocular labor, processed by the spectatorial body without the holistic perspectival "naturalism" of the camera obscura. This is why, for Crary, stereography rather than straight photography is the truer epistemic precursor of cinema, at once a subjective and a somatically dense mode of observed image. Yes, the stereograph was almost always a photograph (or two in overlap)—but an awkward one, binocular now, burdened with an apparatus and overly segregated into receding planes.[31] Crary evokes at length the eerie feel of the stereoptic vista to suggest the drawbacks of its excess, the deficits of its extreme perspectivism (129-34). Unlike the photograph, with its inferentially real gradations between receding depths, the artificially layered planarity of stereographic space, matched by the material conditions of bodily encounter with the viewfinding apparatus, produces a double artificiality, optical and bodily, a double strain. Add to this the social sanction attaching to stereography as a result of its fondness for pornographic images, as well as the ocular frustration that results from the way the image's tease of palpability (too much and too little) exceeds the bounds of verisimilitude without delivering on the carnal—and you have in view not only the sociohistorical impasse of the stereograph but the pressure toward cinema it constituted.[32] Add to this a pointed detail from *Badlands*'s own plot and you have a fuller view yet of the 3-D imprint's historiographic irony in Malick's film. For Holly's father, a taciturn billboard painter, reverses the sketching tradition of immediate natural observation and uses his random collection of Victorian stereocards as the basis for the oversized commercial artifacts, like drive-in movie screens, with which he territorializes (for market share) the American plains. The point is not easily lost in the film's trenchant satire of pop culture. The commercial wedding of updated craft and oldfangled technology, and the consequent translation from one visual medium to another in an ever more public form of image consumption, *is* of course, in a different key, the very history of cinema.

I have been advancing a sometimes invisible distinction between two modes of visual stasis in film, two manifestations of the photogram in its full-screen difference from itself. The one form is a "still" held on by the film, the other an apparent holding still of the film itself. I have tried to show how such motionlessness, of either the first or the second degree, by calling a halt to narrative even as it calls attention to its smallest module, can at times isolate the structure of truncation and stasis—call it mummification, call it death—that film both is based upon and must ordinarily work to erase. When circumscribed in an explicit photographic episode designed to rupture standard continuity, this motionlessness can disclose that "participation in death" from which a whole narrative may not only borrow its elegiac tone but take its formal definition—despite the usual tendency for film to subordinate the photographic dead spot to narrative continuity.

Such a microcosmic sequence in *Badlands*, built upon a tacit ontology of film as well as of photography, is given an extra turn by the later scene in which Kit tosses a number of his and Holly's private "effects," including at the last moment the stereopticon "vistas," into a bucket (fig. 58)—and buries it. Holly tries to explain: "He said maybe we'd come back someday and they'd still be sittin' here, just the same, only we'd be different. And if we didn't come back someone might find them, a thousand years from now, and wouldn't they wonder!" In *Under Fire*, given the posthumous impact of any photograph, the photographing of a corpse was to some extent ontologically redundant. Even more powerful a tautology in *Badlands* is the burial of multiple photographic encapsulations of time past inside a metallic time capsule within the celluloid time capsule that is any film. Safe in that buried tin urn—an unsealed coffin into which the hero has poured his life, at least what could be left of it as trace—there wait somewhere yet, if only in those few late moments of the film in

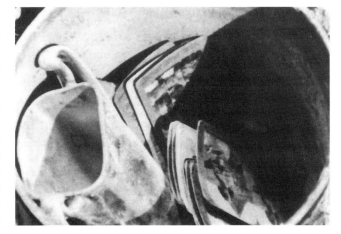

which we will always see them heaped, certain props from that same elegiac film. These are ocular props that stand in for the thousands upon thousands of tiny cellular capsules—or time frames—that make it up.

But it is important to be clear about exactly what this burial scene stages. Kit doesn't hide away some photographs that he and Holly might have taken of each other across the length of the plot, epitaphic tokens en route, deaths in miniature and in anticipation. The buried slides do not insist on such a direct miniaturized relation to the film's collected images. Rather, unknown to him, they are mementos of the moment, indeed the photographic objects that occasioned it, when death first dawned upon Holly's consciousness. In this they stand more for the power of the film's image system than for its representational basis, synecdoches of the cinematographic *effect* itself—apart from its shows of reality. *Badlands* is a film narrative about an antihero's doomed venture in memorializing the self—and about a girl's awakening consciousness of fatality. As a film narrative, an instance of cinematic discourse, it comes to acknowledge these same stances toward time and toward death in its own revised terms. As such a film narrative, its traces are always in the process of memorialization as we watch. This process climaxes in a rite of interment by which the collected signs and insignia of the characters' own defiant plot for their time together are put ceremonially behind them. In a symptomatic psychological gesture on Kit's part that also reveals an axiom of his own materialization to us on-screen, such buried signs and traces crucially include those very photographs that for an earlier few moments have encompassed the film and reoriented it toward the prehistory of its own medium. Yet along with every other photographic frame we see in and as the film, these too, having passed by in series, are finally put back in the can, to show forth at some other and later time, perhaps long after the death of any present viewer, before the "wonder," to quote Holly quoting Kit, of other eyes than ours.

FILMIC WITNESS FOR THE PROSECUTION

That was it, once. But now and then published articles have a way of settling over time into articles of analytic faith (for the author, I mean)—or at least of continuing investigative potential. They certainly do not shy away from subsequent confirming evidence in further primary sources. At some point after turning over to print the conference remarks above, I saw again—and as if for the first time—Fritz Lang's 1936 American debut film *Fury,* with its acid indictment of the scapegoating mentality of a social order rooted in bigotry, violence, and a collective rush to judgment (with clear parallels to the Nazi Germany he had left behind). It is also the only film I know that does not just thematize the ocular force of the freeze-frame but *narrates* that force from within the maneuvers of plot.

Stop-action images projected in a courtroom denouement are the very linchpins in an arraignment and conviction of mob brutality.[33] And anything that halts such ferocity, we are to assume, exalts the medium that intercedes against it. Such, in précis, is the self-cleansing violence of representation that characterizes Lang's entire cautionary fable. Moreover, this last plot twist of cinematic validation ac-

complishes its metafilmic ratification of cinema's power by tacit allusion to an earlier moment of photogrammatic evanescence rather than a stoppage in the film.
This is a moment that pivots around a prominent inset photograph—and its rapid
photogrammatic dissipation.

Illustration leads directly to ramification, especially once *Fury* is turned forward toward that frequent photographic subtext in film noir that Lang's film, like
much of his early work, anticipates by nearly a decade. The first homage to the
1940s and 1950s noir genre in Roman Polanski's later color film *Chinatown* (1974)
results from the black-and-white adultery photographs shuffled through in the
opening shot. A decade later there is the Coen brothers' *Blood Simple* (1984; see
chapter 4), with the snapping of such shots in flagrante. The color stock of such
later treatments aside, even in the original gray-to-black tones of so-called noir itself the evidentiary photograph stands out. Whether as pirated snapshot or newspaper photo, whether transacted as blackmail or used in identification (corpus
delicti or otherwise), the two-dimensional image—in its lifeless flatness—punctuates the receding deep shadows of dark alleys, seedy bars, after-hours offices, all
those nervous, bereft spaces that characterize the genre. Now clue, now fugitive
trace, now fetish object, the inset photograph intrudes upon these penumbral
zones of solitude and disquiet with the nagging black-and-white fact of its captured and often inculpating past. And the more nightmarish the environing space
may look, the more troubling the epistemological anchor of photography can
seem, rooting that ambience in the familiar touchstone of the all too true. Further,
in the morally deracinated social spaces of film noir, part of the impact of the evidentiary photo derives from its sending the private into circulation as public in a
world where that very distinction is compromised by the collapse of a stabilizing
social order and its defining boundaries.[34]

Fury anticipates this photographic swivel between the intimate and the publicly incriminating in a plot that tracks the invasion of domestic desire by a mob
ethos. Upstanding Spencer Tracy is arrested for a heinous kidnapping he did not
commit, then seemingly burned alive (we can only assume) in a jailhouse fire set
by the lynch mob. Early in the narrative, just before he is seized by a deputized
gang, we see a photographic image of him leaning proudly against his new car in
front of the gas station he has just purchased (fig. 59). It is a photo he has sent to
his long-waiting fiancée in a letter announcing that he is on his way to retrieve
her for a marriage he can now afford. But socioeconomic security and its private
fulfillments are immediately threatened by society at large—and en masse. Tracy
has in fact escaped the fire, but to enact his revenge he must pass for dead, pass
from all bodily (hence carnal) recognition. The structural point is unmistakable.
During the course of this twice-postponed marriage plot, all private libido has
been derailed—or sublimated—by a reciprocal public bloodlust.

In between the early letter (photo enclosed) and the couple's bitterly delayed
reunion in court, a subterranean parallel may have insinuated itself upon the
viewer's attention. For that photo of the hero alongside the vehicle of his desire is
no sooner seen than it rapidly lap dissolves into his moving-image departure in
the same car to retrieve his bride-to-be (figs. 60-61). In this edited version of cul-

59, 60, 61

tural typing—the woman waiting, the man on the move—a graphic match on the once stationary, then mobilized vehicle of transport across a lap dissolve cannot help implying that it is the cinematic automatism per se, and in its own interests, that is virtually animating the still image in the process of realizing the erotic impulse as a vector of narrative convergence. This deliberately diaphanous scene change, followed by Tracy's precipitous arrest, is later echoed, askew, in the courtroom climax. Rather than dissolving into montage this time, the moving image is petrified into a freeze-frame. This happens when a projector is wheeled into court and the doctored (i.e., intermittently halted) footage of a newsreel photographer (who, as only we knew, was present at the earlier riot scene) is introduced as evidence against the arraigned lynch mob, picking out the perpetrators from the crowd. Within the photomechanical subtext of the film as a whole, the vaporized fixed image of early photo passing into the automatism of its own (automotive) succession has thus emerged as the model of all photogrammatic advance on the film track. When folded back into plot, this stress on the solitary image in progress returns—like the filmic suppressed from within cinematic momentum—in the form of the evidentiary fixed frame (composed, of course, by multiplied but identical photograms on the track): a frame that now marks the public comeuppance for the previous dissipation of private desire. The judge is given the best seat in the house as the images are projected on the rear wall of the court (fig. 62), between the deco pilasters of its institutional structure (fig. 63), which soon coincides with the vertical edge of our own screen frame. At which point the district attorney begins announcing the culprits as "identified here by stop-action image" (fig. 64)—including a telltale cut to a close-up ("enlarged stop-action") on an ax's cut as it severs the fire hose (figs. 65-66).[35]

It is then that another photographic reversal can occur. Almost sated in his revenge by what the next day's headlines call the admissibility of "movies" in court, Tracy suddenly has his status as incinerated corpse cast into public doubt by the return of that earlier private photograph. It is enlarged and cropped now as a front-page "wanted" shot, under the headline "Is This Man Alive?" (fig. 67), which we again read in the hands of his fiancée. When Tracy, suddenly humanized by guilt over his lust for revenge, enters the court in real time, his image coming back to life as it were—and then again getting instantly converted to image by the flash cam-

62   63   64

eras of the court reporters—only then can the mainstream plot make good on its own original marital (and narrative) contract.

Before this, his fiancée has finally come to realize his deception, his ruse of nonexistence, when an anonymous letter from a supposed witness composed of cut-out newspaper typography is presented in court to confirm his death by fire. The camera once again follows her gaze into a close-up on a telltale malapropism of the hero's own speech, made much of earlier in the light banter of a love scene and repeated in one of his own subsequent letters: the use of "mementum" for "memento" (fig. 68). With its scissored and spliced misspelling of "me" plus "men," here indeed is a marked alphabetic rebus, undeniably called out by plot, of the sort Tom Conley less convincingly associates elsewhere with what amounts to an overstrained, quasi-paranoid mode of spectatorship in film noir.[36] As shot from the heroine's POV for a third time, this graphic pastiche reprises the entire film as a piecemeal textuality filmically severing self from commu-

65, 66

67

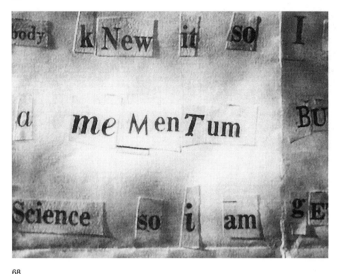

nity (as in the objectified "me" from "me/n") across the very edit (and potential overlap) of its signifiers—and doing so in the process of turning photographic memento on the strip into cinematic momentum on-screen (and back again).

Photography's role in the film, that is, has been encoded via letteral text, script doing the summary work of all composite imprint. And that composite has its own economy. By a systemic symmetry in the undertext of filmic record, the lone early photo of the hero fading away into the generative essence of photomechanized succession has already been linked with the later disjunct frames in the courtroom screening. Material disclosure meets social critique in the meshes of the mechanism itself, where editing once figured even while narrating the very fragility of personal agency and impetus. The ephemera of desire come up against the inexorable in the implacability of the track itself. Following immediately upon that early dissolve from pictured auto to automated picture, a case of false arrest waits to be cured at the metafilmic level by the true arrest of the courtroom's damning frame captures. With film noir in the offing, what has transpired here, in a manner we might call *pregeneric*, is a pervasive and disabling anxiety rescued only through a corrective form of filmic *apprehension.*

Photography's place a decade later, in full-blown film noir, is hardly so symmetrical or reassuring. Before the war, however, the filmic undertext drawn upon (and drawn out) by the fixed imprint in Lang's *Fury* contributes to an almost homiletic thrust. And it does so from within an atmosphere of drastic isolation and justified paranoia that is very close to the noir vision, so close that it seems merely waiting to resurface in more diffuse and depoliticized form after the patriotic communalism of World War II. So what is the technological moral of this story? Whether seeking violent consolidation against a demonized other or not, either a society must suspend (freeze) the juggernaut of historical time long enough to diagnose its own motive force or else the private desires of the individual social subject will get brutally lost in the flux. Photographic imprint, and film's obtruded basis in such imprint, driving a wedge into succession, drives home the point. To repeat a principle from the introduction in the grips of example, we have been concerned yet again with the synthesis between the formal and the cultural under the intermediate and overdetermined sign of the textual. It was, one cannot recall too often, no less a student of structure than Roland Barthes who knew "that a little formalism turns one away from History, but that a lot brings one back to it."[37]

In her book on Lang, Lotte Eisner speculates in passing that Lang's film may have helped clear the way for a wider use of film in court, or "movies" as Lang's headline calls them, a procedure that was suspect until the early thirties.[38] Working from the legal archives, Louis Schwartz has confirmed this suggestion in his recent Iowa dissertation on the juridical use of filmic and video testimony down through the Rodney King trial.[39] Appellate judges, he has found, repeatedly ruled against filmic evidence in the twenties because, unlike photographs, film could not be studied all at once as a portable document—only viewed and reviewed. Pictures on the strip were too small to see, or at least for the jury to examine comfortably, and projected on-screen they were too swift to fix upon. From the avowedly phenomenological perspective of his analysis, Schwartz suggests that judges thus misunderstood the nature of the not yet fully domesticated medium, insisting too much on its sheer materiality: mistaking it, in other words, for pictures in motion rather than a picture of motion.

My point is that this is the way Fritz Lang understood it also, understood the photograph that stands under all motion; and that having known the world before cinema, like those judges, he too had a bifurcated sense of its technology as divided between photogram on the strip and its namesake "frame" on-screen. He therefore meets their not entirely trivial objections by demonstrating an adaptation in the apparatus itself, through optical lab work, to the requirements of inspection rather than spectacle. At the same time, he arranges his probative stilling of frames so that this device—this deviance—will show forth as the exception that proves the rule of cinema per se, cinema as a run and a rush of photographs: a specular effect always edgily in play between the motor drives of plot and, if you will, the *momentum mori* of the fixed trace.

THE END-STOPPED CHEMISTRY OF SELF-DEVELOPMENT

This is the case with a minor classic like *Fury* or with the more recent films discussed in my original article on the engravement of time by photographic instantaneity. In film after film attuned to its sequential rudiments in this way, photographic fixity is lodged in contrast to a span of narrative event that never fully disengages from the suspended ocular moment, whether lost or traumatic or foreboding. Another temporal suspension is at work too. For such films tend, all told, like any film, to fix their own historical period in the sharper perspective of retrospect. It is often said that a given movie looks better now than when it was made. It may also look clearer in its evidentiary relation to its culture. It is in this sense that all films are indeed time capsules. And the clarity at issue is scarcely forsworn by considering such evidence mainly as it has passed through the techniques of representation to become textual—rather than nebulously cultural—discourse. When my 1985 paper originally moved forward from Ophuls's indisputable masterwork to its later examples, I had in mind selecting a recent cult classic like Malick's film—not yet discussed in terms of its photographic arrangements—and a more or less up-to-the minute example in the case of Spottiswoode's little-treated film. Looking back, however, it now seems obvious that *Badlands* and *Under Fire*, exactly a decade apart (1973, 1983), straddle a watershed that the brief remarks on *Butch Cassidy and the Sundance Kid* should have helped bring into more cleanly drawn contour by way of its late 1960s pop-modernist devices and its backdated "road film" (as well as "buddy picture") structure.

Another fateful picaresque, Malick's film becomes, all the more in hindsight, an acute meditation on media history—and well beyond its allusions to film's preconditioning by stereography. Retelling the Starkweather murder spree of the 1950s, the American media's greatest spectacle of serial killing since the historical moment of Bonnie and Clyde, and titling his narrative to evoke the lost days (already lost in the late Victorian setting of *Butch Cassidy* as well) of a frontier ideology, *Badlands* comes at the end—or just after—of 1960s technical experimentation (achieving its great mass appeal with the jump-cutting and slow motion of Arthur Penn's *Bonnie and Clyde* itself [1967]). Malick's narrative thus arrives as a stripped-down palinode for one of its most trusted of mixed (and already self-conscious) genres, the postheroic neowestern, as well as for the cinematographic effects that repeatedly link the metageneric twists of this mode to the metatextual showing forth—and off—of its mediating specular devices. (About their collective status as "period" devices I will have more to say, via Stanley Cavell, in the third chapter.) Belated in content and baroque in form, the self-conscious frontier epic, turned by Malick to psychopathic road picture, had seen its day. Excluded by the deadpan rigor of Malick's technique, the more insistent cinematographic dazzle of the retro western and gangster picture, collapsed into a single postmythic American form, had to be thrown over. From Malick's historical position these cinematic exercises now seemed almost as dated, say, as stereopticon slides.

And closing upon us in the years since Malick, a postmodern aesthetic of dramatically anesthetized pastiche. From *Bonnie and Clyde* to *Badlands* is nothing compared with the quantum leap to *Natural Born Killers* (Oliver Stone, 1994). Short of Stone's brutal spoof of media-circulated violence, there is Ridley Scott's *Thelma and Louise* (1991), the director's most successful film after the postmodern benchmark of *Blade Runner*. An interest shared by both these narratives in the potentially humanizing dimension of the photograph is trumped and undone in the later film through photography's ironic collaboration with the freeze-frame. One is inclined again to generalize. In the decade and a half since *Under Fire*, whenever the freeze-frame enters the realm of postmodernist sensibility, it comes bearing the opposite of scare quotes—more like swaddling: offering a padded intertextual allusion to previous filmic (in some sense quintessentially filmic) treatment. In *Thelma and Louise* the allusion is thematically overdetermined in the

highest degree. For here is Scott's quasi-feminist turn on the buddy-picture crime-spree road western, a languishing form fueled again—and this time in the closural absence of all road—by horsepower rather than real horses. Part of its retro feel in the closing freeze-frame apotheosis, with the heroines suicidally barreling their convertible into the Grand Canyon, comes therefore from a feminist affect that strains beyond *Badlands*'s mordant dismantling of cliché in the neowestern

69

subgenre for an artificial rejuvenation of the form. Photography is one major litmus test of the difference, with Scott harking back to *Butch Cassidy* for the fossil fuel of his closing trope.

Badlands, as we know, excludes any present moment of photographic representation of the hero and heroine for a displaced ocular self-consciousness attached to images of a past not their own. In this ironic respect, Malick's idea is more like Scott's in *Blade Runner,* where the existential dubiety is reduced to a physiological one (replicants or real people?). By contrast with Kit and Holly, Thelma and Louise, like the movie that bears their names, are nothing if not photogenic. The film is so insistent about the filmicity of its myth, the prepackaged genre ingredients it knowingly remixes, that it proceeds by the following photomechanical stages. From black leader behind the main credits, with the roll call of star names, title, producer, and director, a black-and-white moving image slowly emerges of a desert landscape, gradually saturated with color as if it were replaying the history of such sweeping panoramas on the genre screen. When, a few scenes into the plot, the heroines (Susan Sarandon and Geena Davis), car loaded, are about to embark on their road fling, Thelma snaps a picture of the two of them with a Polaroid camera held at arm's length, an image that, in their eager hurry, they don't wait to see gathering shape and color on its white background (rather than the black of the credits). Interceding just here, the first of the film's two stop-action frames—briefly freezing

70, 71

the onset of the snapshot (fig. 69)—has already secured the moment as ceremonial. What *develops,* by elision and expansion of this split second of suspended motion, is of course the entire road plot—ending as it does, just before and then just under the credits, with a double return of the photomechanical moment.

Stretched finally to the optic breaking point, then, is a plot that, when all its directions have been exhausted, reverts to a truncated still image at the moment of certain fatality just before actual death. From the closing freeze-frame of the heroines' car in free fall over the canyon, the image, losing color, rapidly fades back to the white background of an effaced screen (figs. 70 and 71, with this final image reproduced here in mid-obliteration)—in a reversal not only of the gradually emergent landscape at the start but of the self-developing photochemical process over which there was once no time to pause.

72, 73

With Scott's reprise of the freeze-frame apocalypse in a fatal showdown like that of *Butch Cassidy,* this is a final image whose climactic fixity is referred back not, in this case, to a primitive photographic model of Victorian fairground photography (as in George Roy Hill's western) but to the streamlined mediation of Polaroid technology. Moreover, from the narrative's last frame, the reference back has an immediate point of relay. On the evidence of an intercut image just as the women floor their Thunderbird one last time, with a fleet of police cars in pursuit, we assume that these self-conscious heroines must at some earlier moment have taken time to look at that point of no return snapshot, since we finally see the print in their possession. Never glimpsed or mentioned until now, it is the most visible memento caught up in the whirlwind that tosses loose objects from the pile of odds and ends crammed into the back seat of their accelerating convertible (figs. 72 and 73). The lone image returns in this penultimate fleeting moment like the upshot of the photogrammatic undertext—but motivated in context by such an overload of narrative irony that the photo takes part in an inferred visual pun. *Time flies,* to be sure, but more than this conjoint fact about life and screen projection is flashed past by this irreversible transit from disappearing photo to curtailed motion.[40]

The precipitous climax to follow literalizes the earlier remark that in their self-protective violence the female fugitives "have gone over the edge this time." This whole last sequence is handled in a syncopation of dated slow-motion shots of the good cop (Harvey Keitel), running to rescue the heroines, intercut with the full-speed lunge of their car over the cliff. At which point the vehicle of final escape—their feminist chariot of ire—artificially slows in flight toward its front-end collision with that histrionic freeze-frame. Upon the advent of this second stopped frame, the picture is all but over, its image of abandon complete. By the time the frame bleaches quickly to white in inevitable reverse evocation of the death trip's inaugural Polaroid memorial, then, Scott's intertextual summons to that hoariest of closural gestures, the "photo finish," has taken its full postmodern distance from the drama's unthrottled emotional momentum. This is to say that the vanishing of the image carries not only a photochemical but also a media-historical irony. Despite the frozen take, the rhetoric of time transcended no longer holds.

And now for that second phase, as mentioned, of the closing photomechanical—as cinematic—moment. Photographs are funerary, yes, but so too is film, as this film (against the tendency of much cinema theory) knows full well. Swiftly edited moving-image clips of key scenes suddenly begin passing under the final credits, including the scene of the initial photograph being taken—but this time without the ominous brief freeze that had marked it at the instant as a kind of fatality, a break with time to be fulfilled only much later. Nonetheless, the excerpts passing in review perform their own last rites. Brought to the valedictory surface of the text itself, the deathwork of cinema (in reanimating the profilmic lives of bodies lost now to their own time of action, preserved in a memory entirely mechanical) is as clear as even this book could wish. And clear by close connection, better yet, with the photographic instantiation of the same mortal principle. Again like the film by their name, Thelma and Louise are lost but not forgotten; they have left their mark, their traces.

Not only have we seen this in one delimited case, we have been seeing nothing else. Just before the film reviews (without quite renewing) itself in arbitrarily edited segments—as does *Under Fire* with its own coda's archive of rehearsed photo opportunities—narrative, textual, and media-historical indicators have been knotted beyond separation. Yet another "allegory of film" has thus been unleashed by popular cinematic narrative from within a more manifest fable of genre history. Photographic memorialization (the vanishing single shot), that is, has redefined the vector of filmic movement as a death in progress. For in that last glimpsed imprint of the two women when their life was yet before them (the imprint in its later moment of windblown removal), exactly the constitutive photographic image that always disappears in the continuous transformation of strip into track is violently peeled from view as the last loss tallied in the track's own momentum toward frozen closure. To which is appended a rescued duration withered to mere footage. And in this end-title recycling of the already finished, the already dead and gone, the over and done with, lies also the ultimate witness, one suspects, to the narrative's own postmodern stance toward the visual tropes and genre trajectories of past cinematic material.

Just such a stance toward the medium's formal history connects with a broader historical tendency in the period since the heyday of late sixties technical (as well as societal) experimentation. To approach this historical perspective is to return to the texturing punctuation of *Under Fire*. In a long view of cinema's stylistic evolution, the revived and already overfamiliar devices of freeze-frame and photo finish in Spottiswoode's film, which struck me on first release as oddly excessive even in their thematically programmed context (late mannerist one might say), now seem more deliberately hypertrophic and implicitly historicized. Internally sanctioned (I thought at the time) by their relation to the staged photograph of Rafael's corpse, they now also seem quaint, antiquated, almost knowingly so, and for that reason anxious as well. In nearly the full decade between *Under Fire* and *Thelma and Louise,* as well as in the years since, I have seen no American or European films, unless memory fails, that use the device of the freeze-frame with anything like such prominence, let alone integrity—which is to say integration—as does *Under Fire.* This makes our reading, in retrospect, all the more alert to the cost of that last-ditch integration in Spottiswoode's film, well before the postmodernist reworking of the stop-action device by Ridley Scott. Photographic self-exposure in *Under Fire* is so fully naturalized by the story of photojournalism that the styleme has lost most of its textual valence, lodged there as a mere technological datum of a so-called media culture—and threatened as such, in its photomechanical basis, by the newer technology of video, which can broadcast (for instance) a carefully edited strip of photographs (Hackman's murder) so as to approximate the more likely case of continuous digital transmission. If we apply Raymond Williams's categories of residual, dominant, and emergent forms of cultural production to the stylistic element of the freeze-frame, we can see that its use in *Under Fire* (in tight conjunction with the photo of the heroic corpse, and precisely as each invokes the photogram at the basis of film process) enacts the residual last stand of photographicity in the once emergent, lately dominant field of digital representation. This same device of the stop-action frame enacts, in turn, the last gasp of modernist self-reference on the geopolitical terrain of the postcontemporary, where the same technological fillip in *Thelma and Louise* will end up reading like a movie buff's in-joke.[41]

Just here is the link between the textuality of screen rhetoric and the larger history (cinematic, social, political) it inscribes. For to some extent the vast and pervasive cultural fallout from American imperial intervention in the Third World helped sound the death knell of a 1960s film aesthetic reputedly liberatory before it grew formulaic. Clearly drawing on the notion of Vietnam as "the TV war," even while strategically maximizing a graphic alienation effect (in the stop-action italics of the image as image) associated with the European art film and its derivations in the New American Cinema, *Under Fire* works to commemorate the end point of another major "frontier" or border genre, the war picture. It does so precisely through its photochemical nostalgia for the reproduced body of life. It is as if the first widespread use of nonportrait photography, in Civil War reportage, has returned drenched with the associations of a later divisive militarism—but this on the very eve of a derivative medium's own eclipse: on the brink, that is, of cinema's capitulation to the digital. Media wars—where the adjective is no longer a transferred epithet—tend now toward the wholesale computer simulacrum of the same year's *War Games* (John Badham, 1983). The voracious photojournalistic capture of reality cannot, in short, retard the telos of reality's own simulation.

WAR PICTURES

Four years before *Under Fire,* Francis Ford Coppola appears on-screen in *Apocalypse Now,* though still behind a camera, either as himself (a movie director) or as a TV documentarian enjoining his cast from looking into the camera as they rush by in the plot's first beachhead attack. This is only the most obvious way technological mediation is put on view in this film about the war machine as publicity machine. In a parallel vein, the explicit photographic motif—or subtext—of *Apocalypse Now* bears upon the claims of this chapter at least as much as upon those in the next about the autotelic nature of cinema's self-apocalypse.

As Willard (Martin Sheen) probes, over several discrete scenes, the voluminous dossier of Colonel Walter E. Kurtz for any clues to the derangement he is assigned to terminate, the special agent intermittently comes upon eight-by-ten glossies, magazine photos, and press clippings of a younger Kurtz, uniformed portraits of the pariah as former military stalwart. The film fiction suddenly fades back into its own prehistory. For these pictures are, in dawning fact, photos the audience may well recognize as production stills from earlier Brando vehicles in which he played ambiguous and tortured military figures, such films as *The Men, The Young Lions, Morituri!* and *Reflections in a Golden Eye*. The history of the genre in its more psychological variants, a genre Brando seemed repeatedly drawn to, is here recalled on the way to the climax of this war picture to end all war pictures. Only gradually do the photos age with Brando—until we see a swollen, fire-rimmed gargoyle of a medium (faceless) close-up picturing the no longer uniformed Kurtz edged by a satanic aureole (see fig. 76), a pirated picture sent downriver, perhaps, by the crazed photographer (Dennis Hopper) we will soon meet. It is captioned in typescript (tentatively at that: "believed to be") a photo of "W.E. Kurtz," as if to identify, rebuslike, the American audience's own complicity in the rationalized carnage he represents (elliptically, all but preliterately, "We Kurtz").

As it happens, the film audience, along with Willard, has seen one of these dossier photos of Kurtz once before, back at army headquarters early in the film—

setting off the chain of pursuit that articulates the plot. Held up by the general in charge of the secret mission to assassinate Kurtz, after playing Willard a tape of the colonel's genocidal ravings, the backlit image is even legible from the underside—like a translucent photogram writ large—in visible contrast to the general's routine ID photo on his chest in the same shot (fig. 74). We are thus able to study Kurtz's image along with the general as he ruminates all too weightily on that obverse of heroism, the "dark side" of human nature, which becomes the vi-

74

sual and emblematic destination of the plot. When, much later, we find Willard turning over the ominous silhouetted photo to reveal the blank white background—in a frustrated search for further clues—the action momentarily eclipses all of his face except one eye with the image of the colonel's sightless black stare into nowhere (fig. 75)—until the now encompassing image of Kurtz, having filled

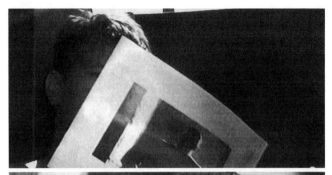

75, 76, 77

the film screen (fig. 76), spills over into the next shot by a fluid dissolve into the rippling current of the river (fig. 77).

Two later cinematographic developments in the film are anticipated here. With the photograph of one man occluding the face of the other, we look forward to the climactic shot plan in Kurtz's temple, arranged as it is to make the two men match, double, and efface each other in a graphic play of displacements.[42] En route to this confrontation, Willard will later stare at that infernal classified photograph for long moments of unsettling recognition—until surrendering its image to sheer memory when destroying the dossier on the way to Kurtz's Cambodian stronghold. Here we approach the second climactic turn anticipated by the earlier lap dissolve of the "superior officer" in superimposition on the precivilian—the precivilized—space into which he has merged.

Most of these cinematographic effects, it should be said, lie beyond the inevitable dictation of theme. The photographic intertext in Brando's career need not, for one thing, operate in view of the film's photogrammatic undertext.[43] Yet it does—and twice over. Eventually a present version of Kurtz's image (not the one of a younger self perused at headquarters in disjunction from the tape-recorded madness run in the background) will have to fuse with the film's own sound track—in the cinematic meld of Brando's voice and image—during Willard's final apocalyptic encounter with the antihero. But this fusion arrives only in the literal wake or backwash of the circumstantial evidence that drives plot toward it. Such, then, is the second level of cinematic disclosure—and the second anticipated visual transformation of the image track associated specifically with the serial study of the dossier. For when Willard has combed the file for all it is worth, his last move on the way to Kurtz is, in the absence of a shredder, to tear up by hand both text and photographs and strew them on the receding waters as the boat plows upstream (fig. 78).

The scene's visual pun is unavoidable, with the secret mission submerging all signs of its classified paper trail in a vanishing inherent file (in French, *défilement*) all its own. Further confirming this sense, the discrete flow of fragmented photos and textual snippets drifting into and beyond screen field—suspended in part by the watery evanescence of lingering lap dissolves—is floated past in a direction that slips away from the still advancing action of plot. This micromontage of lost links to the past not only replays in this way the intermittent reading of the dossier, in bits and pieces edited into the (often dissolving) action of sequential scenes, but captures more generally the channeled route of the disappearing cinematic image in its onward narrative stream. Put simply, film seems to be covering its own disintegrated tracks along the plot's own river of no return. But in this sense, only as always. More particularly, this belated instance of the war film genre is found sloughing off once and for all the photographic traces of its own predecessors in the name of a more thoroughgoing irony of treatment. And in the last fading phase of dissolves, the last image we are given to see—screen center, in superimposition over the reemerging jungle branches—is none other than that demonic photo of Kurtz melting away once more, as it were, into reality (fig. 79). In a film of such visual density and stress, the photogrammatic evidence of the senses, when lifted at least partly from its normative specular suppression, is hard to deny.

What, finally, have we seen about the difference between seeing the screen frame fill with a photograph and, on the other hand, seeing it lock tight on itself? The inset photo locates not the routine dropping into place but rather the putting forward of the single photographic print within a medium that depends on both the multiplicity and the elision of such imprints—their spun subsumption to cinematic image. The freeze-frame, by contrast, is the suspension of all filming in deference to (and apparent detention of) sheer film. Yet the freeze-frame, as much as the filmed photo, continues to repress the photogram it may seem to allude to. Each succeeds only by remaining in succession, only because its specular power r/evokes the photogram—in one case by merely framing its opaque equivalent in the single photograph, in the other by giving the illusion of its separable image from within the continued spin of its duplicates. For precisely this latter reason, more needs to be said about the medium-specific device—and narrative decimation—of the freeze-frame, the complement so far of the filmed photograph in this first stage of investigation.

What if one were pressed to reconsider the general tropology of photograven death, as explored in the present chapter, from a slightly (just slightly) different vantage? What if one were asked (as I was tacitly asked by a journal editor inviting me to pursue the issues of my earlier article) to think of the photogrammatic moment in film

78

79

as a moment explicitly apocalyptic rather than more generally mortal?[44] The results appear in the next chapter, which is really part 2 of this one. In the long run, however, a pair of additional chapters seemed necessary in immediate follow-up to the present one. The first offers a further cluster of exemplification—via cinemato*graphic* reading, again, rather than cinematic interpretation—that locates the apocalyptic overtones of the stop-action image among a wider range of photogrammatic disclosures on film. The next mounts a sustained theoretical rethinking of the cinematic freeze as filmic frame of reference. The first, chapter 2, introduces the specular unconscious of audience reaction into the specialized defect of stopped action on-screen. The next translates this defection from cinema to film, by cognitive inference, to the plane of temporality rather than movement, where subjectivity returns redefined in its specular investment. In both of these ensuing investigations, the "thematic" emphasis often falls on death (as it will again in even more detail in chapter 4). But none of these chapters rests at the thematic level. In each, as in this, we come to find how often filmed death contracts (by assimilation, like the phrase itself) into film death—narrative catastrophe into impacted cinematographic arrest, with inevitable implications for the spatiotemporal coordinates of the whole projective system. After the further distillation of these issues in "Deaths Seen," the remaining three chapters will then move to historicize the photogrammatic crux of cinema as film from three quite different vantage points: first a narratively fabricated future, then a narratively reconfigured past, and finally the actual past of film's technological and cultural emergence as a modernist textuality within modernity.

Apart from links between these subsequent chapters, I had best specify further, perhaps, the line of progression between the first two. Ten years apart in conception as they are, the current discussion opens onto the next by way of a new methodological inflection. Part of what has intervened in a decade of film scholarship and debate is a broadening institutional interest in the recuperative work of Gilles Deleuze in rescuing the so-called movement-images of cinema from anything resembling the strict mechanistic temporality of the apparatus and its racing strip, releasing them instead into an ensemble of figurative temporalities. For my present concern with the generative materiality of the screen image, of course, this is exactly the least revealing direction to move in. One purpose of the coming discussion is therefore to counteract the tantalizing sophistications of this new semiotized phenomenology, where in Deleuze world pictures (from Bazin through Cavell) have been replaced by immanent signs (Peircean "opsigns," "sonsigns," etc.) of movement/time ratios detached, in most cases, from all conceptual contact with the serial track. Attempting to restore some feel for the medium's speeding photograms within their contributory eclipse by cinematic projection—call them optic grams coalesced to optigrams—requires a double step back: not only from screen to track or strip but from screen to audience. This means pulling back toward a textualist understanding of reception itself, with its conscious investment in projected images as pictured world and the nonconscious, instant-swift divestments of the fixed imprint that such yielding to cinematic spectacle depends on.

Here is the motorized subliminality of the screen's textual fix. Here too is where the legacy of the avant-garde offers a bracing refresher course in exactly what is the *matter* with film under the aegis of industrial cinema—and mostly under wraps therein. When, though, in momentarily textualizing its own reception, mainstream cinematic spectacle lowers its guard, weakens its self-defenses in respect to its own propellant materiality rather than compelling immanence, the resulting variety of filmic self-disclosure takes its place in our gathering considerations as follows.

Motion's Negative Imprint

LAST THINGS IN CINEMA MAY REVERT
TO FILMIC FIRST THINGS.

For an apocalyptic model of filmic self-disclosure, one looks elsewhere than to photography's unique purchase on disaster, undeniable as that may be. I refer to the photograph's acknowledged documentary privilege in the recording of lowercase apocalypse, understood in common parlance less in the strict sense of prophetic revelation than as ultimate scourge: everything from Armageddon, genocide, and epidemic to state execution's day of judgment.[1] But the apocalyptic has a longer tradition—as well as a more textual one. It conjures up finish in the sense of revealed end: terminus and telos, death but also judgment. It breaks with history to bend all history into its image, interrupting linearity in order to fulfill it. It inhabits, in short, two time frames, reframes two chronotopes: the temporal and the momentous. That's why *Apocalypse Now* as a title has such an unusual feel, somewhere between the paradoxical and the redundant. Apocalyptic crisis, postponed by the very fact of history, arrives into its own endless present only with the obliteration of the historical then/now. It is all, in a word, written. Hence the textual as well as the metaphysical dimension of the term. And here too lies photography's truest apocalyptic leverage on filmic succession. In the double sense of doom and illumination, the constituent photogram stands to the film track as cinema's ruin and its truth at once. As such, it may intersect at the textual level the narrative drama of apocalyptic violence, however reduced and brutal. Think back only as far as the previous chapter's crude *dies irae* of mob frenzy in *Fury*, where revealed complicity in a fiery day of judgment coincided with photogrammatic first things in those cauterizing freeze-frames. There history seems narrowed to, and held accountable for, the isolated gestures that compose it, gestures whose individual violence cannot be smoothed over by the rush of conveyed public event.

Looking back from the other side of World War II on the genocidal scapegoating perpetrated by the Nazis, Ingmar Bergman's *Persona* (1966) also aligns lowercase apocalypse with the self-revelation of its own medium of record and (psychic) projection. A confrontation with photography provides, twice over, an anchor of the film's emotional transformations. Bergman's plot unites two women in a psychic symbiosis across their common denial of a child—born and unloved in the one case, aborted in the other. It then climaxes in an extended nightmare sequence that submits each to the other's vampiric transference over the torn photo of the one woman's son (first presented in accusation by the other; fig. 80). Earlier, the film's narrative momentum has seemed to stall on the contemplation rather than the rejection of another photograph, this time from Western culture's dossier of atrocity. In this extended, wordless scene, the unloving mother, Elisabeth, turns up a table lamp (fig. 81) to shed more light on a famous image of the Warsaw ghetto (fig. 82), prominently featuring a young boy being rounded up by the Nazis—an image that, further edited in an analysis of its constituent horrors, fills for a long while the projected space of the cinema screen.[2] Genocide is linked to emotional infanticide, mass cruelty to the heroine's private failure of feeling, all across the subjective relays of her gaze. As the camera moves in upon the picture plane, the foregrounded image of the boy is intercut with a closer view of the heroine's fixated stare (figs. 83-84), to which we never return in this scene. She is in every sense *absorbed* by the trauma she peers at—while it becomes for us, as for her, a protocinematic montage (figs. 85-95). The dramaturgically exchanged details and sight lines of its scenic reassemblage, that is, trans-

80

81

83

84

late the tacit scanning of the heroine's POV into a virtual résumé of continuity editing. The induced montage of images circles round eventually to the doubly "arrested" boy who first fixates the heroine's attention, until his image fades cinematically rather than diegetically (with no further reference to her adjusted lamplight) toward a funereal black (figs. 96 and 97).

But not before we recognize his raised hands as echo of the plaintive reach of the equally nameless boy in the prologue, tempting emblem of the other heroine's aborted child, or of both children in one, hovering in an indeterminate limbo of need. When that initiating figure in the morguelike, antiseptic, protonarrative space stretches out his hand first to us and then, by reverse shot, to a twinned full-screen image of the two women in succession and together, halved and doubled (fig. 98), the

82

85, 86, 87, 88

89, 90, 91, 92, 93

94, 95, 96, 97

98

99

film's later interest in a photographic mode of trauma is already being anticipated by a crisis of the image itself that bores through to the very basis of the cinematic medium. As this Eisenstein-like montage-by-collision of the two women becomes at its close a more drastically fixed collage of two distinct faces, each in semieclipse (left half Bibi Anderson, right half Liv Ullman [fig. 99]), the fluctuant transitions of the prologue have sketched in their extreme and schematic point. For film, too, like the psychic repair necessary to mend the son's ripped photo later or to synthesize those female specters hovering before the boy in the prologue, requires the piecing together of images to make a credible human figure.[3] By its default here, the norm is called back to mind in all its textual work: the multiplication of the *imago* into a coherent screen *persona*.

Even before this, the prologue has begun by reviewing the constituent elements and historical precedents of its own medium. Well before it has become a narrative, that is, Bergman's film has flickered into action by backing up its mechanical process to the ignition of the projector's arc lamp and the spooling past of the first inches of strip—the latter effect shown here as two sequential photograms on the film's own strip (fig. 100). Earlier yet, we have seen a few brief gestures, fitfully arrested, from a primitive early cartoon, evoking as it does the most obvious case of filmic movement as differential animation (fig. 101). If the ensuing full-screen animation of the female image had been *singular* in its transfor-

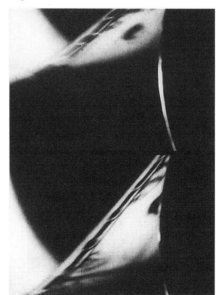

mations, the boy might then have been read as reaching out to bring the maternal ghost alive in his life. But by introducing the psychic rather than merely photogrammatic discrepancy in which the narrative is rooted—in other words, the virtual interchangeability of

100   101

the two female characters—and hence by animating only the dizzying oscillation between their two faces (and finally the perverse fusion in a single composite mask), Bergman's opening confounds its own foundational process in a way that in fact provides the formal matrix of the film's organizing theme. See it like this: Bergman has pursued the cinematic principle back to the interaction of photograms on the image track; in the process, however, he has baffled the ordinary seamlessness of transition by a doubling that is not close enough for comfort to the identical. In ordinary practice, no human images can come before us on-screen, no imaginary investments are possible, without the superimposition of one image upon its near twin. This is the materialist rule proved—if uneasily resecured—by Bergman's not just illusionist but hallucinatory exception. We are always, in watching movies, piecing together successive fragments as if they were simultaneous, always forging a gestalt of movement out of measurable difference.

Here is where *Persona*'s mysterious overture and the later photographic crises come into subterranean alignment with one of film history's most famous "barings of the device." This is the pivotal metalepsis (the invasion of form by content) whereby the relationship of the two women on-screen becomes so searing in its physical as well as psychic violence that the resulting narrative seizure is displaced onto a jam in the projector, making the film itself seem to catch fire under the scorching of its own lamp. The rending of one woman's flesh by broken glass left in her path by the other is transferred from plot to process, to film's material basis in vulnerable celluloid. This is certainly one way to read the violated image, first scratched like a cracked mirror in association with the broken glass (fig. 102), then singed open like a gaping wound (fig. 103). But by the linkage I have in mind, imagistic autonomy rather than mimetic transparency is the material aspect laid open to view—and not just here, in this famous filmic breakdown. It is laid bare as well by the counterplay between portable photographic documents in the plot and the unstable photogrammatic mutation that launches that plot. What has happened is that film narrative, arrested in its progress by its own content, has surrendered to the projector's aperture a single photogram, abandoning it there long enough to let it burn. But then the single photogram is always the end of film.

The whole regime of montage is at risk—here, but also from the first. Bergman's initial sequence of photogrammatic interchange (the collision of visages) has superimposed a difference just a little too great to be assimilated to "lifelike" facial movement. The wavering mismatch has thus disturbed the opening of a film whose climactic scene will imply the needed melding together of photographic fragments to constitute once more an imagistic continuum: namely, the tentatively re-fused picture of the previously rejected son. No longer riven, the optical two-made-one (by collage rather than montage) would, in terms of this particular photograph, recover an image sufficient, like those on-screen as well, to induce projection and emotional investment. The torn photograph seems, therefore, the narrative equivalent of the opening waver (and later fissure) of spliced personae: a severing of the self-identical in the (apparent, the apparitional) name of that yet more vital—or lifelike—reparation known as continuity, human and technological.

102

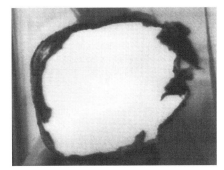

103

PHOTOGRAPHIC GROUND ZERO

Many films, from the popular tradition as well as the experimental or high-art canon, also trace screen spectacle back to the automated succession of the image track. It is no accident that so-called apocalyptic destruction is often the precipitating narrative moment. Just before the bombs are detonated at the targeted ground zero of midtown Manhattan in the nuclear holocaust finale of *Fail-Safe* (Sidney Lumet, 1964), the city's cosmopolitan bustle goes into freeze-frame. This familiar cinematic machination of death's stop-action moment in 1960s and 1970s cinema (as discussed in the previous chapter and again in the next), as well as in its countless TV derivatives since, does two related things in Lumet's early, blistering deployment. It evokes proleptically those photographs of a no longer extant metropolis that may be all history can warm itself with in the nuclear winter to come. It also puts a stop to cinematic representation per se, since everything that makes moving pictures of a place possible is hereby suspended just at the moment of obliteration.

All of a sudden this mainstream narrative film has come to look like an experimental montage. Ten rapid fragments of documentary New York footage, from Central Park and Saint Patrick's through an amusement arcade called Playland to African American children playing in the street to pigeons lifting in flight, are shown in quick cuts timed to the countdown. Splice in an aerial view of the Manhattan skyline along with the final radar scan. Cut again to the same miscellaneous shots we've seen before, though much enlarged now—and only frozen "photographs" this time (all but the first, that is, the birds caught on the wing). With the images pinioned for a dizzying second, one after the other, as if in midzoom, the camera zeroes in further yet—and with a weird mechanical screech on the sound track—on a tighter framing of the already stilled image. (See the same device used in muted form for Truffaut's *The 400 Blows* in the next chapter, though without the collision-course rapidity or the lethal screech.)

Lumet's whole patterned sequence is meticulously blocked out. The camera's scans of the freeze-frames in these chain-reaction zooms are launched by the pigeons whose imminent flight has ended the previous countdown in sync with the pilot's command "Lock" (fig. 104). Their image is reprised now as they burst into moving-image flight, swooping away from the camera toward a blank white billboard gaping behind them like a waiting screen, within whose urban frame some of them are caught when the image freezes (fig. 105). The birds' swift movement away from us seems, in effect, to cut the kinetic groove for what remains, as the camera's inward rush brings the other nine frozen images slamming up against their own two-dimensionality, the world itself cornered, with nowhere left to go—not even on. The visual rhetoric is itself inescapable: photographic stasis mocked by a vestigial cinematic device (the zoom, operated in the lab rather than on location) as if the camera were homing on a fixed target. After the penultimate ironic image of "Playland" has been truncated in close-up to "Play" (figs. 106 and 107) and the children's street game arrested in progress by both a lock and then a zoom (figs. 108 and 109), and just before the final midnight black background of the end

104, 105   106, 107   108, 109

titles, there is an almost subliminal flash insert—a blank white frame, neither photo nor film image—that registers like a burst of shapeless light. As such, it falls somewhere in ocular effect between the eradicating blast of the bomb and the lusterless bright blank of the no longer available world pictures on the strip.

The rigor of this materialist apocalypse, from frozen to effaced frame, is so complete that it has even been coordinated, in advance, with the stopped time of photography itself apart from filmic succession. Following the United States president's command to sacrifice New York City in self-administered reprisal for the accidental destruction of Moscow by an American bomber, we have twice seen the photographic document as a kind of proleptic elegy in the Barthesian sense: the already dead image of those about to die. The American general at Strategic Air Command speaks by phone to his Russian counterpart, just before the bombs are dropped on the Soviet capital, reminiscing about their wartime posts in London, the Russian saying how in a great city "history waits around every corner." Not for long in Moscow or New York. All the while the American general is studying a top-secret dossier that includes an enlarged official glossy of the Soviet general and a small snapshot of his family (fig. 110). The point is no sooner made than matched a scene later by a newspaper headline, with front-page photo, announcing that the American first lady is currently visiting New York City (fig. 111). Representing in sequence the three armatures of our photographic culture, institutional (official or classified document), domestic (private snapshot), and mass-produced (publicly circulated newsprint image), such photos are to be, within moments, all that remains of their subjects—and this by way of an apoca-

110

111

lyptic violence associated, through stasis, with an alternative mode of fixated image in the cinematic freeze-frame. One of the best comments on Lumet's organizing filmic irony comes years later and in a different context. It is no accident of cinematic idiom that in his study of the mediated nature of warfare since World War I, Paul Virilio, writing in 1983 about American tests on the laser-guided interception of missiles traveling at 3,000 kilometers an hour, closes his book with these bilingual fragments of apocalyptic irony and cinematic metaphor: "1984, Scan Freeze, arrêt sur image."[4]

Another narrative from the Hollywood tradition, this time a participant in the 1970s subgenre of "disaster film," manages its apocalyptic overtones with a similar recourse to the photographic basis of cinema. With anxieties over global nuclear destruction narrowed and backdated to a single international catastrophe, *The Hindenburg* (Robert Wise, 1975) actually distorts its cinematic surface with the extruded photochemistry of the processed image itself, not just its resulting visual frame. The film's premise—which makes its historical material over into a *plot*—is that the famous zeppelin exploded because of Nazi sabotage, detected not quite in time to keep the bomb from detonating. Just at the moment of ignition, a shot-countershot exchange of looks between the hero and the Nazi agent ejects them from the saturated color film we have been watching toward the black-and-white documentary aura of the final conflagration. This transition is achieved by the scorching violence of their passage from moving figures on color stock into a freeze-frame negative image switching over all but instantaneously into the black-and-white harbinger of the coming archival footage. In a flash, as the dirigible goes up in flames, the interior image of its melodrama is thus photochemically exploded in the inferno of a frozen split second. The frame itself goes gaseous, fluorescent, spectral, disembodied by optic reversal. The intercut antagonists are bled of color, movement, life, seared into the negative imprint of themselves—and of their own motion. The film's visual trope is remarkably exhaustive. To pass from fiction back into world-historical docudrama, from story into history, from Hollywood film into the look of archival record, the image track must efface its own narrative inventions, must vaporize its characters, triggering their reversion to the rudiment of both fiction and documentary film together: the photographic imprint in its negative origins as inscribed and fixated light.

Here we need to stand back, to hold the film strip up to the light again, to take stock of its material transparency as cinematic stock. This transparency, of course, evokes that other, more fundamental optic sieve: the negative imprint out of which any photograph is generated. Tincture flipped to picture, the photographic print is the destined inverse of its own negative transparency. This chemical fact has a further implication in the filmic sequence. Since film is like language at least to the extent of being based on a system not of double articulation (phonemes/lexemes) but of double realization (photograms/animation), it also rests in this sense upon a double negation. Just as the reversed transparency is the negative of the still image, the photogram on the track is the negative imprint of cinematic movement. In the usual photographic sense, the negative is of course the ghost of the positive—hence its readiness as a trope of death in film from Jean Epstein's *The Fall of the House of Usher* (1928) through Wise's incendiary apocalypse.[5] But so too does the photogram in relation to the generated cinematic image have something of the paradoxical aspect of a vital corpse, whose displacement by another kindred stiff shakes their stasis into life, sparks their flickering kinesis. If not, the photogram negates whatever motion it might otherwise vanish into.

Counterproductive—that's the photogram all right, when laid bare: the decisive piece and the essential decease of film, at once increment and disintegration. But who should balk at the counterproductive these days, the resistant, the estranging? In print media other than film, where there is no literal grain of surface or image to worry about, we call the text-based apprehension of such issues an against-the-grain reading. We institutionalize it as deconstruction. For all its potent phenomenological hold on us in "production," literature throws up little resistance (and suffers no final setback) in being read this way—that is, in submitting to its own unreadability, dissolving from wordsigns, signals of an alternative reality, into mere graphophonemic signifiers. Why not something equivalent in the general practice of film analysis? The gap between literary-critical habits and the heavily marginalized place of deconstruction (even in its heyday) within film studies cannot persuasively reside with the differing level of visualization involved.

Granted that we can see letters on the page, and extricate them from the words that summon mental images, whereas we can never see on-screen the individual photograms in and of themselves, even if we see nothing other than the rushed sequence thereof. But film theory—as textual theory—should long ago have penetrated such naive lines of defense. For grammatological deconstruction has accomplished nothing else for contemporary thought if it has not first of all reminded us that meaning on the page depends not on visible, but only on legible—because differential—signifiers. Film isn't alone here; you can't see pertinent opposition in the phonemic register either, when looking at a word, any more than you can see the single photogram in its displacement by another nearly identical to it. The very fact of signification must be deferred by its effects. Hence the recurrent Derridean figure of textual deathwork, a phantasmal "thanatopraxis" of marked difference, rather than seen marks, out of which the referred word is generated.

Narrative film, as suggested, has never come under this lens for long. Indeed, the deconstruction of its effects—in the name of their fleeting and differential, their (im)material basis—has been oddly resisted in some of the commentary drawn most directly to the vicinity of the question. I must therefore continue to take issue with associations of film with "life" (versus photography with death) in theoretical discussion running from André Bazin through Roland Barthes and Stanley Cavell to Christian Metz and Fredric Jameson and on, most relentlessly (if tacitly) of all, to Gilles Deleuze.[6] In one form or another in all these writers, the trope of immortality (a world viewed in its preserved mobility) wins out all too quickly for film over the constitutive photographic module upon which cinema is occasionally sensed if not quite glimpsed to depend.

WORKING OFF NEGATION

According to prevailing views, we may be ideologically compromised by over-looking the track, duped as usual by the aesthetic institutions of bourgeois culture, but we are not likely to be found challenged by its reassertion in certain film texts. This is the case even in a critique whose blend of *écriture* theory and psycho-analysis comes closest to the bearings of this book. In a brief section of his bench-mark essay "Ideological Effects of the Basic Cinematic Apparatus" titled "Projec-tion: Difference Denied," Jean-Louis Baudry, before turning to his more influential remarks on the psychology of subject positioning in cinema, asserts that film, in regard to the static image or frame, "lives on the denial of difference: difference is necessary for it to live, but it lives on its negation."[7] This is to recog-nize, in other words and in a double sense, that film *works off negation* at projec-tor speed. To add that film "represses" as well as denies and negates its essential differentiations, as Baudry does briefly a paragraph later, is to move more obvi-ously into a psychoanalytic realm. (The complications this introduces into the me-chanical progression of the film strip are ones this chapter will come round to in closing.) Here the sense of filmic productivity as "a system of writing [*écriture*] constituted by a material base and a countersystem (ideology, idealism) which uses this system while also concealing it" parallels the relation of intentional discourse to "the 'language' of the unconscious, as it is found in dreams, slips of the tongue, or hysterical symptoms" (291). In each case "continuity" is "destroyed" before it can be policed into submission again.

The footnote to this paragraph in Baudry is at least as revealing. Derrida's *L'écriture et la différance* has received token mention in the first note of the essay, but the point tucked away later is pivotal: "It is thus first at the level of the appa-ratus that the cinema functions as a language: inscription of discontinuous ele-ments whose effacement in the relationship instituted among them produces meaning" (297). Among them, not immediately between them. This gesture is more traditionally linguistic than deconstructive, for it loses the local force of the trace in the overall abstraction of the sign function. The task of this book, of course, is to find narrative films not only tallying such losses but momentarily re-covering from them at times. It invites the photogram's return to consideration not so much to note its blanket denial in spectation (Baudry's point about the symptomatic "ideology" of screen process) as to register either its allusive sum-mons through inset photography or its own operative recalcitrance, its drag on progression in the (at times) exemplary raggedness of screen imaging.

Both syntactic meaning and screen movement depend not on the wholesale ex-traction of intended effect from forgotten cause but on the point-by-point trans-formation of one thing (phoneme or photogram) into another such thing, each sub-sumed to the third thing—the representational process—that they produce over the dead body of their inscription. In film, one way of thinking about such frictive inscription on the run is that its aggravated, jostled materiality can sometimes goad the photogrammatic stiff at least halfway back to disruptive life. So too in the lex-ical segues of modernist literary practice, where the equivalent of instantaneous superimposition and lap dissolve often press a given syllabic cluster toward its internal breaking point. Through such surface disturbances, meaning is seen to spring not so much from the abstracted relation among signifiers as from the concrete shearing force *between* adjacent letters produced as unvoiced sound cues across the racing strip of script. As movie rather than text, of course, film behaves otherwise, acts as if action were not for an instant rooted in the facts of fixity. But not always—or not all the time. Given the number of films that do foreground the photographic counterpull, do allow a rupture of the cinematic momentum, its ambush or momentary annihilation, what is it about so much film theory that resists keeping in mind the film strip's entropic potential for dissolving back into separate photograms stripping over themselves in the animation effect?

One extended exception is *Screen/Play: Derrida and Film Theory,* but Brunette and Wills develop an argument with limited impact on textual analysis in their own pages and with regrettably little uptake in subsequent criticism. In this study of the referential fallacy in cinema studies, emphasis is placed on the twin fissure between image and world: on the one side, between picture and its signified scene; on the other, between picture and its "postal" destination. Yet in a committed Derridean spirit, this fissure is traced at one point back to its foundations in the camouflaged—or "negated" (their word too)—gap between separate framed imprints in a "paradoxical structure of absence and presence."[8] One consequence is paramount. The "idea of a teleological evolution of reality's representation of itself, like the idea of instant reproduction, can therefore be seen to be a metaphysical overlay" that occludes the "string of contradictory supplements required for the so-called image of the real to appear on the screen" (78). In this same spirit, we continue to inspect those films whose exposed sequential supplements work to peel away this "metaphysical" (that is, immaterial) "overlay" in the roughened byplay of narrative advance. Why—one still wants to know—is this so unusual a tack? To point to a strong phenomenological bias in much of film's best appreciative criticism is not a sufficient explanation. For 1970s film critique (Baudry and others) was ready enough, as I suggested, to see the ideological function of cinema as a deceptive masking of an apparatus in the work of a psychosocial imaginary—and hence quick to insist on anything hidden from the viewer, any illusion in which the subject is stationed to collude. In exploring film's tacit league with the ideological state apparatus, institutional demystifications of this stripe have, as a result, a healthy respect—in theory, at least—for the photogram, the frame in hiding behind the shot. As long as it stays where it belongs. What to say about it when it appears, when it flattens the mirage of the apparatus to sheer imprint, is another matter.

This is a matter that occasionally troubles Gilles Deleuze's otherwise direct borrowing from Henri Bergson. Even when not credited as such, the photogram is there as the very crux (and sticking point) of Deleuze's opening departure from Bergson in regard to cinema's space/time ratio. Here is where Deleuze comes across our path as at once a magisterial signpost and a massive roadblock. He theorizes the photogram, in relation (via Bergson) to the mind's photographic sense of emplaced matter, at a philosophical depth unapproached in previous commentary. But he then fends off its implications in his subsequent work on movement and temporality in cinema *as it appears to view*. The photogram gets lost, as in viewing it must, at what Deleuze everywhere calls, borrowing Bergson's terminology, "the plane of immanence."

FILM'S OCULAR MOLECULE

But to borrow from Bergson at this level is to oppose his own thinking. In 1907, in *Creative Evolution*, Bergson cites cinema as an example of the *illusion* that movement can be captured—rather than merely suggested (or analyzed)—by stringing together points in space as instants in time. For Bergson, movement always eludes us in the interval. It cannot be found where matter has been or where it is going; it can only explain the space, the lag, between as part of a pervasive impulsion or *élan vital*. Movement cannot be observed as such, only noted in its falsely demarcated stages and presumed effects. Its nature therefore is not properly understood as comprising discrete slices or sections of the material world linked by the superadded aspect of succession. This position, Deleuze would have it, prompts Bergson to downgrade the cinematic model too hastily. A decade earlier, just at the birth of cinema, Bergson's arguments in *Matter and Memory* (1896) already allowed for the interval manifested through "mobile sections, temporal planes [*plans*]."[9] This, thinks Deleuze, Bergson must have forgotten in his later critique both of cinema and of the cinematographic model of cognition. "The material universe, the plane of immanence, is the *machine assemblage of movement-images*. Here Bergson is startlingly ahead of his time: it is the universe as cinema in itself, a metacinema" (59).

True, but only when Bergson means it as critique. "We take snapshots, as it were, of the passing reality," Deleuze says, which we make over into cognition when we "set going a kind of cinematograph inside us" (2). For Bergson this is the *trouble* with perception, not the intuition of its fulfillment in cinema. In this way does perception ignore the inherent *becoming* of duration. Real cinema only makes things worse. Even if the mind did not tend to falsify the durative essence of reality in seizing upon its material dimension as it does, the problem with representation on-screen is that it has already mechanized the photographic flow before the mind comes to it. With cinema, we perceive a world in motion already artificially perceptualized. For Bergson, then, the problem with film as a reconstitution of movement is that the conceptual supplement of succession is engineered, the separate loci mechanically vanished. Film thus plays into the hands of our most stiffly schematic views of perception, substituting successive fixities, however finessed into disappearance, for the reality of becoming.

This is no fair objection, according to Deleuze, since what we actually see onscreen is not a false amalgam of position and succession pretending to movement. What we see instead—and for Deleuze everything depends on this—is the fusion of these components in the form of a sectioned duration, a virtual slice of motion, not discretely segmented but registered already as sequence. In a widely shared assumption that needs our further scrutiny, for Deleuze movement is the given, not the claim, of cinema. He holds that "cinema does not give us an image to which movement is added, it immediately gives us a movement-image. It does give us a section, but a section which is mobile, not an immobile section + abstract movement" (2). Yet surely cinema "gives" this on-screen only by having been given in the first place a concatenation of strictly spatial "sections," optic segments, whose mechanization is necessary for them to be projected as movement-image.[10] The image on-screen can only be the result of what the motion of the track does to render the founding imprint's before and after superficially—as opposed to profoundly—continuous. It is a parody of duration rather than an apt approximation or a redeemed and "corrected" (Deleuze's term) image thereof. What appears on-screen in Deleuze is the movement-image, and this is what we need to know first of all, philosophically, about cinema.[11] What appears on-screen in my sense (closer to Bergson's) is something that underlies and allows that image: the perceptible shift rather than the visible blurred shifting (trace rather than tracery) of one photogram in its difference from its predecessor.

This is a predecessor on the track that is simultaneously present to its successor on-screen, overlying it, dividing from it, each as if laminated over and peeling off from the other—or in Eisenstein's sense colliding with and recoiling from its signifying other. This is montage degree zero in Eisenstein's view, and it is an axiom that has been given too little circulation even in film theory broadly indebted to his work: "For, in fact, each sequential element is perceived not *next* to the other but on *top* of the other" in a perceptual "conflict."[12] Cinema is at root a conflictual tension that looks like action. It is, in brief, dialectical. Each picture is available to the eye in this shift, but they are visible only in their difference, a difference itself invisible as anything but a transition, a continuity. Each picture contributes to the mutual and constitutive blur of the movement-image, the imaginary movement. In resisting the drift of Deleuze's thinking, his general subordination of moving pictures to pictured movement, it would be foolish not to avail oneself of what is after all the fullest discussion of cinema's constitutive photograms that I know of in film commentary. These are his pages on the experimental montage of Dziga Vertov. For Deleuze, Vertov derealizes the gestalt of perception only in order to dissect and reeducate it. The discussion of Vertov, in other hands, might have verged on a materialist or even textualist theory of the cinema at large. Not here. It is, first, diverted to epistemology and then no sooner detailed than contained. Vertov's cinematic manner is thus made over into a brilliantly exceptional rather than an exemplary special case, an exception proving no rule about the ordinary suppression of the photogram on-screen. When single optic frames become the detached floating signifieds of a panoptic communal overview in Vertov, it is somehow the "molecular" nature of *perception* itself (rather than the atomistic nature of film's plastic constitution) that appears in a "gaseous" (83) and dispersed, rather than solid or fluid, state.

Writing of Vertov, Deleuze does sound (if only momentarily) like Eisenstein on the medium as a whole, where "montage is introduced into the very constituent of the image" (82). By highlighting the photogrammatic frame in various decelerations and accelerations, including the stop-action image, Vertov seems to foreground cinema's own grounding in an image before movement. To take such practice up into his own theory, however, Deleuze gives it an emphasis all his own. The single disseevered image institutes "the vibration, the elementary solicitation of which movement is made up at each instant, the *clinamen* of Epicurean materialism" (83). The conceptual result of this internal "swerve" from itself of the image? "Thus the photogramme is inseparable from the series which makes it vibrate in relation to the movement which derives from it" (83). In what sense inseparable? Would we not want to put it the other way around as well: that the strip (and its thrown image) is inseparable from the photograms that compose it?

Further, we might want to object that there is no "vibration" in the photogram per se until a multiple set is sent into motion—in other words, until atomized strip becomes track, "gaseously" dispersed or otherwise. Yet for Deleuze, Vertov's own photogrammatic emphases and inflections are immediately referred away from anything like a plastic or textual or medium-materialist phenomenon to a vision of vision per se, isolating "the point which changes, and which makes perception change, the differential of perception itself" (83). Where Vertov's radical constructivism might be thought to intervene against the screened "world" as supposedly received by the passive eye, Deleuze sees instead an analysis of perception's natural limit case. Human vision is distilled as never before to its optic conditions in perceptual mutability—rather than, as could well have been argued, filmically sliced away to its fixed cumulative particles as screen text.[13] Even at its least realistic, then, cinema remains for Deleuze a mimesis of natural perception.

By contrast, to isolate the photogram as the cinematomic unit of all multicellular (or in Deleuze's term "molecular") activity in projection is to insist (varying Derrida) on an inscription before the image as well as before the letter: the materialized t/race behind all screen movement. Numerous films come to mind as motivating—by immobilizing—the photographic undertext of the cinematic chain in ways arranged momentarily to resist the "reality effect" of the movement-image, that primal blandishment of the apparatus. Few films, however, go the whole way (to closure) with this autotropic trajectory, coming to conclusion in a manner devised to question (rigorously rather than merely rhetorically) their very point of departure in the fixed imprint. Three such anomalous films, however, do claim our immediate attention in this respect: one by that prolific student-practitioner of Bazinian phenomenology, François Truffaut; one by a new Australian filmmaker, Jocelyn Moorhouse, who seems to have Truffaut's film in mind with her mordant epistemological inquiry into the very photogravity of existence; and one a metafilmic collaboration between Wayne Wang and the novelist Paul Auster. Three other films will then follow for discussion from a single overdetermined genre. These are films whose photographic self-admissions are caught up in the technologies of visionary science fiction—-and whose narrative finales amount in related ways (anticipating my fuller consideration of the genre in chapter 5) not only to apocalyptic advents but to leveling textual disclosures. For now, the examples of inset framing ahead in this chapter may be said to insist on the photogram by encysting a second-order image of it.

Before these experiments in photogrammatic—because cinemato*graphic*—

reading, it is worth speculating on the underlying causes of the Deleuzian resistance to any such approach at the rudimentary level of the movement-image, a resistance staged most obviously as an objection to Bergson's mechanistic view of the apparatus. More deeply resistant to any Bergsonian cult of creative evolution, in favor of a revolutionary break with the continuum at every level, Eisenstein (as well as Vertov) wanted a dialectics of perception itself, not just of mental reflection. Taking film as a mode of philosophy, however, Deleuze wants only a new kind of thinking built upon a base of normative seeing. So, before pursuing these matters in chapter 3, let me tender a sweeping claim about all Deleuze sweeps under the rug in his first volume. Everything Deleuze resists attributing to the movement-image as an already textured or textualized imprint of the scopic field seems displaced onto the time-image, where betweenness, stratigraphic layering, interstitial and lacunary process, tectonic slippage (I'm faithfully paraphrasing)—where the whole opalescent faceting of indeterminacy is unleashed. According to the unspoken special pleading of this displacement, the movement-image must be constrained to the strictly manifest at the so-called plane of immanence so that it can be credited with nothing more drastic than generating an indirect time-image, time as function of motion, thus preserving inviolate and wild the direct time-image at what we might call the plane of ramification. I will be concentrating instead on the intervallic constitution of the movement-image itself, a thing of strata and lacunae in its own right that alone make possible an imaged temporality within screen motion. At this level the photogram, always forgotten, cannot be ignored.

CHAMBER OBSCURA

François Truffaut's 1978 *La chambre verte* (flatly translated, in English distribution, as *The Green Room*) seems renamed from the Henry James stories of which it is an amalgam ("The Altar of the Dead," "The Beast in the Jungle") in revisionary evocation of the camera obscura—and three years before Roland Barthes's title in the same vein, *La chambre claire* (in English, *Camera Lucida*). Certainly Truffaut's "study" is every bit as much as Barthes's an evocation of photography as a paradoxical death without extinction. More than this, in its updating of the James stories to the period after World War I, it is a reflection on this photographic function as prompted by the "apocalyptic" nature of mass slaughter on the mechanized battlefield. This is a bloodshed captured by cinematography in turn, so that, in Truffaut's montage prologue, his own face in World War I uniform (playing the hero, Julien Davenne) appears superimposed over film's grainy documentary record of the European carnage that robbed him of his closest friends—and with them, his ties to life (fig. 112).

112

A decade after the war and the intervening death of the hero's wife, the plot begins with his devotion to the green room of the title, an upstairs chapel in his home where he has

113, 114

115

enshrined the wife's memory in numerous photographs (fig. 113), including one of the two of them together (fig. 114). Later, when we see the celibate mourner eavesdropping at his office on another widower's conversation about reconnecting with life through a second marriage, the hero appears sealed off behind a rippled glass door pane like one of his own glazed photographs (fig. 115).[14] But camera placement, along with the angle of movement it permits, has even more pointed work to do back in his domestic chapel. When the camera tracks in on one of his wife's photographs, the very movement approaches a diegetic point of no return. As the photographic frame edges forward to coincide with the outer rim of the screen frame (figs. 116 and 117), the moving picture has suspended its momentum upon what becomes a doubly foregrounded glimpse of its own enchained basis in the photogram's constitutive death-in-life. I say doubly foregrounded because not only does a photographically based medium hold on a photograph at the end point of this advancing shot but, blurring the picture slightly, it permits the image to slip out from under itself across a thereby "invisible" dissolve (figs. 118-20). The spatial elision regains focus on the image of another mortuary image in profile, another copy of the same photograph of the wife, this time mounted on her tomb in the local cemetery (fig. 121). It is being viewed at this point by no one on the site, only the retreating camera—doing what the apparatus must always do, imposing motion upon stone-cold imprint. Emphasized in this softened toggle between equivalent funerary icons is the photogrammatic manipulation that alone permits this and any such transition. Montage has at this moment become in its own right a parable: in the interstices of cinema is always lurking—sequestered by negation—the deathwork of the stilled image.

To this sense of cinema as a kind of automatized and ghostly slide show of exchanged fading images, the whole immediately preceding scene has lent a heavily weighted stress. For the ostensible benefit of a mute boy somehow inexplicably in his charge—the wild child of Truffaut's earlier film in a new key—Davenne introduces a mode of inscription different from written language. In projecting for him various "plaques" in a "lantern" (fig. 122)—images, first, of enlarged insects, in which the child shows no interest—he eventually comes to some "beautiful" new ones of corpse-strewn battlefields and dismembered bodies, including in one case a gruesome decapitation (fig. 123). To all of these latter slides the child struggles to offer commentary in a barrage of guttural sounds and sign

language whose efforts, all told, represent the *unspeakable* itself.

It is into the flat depths of photography's own mute eloquence in the matter of death and mourning that the hero now pours what is left of his life. Only momentarily does he imagine other ways of mourning, of keeping the image of the dead alive and with him. After a fire in the green room threatens to destroy all his wife's images, he feels the vulnerability of his hold on the dead and asks a commercial mannequin maker to construct a life-sized 3-D mockup, which in the upshot horrifies him with its funerary waxiness. He will have to settle, monomaniacally from now on, for the two-dimensional imprint, not only of her but of all those whose absence from his life leaves the vacancy of loss. He bribes a priest to deconsecrate a chapel in the cemetery so that he can convert it into a secular mausoleum, with dozens of photographs faintly animated by the shimmering light of banked candles: cinema's flicker effect in macabre duplicate. When the hero falls out of frame from heart failure in the film's last scene, we are left only with his presence in a wedding photograph we have seen earlier and know to be somewhere in the shimmering background of a final prolonged photopan. Thus does the moving image die away into the (at present invisible) still: the mourner mourned in his own favored medium. The more thoroughgoing cinematic illusion generates (above and beyond the still image) an animation effect that carries something of the vivifying emotive investment of the hero's obsession with single photographic portraits. That no one—least of all the hero—is entirely fooled by the flickering candlepower he brings to bear on the plethora of fixed, framed images may be the final thrust of Truffaut's fable. For photographs, it seems, always break the cinematic séance by lifting—or rending—the veil of motion.

116, 117, 118, 119, 120, 121   122, 123

PROVING (INVISIBLE) GROUND

The Green Room seems to have gone as far as possible in marking photography's remove from life—and cinema's with it. Another film, indebted to Truffaut, goes as far as possible in marking photography, from within life (and cinema), as the sole warranty of such life. From the deep-going wordplay of its title forward, *Proof* (Jocelyn Moorhouse, 1991) is a taut study of the photographic imaginary in a bizarre limit case. Its hero is a blind photographer who believes that without his photos the world would cease to exist for him—or at least cease to be credible. This is the premise, and it could just as well be the setup for an extended sick joke—something like "What did the blind photographer say when they told him his work was badly framed?" "Sees who?" The premise is pitched, instead, somewhere between epistemology and metaphysics. On the one hand, it involves the protagonist's sense of the world as ultimately dependent on the evidentiary traces of photography. On the other hand, it turns on a confidence in those traces as the perpetual unseen of existence, its absent cause, its transcendental signified.[15] And as this premise is implemented we get a melodramatic plot—but one that is also a tacit metanarrative about the relation of photographic (via photogrammatic) documentation to the cinema's own imaginary as credited world. For neither the blind man with his snapshots nor the film audience before the screen sees the definitive still images (in our case photograms) whose existence, on filmic stock as much as on paper, underlie in order to element his world—subjectively in his case, objectively (voyeuristically) in ours. Without photographic nodes of record, even unseeable ones, the hero would, he thinks, have no existence—for himself but also, we are made finally to realize, for us.

First, the plot. Martin, a blind young man with an independent income, meets a hapless young waiter, Andy, and they strike a friendly bargain. Andy will describe the photographs taken at random by Martin, so that Martin can inscribe their details on the back of each print with a braille stamp gun. Andy is soon complimented for the simple clarity of his descriptive style. He becomes not so much Martin's eyes as the evocative ekphrastic artist (representing the visual by verbal means) of Martin's photographic dossier, finding economical words for the scenes the camera has transcribed. Yet real bodies get in the way of this strictly representational exchange. It happens that the hero has a mean-spirited housekeeper, Celia, whose cruel passion for Martin is rebuffed with equal cruelty. Jealous of Martin's friendship with Andy, she seduces the new friend in order to come between the two men. The brief affair, which Martin soon discovers, ends in Andy's revulsion when he is invited to Celia's apartment. Since the split with Martin is already accomplished and she no longer needs to hide her secret, Andy discovers the extent of her obsession with his former friend—and hence the fact that she has been using Andy himself in a revenge plot. In terms of dramatic trajectory, this is the film's ironic climax: the revelation—devoured by the panning camera, as if in Andy's eye-opening POV—that her walls are plastered with photos of the photographer in every degree of enlargement (fig. 124), their "candid" nature obviously abetted by his own visual oblivion.

The blind voyeur has all along been voyeurized—and not only by us in the audience, but by a character *within the plot* availing herself of his image. And not just of Martin's image, but of Andy's too. For her jealous realization that Martin has a new friend comes about when she fits together into a composite representation, like a puzzle, Martin's stray snapshots of the interloper's body taken mostly by accident (figs. 125 and 126): a collage by which she then recognizes Andy at the back door in the next scene. Until now, the world is at photographic arm's length from her perverse clutch. If, as one is invited to guess, a good part of her festering scopophilic desire is fueled by the lack of his bodily presence in the pictures of Martin she covets, then her eroticized looking is all the more like that of a film audience indulging in absence. But once her cool lust is removed from the plot (when she is summarily fired by Martin—and never mentioned again), space is made anew for an emotional reclamation of the photographic surrogate.

124

What follows in the denouement is the film's negative or absconded apocalypse of the photographic moment, off-camera, withdrawn to a revelation we realize strangely pervades rather than dramatically punctuates the film as film. The moment is led up to by what we have learned in the story's cumulative flashback structure: concerning the garden of Martin's childhood home, described by his mother in words he could never bring himself to trust; and concerning her death and burial, about which he had only the word of those who sealed and interred her coffin.[16] Absence as death meets absence as immutable mental preservation in the last scene, and then the last shot, of the film. This structuring absence resides in an all-confirming photo of the garden from which the film camera continues to avert its gaze—even when Martin shows it to Andy in a final reconciliation scene. The

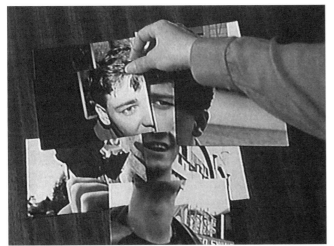

125

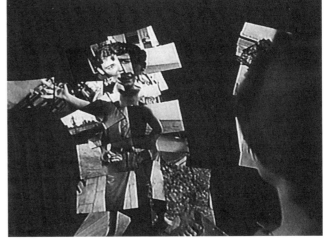

126

object of this confidence is now "read" by Andy in a way that restores confidence in the mother's own original description of the *locus amoenus,* the lost Edenic place whose ingress is only and always through the mind's eye.[17]

To the implications of this elided visual material as the film's title scene, as *proof,* we return in a moment. But to connect this scene with the larger question of photography's relation to film, it behooves us to recall that we have in fact gone to the movies earlier in Moorhouse's film. Midway through the plot of *Proof* it has seemed the logical next step to Andy, as visual translator, that he should mediate the cinematic as well as the photographic medium for Martin. "Has anyone ever described moving pictures to you?" "You mean cinema? No. I hate crowds." So Andy chooses a drive-in screening of an erotic slasher film, and his economical style is especially effective in rendering the naked breasts of the dormitory coed about to be hacked to death by the prowling fiend looking in at her window. In this sleazy *mise en abyme* of reception, Martin's relation to a tantalizing world unseen is, in an oddly inverted way, that of the sighted audience to the exaggerated visibility of cinema: held by the presence of a continuous impalpable spectacle to whose apparent spatial disposition one is denied full access.

For the painfully self-enclosed protagonist, this is the agon of the world's withheld presence. A credible photograph that might suspend this drastic absence, even an unseen photograph but one still portable, a graspable imprint backed by tangible letters (the braille tape punched out and affixed after Andy's descriptions)—an objectified image that can actually be palpated for comfort and reassurance: this is not nothing. But that such photographic solace remains a photoengravement of primal loss is also confirmed by the late scene in which the hero, assured by a gravedigger that there are no empty coffins in the cemetery, runs his hands over the inscription on his mother's tomb—as if inscription were the very proof of death. It is from this graveside flashback that the plot turns to the hesitant reunion with Andy and the exhumation of the original photo from a wall safe. The viewer has ample time, in the scene's slow buildup, to review the epistemological disquisition implicit in the film so far. We are assured (by visual memory) of our life in the world the way the blind hero is assured (by photography) that he has lived: by remnants of a past available to manifestation through means other than sight, delegated in this case to eyes other than his. The world exists, and has existed, because I have photo-

127

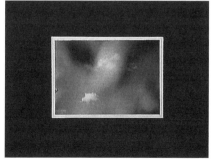

128

129

graphs of it, not that I can see, but that others can. A photograph would in fact dispel the doubt that the world is only in the mind of the beholder, not so much guaranteeing materiality as tending to mitigate extreme subjectivity. The world may be a Berkeleyan mirage, but photography at least testifies to the objective contours of its collective—and thereby communal—hallucination for all observers. More important, not only is the world there in these pictures, but I was there to take them, present to the world even in its visual absence from me. (Cinema backward.)

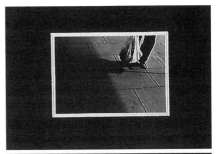

130, 131, 132

As soon as this is confirmed by the verbally depicted and cinematically unseen last photo, filmic picturing returns us in a final flashback to the garden window before halting verbal and visual description together, image and sound track alike, in an abrupt cut to black leader at film's end. In the realization that no more images are to appear, we may be thrown back on the darkness from which, in the form of single photographs, they first appeared. On a black field, even before the credits, the film's first visual material was a random, spaced sequence of color snapshots, nondescript and indiscriminate: tree trunks, the hind leg of a dog, a park bench (fig. 127), flowers out of focus (fig. 128). These are images edging into—or barely caught leaving—the photograph's field of view, as (in the narrative space itself) we will later see Andy diving out of the viewfinder's width of detection (fig. 129). Tossed before us like a miscellaneously cataloged file of snapshots rather than the filing by of film images, and gradually interspersed with the opening credits, these inset images tease us with the sense that their out-of-field space may coincide with the wider optic of the screen's own frame. And when that whole viewing plane is claimed by narrative, cinema seems activated in its explicit departure from the inlaid still shot: burst on us as an almost abstract emblem of vectorized motion. From the automatized parade of photographs, that is, we are precipitated by a shock cut into the surge of a commuter tram speeding by in medium close-up between the camera and a blind man walking down a city street. The photographic series of the credits is displaced on the instant by the sheer instantaneous displacement of photograms—and so fast, precisely, that no illustrative frame could catch it. Further, the last two photographs instantaneously flicked past in the prologue have been timed so that the ill-framed shots of legs and plastic shopping bag (fig. 130) plus cane meeting sidewalk (fig. 131) seem to collide dialectically (as Eisenstein would have it) for the first moving image of the hero making his way along the sidewalk, cane in one hand, bag in the other (fig. 132). Such a synthesis would be italicized by its very speed. In terms of filmic impulse, the rushed transition from sequenced stills to movie offers only the blur of a roaring mechanism producing nothing more—but nothing less—than a reduplication of cinema's own essential flicker effect: namely, the stroboscopically fleeting tram windows through whose lateral cascade we first see a continuous world only by lightning-fast fits and starts.[18] Right from the jump start, then, we know that *Proof* has something to do with the *difference* between photographs and cinema. It now proceeds to unroll itself between the poles of this difference: between the seen world and its discrete still effigies.

Under the dictates of the plot itself, this lurch into motion from the sequential still is soon reversed in a photographically based narrative sequence robbed momentarily of photogrammatic animation. This sequence follows from the film's first

133

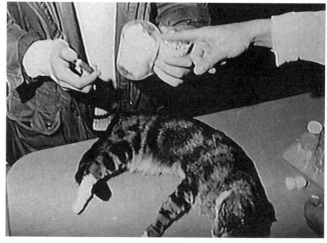

134

135

narrated scene of photography. Andy and Martin have taken an injured cat to the vet, and Martin begins snapping shots of Andy and the limp stray against a bulletin board of similar pet photos (fig. 133). In doing so he might seem merely to be rounding out, with a new prospective offering, the collage of satisfied patrons and animal patients. Not for long. What happens instead is a photo*montage.* For the whole brief story of the cat's treatment and subsequent recovery—all we are ever to get of it—is launched from these initial snapshots in the waiting room. It is a story generated as a quick-cut sequence of his photographs taken in the doctor's inner office (fig. 134, for example). What thus ensues is a narrative told in seventeen separate and frame-filling images whose status—as if just emerged from the camera—hovers ambiguously between freeze-frame and processed still print, like the credit snapshots come (forward, full-screen) to narrative (but still not kinetic) life. Whereas *Persona* narrativized a single picture plane (the ghetto photograph) like a shot plan in action, this "scene" shuttles the planar space of separate shots into a narrative effect. Each filmic episode testifies by default to the full cinematic function it suspends. But the plot's overall thematic of blind faith adds a further turn to this episode of photographic reversion in *Proof.* As Martin's only guarantor of the world, his present camerawork—and not least because of its miniature veterinary fable of tender recuperation for the animal once presumed dead—becomes for a few definitive moments simultaneous with, and indistinguishable from, our film: its own and only proof.

Before its final cut to black, therefore, *Proof* seems deliberately to have sampled every way, other than cinematically, for photographs to add up: as a series of reframed snapshots (in the prologue), as a montage of stills (at the vet's), or as a collage of part objects (Celia's detective work). As a running sum of photograms in its own cinematic right, then, the film must ultimately contend with its own serial fabrication in its last shot, indeed its last frame, where narrative is brought up short as follows. Having just had the garden photo described in a gratifying—ratifying—last ekphrasis by Andy, Martin seems plummeted one last time into his childhood. Yet a fixed frame again prevents his access to the confirming garden, a window frame this time, here translucent like the lit but imageless film frame (fig. 135). This last image is moving precisely in its ambiguity—and stunning precisely in its arrest. Set and lit like the other memory flashes, it sets their peculiar epistemology into relief. Of course memory always tampers with reality, reformulates it at least slightly. Any focalized narrative flashback runs the risk exposed in extreme form here: succumbing to the element of sheer subjectivity that penetrates recollection.[19] But more seems at stake with and in the film's closing image. Here, one last time, is a recovered scene that cannot be strictly visualized as present since it left no ocular trace to begin with. So what are we watching? A last subjective configuration of the always lost visual past? Or more subjective yet, an *image* of reconciliation—one whose best metaphor is in fact the fantasy projection of film, fragile and vanishing as such? The young boy stretches out his hand to touch the window's light-filled pane, and the film goes suddenly to a black screen: the suspended image at the end of all imaging. The hero's dysfunction, transfigured to mere limitation by the grace of restored filial confidence, has of course foreclosed the confirming reverse shot. All possibility is left open, leaving the garden pristine in its absence—in the memory of its invisibility. Echoing the child's yearning reach toward the screened image of the double mother in *Persona,* this closing moment grows metacinematic in the very futility of its urge toward image.

Form implodes upon content—and it is our vision for once, not the hero's, that is lost to blackness. We never get to see the garden either. In the grips of the last shot's poignant image of the craving child on the stretch for his world's retrieved validation, we come slamming up against the narrative's own impasse in the instantaneous convulsion of closure. I can think of no more disturbing or effective cut to black in recent film.[20] In Deleuze's Bergsonian terms, here the "interval" of motion has been snapped short in midspan, spliced away into void, all further images snipped in the bud. And in the recoil of a split-second's reflection, we may well sense that the jolting arrest of the image results from just this deep and otherwise camouflaged fact about cinema. In the context of a single and unseen photographic rectangle certainly (the garden snapshot), but in any and all other cases as well, the cut to black results from the sudden denial of *even one more photogram.* The hero's visual impairment has become our own—but in the absence of that cinematic imaginary that brought us together in the first place.

SMOKE'S SCREEN IMAGES

Of the perplexed subjectivity of a closing "flashback" sequence, there is a more extreme recent example. And on the specific interplay between separate photographic affidavits of the real and the different(ial) evidentiary nature of continuous-action film, there is an even fuller commentary. Both come in the form of

136

Wayne Wang's 1995 film *Smoke*, which is included at this stage by way of summarizing the chapter's main claims so far. On its own terms, the film is certainly a kind of summa: namely, of photography's relation to diurnal reality, to temporality, to narrativity, to death, and ultimately to filmic visuality—and hence to the revealed imaginary of film's mechanized textuality.

The central character of *Smoke*, Auggie Wren (Harvey Keitel), takes peculiar advantage of his tobacco store's corner location as a photographic vantage on its New York crossroads. More than a hobby, his "project"—as he puts it, his "life's work"—is a kind of antifilm carved out of that fixed locus: a series of black-and-white 35 mm photos taken every day at 8:00 A.M. from the same point on the sidewalk, over four thousand in all between 1977 and the film's setting in 1990. Spanning an arbitrary and mechanized interval only a couple of million times greater than the one-twenty-fourth of a second elapsed between cinematic shots, but otherwise following the same logic, these painstakingly collected images have been pasted seriatim into albums. Their discontinuous sighting of the world's passers-by is to be distinguished from film mostly by the distinctness of the separate shots. It is in this form (fig. 136), before their subsequent kinetic transformation by the narrative's own editing and camerawork, that they are displayed, early on, to the film's other leading character, the novelist Paul (William Hurt). He at first finds them "overwhelming" in their freakish irrelevance. He is a professional storyteller, and for him their perverse discontinuity bears no narrative charge. The regularized interval has become a disabling gap. Until, that is, he spots among the photos a shot of his mourned wife walking past the camera's field of vision, perhaps not long before she was accidentally shot (in the other sense, and to death) in a headline-making outbreak of random urban violence. He cannot help but weep at the sting of this image, at the loss its bodily absence redoubles, even as he has already had borne home to him the impersonal metanarrative force of the photographs more generally.

Whether or not we later forget this transformative photomontage, something else remains obvious about the lingering impact upon his storyteller's imagination of the association between photography and death. Out of the blue, the film cuts at one later point into Paul's narrating to a teenage boy, Rashid, an unlikely anecdote (the germ of a story he is at work on) about a young skier who returns to the site where his father was buried by an avalanche years before. The hero of the anecdote finds himself face-to-face not just with a corpse but—like a mirror held up to his own past—with the frozen image of a progenitor younger than the son is now. Nothing is said to link the conceit of this story to photography. Noth-

MOTION'S NEGATIVE IMPRINT

ing needs to be. It drops into place, without comment, as an improbable "natural-ization" of photography's "freeze" framing. And if we happen to remember this digressive anecdote later on, it can only lend a further inflection to the turnabout of the film's twofold closure, where Paul becomes the recipient rather than the source of an equally improbable anecdote from Auggie. The tale is offered up to the professional storyteller—in a prolonged close-up monologue—as possible material for a Christmas story commissioned on short notice by the *New York Times*. Offered as verbal event—and then, as it were, screened by the film itself.

Tendered and then equivocally retracted as a "true story," Auggie's tale in fact loops back to a time before the film's opening to narrate the events leading up to his theft of his precious camera. He tells of having lifted the camera from a stack of stolen goods in the bathroom of a blind African American woman's apartment after having impersonated her thieving grandson, whom he was attempting to track down, through the course of a take-out Christmas dinner with her. Auggie then finds the old woman gone, probably dead, the following year. In this color film's longest shot sequence, we must visualize these events once as he speaks them in increasing close-ups, intercut with the eyes rather than ears of his audi-tor (surrogate for our mind's-eye realization). The surprise is that the film then pictures the events of the story by entering upon a black-and-white replay of their details behind the end titles.[21] This whole coda is not only disarming in its visual rhetoric (sentimentalism one-upped by epistemological quandary) but ambiguous in its cinematographic constitution. Whose images are these—and for whom? Can this black-and white coda be registered as omniscient testimony of the story's ve-racity? Then why risk throwing the color stock of the preceding film fiction into dubious relief? Does the last sequence reject color by some local derivation from Auggie's own daily images, borrowing evidentiary force from these manifest fac-tual documents? Or is the closing footage merely the subjective record of what Auggie does honestly remember, cast up in the look of his favored still medium? Alternatively, are these images Paul's alone, marginally peopled by characters we have seen before, with him, in the film's main diegesis, but assuming new roles by association here? Is this guess confirmed by the fact that the sequence begins as in the black-on-white scripted form of "Auggie Wren's Christmas Story" in a type-writer carriage? Or all of the above?

Ultimately, in the imaginative transfer effected by the scene, it may not mat-ter. In any case, it's too soon to tell. Before we can even begin testing our an-swers—before we can go on to say that the appended montage, whether true or not, imprints a truth about the film as a whole—we would need to look more closely at the definitive matrix of photographic documentation and resultant mon-tage early in the narrative. We must turn again, that is, to the pages of Auggie's photo album. Or more to the point, turn them: producing their sequence like a flip-book animation. But this the film has already done for us—in a two-stage photomontage of first rapidly, then more slowly, overlapped fades closely remi-niscent (and with something of the same philosophical valence) of Marker's renowned technique in *La jetée*, to which I will be turning next.

Paul has thumbed through page after page of mounted snapshots with

137, 138, 139

mounting impatience, finding them "all the same." But wait. Auggie insists that "things happen there too, just like everywhere else." He might have been even more exact. Things, by taking time, *take place*, even as they may be almost entirely displaced from the arbitrary frame. And when these photo frames are cinematized by dissolve, the peripheral achieves the eloquence of the ephemeral. Here Auggie's routine morning efforts edge toward cinema's own mourning work. And all while the wheeling electrical mechanism of a window fan rotates away as synecdochic prop in the background of this emblematic tableau, where two men on-screen, two images imprinted over and over again on a roll of film spooling past us, share the site of photographic spectation in one of the narrative's many long-held, fixed-framed, photolike shots. When, in the inset montage that ensues, photography's random taking-from-place is carried over to the synchronized trace of one image in succession to the next, a further model, though not yet an instance, of cinema is generated by editing. Not just the *figured* evanescence of this montage but its technological *fact* is lifted to view—as each of these same snapped figures in the album now seems either to be captured on the heels of its transformation into another (figs. 137 and 138) or to be fading into the intermittently empty street (fig. 139).[22] Human transience is italicized by its own filmic metaphor. The unsaid punning matrix of the scene—the *pedestrian* nature of these images—is thus one-upped by the itinerancy of the film frame itself.

Here too we cannot successfully discriminate between Paul's mind's-eye view of the process and some shared seeing transferred to him from the intent of the photographer. All we know is that film narrative has carried, as illustrative text, a few minutes of subjectively invested technology halfway along the road toward cinema's immanent motion from its point of origin in the abrupt stasis of photography. This specifically cinematized motion now completes itself in the action of a moving camera when the long-held image of Paul's wife is drawn toward him in a slow forward zoom (figs. 140 and 141)—decelerated elegiac equivalent of the whiplash rack-zooms at the end of *Fail-Safe* (again figs. 106-9 above). Throughout this whole montage sequence in *Smoke*, Auster's deadpan dialogue seems crossed with the intonations of Derridean *différance*, providing a thumbnail theory of the photogram's own continuous self-deferral as screened image: "They're all the same," grants Auggie, "but each one is different from every other one. And sometimes the different ones become the same, and the same ones disappear." He is speaking, of course, philosophically, about presence and loss under the sign of mortal transition, while the film is also ventriloquizing through him not only its own narrative motives but its own motoring technology. An earlier clue to the film's preoccupation with essence as difference comes in Paul's anecdote to his cigar-store cronies about Sir Walter Raleigh's ingenious weighing of smoke as merely the remainder between the measures of unburned and burned cigars. Difference is the concept for which *Smoke* is the name.

If, further, Auggie in presenting his albums is speaking sociologically about a cultural sameness within difference, speaking as a utopianist of eased racial polarities, then his later verbal story—coming to life in an already naturalized black-and-white (rather than black-versus-white) zone of reciprocated imagination—might well be his dream of a humanizing community come true. Not just as a photographer, then, but as an anthropological fieldworker in his own native habitat, Auggie may have tried putting together the pieces of a discrepant social picture from his position as participant-witness at its commercial crossroads. He *may* have, though we will never know for sure. One doesn't have to believe the closing story as true. Precisely not. To hear it as even possibly true, as a wish-fulfillment fantasy of interracial filiation in a world blind to color, and hence to accept its visualization as an act of *vision* (on Auggie's part as well as Paul's), is to appreciate the utopian gesture on its own narrative (and hence cinematic) terms, where every legend of a new amalgamated tribe would have to begin in "sheer" imagination.[23]

Cinematic technology and narrative impulse thus coincide in mutual disclosure when an early verbal evocation of time passing is matched by a full-film coda about the old woman there in her apartment one Christmas, gone the next, released from presence, her space relet to another in that in-dwelling of transience that resides at the heart of life. The still camera alone has been stolen from time, her only memento and her legacy. Whereas photography encases already past images in a text of record, film is brought forth—and here brought out—as *the text of their very passing.* Photogrammatically conceived, film lodges the negative imprint of its own forward momentum: an image always on the way out. Hence, in the end, the dying grandmother revisualized for us only after her presumed demise. Film comes to the screen as duration under the aspect of an apocalyptic (if itself transient and ever renewable) finality. Smoke . . . it all goes up in. But in the meantime . . .

When events are gone by, a fleeting imprint is replayed in reception and identification. Everything about the mechanics of transience in this film is thus circumscribed by its theme of transference, as we might have expected from Auster's early work. Looking ahead to the junctural ambiguities of verbal ligature in the modernist praxis reviewed in my last chapter, we note that in Auster's photographically preoccupied memoir a decade before, *The Invention of Solitude*, reading's phenomenological power is said to open—across the blurred threshold of wording itself—upon "his-

tory" properly conceived. It offers in this way an access not only to the objective past (as in photography) but to the mind of the other, an access distilled in a play on verbal elision that stages in the narrowest possible compass the very cognitive fusion it attributes to reading. Auster speaks of transcribed "memory" as making possible an "immersion in the past of others," a past that one "both participates in and is a witness to"—in other words, in the very otherness of wording to its own signifiers, which one "is a part of and apart from."[24] Such is the phonemic flicker effect whose montage equivalent for film has been activated in *Smoke,* over the wispy evanescence of the photo albums, in the phenomenological exchange between Auggie's split-second historicism and Paul's progressive identification.

MARKER'S MARKED MAN

Before its fuller treatment three chapters away, science fiction rounds out the picture at this stage with its emphasis on the materialized technology of filmic picturing. Here is the one narrative mode that regularly privileges a consideration of mediated reality. In particular, the technofuturism of sci fi's narrative formulas generically overdetermines two aspects of our present topic—both media technology and apocalypse—that are only accidents of the other genres, contingent inventions of their plots. In futuristic sci fi they are often, instead, foundational. And the most daring, pervasive, and definitive fit between the two issues, image technology and apocalyptic figuration, is surely mounted by Chris Marker's legendary *La jetée* (1963), a probable influence, along with Truffaut's *The 400 Blows,* on the closing freeze-frame Armageddon of Lumet's *Fail-Safe.* Marker's is a "film" in which half an hour's worth of photogrammatic track registers for the most part nothing but one still photograph after another, lap dissolved in their emblematic dissolution: relics of a world whose ruin is itself in further decay after World War III. In this strictly residual world, the delayed apocalyptic moment for the time-traveling hero is the revelation (by final freeze-frame) that his flight from inaugural trauma has gotten him nowhere. Via the film's "trick ending," he is immured again in the frozen imagery of his private past, where a proleptic trace of his own end has been lodged. For the death we thought he saw along with us in the opening frames was his own. In the course of the intervening photomontage (or *photoroman,* or *ciné-roman,* as it is sometimes called), each isolated, then overlain, photographic integer, no longer movement-images at all, figures the "scar" left (as described in the voice-over) by memory's impress, then swallowed up by the next one in the ineluctable rush of subjectivity's never better than elusive fixations.[25]

The film begins where *Fail-Safe* leaves off, in the unmitigated, stricken fixity of the nuclear day of judgment. As manifested by the falling away of its photographic glimpses, the aboveground world seems leveled to a disintegrating visual archive of its previous artifacts, with buildings, monumental sculpture, roadways, and airports crumbling grainily one into the other. Where consciousness has become all loss, the slowed photograph in passing, the no longer achievable momentum of film, has become the very figure for life in liquidation.[26] And plot tightens the noose of time. In the face of worldwide technological collapse, the hero is programmed by hostile underground experimenters to transport himself into the future. Once there, he will need to procure an undescribed and portable power source to be sent back through time for the maintenance of the present. Unfilmed in its determining necessity, this essential power source operates an encrypting of cinema itself: the machine that, precisely while we are watching this one proleptic fiction, has manifested the as yet unarrived. But not as we would expect to see it in a genre film—not, in short, cinematically. Warped by the substance of its own prophecy, the form of Marker's forecast is a photographic reversion. Cinema suffers here the onset of its own disintegration, burdened by a drag on the very succession necessary to image the world's nuclear future. At the level of the plot, to keep the present moving forward is entirely in the interests of the future—as the very condition of its possibility; at the level of the mechanism, to keep the present in motion is the continuous losing battle of the film's own textuality. The apparatus seems disabled in its full operation by the plot's own thematic crisis, with the trauma taken out—played out—at the level of the strip itself. Cinema is reduced by Marker to an editing mechanism for single photograms in a clinging duplication capable of sustaining no illusory movement but that of disappearance per se, where death haunts every interval.

Here is where the specular psychology of loss and the scopic rhetoric of prophecy so uncannily converge in this text of decelerated process. For movie sci fi to wax genuinely apocalyptic as genre narrative, Marker's cine-novel suggests, it would have to starve into devitalized surrender its own—as well as to admonish other—technologies of power. It would have to slow down, make plain the losses it envisions, register all presentness in view of its manifest passing, call a halt to unexamined process. Wedded relentlessly to technique, Marker's plot is a perfect allegory of this devitalization. The hero finally decides that the future is not, perhaps never has been, meant for him. Rather than desiring (and so helping to refuel) succession, he refuses it. He flees back to a past recaptured only by a return to—or a return of—an early fixed frame readable now as the scene of his own death. Which, at one level, is only to say that the photogram is always the death of characterization on film, fixity the refusal of all futurity, all space/time ratios.

This is what the entropic montage of Marker's photogrammatic retardation demarcates—and tropes—so potently. Even before the film's self-contagiously punning title will have called itself to our attention under the sign of its fractured modernist gesture in the closing chapter, we note that the voice-over itself describes the hero "ejected" from the present to meet an "emissary" from the future. Bracketed in this way is the etymological middle space (in French as in English) within which any emitted image is sent, thrown, into receipt. Among the title's palimpsest of associations (including the airport jetty of its first and last frame), *La jetée* impresses us further, by imprinting it before us, with the fact that "the thrown away" on-screen is always *la photogramme:* the ejection from the apparatus of one image after (and by) another. Posed here by the counterweight of mere photomontage, the question is only whether the specular suppression required by the apparatus will go so far as to sustain this loss in the form of a motion picture.

142, 143

In *La jetée*, when film comes awake to its own possibility as movement, so to speak, it does so only after considerable struggle—and only to give way again, give out, to mere photography. I refer to the hero's dream woman coming awake in real time under his own seeming glance by the faster and faster overlap of photograms. But the contributory still imprints (figs. 142 and 143) are not forgotten in the kinetic effect that results, even before they again swamp those few seconds of movement with the prevailing overlay of phased stasis. Too much of reality's image has been undone, too often, for us to relax fully into the emergent cinematic illusion. In the earliest stages of underground experiment, for instance, the hero was meant to summon up images of "real birds" (fig. 144), a shot whose petrified wings anticipate the New York pigeons whose flight is stopped cold by the dropped bomb in *Fail-Safe* (fig. 105 again). When, in the company of his dream woman, the hero of *La jetée* later visits a prewar natural history museum within the gallery of his artificial memory, the real birds he sees there, stuffed (fig. 145), carry over with them no more momentum from their unembalmed previous reality than do the photographs that materialize these exotic specimens in the evanescent museum of Marker's degenerated cinema.

Marker's micromanagement of duration figures life's sequential past ages as stages sundered one from the other, stacked, layered, lingering, but (except on pain of death) irreversible. Life is more like a photo album than we want to think—or than we think from the midst of our wanting. For Vivian Sobchack, by contrast, Marker's anomalous film enacts the phenomenological pressure upon the photographic element within cinema: the pressure toward a movement that for her grows ontogenetic. If no other film criticism existed that was bent on dismissing the photographic basis of film from screen consideration, Sobchack's unique way of including it in this one atypical case would alone be enough to call up the present book in rejoinder. For it is exactly the phenomenological thrall of cinema, its illusion of existential immanence, that my chapters find certain films willing, instructively, to suspend. These films are willing—and able—to do so precisely in their reversion, momentary or prolonged, to the photographic undertext. Completely unlike film in Sobchack's view, however, the photograph is in her terms "transcendent" in relation to the time of its taking.[27] With an unacknowledged Bergsonian emphasis on becoming rather than being, Sobchack says that the photograph, in diametrical contrast to film, "never presents itself as the coming into being of being" (59). Somehow, we are to think, film does.

Hence Marker's halfway house as her chief exhibit, where there is no doubt that such ideas of cinema's ontological animation effect are put into thematic play.

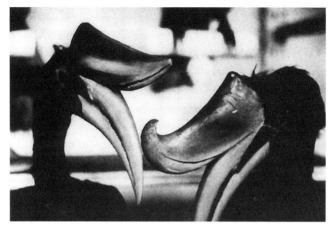

144

145

But for Sobchack these do not remain at the level of narrative figuration. Instead, they remind us of the nature of the medium at large. Photography struggles to arrive into the fullness of a moving presence, where, for Sobchack, image seems to inherit (or mime?) the durative essence of the thing it pictures. In her expanded formulation, "film is always presenting as well as representing the coming into being of being and representation" (61). Her stress on film as a simulated world space ripening before us into its own continuous being (in ways that would ultimately contradict rather than revealingly accrete its photographic increments) leads her to discount, after all, the full weight of the stilled image's inertial moment within the balked momentum of Marker's exemplary plot. I wholly agree that it is a metaplot, an allegory of the apparatus. What it figures for me, however, and by its own defaults, is just this: that the only *becoming* we ever see signs of on-screen is the very moment—one, then the next—of the photographic strip's becoming film track. For Sobchack's phenomenology, this won't do. According to her exaggerated ontological rift between the two media, only the latter has "being" at all. In her telling personification, film "possesses its own being . . . in the sense that it *behaves*" (61; her emphasis). This is thought to distinguish it absolutely from the still photograph that only "waits—as a vacancy—for us to possess it" (61). In objection to this divisive personification, one feels bound to say that the only behavior film exhibits in its own right is the constitutive necessity for *behaving itself* as a string of stilled dim prints lying in wait for projection—or toeing the line in the event.

COUNTERPROOF: DECONSTRUCTING
THE HOLLOW GRAM

To continue with exhibits from the genre of science fiction is to extend my emphasis on the materialist apocalypse of the filmic within the filmed—even while postponing, till the fifth chapter, a fuller analysis of the genre at large and its *fin-de-siècle* mutations under pressure from digital technology. An even more explicitly cautionary sci fi narrative than *La jetée,* the 1986 Argentinian film *Man Fac-*

ing Southeast (Eliseo Subiela) concerns a self-purported extraterrestrial hero who arrives by holographic incarnation to avert the nuclear collision course of earthly history. Insofar as this oblique, meditative work is nonetheless a genre narrative whose extrapolation from present to marvelous future technology turns back on the very image mechanisms that generate it before our eyes, it offers a late instance of a long-standing motif of technological self-reference in film science fiction, where movie futurism often turns at the plot level, as well as in the *mise en scène*, on the postcinematic future of the moving image. Insofar as Subiela's film goes on to relate a postcinematic technology of immanence—laser epiphany—to the disruptive temporal status of photography itself, it joins *La jetée* in a tacit investigation of film's own material basis.

The plot concerns a putative holographic messiah whose apocalyptic visions are rendered finally irrelevant by way of the conservative countertechnology of mere photography. Into a mental institution overseen by a jaded psychiatrist, his own family life in shambles, comes an affectless young man who claims to be a computer-generated agent from another world. He declares himself one of many on a similar pacifist mission, a virtual army of "cybernetic Christs," as the doctor satirically calls them. Believing not a word of what he takes to be the young man's schizophrenic delusions, and increasingly sealing himself off from their evident emotional impact, the doctor brutally proceeds to normalize by stages this intractable Christ figure, who finally dies during electroshock treatment. In retreat from the power of this visitor, the divorced doctor seeks refuge in home movies of his once happy marriage. Anything seems preferable to what the holographic Christ has claimed about his own apparition: that he is "a type of photograph obtained through a laser beam. . . .How can I explain? We have been able to have those images take shape in space by means of what you would call a large projector." The laser emission, the alien emissary, would be a kind of homeless movie in search of reception—and response. Against this the doctor must at all costs inoculate himself.

Once the pacific visitation of otherness has declared himself as a bodiless incarnation, then the best evidence to the contrary would be his disemboweled remains, the evisceration of exactly those insides he pretends not to have—which is what eventually happens on the dissecting table after his death, as disclosed in the doctor's voice-over during the long-held final shot. What the camera hovers upon in closing, and lets fill its own frame, is what another (still) camera has once before brought into its scopic field. A latent photogrammatic irony is now complete. The film itself, a technology of image projection as illusory in its way as holographic manifestation, is made to coincide here with its own negative imprint in arrested presence. The logic in inexorable. Justifying the reported sacrificial abjection of the interloper's bodily form in the hospital morgue, the nearest earlier proof for the doctor (that the self-annunciated hologram is not the recently manifested space projection he claims to be) is this discovered photograph of him and his sister, another self-declared alien, both seemingly younger and standing solidly on earth. They are pictured so that falling alongside them is the shadow of an unseen figure whose peripheral place just past the limit of this visual transcription has been, it seems, implicitly excised by ripping off the far edge of the print—as if the image plane were as extensive, say, as a wide-screen movie rather than a three-by-five photo (fig. 146). As emphasized by this jagged melodrama of out-of-field space, what necessarily falls just beyond view is an undetermined figure that the doctor, grasping at straws, races to assume is their alcoholic and psychically crippling father: the generative origin that, in another sense, is always beyond range of picturation in any photograph, as well as any projection.

146

The doctor insists, in effect, on that implied ontological vanishing point of the recorded human form that appears as a recurrent inference from moments of photographic regress in science fiction film (see chapter 5): the original bodied presence that grounds any photomechanical index. But his hasty conclusions backfire at the metatextual level. In the long run the hero, even if psychotic, cannot have been altogether wrong about his projected nature—though he has paid the price of being sacrificed to his own mediated condition not as laser but as cinematic (and hence photographically based) mirage of presence. There is, moreover, a strange foreglimpse of this tacit cinematization of the organic body in an eerie slow-motion sequence midway through the plot. Here the filmic refigures the cinematic as metaphor for the latter's own deathwork. What we see is an open coffin being dragged down the steps of the hospital, the limbs of the unknown corpse undulating in viscous ripples of loose flesh. Call it a body already dead but animated by projection into a decelerated semblance of life and you have an apt description of the film's slow-moving, increasingly comatose hero gradually devitalized over the prolonged course of his (screen) treatment. Like all cinematic bodies, he is himself cast into the seen world, feasibly rounded in his movements, evidently at home in a certain depth of field.

The logic is, I will say again, inexorable—and its irony self-engulfing. It seems to require an isolated photograph (rather than merely the slowing of the cinematic image toward the disclosed filmic frame) to prove once and for all that, though he may be a film character, our hero is at least not an astral visitant—to prove that, even if only a figment, at least he has a routine photogrammatic basis rather than a preternatural laser one. In suggesting as much, this one film narrative seems finally to have arraigned its own conservatism (more as medium than as genre) as the very enemy of visionary credence. But not as a medium inimical to the suspended disbelief of sympathetic identification. Nor to the drama of its withering failure. For until he sets it aside on a table for its last dilatory close-up, the doctor has been looking on with us, bereft, at the film's final photographic icon—autopsy and tomb at once—of the slain hero whose credited three-dimensional presence in the world is now only a memory trace.

In this last prolonged and nearly screen-swallowing image of generically counterapocalyptic disclosure may well be revealed, yes, the illusion and the subterfuge of all screen incarnation. But to claim that this subtracts nothing from the plan-

gency of the image in narrative context is only to stress again that we have been
speaking all along about the installation of the photogram within the apparatus of
cinema's psychic investments. And not the least of the clues to this is the sense we
get, with the closing mutilated photograph, that the return of its missing supplemental margin would, again, complete its "unrealistic" rectangular format in the
image of a wide-screen rather than a commercial snapshot ratio. Thus does the variously mystified nature of this inset photograph, the longer the film's camera seems
glued to it, come as close to a certain kind of photogrammatic revelation as any single shot I can recall on film: the lone truncated imprint ripped from origin and succession both. This chapter's next and last sci fi example lifts the isolation of the discrete imprint from the level of mortuary photo inlay to the whiplash reflex of
interstellar velocity upon the abrogated motion of extratemporal freeze-frames.

SPEEDS OF F/LIGHT

Nearing the mysterious close of *2001: A Space Odyssey* (1968), four momentarily confessed and arrested photogrammatic frames are spewed up from the visionary flux of light and image. They arrive as if to mark the immeasurable
lengths by which photography's mere mechanical technology is being outdistanced through apocalyptic visualizations. Cinema is caught, in convulsion, outstripping its own constituent cells, leaving them *manifestly* behind—as of course
at a lower level it always does. But before these arrested images bring filmic textuality to bear on specular transfiguration from the underside of its ravishing visionary sheen, certain old-fashioned photographic moments within the plot have
led the way. En route from the moon base to the exhumed site of the buried monolith, the American reconnaissance crew examines aerial photographs of the
epochal dig. Once landed, however, they seem in the mood for a more personal
record. In front of the exposed black entity—object, machine, apparatus, there is
no telling—the helmeted spacemen gather in pantomime, an idle film camera in
the background, so that one of them can take a corny tourist-style shapshot of his
cohorts bunched together before the baffling form, one for the folks back home
(fig. 147). A high-frequency emission interrupts their efforts, however, and we cut
to the final Jupiter leg of the mission. But not before the monolith seems to have
laid superintending claim to the screen plane with a transitional agency all its own.
On the brink of scene change, the impenetrable slab blocks out with its foregrounded shape a kind of giant antiquated "wipe" that usurps half the peopled
image field, along with the enacted scene of visual recording, on the way toward
the total eclipse of human subjectivity (fig. 148).[28]

Bowman (Keir Dullea) is of course the scapegoat of this last transition. Taken
to the far edge of a corporeality that will shortly desert him in marked stages, he
is funneled through a high-speed chute of luminous graphics (the "stargate" transit) on the way to the film's enigmatic coda. There a fourfold transfiguration in a
mystic bedroom suite will reveal him aging by displacement before his own eyes
until, after a symbolic last supper, he will be delivered (in every sense) from near
corpse to the apocalyptically self-manifested origin of his own new species: the so-

called starchild. Metaphysical hokum or the hocus-pocus of a sublime metacinema? The least cogent or the most majestic single sequence in contemporary cinema? Or the one because the other: pure cinema?

147

In any event, Kubrick's closing sequence mounts an assault on normative screen temporality. One critic has called the simultaneous avatars of the aging self a breakthrough from cinematic into "photographic time," where the past is made technologically visible to the eyes of the present.[29] But I would reserve this designation for a preceding two-stage effect that throws this final sequence into relief, an effect we are now approaching at the speed of light. First, a close-up of Bowman in his space pod—to which the whole stargate light show is an intermittent and prolonged reverse shot—shows him in a paroxysm of what *Star Trek* lingo would call warp speed, his whole body in convulsed overdrive. Human presence has become a rending internal velocity. Something like the opposite happens in the subsequent climactic sequence. Beyond the speed of light, plummeting through the abstract corridor of materialized temporality, Bowman is soon to be shunted out of normative time toward the apocalyptic upshot of his last fourfold

148

mutation in the galactic bedroom, his self-observed passage from present to older to aged to dying and reborn self. Here is exactly where, and why, one might resist the notion of a character's seeing his own future body as a bending of real toward photographic time. It seems instead the opposite: an attempt to reverse photographic time (where our past is made present again to us) in the direction, and service, of epiphanic—another word for apocalyptic—time (where our future is made present in revelation).

Photographic time is what the closing episode has in fact to overcome across the elided leaps of its transformation. And that outdistancing of the photographic moment is actually measured against photogrammatic markers, as I mentioned above, that have recently preceded its final overreaching. Four times before the coda's own fourfold displacement of body and subjectivity in its fast-forward aging, that is, Bowman is lifted out of ordinary succession into disclosed photographesis. Four times over, with the light show flooding the intervals between, a freeze-frame close-up on his desperately racked face (figs. 149-52)—an iterated and punctuating photogram—seems to reprise by allusion, and at approximately the same scale, the previous shuddering close-up in its punishing vibration. The linked effect is closer to Vertov than to traditional sci fi. Frenzied motion agitated to furious blur meets its antithesis in the segmented increment of screen kinesis, with the arrest of human animation seamed over only by the rarefied continuity of an otherworldly electronic score. If only for these four instantaneous moments, the character's being in the world is caught in the temporal essence of its passing, a mere moment in eternity.

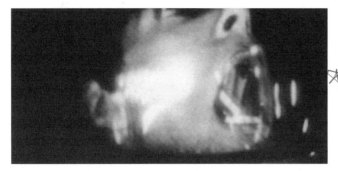

149

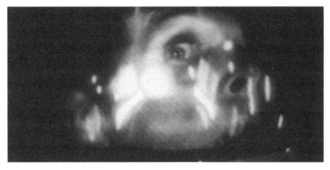

150

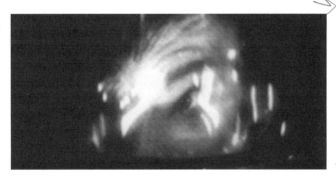

151

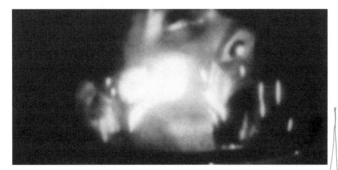

152

In his preoccupation with time signs, Deleuze treats entirely different aspects of Kubrick and this film.[30] This is not surprising, given the way even his second volume, on the "time-image," so completely ignores the deviant temporality of the freeze-frame. Yet as we will see more fully in the next chapter, he gives us many of the terms we need for its consideration. When a slice or sectioning off of space is multiplied to suggest the sustained image in arrest (as a prelude to transfiguration or otherwise), to evoke by instantiating a stalled action (whether in the latency of its renewal or the very picture of its cessation), what is this but a special case of the "time-image" in the aberrant mode of sheer prolongation? Through such means does the disclosed photogram erupt as irreducible unit, and linchpin, in Kubrick's textualization of the visionary. In this node of crossing over, this momentary persistence within obliteration, the seen human subject within the all-seeing scopic field lingers within the eclipse brought on by its own evolutionary elision. It lingers there as a momentary endurance within duration per se. In a last and climactic association with the arrested cinematic photogram, and so in turn with film's own technological prehistory in still photography, all such parochial technology has been suspended.[31] The photographic tools that first served to locate the monolith but were then abrogated by it have been turned back upon its human operative. With subjectivity itself subsumed to the monocular Medusa stare of Kubrick's visionary medium, barely extricated by now from the related panoptic stare of Hal the Cyclopian computer, the final upsurge of photograms in those four freeze-frames appears to figure the last familiar trace of traditional human record. This, and something more: something that would escape the historical altogether. The evoked vestige of mechanical imaging—in its inevitably inbred allusion to media history's now superseded photographic moment—shows the astonished spaceman stared into stone-cold fixity. With his persistence isolated as a mere cinematic integer, what there is left to do with that image is entirely up to visionary (call it apocalyptic) cinema. In film's unprecedented editing for the last transmogrifying sequence of shot/countershots (aging space traveler seeing his own time slipping away into an older self), suture is about to bear witness to evolutionary time. On the threshold of this sequence, Kubrick has the spaceman just where he wants him, entirely spatialized as a single unit of film: a still image, an image still, the manipulable photogram of all film alchemy.

BEYOND PHOTOGRAMMATOLOGY

Once again, if this isn't too feeble a way to put it, cinema tutors the viewer in its underlying constitution. It does so while putting its material basis to work as narrative matter. Cinema, I have said, *thematerializes* itself as film. What we find over and over, with one image always overrunning another unless braked in progress, is that film can at any moment strategically bring forward its own photomechanical origin in the process of advancing a given plot. What stands to be revealed, brought to (projected) light, at such pressure (or puncture) points—and by a violence to textual continuity not unlike apocalyptic manifestation in other registers—are the elementing laws of film's whole universe. These are the ruling images that imprint its imaginary in their very negation of its fullness. A powerful textual homology, therefore, binds the logic of apocalypse to a dialectical interplay of the sort tracked here. Etymologically, the Greek root of *apo-calypse* suggests the removal "from-" something of its "-cover" (*Discovery*, as it happens, being the name given to the last of the spaceships, the Jupiter probe, in *2001*). The cover is protective, its lifting a shock to the whole system. Thus do photographic form (underlying) and film content (overriding) recover under narrative pressure their essential tension. The revelatory unveiling of the scheme of things, manifesting the very shape of time from within the content of its succession, requires nothing less than submitting duration itself to the apocalyptic equivalent of formalism's "baring the device." We can therefore usefully conceive the mode of revelation by which the withheld ordering principle burns through its phenomena, in fury or clarification, by analogy with the surfacing of photogrammatic necessity within cinematic flow.

Photogrammatology, for short. But beyond it—what? The remaining chapters should answer by example. I might anticipate for now by suggesting that the photogram's assault on both visual coherence and narrativity, on medium and message at once, induces an analogous upheaval in the zone of reception. Blending psychic and ocular models, we can locate such disturbance in the always twofold effect of the apparatus: a kind of depth physiology of the scanning glance. This is the cognitive slippage for which Freudian depth psychology comes into play as metaphor. Its figurative use has a rich, but no less elusive, history. Walter Benjamin understood photography as giving us access to visual material lying latent in our ordinary scopic field. These were optical facets of the world that the perceptual demands of ongoing "reality" often foreclose or suppress. Benjamin had, as a matter of fact, what seems an almost Bergsonian (or Muybridgean) interest in the very intervals of movement. He was quick to see photography's role in restoring to us "the positions involved in the fraction of a second when [a] step is taken" (203), an effect he later associated as well with such devices of the motion-picture camera as slow motion.[32] Instead of being a mechanical prosthesis of seeing, the photographic—and in turn the film—camera is an analytic (even a quasi-psychoanalytic) apparatus. Benjamin called the historical and technological innovation inaugurated by photography, its unprecedented level of revelation, the emergence of an "optical unconscious" (203) of quotidian sight. Though it gives the title to Rosalind Krauss's book on the modernist avant-garde in painting, this borrowing from Benjamin is acknowledged for the first time only midway through her study. Her use of his phrase to describe the formal inferences (rather than unexamined authorial motives) of modernist visual textuality is by that stage, she assumes, quite clearly meant "at an angle to Benjamin's."[33] But more than this, she even seems to doubt the applicability of his phrase in the first place: "Can the optical field—the world of visual phenomena: clouds, sea, sky, forest—*have* an unconscious?" No, but then this isn't what I take Benjamin's adjective in "optical unconscious" to mean or, for that matter, what one would think Krauss's own "optical field" suggests.

Benjamin's notion refers to the underside not of the phenomenal world but of its visual cognition. To make this inescapably clear, one should return to the quotation in context. Benjamin has just mentioned that we "know nothing definitive of the positions involved," for instance, in the simplest human movements.[34] Thus his main point about the photomechanical media: "Photography, however, with its time lapses, enlargements, etc. makes such knowledge possible. Through these methods one first learns of this optical unconscious, just as one learns of the drives of the unconscious through psychoanalysis" (203). In fact Krauss's textual emphasis seems closer to his paradigm than she is comfortable admitting. The difference can be bridged as follows: Photography, by bringing to light phases of cognition that are disallowed in ordinary vision, gives us not the optical repressed of the object world but the underlay of subjective vision itself, where the notion of apperceptive forces moving beneath consciousness is hardly so puzzling—and not at all foreign to certain theories of the textual phenotext and its underlying genotext.

Over against Benjamin's metaphor for the photographic supplement of perception, I am now ready to venture instead (and with full acknowledgment of its equally metaphoric status) the *specular unconscious* of film viewing. And *that* stratum of specularity is photography itself: the unseen elisions of imprint that are materialized only by way of the (not necessarily Freudian) condensations and displacements to which the photogram submits in multiplication on the strip. When it puts up resistance, throws itself up in the form of resistance, that is where analysis is enlisted from within passive spectation. Whenever such a negative revelation takes place (through photogrammatic advent), film offers up one investigative paradigm for apocalyptic disclosure—as well as for what we will come to see as a mode of cognitive transference. In the shock of recognizing the suddenly unavoidable open secret of photogrammaticality, viewers cede back to the film medium itself an uneasy knowledge they were only too ready to forgo in going forward, to bury in the pleasure of the frictionally vivified interval. In the freeze-frame, for instance, the dramatically resurrected but artificially deanimated (multiplied) photogram is, we have seen, the tomb of the motion it has otherwise propelled. In this, however, it is only the unflinching reverse face (or negative imprint), as well as incremental facet, of a long-averted fact. What appears in arrest is only what filmic momentum everywhere rests on, what it thrives on denying, the photogrammatic loses it regularly recovers (covers over) by arranging for us to invest in. This is the first, or last, of the reasons why reading a film, above and beyond—and beneath—merely viewing it, can become in its own right an act of proleptic mourning for the already passing. The seen world comes to be fully known only in going. Apocalypse is merely one of the most venerable names for such an ultimately textualizing process. Within this process, what a prophetic epic like *2001* brings to hypertrophic view is the way cinematic *speculation*—powered by, until collapsing into, both fixity and absentation—may carry itself at once to the inner and the outer limit, the weld and the far verge, of filmic inscription. And the tour de force confirms the norm. Only by maintaining the photogram under erasure within cinema's specular field can a given film be kept alive and flicking. Building on previous evidence, the chapter to follow concerns what happens otherwise.

I defer such consideration for a few paragraphs only to secure terms for it. The freeze-frame, to which I am about to turn, draws a good part of its textual charge from a relation between cinema and photography that Benjamin has taken us only part of the way toward elucidating. Without starting over, we need to step back and move a little more slowly. Mental images may be gone but not forgotten. Photographs in the screened form of photograms, however, are ordinarily forgotten even before they are gone. We have seen them, but no one of them—and never any longer. We know one of them after another has been there, but we must contravene this knowledge so as to relax into a continuously received world picture. There is no denying it: this is a kind of denial. But what kind? As some such, it might be taken as the synecdoche for all the other denied things, many offscreen, that help bring the rush of photograms before us. If we more actively "repress" this larger field of knowledge (lighting crews, production costs, editing labs, star contracts, the politics of the studios, marketing tie-ins, the ideological freight of international capital), and if "repress" is indeed the word for it, what at the level of the track itself is the word for all we keep from consciousness? Are photograms "repressed" in cognition or simply assimilated indistinguishably at the very threshold of perception, their singleness censored involuntarily, mechanically? What kind of nonconsciousness, then, are we concerned with at this rudimentary stratum of screen spectation?

In one sense the scene of production must, of course, be blocked from our awareness in movie watching, framed out. Only in this manner can the transmitted film image, free of encroaching industrial clutter, become Benjamin's famous "orchid" in the tangled garden of technology.[35] In another sense, those moments in a given film event that invoke the wider conditions of production under commercial capitalism are what we have seen David James, his attention crossing between avant-garde artifacts and modernist inflections of mainstream film in the 1960s, call "allegories of cinema." No matter how abstract or minimalist, films of this stripe operate as such only by springing "the return of the repressed milieu"[36]—repressed by the text, that is, in our immediate interest as viewers as well: the milieu both of production and of cultural context. But in our present concern, from the ground up, with what we would instead have to call allegories of *film* (the medium) rather than allegories of cinema (the industrial product), the question remains: Out of what zone of denial or negation does the photogram "return"? Does Benjamin's "optical unconscious" really point us toward the answer we need?

I think so, but only if we aggressively press it to confront its origin as a psychoanalytic metaphor—and only if we then use it to pursue further the circuits of transference that photogrammatic reading calls out. A photograph can mechanically capture and manifest what has been ignored in the fundamental overlooking that is part of everyday seeing. Given the visibility of the photograph, however, its relation to an "optical unconscious" must be that of something suddenly released (therefrom) to consciousness. One level up in the complex mechanism of cinematic seeing, of course, the photographic unit on the strip is the very thing forgotten in turn by automatism. When it surfaces to scrutiny, in just what terms might we best describe that aspect of cinema's specular system, that aspect of our spectation, that seems thereby to return? The answer can lie only in a variable collusion—as hard to denominate as it is difficult to dismiss (or resist)—between projection and introjection. We must look to the transferals of affect and recognition that these relays of looking depend on. To get this under real terminological control will take some further work, after many further examples, in this book's final pages. But there is this much we can expect tentatively to settle (on) at this stage. Faced with Benjamin's resonant analogy from psychoanalysis, we must query the true application to film's technical basis of the surface/depth paradigm inherent in "the optical unconscious," drawn as it is from Freudian topographical schemata. Down, under, or away, what is driving perception where?

One might object that Benjamin's sense of the photographic intervention in normal sight, in and before film, can properly involve only what Freud would call the "preconscious" rather than the "unconscious." Isolated as such, in the cinematic mobilization of photographs, would be the level of perception that passes away without recognition—but that passes nonetheless into cognitive experience. Such continuous inhibition of discrete photographic notice would be film's inherent defense mechanism against its own mechanical basis. This potential revision of Benjamin has its immediate appeal, especially since it does not require giving up something like persistent *suppression* as an explanatory category. At the level of the preconscious in film viewing, there is indeed a kind of perceptual policing at work, not so much by the subject as by the apparatus itself—but one that has to do, following Freud's notion of "secondary censorship" in the preconscious, more with a blanketing *distortion* than with protective selection and deletion. Supervening here is a continuous inflection (the sequential integer skewed into moving image) rather than those tactical interdictions we associate with psychic material hounded into hiding in the unconscious.

So far so good. According to the most potent insight behind Benjamin's analogy of the "optical unconscious" when that insight is applied to film, we are kept from perceiving the increments involved in represented motion in order that such suppressed discreteness can generate the image of objects *in* motion. This sense of perceptual elision is exactly what is needed to explain the force of surprise with which the photogram emerges (rather than reappears) to consciousness in exceptional film moments, moments prizing open the very interval that the photogram usually vanishes into. But it must be stressed that when we translate Benjamin's "optical unconscious"—that pervasive unawareness in the working of normal vision, a perceptual slumber that the photograph snaps us out of—to the kinetic mi-rage of cinema, the mechanistic adjustment this entails shifts the terms by which spectation can be characterized. Our strictly ocular *non*awareness of those tiny cognitive impressions that make up the "single" everyday view is now redistrib-uted in film across a sequence of photographs whose sequentiality is itself cen-sored by speed per se. Not repressed in the true psychodynamic sense but rather automatically suppressed (by the apparatus of projection itself, again, rather than by the receptive psyche), suppressed at the very brink of perception, photograms are driven automatically from view—and from mind—-by the mechanism that necessitates them and by the picture they manufacture. Hence the photogram is to the single moment of screen image as the photograph is to a single normal sighting: the *return of the suppressed.*

In adapting Benjamin, I therefore retain the topographic notion of some sort of *sub*conscious (if pre- more than un-), subliminal and perceptually self-elimi-nating, as the undertext of screen reception. This is a "specular" (in other words filmic) rather than strictly ocular matter because the automatized suppression of the increment—by the mechanism on our behalf—produces on-screen the ghostly counterpart to the eye's normal override of intervals in perceived motion. Realizing why the psychoanalytic metaphor can never be more than metaphoric also highlights this metaphor's formal utility in analysis. For it is not the *content* of the image that brings disturbance in its recursion, as with interdicted traumatic material in Freud. Precisely not. What recurs from specular suppression is the very structuring of the screen image itself: its elided photographic form. (In not-ing further that the relation of *langue* to *parole* in Freud, of the verbal fund to its local instance, is also a matter of activating the linguistic "preconscious," I am looking ahead to the negotiations between filmic and literary models of textual os-cillation in my concluding chapter.)

At this stage, resisting suppression may perhaps sound too liberatory for the textual gestures this book is preoccupied with. It shouldn't. Call such a filmic per-ception of the cinematic artifact by any other name, and it would seem just as much a flouting of the routinized norm. The difference is that this liberation too is mechanized. If being "forced" by the track to overcome the usual photogram-matic suppression it induces through us is to see more clearly than a given screen sighting usually allows, and if the return of the elided photogram is to this extent always at least distantly implicated in a politics of ocular therapy, as we will per-mit ourselves to imagine in closing, then the lifted ban on the static filmic incre-ment momentarily rescues the medium from its own most intransigent deceit of seamlessness. It is in this specialized sense that even commercial screen narrative can generate an allegory of film's resistance to passive inspection in a commodi-fied culture of naturalized visual intake. The freeze-frame, as we are to find, is in one sense the purest form of this resistance. Undoing the moving spectacle from within its own photographic visuality, its peculiar return of the suppressed stands in for all the other ways our eager hold on the projected scene is never better than fragile and contingent.

THREE

Frame of Reference

THE FILMIC EXCEPTION TO SCREEN MOVEMENT
REPROVES ITS CINEMATIC RULE.

Like many of the films previously discussed, this chapter temporarily freezes progress to highlight an undergirding element in the larger picture it is working to unfold. What results is the theoretical fulcrum of my whole argument about cinematic textuality. And there's the problem right there. No textual articulation, as we have already seen, is more resistant to recognition *as such* than is narrative film. If the understanding of any medium is to include what stands under the motions of story, narrative involvement gets in the way, as it must, of the textual operations that convey it. The medium's very materiality lies mostly in hiding behind the viable otherworld of film. It's murder to dissect. Yet sometimes a cinematic narrative performs its own vivisection with a single quick cut to the artery of all flow, a slicing off of motion itself from the projected image. Either this or a sudden stagger in film's pace, sequence grinding to a near standstill, opening the wounds of the photogram as blurred d/rift of the consecutive. Slow motion, skid editing, step printing: they are all surgical interventions, and not always antiseptic. Sometimes they begin to poison the whole stream of images—even without damming it up altogether, as does the so-called freeze-frame.

And so a first distinction. Devices other than the freeze may still seem, briefly, like something that is happening in and to the film's world space. A decelerated world, for instance, is a world that may have gone mad—or to sleep—but is still in a sense going on. It is still imagined to be *out there,* even if suddenly projected in the mode of flagrant subjectivity (all in a character's head). On a technical continuum with such retardation is its end point in the freeze-frame. At the specular level, however, the whole picture changes when the world's image no longer changes at all. Isolated in such stasis is the abdication of filming to mere film, or we might now say of the filmed to the filmic. Screened reality is no longer out

there. Only its image exists—and only *up there,* a return of the specular suppressed in the mode of checked motion.

If we might want to call such a moment the textual apocalypse of the world fiction, when not of the fictional world, as I did in the previous chapter—or more generally the photographic block to phenomenological persuasion—what does phenomenology itself want to call it? As terminus ad quem for all deviations from the
illusionistic space/time ratios of recording and projection, the freeze-frame is the
preeminent challenge to the view of cinema as a world in view. Equally, as we will
see via Deleuze, it defies—or deflates—our ready acceptance of cinema's "immanence" as a ruminative mental construct of mutable temporalities. In confronting
the freeze's radically materialized discreteness, we recognize among other things
the deep misnomer of the very term "freeze-frame." Certainly two of its likeliest
meanings must be ruled out. Nothing is "frozen" or fixated on the strip, since the
stop-action image can be projected only by the wheeling past of identical frames (or
photograms). Nor does the notion of a freeze "frame" single out any unique motionlessness in the screen's border not called upon elsewhere, a border that can remain static even in the most frenetic and volatile of scenes. We come in this way to
the phenomenological impasse. For if the "frame," both on track and on-screen, is
conceived to be a world picture actualized in embodied reception, both an aperture
and a view at once, the notion of a "freeze" defeats this conception *from within.* It
is the one sure moment in film technique that cannot be imagined to tamper with
anything that is not entirely determined in advance by a chemical imprint and its
unvaried duplication. I mean "in advance" in both senses, the one because of the
other: *before* any plenary world is materialized for us; and by the illusion of stasis
in advancing the frame to an unvaried duplicate. That is why one does for once
want to call this device, as students have sometimes misunderstood me to be saying, the *frieze* frame. To say the very least for this punning alternative to the reigning technical argot, the notion of a "frieze" better recognizes, in such a photo-
graphic moment, the advent of a seemingly plastic manifestation on-screen rather
than some peremptory event (or untimely disruption) coming to pass either in the
fictional world or in its simulated subjective cognition.

But the question remains how phenomenalist approaches to the cinema might
tackle this limit case for the immanence of a materialized world. In which terms
might they seek to recuperate—or exempt—what a textual theory of film might
call the imposition of material enunciation upon enounced world? More than time
lapse or slow motion, more than pixilation or colored filters, more than shifts of
focus or tricks of editing, more than anything else the cameraman or the laboratory technician puts in the way of the normative kinesis of projected film, the
freeze-frame—precisely because frieze frame—remains the last frontier of film
phenomenology, its ultimate affront and greatest challenge. How the challenge is
allowed if not exactly met, how confronted and finessed, how theorized and historicized—or not—is one topic of this chapter.

The film scholar who wrote the book on these phenomenological matters, Vivian Sobchack, no doubt knows the enemy when she sees it. In her hands the
freeze-frame suffers the ultimate suppression, banished to a footnote and dis-

placed there onto another medium entirely.[1] The move is nothing if not bold. Sobchack considers only the voluntary and adventitious "pause" of the videocassette playback in this light, ignoring the inherence of the device within her favored medium of film. Long before they fall into the remote hands of the VCR operator, however, certain films have already done themselves in by these same means of arrest, and what has happened to their imputed world vision gets no mention in Sobchack's study. Nor does the freeze-frame offer quite the trouble it might to the more broad-gauged phenomenologically oriented approaches of Stanley Cavell and Gilles Deleuze. Nor yet, in a different tradition, to the pioneering work, before them, of Rudolf Arnheim. In all these cases there is a tendency to quarantine the systemic (or photogrammatic) contagion that consideration of the freeze-frame might otherwise lead to. This chapter, therefore, lets the freeze give the pause it should to all assumptions about the screen image as either the world's body in display or the playing of memory upon it. Discussion will hold on the freeze until the full threat of the stilled image is registered, the phenomenological damage tallied, the textual clarifications achieved, the photographic disclosure owned to—and recirculated through the entire material system.

A definition, loaded enough, can get us started. Freeze-frame: the abortive cut on action that merely plunges us into more of the track's motion as a strictly fixed image (or frieze). Seen as a cut *from* action rather than a hold on it, if only a cut into action's own afterimage, the freeze asserts itself as montage degree zero—or minus one. Going nowhere as they do, where can the contemplation of such images take us? Two chapters so far have attempted a split-level photogrammar of film that would hold together—within the same textual system—the photographic frame of the film strip and the reframed photograph on-screen. The second of these has related this textuality to a classic prototype of disclosure in a lowercase "apocalypse" of first and last things. Both attempts have crossed paths, in turn, as will this chapter, with the complicated interrelation among photographic fixity, filmic flow, and the complementary logic of death and immortalization associated with the distinct but kindred temporal registers of photography and cinema.

Even in its attempt to knot off previous strands of discussion, this new chapter starts small. It is a kind of minority report from the underside. It salvages from infrequency what is, in the main, an occasional and period-bound stylistic device. It does so, however, not just to get some conceptual satisfaction about a dated but nonetheless still available "styleme" of the movies. Well beneath the level of the seme or shot cell, well before screen representation in its least divisible segments, this chapter has in mind—in mind only, because never quite in separate view on-screen—the fragment upon whose suppression the cinema's whole visual system regularly depends. In familiar enough film terminology, this is, of course, the photogram, rendered imperceptible on film in order to make cinema visible. But its nearest—if never complete—manifestation on-screen may help fill a terminological lack in the semiotics of cinema. If the present chapter has something wholesale to add, it would in part involve just this. For the micro and the macro, the photogram on the track and the image on-screen, technological cause and phenomenological effect, most nearly converge (as, indeed, do movement and time in their twin suspension) within the image as declared photographic freeze. Under pressure of this approached convergence, then, there is forced into view the role of the photo cell on track as the revealed *photographeme* of the cinematic process: the film text's irreducible, yet separately imperceptible, signal. As intermittent frame of reference for the whole machination, the freeze-frame takes its place by negating the system whose logic it all too baldly inscribes. In its photographicity, it breaks from those timed mechanic crises of continuity out of which, alone, the filmic rises.

This is hardly to deny that for most of us, most of the time, what we see is what we get. We all can imagine our way into the "world view" of the cinema, even if we don't take that view in our more hard-nosed (or cold-blooded) analytic moments. The result of this double vision is a conflictual apprehension of the medium. This is as it should be, since nothing is truer to the dialectic energy of its founding materiality. Yet matters still need to be gotten and kept straight. In attempting once more to account for the vicissitudes of any such material emphasis—and hence for the variable fate of the photogram—in the body of film theory, we had best begin with the influential writer whose groundbreaking work often seemed to take a forked path on just this undervalued problem of the single frame.

MATERIAL THEORY AND THE CONSTRAINTS OF THE AESTHETIC

Rudolf Arnehim is the writer whose aesthetic vocabulary, along with Siegfried Kracauer's, lends itself to Dudley Andrew's emphasis on the "formative" (rather than the formalist) tradition in film theory.[2] But Arnheim is only typical of film theory at large, even antirealist accounts far afield from his own, in his equivocation on just the point of film's essential formative elements. These seem at one moment to be the structuring modules of the strip, at another moment the formal features of its aesthetic effect on-screen. All film theory priding itself on a medium-specific account must, of course, work to hover, trying not to waver, in this conceptual space. Film as art, art as the resistant compliance with a medium's self-imposed limitations: such is the starting point of Arnhein's "material theory" of aesthetic force in film.[3] Though cinema, like any other art form, is bound to respect, and may be found to thrive within, its inherent constraints—call them its enforced exclusions—this understanding does not bind Arnheim (or later commentators in his wake) to any stable orientation with regard to the structuring "materiality" of the medium itself. This fundamental filmic matter seems now in the camera, now on the screen, now somewhere between.

Arnheim writes at one point that the formative dimension of film makes itself felt above and beyond the automatic or mechanical dimension only when, with montage, the recording process can no longer be "regarded superficially" (88) as a mechanical reproduction of nature. As he has it later, however, film's "dividing of the [recorded] movement into single 'frames' (just as their subsequent unification in projection)" can properly be dismissed from consideration as "nothing but a technical detail" (178-80). So far beneath the superficial as to be negligible because merely technical (rather than phenomenal), the photogrammatic moment of film is put beyond attention. One can see why. Or let us say that one can see only by such denial. It all depends on what we are calling the frame of reference. Fixity, stasis, originary photochemical arrest and its radically pluralized "frames," the very intermittence of the strip—these are not for him the constraining conditions of the filmic impact. They may be thought of as first or efficient causes—vanished without effect, screened out on-screen. Arnheim gravitates instead to the alternative and prevailing use of the term "frame"—and for reasons it is easy to appreciate. Things pass out of frame, flash into it; the frame itself sweeps, zeroes in, retreats; characters are framed by it in close-up or not. The whole catalog of effects gets referred to by apparent derivation from the camera's selective *framing*—understood to mean more a bracketing than a swallowing whole. That such an understanding depends upon—in action—what appears on the celluloid strip, depends upon "frame advance" in a more rudimentary and rather different sense, upon what Eisenstein called the "little frame," is a fact both technically unseen and conceptually lost sight of.[4] In most cases the very vocabulary of the imprint gets translated to that of the window.[5]

The bearing of all this on Arnheim's unsaid presuppositions is that only the latter sense of frame counts for him as an aesthetic constraint of the medium. Setting aside the extent to which the photogram as frame may constitute the technical essence of film, it is only by the framing of the image itself (thanks first to the camera) that film technology passes over into technique, into cinema as art. Arnheim's unspoken wish seems to be that his account should preserve some of the astonishment of the technology without letting its brute fact enter into the material consideration of the artifact per se: the aesthetics of its visibly mastered, rather than tacitly overthrown, limitations. To appreciate the attempted equilibration of his position, one must recognize that the level of emphasis is everything—and that nothing can be relied on to fix our double vision about the medium as material.

To Arnheim no less than to anyone else, film looks different from different technical vantages. The theorist who, championing montage, sees the principle of "stroboscopic fusion" between "objectively separate stimuli" (95)—a phenomenon underlying the "whole existence of the motion picture" (99)—as in effect a "montage of single frames," an "imperceptible montage," and who thus finds this principle carried over "to the macroscopic" in montage editing, couldn't be more in sympathy with Eisenstein's claims. Yet this is the same theorist who elsewhere settles for an account based on the perceptible rather than fully perceptual nature of the moving image, who stresses that in the viewing event "there is no synthesis of phases but an indivisible continuum" (169), with "synthesis" thus reserved for the special case of edited separate shots. This is because "the principle of synthesis reappears in the movies only when scenes that were taken separately are spliced together in montage" (169). If so, "principle" can only mean aesthetic rule rather than technological explanation, the latter never allowed to "reappear" from its continuous and constitutive suppression. And in this case, what does Arnheim mean by the "imperceptible montage" of the "single frame" being "carried over" to editing? Transported at what level? If it is merely displaced without manifestation, doesn't this sound like the work, once again, of the preconscious? In sum, Arnheim's aesthetics can afford to elevate neither photographic succession nor the individual photogrammatic cell to one of the pertinent limitations or "molds" (3) that make for the perceived art of cinema. This is why the category of aesthetic constraint seems finally a restraint imposed by aesthetics itself on material analysis. At the very least we should be able to agree that his sense of a "mold" tested by resistance—in the name of ultimate submission—certainly favors the "frame" on the screening-room wall over the one on the reel. Thus does Arnheim's project end up more like "materialization" theory than an account of film's complex negotiations with its own "animated" plastic material.[6]

Certainly we need to lay the conceptual waffling of Arnheim's collected position papers at the door of no peculiar sloppiness in his own thinking. One chalks it up instead to the differing levels at which any of us does inevitably think about film—about film within cinema or, put otherwise, about film as *both cause and effect* of projection. Yet we may still wish to keep the basis in mind as we heed the manifestations that keep it from view. That's one of the things that would differentiate film theory from film viewing. Here, however, we come into collision with an influential recent polemic. Impatient with "medium specificity talk" in connection with artifacts in any medium, Noël Carroll sets out, across three overlapping and reiterative essays, "to discredit the philosophical foundations of such talk" (3), characterized (so he finds) by a false purism of either the montage or the depth-of-field schools (Arnheim vs. Bazin).[7] Carroll sees this as the "essentialist" bent of film studies before its turn to semiotics and politics (6), a clear derivative of "Greenbergian modernism" (7). Hoping to undercut Arnheim's influential position, Carroll enters this debate at just the point of Arnheim's own occluded view: "Arnheim says that cinema has a special capacity to represent animated action, but it is not apparent how that follows from the representational limitations of the medium. Indeed, isn't this very power the opposite of anything we could meaningfully construe as a limitation of cinema?" Yes—hence the stress in Arnheim, not in Carroll, on the framed nature of these animations.

In another of these essays, Carroll allows that "if anything can lay claim to being the physical trait that essentially defines film, it is its flexible celluloid base. But what does this suggest to us about the kinds of things that could or should be represented or expressed in the medium?" (26). Precisely nothing, as Carroll can show. Out, therefore, goes any aesthetic *imperative* attached to a medium's essence. This is not all. By now Carroll is no longer interested in the essential material of the medium on any score. In order to prove that "medium specificity" (such as it is, and partial contributor as it may be to the overall impression of film as hybrid narrative art) is not its definitive aesthetic factor, Carroll has ruled it out of consideration altogether, as if there were nothing of worth in the conceptual approach to film besides an immediate encounter with the artifact. Hence, against Carroll's view, the need for a film theory that resists being subsumed by an aesthetic philosophy where anything but the intentional or expressive value of an individual film gets relegated to a distracting technicality.

MENTAL SYNOPSIS VERSUS OCULAR SYNTHESIS

From the major early theoretician of cinema, Hugo Münsterberg, to the latest cognitive revisionists, much energy has been spent defending screen action against the charge of artificial movement, even lately against the "persistence of vision" thesis that once hoped to explain and "naturalize" such movement. From early screen psychologism to the latest motor response studies of the physiologists, as we will see shortly, movement exists somewhere above and beyond, not just between, photograms. It is a third thing other than the differential's structuring pair. Eisenstein, though seldom combated directly, must be wrong. Screen movement— so the argument goes—isn't just dialectical, but rather a kind of diacritical inflection of both images together, a thing superadded (an independent variable) rather than merely the reciprocal supplement of each in sequence. Whether for Münsterberg in the teens or for essays of the 1980s included in *The Cinematic Apparatus*, however, movement, even if it transcends or exceeds or transforms the mere strip of photograms, is still available to recontainment on-screen.[8] So for Arnheim as well. So for Cavell and Deleuze later. Whatever the nuances of their philosophical or semiotic allegiance, this consensus makes connection with the absolutist phenomenological argument pressed by Vivian Sobchack.

Cued by Maurice Merleau-Ponty's phrase, Sobchack claims that film is the "abusive transformation" of photography into film, generating (in her words now) "cinematic situation from photographic point of view, and cinematic momentum from photographic moment."[9] This abuse of origin—this disfiguring use of multiplied single images—derives from the fact that film adds to the photographic object of vision a *subject* of vision as well. Why the moving camera "eye" needs personification in this way, over against the photograph's point of view, is not argued, just asserted. Leaving that aside, it is clear that whatever lends subjectivity to the conjoint movement of image and its framing on-screen cannot, for Sobchack, keep company with film's photogrammatic base. The movement visualized must be freed from machination so that it can be a movement *seen for real*— naturalized by the receiving subject. To this end Sobchack adduces Münsterberg on the independent perception of movement apart from bodily displacements in the photogrammatic sequence (207), but with italics (unadmittedly) all her own: "The perception of movement is an *independent experience* which cannot be reduced to a simple seeing of an series of different positions" (quoting as Sobchack does the Dover edition of Münsterberg, which, like the original, has no shift in typography).[10] I call out this citational variance not to fault Sobchack over what was no doubt a mere slip of transcription but to suggest that this is in fact not the really emphatic point for her predecessor.

Münsterberg's sense of the ocular subject is different from Sobchack's. When viewing film, our perceptual center is in its own way constructed, made and not begotten. On his showing, what we see on-screen seems for all practical (receptive) purposes to be real motion, but it is in fact created in the spectator's own mind. This is a point he *does* make in italics: "*Depth and movement alike . . . are present and yet they are not in the things. We invest the impressions with them."*[11] However exactly that investment is transacted, the choice of the term "impressions" seems just right for both the cause and the effect of filmic actions, the cellular imprints that conduce to our perception of movement. By such means "we create . . . the continuity through our mental mechanism" (71). As for Kracauer a decade later, here is, for Münsterberg, film's deepest association with the subjectivity of the dream state.[12] Formulaic or coded shot sequences make the point at the macro level. A flashback, for instance, must in its presence before us be subjectively envisaged as past. Like other cinematic techniques, as well as like dream visions, it images an alternative reality bent to our optic will: "It is as if the outer world itself became molded in accordance with our fleeting turns of attention or with our passing memory ideas" (95). This is, to say the least, far too psychologistic for the ontological (and often deliberately redemptive) autonomy imputed to the screened world by the tenets of phenomenology.

Münsterberg can insist on this imbrication of attention in the scene received because he does not need to take his case for film's embodied subjectivity as far, for example, as Sobchack does. Still, he certainly leaves no mistake on the point of movement's only partial constitution by the photogram. The higher-level cognitive phenomenon of perceived motion is more, for him, than the sum or synthesis of its parts, more than a response to separate successive positions. At the same time, it is not real as given. As against movement on stage, movement on film is constituted by the mental work of watching. (In this he is very close to what Eisenstein calls the "intellectual" dimension of movement as a montage of adjacencies in the form of overlaps.) Sobchack will not go this far. Without acknowledging any difference from her predecessor on this one point, she holds that screen movement "*is* real movement" (her italics) achieved "through the film's existential activity," a movement generated not by the mind of the spectator but "introceptively perceived . . . through the camera and visibly expressed through the projector" (208). One can be forgiven for finding this more like a personification allegory than a technical or material account. In her eagerness to save the phenomena, she must resort to a deus ex machina: a subjectivity recruited to figure the mechanism itself, rather than merely brought to it from the audience. A false analogy comes to her dubious assistance at this point. The "segmented and rhythmic activities" (207) of lungs, heart, and eyelids don't trouble us in normal life, so why should the equally unnoticed pulsing of the screen frame disturb our sense of uninterrupted activity in time? "As do our own bodily mechanisms, the film's bodily mechanisms co-operate and synopsize their functions into the co-Herence [*sic*] and comprehension of a significant lived-body experience" (208). Yet film, unlike the organic body, can forge its synoptic existence only by effacing, rather than simply forgetting, its rhythmic segmentation. It must generate its coherence out of a synthesis of recorded being and instantaneous cancellation, of projected presence and absolute absence, whose radical binarism must be denied for the lifelike image to survive.

Whether or not suppression (or unconsciousness) is the best word to locate such denial in film experience, the effort of this chapter so far has been to make it as clear as possible, from amid the polemical cross fire, that the eye's necessary override of single frames in film movement cannot be used to discount the contribution of just those frames to just that movement. Whatever it is, they are all it has—until the mind goes to work on them. And recognizing this fact should help us to where we are headed next: to the theorist who most subtly confronts the tensions between projected world and its "acknowledged" basis in plastic and mechanical fact.

WHIRLED VIEWS: SKEPTIC OPTIC VERSUS SPECULAR IMPRINT

At just this turn in drafting the present chapter, I needed to return to Stanley Cavell's *The World Viewed*[13] to address the ways my argument departs from his essential persuasion about film, his philosophical insistence on the heuristic distanciation of its world pictures. In returning to this landmark book—a book that I long ago read, reread, quarreled over with friends, indexed in memory before (in its revised edition) it had an index of its own, and reentered again and again from new angles for a freshly energized sense of what one could say on the occasion of a film among films—I realized that what most of all I had forgotten was the decade-turning immediacy of Cavell's film viewing and his film views. The year of publication was 1971. John Schlesinger's *Darling*, Sidney Lumet's *The Pawnbroker*, Larry Peerce's *Goodbye, Columbus*—these and many other films of the time, films (we now know) only of the moment, exercised Cavell's wry appreciation and his high ire by turns. But they did engage him, or he them—and most of all in the theoretical climax of the book. I had forgotten, that is, how much *The World Viewed* was willing to view with patient speculation the slick, experimentally derived but mass-packaged uprush of "technique" that cut across national boundaries and genres beginning in the middle to late 1960s—the whole diffuse fallout of what Deleuze, Jameson, and others have emphasized as the postwar international modernism of cinema's most achieved aesthetic phase. Not for a moment did Cavell shy away from the affront this hypertrophic technique posed to his Bazinian preferences—and their triumph in a cinema like Renoir's, with its more rather than less free registration of the world in long takes. *The World Viewed* thereby put its judgment before its taste in order to embrace for consideration, without cottoning to as art, the flash, dazzle, and graphic panache, the sporadic self-fetishizing, and sometimes the pervasive self-scrutiny of a medium convulsed by its own capacities. "If the presence of the camera is to be made known, it has to be acknowledged in the work it does. This is the seriousness of all the shakings and turnings and zoomings and reinings and unkind cuts to which it has lately been impelled" (128). The issue is all the more crucial when Cavell moves from film's nervous addiction to a hyperkinesis of the shot to the reductive dynamisms of the moving image itself, either the negation of the image in the freeze-frame or its devitalizing mutation in slow motion. What these new labors of camera*work* were meant to acknowledge, from the midst of their expected visual witness, was for Cavell the event of ocular mediation per se. Why he did not include within this self-responsiveness of the medium an awareness of film's underlying photogrammatic basis—beneath the deviant speeds or downright snags of its normally self-vanishing flux—awaits a fuller estimate of Cavell's phenomenological assumptions.

Toward this estimation, the double-hinged grammar of two late chapter titles in *The World Viewed* is especially revealing. "The Camera's Implication" is not primarily about the inferences derived on-screen from the invisible agency of the camera, but rather about the visible implication of filming itself (as object of scrutiny) in screen manifestation. Yet camera rather than track is still the focus: sighting rather than filmic textuality. The bifocal title "Assertions in Technique" evokes both the narrative emphases conveyed by (and hence motivating) technical ingenuities and also the assertions per se of the cinematic devices involved, their bringing themselves forward for scrutiny. Here we move further from the recording of a view, since these are devices that seem almost to spring from the engineering of the image track itself. They include slow motion, freeze finishes, flash insets, split and interruptive freeze-frames. But in their excess they also subtract.

For whatever else such obtruded visual declarations acknowledge (for Cavell it is never explicitly the photogram), they tend to wrench loose the image track from the temptation, the very possibility, of sound synchronization. You cannot plausibly have slow-motion and certainly not stop-action dialogue; it is only noise—or nothing. "You cannot freeze a word without losing it" (149). According to Cavell's ontology of the medium, wrenched *free* might be just the phrase for what happens in the delinking of image from sound. From within their modernist (or at least "mod") ambitions, however routine or meretricious, such self-assertive devices provide, on Cavell's view, the partial release back to a founding authenticity of the medium in silent film: namely, the projected world's distance from us even in the moment of its wholly intelligible disclosure. Most films of the late 1960s boasted a quite different aesthetic. "The massiveness of sounds and amplifications of figures in works like *Point Blank* and *The Dirty Dozen* are as if so maddened by the threat of nature's withdrawal that they would in vengeance blot it out on the spot" (131). By contrast, silence on film, even when coming at the cost of a mechanical tampering with visual continuity—whether in acceleration, arrest, or disjunction—expels at least one of the impediments (adventitious noise or dialogue) to the world's exhibited presence.

But exhibited, not inhabited. Displayed as one might display the world in a museum. There is the true force of Cavell's chosen term ("Exhibition and Self-Reference," chapter 16), and it harks back to his very definition of the medium, reiterated in this chapter: "a succession of automatic world projections" (146). When the sound track is thrown out of sync, then, film retrieves almost by accident its native hospitality to the wordless exhibition of its world views. In just this way, modernist film is working well within its foremost obligation in the matter of acknowledgment—namely, the requisite admission of "its own limits: in this case, its outsideness to its world, and my absence from it" (146). Here Arnheim's lateral frame as foundational limit seems rotated ninety degrees into the axis of spectation itself. For Cavell, film must contrive to realize itself not so much within its peripheral exclusions but in terms of the wholesale *distance* that constitutes it. It is an emphasis reiterated in Cavell's appendix, "More of the World Viewed." Film, by holding up only the world's image, "withholds reality"—but withholds it not just from us but perpetually "before us" (189). And if the filmed world may be all the more strictly and purely visible for and before us—even though momentarily stilled, distorted, or set to a perverse tempo—by being unbothered in the very process of exhibition by the overlay of sound, that does not bring such a world any closer. This is why silence is golden in the modernist cinematographic extrusion. It redoubles the remove of attention. The result is, in short, less an immediacy lost than a distance admitted.

Quite apart from the important place of this notion in the problematic of skepticism, the technical point itself—about the inherent silence of such cinematographic deviance—is one I have never seen made elsewhere than in Cavell, let alone made so much of. For him to turn the exploded image of continuous world pictures (in various baroque machinations of the track) to its own advantage by recovering from the debris a few shards of projected reality's essential silence would be a mere conceptual stunt if it were not so true to the cinematic mechanism itself. And it is a fact not seriously compromised even when the necessities of silence are overridden by the "fake" continuance of a sound track, as when the bullets that riddle Bonnie and Clyde are audible in the real time that has fallen away from the slow-motion corpses. Exceptions aside, though, why not let the general fact about a necessary detachment or evacuation of sound from tampered image tracks urge us to a full materialist disclosure—one in which silence approximates the condition not of aberrant mechanics alone but of photochemistry itself? We will eventually let Cavell take us very near this point at his own level of investigation.

Approaching the close of his appendix in the revised edition, Cavell speaks at last in German to unleash the underlying pun of his title, *The World Viewed*. The particular historical moment of film's "moving image of skepticism" (188)—of a world in denied intimacy with us—is coincident, for him, not only with the tail end of modernism in the 1960s and early 1970s but with a broader epoch of the spectacle, of a life already theatricalized. For cinema "entered a world whose ways of looking at itself—its *Weltanschauungen*—had already changed, as if in preparation for the screening and viewing of film" (226).[14] This telos of the spectacle makes film a last capitulation to, even when also an exposure and critique of, this whole mental disposition, this view of the world as primarily a scenic display. That film can be both a surrender and a diagnostic rejoinder to this specularized modernity suggests the full weight of its unsettling intervention. No sooner do we insist that the distance between us and the screen world makes the latter unlike life than we need to defend the implied boast about our participatory hold on *the* world, rather than just our place in an audience before it. To the further implications of this I will return, via Siegfried Kracauer, in the coda.[15]

Let me extract from the annals a luminous illustration unused by Cavell. Doesn't something like film's revealed distance from—and on—the world, as it figures a definitive human condition, signal the final brilliance of the final mystery in Kubrick's *2001: A Space Odyssey*? Isn't something like this the destination of all extraterrestrial quest in the revelatory estranging of the world space itself?

However we understand the astral fetus whose englobing look anchors the film's last views (fig. 310 and 316 below), and whether or not it is thought to stare only with the blind eyes of the newborn, the world it seems to peer at is entirely removed from any dawning mental presence. The world floats at the distance of a sighting, by no means the newborn's native—or natal—scene. Thanks to Richard Strauss, this is one of the least silent climaxes in film history. But it *is* wordless, as the whole film has been for the last half hour and, except for one tape-recorded message, for many minutes before that. And would, at the end, *have* to be: a necessity thrice over. Here, at the close of Kubrick's masterwork, the gap between diegetic and nondiegetic sound, narrative noise or utterance and imposed orchestral accompaniment, has widened to cosmic proportions. On the one hand, the fetus (*infans*) cannot speak. On the other, the distance of the world prevents audition. And between them is a galactic vacuum that denies the transmission of either speech or sound.

This vacuum is also a conceptual space, and across it we sense the intersection of epistemological and apocalyptic templates for the visible universe in its availability to perception. All that Kubrick's genre apotheosis has done is reverse certain rudimentary associations of a specularized world. For in *2001* the visionary escape from the impasse of technological history is ultimately to rethink the world's deathlike removal from you as your birthright in coming, open-eyed and always at a distance, toward it. Skepticism is inverted and redeemed by outrun narrative expectations within the quintessential genre of suspended disbelief. I might now put in Cavell's terms (stretching them in just the direction we must next pursue them) the point made about this film in my previous chapter. Our eyes are again fixed upon this last confrontation of planetary and cognitive body. Thinking of the film's mandated final soundlessness in material terms, we realize we have met it once before. For it is an effect closely akin to that brazen occlusion of the reality effect achieved by the fourfold freeze-frames ushering in this climactic episode (figs. 149-52). In both places the optical effect outstrips the electronic or orchestral score intruded to mute the roar of such silence. As anticipated by these previous freeze-frames in their inherent prevention of synchronous sound, the last pregnant moment is also big with the photographic hush itself.[16]

The question lingers: Why the absence of the photogram in Cavell's leap from device to its silence, from exhibited track to its constituent lack of sound? Why wouldn't his wary interest in the freeze-frame lend emphasis to the module it *almost* holds up to view? With an early chapter in *The World Viewed,* called "Photograph and Screen," Cavell no doubt means to settle the matter before the unsettling effect of the fixed frame has even begun its cinematic—or filmic—work. According to his phenomenalist axiom, however, the actual photographic imprint (unmentioned) appears subsumed a priori to the succession of camera-framed shots, as these are contained in turn by the screen border: "The fact that in a moving picture successive film frames are fit flush into the fixed screen frame results in a phenomenological frame that is indefinitely extendible and contractible" (25). Just his idiomatic locution—the synecdochic "moving picture" for its constituent moving pictures—has, apparently, the final word on the matter. In any case, this is the last Cavell has to say directly about "successive film frames," whether he means framed views or viewed frames (photograms), whether they are fit flush to the aperture or not. From this point on his philosophic sights are trained on the screen, however jagged or distorted its manifestations. Fair enough for most purposes. But when the modernist pressure in film is taken up under the sign of an "acknowledgment" of the medium in which it works, one wants to ask why one of the things worth acknowledging, since it is certainly one of the things sometimes foregrounded, is not the photographic thing. And we can ask this, I trust, very much in the spirit of Cavell's largest argument about film's destabilizing relation both to skepticism and to its presumed transcendence.

To make a point (of differing emphasis) as clear as possible, we might attempt the question from another angle. Why should the fact that the manifested world is not a space to which I am manifestly present count so much more than the fact that the apparent motion of this world is constituted by processes beneath my recognition? The aspect of its exhibition that, for Cavell, makes film nothing less (I quote again) than "a moving image of skepticism" (188, in the double sense of that participial adjective) is just what makes regarding film as never better than an "illusion of reality" amount to a "farce of skepticism" (189). That aspect is this: "The basis of film's drama, or the latent anxiety in viewing its drama, lies in its persistent demonstration that we do not know what our conviction in reality turns upon" (189). *Turns upon*, I would add, in the sense of "pivots upon"—from instant to instant. Film satisfies certain conditions of skepticism, for Cavell, because "not only is there a reasonable possibility, it is a fact that here our normal senses are satisfied of reality while reality does not exist—even, alarmingly, *because* it does not exist, because viewing it is all it takes" (188-89). Especially in light of current technology, we may want to shift the grounds somewhat. One may well admit that in "virtual reality" some further "normal senses" are enlisted that film leaves alone, leaves out of the picture. But since film is known to exclude such registers of sensation (the arrows that never graze your skin, the arriving kiss always deflected by a cut), are we not further encouraged to rachet down Cavell's model to a more foundational level of the photogrammatic apparatus? Wouldn't film's most deeply latent anxiety reside in just this: that even though screen images ("automatic world projections") *look* like the world, or at least *a* world, and continue to do so even though we know it isn't (because they aren't), still we cannot rest easy even in the way such a specular semblance is constituted? Or let us come nearer yet to Cavell's own formulation, adding only one phrase to it. We do so by admitting that on film we forgo knowing what our conviction in *the appearance of* reality turns upon—whether in regard to the particular look of it or to the general visibility of it from second to second.[17]

A symptomatic moment for Cavell's overall argument occurs in his treatment (via self-"acknowledgment") of the shopworn popular trope of "freeze" closure, or what I have called (stressing its constituent) the "photo finish." Commenting on the "uncontrollable tic of the freeze finish, apparently part of the contract in television drama," Cavell relates this arrest of movement to an older and overt rhetoric of mobility in the form of withdrawal: "The outside pull-away, up from

the house or neighborhood in which the drama has ended, letting the world return, is now replaced by stopping the departing subjects in their tracks—partly returning the figures and their world to their privacy, but unable really to let them
go, since otherwise you wouldn't be convinced they had ever appeared" (135). Yet
why shouldn't the clutched last view of such characters, snatched from plot into
the plane of mere image, be recognized, after all, as in the best faith possible, however clichéd in execution? Only given a glimpse into their material constitution,
in exit, could we indeed "be convinced they had ever appeared"—appeared in their
true form, as a race (a rush and a species) of images waiting to be taken up as a
story. That this conviction rests now, in the freeze finish, upon a cinematographic
blockage and arrest is scarcely negligible. That it rests in this way on the exposure
of the very thing we have found easy to forget—namely, the photogram in motion—might well be taken as the most authentic skeptical residue of film's scopic
regime. Or if not, why not? Why wouldn't the uneasy sense that manufactured
stasis underlies immanent motion, a fixity secreted beneath flux, be at least as unnerving to epistemological confidence as is that absence at the back of exhibited
presence?

In regard to the aesthetic "constraints" confronted in such moments, we know
Cavell to highlight the *outer* limit of the film world, all told, in its difference from
us in ours. Yet what about the *inner* limit, if I may call it that, of filmic montage,
not its impinging integrity or conviction as world but the seam of its every optic
fragment: the photomechanical border of its enchained rather than screened
frame? We can now see better what is at stake in the dubious but never quite dismissed stylistic exercises Cavell considers, including slow motion and split screens
as well as held frames—even when these techniques are only flashes in the (developing) pan of 1960s visual chic. What emerges as their conceptual pressure
point is the lone image itself to which the whole automated projection of reality is
loosely indebted and by which, in the shuttling of such images, it is induced. This
is a debt called in especially by the freeze-frame, and even more especially by the
freeze finish. But this is only to say that such stasis testifies to the motion it suspends from within. What is fastened on is what has elsewhere spun past faster
than the eye can see. And if that single fixated imprint is not just the cancellation
of the movie but its prime mover and efficient cause, then it must partake, at the
lower limit of sequence, in that porous spillage by which all images pillage their
immediate neighbors in the supple plunder of movement's undertext. In so con-
fessing its operations, this admitted flux reminds us not only that the separate imprints were there all along, but also that, as images, they came (or went) before us
in the mode of a unique kind of movement. This too, finally, is a movement as true
to the world in its way, and to our philosophical views of it, as is the silence (read:
distance) that may accompany such sighting. For this is the mode of the always
and already disappearing, an almost tangible vanishing.

That this may be an un-Cavellian thing to note about the stripping away of
the track—without being in the long run an un-Cavellian way to think—is suggested by his early distinction in *The World Viewed* between photography and
film on the score of mortality. "The nostalgia of old photographs is the perception

that mortality is at some point to be stopped in its tracks" (75). Add to this thought its corollary and complement—depending on the other sense of the term "mortality," referring not to life but to its definitive condition in terminability— and you have Roland Barthes's guiding notion of a decade later: that photography installs one version of the death it always at the same time forestalls. Returning to our opening text, *The Asphyx,* we find that this is exactly the effect transacted in the freeze on the colliding autos in the last shot, halting (once again) a death in progress. When the stilled image of the ancient man caught between them is accompanied on the track by the sound of their collision, this forced and illogical division of narrative labor only further exacerbates the artifice of suspended mortality. Even Sir Hugo's own film within the film of his son's death marks the moment of fatal impact, also illogically, with a closing freeze-frame— as if we are to believe that when filming stopped in panic, the image persisted, deathly in the very fixity of its frame. To this equation of fixity and death there is a striking point of contrast, and confirmation, from the same year as *The World Viewed.* Multiplying the familiar device of the closural freeze, including several shots locking on the hero in his flight from the police, *Sweet Sweetback's Badd Asssss Song* (Melvin Van Peebles, 1971) lodges a symmetrical reversal of this trope in its opening scene, where the hero gets his preteen sexual initiation with a prostitute. Her orgasmic pleasure is punctuated by half-a-dozen freeze-frames—the *petit mort* cinematically realized—that end with a cut to the adult hero topping the same woman. Plot itself has thus been initiated after the film's opening lines, where the passive boy is ordered to throw himself into the act: "You ain't at a photographer's. You ain't having your picture took. MOVE!" The stop-action ecstasy to follow will only briefly interrupt the fundamental antithesis between photography and pictured motion.

Contrasting the two media, Cavell wants to emphasize, as did Bazin before him, the prevailing lifelike kinesis of film (prevailing both as persistent and as winning out in perception), over against the stasis of photographic mummification. On Cavell's own account elsewhere, though, something like the death of presence may emerge from its counterpart in the happily ever after trope of marital closure—when such a trope is submitted, that is, to the negative imprint of its own tacit momentum. When the wedding party at the end of *The Philadelphia Story* (1940) is snapped by the uninvited camera of the *Spy Magazine* editor and converted to tabloid print, we get a freeze-frame passing back into inset photographic object, as in the "Caught in Love-Nest with 'Singer'" headline for the same year's famous transitional moment in *Citizen Kane* (or of course in *Under Fire* later). For Cavell this "turn to stillness" breaks the dramatic illusion of our presence at the wedding.[18] It thus operates to divorce us, so to speak, from the thrall of the medium's prevailing effect. It leaves behind all narrative temporality for the flatness of an after the fact revisitation: eros become archive. As such, and here I enumerate suggestions not developed in Cavell's analysis, it also travesties the closural stamp of marital comedy with the undisguised rhetoric of fixity. But as such, it yet again returns film to the condition of its own record and dissemination as sequenced photographs, canned if not candid. These are images normally read when scrolling past the eye rather than, say, by the turning of a textual page—a page such as the one that brings us, as the last image of *The Philadelphia Story*, a second discrete wedding shot as printed in the invasive magazine.

Let me be entirely plain. As a guiding concept in his ontology of film, Cavell's notion of "acknowledgment" directs us to all we can expect in advance of a given film in the way either of intertextual self-reference or of more profound disclosure. In acknowledgment, the medium is found calling out its own process of intermediation. It is only theory or material analysis, not the individual film text, that may be obliged to go further into the recesses—and staged recessionals—of constitutive textuality. As one might well expect, screen examples of this burrowing reflection are not everywhere to be found, and one seizes the moment—in this case the moment of seizure (as with *The Philadelphia Story*). If the freeze invokes primarily the photomechanical basis of film, then it thereby inscribes and reexhibits not so much the mediating as the constructivist function of cinema. The appearance on-screen of the single fixed image is not an acknowledgment of film's conveyance to us of the moving world, but rather the end or suspension of all movement, the obtruded intervallic origin in itself. The freeze is cinema in little and cinema in cancellation at once: the photogram in motion, minus change—or, more accurately, change without difference, pure *exchange*. This is the chief point so far, yet it leaves an additional speculation in its wake. If the freeze borrows something else from the real world while surrendering the world's motion, if it borrows—or steals—real time from within narrative time, this is a thought that needs some further philosophy—converted to some further film theory—to bring out.

FRIEZE FRAMED

By the punning analogy with plastic relief, one gets at the way all flow is dammed up in a mechanized tableau. This has nothing to do with characterizing cinema as "sculpture in motion," as did the poet Vachel Lindsay in a chapter of his 1915 book *The Art of the Motion Picture*.[19] Paradoxically, cinema approaches the sculptural only in one limited sense when it flattens itself, by stasis, into the strictly filmic. In this sense the optic freeze illustrates to perfection the formalist "baring of the device" within an aesthetic "alienation effect." It ostracizes movement from the projected effect of the photogrammatic chain. It is a glitch that suddenly—instantly—exposes the nature of this chain as such: a mere mechanized concatenation of pictures produced as moving image only by the overlapping g/round of their differential perception. But that is not the level on which to leave this device—any more than our discussion of it. More fundamentally, as we have seen, the freeze-frame estranges movement *from within*, from the surge of the interval itself, and thus lays open the grounds of movement's very possibility as screen image: its always subdivided instantaneity, the paradoxically splintered integer of all screen action. In the misnomer of a frozen moment, film abruptly hides and denies, rather than annihilates, its own motoring technology only to invoke (without executing) the act of curtailed process. Once again, the multiplied photogram on-screen freezes over nothing. It simply refuses to melt away as usual, to meld into difference. It resists, in short, the rush of time to which it has previously been synchronized. Its resistance takes the form of removing the *moment* of movement from the gestural act thereof. Subtract time from movement and you have the pose—or, more to the point in cinema, the fixed picture. In such subtraction, the fractionalized stage of a motion seems peeled away from the ongoing vector of imagined live action (world action) and pasted before us, fixed and transfixing.

More, too. There is a third level (or a fourth dimension) of this process. First, as we have seen, movement is called off even while the mechanism of its presentation is called out. Thus, and second, movement is reexamined from the inside out, gesture reduced to always schismatic integer. Third, as the rest of this chapter will show, there emerges from this textual self-investigation the time (rather than the spatial image) of cognition, reception, audience reaction, however much artificially distended. And this temporality seems to fill a sudden vacuum as well as relieving—while extending—a sudden arrest. Not only is movement removed from the freeze-frame, but in the device's foregrounding of the photogram—the bringing forward of the ground itself as figure—something else happens. One facet of the former illusion, depth of field, is flattened to the surface of the screen's own spatial coordinates. The previous inference of three dimensions, generated by an apparent mobility along the axes of all three, shrinks on the spot to the photochemical manifestation of two. Recovering a (fourth) dimension of quite another sort in lieu of the forgone spatial illusion, recovering time from within its breached interval, may be the ultimate work of such a stilled image.[20] Where motion only *seems* frozen over, in fact a dilatory space for reflection is thawed out. In the theft of what is photographically "taken" (both senses), there is, in other words, a compensatory impulse to replace the voided element with a residual facet of photography's precinematic manifestation: namely, the time of contemplation.

What exactly is the feel of this temporal quality, or perhaps this quantity, of continuance beyond succession? Examples need be no more than briefly misleading. When noting the "photo finish" of certain films, it is tempting to think of the freeze as the cinematographic equivalent of a stopwatch, where watching may then outlast stoppage. This would be especially tempting in a freeze-frame closure like the end of Peter Weir's *Gallipoli* (1981), where former long-distance runners from Australia, fighting the Turkish campaign in World War I, make their last sprint to extinction like a race won, the film holding on the penultimate moment before their certain deaths. The finish line is drawn at the frame break itself. But what we get is not an image of agents no longer in action, since, at the very least the slain runners would complete their grand dash within the diegesis by falling forward dead. Instead, the freeze constitutes in and of itself the photogrammatic mourning work of images deactualized, denied their inevitable succession by the seamless alternation of the same. An effect like Weir's operates, of course, to thematize rather than to theorize the device.

To pursue instead the theoretical effort, we cannot afford to skim over a premise. So I repeat: The freeze-frame brings forward the cinematic ground as figure. I mean by that the photogrammatic ground, the photocmechanical series that makes any figure go round the reeled strip on its way to projected motion. What do I mean by figure? The figure we see—let's say Antoine Doinnel in midstride, beached and stranded on the shore of his unrealized future at the frozen close of Truffaut's *The 400 Blows* (1959)—this represented human figure hasn't changed, except in that it has stopped changing in representation, has been struck still. But it has become figurative as well as figural, or we might say emblematic as well as representational. Yet not just emblematic of the plot's or hero's posture, here (in Truffaut) on the bridled verge of a perpetually latent transition. Whatever its metaphoric discharge within plot, the freeze figures the place of the image in the rendering of, rather than the rendered, event: the deconstruction of narrative vector into optic sector, of the filmed into the filmic.

This is a fact we may assume Truffaut wishes to underscore by a seldom remembered aspect of this famous closing shot, to which I will soon return. The last held image is more than ordinarily objectified by being taken as object by the still moving camera itself, which (through an intervention of the optical printer) closes in on the suspended image by an extra second or so of inward tracking (looking ahead to figs. 162-64 below).[21] Such a rapid zoom is already familiar in these pages from its later, and again closural, use in *Fail-Safe.* Its effect does not in the least spare the cancellation of narrative drive, but it does show forth a given narrative device arranged to outlast the suspension of plot long enough to take its leave of the diegesis with a last spasm—a last reflex—of enunciation. Once again, then, the stuck (reiterated) photogram, rephotographed in multiples, becomes less a freezing of the imaged action than a lingering, numb cinematization of a photographic *frieze,* with the residual narrative (as well as pictorial) apparatus often powerless to get things going again.[22]

Finally, that is, the cinematic freeze has as little to do with arrested motion as a frieze in plastic art. Fixation is more the double-faced term for it, inducing an enforced fascination with the affixed. And in that summoned attention, one comes to see, as in veined marble or pocked granite, the grain of the photogram as well, another figuring forth of the material ground as part of the figure of distended attention. This is why one can usually spot a freeze-frame even when it transforms a stationary shot of a static scene—blank wall, empty street—into a tableau. The limited clarity of the image, its nature as inscription rather than immanence, a condition otherwise masked by rapidity, is now part of the view. There is too much time to deny it, and it represents a detraction—a loss of innocence in its own right. This seems preeminently the case for the arrested development of the teenage hero in *The 400 Blows.* The way Truffaut stages this closural holdup, this negation of space's essential maneuvering room, connects directly, we will find, with the photographic fetish and the mechanized analogues of its cinematic evolution evoked along the course of plot. Yet it is less toward the photograph that the film ultimately reverts than toward the photogram in stalled transit, in canceled action: the frieze of inaction installed under the lengthening duress of the same.

TRUFFAUT'S PHOTOGRAPHIC G(O)ROUND

Antoine Doinnel: the echoic feel of the hero's own name in *The 400 Blows* tells half the tale of the rut in which he keeps finding himself. The rest is spelled out by the film's tracking of its own photographic motif. Without at any point bringing an inset photographic image into full-screen equivalence with the cinema frame, as he will later do in *The Green Room*, Truffaut's debut film comes as close as it can to aligning the two media across a subtext of graphic textuality itself, optical versus scriptive. To watch the way this takes place as the very armature of plot is to appreciate once again, as in my first chapter, the mostly overlooked connection, in this classic instance and elsewhere, between the reframed inclusion of photographs and a film's own strategic reversion to photogrammaticality.

153

After establishing shots of the boy's regimented classroom, the first fully narrativized image on-screen, impelling the first movement of the plot, is the disclosure of a photographic image slipped out from under a writing desk. It adorns the exposed page of a girlie calendar, fixating attention even as it offers, below the image, the neutral template for an ongoing chronology, days on end. Where words should be generated on the desktop in their proper succession, an image appears instead—as if to lay bare the underlying desire of all text as well as the eros of temporality itself. The rapid inspection of the erotic photograph by a nameless schoolboy begins the chain reaction by which the photo is shunted from desk to desk among the pupils. Not only differentiated from the material basis of the assigned writing lesson, the fixed photograph emerges into distinction from the filmic chain whose plot it precipitates. The photograph in motion, where there should only be scriptive text production, now stops dead at the desk of the hapless hero, intercepted there by the instructor just after Antoine has exercised his spontaneous iconoclasm even on this fetish object and regendered it with a mustache (fig. 153). The strong arm of the teacher is at this point the first of the film's many punitive interventions on the part of authority, arresting desire in action. It is a pattern that eventually ends in the hero's consignment to a reformatory—from which he attempts his final escape, only to be arrested this time by the apparatus itself.

Playing hooky from school in an earlier scene, Antoine has launched his career of escalating petty larceny by abetting his friend's theft of a pinup publicity still (from Bergman's *Monika,* as it happens) outside a movie theater (a pilfering caught on the fly by the camera, fig. 154). This is the circulating sexy photograph in a new mode—shown here in its own redoubled form as a cannily chosen production still from Truffaut's own marketing effort (fig. 155). This same day of dedicated truancy also puts Antoine's own person, rather than merely a photograph, into accelerating motion inside a "Rotor" at a local amusement park (fig. 156). The optical deliberation of the unfolding episode may be without peer in narrative film. Racing circular motion, when photographed in sync by the rapidly spinning camera, offers by optical illusion the virtual stasis of the rotor drum's separate rectangular panels.

154

156

155 (Courtesy of the Museum of Modern Art Film Stills Archive)

157

158

Within one of these demarcated (wooden) frames, Antoine inches his way, against
the centrifuge's slamming pressure, into various shifts of posture in the only movement made visible to us (fig. 157). As with the cinematic apparatus obliquely modeled here in carnival prototype, the rotary motion behind the effect—as we are only
next given to see it by the centrally stationed camera—disappears into the artificially delineated and constrained human motion of the blocked-out character in the
drum's subdivided rectangles. We know he is spinning, but we see him holding still
before us, in a frame of his own within our screen frame. This, as suggested, is only
the half of it. In the reverse shot from the revolving subject's own point of view, the
adult spectators ranged in a circle above the pit are spun round and together in a
flickering blur of interchangeable disappearances.[23] At peak speed, the camera's full
rotation goes so far (and so fast) as to double a single onlooking figure as its own

afterimage within our perceptual field (fig. 158). The effect is to reverse the axis of cinematic analogy and to turn the spectators' fleeting images into photogrammatic stand-ins—each for the other and all, together, for the whole apparatus being emblematized, as well as for an adult world of dizzying irrelevance to the adolescent on the run.

The rotor episode is as literally rounded—and self-contained—as any "acknowledgment" of the cinematic mechanism could be. But in its evocation of the photogrammatic oscillation as well as the spinning axis of the apparatus, it soon connects with the whole photographic subtext of the narrative in its drive toward the final calling of a halt. Not just watching a movie (as Antoine's flickering face is seen to do in one later spell of truancy), but caught up in a mechanism comparable to it, the actor as screen character, submitting to the relativism of imaged motion and its reciprocated illusions, has been pinioned by the gears of the machine as surely as was his great predecessor, Charlie, in the claws of the engines in Chaplin's *Modern Times* (1936; see chapter 7). And again the rule of narrative, under the sign of law, has helped ensnare him there—in Truffaut's case, a narrative inexorability associated at every turn with photographic arrest.

The traps of plot in *The 400 Blows* are never far from the machines of motion and its capture to which the film continually alludes. The errancy of Truffaut's hero, once he has first been distracted by the lure of the visual image from his task of writing, leads to his own theft of a machine of text production—a typewriter, no less—for which he has, of course, no use. We are reminded that someone else is scripting his story—and under the gaze of another, not himself. Moreover, it is because of his attempt to return this useless textual appliance that he is apprehended, jailed, and shipped off to the reform school—but only after he undergoes two forms of enforced imprinting. A fingerprint session quickly dissolves—by thematic association—into a police photographer's studio (fig. 159) where Antoine is to have two mug shots taken, one frontal (fig. 160), one shifted violently to a profile shot by the bullying hand of the law (fig. 161). After an initial blink of the boy's eye, the second shot is held still on-screen for six long seconds, having been tricked into fixity by the substitution of a repeated photogram for the otherwise continuous record of an obedient pose.

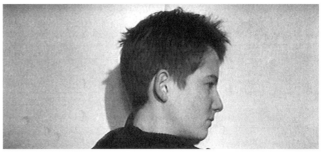

The fugitive hero has been policed into stasis as character in order to be photographed. More than this, though, he not only now *has* a record, he has *become* one, a mere forensic imprint in the form of the film's first of two freeze-frames. All that remains, as anticipated in front of the disciplinary lens at police headquarters, is that the boy's photograph, as screen actor as well as cornered charac-

162, 163, 164

ter, be definitively locked into place as image—and the film is over. This time it is the intervening hand of the director, rather than of the police, that forces upon the boy a frontal rather than profile shot. At this final turn (toward the vacant prospect of the camera—and the audience invisible beyond it), the optical textuality of the narrative arrives for a second time at the breakdown of cinema into sheer film. After racing toward the beckoning horizon of the beach, Antoine turns from the water's edge to face (down) the camera, having nowhere left to go. Only the camera, as mentioned, has the energy left for an extra lurch: a vestigial gesture displaced from the running body to the still-running mechanism. Moving in for an enlarged shot of the hero's narrowed options (figs. 162-64), the camera locks onto a full close-up over which, almost at once, FIN appears blocked out in the script of an overseeing authority—a tonal if no longer narrative authorization imposed upon the running in place of photograms going nowhere.

With Truffaut dedicating his film in its opening titles to the memory of André Bazin, the narrative has articulated its indebtedness by entering one of Bazin's abiding themes—the ontological divide between photo and film—and extending that difference over time, yet still within textuality, as a plot. This is a story in which the photograph that starts the film rolling anticipates the fixed image into which plot will unravel at its point of impasse. This last is a photographic stasis whose look—whose abrogated narrative *appeal* in both senses—is rendered sightless in its fixity and that we, at the same time, are impotent to return or appease, a look unsettling precisely by its continuing availability to us. As with the titillating calendar under the impress of the hero's irreverent pencil in the first scene, the film's most plangent image is now partially defaced by orthography (FIN) in the very act of being claimed as inscription, stopped dead by disclosure as such, by disclosure as sheer imprint. What condition of (the) film as a whole, what "limit" in Cavell's sense, is reframed by this frieze, even as it is reshot in its fixity by a progressive close-up? Our distance from it, tying the hands of compassion: this would be one ready answer. But such an aesthetic of ironized empathy would await fuller contextualizing within a materialist aesthetics of the medium itself. What does such an optic frieze tell us about its governing antithesis in invisible speed? Contemplation is the mode of sculpture's moment, not haltedness. So with the cinematic frieze. Cinema minus the motion of its track enters in this way, after all, the temporality, even the materiality, even in a sense the plasticity, though not of course the solidity and roundedness, of sculpture. It does so by carving out from its celluloid process a so-called *space in time*. In passing from the split second to the distended moment of a canceled differential interval, a petrif/action on-screen, persistence of vision has become the vision of its own persistence, motion removed from the cinematic to the strictly filmic register. As residue of a world once credibly on view, such an effect has to be seen to be disbelieved—seen in its radical conflation of real time with screen (no longer plot) time.

THEN/NOW: FROM PUNCTUAL JUNCTURE TO PUNCTUATION

One way of noting what is breached by stasis at the end of *The 400 Blows* is to observe the suspension of all possible suture, the cornerstone of enunciated subjectivity in film theory. Even if another character were imagined present on the scene, no glance back at Antoine—given the arrest of all sequence—could ever stitch together that plenary exchange of looks that "realizes" narrative space and emplaces our own subjectivity within it. No countershot will over carry us back again to the shot of Antoine as if he were still there to his world. This whole triadic reciprocation (the seen/the looking/the looked-upon, each shot presuming and so "signifying" the next image in sequence) is forsworn by the freeze. So is another triadic possibility, one named by Deleuze with no allusion either to suture theory or to the truncation of the stop-action image. For Deleuze, the movement-image has three facets that are also "avatars" of subjectivity. The first "material aspect of subjectivity"[24]—as a veritable function of movement over time—is the perception-image, accompanied perforce by the action-image, by which he means the self-imaged reaction in the mind to a given perceptual stimulus. To the resulting gap between perception and reaction, Deleuze also gives a name: "Affection is what occupies the interval, what occupies it without filling it in or filling it up" (65). The affection-image, "third material aspect of subjectivity" (65), is what prevents perceived movement and instigated reaction from seeming "incommensurable" (66). It is an image associated most obviously on film with the expressive capacities of the human face, the exteriorized sign of internal reaction.

But this Bergsonian subjectivity constituted on-screen around a "center of indetermination," every bit as much as the signifying exchange of the gaze that "sutures" the viewer's subjectivity into constitutive relays of identification, is brought to a halt—and an ontological deadlock—by the freeze-frame. As the residue and antithesis of movement, the held shot passes over in its photographic aspect from partially (and vanishingly) indexical trace of movement to entirely iconic status.[25] In the process, the freeze seems to congeal all three facets of the movement-image at once—perception, (re)action, affection—while passing beyond their determinants to trespass upon the terms of Deleuze's second volume, *The Time-Image.* How so? This is because what rushes in to fill the vacuum of motor stimuli in the freeze-frame is nothing less than time, our time. This is also why, though elided from the diegesis, the mediatory affection-image seems to suffuse the whole perceptual trans/action of the freeze-frame as a kind of punctuation. The freeze becomes the italic font of the cinematic register. Like italics underscoring the word *as word,* the freeze highlights not the image as world picture but the image as imprint. Retention of the image in transit is subsumed to height-

165, 166, 167, 168

ened attention. Sequential temporality is held hostage to the suspended interval of, in common parlance, "reaction time"—and in the radical absence of any further "reaction shot."

The clearest example I know of this temporalization of stasis comes very late in the late modernist day. It is a photo finish that plays upon just that suspension of synchronized sound that is Cavell's best excuse for the device—and does so within a postmortem fantasy of erotic suture, gestured at but never realized. In the 1976 *A Star Is Born* (Frank Pierson), Barbra Streisand, singing her dead husband's signature song at a memorial concert, closes no doubt the longest fixed-frame close-up in popular film (seven full minutes) with a stasis that finally invades the whole image plane. This happens with the onset of a freeze-frame just after the repetition of a last question to the dead (for whom we in the movie theater, proxies for the never again seen diegetic audience, are in turn placeholders). The question: "Are you watching me NOW?" It is a question to which no reverse shot could ever deliver a fit response. As the singing image eventually passes under red filters to a memorial frieze (see fig. 168), the sound track (though overruled by stasis in narrative space) nevertheless brings up the character's (and star's) own signature song, "Evergreen," over the end titles, at which point the stop-action image has become more logo (or record cover) than therapeutic icon—but not before it has arrived to figure a time beyond time.[26]

Everything has conspired in this figuration. The escalating pop catharsis of the scene has built toward the release marked by the last throw of Esther's head (figs. 165-67), the final "now" delivered at the top of its arc in a way that exceeds the diegetic climax by escaping altogether the range of her hand-held mike. Accident or thematic license? Slip or further figure? Whether Streisand's last "now" is suddenly miked from above in this live-concert footage, off-camera, or dubbed in later, the only way to "read" this final moment of the freeze is that the fictional context of her character's own live performance is transcended by a note conveyed by narrative alone, not by the narrated equipment on the portrayed stage. Sound track is thereby set over against image track in their mutual tampering with both the audiovisual and the spatiotemporal continuum.[27]

What I need to stress again, and am now ready to bear down on, is that given time to think in this way, dwelling on a moment that swells before us, we think in part of time. We do so by finding time implicitly pictured for us. Like any film image, only more so, every freeze-frame asks us to "watch . . . now," even as the now has already been surrendered to by a then without difference. Sequential temporality gives way to a forced presentness of imprint: then/now as the now. By the cinematic frieze, that is, we are *put in mind of time,* delivered into a temporality that has its own cognitive—and ultimately psychological—emblem, to which we will eventually be able to give the name of a specialized sort of duration unapproached by Deleuze's Bergsonian categories.[28] From the fast-stripping intermittent rips in continuity, inch by inch, to the stable image of temporal discontinuity, from the punctual to the punctuated: that's the change made by fixity, by the irruption of the freeze-frame as an isolated slice of motion. Let's call it, once more, a crucial *textual* moment of cinema—and textual according to a

provisionally psychoanalytic model of generative significance. Here, as we have
seen, is a device that stretches the diegesis so thin as to breach its illusion, revealing below its surface the specular unconscious of all photogrammatically received images, the ground beneath all screen figuration. To the fuller use of the
psychoanalytic model of surface and depth, in unexpected connection with
Deleuze's mentalist (and immanentist) approach to cinema's thought machine, I
will return at the end of this chapter when the materialist determinants of the
screen image are more firmly in place.

With this on hold, other theoretical voices, those of Barthes and Bazin, may
profitably rejoin the debate. For the freeze-frame allows back into cinema, with its
special case of reduplicative automatism, what the mechanization of the photograph originally drove out: what Barthes calls the meditative "punctum" of the
photograph.[29] Different for each viewer by definition, this is the contingent sub-
zone of the still image that grabs us, pierces us. Not a pictorial effect, it is an affect
beyond the instrumentation of semiotics to encode, the punctuating detail that reflection alone gives time to make salient. As such, the photographic punctum
marks the latent dramaturgy of the *trouvé en scène.* And on film? On-screen, at
least, the freeze *is* the "punctum," an arrest and retention that translates, further,
to an image of the very time we are surprised to find for looking, a time associated
with photographic contemplation and hence with the structuring opposite of the
cinematic image in the discrete still.

Here is the movement-image of Deleuze attenuated on the spot into a sheer
perception-image—and so radically prolonged in this aspect as to denarrativize
perception itself, leaving only the emptied, nonpersonified locus of affective re-
bound. What, then, is the cognitive charge of such discharged movement—such
negated change—but an instance of self-generated "memory" from within the dilated instant itself, the unnerving onset of a nostalgia for the present? This is not
a "sheet of the past" as adduced repeatedly by Deleuze in *The Time-Image* but a
sheet of the present, sheared off both from the true past into which it cannot quite
lapse and from the future it bars. All succession is displaced upon spectation.

TIMECHANICS: FILM'S SPECULAR UNDERTEXT

My goal has been twofold, my trajectory forked. Only one phase of this branched
purpose remains to follow out. Having situated the freeze (uninvestigated by
Deleuze) within a system of animated immobilities (a montage of fixed sections of
movement), or in other words having understood its relation to the photogram as
particle or articulatory hinge of movement, I have also been following the device
along the path of temporality, which of course it only seems to halt. Here, as implied, Deleuze neither leads nor blocks the way, for his approach to the phenomenal immanence of the screen image (even when sophisticated by Peircean semiotics: made signifying rather than merely manifestational) locates the question of
time primarily within the content (however abstract) of the shot or the movement
between shots rather than in the persistent form of the image. Yet the two modalities of the freeze-frame, space and time, not only are complementary at the level

of effect but also record equivalent recognitions of the medium's own bases in motor tension (difference) and temporal extension (persistence).

We may return again here to Bergson. As always, his resistance to cinema's fabricated mobility is lodged in the name of time, of *durée.* In a passage not mentioned by Deleuze, however, Bergson actually discusses the cinematograph itself rather than just the cinematographic model of cognition: "Suppose we wish to portray on-screen a living picture, such as the marching past of a regiment."[30] The most efficient way is "to take a series of snapshots of the passing regiment and to throw these instantaneous views on the screen, so that they replace each other very rapidly" (331). His example is no accident, the regiment offering a kind of *mise en abyme* of the whole mechanism in its filing past of "superposed" (340) and mechanically self-regimented photograms. Against the so-called illusion of movement, Bergson insists on movement's *invisible* presence—as never more than falsified in screen realization: "In order that the pictures may be animated, there must be movement somewhere. The movement does indeed exist here; it is in the apparatus" (331-32). What appears on-screen is disjuncture masquerading as a parade of continuity, fracture as duration. The film's life f/lies all before us, dead on arrival, each image riven by its own rival, ghosted by its own double. Real movement vanishes in the intervals whose optically traced poles of difference, traced by superimposition itself, hallucinate another kind of movement—or, in the case of the freeze, mime its own foreclosure.

Between the fixed points of any and all such intervals there is for Bergson no becoming, no ripening, only the artificial gap—turned span—between immobilities. The no longer spaced time of the frieze—the erasure of the interval (however artificially, given the still racing strip)—takes us forward from Bergsonian to Bazinian time from a helpfully skewed angle. In a discussion titled "The Concept of Presence,"[31] Bazin considers the stages of photographic advance within the history of plastic arts as narrowing the intermediary distance between presence and absence, with cinema ultimately overcoming the "piecemeal" nature of photographic realization (96) to produce "a molding of the object as it exists in time," thus generating (as Bergson would deny with regret) an "imprint of the duration of the object" (97). This is a notion carried further, and with some mystification, in Bazin's metaphor for cinema as "a mirror with a delayed reflection, the tin foil of which retains the image" (97). These figurings of cinematic duration as optic "mold" rather than fleeting trace are continuous with the language of the more famous "Ontology" essay, where photography is said not to "create eternity, as art does"; rather, "it embalms time, rescuing it simply from its proper corruption."[32] Breaking through the deadlock of baroque aesthetic aspiration in a teleology Bazin may be thought to draw directly from Malraux,[33] cinema arrives so that, for the first time in representation, "the image of things is likewise the image of their duration, change mummified as it were."[34] The heuristic force of Bazin's metaphors is not to be forsworn lightly—as long as one realizes that, even as figures of speech, they have to do precisely *not* with "ontology" (the true "being" of time, say) but with the illusory effects of mechanic phenomenality, not with the essence of the photographic object, and certainly not with that of the cinematic "image" on strip or even screen, but rather with the *apparency* of their mediated presence in (or across) time.

Within what alternative framework, therefore, might one better convey the complexity without obliterating the mysterious spectrality of cinema's temporal coordinates, its ostensive durations? The pieces of an answer are arrayed before us, as it happens, in our local consideration of the freeze-frame—as soon as they are submitted to a certain conceptual reformulaton. If the freeze (though not mentioned by Bazin) may be thought, first and foremost, to catapult the screen image back to that "convulsive catalepsy" (15) of baroque art's contorted gestures at motion, this prolonged instantaneousness is nonetheless a very different thing, we have seen by now, from any sense of time standing still. In its extreme case of the ontological aura displaced onto pure phenomenal affect, the freeze discloses the conditions of its own deviance, of its insistent rather than relaxed and vanished fixity. Photograms grabbed one after the other by the clutches or claws of the mechanism and plastered (over each other) to outlast all difference: such is the freeze or frieze in (suspended) action. Induced thereby is instead sheer, sheeted *protraction*, inducing in turn a reactive quality of temporality: the irruption of the pure durative, bred of repetition, amputated from all change.

But this perceptual purity can result, as we have seen, only from the negation of a negation—and twice over: the canceled erasure of an original stasis on the strip, which was in turn the cinematographic negation, frame by captured frame, of an initially recorded movement. What comes through in the end is a twice removed image of the original photographic moment itself, indistinguishable for once from photogrammatic advance. To call this the pure duration-image in reception is not to suggest, of course, that it extends to us in any sense an image of objects in their durative essence (Bazin). It holds out, instead, duration itself objectified. We have noted that the mode of retention exhibited by the freeze-frame can be seen as that of a desubjectivized memory: an immediate afterimage that prosecutes the *subjection* of space to time without the intervention of a rendered consciousness. And such enforced recourse to the time of viewing puts us in mind of the thing viewed at a new level. If ordinary cinema ensures continuance by sending the photogram into serial cancellation, the freezing return of the filmic upon the cinematic brings the photographic underlay of the medium at large to unwarranted disclosure.

Within the frame of reference provided by the stop-action image, then, we are now prepared to tighten the analogy between filmic animation and mental life (rather than living motion) advanced in the previous chapter. For like cinema *as film*, the psyche is founded on the gap between conscious unitary impulsion and unconscious fragmentation, between synthesizing drives and their potential breakdown. Such a psychic prototype for reception is not designed to reengage with or debate various neo-Lacanian accounts, for instance, of the male-gendered gaze and the spectator's constitution by it. Rather, the generative binary of surface and depth is introduced to recover a textual deep structure in cinema's repressive perceptual (rather than representational) order—a scopic order imposed perforce upon the machinated chaos of the photogram. I have been concerned with a suppressed underlay in cinema's plastic automatism and those occasional blockages that perturb the medium's image-summoning power. For Walter Benjamin, as discussed in chapter 2, instantaneity is the optical unconscious of normal vision. As traumatic limit case of a world view, it is precisely the filmic work of the freeze-frame (whatever its narrative labor) to access *that* unconscious in its screen equivalent: the photogrammatic undertext of reception.

It is in this sense that the freeze provokes a unique intersection between the movement-image and the time-image. It marks at once their node of reciprocal interference and their mutual vanishing point. So back to Bergson once more, whose objections to cinema came down to this. Brute perception cannot engage *durée*, which is lost to cognition's false reliance on the instantaneous sense of positioned matter. Hence Bergson's complaint about cinema as a machination that only repeats the mental error of conceptualizing the world without a true continuum. Deleuze, we know, wishes to intercede against the overscrupulousness of this complaint. He not only claims that cinema rectifies the cognitive error isolated by Bergson, giving us (not just instigating in us but giving to us) new ways of thinking the world in its durative continuities. Further, he proposes that Bergson would have been likely enough to have seen this for himself if he had written from the vantage point of the medium's later developments, when motility had become part of the art rather than the mechanics of cinema,[35] one of its freed-up but still definitive "constraints."

But if one is encouraged by Deleuze to contextualize Bergson's alleged blind spot, his limited purview on the full unfolding of cinema's technical repertoire, then one ought to begin by historicizing Bergson's explicit dissatisfaction as well. He was there when cinema was not, and he therefore saw it burst onto the scene from its origins in a culturally pervasive fascination with the single photographic print. Oriented toward the new medium by its immediate descent from serial imaging (Muybridge), from overlapping chronophotography (Marey), and from instantaneous snapshot technique (Lumière's latest developments, as Tom Gunning will help us understand them in chapter 6), Bergson was historically disposed to resist what cinema would pass off on the public at the plane of its own artificial manifestation: the suppressed but essential discontinuity of the image. Deleuze might have been on somewhat firmer ground, however, had he suspected Bergson's allergy to cinema was occasioned by a primitive phase of the medium not so much before the mobile camera as before the muting of flicker by both a sophistication of the shutter and the increased speeds of frame advance. But even in view of these developments, Bergson would have had his sticking point—in the fixed image of the strip, ingeniously slurred over or not by the mechanics of projection.

In wishing to situate Bergson's animus against cinema within turn-of-century European culture, additional scholarly evidence comes conveniently to hand. A recent essay on temporality as a quintessential modernist problematic helps triangulate Bergson's historically conditioned doubts about cinema with those of both a photographic practitioner and a theorist of mind. In their reasoned resistance to motion pictures, Mary Ann Doane sees a rare point of convergence between Bergson and Freud—and of each together with the late nineteenth-century master of serial chronophotography, Etienne-Jules Marey, his photos an overlapping blur of layered and terraced gestures attempting to capture time, so to speak, in action.[36] The gist of her complex argument is as follows. Each of these analysts of time and mind resisted cinema for different, even opposite, reasons. Marey and Bergson both respected time as an absolute duration, a continuum that Marey struggled to parse and transcribe in exactly the way Bergson would have thought destructive to the transformative continuities of élan vital. Freud, by contrast, believing time to be at base a disjunctive and piecemeal construct of consciousness, a kind of "symptom" of underlying psychic causes (324), would have found that Marey's effect to capture it by rationalized subdivisions was only a trivializing reduction of time's more inherent and profound discontinuity. None of this warmed any of them to the spatiotemporal automatism of cinema. Each found it conceptually wanting, artificial, because it pretended to capture either a suppositional and nonexistence plenum (Freud) or a real but elusive continuum whose mechanical reconstruction could only, if for different reasons, falsify its homogeneous essence (Marey and Bergson). For Marey, cinema returns the eye to its own lulled imprecision about movement through time. For Bergson, cinema's inherently mechanistic reconstruction falsifies the seamless durative essence of time. For Freud, whatever its other problems, and however ineffectively, cinema still participates in the myth of objective time, masking traumatic discontinuity as an effortlessly directional representation of desire and act.

Enter again Deleuze—and not just in his explicit contest with Bergson. For Deleuze's sense of the ultimately disjunct and almost schizoid potential of the time-image, if it could only be delinked in his thinking from the vaunted "plane of immanence" (or screen manifestation) and returned in part to the undulations of the undertext, might be used to break down the terms of Freud's own resistance to cinema's supposedly figmented (rather than deeply fragmented and schismatic) continuum. For Deleuze, time is where the real action is. The movement-image is its mere support, launching pad of temporality's salient conceptual deviances. Bergson ought to have settled for the movement-image as given, Deleuze thinks, so that cinema, as philosophical object, might have provided him with the evolutionary sense of duration he found lacking in the medium's nascent phase as mere attraction. Accepting on Bergson's own terms the sense that the world's received presence actually constitutes human consciousness in the interchanges of sensorimotor engagement, Deleuze interposes cinema in this process without due qualification. Because the world can already be understood as a decentered "metacinema" in Bergson, Deleuze goes on quite literally to erect this "plane of immanence" into the screen rectangle, immediately dissolving its artificial verticality, however, into the flows of motion intersecting it from every angle—even from the multiple axes of time itself.[37] This is what I have called Deleuze's resolute phenomenalist approach.

Duration is thus reclaimed from its supposed evasion by sheer mechanistic visualization and given a twofold force—first within the time of the moving shot, then in the time negotiated between shots. These are the two chief aesthetic refinements of the medium, beyond its primitive mechanistic stage, that might well have changed Bergson's mind, Deleuze assumes, about cinema's failed adequation to the genuine psychic interdependence of matter and memory. Well before midcentury modernism, these refinements are the first promise of cinema's "time-image," insinuated respectively by camera movement and montage. The so-called motion picture, as strictly a technology of animation, would be more vulnerable to Bergson's critique, that is, if cinema were only, as it once was, the fixed-frame agitation of bodies and objects in simulated motion. But when the movement-image ends up fulfilling cinema's potential by way of tracking and cutting, it reveals the whole plane of immanence as saturated after all by *durée*, in ways that postwar modernism can thereby maximize and philosophically exploit. Even early on, therefore, the movement-image has already ceded considerable screen ground to the time-image. But it might also be said that this is just the point where technological figment—the mirage of motion—passes over to figuration, or in other words where ocular mechanism becomes, as never admitted in Deleuze, something best understood *as text*. When the movement-image comes of age by exceeding merely the image of movement to include the movement itself of the image plane, then it is no longer a picture of something (image in this sense) but rather a figure (image in the other sense) for something else, transpiring in the ocular hinterland between a metaphor and a metonymy for the operations of temporality per se.

With the encroachment of the time-image upon the framed field of cinematic motion, the filmic rudiment (or "little frame") can be swept away only in the immediate generation, not in the proper and full estimate, of cinema's screen action. A categorical discrepancy is already apparent in Deleuze's initial sketch of the issues at the opening of his first volume. There, by way of an undue conflation, the "immobile" sections of the strip get too quickly assimilated to the sectioning of space by the immobile frame on-screen. The persistence of the same term, "sections," yet in different understandings, may make this categorical elision either easy to miss or easy to spot. In any event Bergson, as is noted later with regret, "only considered what happened in the apparatus" rather than on-screen. At that level, Deleuze is ready to agree that cinema "proceeds with photogrammes—that is, with immobile sections." Within a page, however, cinematic evolution is understood, from Bergson's day forward, as the gradual "emancipation of the view point," which would become "separate from projection," with the result that "the shot would then stop being a spatial category and become a temporal one, and the *section* would no longer be immobile, but mobile" (emphasis added, to highlight the false parallel across the two passages).[38] What Deleuze never acknowledges is that there is a wholly different level of perception involved in moving from the photogrammatic to the projected section (the latter closer to what we saw Cavell mean by the "phenomenological frame"),[39] a different definition of "frames" themselves. So that the eventual ocular or scopic mobility prized by Deleuze cannot rightly dismiss from consideration the optic or plastic fixity that permits it. Even the most advanced and adventurous montage of the time-image "proceeds with"—and proceeds *from*—those same activated fixities that Bergson, had he written later, might still have found every reason to continue bearing, with disquiet, somewhere in mind.

Bergson aside, the important point here is this. What Deleuze will later celebrate as the deterritorialized flux and quasi-schizophrenia ruptures of the time-image can be understood from the start as a function of the strip as well as the screen image. To film's further function as a tacit critique of both centered consciousness and a falsely totalized social real we will be returning, via Kracauer, at the end of this book. For now we need only see how tellingly Deleuze is drawn back toward the procession of photograms even in his veering away to a plane of immanence where movement goes—and comes—without saying, without primary articulation.

This return to the strip happens, early on, as follows—and with nothing allowed to follow from it by way of theoretical reorientation. When drawing on Jean Mitry's refusal of the term "shot sequence" to describe a continuous camera movement, Deleuze admits the "justification" in thinking of that movement as a series of separate shots. Looking at the film strip would only (I hasten to add) bolster this point. Such, indeed, is the final implication of the "photopan" I began with in the introduction: the moving shot of stilled photos that never dissevers itself entirely (as photograms in action rather than photographs at rest) from the tug of the singular. When Deleuze asserts that the sequence shot, as sequential reframing, "inherits the movement and duration" formerly confined to (because within) the movement-image, we wonder about the line of descent or derivation. Why not the other way around? Isn't it more accurate to say that the moving screen frame inherits its sliding positionality from the incremental ingredients of the strip? So too, and even more obviously, with that other form of movement-image rather than sheer imaged motion Deleuze adduces in countering Bergson: the rudimentary montage cut. Here, as with the tracking shot, the strip itself reveals even more obviously the differential cleft that gets (for once) transposed directly to the screen (as in extreme form with the cut to black at the end of *Proof*). One frame on the strip abutted with another not at all like it makes on-screen for a visible (rather than an imperceptible) movement *of* rather than *inside* the very "plane" of vision, its touted "immanence" never more contingent or textually marked.

I do not mean that tracking and montage can in any sense be reduced in reception to the mere track (the moving and projected strip) from which they "inherit" their inherent possibility. It would be crucial *not* to say this. I mean, rather, that their homology with the track, when sensed, serves to recruit the photosynthetic differential as filmic model—within cinematic mediation—for the peculiar kind of spatiotemporal field that motion pictures construct, as well as for the particular kind of thinking (epistemological and ontological and often, one should add, antimetaphysical) they may induce. Such is a thinking (and here lies both my main sympathy with Deleuze and my chief departure from the level at which he is willing to entertain it) that draws part of its power from its tension between overt manifestation and the fault lines of reception's specular unconscious, where the track returns from constitutive suppression both to indemnify and at times to unravel the cinematic construct.

The textual (rather than linguistic) analogy again comes to the fore as a materialist ratio. The supposed membrane of immanence in screen experience, the phenomenal image, stands to the elementing members of the chain as a literary message stands to the phonemic undertow that sometimes erodes our conscious sense of discursive intent. The whole vibratory, fibrous nature of experimental verbal texturation finds in this way its modernist complement in the (for the most part) *invisibly* rippled stream of the cinematomic aggregate. On the one hand, then, Bergson was by his own lights perfectly right to distrust cinema at its cognitive basis, even if he missed its "imagistic" or figurative reverberations (brilliantly teased out by Deleuze) for a nuanced apprehension of *durée.* On the other hand, that antithetical modern thinker, Freud, was far too quick to write cinema off as a meretriciously seamless skein of duration false to the definitive clefts and irregular sedimentations of mental life. These disjunctures not only manifest themselves, for instance, in the condensations and displacements of punning verbal amalgams in dream's chaotic montage, where they are open to literary theorizing in connection with the inherence of the sliding signifier in the unconscious. The cinematic apparition also offers on its own terms, in generative tension with the buried play of the filmic apparatus, another revelatory psychomechanic analogue, along with modernist literary writing, for the oscillatory reciprocities between consciousness and its own undertext.

The rightful place of a surface/depth model for cinema's perceptual investments, its fit place at the end of a chapter on the stop-action image, should now be apparent enough. The freeze-frame has emerged from our earlier discussion as what might be termed the negative asymptote of the movement-image and the time-image together. Deleuze's own simplest and typifying cases of motion picture technique—tracking and montage, each offering both a movement-image and a time-image at once—can now be compared to the mutual reduction of both devices in the anomalous limit case of the freeze shot. This is the seized-up frame that can neither spring movement from within its own circumscribed field of view nor move on to a different field. If the supposed misnomer of the sequence shot refers instead to an imperceptibly graduated series of microshots, so does the misnomer of the freeze-frame, but in the latter case as a sequence blocked from "creative evolution" by sheer repetition. In a complementary sense, the freeze-frame also constitutes a montage cut that gets choked off on the brink of transition, ending one shot but going nowhere next. It is also, of course, going nowhere fast. In both respects, it questions the very notion of a plane of immanence. Its strictly receptive duration operates, in cognitive engagement, as the materialized return of a filmic preconscious, entailing whatever degree of unconscious cathexis in the process.

For Deleuze, cinema is a way of thinking philosophically about human action over and within time. But with the freeze-frame, cinema's putative brooding upon time has become only our brooding upon its, upon filmic time per se. The sponsoring thought of Deleuze's whole project (in two volumes that are, of course, its own best proof) amounts to the philosophical premise that cinema itself innovates thoughts—and thought processes—before our eyes. If so, it must be that reception is then necessary to think them through, or in other words to *think* through them. Cinema may in this sense be said to have a mind of its own, but one that spectatorial consciousness meets halfway. In the different emphasis of the present photo-synthetic account, however, cinematic spectation can never fully know its own responsive mind. Where cinematic technology forgives the interval, reception must forget—if, in the long run, never entirely. The photogrammatic moment on-screen is the jogging of that repressed trace memory, summoning the undertext from the field of its exclusion, returning the motorized imprint to the frame of reference for all screen spectacle. That this too gets one thinking—but thinking in part about a fabricated sighting one is otherwise so oddly ready to accept as a world in view—is the continuing thrust of the chapters that remain.

For now and in sum, the very thought of the freeze chills the veins of portrayed duration. Fixation grows contagious, taking the spectator's time in tow. As the visible becomes merely visual, becomes strictly scopic, the viewer seems no longer so free to look but feels, rather, as if tethered to the apparatus for the length of attention it both permits and *inscribes*. And this optic coercion, before it can be fully assimilated to screen rhetoric, involves a lifted suppression as well as a new compulsion. Suddenly the screen frame seems to burrow back to its unearthed origin in the no longer paradoxically riven integer of the track, the no longer schismatic rush of difference. But in the mock candor of their fixity, such iterated photograms blow the cover of our simply looking-on at a world in view. A false model of skepticism may be one enlightening consequence. There are others. When the operation of the photogrammatic increment is no longer narratively motivated but textually exposed, other motives come to the fore: the only ones left, the desires that feed, and feed on, the specularized world. Why shouldn't these desires, as occasionally deprogrammed by photogrammatic recursion, lead in the long run to a fuller psychoanalytic template? In the meantime, where does it tend to stop or falter, this scopic attachment to mediated reality? What are its definitive limits? How does death, as one of those limits, come back into the picture, the moving pictures, from beneath their sequencing? And when it does so, by what internal wrench to spatial succession must the movement-image yield—whether violently cede or effortlessly accede—to the time-image? The next chapter awaits us on the score of such questions.

FOUR

Deaths Seen

DEATH IN CINEMA REGULARLY TAKES THE FORM
OF PHOTOGRAPHIC FORM ITSELF.

In disengaging from the freeze as lingering frame of reference at this point, I am
trusting that some analytic pressure has been built up by the conceptual stock-
taking of the previous chapter. We found that the temporality of mechanized arrest offers its own typifying disclosures about the spatiotemporal arrangements
of the entire cinematic medium as a specular event. Such a freeze becomes the duration-image not of the world's retention on film stock but of our held attention
to it as sequential imprint. If film in its function as cinema is more than a strip of
fixities in motion, then the freeze-frame immediately justifies its role as exemplary aberration. If, that is, cinema as film offers the sheerest trace of stasis, the
freeze performs the masquerade of that stasis.

As it happens, I have just stumbled upon an unexpected way of putting this.
In doing a routine computer spell-check on a preliminary version of this chapter I
was, strangely enough, offered "phaseouts" as a lone alternative to the eccentric
plural "fixities" in the last paragraph. So be it. But the freeze-frame makes the fixity and its phasing out, each in its own way, integral to the filmic process—and not
just instantaneously but simultaneously. The reiterated photogram, as we saw,
jams the system in order to block (out, into the open) those anomalous moving
frames that, in seeming for once to hold still, actually preserve their vanishing
separateness while surrendering only their usual difference (one from the next in
the chain). The photograms that together compose the freeze accomplish thereby
the erasure of an erasure, the masking of a motion that ordinarily masks the stasis at its base. The stop-action image blots out all transit in a new specular transaction with the same. Such images no longer perceptibly come and go, no longer
edge each other along and out. They simply *return* from within, one upon the
other, as if from the suppressed undertext of the coherent screen image.

I continue for a moment more to renew conclusions we have previously reached. The time of these sequential photograms is the time of a persistent self-eclipse, the accession to the other in the form of the same. For the spectator, the odd time entailed is the time of looking divorced from all narrative temporality, the return of the photochemical provocation from within cinematic manifestation. Picking up again a recurrent metaphor from image theory, we realize that if photography is a corpse, film is, by contrast, a finality always on the cusp of revival, or otherwise a vividness always in passing. And so we are back where we started, under prompting from *The Asphyx.* To repeat: Photography is a death in replica, cinema a dying away in progress.

We are now in a better position, however, to weigh these and similar figures of speech as they proliferate unchecked in the commentary on film and photography. If such determinations are *only* (as well as patently) metaphoric, and thus seriously compromised for any ventured theory of the filmic text, their ultimate frivolity should find its severest rebuke in the consequent theoretical redundancy of an actual dying on-screen. If not, if literal death within plot works to clarify the metadiscourse of photomechanical mortality, then we may well be on to something after all—and with some distance yet to go along the road it marks out. Much depends on where absence is understood to have set in: whether between profilmic temporality and its mediation by image in the first place or between one filmic imprint and the ousting adjacency of the next in line—or both. The one absence tends to mark the heft of reality given over to the photographic theft of presence, the other the fugitive feel of presence on the heels of its passing.

Either way, filmic textuality has one foot in its own graven image as photogram. Such recourse to the rhetoric of mortality has little to do with borrowing the funerary luster of theory's higher melodrama, from Blanchot through Derrida, for instance, and everything to do with specifying the material recognitions—not only within but across media—it issues from. A statue, for instance, understood suddenly as marble carving rather than human figuration, may well stone to death its human subject. But the incisions of print textuality, literary and filmic, cut more deeply than the sculptor's chisel, even if only in two dimensions. They constitute the very medium rather than just realizing the contours of its representation. Prose, to be sure, can be called sculptural, just as film can be praised or blamed as painterly, but each metaphoric descriptor belies the linear temporality and irregular surface inscription of the material medium in question, the ridged rigidities of script or the barred cells of image. No matter how lapidary the style, film and writing are in essence partly lacunary. Their incised units of effect mark the slicing off of those respective frames and lexemes that make for continuous representation—even as they unmake it when their own cracks show through. If death in film and literature often finds itself figured as the moment when textuality erupts from beneath mimesis, this is not only because of the medium's lifeless materiality, then, but because of that medium's own intermittent presence in reception. Lexical blanks and photogrammatic bars, phonemic juncture and cellular juxtaposition, or in other words traversed intervals: such define the pulsing oscillation whereby chasm and glyph, gap and impress, mark the alternating current of the representational continuity they generate.

In cinematic narration, this is why the edited gap within a given scene—the cutaway, sometimes the reverse shot—is often the decisive inscription of the death moment, where the intermittent nothingness of the strip may for once burst through on-screen as figurative hole in human temporality. The cognitive abyss of truncated human seeing may become a *mise en abyme* of the medium itself reduced to sheer materiality, compact of dead spots and the signals they organize. Short of this, on track rather than strip, death may already have confounded the system at the level of montage. The strip's fundamental intermittence remains the register of a specifically filmic—or photomechanical—operation. For *cinematic* rather than filmic death to engage fully with the thematized absentations of screen plots, the codes of narration must intersect the conditions of serial record and sequential animation. The metatextual dynamics of a death *scene* (and thus seen) must carry the spectator past a strictly successional dichotomy (or dialectic) between the ongoing and the elapsed at the microstratum of frame advance—if only to return there in the end—in order to enter upon the screen's edited displacements from the immaterial subjectivity of the here and now to the objectivity of the gone.

Maximizing the latter dichotomy on-screen, the work of such different narratives as *Citizen Kane* and *The Shining*, discussed at length below, is to pitch the preternatural form and content, respectively, of their deaths-in-action—their calibrated negations of the subjective—against the unnerving objectivity of the photograph as both historical record and funerary icon. It is from such photographic associations that the further photogrammatic inference then slips into place. This pairing of cinematic death scenes (and the photographic moments that contextualize them in their respective narratives) has an additional advantage as discussion fans out into the conceptual space cleared by the previous chapter. In bringing together two of Deleuze's favored masters of the time-image, Welles and Kubrick, I will be monitoring closely the evoked persistence of the single frame when it returns impertinently as the swivel between a movement-image blasted open and a time-image closing down. This happens, I suggest again, when death assaults the projected track at the level of the strip as well.

So it is that to inquire more closely into the structural force of the death scene in levering open the entire cinematic system is to pursue our continuing inquisition into the invisible constituents of the photogrammatic screen image. Nagging questions shatter any premature complacency about the approach so far, even as they may finally be seen to support it. Can the strictly *ob*scene be made seeable? Can life's ultimate offstage moment, rather than the corpse it leaves behind, be caught on film? And if so, does it thereby grasp at what is always caught in passing on film—a temporality not quite present and no longer backed by presence? As my title lets slip, this chapter is about the cinematic death scene as multiple specular crisis. If *The Asphyx* offered an initial set of terms for death as both sponsor and by-product of the photographic-become-cinematographic apparatus—the ghost it produces and the corpse it overcomes—this chapter enters upon the textual inversion of those terms. For at critical moments of self-disclosure on film, deathwork as figure for the temporal violence of the cinematic machine is joined by optical disruption on-screen as a variable metaphor for the intercession of fatality within narrative. Variable, because in the evidence of this chapter we leave behind the exemplary drag on succession—and theoretical anchor—of the last. From the freeze-frame, that is, we return to the correlative device of the opening chapter, the inset photographic image, but this time within a fuller spectrum of ocular disturbance and tricked specularity.[1]

We are concerned now with the visual phenomenon of death as only cinema, never photography, can capture it. By contrast with the photogram's elusive traffic in fixity, we might say that what is most lifelike rather than deathlike about cinema, about film on-screen, is precisely that it can show a dying as well as a corpse—and moreover from inside as well as outside the gradually expunged consciousness. Cinema can, in other words, kill off the narrated beholder as well as the seen body, arresting the envisioning as well as the visible agent of a framed space. My largest subject in the present chapter, then, is the seeing subject—the bearer of the look within the scene—consigned to visible annihilation. How to show this on film? How to see it as the absentation of the subject's own sight? How to picture just this departure as the moment of the character's conversion from subject to object? How, in certain cases, to link this as well to the related encorpsing of the scopic object—the visible thing rather than the ocular moment—in photographic arrest? And in any case, after the scene of obliterated subjectivity has been played out, how to motivate the screen's continuing image as a survival of such death? If the moment is not fixated from without in a freeze-frame, how to manage it as the eerily prolonged registration of an external world that—as the veritable proof of a self's absence from it—persists beyond human cognition? Or if not given over to such persistence, how by the relays of editing to withdraw cognition so that the world vanishes from the spectator's vision—as from all narrated consciousness— in such a way that blankness itself becomes a trope (if not a picture) of the very death that can never be lived *through* from within a focalized point of view? Such questions should be enough to prompt a chapter. That the evanescent density of registration in the scopic relays of a death scene is so often found in thematic if not narrative proximity to an ironized photographic portrait should further be enough to demand such a chapter in a book like this.

Even classic film theory has touched on this subject, I now find. The problem of death in representation always leads straight to the question of form. As early as 1932, in a brief and only recently translated essay called "Death in Film," Rudolf Arnheim, commenting on the trend toward cinematographic exaggeration in the treatment of death, notes, with no film titles mentioned, how "the dying man departs from life in close-up and in slow motion."[2] These are the manipulations of space and time, respectively, or of scale and speed, deployed to evoke what amounts to a medium-specific inhabitation of death. The close-up can pull us toward a liminal zone between the subjective and the bluntly objective, between a searching last glance and a sightless corpse. And well before slow motion's bravura use by Akira Kurosawa and Arthur Penn and Sam Peckinpah (and the endless TV derivatives lamented by Cavell), this device casts the mortal subject into a time out of joint. Each manipulation foregrounds the filmic (photographic distance and camera speed) to maximize cinematic access to the always unseen. The nature of death as absentation is indeed what lends the hypothetical slant to the last phrase of Arnheim's essay, when a particularly naturalistic death scene on-screen seems to validate at least one film's oxymoronic status as ("if we can allow the phrase here") a "documentary film on the topic of death" (74). More often, or at least strictly speaking, death (if not dying) turns its back on visual documentation. It cannot be seen to be believed. Hence device itself must bring death off, carry it over from drained content into figurative form.

It often does so in an extreme version of what I have noted elsewhere as film's thematerialized inflection of cinematic spectacle. In the introduction I suggested how the "two-way street" linking textual analysis and theoretical abstraction operates, in cinema, by a conceptual transit between the generative levels of strip and screened track—or, I might now add for literary writing, between clustered phonemes and the lexical regimen of narrative syntax. The narrative moment of death often seems to plot that transaction into the open, so that systemic crisis registers as a representational impasse. This is why, in sum, poststructuralism's general gravitation toward the rhetoric of death (especially in deconstructive reading) can be pressed to new and twofold clarity in the narrated scene of departing consciousness. What Joseph Conrad called the pivotal event *in articulo mortis* often exposes, that is, the articulatory hinges of an entire inscriptive system, whether literary or photomechanical.[3] With a jolting short circuit at the level of representation, textuality may get openly plugged back into the sequential basis of the medium itself. In life, death is the debt called in by time. In narrative representation, death is often a toll exacted from the realist continuum by textual succession per se. In the exorbitant return of textuality upon mimesis, as I have been suggesting, narrative death comes before us under a double description. Death's twofold abrogation of continuous presence is based at once on what we might call external and internal evidence: the vacuuming out of world from its imprint and the revealed vacancies in the latter that have previously served in sustaining the manifestations of the former. Call this the difference between absolute loss and constitutive fracture, wholesale absence and serial gap. But of course this difference, along with each aspect of disjuncture (*from* the world and *between* the markings that would collectively manifest it), is usually veiled in its textual fabrication by the woven spell of representation. When the cinematic guise of continuous presencing is actually unmasked by its own origin in the filmic assemblage, though, it is in this sense, as in many another, that death may be called a strictly theoretical experience.

BLOOD COMPLEX

We can start simply. The world's abrupt removal is the flamboyant figurative device chosen for closure by the Coen brothers in their debut film of 1984, *Blood Simple.* But its last-ditch trope of precluded suture—inscribing the death we can never quite look into, the blankness that alone stares back—works in consort with an explicit photochemical figuration of death earlier in the narrative and with a satire of portrait photography earlier yet. Whatever else this offbeat film may be up to in its perverse local colorism, it comes across as a morbid travesty of the "mummy complex" that Bazin associates with the evolution of representational arts into the technology of automatic imaging—first the photographic relic, then the "embalmed duration" of the moving image. As its central plot twist, *Blood Simple* hypothesizes the faking of death through a merely photographic finality. And it is this strictly photographic engravement—the subterfuge of the "doctored" death shots—that complicates the ontological ironies of the final bloodshed and its capping death scene. The main points do seem simple enough when made to face each other in this way. Photographs always resemble the deaths they may be commandeered to dissimulate. Movies sometimes simulate that aspect of death that necessitates the surrender of consciousness on the brink of its extinction.

The latter emphasis first, in a closural scene that operates by the apparent condensation of several visual puns. Just after the film's bloodbath finale—in a bathroom no less—the slain detective, lying under a washbasin, looks up through the camera's eye—or it through his—at the intermittent drip from a leaky pipe on the underside of the sink. Like some temporally compressed variant of a Chinese water torture, as long as his POV shot seems lingering in wait for the next release of a pendulous drop, the onlooker is not altogether lost to the flow of time. The last dilated shot pauses as the drop hangs poised for descent: for the arrival, that is, of a sensation the dying villain could perhaps still feel if he were able to watch it fall toward his face. A freeze-frame here, though hard to read as such, would have been the film's last sick joke. Instead we get a cut to black leader for the eventual end titles. In this thriller plot that has come down to a single suspended dribble of action, death is the cognitive blank that ends all suspense. Borrowing as it does the cut-to-black closure from a film like *The Parallax View,* we may call this the textual parallax of death's filmic sighting: measured in its canceling distance now from the diegesis, now from the exposed film strip. Death, in short, penetrates from plot to track, figuring by an effacement of the photogram the narrative's designated fatality. Such is a fatality that, in the interrupted suture of its structuring gaze, also serves to expose—by the mechanical cancellation of subjectivity in the edited POV shot—the inherent constructedness of all such subjectivity on film.

As suggested, this truncation of the screen image completes an oblique link across strata of mediation in the film. Within plot, photography (as opposed to the photogrammatic track, but in a strange approximation of its sequencing all the same) has been explicitly used to figure death, to substitute for it in a criminal ruse. Our low-rent detective, having photographed an adulterous tryst, is paid by the cheated husband to become a hit man. Instead of killing the couple, however, he photographs them in a motel once more, asleep under the sheets, and tricks the image (fooling us as well as the husband) to suggest the puncture wounds, powder burns, and spilled blood of his job done. It is only at the later point of revelation (to us alone) that we may be likely to recall an earlier, oddly prolonged episode in which the wife's new lover stares at a domestic gallery of professional and amateur portraits of the once happy couple (figs. 169-70) and is found touching (rather than touching up) one of the poses as if to see whether it—whether they—could possibly have been real. The

169   170

present lie of a past amorous bliss, now dead: such is the photographic cheat that comes back to haunt the husband, the lover, and the plot itself.

Concentrating these ironies, the film's central episode works to travesty the familiar trope of photomechanical death in two installments. First, in a POV shot from the detective's lurking vantage, and with no camera in sight, the flash of his voyeuristic photo through an uncurtained motel window resembles a burst of gunfire in no particular way—except by the cultural cliché of photographic deathwork, the "shot" that stops you live in your tracks. The knowing film audience is, in short, all too ready to take the burst of light as the elliptical sign of an assassination. Having seized a moment from the lovers' unconscious time, the detective now pretends to have taken them from time altogether. And since the audience is not let in on the counterfeit until much later, the photo of the bullet-riddled bodies—seen by us over the husband's shoulder ("Dead?" he asks, followed by the detective's scrupulously accurate ironic reply, "So it would seem")—only confirms for the time being our association between two kinds of shooting, the one as witness to the other.

Only much later, when the detective is seen destroying the evidence in his photo lab, does a further bizarre twist emerge beneath the level—and against the very logic—of plot. This is the second installment in the sardonic parable of mummified time. It turns out, for no good reason (except to continue the metonymic slide from shooting to photography and on into film), that he has staged the murder *in stages,* narrated it rather than merely mocked up its document. Here is the real surprise behind the shock tactic of this plot twist. The detective has rehearsed the death—has, if you will, gone through the motions of death—via a needless *series* of photographs that indicate the progressive dripping of blood over the bedsheets. It is only the last and most gruesome of these images that he has given to the husband before taking his money and (actually) shooting him dead. In the subsequent scene of technical disclosure in the photo lab, however, we spy on the now certifiable murderer as he burns up his incriminating prints one after the other (fig. 171), like photograms exposed too long before the lamp in the artifice of their seriality: first the original sleeping couple (fig. 172), next, in reverse sequence (as if to make the artifice clearer to the viewer), the heavily bloodied (fig. 173) and then only bullet-punctured sheets (fig. 174).[4]

In any realistic sense of this sting operation, all lab work would of course have been done on a single negative or print—or only by random trial and error on

171, 172, 173, 174

175

more than one. The retouching dye did not need to enter temporal succession like the death scene it dupes. Unless of course this antidetective, this falsifier of evidence, was introduced to approximate the ordinary work of filmmaking violence in the photomechanical animation of a merely fictive bloodshed. Which of course he was. And by the optic economy of this one screen text of photographically based temporality, he will pay for his bloodletting (faked at first, later authentic in the murder of the husband) in exactly the right ironic currency, submitting in the end to a different kind of dripping—over (and beyond) time. At which point the film whose opening montage of Texas landscapes included most prominently a blank drive-in screen catching the dying light of a sunset (fig. 175) will, as we have seen, go blank on its own terms, occluded by the negation of the sequential photogram. Put out the light, and then put out the light.

DAZE OF HEAVEN: THE POSTHUMOUS GAZE

Fatal bloodletting may not get any more complex on-screen than in the Coen brothers' epistemological tour de force. But dying does. I return briefly to the work of Terrence Malick. There again we can try thinking out the difference (in this case across two separate films) between the still as corpse of mobile being and the edited film track as an enactment of mortal removal—each within the law of the photogram as intermittent filmic undertext: the photogram, in this case, as imprint and switch point of any sutured gaze. Following *Badlands*, a film preoccupied with the relation between photography and death, came *Days of Heaven* (1978), where the relation of death to the held shot has visibly infiltrated the very weave of cinematic narrative. The cognate recessional of stereopticon slides in *Badlands*, as a mortally contaminating trace of the lost past, becomes in *Days of Heaven* not the freeze of truncated action but, rather, the evacuated shot/countershot pattern as a truncation of embodied sight: the seer removed from the scene. This is what happens to the optic of identity at the moment of death.

Badlands was about the desecration of the American Great Plains by the random exploits of a psychopathic drifter. *Days of Heaven* backdates that violence to a formative moment of western settlement: the rise of a class system on the prairies, where a migrant worker (Richard Gere) kills the landowner (Sam Shepard) in self-defense when about to be shot after he is discovered in a liaison with the owner's wife. Furthermore, death and retribution are silhouetted against a backdrop of natural catastrophe in a biblical infestation of locusts and the scourge of an out-of-control fire meant to contain them. The pivotal death thus arrives to shadow the Edenic title with the apocalyptic overtones of the *dies irae*. Just before the Shepard character can pull the trigger in their confrontation scene, Gere jabs a screwdriver into his chest and runs off toward a cluster of horses on the smoke-shrouded horizon. My metaphor is the film's own as well: the veritable pall of death descending, seen through a POV shot from Shepard's fallen position, laid low on his own scorched land. The stunned victim looks on blankly, dazed by death (fig. 176), in a transfixed stare that might have seemed like a freeze-frame except for the smoke slowly churning behind him. As if answering to this fixated gaze along its own line of sight in the countershot, the fatal other looks back and then flees, scattering the horses (fig. 177). With more billowing smoke gradually occluding the view (fig. 178-79), we are still watching from the site (and sight) of the fallen man. Or so we can only assume. But this reemphasized metaphor (blackness as the subjectively registered emblem of death) dissolves back into narrative metonymy (blackness as index of doused fire) at the breaking point between the dying mind and the world's continuance. Once returned to sequence, that is, the gap opened by this last image seems almost to literalize rather than to figure death. For at some indeterminable (invisible) point of transition, this sustained POV shot has surrendered—it turns out in immediate retrospect—any point of consciousness from which it can originate. When we cut back to Shepard's looking rather than his last view, the dying and now dead man is seen supine and sightless (fig. 180). He is already gone. For however many seconds, the vestigial look we have shared with him has grown posthumous before (and through) our own eyes. It would be hard to exaggerate the cinematic, the systemic, tremors of such an effect.

As a breach in the enunciative system of suture, we have watched his going— through his own eyes for as long as possible—as follows. His initial glazed look "signifies" the world's persisting presence as image. The shot of what he has been seeing, as referent of the first look, then takes up its place, in turn, as the signifier of his still looking on (his continued signified attention as well as a figure for death as life's ultimate clouding over). No sooner do we decode that signifier in relation to its presumed referent than we expect a return to the image of his signified looking, a return to death as a last *recognition*. But the chain is suddenly broken by the sight of his averted gaze, the suture undone. *L'absent* (the sliding signifier of the look in the founding terminology of this theoretical account) has passed from the absent one to the merely absent. Within the full spectrum of the Deleuzian movement-image, turning on the absentation of a rhythmically predetermined exchange of POVs, the "perception-image" is in this case detached from all "action" (reaction) and "affect" together in the moment of death: the moment, we may say, when suture's ideology of presence is no longer *personified* for us.

What results is not only a crisis for the phenomenalist approach to film but a disjunctive trope in its textual system. In a pattern of ad hoc generalization that has already become familiar from the mounting evidence of this chapter, we may say that *death takes visual definition* from the self-apocalypse of the medium's own representational limits, here of the shot, later of the frame. Death is defined in situ, that is, as the moment when the fiction of a camera angle assimilated entirely to the organic agencies of the diegesis can no longer be sustained, when seeing (recording) is made to persist in the evacuation of the gaze. Well before his own book on the photographic death moment, *Camera Lucida*, Roland Barthes had seen through his usual aversion to the naturalizing powers of cinema to something more film specific than his preferences appear to realize. In celebrating the estranging tactics of Brecht and Eisenstein, Barthes stresses the "law" of representation, which can be violated at a price "no less than death." Hearsay evidence confirms: "In Dreyer's *Vampyr*, as a friend points out, the camera moves from house to house recording *what the dead man sees*; such is the extreme limit at

176, 177, 178, 179, 180

which representation is outplayed; the spectator can no longer take up any position, for he cannot identify his eye with the closed eyes of the dead man; the tableau has no point of departure, no support, it gapes open."[5] We have been interested in the advent of transgression rather than the illicit void itself, the interplay of the sutured shots that only gradually "outplays" its own rules. And in the first signs of Malick's "gaping" tableau, the first irreversible slippage of the signifying look, *Days of Heaven* reaches not so much an "extreme limit" as an internal delimitation of the medium as a play of absences.

But questions again collect. How is Malick's jolting elision of sight lines linked to other manifestations of death as structuring principle in filmic succession as well as in screen narrative? How does the death moment tend to emerge not only as a function (through editing) but as a featured recognition (through photographic inset) of photochemical mediation? How, in short, does on-screen death come forward as a filmic as well as a cinematographic event? The categories of such questions are by no means new to this book. For their renewed pursuit here, however, we have use for film exhibits different from those adduced in the past three chapters. More than before, we need films whose negative imprint in sequential engravement—whose disclosure of their photo-synthetic basis—does not just trope death by optical emblem but enters the cinematic death moment as it transacts the very difference between moving picture and photogram, between kinesis and that fixity to which it may at any moment revert. Only in this fashion can we continue to wear away at the inert truism that has cinema side with life, photography with death.

Whereas the previous chapter sought out the theoretical resonance of the freeze-frame as a simultaneous scandal to both inhabited space and progressive time, this chapter concerns something like the melodramatic near miss—the cued avoidance—of such rhetorically loaded fixity in film's attempt to capture the psychic voidance of death. The stopped frame is the decisive and incisionary sign of finality repressed by rule—by "law," Barthes might say—in cinematic enunciation but gestured at in certain cases through the strangest of optic contortions within the racing chain of the ongoing cinematic image. How might this happen? Two very different screen moments should clarify the collapse of perceptible movement into cognitive stasis apart from the petrification of the frame: one an internal split between the fixated human image and the action it precipitates within the same shot, one the figurative subtraction of all human mobility from resumed camera movement in the voided subjectivity between adjacent shots. These moments come, respectively, from two of the most extravagant death scenes in film history, at the opening of Orson Welles's *Citizen Kane* (1941) and at the close of Stanley Kubrick's *The Shining* (1980). Under analysis here, and against prevailing arguments for cinema's vitalistic rather than funerary cast, they should help get us beyond the strategic rhetoric of the freeze-frame to a more deeply struck bargain between mortal absentation and the very law of montage.

The disparate character of my chosen examples, in tone and technique, is exactly their secret advantage. Let me anticipate. If death in these two widely divergent films, each with its own simultaneously evoked and deflected stasis of a fixated human subject, can be seen, in the fullest possible narrative context, to reveal the unconscious photo synthesis of film viewing, then our excavation of these very different filmic sites will have been mining common terrain after all. And if they are found to tap this unthought photo-synthetic fusion of our screen view without depending on (even though partly alluding to) the jammed photograms of the freeze-frame, then this book's largest point—about the functional force of just such an unconscious textual engagement even in its more typical suppressions and oblique returns—will be well on its way to being carried.

In an untranslated article by Bazin, "Mort tous les après-midi," an essay that explicitly distinguishes filmic time from "Bergsonian '*durée*,'" Bazin writes of death, made repeatable on film, as "one of the rare events that justify the term, dear to Claude Mauriac, of cinematographic specificity."[6] Death "marks the frontier of conscious duration and the objective time of things" (68), and on this score photography must cede to the greater powers of cinema. Photography is able to represent the death agony or the corpse, "but not the unseizable passage from one to the other" (70). Bazin means that the death moment is ungraspable from an exterior perspective, so that for him the ultimate cinematographic "obscenity" (69), in other words cinema's "extreme perversion" (69), is to run the footage of death in reverse, bringing the corpse back to life. The filmic arises in other ways as well to meet the challenge of cinematic mortality. Apart from any suggestion of this sort in Bazin, the specific burden of this chapter is to explore the way cinema works to "seize" the passage from dying to death from the inside out, by a seizure in filmic subjectivity per se.

"EXCESS OF SEEING": DEATH IN THE EYE OF THE BEHOLDER

In a suggestive comment about the narrativity of the novelistic death scene, Mikhail Bakhtin's dead metaphors of omniscient *sighting* seem to invite literalization by film narrative. "[The narrator] will seek to consummate the hero's life from a point of view which is in principle different from the way that life was lived and experienced by the hero himself from within himself."[7] Fiction thereby attempts "to utilize the narrator's *fundamental and essential excess of seeing;* . . . the author's gaze and self-activity will *encompass* and shape essentially what constitutes *in principle* the hero's *limits with respect to meaning* at the point where the hero's life is turned outside itself" (166; Bakhtin's emphasis). We have already seen such an "excess of seeing" in *Days of Heaven,* in the exceeded—or in Barthes's sense "outplayed"—optics of human consciousness itself. A yet more excessive involution of ocular dramaturgy awaits us in *Citizen Kane.*

We begin with what must be the first certifiable time-image in what Deleuze nominates as "the first occasion on which a direct time-image was seen in cinema,"[8] namely Orson Welles's debut film. From the ominous gothic lair that provides the film's initial interior, there is a dissolve through falling snow to a fake winter scene with an artificial log cabin; then a reverse zoom to a broader shot of the glass globe that contains that scene, held at arm's length on a bed over which snow again seems to be falling (as if for the start of a second transitional dissolve,

181

182, 183, 184, 185, 186

fig. 181); then a huge close-up of moving lips forming the word "Rosebud" beneath the same fall of snow, whose transitional status is no longer confined to the film's grammar of advance but extends to the narrated mind and its own dissolution. Across the swollen temporality of this distended death moment, the superimposition of a "special effect" from the glass toy upon the realm of the dying subject has suggested not so much the encroachment of its interior upon his as his removal to its space.[9] As such, narration performs a displacement in—and as the visual definition of—the onset of death, accompanied by a letting-go both literal and figurative.

In the second dissolve to more of the same falling snow, metonymy (sequence) is thus instantaneously converted to metaphor (equivalence): the chill descent of death. So that when the glass trinket is released to its obliteration on the floor (figs. 182-85), there is a further explosion of figural clichés that cannot be evaded: as he loses his grip, Kane's world, slipping away, passing beyond grasp, has gone to pieces, its bubble burst.[10] Retrospectively understood, from the perspective of death's aftermath, not only as a "peak of the present" but as a "sheet of the past" (the titular opposition of Deleuze's fifth chapter in *The Time-Image*), this stratigraphic lamination of snow within the ambivalent virtuality of a "crystal image" lingers so decisively across the death scene as sole marker of subjectivity that the eventual removal of its strange overlay, just when the glass shatters, seems inescapably to signal the presumptive *instant* of death.[11] What we might call the extruded subjective shot that has preceded this instant, in which we see Kane as he might be imagining himself in the process of dying away into a remedial fantasy landscape, becomes now—in the very next shots—a perspective instantaneously extrapolated beyond the confines of subjectivity altogether.

What exactly am I pointing to? We will be keeping our eyes on the glass totem. Slowing down the image of the crashing globe reveals unmistakably that the released liquid, in which the snow was formerly suspended, contributes to the sense of explosive disintegration by splashing in dozens of droplets against the camera lens (fig. 186). If noticed at all in the rush of this narrative transition, such (accidental) foregrounding of optic technology and its contingencies would only italicize the functional transfer from one molded glass surface (globe) to another (lens). Furthermore, it would do so just before the glass globe phantasmatically returns from destruction to reduplicate not only the curved arc of the camera lens but an improbable focal point previously linked to the last clutches of subjectivity.[12]

This happens in the fleeting spectral shot, from amid the debris of the broken glass paperweight, that further confounds the nature of inner versus outer in connection with the now shattered sphere of the dying man's fantasy (figs. 189-90 below). There is nothing about this perspectival oddity in the shooting script, only the following gloss from the cutting continuity about the opening frames of the sequence: "distorted reflection through broken glass ball—camera shooting through enormous bedroom to door in b.g.—nurse coming in" (308).[13] Even the phrasing is curious, let alone its dubious match with the image as we have it in the final print: "reflection through"? Rather than "in"? In any case, from the dying of the body to the shrouding of the corpse, all action now takes place half reflected upon, half filtered through, the ocular emblem of this sudden shell of a life: the convex former site of conferred subjectivity. As such, the "distorted reflection" has been meticulously prepared for. To begin with, the paperweight has already been visible in Kane's hand even in the establishing shot of him supine on his bierlike bed, arms tight to his sides, the glass not really in his line of sight. When we first see the encased snow scene in close-up, therefore, as intercut with Kane's dying utterance of "Rosebud," there is no necessary suggestion that he is himself looking down at, rather than merely thinking about, the object that has just claimed our attention. The distance between his exhaled utterance and the artificial winter scene is thus both bridged *and kept* by editing alone, rather than linked by a motivated eye-line match. With the object of underspecified desire first held and then lost at arm's length, what follows after the paperweight hits the floor is an unsettling mix of the virtuosic and the blatantly impossible. In a two-step disclosure paralleling the initial reverse zoom from close-up to medium shot of the paperweight, we now see, first, a slightly distorted full-screen image of the closed door (fig. 187), with the nurse immediately opening it and entering the room (fig. 188). This is followed, second, by a cut to a baroque shot that has pulled back to locate this image within the still magically intact lower half of an (apparently hemispherical) glass fragment, with the toy cottage turned on its side to the left of the frame in that gargantuan close-up (figs. 189 and 190 again). While the predominant bottom sector of the image captures (by reflection) the nurse striding across

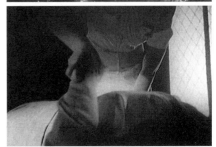

187, 188, 189, 190, 191

the room, as if from behind us, the fixed rather than kinetic image of the upper third is not a reflection at all. This visual segment—as itself a window rather than mirror—is taken up mostly by the gothic windows through which, by an inverted match cut, we have originally gained admittance to the room ourselves. Together, then, door and window figure the convergence of a double cognitive access upon the emptied space of the no longer cognizant subject.

The studied "tricking" of this vertically bifurcated image plane only compounds the preternatural quality of the floor-level shot to begin with.[14] The mind's eye of the dying man—having appropriated the landscape of glassed fantasy only a second or two before, englobed as he visibly seemed in its not entirely contained zone of escape or nostalgic regret—is a mind's eye that still hovers instantaneously, if only by association, amid the splintered remains of that fantastic space. Enter merely external ministration—and too late. The floor-level angle from which the nurse's arrival is seen in reflection provides, then, what we might call a *displaced* out-of-body shot, the merest ghost of a ghostly purview. It is as if the object of desire now looks back toward the displaced subject of the original mind's-eye glance. Whole or in splintered bits, the fragile globe has marked that lingering within disintegration that captures the mind's slippage into death. In its transitional station on the way forward into the reverse unfurling of plot with the coming newsreel, the globe's paradoxically fractured integrity also begins imaging the prismatic, refractive, mosaic nature of the orchestrated narrative fragmentation to come.

Just as the literary death scene tends both to evince and ultimately to characterize death in figurative terms—as the moment when all subjective representation turns metaphoric, there being no worldly referents left for mimetic report—so film tends not just to render but to *define* death in specifically cinematic (hence metatextual) terms.[15] Your death *is* the moment when whatever seeing or hearing continues to exist can no longer be yours. Just as literature broaches death's epistemological vacuum through rhetorical deflections of various sorts in the moment of canceled subjectivity, so film can evoke the occlusion of the visible in the moment of death: the arrest, emptying, or reassignment of the POV shot—or, as in *Kane*, the superimposition of the unreal in an encompassing subjective snowscape. This in turn is an extroversion of the inward gaze that becomes instantaneously vestigial in *Kane*'s next shots, when the residue of the hero's consciousness seems caught a split second after its explosive descent into the void. For the life that has hit bottom, the POV is suddenly DOA. In sum, we do not so much see Kane die as see the evacuated traces of his own seeing.

But wait—as we just barely have time to do in this held shot. There is something more there in that vertical diptych as hinge for its irony (figs. 189–90), a detail of the shot regularly passed over in commentary upon its convex distortion. It is this and this alone: the dead body itself. For the transparent rather than reflective upper part of the frame brings to view at its lower border the enlarged (and at first hard to read) image of Kane's hand, empty now but still in place on the edge of the bed, his fingers rigidly outstretched and dwarfing by anamorphic distortion the profile of his head off to the right of the bent image. What we have noted already as a kind of dialectic ideogram of death plus its recognition, collapsed upon a single impacted frame, is therefore also an ocular emblem of death as divisive bar to desire. We can also cast up the implications of this manifold shot, with its horizontal thrust of the glimpsed corpse, in the familiar paradox of the container contained. The glass ball once held by Kane's living hand now holds the same hand, dead, within its own improbable scopic field. In Deleuzian terms, there would be a further dimension to this irony. The pure Newtonian intervals of the movement-image (in the vertical calculus of falling matter) have been deflected into the horizontal axis and realigned around an unprecedented 180-degree depth of field. The result is that the spatial interval has been shifted or torqued into the temporal lacuna of the time-image: the instantaneous gap between deathbed sighting and seen death. This has happened in such a way that its visual logic of containment may be found to reinscribe in extremis that deepest Bergsonian question in Deleuze: whether time is in us or we are in time. In any case Kane, dead, is now the plaything of replayed chronology. The hand that has grasped and lost is the same hand that the nurse finally lifts across Kane's chest, his head out of frame by now, before putting his body, and with it his life's secrets, under wraps (fig. 191). Cut to the blaring superficial reconstruction of "News on the March," subsuming temporal consciousness entirely to the replay of history's mechanical (edited) time, a time (following Bergson) robbed of duration and substituting a public masterplot for life's true and inward evolution.

Form has once more been tested, stretched to its internal breaking point, by terminal content. Just before the fabricated chronological continuities of the newsreel, it is the microgrammar of editing itself, then, along with the temporality of succession, that has been pointedly internalized in a bipartite shot that seems hinged, almost subliminally, around the embodied fact of death. In that image of the unseeing corpse hovering *above* rather than superimposed *upon* the nurse's advent, the linear stretch of Kane's body athwart this frame helps explain why that body is so easy to miss on first glance, so easy to elide in its horizontal insistence. Its elongated, fixed mass may seem to the rapidly scanning eye like merely the blurred *difference* between the upper third and lower two-thirds of the image, the former windows we recognize and the new arrival we attend to. And at one level of conceptual recognition, it is indeed *just* this difference between a past and its aftermath. The contraction of the torso between foreshortened hand and skewed profile of the head contributes to this more abstract sense of a mere transition in the visual field. In a mockery of levitation, the very image of death is manifested as a border or bar delineating not so much the outstretched corpse as its representation's own anamorphosis, the attenuated liminal zone between seeing (the nurse in haste) and seen (the noticed body in arrest).

One of course no longer uses the term "anamorphosis" lightly in such a context. According to Slavoj Žižek's attempted deployment of this psychoanalytic concept for film analysis in *Looking Awry*, "Lacan's constant point of reference is Holbein's *Ambassadors*."[16] Seen from a skewed angle, the worldly opulence represented on that fabled canvas reveals a human skull where there seemed at first merely a blot or stain. This is what Žižek isolates as the "phallic signifier" (91) that enforces upon spectation "the nullity of all terrestrial goods" (91) in Holbein's humanist thematics of mortal vanity—and, by psychoanalytic extension, the nullity of the acquisitive, because always lacking, subject inscribed into the language and the law of desire. The look that reveals the skull where there was otherwise only a certain confusion in worldly seeing is thus associated with the gaze of the other that everywhere, and invisibly, is taken to fix the symbolic horizons of the self. With Holbein's canvas, what is in fact revealed by this canted angle of vision is human identity's inherent (rather than eventual) vanishing point in death, the hollowed inverse of any transcendental backing for the desiring subject.

Much of this is left implicit in Žižek's mention of Holbein. And when he turns to individual films, he recurs to such phrases as "anamorphic deformation" (91) in only a very loose or metaphoric way. What concerns us about Welles's floor-level shot, however, is the way it may be read to materialize just such an anamorphic effect at the scopic as well as the thematic level. Kane's bald pate, seeming more than ever a skull-like blot within its compressed zone of the image, certainly serves, if seen at all, the immediate and time-honored purpose of memento mori. But there is a difference from canvases like Holbein's that goes to the heart of Welles's effect. Where in traditional instances of this visual topos, the death's-head alone is rendered as an anamorphic smudge on a realistically disposed scene, here the entire visual field is warped, with the fated body only one element in a space bent altogether to the mind's extremity. Such is the exhaustiveness of Welles's trope: death as an instant global and engulfing.

To borrow Barthes's terms once again, vision has so far exceeded itself that the usurped vantage of absented consciousness has "outplayed" the "law of representation" even while perversely reinvoking, we are now to find, the abiding rule of montage as a function of the strip itself. This is to say that the optic mode of this visual figuration taps the more fundamental and specific cinematic structure of what Žižek, in another context and in his one passing allusion to Welles, calls "inner montage" (95). What he must mean to evoke by this notion is Welles's systematic mastery, within a single deep-focus frame, of spatial continuity through perspectival contrasts of scale and distance, as if the single narrative space were every bit as dialectically analyzed as in an editing sequence. We are now concentrating on a moment when this touted innovation of Welles's film style appears both to advertise and to mock itself by exacerbated foretaste. It does so when a subsidiary and curved image surface (the fractured transparent sphere) is stationed to intersect a given depth of field, thereby producing a visual anomaly in the vertical axis. The shot may in this manner be said to "edit" its own component images. With the eye pulled toward the point of movement at the opened and entered door, and then between it and the bright window opposite/above, it is somehow as if a shot and its reverse shot were, in filing past the aperture, caught and projected together midway between frames. Imagine an analogue: the slowly dying landowner in *Days of Heaven* in a vertically split screen image with the demonic billows blanketing his world. What we see in *Kane*, in other words, is a simultaneous rather than sequential view of a scene (deathbed) and its seeing (nurse arriving to recognize it as such), a sequence sutured together in the same visual

field. Montage is not simply interiorized but is pitted against itself: a visual impaction coinciding with a death moment diagnosed as, in its own right, a violent
short-circuiting of the look. If this is the film's first instance of deep focus passing
over from spatial disposition to figurative time-image, as it no doubt would be for
Deleuze, it is also something more—and more material. Tacitly manifested by this
disjunct continuum in supposed deep space is exactly that one and only optic plane
on which a shot and the onset of its countershot can ever truly cohabit, not the
"plane of immanence" so much as the cause of its effect: the vertical plane of the
film strip in its sequential linkages first of modular cells, then of aggregate points
of view. The larger irony is fueled by this microcosmic oddity. To shift the Lacanian figure of the "big other" and its presumed shaping overview into a cinematic
register, we here confront the site of Kane's death within that big picture that is
phantasmatically presumed at origin, like a cinematic projection, to hold in view
the very subject positions it generates—and eventually eradicates. More arrest-
ingly, though, we confront this external, denaturalized, and uncanny gaze at the
level of the strip itself for a moment, filmic equivalent to the sliding signifier of
the unconscious.

At this point we grow alert to a curious historical involution in the very fate
of formalism, one that bears directly on this transitional death moment in *Citizen
Kane*. As we have been noticing, in order to delimit the floor-level shot's metaspec-
ular point of no return, the glass globe has been doubly recruited. The once sub-
limed object, released from the hold of the body's desire, has been lost and instantly remade as the all but subliminal (because so briefly visible) *objectif* or
lenslike site of posthumous focalization. Its wreckage marks the spot of a supervening vantage. It is in this sense that the literary supplement accounted for in the
work of a critic like Bakhtin—by which a dying character is at once emptied and
fulfilled, both exceeded and consummated, through the greater "seeing" of the
narrator—can be found to have mutated over time from posttheological aesthetics to psychoanalysis. Life once again imitates art, though here in the key of potentially traumatic recoil. For narrative's ongoing formalist dispensation has become, in short, nothing less than the ultimate anxiety of the subject in
poststructuralist psychoanalysis: the never completely repressed sense that consciousness is nowhere present to itself except as already emplaced in the regime of
the symbol, already written and read by another's fixing gaze.

And so *Citizen Kane* instances a further definition of death, of human subjectivity in filmic as well as cinematic cancellation. Death comes forward as the
pivot point where the seeing subject must cede, in the instant of its no longer de-
niable absentation, to the fantasized and irreversible gaze of the other. Such is precisely that gaze assumed all along to inscribe this subject into, even while voiding
it within, the symbolic order. The wrenching torque of death thus warps the subject into its own, in a word, anamorphosis, the fatal blot on desire. Following
through on just such a logic, the subsequent momentum of the film toward closure, its own death drive, seems almost to require the full exposure, the analytic
dismantling, of that symbolic order: the full deconstruction of the very name of
desire. Moreover, as if sprung from the conjunction of the utterance "Rosebud"

and the internal fracture of montage to follow, this resolute pursuit of the signified will operate in continued association with the reduction of the cinematic plenum to its photographic basis in manipulated frames as well as its links to separable photographic images in public dissemination. This process will be completed in the climactic and equally disembodied imaging of the incinerated sled, alias "Rosebud," an overhead POV shot aligned in its eviscerated subjectivity to the very images that first sent the film in quest of it. Toward this final test of the "author's gaze" (Bakhtin), in its radical otherness to desire (Lacan), the whole narrative is now propelled headlong.[17]

As a first stage in this progress, however, we are precipitated into its veritable travesty in "News on the March." Like the artificial out-of-body shot that precedes it, here is an extruded subjectivity in review—complete, as we are to see, with its own photographic intertexts and subtexts. The shock cut that plunges us into its heavily edited narration seems to turn Kane's emptied present inward upon his own life in retrospect—but to do so in the mode of parody. This is the oldest trick in the book (certainly in the classic novel): a death by epitome, extruded here in the melodramatic form of yellow screen journalism—as if this were just the way the sensationalist editor's life would flash past him at the end, in the movie equivalent of a tabloid obit. The mechanism of temporal retrospect may deliberately clank here, but its assumptions are widespread, shared by speculative theory (Bergson, André Malraux) and popular media alike. In a quite different context, chapter 6 will consult Malraux as theorist of both the photographic origin of cinema and its superadded kinesis of view. To anticipate his emphasis on discrete and mobile planar spaces in relation to Deleuze's concern with "sheets of the past" may well serve at this point, however, to gloss what is no doubt more than a passing metaphor in Malraux's memoir, *Lazarus*. Remarking on his own near approach to death, Malraux remembers hearing that the dying subject is supposed to see "one's life unreel before one when one loses consciousness" and wonders why he was not granted "this vertiginous film."[18] It is a trope of mortal retrospect that has earlier been deployed by Walter Benjamin as well—in connection with what we have seen him elsewhere call out by way of cinematic prototype: namely, those "photo booklets with pictures which flitted by the onlooker."[19] Malraux too may be speaking as an erstwhile film theorist as well as a disappointed visionary, distantly connected to Pasolini's later view, as quoted by Deleuze, that "death achieves a dazzling montage of our life."[20]

This sensed residuum of genuine film theory in Malraux's offhand remark results not least from the fact that one of the ways he might have gleaned rumors of the death moment's vertiginous rerun film would be from reading the French philosophical tradition and its cinematic analogues. Bergson himself—for whom the intrinsic seamlessness of becoming is at odds with cinema's discrete elements on the photogrammatic strip—naturally enough, and outside of cinema, sees the death moment departing from the vital succession of the lived world. Retrospective juxtaposition replaces inner evolution. From this we might well infer that death pries open, after all, the one appropriately cinematographic node of temporality in a profound continuum ordinarily betrayed by analogy with the appara-

tus. In this regard one looks to Georges Poulet's untranslated appendix to his phenomenology of Proust, "Bergson: La thème de la vision panoramique des
mourants et la juxtaposition."[21] In view of such terms from Bergson (alluded to
briefly by Deleuze in connection with deathbed vision and the technique of superimposition in early expressionist cinema [55-56]), Kane's truncated bid for a
deathbed's panoramic overview (in summoning up a fantasized snow scene of his
childhood) seems more like a sudden tunnel vision into a past that engulfs him. It
is followed in the newsreel by a past that survives him—but only via a steamrol-
lering of interiority across the hyperkinetic juxtapositions of bombastic screen
montage. And this is followed in turn, across a distended chronology of retrospective segments in the main plot, by a detective trajectory driving back toward the
lost object named just before the newsreel and everywhere absent from its own
thin documentation.

In the scene that leads us out of the newsreel and back into the separate eye-
witness testimonies to Kane's past, the producer of "News on the March" sums up
the mandate to his crew in a bounty hunter's cliché: "Rosebud dead or alive!" As
a signifier, it can never be other than the former, never be anything but the inert
material mark of an absent life.[22] Referring to the explanatory blank its name
leaves gaping in the newsreel overview so far, the producer insists that "all it [the
film] needs is an angle" (322). As it happens, the slant needed has already found
its cinematic prototype (its formal model as well as the broken traces of its elusive
content) in the defiantly "angled" shot, first of many to come, that directly precedes the newsreel screening: the upward view of the arriving nurse seen from the
proximity of the once ambient (if merely virtual) space of a winter without season—the sled a perennial absence within it, time out of mind. The overhead
purview of the plot's last shot (before the exterior coda at Xanadu), a shot disclosing the object "Rosebud" to no viewpoint but the camera's own, is the long-de-
ferred and answering "angle" to the floor-level emphasis on the fatally missing
referent. Otherwise, it seems, merely looking straight at the world never shows
you so clearly the absences that constitute it.

In a manner that can only enforce this inference, *Citizen Kane* grows unusually concerned in its climactic sequence with precisely the arbitrary means by which
words (significance of any kind) may be attached to things on film. The totemic
word "Rosebud" will be disclosed, in fact, only in the very process of severance from
the thing it names. In their search for the mysterious "meaning" (sheer signification) of the dying word, the film journalists, like Kane himself in every other sense,
have come up *empty-handed*. Only the disembodied moving camera picks out the
lost object amid the bonfire of Kane's vanities, an object exposed there—in connection, we will find, with photographic as well as verbal and three-dimensional objects—as an entirely arbitrary sign. For what the film spectator finally sees through
the illuminated threshold of the furnace door, as through a framed lit screen (fig.
192), is the very objecthood of the signifier, vanishing—as always on film—with
no more than a (pulverized, molecular, ashen) trace.

As the camera lens seems zeroing in and holding on the burning sled, at a distance from the flames that no living spectator could sustain (fig. 192), cinema thus

192   193

declares itself twice over, once as apparitional phenomenon, once as ephemeral inscription.[23] Superimposed upon the photographed surface of the discovered
"thing" is, first, the arbitrary (symbolic) seven-letter signifier R-O-S-E-B-U-D, and
a second decal below it that shows a linguistically redundant rosebud. In this tautological compress of the full representational spectrum, the iconic sign, the pictured bud, is no sooner melded with the orthography of symbolic signification
than it is melted away along with the spelled name from the tabula rasa of filmed
sled—as if they were all celluloid signifiers submitted to the withering light of
their own manifestation. So, too, another possibility comes to mind. In either a
send-up or a funereal thematization—or both—of the film's own frequent editing
style, with its tendency toward dilatory and lugubrious fade-outs (over a dozen in
the opening Xanadu sequence alone, just before the death scene, with more to
come in reprise at the end), are we not invited to read these dissipating signifiers
in the furnace of transitory meaning as thinning from sight in something like an
unedited and nontransitional travesty of a *dissolve*? If so, the effect is an instance,
again, of formal tendency imploded upon local content.

In any case, what is certainly clear by now is that Rosebud as much-debunked
"literary" symbol is subsumed—by consumption in the flames—to a strictly
semiotic symbol, yet without forfeiting its psychological reverberations. Even as
designated, the wooden plaything is operable only as the signifier for something
else, something never named, forever deferred: sign of the dramatized absence at
the heart of all nostalgia and all want. If, following Lacan, following Freud, we
wish to say that the unconscious is structured like a language, so therefore can the
return of blocked desire find voice in a single metonym or metaphor, condensing
all lack into life's exit line. Heard in this way—as only the audience can once have
heard it and as only that same audience now sees it—"Rosebud" captures subjectivity itself as the vanishing trace of that lack whose designation can only coincide
with the effacement of its supposed object. In the process of its absentation, and
hence rehearsing the scene of death that launched its signifier, "Rosebud" stands

revealed as the very name of absence. The verbal privilege accorded to a canonical literary death scene is, in short, divided in Welles's film across the humanist resonance of a dying word and the concerted perplexing of this trope—right through to the furnace shot—by the film medium's own thematerializing of a death seen. When we cut back now to the opening exterior shot of Xanadu, we realize too how the rising pillar of smoke serves to complete the ironic anatomy of the signifier set in motion by the film's first dramatic scene. For in semiotic terms the smoke may be identified (*within* the representation this time, rather than solely in regard to its photographic medium) as an indexical sign. As such, it is an index not just of fire but of the sled itself among the other combustibles: Rosebud's last—and finally nondifferential—trace.

PHOTOGRAPHIC CAPTURE AND THE CAPTIVE AUDIENCE

Supporting the thematics of enciphered absence in connection with the "Rosebud" signifier—and in fact narrowly averting collision with it in the end, as we are shortly to see—is Welles's tactical use of the inset photograph. Here lies the final bearing of *Citizen Kane* upon a theory of cinematic photogenesis and photo synthesis. Here too is a further context for everything noted so far about the death-cued spatiotemporal rupture of the visual plane. Photographs in this film render nostalgic the losses their images can only underwrite, never overcome. And Welles makes strikingly elusive use of such inset images in their relation to the film that reframes them: now in direct connection with the transitional freeze-frame, now in oblique avoidance, now (as framed portraits) in unsettled distinction from it. Many of the examples are renowned on their own terms. Early on, the bravura sequence freezing on a framed publicity photo of the blue-ribbon staff boasted by the *Chronicle* in its office window, and then reanimating it as a co-opted gallery of talent later being rephotographed for the self-promotion of Kane's own *Inquirer*, displays only the most legendary photogrammatic prestidigitation in the film. Recall too the exposé of Kane's mistress, where a freeze on her apartment building becomes, when transformed to newsprint reproduction, part of the "Love-Nest" headline the morning after, killing Kane's political hopes. Live by the disseminated image, die by it.

The death can be literal as well. For Kane as preeminent manipulator of public images is a man we first see in his prime (in the early newsreel sequence) as a screen-filling newsprint photo in the obituary headline of his own paper. His image there is part of the flip-book shuffle of the world press, one headline removed from on top of the next to generate a discontinuous text narrating (as if from different perspectives, like the film as a whole) the same fatal event—and often accompanied by photographic poses of the deceased. As the single-shot equivalent of the hoary newspaper-film cliché—the press montage—this mechanical peeling away of layers in a sequential disappearance of the photographically inflected text does the work, within the film within the film of "News on the March," of a further filmic narrative in little. Yet amid all the headline signifiers

Charles Foster Kane's young son and wife with him out

194

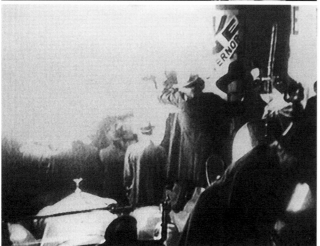

195, 196

in different languages, what sticks with us in the flood of ephemeral commemoration is the first and screen-engulfing memorial photo: objective correlative of exactly that dying away from subjectivity that the *motion picture* camera has just attempted, in the opening sequence, to look into and see through, at peril of its own spatiotemporal continuities.

Renormalizing both deep focus and montage from there on out, the rest of the film is a sustained attempt to *motivate the photograph*, to put in play the single image or shot (as behind it the photogram) within an explanatory (or at least signifying) system. In this way do the opening death scene and the newsreel's funerary photo icon install comparable nodes of drastic absentation, the first turning on the fixity of the corpse in counterpoint to the rush of posthumous ministration, the second on the once living body that succeeds itself only as fixed image. In so doing, they call to and gloss each other across the gulf, once again, between the going and the gone. In further connection with the spatiotemporal rupture of death, the pronounced photogrammatic segues noted above (*Chronicle* portrait, "Love-Nest" headline) also prepare for subsequent moments of reflex textuality where the still image obtrudes both as constituent of and as irritant to the smooth rule of cinematic illusion. What *Citizen Kane* actually images at these later moments is the photographic underlay of its own flow, once in manifest connection with death, once in sly alignment with the spectator's assessment of death's meaning. Again, a brief recognition of each instance is a comment on the other as well.

In a fleeting, devious gesture of the filmic undertext, *Kane*'s scissoring out of a potential photogrammatic frame in an anticipated freeze on action leaves a wound in the text that has actually found previous materialization as fixed imprint in the opening film within the film: the second mortuary image in the newsreel. The irony of this optic syncope turns on the shot of Kane's wife and son greeting him at a political rally. As a headline photo for the "Victory Speech" edition of the *Inquirer*, the shot serves an obituary role in the newsreel's brief mention of the subsequent death of both wife and son in 1918 (fig. 194). Much later, in Leland's segment of the flashback plot, we finally see in live action, as it were, the actual meeting of the Kane family in front of the convention hall. Kane greets Emily and takes his son up in his arms, and as one of many gathered photographers says "hold it," the three are in the process of striking the pose we have already seen (fig. 195). But this happens as we cut directly into a long shot of the crowd—and this in turn just an instant before the photographer's spreading flare (fig. 196) precipitates a glowing microsecond of blank screen. It is almost as if a frame of the film (the freeze-frame we might ex-

pect of the artificial family tableau) has been excised and displaced—under cover of the blinding flash—in such a way
that the missing arrest of action is now read back in retrospect as precisely that obituary icon strategically placed
within the newsreel: the journalistic photo reframed all but
full screen in a film documentary. Only much later, of course,
can this shot be recognized as an elided frame of the cinematic narrative itself, the hole in continuity its deflection
backward (to the newsreel) has hollowed out. In this sense,
then, death comes to definition at the material level of textual drive as that radical gap in continuity to which the apparatus may blind us in progress—either through editing or
through the hypnotic brightness of projection itself (redoubled in this case by the intrusive flash). But such is a death by
disjunction that is always there waiting, dogging the foot-

197

steps of all action, haunting the tread of plot. Such is the death of (or into) fixity
that may emerge under narrative stress, at however far-flung a remove from the
actual scene of dying, in its purest—because photographic—form.

   Photomechanical associations thus cluster and reroute attention beneath the
surface work of plot—until the convergence of the two, of narrative drive and
photochemical arrest, in the final sighting of Kane's boyhood sled amid a clutter
of, among other things, old photographs. Once these reminders of picture taking
are associated with the forgotten object whose overhead framing they share, and
hence leagued with the soon arrived vanishing point of our ongoing curiosity
about "Rosebud," we may also link these discarded photographs to the virtual picture taken of our own continuing hermeneutic participation just moments before
in this same scene. The full implications of this aggressive rent in the enclosed
world of representation by yet another blinding flash—as we, this time, are sutured under erasure into the panoptic impetus of narration as a whole, its "excess
of seeing"—are implications that derive not just from the local gesture's ocular affront but from a certain subset in the backlog of photographic (as well as photogrammatic) allusions in the plot so far. The most important, and easiest to miss,
of these precursive photographic moments has served to associate the sealed glass
sphere of the past with the time capsule of photographic imprint. In the earliest
sighting of the glass paperweight on Susan's dresser (which no one could be expected to notice on an initial encounter with the film), the inert transparent object
is visible to one side of a mirror image of Susan staring up at the towering gentleman she has just met (fig. 197). Next to that mirror self, behind the childish
crystal, is a Victorian photograph, no doubt of Susan herself as a young girl. The
photo thus provides her own equivalent of Kane's ironically characterized
"search" for "my past" at the Mid-Manhattan Warehouse from which he has just
been diverted by his accidental meeting with Susan. The sliding association between the glass paperweight and photography's reverse crystal gazing (into the
past rather than the future) is completed only at the end of the film—and by a
metonymic double reversal. There the fragile sphere that has come to evoke for

198, 199   200, 201

Kane, after Susan's desertion, not only this but all previous losses is itself lost. And when it is replaced, finally, by that real sled always absent, even in miniature, from the glass toy's imaginary snowbound past, that childhood relic is in turn almost displaced in climactic prominence by a photograph of a yet more primal loss.

The melodramatic subplot of this particular photograph has unfolded as follows across the temporal backtrackings of narrative chronology. Had Kane managed to recover his mother's effects, he might have found, among such remains, the very photograph of mother and son that will eventually be used to signify their relationship in the obituary newsreel. We end up knowing (if only, again, in retrospect) how little archival privilege is accorded to this photo document, since in the last sequence it will be spied among discarded junk next to the sled and only accidentally spared from the flames. At that point we may even remember the kinetic irony of its first appearance. Reframed by the newsreel screen in a reverse dolly shot is an image of the proud young boy (fig. 198) gradually seen *looked up to* by his seated mother (fig. 199): a professional photograph no doubt taken after unexpected wealth had begun to disorient the normal relations of dependency and affection. This long ago semicinematized (or narrativized) photo—as part of the mobile rhetoric of newsreel style—is the same photo, differently cropped, that we may well expect the arriving workman in the finale (as he comes into frame knee first at top center [fig. 200]) to reach for amid the stockpiled debris—until he veers to his right and goes for the sled instead (fig. 201). The apparent false lead is a deep-dredged clue, since the brief uncertainty could never amount to a full narrative ambiguity. The point would be much the same one way or the other if we associate each object (photographic record of the mother, forgotten plaything)—in their posthumous proximity—with its equivalent and irreversible distance from the past. Like the several photographs in disarray around it (the one of Kane with his mother being only the most prominent among them), the sled too, in its freighted role as signifier, is merely an *image* of the irreversible in the long downhill slide of Kane's life. As a sign consumed in the same fire that brings it to light, "Rosebud" as readable textual datum leaves only our interpretive energy in its wake.

Which brings us back a couple of shots to the penultimate photomechanical—and finally photogrammatic—irony in the narrative. To distinguish the scene of biographical interpretation from the posthumous images that prompt it—while bonding each to the other along the specular track of filmic enchainment—is the charge of this moment, its obligation and its jolt. Just before we are put in position to notice the sled in the overhead shot, we have been momentarily accosted by one of the press photographers turning her flash straight at us before firing it (fig. 202). The textual rent of this scopic (and narrative) snap thereby recalls that earlier shot transition (and mortuary prolepsis) at the political rally, where a cinematic elision at the moment of the flash precipitates a narratively mobile photographic engravement of the Kane family. With the later spectatorial flashpoint at Xanadu, cinema as film again disappears from view in the triggering of an all-white frame: the sign of light's excess exposure. In this way the ignited image, as its own blanched afterimage, inscribes what amounts to a subjective reaction shot from within its own blind and now blinded field. For on the one hand there is nothing film can record per se of its own audience—only an awaiting blank. On the other hand we are, as readers of word and image, all the film has left at this point. Anticipating a category of effect introduced in the next chapter, here is an extreme "negative regress" of cinema's filmic basis in photogrammatic progression. For a few frames (on strip), and in only a glaring void—or voiding glare—on-screen, we have entered for a split second upon the *mise en abyme* not of cinematic narrative but of filmic projection itself, laid bare by nothing less than diegetic (as well as cinematographic) overexposure.

Placed as we are on illegible record as part of the scene's scanned inventory, we may well be reminded of the striking "experimental" moment in Bergman's *Persona* twenty-five

202

203

years later when the mute actress pops up into frame on a beach to take "our" picture (fig. 203), suturing us into a countertransference whose equivalent she has been perpetrating on her nurse-analyst. With a similar alienation effect in *Kane*'s climactic burst of spectatorial self-exposure, one aggressive crew member of the film within the film is found straining to capture your own invisible *affect,* your own remaining curiosity for instance, as prelude to the otherwise empty significance of "Rosebud." The difference from *Persona* is that, since you are now inside a darkened cavern of a space (as of course you are when watching a theater screen), the flash is required—even at the cost of losing the next image. Hermeneutics—and its own transferential investment—is all that remains. You (unseen but inscribed) must transfer to the subsequent shot of the sled (the sled rather than the maternal photograph) whatever meaning it will unfurl. To be brought face-to-face with your constitutive participation in this way, however, is to be reminded of that specular unconscious of cinematographic manifestation that brings the images to you in the first place. It is as if, impossibly, you were being made present to them; as if they themselves were recording, here at the close of plot, your own all but spent narrative desire perfectly emblematized in the stalled temporality of a single flashbulb shot—and the resulting effaced photogram(s). Long taken with the narrative, you are now taken by it. The photomechanical abyss is a projective mirror after all. Building on the numerous inset photographs along the course of the plot, and just before the camera's final scavenging of a few more, the tacit reverse shot (blank, strictly latent) of your own attention is for a severing split second—inducing a literal blind spot on-screen—the internal duplication of narrative reception and its rupture at once. As a syncopated gap in the run of frames, yet as the inferred function still required to fill in all the remaining interpretive blanks, the interface of spectation, momentarily foregrounded in its structuring absence, cedes again to its latency. Subject *position* disappears once more into mere reading stance. Once you and I have been photographed in the space where we are, strictly speaking, not to be found, all that is left of the onlooking agency is the work of the roving, disincarnate camera, impersonal in the extreme—but interpretable through and though.

LAST SEEN AT THE OVERLOOK

Authorial oversight as the gaze of the other: this is the concluding irony of Kubrick's *The Shining* as well as of *Citizen Kane,* a life summed up in terms not its own, superseded by an "excess of seeing" to which the removed subject can neither now nor ever before lay claim. Such a life is in fact imagined, in the fantastic premise of Kubrick's film, as no more than an animated (reincarnated) trace to begin with. And this trace carries no residue of mystery except for the bizarre logic, indeed the paradox, of this reduction—since (I give away the plot) the adult image of the protagonist, a framed photograph on the wall of a deserted hotel, will end up having preceded the adult corpse of the same body by half a century. The self reverting in death to a framed image comes to seem like the filmic—within the cinematic—equivalent of the epitomizing literary death scene of classic narrative: selfhood reduced to truncated quintessence, though here in reversion to a *previous* self. Much supernatural exertion is needed, therefore, to pave the way.

A "normalized" version of the same relapse to photography after a psychotic break may be instructive, precisely for its absence of supernatural suggestion. As indicated earlier, death on film is often in the eye of the beholder. *Repulsion* (1965) begins with the minutiae of ocular movement in anatomical close-ups of a woman's left eye, its blinks and twitches, its veins and vitreous surface, only to freeze on this specular emblem just as "Directed by Roman Polanski" slices horizontally across it from right to left. The entire direction of this movie is, indeed, toward the dissection of vision itself, but without the necessary return of the stop-action image. When, much later, the woman's body is lifted away from the mayhem she has caused in her delusional confinement, we see her limp in the arms of her sister's lover, an open-eyed corpse. Only the camera remains behind to pick out on the floor beneath the TV a family photograph that shows the heroine as a young girl looking aslant at the camera, favoring the same left eye from the title sequence. On this evidentiary photograph the camera zooms in until the graininess of the girl's eye, in anticipation of her *Psycho*-like blank stare as corpse, expunges *our* vision of *it*. In their troping of human removal within narrative, photography and freeze-framing thus collude once again. By contrast, *The Shining* does its work without the latter in order to highlight the uncanniness of the former.

Jack Torrance (the torrential Jack Nicholson) brings his wife (Shelly Duvall) and child to an isolated mountain site to take a job as winter overseer of an evacuated summer resort hotel, so as to free up some mental space in its deserted roominess for work on his novel. There are problems. Unbeknownst to his parents, the child is cursed with telepathy. Unbeknownst to his wife, Jack is so blocked as a writer that his daily output consists only in repetitions of a single numbing sentence. Unbeknownst to either wife or child, Jack has heard that a former caretaker (who reappears in ghostly form as Jack's spiritual adviser in the handling of family tension) had years back, in an extreme bout of cabin fever, hacked to death his wife and two daughters. Unbeknownst to the son, this is the violence he keeps seeing in flashback, even while his father is now in secret dialogue with the ghost of this murderer. Unbeknownst to all, even Jack, and disclosed only by the camera in the last shot—like the sled in *Kane*'s closing conflagration of the signifier—is a single photograph, among the scores of them that adorn the vast walls of the hotel, of Jack himself among a group of party revelers in the grand ballroom. Problems persist. The trouble here is that this date-captioned photo was taken, as noted above, over six decades before. But this is no longer a problem for Jack, since he sits frozen to death in the labyrinthine maze that adjoins as well as refigures the reticulated interior halls and time-warped corridors of the hotel.

As the film plows toward Jack's death in the snow, a death transpiring finally across the disjunction between a long shot of the just collapsed body and a medium close-up of the iced corpse, then flees the deserted body for the imprint of that body's previous incarnation in the photograph, a proleptic irony of the film's bared narrative works has been fulfilled. Something was wrong with its temporal progression from the start, as marked by the sequence of wholly unnecessary intertitles from "The Interview" through "Closing Day" to "A Month Later" to the disengaged pointless specificity of "Tuesday"—the last detached from any progressive calendar but the diurnal round of mounting repetition. It is only right that the titles should then have been dropped altogether in the shapeless waking nightmare of the last phase. Time is no longer a narrative's to control—or contain. Time has become history, present vaporized by the past.

For Fredric Jameson, Kubrick's film is the encoded fable of a particular historical anxiety: a would-be novelist's repressed nostalgia for a period of American history associated not only with the myth of the great American novelist but with the relaxed stability of class boundaries, where hierarchies were assured and where leisured wealth was content in the uninhibited spectacle of its display. The ballroom photograph of such celebrated luxury at the Overlook Hotel that closes the film, and that has irreversibly swallowed up its hero's present life into a past existence in the same hotel, is thus the gothic transformation of a socioeconomic wish-fulfillment fantasy.[24] Such an allegory, with its sense of plot's hidden agenda, builds on the rather salient false expectations of plot itself. For Jameson the telepathy material of the film's very title, as the first sign of gothic convention in the plot, is a generic decoy. Nothing much comes of it, except for what it throws into relief by contrast. It masks the true nature of the film as participating in the dated genre of the ghost story, with its special relation to the past and its haunting of the present. One can readily agree here, but only if allowed to add that the appearance of this telepathic subplot, before it gets swept aside by other preoccupations, has been explicitly inserted to figure the cinematic procedures of the narrative both during and after its misleading thematic sidetrack. Montage becomes another name for second sight, parallel editing for telepathic transportation, identification for thought transference, flashback for the irruptive traces of a never before experienced scene.

We catch on right away. Anyone with the power "to shine" is, in a word, a medium. When the chef at the hotel (Scatman Carruthers) first makes subvocal contact with the son, Danny, offering him ice cream without moving his lips to deliver the invitation, he is of course ventriloquized by the film's own sound track, where voice and image are always separable, commutable, transferable. When he tries to allay the boy's fears by suggesting that his seeing things is only natural, since many things that happen "leave traces," he resorts to analogy, to the effect that such visions are no more real than "pictures in a book." (To be more specific, this is what Danny later remembers him saying, although it is a remark that we have never heard in the scene of their only meeting: a message perhaps relayed, therefore, by ESP meant to take place entirely offscreen.) Given the reality effect of such "pictures in a book," the chef must have meant photographic plates, not drawings or paintings; he might as well have said photogrammatic inserts in a film, traces that recur by being edited into present reality. And when this same character, on vacation in Florida, sees by second sight the dangers besetting Danny back at the hotel, his access to the absent scene is visually punned upon as an explicit mediation. We cut unexpectedly from Nicholson growing progressively more psychotic to a full-screen TV, indeed to the split-screen title sequence of a Miami news broadcast about a dangerous Colorado blizzard. Here, as in all the scenes that link the chef's psychic powers to Danny's, the routine devices of parallel editing take on the aura of supernatural omniscience. As if specifying Deleuze's emphasis on Kubrick's work as a "cinema of the brain," of the disembodied world mind (see chapter 2), cinema emerges from its own plot as a telepathy machine, thematizing its own coherent access to widely divergent sites. Everything takes place within the specular regime of the so-called Overlook. Through the ability to make absent space present (as, elsewhere in the supernatural genre, through the telekinetic ability to instigate motion at varying distances from its willed origin), the screen image—with its induced glow of communication at a disembodied distance from its source—is the real shining.

REPETITION IMPULSION

One other dimension of the plot, in its metafilmic parameters, needs mention before we submit at length to the specular self-admissions of its closing shot. If this is a film whose last sighting (of a professional photograph long ago preserved under glass) is in part about the photogrammatic basis of all cinema, then the best evidence for such textualization of the narrative appears *en abyme* in the form (the very *form*) of the plot's one included verbal text: namely, the hero's long withheld but eventually confronted narrative typescript. This is to say that *The Shining*'s climactic transition—the cut from a frozen corpse to a mechanically scrutinized photograph—converges on the disclosure of film's own materiality, its photochemical materiality as text, in ways that have been indirectly prepared for by this earlier turning point in front of the typewriter, easily the film's most harrowing scene. At oblique issue, we may be surprised to find, is the very photographesis of the filmic chain.

Discovering Jack gone from his typewriter, his wife approaches the lone page in the carriage. In horror at its empty self-referential inscription, she turns to the collected manuscript in a box to the left—only to find more of the same. "All work and no play makes Jack a dull boy." Jack Nicholson, alias Torrance, is in fact the latest manifestation of a proverbial cliché, the self a derivation from a long-suppressed matrix in the infantile and regressive nursery bromide. As content, therefore, this typescript all by itself sums up, by anticipating, the derivative nature of its productive subject. This is a human subject photographically archived in the last scene as having been there once and long before, a fixture deprived of present vitality, a mere iteration of himself. But it is with the exact form taken by the aphoristic matrix that we are finally concerned. For the bald monosyllabic sentence is repeated dozens, hundreds, thousands of times, unvaried in content, ramified only by different graphic shapes. And the excruciating scene is protracted long enough, longer than any other director would have seen fit to insist, so that we register all this in precisely its mechanical (as well as maniacal) typographic registration. When I called it emptily self-referential, I meant to suggest that as a writing about writing it is a virtual parody of the film's own metatextual trajectory, an impasse Kubrick's own disclosures will need to outdistance. For something more to be made of it in context, this desperate, unchecked textuality would need to route its own self-collapsing irony through the photogrammatic inscription of the filmic text as a whole. This it does.

The message, as text, is at various points separately lineated or run together, paragraphed or not, now punctuated, now not, here with typos that confound word breaks ("Al lwork") or swell a spelling ("Alll work"), there with aberrant capitalization. At times the text is indented as its own self-citation within wider margins that are filled up, above and below, with more of the same numbing enunciation—as if the indentation offered verse to an identical prose: the nugatory art within its reduplicated commentary. At other times the text appears in the upside-down triangular form of some self-imaging pattern poem, emblematic only of its

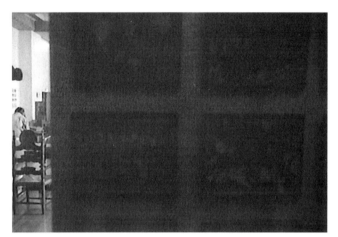

204

own unbalanced emptiness. Three levels of typographic impression need to be sorted out. The message is that of unrelieved labor. The form of that labor is a repetition compulsion that folds back into the message to anticipate the closing revelation of the self as its own historical repetition. But the metatext of this form is a graphic patterning that carries us deep into the heart of the film text as medium: a medium of just such fractionally varied differential imprints. (Consider the effect this way: If Jack's workaday text *were* literary, rather than the default of all literary originality, the served-up materiality of its production would make it an exemplary modernist text of just the sort the filmic track will be found to resemble in my final chapter.)

What happens next may operate on the viewer to confirm this sense of the madman's text as protofilmic inscription. We cut to a long-distance shot—through one of the lobby's huge square portals—of the wife's horror over the discovered typescript. It is a shot that slowly gives way to a lateral pan momentarily darkening the screen with a shadowed wall of the lobby (fig. 204). Our own rectangular "text" goes nearly blank for a moment just as Jack's has been discovered empty of reference beyond itself. But not for long, since the obscured screen image is soon occupied—and motivated in its traveling POV—by Nicholson's head appearing in silhouette against the briefly occluded spy's-eye view of the trauma his typescript has induced. I say the screen goes *nearly* blank because of the second aspect of this occluded long shot that happens to ratify our sense of Jack's sheer *writing,* rather than the content of his narrative, as a reductio ad absurdum of film's own sequential imprint. On anything but a first viewing there is a good chance we will notice that the obscuring wall across which the camera pans is arrayed, like so many in the hotel, with more of the same framed photographs that are ranged one after the other within the narrowing frame of the film's final shot, closing inward upon them (e.g., fig. 211). In the present and pivotal episode, the eye skims over these photographs in deep shadow; at the end we rush in upon them in clear light. In both of these scenes, and in others like them, each successive framed module of documented hotel history is an image of the same closed world. Each captures a space just a little differently populated over time, so that together they tell a story (if not much of one) only by running together their visual information as serial data. Yet even as they may register a difference over the decades of guestbook temporality, the whole sequence is threatened in this sense of historical overview—or panoptic overlook—by the mortal fixity of each frame in turn. History has become the disbanded and redistributed strip of a time-lapse film.

DEAD IN ITS TRACK

Fixity, in the mode of fixation, is indeed one name as well for Jack's psychosis, which the rest of the plot must play out to its gruesome conclusion. By which point film

itself has confessed to being the instrumentation of ghostly sight in the sudden vacancy of all immediately seeing eyes: again, a shining—and again equivalent, at another level, to the normative operations of the medium. Clubbed by his wife in timely self-defense and then left trapped first in a food locker, then in a blizzard within the vast shrubbery maze alongside the hotel, Jack is found in the morning light by the camera, after a jump cut from his collapse in the snow the night before, as an ice-shagged corpse in medium close-up, his eyes rolled up under frigid lids (see fig. 207). As suggested by this unnatural wrench of his glazed eyes (at least in the context of the scene's photomechanical aftermath), his inert body seems struggling to look inward and behind itself to some lost—or recovered—past. And just to assure us that the uncanny prolongation of this frozen pose is not a freeze-frame *trucage*, a drop or two of water released by the sun's light (under the spotlights of the set, that is) drips down his cheek like the tear it is all too late to shed. Such is the cheek, we can only assume, of a perfect mannequin replica of the actor who, living, could never perform such contorted immobility.[25] And as we study his preserved form in the deep freeze of the maze, we may recall the climactic encounter of the previous stalking sequence. Jack's armed wife is fleeing from his homicidal rage. In a single shot/countershot exchange, we see her framed against yet another wall of photos (fig. 205), then intercut with the hollowed stares of the skeletal originals—or their interchangeable equivalents (fig. 206). These are the suddenly materialized ghouls who represent, in contrast to the photos of registered guests just like them, the *decayed* remains of a past that is otherwise photochemically embalmed.

Jack's body will be preserved only until the spring thaw,

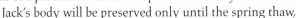

207

by which point it will need burying (once more). So back to that second jump cut—this time from stop-action corpse (fig. 207 again) to the immediate shoving off of the last of many tracking or dollying shots in the film. This previous obsessive movement of the camera has by now become abstract rather than paranoid or voyeuristic or predatory, given over to a purified cinematicity in the sumptuous smooth groove of this last processional through a cognitive vacuum. What takes place, via displacement, as we close in on a single framed photograph—zero in on its rehearsed zeroing out of human presence—is a lethal transition hinged by a twofold play on cinematic device. The previous shock cut to the frozen figure without exit route completes a punning turn that includes the footprints in the snow by which the hero, the camera trailing him, has failed to *track* his way past death's impasse. In the subsequent shot, the final tracking in on a less vulnerable icon of the self (the photograph rather than the self-congealed statue) requires penetrating to a different chronotope altogether, the time-space of the imprint. Between these poles, in the excised death moment of the organic rather than photographic body, there is the elided specular pun on the freeze-frame, which the stiffened, crystal-sharp image of Nicholson can no more than partly evoke. As with the smashed globe in *Kane*—marking the lost grip of his will and the burst bubble of his illusions—the blunter the visual pun, the sharper the ironic stab.

In the unkindest cut of all, Jack's corpse is tossed aside for the reclamation of his past image. When we seem to enter (as if already in progress) this last long and rolling take, the dissociated camera is already barreling weightless across the main lobby of the hotel. With the screen's inner space reframed by two pillars (fig. 208), the camera passes through the curtain-draped, theaterlike proscenium of the adjacent hall gallery (fig. 209) and edges rapidly in upon the three rows of seven photographs each on the far wall (fig. 210).[26] Floating closer still, it singles out the middle one until that image fills the frame (figs. 211-13), equivalent for a moment to the film whose ambient space it has engorged—until, in turn, cinematic device seems almost to reassert itself (within the photographic frame) a moment or two later. We have, as mentioned, seen these carefully framed photographs, and dozens more like them, at least a dozen times before in establishing and transitional shots—though never within range of the images' separate legibility. Now at last, as in the last of *Kane*, we read—and in a suddenly double semiosis—the indexical as well as the symbolic sign (optic trace and scripted legend) of photograph and caption together, the one posing the impossibility of the other within the supernatural premise of the emergent ghost story (fig. 213). How can our protagonist, so recently become a corpse, have been there then (4 July 1921) as well? Only by the fatal exclusion of that present-day self (also photomechanically generated), the self whose decline into psychosis we thought we had been tracking. In one of his leading Weimar essays, "Photography," Siegfried Kracauer evokes the common figure of the doppelgänger from German cinema of the period, without explicit mention, in giving his own spin to the familiar trope of photography as a shooting unto death: "The photograph annihilates the person by portraying him or her, and were person and portrayal to converge, the person would cease to exist."[27] Such an uncanny proposition reads like the hypothesis behind the whole displaced "freeze" of *The Shining*'s asymptotic destination.

With the growing orchestral sound of "Midnight" on the track, as if issuing from the inner ballroom scene of the photograph itself, the camera locks momentarily on the image of the star in costume for a time not his own. "Your eyes hold a message tender, saying I surrender" is a lyric that then coincides, in the film's final fade to black, with our recognition of Jack's sly glint from out of his own surrender to history. In between, the image plane has been mutated by editorial device, the filmic asserting itself from within a seeming cancellation of the narrative field. Just before the "Midnight" lyric, a final pair of lap dissolves—cinema in its most typical filmic (or photogrammatic) machination—has carried us beyond the coincident framing of the framed photographic object farther into the imaginary space (or closer to the grain of its detail) in order, when each dissolve comes to resolution in turn, to scrutinize more closely Jack's earlier incarnation and original (photo-engraved) corpse (figs. 214-16). Photographic time is the proleptic stopped time of one's eventual death: once long ago for the deco swinger, and once just now for the ax-wielding madman. And in these last tiered dissolves, the full-screen face of the past is gradually singled out from the crowd—identified by

208, 209, 210, 211, 212, 213, 214, 215, 216

the ghostly icon of its own absence. This happens in such a way that the film, having reverted to photography, has in fact (via superimposition) cinematized the visual stasis of such still imprints into a kind of spectral transition. Once again photography comes forward as the grave of motion, film (through editing as well as through the rudiments of projection) as the never better than artificial resuscitation of any such movement, any change whatever over time. This is to say, yet once more, that cinema puts itself forward as the illusion of fluidity between fixities, the intervallic specter of all action—haunted by the absentations it can never seek to erase entirely.

No one, I'd bet, stirred by the supernal glide of the film's last shot and its penetrating continuance through editing, with its axial symmetries and balletic cool, could fail to find its lucid power residing in some force larger than the trivial plot twist that parades it as a revelation. One possibility is that the true residence of its chill beauty lies in some tacit reciprocation with the great intertext of closure in *2001*. I refer to the last dolly shot coasting in upon the self-transfigured field of screen-encompassing vision—the vertical monolith that rapidly fills the approaching horizontal frame—before an instantaneous dissolve to the pellucid sublunary overlook (cf. figs. 311-15). In the very transit from planar surface to purportedly deep(er) space in the closing moments of both films lies the switch point between the genre deployments of this shared cinematographic device: a surge through obdurate blackness into luminous destiny in the visionary narrative (see more in chapter 7), an inching across the plane of representation into the imagined space of deadly record in the supernatural thriller. Having, like Kane, inadvertently broken a crystal emblem of time's own fragility (the wine goblet of his last supper), the dying astronaut in *2001* gives up the ghost (and the POV) by yielding to an image of his own renewal in the eye of omniscience. This disincarnation of the POV is the ultimate cinematographic model for the last-gasp plunge into the impenetrable surface of the monolith, where one black photogram evolves on the cut from steely plane to midnight cosmos. Transfiguration from two to three dimensions (primal rectangle to "space") in the one genre is the visionary opposite of transfixed stasis for its gothic counterpart in *The Shining*, where the widening borders of a two-dimensional photographic image are invaded by the dissolutions (lap dissolves), and then granted the restabilized frailty, of the filmic track alone.

In comparison with Welles's masterwork as well as with Kubrick's, another aspect of *The Shining* comes to the fore. The elided and displaced death moment we have considered in each depends once again upon different but correlative senses of the cinematic frame. Death comes with a force that seems to split the screen frame in *Kane*, whereas in *The Shining* death drops through the brutal lacuna between successive frames—in a double hurdling from ended frenzy to static corpse to a long view of the corpse's photochemical double. In the case of Kubrick's climactic jump cut in *The Shining*, another way of saying what we don't see is that death evades the frame advance—only to return framed as visual metaphor in a still photograph. This is the true (and inverted) ghost story unmasked from within this last spurt of what we might take to be a postmortem telepathic transference. In this sense, as in *Kane,* the intensity of the death moment overflows into camerawork alone as the last emptied vestige of an effaced consciousness. Still at work in the Overlook's maze of representation, in its tomb of presence, is a scopic drive that seems itself, in a word, ghostly. Its fit object, which it both collides with and penetrates, is the mummifying photochemistry of a single lifeless imprint.

Haunted by specters from the past is one thing: the formulaic thing. Here is its fantastic obverse. The plot's chief human agency is at the moment of death, and always has been, nothing but his own dead—and extraneous—double: again, Kracauer's nightmare scenario come true. If the self is no more than a haunting of the present by a past image, this trope—like a parody of the view that we are wholly composed by our own memories—has eviscerated identity itself. It has also provided what the next chapter will explore as the "negative regress" of the film's own shining forth in artificially projected presence. The inference is hard to avoid. To discover in death, with no one left to focalize the discovery, that the animate present being can be factored down to single "traces" from a past instant ("like pictures" in "a book"—or a text) is to submit film narrative once again to the disruptive return of its own intrinsic negation, its own negative imprint.

If this view of *The Shining* constitutes an allegorical reading, is it a less culturally embedded one than Jameson's? Does the addition of something we might wish to term photogenesis to Jameson's emphasis on "historicism" result in the text's undoing as social discourse? Not if one thinks of Jack's problem—his fantasy of himself as a writer, his will to inscribe himself into the American success ethic—as a problem of what an advertising culture calls self-image. And if this is a further link to *Citizen Kane* as a quintessentially American narrative, *Kane* the mythic obverse to *The Shining's* gothic satire, then so much the better for the gravitational field of the present analysis. In Kubrick's film, every bit as much as in the newsprint manipulations of *Kane's* image track, the overt reversion of the cinematic to the photographic, followed by its last-minute reinflection by the filmic (in the closing dissolves), works to locate the narrative squarely—precisely because unstably—within cinema's own manifest participation in a devitalized (however animated) culture of the image. In this sense too, as in so many others, Kubrick's unorthodox gothic is the generic corollary of science fiction in the latter's pervasive—and often two-faced—concern for both the future technologies of the image and the societies of its dissemination within the genre's self-celebrating critique of the seen. These are future technologies and societies—as the next chapter will revisit their screen conjurings—where at times death is no longer to be seen, life no longer to be trusted on sight.

Correlations as various as those attempted by this chapter deserve the extra labor of summary. The effort of our long look at *Citizen Kane* was to see how and why—on the film's own terms—the fractured optic that locates the very moment of death, severing the body from its own vanishing oversight (or undersight), could scarcely avoid connection with the photographic relics lost to human view along with the sled at the end. For this was a connection relayed across the length of plot by those associated moments of overt textual discontinuity (mortal or otherwise arresting) sprung either by the eruption of a freeze-frame or by its strategic elision in a jump cut. Relayed like this: Kane dies attempting to close the distance between desire and its object. Failing this, he seems to project his will beyond consciousness into its *recognized* cancellation. The objectification of desire that marks the superimposed death shot (of an inner storm descending upon a radically outered body), as well as its immediate aftermath in the floor-level contortion, works to contaminate the photogrammatic extrusions of the track in later episodes, linking the stopped image of the posed body, again and again, back to the externalized image of the self as corpse.

No such relay between the internal fracture of a death seen and the photographic affront to cinematic motion is necessary over the course of *The Shining*, since the two modes of disjunction, separately manifest, collide in the last sequence. All the photographs hung upon all the statically glimpsed or laterally traversed walls of the hotel, even the rotted corpses intercut with their presumptive photographs (or those of others like them), merely build pressure toward the final and reciprocal rupture of self from its frozen body, of self from its fixated image. And so the often personified force of the traveling shots in this film, repeatedly motivated through the POV of one among the characters, comes home to roost in a disincarnate form: the preternatural will to scopic dominance—at least continuance—as it superannuates the very self whose desires such continuance might otherwise implement. *Kane* begins with an out-of-body shot that seems to distort the whole system of representation by looking at the passing present from the denatured POV of the past (and absent) object. *The Shining* ends rather than begins, we may want to say, with another ceding of the POV in an out-of-body shot that, rather than aching for the unretrievable past, succumbs to that past as its only present. In the thriller and the biopic alike, the effect is peculiarly the same. Through the desertions of plot by sheer camerawork, the liminal has become a kind of scopic limbo. The spectatorial privilege is impelled forward somewhere in the narrational hinterland between Bakhtin's "excess of seeing" that eclipses a hero by the very apparatus of his rendering (the ironic overlook, for instance, of Kubrick's camera) and Barthes's "outplaying" of representation altogether in an impossible POV. But it all depends on photography, all (we should more accurately say) depends *from* those single photograms on which cinematic motion is hung and by which it is strung along.

Even summaries may stand in need of a summation. In the end, Kane is lost to the present. In the end, Jack is claimed by and as the past. In each film, such absence is the very definition of photography and of death. The cinematic process that would attempt—again by definition—to overcome mortality through imaged movement, to best death by a procession of ocular fixities sped by in transit, has thus entered upon a contradiction in quest of a dialectic. The next-to is annexed and assimilated, the pose opportunistically subsumed to the moving picture. One after the other in the blurred lure of illusory movement, the two-made-one of forgotten contiguity becomes the tomb made of motion itself by the passing imprint. In this sense, with its ribbon of self-displacing photograms thrown forward into spectral screen presence, cinema is nothing more vital than death thrown for a loop. Once achieving such photofusion, such synthesis, embalming time itself (as Bazin would have it), any film that would then turn its hard-won dialectic (or gestalt) of motion inside out to obtrude the photogrammatic undertext, either within a scene of dying or in association with it, has fostered once again the return of the specular suppressed. Either way, death marks the spot.

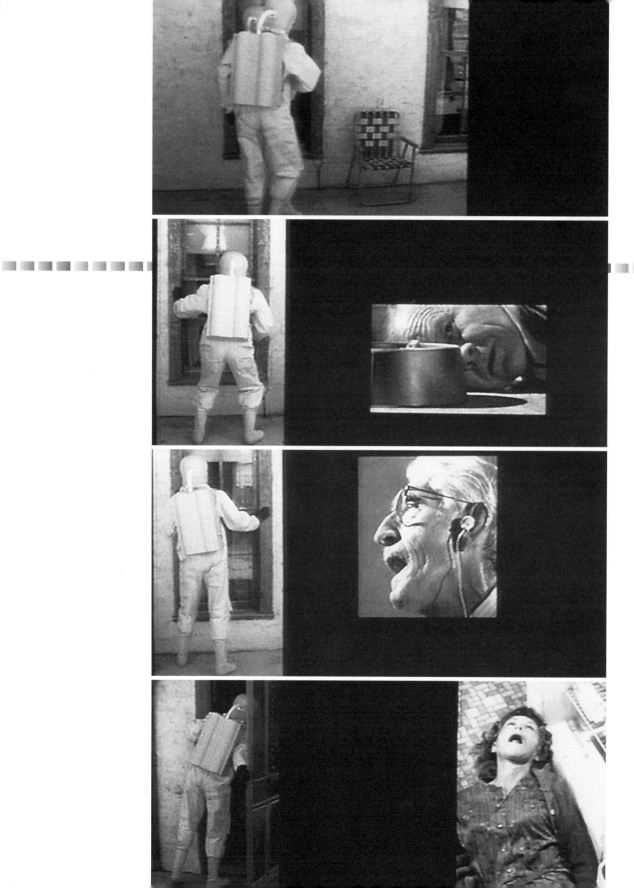

FIVE

The Photographic Regress of Science Fiction Film

THE MEDIA TURN OF FUTURIST FILM FICTION
ADDRESSES THE POSTPHOTOGRAPHIC SCIENCE OF
CINEMA'S OWN DUBIOUS FUTURE

Science fiction cinema is the time-honored genre of the special effect. What science fiction on film in fact tends to do is to render the most general effect of cinema special again, denaturalizing it: the photogrammatic effect of ostensible secondary presence. Photography indexes objects and bodies in place, cinema objects and bodies in motion, each in the absence of the things themselves. But on-screen the illusory image remains for the most part plausible. This is film's ontological promise—and compromise—in reception. Science fiction, always and increasingly, calls the bluff. Almost by definition, it has traditionally sent impossible objects and bodies before us with the same photogrammatic status as their cousins from the real. Though originally anchored in the unimpeachable photographic index, the celluloid strip thus surrenders its status as a litmus test of original presence. This is the genre's ontological challenge. Further, in the last decade and a half, the digital revolution in sci fi not only ups the ante but changes the ground rules entirely, undermining the photomechanical ground of the image itself.

With the previous chapter behind us, we are familiar with terms readily applicable to the strictly photogrammatic phase of the sci fi genre, long before electronic intervention. Like death, the photographic image is the human body's irreversible limit case. At a given instant in time, that photographed body, along with the objects around it, has passed unrecoverably from being to image. In the plots of film science fiction, more suspect "beings" as well as more impalpable ocular technologies complicate this photographic removal from the real. One result is that sci fi often tacitly asks how the human body's organic form, absented of course by representation, might serve to measure the humanist deficit of other illusionist systems projected (both senses) into the imagined future of the image—and might do so all the more decisively in the face of those newer visual technologies anticipated by, and increasingly incorporated into, sci fi narratives, technologies that are leaving the human body more radically behind, not just at its point of no return but at its point of replicated origin. The isolated photographic memento, we will come to find, is repeatedly the mark of this ontological vanishing point.

Beyond this localized emblem, a more general tendency is hard to miss. The technological predictions this genre thrives on may at any point turn on their own present medium. Science fiction has always been the one screen mode that institutionalized the foreseen—and now even exceeded—limits of its photographically based representation. Within this general tendency, a rooting sense of human presence is, as suggested, among the first sureties to succumb. But there are others. By way of narrative motifs prevalent in the genre's literary forms but given new edge in sci fi film, the mortal body is attenuated to a frail placeholder for the human spirit amid a swarm of ontological subterfuges. Duplicated or mutated, ejected or projected, vaporized or remade, cloned, morphed, sloughed off, beamed up or otherwise digitally repossessed, the organic body as locus of consciousness becomes more like a phantom, a vestige, or at best a leaky vessel. With that body registered on-screen, where all bodies are figments anyway and already, the genre is tasked with unusual reflexive obligations by its own fictive projections. This has always been the case. Now, though, technology has overtaken narrative material (and materialization) with a vengeance, so that electronic device infiltrates photochemistry in the filmmaker's own scientific laboratory. After a review of the genre's long-standing relationship to the photographic moment (via the thematics of mediation), we will therefore confront the latest wave of narratively digitophobic—but technically complicit—sci fi narratives. Here are films that may implant the loaded photographic vestige as humanist checkpoint even while supplanting the very filmic medium once built up around it.

The pervasive generic tendency is as simple in the setting forth as it is complicated to bear out with illustrations. When, in film science fiction, the plot itself as well as the apparatus renders the bodied subject potentially unreal, the photographic trace of an actual human body may return to weird salience in a screened world of simulacra. Located thereby is a vestigial photo-ontology under pressure from the digital figment. Estimating fully the beleaguered role of the photographic throwback in the escalating digitophobia of screen sci fi, however, requires attention once more to the filmic undertext of the cinematic image. We are dealing yet again with the special case of a general principle honored more in the deviant breach than in any normal visual observance. The corporeal subject on-screen, supposed host of human subjectivity, is always the lagging ghost of itself in the file of photograms. As we know, photomechanical materialization on-screen (the appearance of the photographic as such) either infers or temporarily defers—either alludes to (by reframed inset) or precludes (by reduplicated frame advance)—the ongoing cinematic illusion otherwise empowered by photographic technology. Taking as already established (by chapter 1) the complementary systemic difference between the inclusion (inlaid framing) and the recursion (reflexive framing) of the photographic image within or as the screen frame, one anticipates a likely generic bias. You would indeed expect to see more of the former than the latter, more diegetic photographs than freeze-frames, in a genre staked on the visionary access to the future rather than the cinematic production of it. With a narrative mode devoted to ocular astonishment within the diegesis, too much disclosed image manipulation would be counterproductive—or genuinely apocalyptic. In *2001: A Space Oddysey*, for instance, the freeze-frames near the end tell us that something is catastrophically awry in the whole supposed "world" that has engulfed us.

Photographic evocations of all sorts carry us back to the historical moment when bodies were first automatically captured in the precise form—if no longer the duration—of their being. The time of being versus the time of image is in fact the subject of one of the earliest instances of the genre to conceive deviant science in terms of an explicitly cinematic manipulation. In a landmark intersection of science fiction and cinematic modernism, *Paris qui dort* (René Clair, 1922; in English, *The Crazy Ray*), the deranged Dr. Crase is able to make the world stand still by turning a giant lever in his laboratory. What results in the ensuing montage is a number of seriocomic freeze-frames of Paris scenes, some obvious camera or lab tricks, some looking more like held (refilmed) photographs of deserted streets. A typical hypothesis of the whole conjectural genre is here on view. What would happen if a perverse (often future) technology could do to the world what a director can do to its simulation on film, manipulate and distort our spatiotemporal relation to a surrounding environment? But from here on out in the evolution of film science fiction, at least until lately, the tricks by which this is accomplished are usually contained within the scientist's laboratory or the ambit of an alien spacecraft's force field rather than being trumpeted as the anticinematic (because, for instance, world-fixating) work of the filmmaker's own lab craft run amok. It is usually by means other than the violation of screen montage itself, therefore, that the cinematic analogue enters plot as either an imagined facilitation or a foreboding trope.

The genre's typical *mise en scène* is replete with viewing screens that function not only as tools in the narrative but as icons of continuity with the present-day science of communication or surveillance. In this way the imaged future repeatedly looms as the intimidating future of the image, the medium's state of the art extrapolated into the art of some future state. Alternatively in the genre, a given film's present visual achievement may be measured against its screen predecessors, as when DeMille's parting of the Red Sea on the hero's TV establishes a baseline for the one-upsmanship to come in *Close Encounters of the Third Kind* (Steven Spielberg, 1977). In all this *The Asphyx*, as a science fiction metatext about media invention, stands forth as both the anomaly and the model. With dizzying historical irreverence, its Victorian film fantasy rewrites the medium's own prehistory, translating death's relation to photography into a founding relation of the mortal body to rudimentary film technique. By contrast, ordinary science fiction film takes present visual technology as ground zero and prognosticates a technological advance upon it that again throws into question the very limits of the organic human body and its representations.

In chapter 2 we considered in brief the disruptive ontology of the photograph within the genre of science fiction: most pervasively in the photomontage of *La jetée* (with its variant in the apocalyptic climax of *Fail-Safe*'s day-after-tomorrow futurism), most disruptively in the freeze-frames of *2001*, most dramatically in *Man Facing Southeast*. Each case involves the negative imprinting of the moving image, whether as inset photograph or as reflexive fixed frame. The first two films strategically dismantle the filmic apparatus as a machine of motion, either through-out (*La jetée*'s edited stills) or under split-second thematic pressure (the late freeze-frames of *2001*). Although confining the disruptive photograph within the diegetic field of plot, *Man Facing Southeast* does all the more damage to the narrative genre of science fiction by attempting to rob its holographic hero of his extraterrestrial credentials, however suspect this debunking. Apart from the extreme foreground-ing of these examples, how does the photographic moment fit within the flood of other media technologies that engulf the future from the earliest instances of the genre down to its second renaissance in the 1970s—and beyond?

In science fiction film, one crux, both narrative and formal, regularly takes shape at the crossing between the seeing body and the materiality of the seen world. The body is the transit station between inner and outer, between the seeing and the seen. When it functions only as a thing seen without sight of its own, the body has instead been translated to either a corpse or a photograph. When func-tions in both ways but only artificially, the body has been replaced outright by a simulation. The oppositional categories of this chapter are now before us in the impure distinction of their mixed coordinates. Along the same axis, another dia-metrical contrast immediately comes to the fore. Stopping time, the photographic body does battle with death, but on death's own terms; with the simulation there is, strictly speaking, no death left. Yet it is up to the plot of film after film to *figure* the simulated body as the death of the human, whatever its ghoulish afterlife. In descending order into the postmodern, then: Embodied world. Perceived phenom-ena. Visual transmission. Visual illusion. Simulation. Human cancellation. It is one assignment of this chapter to discover whether it is more than coincidence that the photogrammatic aspect of film operates to reverse this trajectory point by point when moving from the mechanical to the phenomenal level: Shot. En-corpsed Image. Illusory Body. (Re)animation effect. Projected world. Virtual real-ity, by any other name.

The work of a single critic slices across several of these issues at a revealing (if skewed) angle. Vivian Sobchack's whole polemical challenge to text-based film studies is there in her 1992 title. *The Address of the Eye: A Phenomenology of Film Experience* implies not the spectacle's rhetorical address *to* a viewer, its enun-ciative and suturing maneuvers of interpellation, but rather, by way of reversed priority, the optically disposed stance the eye takes toward a credited reality on display before it.[1] Text disappears into a corporeally centered world view. The ti-tles of her previous books on science fiction then fall into place with a comparable story to tell—or a story and its reconsidered sequel. Under the influence of Guy Debord, Jean Baudrillard, and Fredric Jameson on the postmodern epoch of the spectacle, 1980's *The Limits of Infinity* became 1987's *Screening Space*. In particular, the revised volume is concerned with the deep space of a far future fore-shortened now to the computerized grids of a radically dimensionless site, a zone of sheer electronic spectation screened from all illusion of presence.

In her new argument's responsiveness to present (post)historical conditions in the depthless and gravityless interspace of the chip, however, Sobchack minimizes a similar diagnostic at work in the sci fi tradition from the first.[2] The leveling emblems of the postmodern that preoccupy Sobchack's appended chapter, the hollowed frames of monitored cyberspace, have all along in different forms—through the boxing off of the absent or unreal by whatever mediated means—been a structural (and hence textual) feature of the genre. Such screens within the screen have always played their part both in the genre's formulaic *mise en scène* and in the plots that often seem working, in rather perfunctory fashion, to motivate such settings. Further, these internal frames have kept from full suppression, if I may put it this way, the single framed image that motors film in the first place: the photographic imprint on track.[3] Lately the encroachment upon the screen's inclusive frame (rather than just within its internal monitors) by the upgraded *trucage* (trick effects) of digital technology is the genuinely new turn. Morphing is the cinema's true invasion of the body snatchers, whereas the prototype for the insertion and framed containment of mediated amazements had long been in place. The technical iconography of the genre has repeatedly been marked by what we might call a postcinematographic iconophobia: a fear of images either more or less dependent on mediated presence than are movies themselves, images either mesmerizing in their artifice or delusory in their surrogate force, openly simulated or too close for comfort to the real.

This is to say that the most recognizable settings of screen science fiction have always tended to cast into relief, by their own recession, the filmic origins of their cinematic manifestation. Consider a production still from an influential early entry on the roster of the genre, an image patently designed to set off the set decoration of James Whale's 1935 *Bride of Frankenstein* (fig. 217). Melodramatically positioned behind Frankenstein's head is one of the outsized pulley wheels that will lift the dead body of his Creature into galvanic contact with the lightning rod on the laboratory tower. Rimming the very source of the demented scheme, as if by a technological metonymy for the wheeling brain of the mad scientist, this giant spool also evokes the rotary device of the film reel that, through the wattage of projection, brings Frankenstein to animation as much as his Creature. Such is the true tool for the multiple raising of the photographic corpse—in a metanarrative not only of this one cinematic genre but of its underlying filmic track. (Recall Noël Burch on the "Frankenstein complex" of all bourgeois mimesis, including cinematic reproducibility.)

Far more unmistakable as metatextual decor is the set design in a production

218 (Courtesy of the Museum of Modern Art Film Stills Archive)

219

220

still from a decade before *Bride of Frankenstein,* picturing an explicit monitor within the narrative frame. The screening of Fritz Lang's *Metropolis* (1926) is optically punned on in respect to the materiality of its very mediation. With a mesh of diagonal wire crosshatching the overlord's internal viewing panel, as faintly visible here (fig. 218), the "screen"-like bracing of the image plane emerges along with the suggestion that the workers' underground city, brought to view only across the safe distance of transmission (in a prophecy of closed-circuit TV), is a space safely caged away from the control panels of power. That this is a quasi-cinematic rather than a fully televised space is further suggested by the improbable lap dissolve between one accessed scene and another under inspection by the master Frederson (fig. 219). He thus achieves an overview of his proletarian underworld not from a stationary surveillance console but through an editable multiplicity of camera positions. Moreover, when we first see the foreman who later materializes on this monitor to announce the revolt of the literalized "lower" classes, the console of his eventual transmission—glimpsed behind him at his bodily entrance into Frederson's space—is dwarfed above by the more obvious movielike screen of its presumed magnification (fig. 220). In the power plays of the future technocracy, the more direct the offshoot of the cinematic apparatus (whether in sheer scale or in the multiple perspectives of editing), the closer to the bone is its irony.

To be sure, the inlaid screen is one kind of cinematic synecdoche: the rectangular part standing in (via whatever differentiations) for the enclosing whole. But the photogram on the strip is another: the rudiment of the whole, of cinema as film, without being its replica. The photogram is so inherently the *pars pro toto* that the part disappears into the whole. What, we need to ask, signals the interrelation (either necessary or at least typical) between these part-objects—one on-screen, one on the track—within the narrative system of a given genre film? And how might a reframed single photograph on-screen (rather than photogram on the strip) offer a point of discharge for the force of this latent relation?

NEGATIVE REGRESS

Although Lucien Dällenbach's structural study of internal *reflexion*—or *mise en abyme*—nowhere mentions film, transposition cannot be ruled out on any good grounds.[4] Rather, it seems invited along a ready chain of associations, starting with the ocular resuscitation of his dead-metaphoric title, *Le récit spéculaire.* Cinema too can surely provide its own reflex speculum. But by the still as well as the moving image? On the face of it, the photographic regress—which in some sense negates rather than mirrors the ocular kinesis it engenders—might seem to have no place in Dällenbach's internal mirroring, subdividing as he does the universal set of inset textual determinations into a fivefold overlap of possible compressed replications. They are these: fictional, enunciative, textual, metatextual, and transcendental. They have to do, respectively, with the story or plot, the discourse of its articulation, its compositional assemblage, the codes of reception, and finally the contradictory glimpse from within the system of what lies outside and before it. Retrieved in this last case is a text's preceding point—internalized as narrative node—of origin: an improbable forefronting at the surface of the text of its constitutive (hence precedent) ground. In sum, then, whether as story, as enunciation, as text, as implemented code, or as underlying intentionality, the narrative is paradoxically reframed from within, the whole recontextualized by its part.

In grasping the force of the "transcendental" reflection, one may think back to the screen within the screen of *Metropolis.* Addressing less an authorial than a historical and political first cause, this metafilmic moment puts into *abyme* the plot's sponsoring motive as an intervention in Germany's contemporary social unrest: its ameliorative telos of a redemptive liaison between the superstructure of complacent power and, at its volcanic base, the "broadcast" spectacle of an underclass in eruption. At this level the monitor is not only an instance of filmic but an emblem of narrative *mediation.* To the extent that this operation is at odds with its coercive deployment within plot, however, the "reflexion" of this abyssal screen may begin to suggest, beyond Dällenbach's categories, the need for a reverse or negative regress in textual semiotics.

The need may be easier to detect in the realm of obvious satire. At the outskirts of science fiction's genre material, and building on the thematics of oppressive surveillance in *Metropolis* to which it is no doubt indebted, is the film within the film a decade later in Charlie Chaplin's *Modern Times* (1936). Again, its technophobic projection into a dystopian near future transpires at the level both of the narrative and of the enunciation. Science fiction invades Chaplin's episodic comedy in its first factory episode as one unmistakable measure of the celebrated retrogression of the star-director's own aesthetic. Sound had long ago come to

221

222

223

film, and Chaplin had long famously resisted. He now turns
voice on-screen over to the unfeeling syllables of the factory
president at the controls of the parodic conglomerate Electro
Steel, manipulating his panoptic console (fig. 211) in bleating
out orders to speed up production (fig. 222)—or spying on
and curtailing the workers' toilet time (fig. 223). Together
with this vocal transmission, the giant screen predicts two-
way video technology (television itself then in the developmental stages), even while it comes before us by the obvious
trucage of rear projection. Such surveillance monitors are in
this sense nothing but bad, mechanical movies—in short,
talking films. The fictional level of mass mechanization thus
reverberates one level up at the stratum of enunciation,
which has contaminated the message circuit with the de-
tested new modes of mechanical voice recording. The abyssal
film hectors its internal audience into subjection, as Chaplin
resisted doing to his own. His art getting "transcendentally"
rehearsed in this negative node of resistance (performing its own prompting animus by example), Chaplin enters the talking era only, as it were, tongue in cheek.
Again, it is in just this regard that such an abyssal effect as the president's talking
screen is stationed not to replicate but to *throw into relief* the superannuated purity of the film as a whole. In the confines of negative regress, the reflexive inset
functions as the offset of the whole.

If the abyssal device, in all its manifold functions, operates *tout court* (according to Dällenbach) as an instruction to the reader (or viewer), replaying the narrative to outline more clearly its proper acceptation, then what I am positing here
as the negative regress also fulfills this overarching function. It services structure
by the very difference it induces us to recognize. It undoes by redoubling the
whole, reflecting it at odds with itself, and so reconfirms it. As a compressive

episode, such a negative *abyme* works
to set on end the structure that encysts
it. Like a mirror, a true *récit spéculaire*,
it reverses the image it is turned on.
Only with such a category in mind can
one open up conceptual maneuvering
room for the still or stalled image—the
single photograph or the "frozen" photogram—as skewed reflex of the animated filmic whole. It is just this reverse or reversion that is at crucial
moments effected by the photographed
human body in a futurist film genre
that imagines the outstripping of the

224

human by its engineered image, by electronic replication. This we have seen, for
instance, in the freeze-frames of the astronaut's face in *2001: A Space Odyssey*.

Earlier, negative regress has operated in *2001* by a metageneric as well as a
metafilmic reduction: a blanking out of all sci fi visuals. It does so in the scene immediately preceding the astronauts' photo session and its preternatural truncation
(both as episode and frame) discussed in chapter 2. The habit of the futuristic
screens within the screen was so generically ingrained even by the late sixties that
one detects its send-up, rather than mere thematic evacuation, in the film's most
dramatically inert scene. This is where American scientist Heywood Floyd addresses the assembled top brass on the Clavius moonbase about the mysterious appearance of the monolith, his lectern backed and flanked by the luminous walls of
a blandly improbable set (fig. 224), more like an outsized gallery installation in
some conceptual art exhibition than a feasible narrative locus. In one of those turns
of fierce minimalism that drive Kubrick's film to the near edge of avant-garde practice, the inferential absence of every movie set's invisible fourth wall, enabling the
camera's access—and opening in projection upon our screen rectangle—is internalized and tripled in the briefing room's glumly luminous wall panels cut to the
measure of the cinemascope ratio yet glowing only with a dull, migraine-inducing
intensity. Indeed, in the film's original road-show venues, the three panels of this
stark set may have recalled the earlier manifestations of Cinerama, whose original
three-projector process was geared to the screen's exaggerated curvature. Not credible as slide-projection screens, these translucent panels look like nothing so much
as latent, disengaged surfaces for the rear projection of some engulfing special effect—for, in other words, the potential disclosure foreclosed by Floyd's bland cover-
up. With all images removed, bleached out, this folded triptych of tabulae rasae thus
turns inward upon itself as, one suspects, a visual pun for the glaring whitewash
that Floyd delivers from the podium. In a closeted space whose very parameters are
cinematized, the briefing becomes the *screening out* of all information, all revelation. Only the very different wraparound apparatus to which we return from the
empty brightness of this hermetic chamber will alleviate its denials—namely, the
maximized visionary spectacle of the wide-screen epic.

Then, too, hovering implicitly somewhere between the metatextual and the transcendental *abyme* is the further r/evocation of the unexposed 70 mm photogram itself. This is the single serial imprint that would alone permit, from within the ongoingness of a film track, the lit elision of all image. At the back and basis of the scene, then, is both the molecular and the monolithic first cause of the film's whole visual trajectory. For each of the three panels, anticipating the (often vertical) dimensions of the black monolith in its own remaining three appearances in the film (in the following scene at the moon crater, in Jupiter space, and in the final cosmic bedroom), reads as the bleached negative image of the film's prime mover: the midnight-black rectangle of galactic revelation, which coincides with the lateral reach of the screen frame in the film's penultimate dolly shot. It should be clear yet again how only a model of abyssal recession that tolerates the notion of negative mirroring (here, for instance, the film track under cancellation as unexposed units of the strip) would be flexible enough to entertain photography (let alone the photogram in series)—in just its difference from cinema in action—as among the potential emblems of film's mimesis in condensed reflexion. In positing this enfolded negation, this encysted contrary, as a regress ingredient to the very genre of science fiction on-screen, let me give, for now, one more example of its photogrammatic evocation before turning to the more common photographic instances.

IN VISIBLE RAYS: THE BODY MANIFEST

Indeed, Kubrick's knowing allusions to the symptomatic screen within the screen send us back across the history of the genre once more. In the film version of H. G. Wells's *The Shape of Things to Come* (William Cameron Menzies, 1936), one of the most visible signs of the coming times is the proliferation of optical technology cast forward to 2036 from the film's date of production a century earlier. At its climax, the film concerns in good part the shape of screens to come. The future's image technology includes a massive statewide network of visual transmission that somehow permits the simultaneous broadcast of the human image (fig. 225)—though neither projected (as in film) nor generated from a sequestered apparatus behind the viewing panel (as in television). Rather, such images of the live body are materialized as translucent pictures from within transparent plates or as "windows" that punctuate the airspace of the gleaming metropolis, appearing even in milky three-dimensional forms within quasi-holographic cylinders. We in the audience know, of course, that we are watching film technology operating by *trucage* (mattes, rear projection, etc.) to simulate its own outmoding by electronic magic.

What is more to the point, that knowledge is not entirely overridden by plot. Even with no ordinary image projector in sight, still the basis of the photochemical procedure remains approximately intact. In the control room during one of the mass media broadcasts, we are given to see the mechanics of mediation by which the human image is multiplied, to see it not only in dissemination but in production, for racing across an inset groove on the broadcast console is a chain of single images like a outsized film strip—filing by as if on a flatbed editing machine (fig. 226). In 1936 the democratizing wonder of worldwide simultaneous broadcast can be

225   226

summoned up for us, it seems, only as a technology of analogous rather than electronic representation, frame by still frame, even as the time necessary for photochemical development has been elliptically dropped out. The moment bears
dwelling upon. More is at stake than technology, because more is at risk than the
image. The human body is figuratively on the line in the defile of these oversized
photograms. The quaint anachronism of this technological amalgam, with its pictured nostalgia for the photogram itself, reads to the postmodern eye like the return
of a repressed technological conservatism from within the adaptation of Wells's
anything but monitory futurism. This third-millennium projection booth, that is,
houses nothing less than a vestigial feeling not just for the body's original presence
to reproduction, microsecond by microsecond, but for its need to be taken down
whole rather than by digitalized bits. For all the electronic mystification of the future viewing panels, the integral body remains even here the imprimatur, the foundational validation as optic imprint, of even the most advanced specular projection.

In *Things to Come* the body has to have been there for the image to take, its
ghostly multiplications notwithstanding. In a lower-budget science fiction film
from the same year, *The Invisible Ray* (Lambert Hillyer, 1936), the body provides
both the aperture and the surface of the *retained* image—and does so as an almost
redundant diversion from a loony pseudoscientific fantasy about the universe itself as both a virtual movie camera and an infinite scroll of exposed film stock. First
things first. According to the film's mandatory mad scientist (Boris Karloff), the
cosmos is one huge optic imprint, the post-Gutenberg equivalent of nature as
God's book. Every ray of light ever fallen upon an object "has left its mark on nature's film"—if only science could "reproduce what is written" on this infinite
text. In an expository sequence of inspired, doggedly elaborated claptrap, we learn
that our scientist antihero has developed an optical decoder to do just this. Having
captured a beam in the galaxy of Andromeda, his machine is able to travel back
along the trajectory of its single ray—emitted centuries ago from earth—and recapture the optic event at its source, an exploding meteor reseen as if in real time.

227

228

229

To recover the event once present to the distant light ray that still retains it, the scientist's projector-like device (fig. 227) must somehow pivot its optical field 180 degrees. With the diegetic audience attending his demonstration from behind a transparent protective shield (fig. 228), we get the point at once. Some visions are so intense they have to be screened. Here too cinema's own film rather than nature's film is placed under laboratory analysis. For the openly cinematic means of this galactic reversal (or the figuration for it) involves the now dated device of the ripple effect. This is not a full horizontal "wipe," clearing the screen entirely, but a striated dissolve (fig. 229)—as if it were, within plot, the marvelous effect (rather than cause) through which the vector of the light beam is torqued into reverse by this cosmic "editing" apparatus. In this way the very photogenesis of the cosmos seems recapitulated by a genre's primitive battery of special effects: one of those stressed admissions of montage as its own *trucage* called to our attention by Christian Metz.[5]

Once contaminated by radiation from the discovered meteor still buried in Africa, and having become a lethal weapon in his own right, Karloff, like any screen actor—and then some—glows in the dark (even as he is able to harness the ray to cure his mother's blindness). All this is, again, the effect of a deeper cause also plumbed by metatextual regress: his availability, as real body, for filmic registration in the first place. Improbably enough, no sooner has the protagonist become a living ray than his first victim becomes a camera for recording that ray. The film draws here on an overturned theory of nineteenth-century medical and forensic biology, explicit in the mouth of one of the characters (and familiar to us from *The Asphyx*), that the eyes of a murdered man may retain the image of his

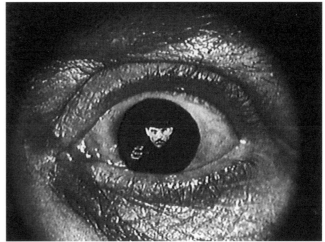

230

231

nemesis.[6] In *The Invisible Ray*, the unspoken and discredited term *optogramme* is given an additional sci fi twist, because the image from the retina of the corpse can indeed be recovered by media technology. It can be rephotographed from the material body of its first imprint "before the eye tissues glaze over." In one of the most deliciously absurd lines in all talking film, a scientist (Bela Lugosi) in the murdered man's bedroom asks the widow, with time running out, if "there is an ultraviolet camera here." Sure enough—and the result, when the open eye of the corpse has its carnal film transferred to celluloid for detection (fig. 230), is an image of the scene we have missed. In a somatic point-of-view shot seared upon the body in the very moment of its choked-off subjectivity, we look upon the crazed scientist strangling his victim in an irradiated death grip (fig. 231). Accidents will happen, however, and Lugosi smashes the photographic plate that has preserved the now vanished corporal image of the crime. Forensic technology is absorbed by cinematic technology. The image is now for him what it is for the film viewer, merely a fleeting ocular trace.

Inferences continue to mount around the film's pseudoscientific notions. *The Invisible Ray* envisions a universe whose conditions are all radiant, specular, photogenetic, whose motions are all optically captured and indefinitely retained: in short, and by any other name, a film world, however fleeting its image may seem in the moment. But this emblematic configuration has one more twist. For here is a world where every trace of life, held in and by light itself, etches the moment of a death. Such is the weight of the film's opening parable as well: the universe as the scopic tomb of its own prehistory. The metaphysical premise of *The Asphyx* once again comes to mind. But here every corpse is a photograph rather than the other way around: a photograph not of itself but of the advent of its fatality.

In *Things to Come* the imaged body, stilled in the moment of its captured motion and resynthesized for transmission, is the ground-zero of image production, the carnal given of all simulation. In *The Invisible Ray* the body is so entirely the measure of all imaging that it is both beam and plate at once, source and trace of ocular energy. Between them, these films offer a bioptic conflation that forms the seedbed of an entire sci fi motif. Film after film in the subsequent decades of the genre, reflexively prefiguring whatever variety of future image system its plot may concoct, will come round once more to the body not only as a mutable ingredient in the narrative but as the primal (if often forsworn) organic touchstone for the artificial projections of the so-called *biograph* itself.

This is the body, the photographable envelope of self, as point of departure (in both senses, historical and mortal) for all scopic prophecy in science fiction. It is not far from the body whose semiotic valence Dällenbach has in mind when he identifies such corporeal incarnation as the most likely site for the reflexive duplication of an "organic" textual system (96). But for Dällenbach the semiotic body, however probable a candidate, does not often fill this bill. Even where textuality is understood according to organicist models, "the textual *mise en abyme* seems unable to use the symbol of text-as-body" for the very reason that it is "difficult—if not impossible . . . to introduce into the diegesis" (96). It is less difficult in film, though, especially once the body is transcribed by a photograph. In a genre preoccupied with the organic body as a limit case for humanity's subjective incarnation, and in a medium in which the body is always and already textualized not as mere arbitrary sign (as in literature) but as picture in movement, its role is more active and frequent—and often linked with its photographic trace. Further, this delimited trace or imprint is all the more likely to drop into negative regress within films of a depicted future where the lived body no longer grounds the simulated corporeality of its own electronically mediated or downright illusory presence. In such films the functional absence of the body outmodes its own death. In them photography stages a double mourning, including a retroactive lament for the brute fact of the human corpse itself. My exhibits come from both the first and second wave of 1970s and 1980s cyberphobia. I will then bring them hastily up to date by two examples, from just last year, of all they feared: a future not just of genetic tampering but of digital co-optation that may at any moment threaten to eviscerate further the already disembodied medium that envisages it.

CORPUS DELICTI AND THE PHOTOGRAPHIC TRACE

The relation of corpse to photographic inscription may never again be so direct in mainstream science fiction as in *The Invisible Ray*, where the body itself offers the stained plate—or retinal membrane—of a mortal imprint. Yet the body returns again and again as the site of a photographable relation to the inhabited world. Three decades after *The Invisible Ray*, the displaced and finally evacuated self-recognition of a single human subject is carried out, in a more venerable sci fi film, through climactic references to photography that mark the hero's flight from a panoptic dystopia. The film is François Truffaut's adaptation of the Ray Bradbury novel *Fahrenheit 451* (1967).

In the future police state the film envisions, where large wall screens have replaced outlawed texts, the media assault on literacy is driven home at every oppor-

tunity—quite literally home. Domestic privacy consists for
the most part of sitting listlessly mesmerized before these
giant TV screens, the audience caught up in interactive dramas where space is made for their pointless response and
where frontal camerawork and direct address repeatedly "in-
terpellate" the viewers into scenarios not their own. That the
video image is a kind of policing mechanism is shown by a
compound irony of "frame up" at the film's climax, as it harks
back to a scene of photographic allegory early on—and summons back, in further replication and reframing, that scene's
own multiple images. This earlier episode has been detailed
and precise. In a world without reading, the only identifying
legal mark is not the signature but the photograph, as Montag discovers in the dossier kept on him at fire headquarters
(fig. 232). It contains rows of serial snapshots of his head in
profile and a similar strip taken, oddly enough, from behind.
Like a signature to this extent, the nearly "effaced" iconicity
of this last string of photographic documents is only a kind of
arbitrary signifier of the social subject rather than a picture of
his existential presence. More than this, the faceless shot is,
for all intents and purposes, the most thoroughgoing ID of the
managed human pawn in a society that places no value on
self-identified subjectivity. More, too. The System is always,
in effect, looking over one's shoulder, keeping its unseen eye
on the social agents it subjects. And it is upon one of these reverse human images that the film camera zeroes out at the
end of the sequence with an anachronistic iris wipe like some
kinetic magnifying glass (fig. 233).

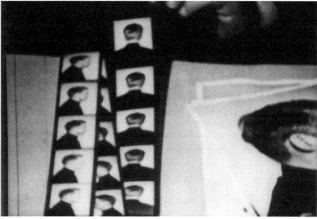
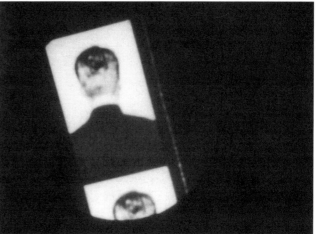

232, 233

What more remains of this photograph in recess as the film's own negative
signature awaits the climactic sequence of the narrative. When the traitor to surveillance takes flight to the forest hideout of the Book People, his role within society is brought to closure, just before his simulated death on camera, by a continuous screening of those early ID photographs as part of a broadcast TV
manhunt, including the otherwise useless shot of the head from behind—as if it
were now the stigmatizing insignia of a turncoat in flight. In the midst of that
flight, Montag is pulled up short by these multiple photographic images reduplicated many times over by a bank of TVs on display in a storefront as he runs past
(fig. 234). As the TV camera closes in on an isolated single image, we seem confronted by a kind of deconstructed freeze-frame (with its intertext in the final, albeit frontal, shot of *The 400 Blows*), each photographic piece in sequence rather
than laminated into duration. In Montag's case this is the last snatched and iterated glimpse of the one who turned his back on the system, the one who got away
(fig. 235). In what might otherwise evoke a sort of Magritte-like reverse mirror
(of the man confronted, as if from behind, by his own facelessness—or poised in
his depersonalized social life under the sign of the overseen) is instead, at least by

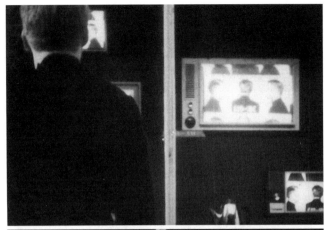

234, 235

236 (Courtesy of the Museum of Modern Art Film Stills Archive)

now, a pictogram of the self refusing social picturing in the reclamation of his willed identity. For this is an identity founded, we viewers too should know, on an ability to identify with others through narrative—in his case, to "become" the books he flees to read.

Surveillance has passed beyond the need for any photographic dossier into an electronic penetration of the private life so extreme in George Lucas's *THX-1138* (1971) that at one point we watch (along with neural technicians on a video screen) the body of the hero digitally programmed for experimental shock therapy. Within this dystopian vision of perpetual monitoring, the fixed photographic icon is meant to provide soothing relief, even if it pretends to be looking back at you. I allude to the supposed panoptic godhead of the underground metropolis: the Christlike image of Big Brother called up in electronic confessionals as the fountainhead of abjection in this narcotized society. This putatively omniscient presence is in fact the opposite, merely all-seen. For at one point the hero accidentally breaks into the throne room of the deity and, before being accosted by robot police, discovers a giant, screen-sized photograph of the deity's image stationed before video cameras in the process of transmitting the opiating icon to its numberless auratic sites (fig. 236). In this ultimate *mise en abyme* of the film's illusional world system, as well as this empty center of the plot's own sociology, its hero has come upon the transcendental signified of totalitarian ideology in an empty photographic signifier—and hence, in this case, the negative regress of kinetic illusion. God is dead, become a photograph of himself—and in a genre increasingly concerned from here out with the death of man.

In Bertrand Tavernier's *Death Watch* (1980), Romy Schneider plays the dying heroine with the doubly punning surname Catherine Mortenhoe, whose death is being recorded on national TV in an ongoing soap opera of morbid video verité. Not only is she tortured by this merchandizing of her decline, but her attempted flight from the panoptic autopsy of her last days is for a long while compromised by a false friend and traveling companion in the person of Harvey Keitel, who helps in her escape while secretly recording it for the climax of the TV series. I said "in the person" of this character, and the preposition has an unnerving ring in this case. For the source of Keitel's falseness to her, his betrayal, is indeed inside his body, in the video camera we have seen surgically implanted in the film's opening scene to replace his right eye. With nature's own stereoptic vision losing its three-dimensionality as a result, his monocular recording device is like a parody of the documentary trope "I am a camera." Overcome by empathy and guilt near the end, Keitel is willingly blinded by the removal of the camera—but rehumanized in the process, demachinated. Uncoupled from his prosthetic instrument of surveillance, he can thus be recoupled with his estranged wife, whom he introduces to the dead heroine's ex-husband in the film's last frame.

One can be this precise about the film's last shot because the frame stays there before us, frozen in mid-handshake: a gesture of return to community that suspends even the cinematic viewing that has been tainted throughout by ironic contamination with the exploitative TV serial. The heroine having exorcised her video ghost by at last taking her own life offscreen, a further way to respect such human privacy is thus troped by a visual stasis that suspends all cinematographic record. In a metaplot of such perverse detection, the narrative track has finally been lost. Only the photomechanical trace remains. And is named as such. For the last word we hear on the sound track, before the freeze suspends all dialogue, is the nickname of Keitel's wife, Trace for Tracy. Where before it was his seeing, here it is his external sighting that is aggressively automatized. Yet in a sense the single photographic image feels redemptive too, after all that digital prying: a moment that honors, that might genuinely elegize, the absent bodies whose surface images its chemistry can duplicate.

Photography can be as much a symptom as a palliative, though, in this brand of premonitory sci fi. In the reduction of the human to its manipulated image within a culture of surveillance, a compensatory (even narcissistic) scopophilia—enhanced by photochemical mediation—may provide the suspect reverse face of society's invasive eye. In the paranoid conspiracy plot of Nicholas Roeg's *The Man Who Fell to Earth* (1976), photography offers in this way a further measure of the body's technological alienation—and from its own focal (as well as social) place. The film's extraterrestrial hero (David Bowie) comes to earth bearing the scientific expertise of another world's visual culture. This includes designs for a camera that can photograph the operator himself from a vantage point outside his own body. Once marketed, the portable camera is first seen tested in a sexual tryst in which a character is able to take pornographic shots of his own lovemaking with his mistress while she is holding up—at a mocking further distance from their self-voyeurized desire—a framed photo of his wife. All things traditional are cast into negative relief by the new scopic kink. Here also is the very science of self-alienation in a single distanciating device: a prosthesis of desire as disengagement.

In similar cautionary fabulations of the 1970s and 1980s, the photograph frequently appears as either elegiac emblem or stopgap document in an outrunning

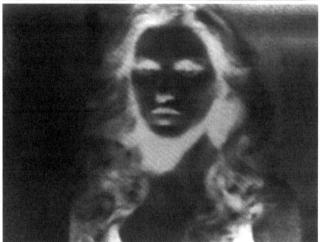

237, 238

of the human by the bodied offshoots of subsequent visual technology. *Looker* (Michael Crichton, 1981) works to allegorize the elegiac effect in an explicit play between the technical rudiments of both photography and film, overridden together by digital simulation. In the process, such scopic ironies divert an ongoing melodrama away from its main theme into an extraneous bit of technological business (involving a tool accessory to murder: a kind of photoflash stun gun) that ends up inscribing a negative regress of the film's whole plot of lethal electronic co-optation. *Looker* names by perfect title both the object and the subject of the mediated and fetishistic gaze, the so-called photomodel and her transfixed audience. The plot has it that star models are being killed off as soon as their computerized holographic images have been fully synthesized for TV transmission. It is a plot discovered by none other than a Beverly Hills cosmetic surgeon (Albert Finney), as if the whole phobic fantasy were an extended pun on a reconstructive surgery so complete that it ends up deplasticizing the body altogether: converting the female model into the sheer and perfect image.

None of this should depend on any particular mode of assassination. But the means of death remains overdetermined nonetheless. The photo models are not, as it happens, just murdered. They are, as it were, shot to death first. In order to confiscate their bodies so as to perfect their images, they are frozen by a newfangled electronic weapon that operates like a blinding photographic flash. But this device actually arrests their persons, not their images, rendering the women unconscious (suspending their subjectivity) long enough so that, lest they should compete with their own surrogate images, they can be brutally removed from all further public sight. To demarcate the very instant of that removal, that photographic exclusion, the medium close-ups of the victims on-screen, already "sized up" for holographic replication, are seized up as photogrammatic reductions of their own filmic presence in a strictly photochemical reversion. This is brought about by having a brief freeze-frame on a stunned face (fig. 237) immediately dissolve to negative image (fig. 238) and then instantly cut away to the next scene, while the "model" for all subsequent commercial images is being done in offscreen. Form infiltrates content yet again, as the elliptical becomes lethal. The inference all but spells itself out: where there might have been a new photograph developed from its own full-screen negative imprint, there is instead a death. In this way the aggravated vestige of the photographic apparatus clinches the film's satire of the hollow feminine image. The principle of corpus delicti requires the presence of a demonstrably insentient body for the charge of murder. But the stun gun allows the removal of the body from the scene of consciousness, the "models" remade as replicas of themselves on the trace of their own annihilation. It would only be necessary to press this extrapolation from our present image culture one notch further to foresee a time when the bodies of such murder victims would be submitted to biosynthetic rather than merely digital duplication: "morphed" in person, as it were, rather than just on-screen.

The specifically photographic measure of this outdistanced real emerges only in the sequel to Michael Crichton's *Westworld* (1973), the bluntly titled *Futureworld* (Richard T. Heffron, 1976). Both titles designate, in fact, the trademark locales of high-priced, high-tech theme parks featuring the lifelike thrills of robotic interaction. In *Futureworld* the managers and operatives of the corporation are no longer in danger of being sabotaged from below, as in *Westworld*, by their cybernetic underlings. Rather, it is the customers of the theme park, in this case the world's political elite themselves, who are at peril of death and replication. One ferrets out a shadowy parable: indulging such electronically aided fantasies as virtual-reality vacation centers will eventually, like the primitive rituals of TV before them, robotize your imagination. At the level of plot, the idea is to turn these moguls and power players into mere images of themselves, automatized puppets, thus normalizing international relations so that the flow of postindustrial capital will remain unimpeded. The notion of the corporate figurehead is literalized in the corporeal simulation. Recorded images of the arriving dignitaries are submitted to three-dimensional computer analysis to produce electronic replicas of these so-called world-stage figures, dummies indistinguishable from their originals except in their hardwired determination to keep an economically serviceable peace. The first programmed action of each of the electronic replicants is, we soon find, to assassinate its prototype. Thus does the image, the simulation, come into presence as the violent absentation of reality, the very death of its referent.

The logic seems irresistible. Electronic surveillance leads to the electronic contrivance of the scanned subject. Devious mimesis comes of age in total substitution. The film has opened with the murder of an informant from Futureworld who has tried to tell the investigative journalist-hero (Peter Fonda) the inside story of the transnational corporate plot. A close-up photograph of the dead man—discernible only as open-eyed subject rather than corpse—is later shown by the journalist seeking information to one of the robots on duty at the theme park, as if it were a perfectly normal portrait. No recognition is forthcoming. Indeed, the photo is immediately stolen from him, its very existence subsequently denied. But there before us for a moment, in the negative regress of the fixed print, is the once lived rather than wholly simulated body stilled in a double last rite: funerary icon for the death (the stolen ontology) of animate presence and of organic basis alike. Turning almost unnoticeably on this photographic pivot point and its denied recognition, film technology is now mobilized to narrate its own overthrow by less candid representations of reality.

In the "theater" of international intrigue enacted by this one cinematic plot, and in this *last resort* of the human body itself, actors no longer present but replayed by optical illusion on film (the cinematic given) are seen playing first characters and then indistinguishably (by the trick photography of the double image) their replicants, as if those electronic substitutes were no longer credible beings at all but only tactical illusions. Nonetheless, as marked by the negative regress of the photographed corpse, the film participates in a certain entrenched defense of cinema (in its photographic, hence human, basis). It is a line of defense hardly foreign to the sci fi genre. The line is held not only against video (in its capacity for secret surveillance and transmission) but also against other electronically derived and fiendishly sophisticated technologies of deceptive (rather than merely, we are to think, entertaining, informative, and premonitory) simulation. By the next decade this line will be harder to draw. By then films have begun to incorporate in their own method the very threat of the digital they still seem rhetorically bent on staving off.

BEYOND THE SOMATOGRAM

In *Brainstorm* (Douglas Trumbull, 1983) it is not the lived body that is at risk so much as the so-called autonomous subjectivity (and sensorium) it was once assumed to house. Financed without their knowledge by the CIA, a cadre of advanced computer engineers has developed a tape-recording apparatus for laying down on multiple tracks the full psychoneural web of human cognition. Generated thereby is a virtual-reality playback that is never projected outside of the recipient's body but, instead, is internalized by it through computer-driven headsets.[7] In the film's closing sequence, the surviving lead scientist (Christopher Walken) attempts, against the armed prohibition of the government controllers, to complete the playback of a tape left behind by the device's coinventor (Louise Fletcher). But this isn't just any laboratory recording. It documents—if that is even the word any longer; better, it occupies—the throes of a fatal heart attack whose symptoms, as well as whose visions, his colleague managed to record in the grip of her agony and release. Art's millennial charge, the representation of death's ultimate otherness to the surviving consciousness of the living, is here technologically abetted. If one could—such is the film's premise—disengage the physiological from the visual track of this Brainstorm device, one could *see death through* without having to experience it. Yet this in its own right seems to be a fatal withdrawal from the world, from which the hero has to be pulled back in the instant of dissolving consciousness by the still bodily presence of his wife (Natalie Wood).

Portrayed here is, in fact, the second conjugal reunion in this version of Cavell's "remarriage comedy," a final embrace accomplished to foil the technology that has recently (and quite indirectly) brought the couple back together.[8] Obsessed with his work according to genre cliché, Walken has gradually become estranged from his wife. Unexpectedly, on the eve of divorce, they end up rekindling their love through the accidental mediation of the Brainstorm device when it was set to record the wife's reactions to an album of marital photographs. We see these first through her eyes as she inadvertently transcribes her present emotional rush and the moving-image memories it triggers. When the tape is played back by the scientist husband, his own invention ends up not blocking or sublimating desire this time but freeing him to feel once again. By the images made available to him he is able, that is, to relive an image of himself as loved by another that he had lost sight of. As salvaged photographs are "animated" into whole recaptured scenes, it is as if the affective equivalent of old-fashioned movies has intervened between photography and digitalized cognitive simulation. For as we see with the heroine, then the hero, their past photographs come to life in moving-image scenes, the shots they have once taken are spun out from memory in a form of affect most nearly associated with—and in fact generated by—the work of traditional movie flashbacks.

Under the onslaught of the virtual, the cinematic has found its loophole in the filmic. Which is to say that the negative regress of photography has dropped through yet again to a more fundamental textual stratum within cinematic effect. The technology that is being secretly co-opted by the CIA for experiments in psychological warfare is hereby redeemed in a therapeutic reversal. Extrapolating from simple snapshots in such a way that they become the textual counterpart of cinematic "sheets of time" (Deleuze), the work of the Brainstorm helmet is then to project them intersubjectively. A definitive requirement of phenomenological transfer is thus met. "I have the thoughts of the other," writes Georges Poulet about the psychodynamics of reading, "as if they were my own."[9] In *Brainstorm,* I see the memory flashes of the other as if they were my own lost memories of a better self. In this sentimental cross-identification, the marriage photographs generate moving pictures that are then internally transmitted as the abyssal equivalent of films within the films, albeit "inhabited" rather than merely framed for the participant observer. The retrieved mutual gift of memory is, however, given for *us* to see (all digital technology aside) in the form of atavistic photochemical devices (photography, then cinema) whose recognition—even in this romantic cliché of "the way they were"—does not rest with plot. It ends up warming us more to the film we are watching, with its own powers of identification, than to the future invasive technology it renders.

A broad theoretical point has been waiting to emerge from this sampling of recollected textual evidence. It has to do with mortality as common denominator of various photographic and photogrammatic "reflexions" of the track: mortality in a double sense—the body born to die and the very death, through simulation, of that rooting human condition. Photography is the recurrent trace, evidence, or residue of just that body. The photographic portrait, or the technology behind it, is often seen to function—either metonymically across plot (as in the homicidal flashgun blackouts of *Looker*) or metaphorically in a single emblem (as in the open-eyed corpse in *Futureworld*)—within a film narrative more obviously concerned with the primary rather than the secondary reproducibility of the human organism or image. *Fahrenheit 451* and *The Man Who Fell to Earth* also insert the photographic trace in relation to the alienated image within a culture of voyeurism and mediation. With these two films, the unnatural photographic vantage (the ID from behind; the self as its own camera subject) actually plays between a metonymic link in the plot and a metaphor for its entire thematic of cultural estrangement.

In all such cases, the two poles of the spectrum of investigated technology— a spectrum running from the photograph that precedes cinema to the future mimesis that outdistances the so-called motion picture—come into perspective in connection with the regime of the simulacrum. For its leading theorist, Jean Baudrillard, this simulant reality is as much a mode of death as is, elsewhere in French theory, the photograph. But for Baudrillard the simulacrum institutes a more drastic (because historically irreversible) order within the history of representation, where ontological presence seems simulated at its source: "Never again will the real have the chance to produce itself—such is the vital function of the model in a system of death."[10] What, we continue to ask, is the relation between the "embalmed" life of the photograph (or its duration on film) and the simulant body of the hyperreal? At least we are confident in having chosen the right genre for the pursuit of the question. In his "Conclusions" to *The Time-Image*, Deleuze decidedly does "not claim to be producing an analysis of the new [electronic] images" (262), but he has in fact much to say on their relation to cinema in the latter's role as the projected "psychomechanics" of a "spiritual automaton" (262) that thinks, conceptualizes, dreams, and free associates for and before the spectator.[11] "Hence there is something specific to cinema which has nothing to do with theatre. If cinema is automatism become spiritual art—that is, initially movement-image—it confronts automata, not accidentally, but fundamentally" (263). This is to say that cinema confronts artificial being as its own double. Deleuze has in mind primarily the lineage of somnambulists and hypnotized agents from German expressionism (Dällenbach's "organic body" as *mise en abyme* of the text, by any other name), but he might just as well be making a genre-specific point about science fiction when he adds: "The man-machine assemblage varies from case to case, but always with the intention of posing the question of the future" (263). Such is the intention, as well and at large, of the human as mechanic assemblage, the human as film montage—and all the more decisively when the nature of cinema's spiritual automaton is demystified from the photomechanical (rather than just psychomechanical) ground up, a process that Deleuze's commentary everywhere resists.

THE VIVISECTED PHOTOGRAM

One film, at the lower limit of the sci fi mode, executes this procedure with clinical precision. With its just barely futuristic premise, John Frankenheimer's *Seconds* (1966) inhabits the thematic interspace between self-image and the surveilled body. By contrast with *Death Watch*, here a surgery and its attempted rectification do their work not on the hero's ocular functions but strictly on his image in the eyes of others. Here too a photomechanical trace is all that remains in the end, in this case an actual photograph fixed and mortuary: negative regress of a plotlong bodily reconfiguration. This photo is the image of the earlier self preserved without mourning in the glass coffin of a mantelpiece frame. And in the denouement following this emptied epiphany of the self as other, a photogrammatic reduction of the hero's current rather the past body is the final narrative turn. In its disjunctive imaging, the barrage of jump cuts in this merciless closing sequence catches the very incision of fatal rupture on the way to the hero's surgical murder.

Shot throughout with macabre bravado in (already superannuated) black and

239   240

white by James Wong Howe, Frankenheimer's film recounts, in a ghoulish mix of
black comedy and urban gothic, one of the great conspiracy plots of the cinema. It
begins with the unadvertised services of an underground corporation that, for a
huge sum, will stage your death with an untraceable corpse, see you through not
only reconstitutive surgery but psychological rehabilitation and vocational training as well, and then comfortably fund your relocation in a fantasy life. When the
emotionally drained banker protagonist is forced to sign off on his own life after
watching staged blackmail footage of his drugged sexual assault on an unwilling
woman, this filmic embedding actually fits flush with the logic of the whole: a
pornographic displacement of identity that is the summation as well as the trigger of the bargain he is made to strike. So will the rest of his life as a dashing minor
painter in Malibu provide, arranged sex and all, nothing more authentic than a
lead role in someone else's movie. And not least because, when Arthur Hamilton
(John Randolph) becomes Tony Wilson, he will also, in an inspired bit of casting,
become Rock Hudson, whose stalwart heterosexuality on-screen (as well as in the
publicity magazines) was by this time widely recognized as one long assumed role.

    Taking flight from his Malibu beach house back to the former Scarsdale home,
Wilson visits his widow for a retrospective glimpse into his own former self. Awkwardly explaining his identity as a friend of the deceased, he stares in covert nostalgia at the wife's apathetically enshrined photograph of himself as if across the
distance of the grave. Wilson's epiphany of his former self as photographically
foreseen corpse only reduces the mortal trope of photography to a perverse fact.
The camera shifts from a close-up of the glassed photograph of Hamilton with the
reflection of Wilson overlain upon it (fig. 239) to Wilson's staring in the mirror at
his own cosmetic remake (fig. 240)—twin doublings of the undone self.

    Knowing that there is no going back, Wilson at least wants to try again. Just
after it is too late, however, strapped to a gurney, he realizes he has been requisi-
tioned by Cadaver Procurement instead. He will become not even the body for another's implanted dream but a mere alibi for disappearance, the disfigured and thus

unrecognizable corpse of an untimely fatality. It is at this stage that the film's own photogrammatic textuality comes under duress—and snaps under pressure—of the plot's last bitter twist. In his status as film image as much as in his role as doomed character, Wilson as his own surgically remade double has all along been a "spiritual automaton" laying no claims to a fully inhabitable space. As if to enforce this

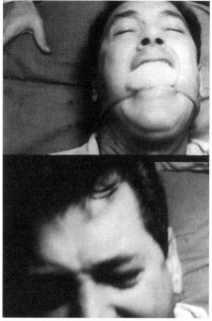

point at the end, the film discloses its concern solely with the sliced, spliced, and sutured body, not the enworlded one of phenomenological persuasion. To think otherwise is to make something like the hero's mistake, to believe that one can see through eyes other than one's own: that the POV does (automatically, as it were) tether the world to a proven subjectivity. Under orders from the film's guiding irony, we cannot accept embodiment through Rock Hudson's looks (in either sense). We can only live on and in borrowed time, through an optic not our own. And in the end we are thrown back in paroxysm to the photogrammatic chain itself, to the material body of the screen image before the apparatus of psychic investment. The effect can be characterized only as subliminal, a jar on the nerves of spectation, a convulsion of film's specular unconscious as the hero is hacked to filmic bits. Along the cinematographic underside of the traumatic spectacle— in a protracted scene of agonized recognition as hard to watch as any in Hollywood cinema—the play (or better, the slack) between photo and film is made visible, that is, in the return of the latter toward the virtual photogram of its constitution. As Wilson in close-up flails in rage on the gurney, the continuous record of his tossing head is shaken loose into a series of discontinuous shock cuts reproduced here, in their inherent discontinuity, by adjacent photograms on the film strip (figs. 241-44). Visual rhetoric passes over into cinematic confession. On view and in crisis

241, 242, 243, 244

is a metalepsis of the track itself, where the emotionally shattering is conveyed by the always and already piecemeal. No autoallegory of photogrammatic machination can detract from the existential melodrama of the moment. Technological form has sustained an unholy marriage with genre content in the barely fictional science of this harrowing fable. Watching the hero confront his surgical destiny, we watch the otherwise seamlessly paced race—and cloven trace—of the film strip at last ripped open to disclosure. A surgeon's scalpel could scarcely be more lethal than the editor's blades to the tissue of illusion stretched thin and spinning in the projector: this perpetual rebirth of photogrammatic leavings in the form of a vanishing second time around. At such a moment "cadaver procurement" becomes just another name for the material operations of cinema itself—especially when the imaged bodies on-screen, the part objects of their own continuity, are reassembled as the lifeless spectral site of projection for fantasies other than their own.

Two other screen moments come bearing down on the gaps sprung open by this climactic jump cutting. One is from this very film, one—more famously—from another of the same year. In the earlier, multistage shot transition across the transformation of Arthur Hamilton into Tony Wilson, there is a metatextual shock cut from the bloodied instruments of surgical incision to the splicing-in of a full-screen photograph, illustrated here again by adjacent photograms on the strip (fig. 245). This inset image is the respected citizen's newsprint obituary photo (the same picture, we will later discover, resting in state on the mantel back home). On-screen, the passing of self to mere photograph takes only the leap of a single photogram on the strip. As the camera next pulls back to reveal the obituary headline, "Noted Banker Dead in Hotel Room Fire," there is another jump cut to the bandaged brow of Wilson (fig. 246), whose fully effaced visage then continues (by vertical pan) its swathed arrival from behind a darkened rectangular shelf in the recovery room (fig. 247). The resulting bisection of the full screen image looks like nothing so much as a black frame passing out of view with preternatural slowness, like some stalled "wipe" from an older arsenal of editing devices—or, of course, like the vertical relay from one photogram to the next in line.

Also from 1966, Ingmar Bergman's renowned meditation on the face (or mask) in cinema also involves a metafilmic—because microanalytic—jump cut. In the hallucinatory prologue to *Persona*, the interrelated and mutually

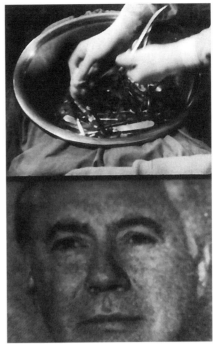

245, 246, 247

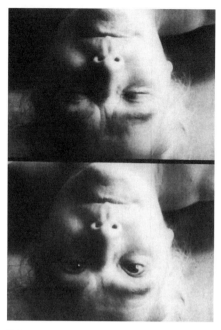

248

unresolved faces of its two protagonists are preceded by an upside-down shot of a corpse in the morgue—or is it merely an old woman asleep under a surgical sheet? In any case, she goes from a closed- to an open-eyed body, vivified by sight itself, not as a represented living actor would mime a character's coming awake or to life but only by the galvanic start of a nonanimated shock cut—across, that is, a single frame advance—from sealed to staring eyes (fig. 248). It is the photogrammatic difference per se, Bergman's textuality seems to assert, that alone gives life to the encorpsed human figure on-screen, alone turns image into persona within cinema's morgue of Bazinian embalmed time.

In this sense the jump cut—dependent on the photogram whose *disappearance* rather than prolongation is made anomalously manifest by it—emerges as something like the material correlate of the freeze-frame. Returning to *Seconds,* we find, in sum, a strained variant of that systemic interplay between internal stills and stop-action shots pursued in my opening chapter. Just as the body of Wilson was about to debut, Hamilton was seen to exist only as a photograph; just as the body of Wilson is to be jettisoned, that body has become all severed photograms. So, too, we add another metatextual death scene to the exhibits of the last chapter, rounding out the paradigm of narrated death as *the* filmic moment within cinema. *Citizen Kane* cites death as the elision of consciousness between the seeing and the seen. Hence, compounding the wrench of superimposition, we get the warping rupture—by tricked reflection in the fallen glass—of the whole shot-countershot system. *The Shining* cites death as the elision of presence between the fixated body and the fixated image. Hence the structuring absence of the freeze-frame as a kind of elided technical pun. Welles works in this regard at the level of the shot sequence collapsed inward upon the single overloaded frame, Kubrick at the level of the image track collapsing back upon the gradual magnification of a synecdochic photo.

And Frankenheimer? As the hero's impotent, concussive rage breaks through to the level of representation's own pulverized duration, *Seconds* operates its visual irony at the level of the dismembered track itself. Where Welles inscribes death somewhere in the vanishing interval between normally sequential (but suddenly simultaneous) frames, and Kubrick in the preternaturally suspended temporal disjuncture between successive shots (corpse and old photo), *Seconds* ends up citing death in the internal noncontinuity of the single shot—in other words, as the photogrammatic lapse from continuous materialization to mere inanimate material. Death is, in short, the former power of cinematic presencing reduced to a mere stagger and gash of photograms: once again, the return of the filmic suppressed. Even in disintegration, and even under ironic erasure as authentic subject, there is more of indexed corporeal presence in these last microseconds of the severed dead than in the later reign of the electronic. In order for cinema to accomplish any such materialized death as we see at the end of *Seconds,* that is, as opposed to electronic derealization in the simulacrum's "system of death" (Baudrillard again), a living body had once to be put on the line.

BODY IMAGE: FROM ID PHOTO TO COSMIC CENTERFOLD

Along with their associated photographic traces, such certifiable organic bodies are, as we have seen, at a desperate premium in the latter-day forms of sci fi: the human organism as the last of industrial society's vanishing natural resources. I return, then, in conclusion, to the recent spate of cyberphobic narratives, where computerized doppelgängers have emerged in untoward numbers as a negative apotheosis of 1980s fitness culture. Enter Arnold Schwarzenegger, not as body-builder but as built body. When the paradoxes of photographic temporality (the "then" that is always "now" and always gone at once)—paradoxes that appear as such mostly in light of the irreversible temporal constitution of human mortality—collide with a time-loop sci fi narrative like *The Terminator* (James Cameron, 1984), the inferences for the reanimation machine of cinema may be pressed to new emphasis. When these elements collide at the same time with a computerized cyborg plot, the metafilmic and the postorganic come into unusually stark confrontation. The photograph as the negative regress of an electronic virtuality works overtime to situate cinema along the very spectrum of similitudes that the film itself is busily narrating.

Four times over, a portable photograph of the heroine, Sarah Connor, appears in *The Terminator*, with the first in every sense an evidentiary setup. It is because of her college ID photo (fig. 249) that the newly arrived Terminator can match her face with her name in his quest to assassinate her. The second photograph of Sarah is recalled in flashback (flash-forward in the time-loop narrative) by the character (Reese) who has tracked Sarah back into the present in order to head off the cybernetic nemesis. He has been impassioned to do so by the hero of a postnuclear resistance movement, John Connor, who was in fact conceived by the time traveler to make possible Connor's own future and the liberation movement he (will have) galvanized. That wrinkled, timeworn photograph, which has stirred Reese's desire as well as his admiration (fig. 250), is next seen when it is blasted from him by a Terminator assault (still remembered from the future) and is framed by the camera shriveling in flames (fig. 251)—its "skin" buckling and peeling like that of the cyborg in the tanker-truck explosion at the end.[12] After the later (former) night of love with his hero's mother and Reese's subsequent sacrificial death in the destruction of the Terminator, whose own human surface has now been burned away by flame to reveal merely an ambulatory metallic skeleton, we see that same photograph actually being taken by a Mexican boy near the Arizona border. Just before the film's last shot of her receding Jeep, Sarah slips the rapidly developed Polaroid print under the tape recorder on which she has just left a funerary message to the future (fig. 252), promising to tell her unborn son about his father so that he will one day permit his compatriot's return through time—and hence allow for his own possibility. Together with the sound of her voice (which we know from an earlier scene that the Terminator could readily dupe, like any aural data), the still image completes this double and mediated prosthesis of the human at its point of transmission—and this in contrast to the Terminator's originally

249

250

251

252

simulated body and its illusory apparatuses: the cyborg a prosthesis of himself at point of manufacture.

A photomechanical parable once more glimmers into view. A single photograph in frame, then seen vanishing in a liquidating brightness (fire, lamp), but yet (again) imprinted and rapidly materializing into view, while accompanied by (without being fully conjoined to) the voice of the subject: this is all the future will have of its mythic heroine, just as in another sense it is all the film audience has of our own in the narrative's machinated progress. But we know that this underlying filmic materiality guarantees the body, know that the present of film always photographically testifies to the past of its actors. Not just the plot's first, but all subsequent photos, and precisely in their disappearance and reappearance within an unstable temporality of the foregoing and the oncoming, are in this sense ID photos: witnessing to the surviving fact of human identity even under the electronic stare of its cyborgian double.

The Terminator is no doubt the paradigmatic film for the subsequent decade of biotech action picture and the mayhem of electronic predation. We find continued—if divergent—signs of this cautionary strain in two films of 1997. One of them, *Gattaca* (Andrew Niccol), tactically eschews the *trucage* in which the other more predictably wallows. It thereby works to confirm my argument about screens within screens in the monitor-laden sets of the genre, to say nothing of freestanding optical illusions, by mostly negative evidence. *Gattaca* concentrates on the genetic engineering rather than computer simulation of the organic body, with the usual digitalized decor of science fiction thus held to a minimum. Optical displays and illusions are internalized as cosmetic and constitutional advances in human biology itself. The visible surface of the human organism is therefore not at immediate peril, only the "faith born" body willing to take genetic risks.

True to genre form, however, photography remains the yardstick of its own outdating. To measure the future's distance from an image culture that once fetishized the undecidedness—hence mystery—of the human body and its fate, *Gattaca* portrays a world in which "no one looks at photographs any more," only at the indexicality of the genetic code—as "read out" by portable blood scanners able to download in the process, almost incidentally, a video image of the identified subject.[13] By contrast, the "de-gene-erate" or "nonvalid" hero, born without genetic intercession, is seen leaving his family after ripping off his own corner of the family portrait. It is the photographic image of a self more authentic, less constructed, than his genetically programmed younger brother, an image of himself he takes with him into the unforeseen.[14] The inference goes in two contradictory directions. Carrying the fragmentary photo away with him into the main phase of the plot, the hero may thus be thought to keep his image in motion, as if to privilege film itself (and its ties to a visualized narrativity) as the apt model for a life always unrolling rather than locked into genetic predestination. That this is only a *ruse* of the indeterminate—in an already scripted and shot narrative from which all accident has in fact been removed—is an irony the film does not openly contemplate. Nonetheless, its genre status lends weight to this sense that the engineered rather than contingent lifeline is closer to a movie than to what we like to call life.

Whereas in *Gattaca* the individuations associated with photography are marginalized by a culture of perfection, another and more typical genre exercise in apocalyptic space travel from this same year deploys photographic images in brutal subservience to their digital successors: a film reveling in the loss of that human index that its computerized special effects both permit and, in bad faith, contrive to lament. In the dreary *Event Horizon* (Paul Anderson, 1997), morphing technology as *trucage* has entered the diegesis in the ambiguous form of hallucination or premonition. Characters thus bear the burden of the technology that materializes for us the lethal disfigurement of themselves and others. When, for instance, a crew member sees the deformed and bleeding body of her son (whom we know to be back on earth) floating in the onboard laboratory before her, the film's trick effect has become her traumatic vision, so real that she (and not only she) can no longer tell the difference. In the bludgeoning home of such epistemological ironies, this overwrought narrative pounds the whole logic of *trucage* into the psychic chinks and crannies of the unconscious. The subjective flashback is indistinguishable from the apocalyptic blitz, so that volcanic memory bursts and the onset of destined terrors exist on the same time-warped plane.

The nominal "event horizon" (technical term for the liminal zone that rims a black hole) names the limbo and holding action of the plot. A gravity-warp supership was lost in Neptune space in 2040 when attempting its first effort at "bending timespace" and transmitting itself to a distant galaxy. A rescue mission seven years later, led by the ship's inventor, Dr. Weir (get it?), slowly uncovers the grotesque results of that experiment. The electromagnetically self-generated black hole through which the ship is designed to plummet, via a fold in time, has spit it out again from the unspeakable (but gradually all too visible) abyss of hell itself, the ship's mechanisms now transformed into the living being of evil incarnate.

Such developments cannot be taken in all at once, by us or by the crew, even as a previously recorded revelation. So narration needs the digital update of the evidentiary film within the film or the stash of verifying photographs. As it happens, disclosure occurs in stages as the ship's log is downloaded from its CD-ROM storage in order to monitor (to screen) in retrospect the moment of the ship's first disappearance. Just as it took the plunge, the roar of the Underworld has intervened and blocked digital transmission—after a few words of warning in Latin, apparently the devil's own tongue. Only much further along in the present-day reconnaissance plot does the rest of the video disk become suddenly readable as the mayhem of the pit: electronic equivalent of an old-fashioned internal film screening (or video playback) of previously sighted visitations. Though intended in a different sense, from here on out this film is hell to watch.

Since so much of what we now see on the genre screen of this or any sci fi film—just over the far horizon of any real staged event—is digitally induced rather than photographically reproduced, the narrative convergence marked by CD-ROM retrieval constitutes a textual disclosure as well as a plot revelation. And against its onslaught, ordinary photography—as so often in the genre—is only a frail stopgap, dated, temporary, atavistic, and ultimately ineffectual. Once again, as in *Futureworld, The Terminator,* and *Gattaca,* photography offers a frail hedge against the hyperreal—until the photographic image itself is bent to the will, in this case, of the electronic countersublime. This contortion of the photographic role takes place in two cumulative stages. After the first scene of violent shock, in which Dr. Weir is accosted by his wife with bloody eye sockets, he turns out to be awakening from a "mere" nightmare. Damnation, we later find, will be no more than the bringing true of these and other fears. Lurching to consciousness, he reaches out for one of many photographs of the wife, eyes intact, on the wall next to him, stares mournfully at it (we later learn she has committed suicide in the face of his scientific obsessions), and deposits it on a dresser full of many more such snapshots. The camera eye of photographic registration assures us of the former autonomous presence of the sighted body (both senses) before its duping and desecration. This is the first stage in the counterpoint between technogothic conjurings and photographic documentation. The next takes a turn from funerary fetish into locker-room sex comedy.

At the point where Dr. Weir is forced by the rescue team to explain the scientific basis for the ship's electromagnetically manufactured black hole, he returns to the erotic and ontological consolations of photography, while warping them to his own purpose. When all the gobbledygook of standard Hollywood astrophysics is rejected by the crew as impenetrable, Weir grabs a *Playboy*-like centerfold from the cubicle of an irate crewman—"Hey, leave that alone, that's my Vanessa"—which he stabs at two points (the pinup pierced again) and loops together as a band. He wants to illustrate that the shortest distance between two points is not a line but a reduction of the distance to zero: a veritable fold in time. His need to deface and render illegible the two-dimensionality of a photographic image in order to suggest the fourth-dimensionality of infernal metaspace (and its coming digital simulations) is the film's fullest measure of its own prognosticated (and soon paraded) technology. For the viewer of *Event Horizon,* the bodiless scopic spectacle to come is meant, of course, to be no less of a turn-on than the former photographic centerfold sacrificed to explain it. But this is only to say that sci fi spectacle, no longer entirely generated but only transcribed by the photographically based medium of cinema, continues to indicate vestigially, if no longer to mourn, the photo-ontology of its original magic.

GENRE IN EXTREMIS

How did we get here from there? Let me attach summation to a last pair of examples. To clear the head after the lurid murk of *Event Horizon*, we may recapitulate the place of the photographed human body in the sci fi genre by way of two very different films from its 1970s revival. These are narratives whose opposite apocalyptic visions are respectively ecstatic and foreboding. They thereby offer, in review, the sharpest polarity between two antithetical valences that attach to the photographic trace of bodily presence in the genre: the missing but represented person as either a crisis for or a transcendence of the species and its mortal basis. To work back from the less frequent (because celebratory) mode of alien intervention, we note the insinuation of a double photographic benchmark at exactly the visionary climax of Spielberg's *Close Encounters of the Third Kind* (1977). In that epic of extraterrestrial bonding, the displacement of funereal photograph by inhabited body, rather than the other way around, enters the genre as a comment on the space/time relativity of its own fantastic premises. At the apex of the film's rhapsodic finale, while giant government cameras record the alien visitation on the landing strip, the heroine is seen in close-up snapping with her Instamatic what the novelization by Spielberg calls (modestly) "the last of the most important pictures in the history of the world."[15] Each of her snaps is answered on the click, in the reverse shot, by jump cuts that mark the serial transcription (far slower than the movie's own, but not unlike it) of the alien bodies circulating before the onlookers.

The process is in a sense the normative inversion of the previous scene, with its photographically marked homecoming of the ship's human passengers. There, rather than a capture of the other in a rapid sequence of stilled moments, the same is returned again into the differentials of human temporality. As the mother ship disgorges her assorted crew of previously unexplained missing persons, that is, including the 1940s military pilots whose antique prop planes, also never accounted for, had been deposited back on earth in the prologue, one of the presiding officials, turning to a display board of improbably (if metacinematically) backlit memorial photos, some necessarily black-and-white, tapes them over in sequence, as if x-ing them back *into* life (fig. 253). "They haven't aged a bit," we hear in passing. "Ein-

253

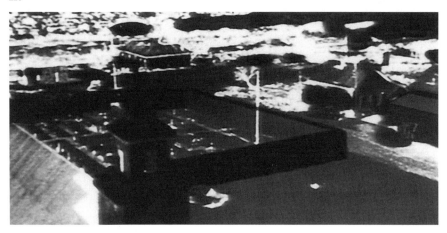

254

stein was right." In the living body's absence from discernible time and space, the photograph (brought to view now like a lamplit photogram) has stood in for the hypothetical death (the arrested development) of its subject. Emerging by another backlit manifestation from the blinding portal of the alien ship, these revenants no longer need their photographic proxies, no longer need any but cinematic representation. Real time has resumed, to be suspended only for other galactic vacationers, our hero included, who now elect their own exit at the speed of light.

At the other pole from Spielberg's literalized uplift, *The Andromeda Strain* (Robert Wise, 1971) deploys both the moving and the still image as preternatural indexes in its autoallegory of alien(ated) biology. The plot has slowly disclosed a top-secret "Scoop" mission designed to retrieve foreign organisms from space during early lunar probes, for potential use in germ warfare. When one such extraterrestrial microorganism kills all the inhabitants of a desert town, the first phase of surveillance in a night flyover is to gather "film evidence of unnatural death," both "infrared and fluoroscope." In time-honored genre fashion, the film moves at this point to borrow (and refigure) its own medium for thematized mediation. Almost identical aerial footage of the corpse-strewn village, ending with the church cemetery that sums up the graveyard the whole town has become, is run through twice, first as representing infrared recording, then in a spectral negative version meant to suggest some kind of X-ray (i.e., fluoroscopic) analysis of the ghostly—because supranatural—truth behind and beneath it all (fig. 254).

In the second phase of reconnaissance, we move more deeply yet into the constituents of sequential imaging to its sine qua non—and lethal negation—in the still imprint. This move takes shape as an almost unprecedented modernist distanciation in the sci fi canon, with cinema itself partly undone by the devastation it must give witness to. Scientists rapidly dispatched to the village, suited-up like spacemen for their contact with this new form of invasive extraterrestrial debris, search for human corpses in a morguelike apartment row. As they begin staring through their helmets into a series of windows, a lateral wipe edges the whole image—not theirs, but ours of them—toward extinction (fig. 255). This startling effacement stops short at screen left, leaving only a vertical aperture of diegetic space that reframes one window after another inside the plot (figs. 256-60). To the right, inset and reframed by the mortuary black border of the remaining screen rectangle, severed from the logic of all point-of-view editing, photographs of the bodies in room after room suddenly flash into frame. Shot from a variety of angles and distances, they are displayed in sequence for visual autopsy rather than rendered as seen on the spot.[16] As contrasted with the earlier narrative ligature of

255, 256, 257, 258, 259, 260

the negative film stock, this subsequent series of posthumous stills does not carry the proleptic suggestion of filmic
evidence (slides, say) examined later by the mission command. Rather, the still
frames threaten to deconstruct plot and diegesis together with their photomechanical proof of "unnatural death." This is a proof unnaturally displaced in its
own right from the immediate scene of narration: dislodged from plotted action by
virtue at once of death's evacuated life and its abrogation of human time. Recalling the terms of the second chapter, one senses that a kind of apocalyptic pity has
withered the cinematic image from within, now squeezing it toward obliteration,
now factoring it back to its cancellation in the isolated filmic frame.

The immediate context for this contraction of the cinematic image carries a
narrative force all its own. Dialogue just before has ruled out coronary arrest as
the cause of death, because from the looks of the bodies it must have happened too
fast, without pain. "These people were cut down in midstride"—in an instantaneous freeze, we later find, of their very blood. Once again a metafilmic premise
of the genre is borne out by plot, with alien "biotechnology" imaged by analogy

with film's own laboratory craft. We have in fact come full circle, half a century back, to the mad scientist's freezing of the world in *Paris qui dort*. In the self-declared *trucage* of the inset still shots in *The Andromeda Strain*, imposed photographic stasis alone (rather than continuous film recording) can render death's preternatural stoppage on the spot, the open-eyed stare of awkwardly fallen bodies. Not only has Bergsonian *durée*, as the very foundation of human existence, been violated by the backlash of such incipient "biological warfare," the temporal violence has been visited in turn on the image system per se. Gone from the narrative apparatus for the most part, with only a vestige of plotted action in counterpoint at screen left, is the very biological basis of the human form. This is the lived body as it has been traditionally mourned (but not forgotten) by photography, mourned in the arrested death throes of that medium's own inorganic stasis. *The Andromeda Strain* thus delimits a point of no return in the metafilmic evolution of its genre. This in turn marks its cinematic poise on the verge of the postmodern. Thereafter, the human image on the motion-picture screen will increasingly do battle with its own digital simulation rather than its funerary photomechanical index, as anticipated in this one film when the entire narrative frame surrenders at the end to an engulfing video screen for the last computerized "message": DISENGAGE. END PROGRAM. STOP.

Some genres find their evident destiny on film, and none more than science fiction in regard to (if not for) the imaged human body. Once a solely literary genre, science fiction was disposed by nature to forecast machines of visualization unknown to its nineteenth-century print audience. Yet something of the intimacy and private imaginative manufacture inherent in reading kept these mediations at a structural distance. When audiences were later congregated in theaters to watch the prefigured technological legacy of a fledgling film genre, in all its mutated scopic forms, such media-saturated futures nonetheless continued to take a backseat to the immediacy of the cinematic experience. As the most durable of screen genres in the second half of this century, science fiction has continued, more and more vividly, to imagine the technologies that would outdo it, do it in. In the digital era, however, futurist cinema has for the first time mobilized rather than merely evoked its own self-anachronizing upgrades. Engineered by computer enhancements, the superannuation of a suddenly hybrid medium has become a manifestly planned obsolescence, performed from within rather than simply foreseen. The technological overkill has spilled back into plot as an ontological dead end.

Building on the tradition of reflexive parable in sci fi narrative, screen plots still find ways to refigure as a crisis (rather than just to deploy) what we can only call this invasive present eventuality, this haunting of projected photomechanical space by the specter(s) of the digital. As evidence has shown, the incorporated foreign body of electronic simulation, infecting the filmic system by design, takes its greatest toll on the corporeal integrity of the represented human body. In everyday social space, environments can often be artificial—but not as a rule the agents that "people" them and receive their stimuli. It is one thing to say that science fiction film always glimpsed the dystopian shadow of its medium's eclipse as a privileged representational system. It is another to suggest that the genre contemplates the metamorphosis of its own viewing subject to mere simulated being, a receptor without presence. Long the lodestone of all representational arts, the depicted "mortal" body, despite its continued attractions for the camera, is losing its humanist draw; not only spiritually evacuated, it has surrendered its inherent animal magnetism as well.

In response to the technological proliferation it has always thematized, that is, sci fi cinema has devolved to the point where so-called human representation is not necessarily derivative but often original, the mobile body become merely the sign of itself at its source. One result, perhaps the most obvious for narrative plotting, is that the site of bodily death is no longer the certified *mise en abyme* of secondary visualization in a photographically based medium, no longer the place where a constitutive human absence finds its nodal trope. Nonpresence has become the potential content rather than just the representational form of the humanoid body, displayed on-screen by an electronic science no longer fictive but immanent. What is often revealed by such display is that being absent has passed from a condition of mediation to a virtual fact of life in the new simulated world of absent being. As before, only more so, the photogrammatic medium of sci fi cinema keeps pace by putting into marked narrative recess the signs of its own ontological as well as technological supersession. In the future that is now, the photographic image is held hostage to a pervasive cultural nostalgia for the very bodies its chemistry used to embalm.

The original locus for any such technological nostalgia, isolated and reclaimed as historical spectacle, is one recurrent emphasis in a seemingly divergent but in fact complementary tendency in recent narrative film. This is the anxious eroticism of Victorian costume drama, especially in its response to photography and the first stirrings of cinema. The motion picture's uncanny animation of the discrete human image, recent period films suggest, could only have made the lived body doubly nervous on the eve of cinema's commercial advent within an already nervous culture of photographic record and exchange. One route, then, by which to approach the relation between contemporary genre trends in the last decade of the twentieth century—futurist sci fi over against Victorian melodrama—is to remember that cinema itself would have been included among the science fiction fantasies of Victorian narrative until the sudden disconcerting breakthroughs of the nineteenth century's own last decade. This double perspective is not easy to formulate and will take an entire chapter to sort out. As tacitly evoked by certain photogrammatic moments in the latest Victorian nostalgia films, one way to put it is that photography's mutation into cinema impinges, as both the future of the image and the image of the future, from within a fraught vision of the unsettled present, a present replayed by these period narratives as our collective historical (and media-historical) past.

SIX

Cinema's Victorian Retrofit

RECENT PERIOD CINEMA TURNS A
REAR-VIEW MIRROR UPON THE WHOLE COURSE
OF MUTATING FILMIC TECHNOLOGY

There is nothing about history films that necessitates historical thinking. Deliberately or not, they often seem to disable it. Films concerned with the period of scopic ferment that led to cinema need be no exception. Some, however, are. In respect to this imminence of cinema, certain history films among the latest spate of turn-of-the-century screen melodramas do begin to seem genuinely historical.[1] Connecting us again with such visual precursors of cinema as locomotion, stereography, the ocular tricks of fairground attractions, and the craze for spirit photography, these new films lead toward a fuller treatment in the next chapter of kinetic spectation as a modernist precondition—and to the recursive place of the cumulative imprint in modernism's filmic register. But there is another reason for attention to such films at this turn, having to do with media culture's own technological mutation at the end of the twentieth century. Here the latest period films assume an often tacit media-historical cast that brings them into polar alignment with their genre counterpart in the coeval flood of high-tech sci fi. In view of the previous chapter about cinema in partial digital eclipse, so-called heritage films seem concerned anew with film's own specific heritage as plastic medium, including the legacy of the photograph: a casting back to origins (or at least predispositions) rather than a computer-driven obituary.[2] As never so prominently before, that is, Victorian costume dramas of recent years have gravitated toward the uncanny mechanism or the social circulation of photography in an envisioned past ripe for cinema's industrialized new looking. But if cinema's institutional embrace of the electronic juggernaut a century later (and of a sci fi genre that capitalizes on it) seems to invite consideration alongside the alternate tendency of period film nostalgia, the apparent counterpoint needs more formal specification.

Alas, no satisfying vocabulary comes to hand. Anachronism isn't exactly the term for it. Yet the viewer may occasionally be made to sense a faint disjuncture at the level of form rather than content, or medium rather than scene, in watching movies either about a time just before movies or about the coming of cinema. Content lags behind form—or sometimes collides with it, in a curiously staggered or layered fashion, at dramatic moments keyed by marked filmic inflection. In the double historical context of such moments, their then and our now, form interpenetrates content not just synchronically, by stylistic distanciation, but with a diachronic overlay as well. Again, there is no good term for this. When that overlay operates as a hovering technological discrepancy—in cinematic evocations of a precinematic era—the tacit gap is obviously authorized by the blanket poetic license of "restaging" rather than documenting the past. But when the gap narrows to movies about the cinema itself or its immediate antecedents in ocular experiment, the question becomes harder to evade. How, then, when the prevailing discrepancy between mediation and its material is not just suspended or neutralized in a more or less transparent camera style, is it returned directly to questions of media history from within certain texts themselves, as the conceptual residue of their *worked* rather than ignored filmic mediation?

To some extent the formal disjuncture must return in kind—formally. Coming to these films expecting that photography will take its place in their period *mise en scène* makes sense enough. Finding in them, however, not just the photographic but the *photogrammatic* moment is more of a metafilmic surprise. And it tilts the emphasis on imprinted imagery, by way of historical precursion, over from the strictly photochemical toward the more aggressive mechanizations of the cinematographic. In so doing, the filmic recursion—the textual upheaval of the photogram—distills the larger argument of this book so far, even while urging it forward again toward broader media-historical considerations. Recent cultural theory wishes to distinguish certain ruling *techniques* of the precinematic gaze from the strict *technological* lineage of visual instrumentation. This way, the coming of cinema might properly be seen to promote a cultural disposition—a whole epistemic regime—rather than just to machinate further a previous visual device. To borrow Jonathan Crary's title, cinema is best understood (and placed) as one more "technique of the observer" in a visual economy of the unfixed and circulating image rather than primarily as the latest refinement of a long-standing technological experimentation. A powerful incitement to new thinking about the rise of cinema, this history of vision approach does tend to downplay, however, cinema's invisible (imperceptible) dependence on the constituent photogram. As expected by now, this chapter puts the photogram back into play, into the play of images, even as the tension between the ingredient and the aggregate is historically reimagined by the heritage text. Stepping aside at once from technoteleology and from the psychoepistemology of gaze theory, my emphasis falls instead on a third and slightly different thing: on the return of the *technical* suppressed, the incremental photogram, within the kinesis of the cinematic frame, a kinesis not only of view but of bodies and objects. When this automatically suppressed single integer of screen illusion is lifted to view, however, to what extent does it drag with it the historically forgotten or overcome? In such technical recursion, what techniques of observation and what technologies of imprint may be summoned back and summed up?

And how can this broad question be most usefully aimed? If current sci fi witnesses cinema's institutional surrender to electronic industries—is a kind of corporate merger for which human corporeality is the representational scapegoat—does the Victorian body on contemporary screens, the body as it was first available to mechanical representation, offer an ontological counterweight? Then what about its own anxieties of technological modernity and mechanical reproduction? How are the photographic moments of heritage plots arranged to anticipate, whether sanguinely or not, the human body's coming disjunctive mutability, as well as its erotic license, on the cinema screen? To have demonstrated that movies about the future tend to concern the future of movies does not require immediate assent to this new and related proposal: that movies about our fin-de-siècle past tend to posit movies *as* the future. Not, at least, until the evidence is in. But let me anticipate this evidence as follows. In science fiction the photographic moment, variously circumscribed, provides a hinge between the prehistory of cinema and its future etiolated forms. In the alternative genre of Victorian melodrama, the photographic moment—along with its associated photogrammatical distortions—is the harbinger at once of modern image culture and of the specific self-congratulatory promise of the cinematic mirage. The various failures and defeats of the Victorian self, suffering what Thomas Hardy famously thought to call the "ache of modernism," cheer us in the contemporary film audience only by their appeal to all that our century, and cinema with it, stands for.[3] Over the dead bodies or dashed options of the past, it is as if modern desire is redeemed in part by the first stirrings of a cinematic dispensation. This is to say that, by a curious introversion of effect, the very fact of cinematic form, in collision with the historical material, outstrips content as its manifest(ational) destiny.

This is also to say something more specific—and to point to something more curious—than the generalized false consciousness of any mainstream film formula. By the logic of popular media escapism, any fetishizing of Victorian luxury on film, let alone any latent idealizing of the period's well-ordered hierarchies, must be matched by a distancing of the age's blinkered stability sufficient to return viewers to the present with equanimity. In this sense cinema's recent Victoriana does function like a kind of genre, suspending cultural contradictions (here mostly in attitudes toward rather than within the past) to permit a temporary reconciliation—not of characters or forces within the plot but of the audience's stance toward that plot's seductive spectacle. This much we can provisionally grant for now, before finding it confirmed by unexpected material detail. But my differing emphasis begins with precisely the lure of a comparable spectacle, including the specularized body, for the Victorians themselves—for the nineteenth-century subject, that is, both on film and in history. The premise is a simple one. We respond to Victorian photographic images with a kind of displaced identification. It is not so much that we see ourselves in the Victorians. Instead, we see them as they, for the first time in history, could see themselves. In scenes structured around the localized photographic moment, period films that visualize the broader historical moment of photography may in this way call up unsettling recognitions about human presence in representation. In film after film of the past two decades, these recognitions seem deliberately located on a continuum with those induced by the equally epoch-making fact that the late Victorians were also the first generation to see themselves in cinema's perpetual motion machine. When photography is found dropped into recess by screen Victoriana, its impact is seldom isolated for long from this media teleology. As represented within plot by everything from the daguerreotype to the stereograph, the mechanized forms of Victorian image culture are often asked by the films that recover their era, as most blatantly in *The Asphyx*, to press from within for just this cinematic eventuation. In such simultaneous acts of historical recovery and cinematic anticipation, a nostalgic patina may end up attaching to the rudiments of the motion-picture medium itself, the lost charm of photography's original wonder, rather than to the social world once captured by such images and now fictionalized by their sequential automation.

We can begin illustration with a single film's effort to situate such a photographic moment and its documentary charge as the foundation for its own historical material. Early in their collaboration, and with a self-conscious cinematic gesture all the more salient for the staunch classicism of their usual style, Ismail Merchant and James Ivory show us the suffragist collective in *The Bostonians* (1984) having a picture taken after an early rally, with the cinematic image freezing at the photographer's flash. As the fame of its spokeswoman, Verena Tarrant, continues to spread, we see its members pasting newspaper photos of her into a communal scrapbook. (From the real-life counterparts of such documentation, the costume drama has of course taken its own inspiration.) But when, in the film's last scene, Verena deserts the movement for love, and Olive Chancellor (Vanessa Redgrave) is forced to take the stage in her place, the double-pronged effect of her last audible line, " . . . and we *will* be heard," marks not only the will to voice within the Victorian women's movement but, in the future tense, its projection a century later into contemporary feminist activism. Image now italicizes dialogue. At this closing moment of the film, a freeze-frame on the assembly hall that doubles for our movie theater coincides with, even as it outlasts, the internal audience's mounting applause on the sound track—a fixed image recalling the newsprint clippings gathered earlier in the name of the cause. At the photographic basis of cinema, yes, is the impetus to stop time, frame by frame, in order to enter history in the form of record. Thematically, too, "the cause" is vindicated in its ocular effect. In brief, the abrupt filmic inflection, returning from within the cinematic by association with the photographic moment, has come to the aid of "the movement's" own longevity by way of imprinting its heroic icons.

Often, film Victoriana's photographic index is more directly eroticized. The pervasive sexual unease—whether through repression or hypocritical indulgence—that becomes the cinematic hallmark of Victorian self-deception encounters various ironic wrenchings of narrative pattern, of closure especially, that also take their revisionary toll on inherited plot formulas. Such a structural tension is found repeatedly discharged around the metatextual node—and frequent erotic disquiet—of certain photographic moments. These are moments that arrest film narrative with a glimpse into both the single-frame basis and the media history of its own image system—not just as a technology of projection but as a representation of the sexual body, whose availability to the camera is further eroticized by the very mode of automated, impersonal looking that permits it. Related to such photographic regress are other disturbances in the complex mimesis of cinematographic registration, we will find, that also open upon the technical basis of the medium. What results, under examination, is a complicated new stylistics of Victorian culture on film. At this stage, however, two films of typifying interest—for the psychosexual cast of their social representation—need retrieval mainly for their alternative models of the photographic emphasis per se in Victorian retrospect. They illustrate the photomechanical experimentation of the period on the one hand, our photographic access to that past itself on the other. In so doing, they sketch in advance the double perspective of this chapter.

SOMEWHERE OUT OF TIME

In the 1981 Karel Reisz adaptation of John Fowles's *The French Lieutenant's Woman* (1969), the added film within the film format is matched with a further level of reflection on the origins and nature of the film medium. This level consists of images that insinuate the photographic document either as epistemological touchstone (documentary imprint) or visual increment (sequential photogram) of the cumulative film track. At the same time, these pictures are the film's way of probing the Victorian roots of its own technology—and are more effective in passing than the whole film within the film structure. Visiting the apartment of the brain pathologist Dr. Grogan, the hero Smithson sees scrapbooks of Charcot-like photographic studies depicting patients in various stages of melancholia. Later, in Grogan's office, he sees rows of such pictures pinned to the walls—as well as the camera that has recorded them. Tainted with the sense of professionalized voyeurism and the coercive medicalization of the body, these images are clearly used to study the nuances of mentality in facial manifestation. Yet we also sense something more. The rank and file of such photographs, barely distinguishable from one another at the range of a middle-distance shot—or spread across a wall in serial fashion—are likely to evoke the contiguous frames of a potential film strip. Calling to mind the protocinematic studies by Eadweard Muybridge of the body in action, here different rather than identical bodies are ranged in differential sequence. They provide in this way a virtual analytic breakdown of the sustained mute eloquence of the cinematic close-up, let us say from Lillian Gish to Meryl Streep. What Eisenstein saw Griffith lifting from Dickens's eye for detail in the technique of the close-up, we may here find tracked even further back—behind Victorian narrative, as one of that literary system's underlying funds of figuration—to the link between photography and phrenology, where physiognomy is made semiotic.[4]

Photography has other ways of entering the visual treatment, if not the scene, of Victorian retrospection: tipping its hand as our most direct mode of access, even before cinema, to the visual memory of that past. If we wish to say that cinema builds on photography to perfect its own version of H. G. Wells's time machine, then a contemporary film that catapults Wells himself from the London of 1894, on the very eve of cinema's invention, into 1970s San Francisco also goes out of its way to secure that analogy between the productions of Victorian fantasy and its own apparatus. Chasing Jack the Ripper through history in *Time after Time* (Nicholas Meyer, 1979), Wells ends up crossing the threshold of the present in a museum display of the very time machine in which he arrives, surrounded by a retrospective exhibition—of his (yet unwritten) work—blazoned as "H. G. Wells, a Man before His Time." After the Ripper has been foiled in his scourge of the modern-day "singles scene" (with its feminist-sanctioned release of the female libido) and a triumphant Wells has escaped into the past with his erstwhile feminist mistress, who thereby surrenders some of her commitment to historical advance in order that the eventual great man should get his books written, we revert to a full-screen photograph of ambiguous provenance. The film, that is, locks tight its gaze (behind the end titles) on the enlarged photographic wall mural of Wells's London neighborhood (site of the opening murder scene of a prostitute going her rounds). It is a mural mounted as backdrop at the museum exhibition from which the socially atavistic couple has just fled in the time machine. All we are left with is the full-screen image's double and undecidable fixation. Is it a long-held shot of the photographic mural or, eventually, a freeze-frame? Does its graininess suggest merely the magnified print of an extant Victorian neighborhood or an actual Victorian photograph? All we are left with, in other words, is the scene of history itself in a two-dimensional media manifestation. The film is indeed back where it started: representing the environs of male industry and advancement, all women safely behind doors and out of sight—except, at any moment, for one of those marginalized and doomed figures who walk the very street we stare at, premonitions of a more programmatic vulnerability (incautious feminism) yet to come. As with the last frame of *The Bostonians*, photographic arrest abets the cinematic rendering of history as a staged evolution, whether progressive or regressive.

Compared with the comically finessed capitulation of the modern feminist heroine in *Time after Time*, the closural conservatism of *Somewhere in Time* (Jeannot Szwarc, 1980) seems almost disguised. To our purpose here, its Edwardian plot also conflates the photographic recovery of a documented past world with an explicit metacinematic icon: the manifesting beam of cinematic projection. Christopher Reeve is a collegiate playwright who is visited upon graduation in the 1970s by an old woman who gives him an antique watch and says spookily, "Come back to me." Back indeed. A few years later—his plays a success, but his girlfriend having left him (overdetermined sign of the transience of modern sexual relations)—he drives off toward his old campus and detours for a stay at the nearby Grand Hotel, to which we happen to have seen the mysterious sibyl return after her visitation. There he stumbles upon a photograph of a beautiful and once renowned actress (Jane Seymour) taken in 1912 before a performance at the hotel theater. Approaching the framed photo, at first as if it were a projected film image in a diagonal beam of light (fig. 261), he soon stands close before it at every opportunity, the camera eventually catching his own reflection in its glass (fig. 262). Mesmerized from the start, he has already begun searching for clues to his inexpressible sense of déjà vu, ultimately finding his own signature on the hotel reg-

ister for the very days in 1912 that coincided with her stay.[5] He soon clears
his room of all contemporary artifacts
in order, by self-hypnotic force of will,
to burrow back in time. Once fled—that
is, projected—into the past by means of
this ocular cleansing, he of course
meets the actress, charms and courts
her, and discovers that what had originally riveted him to her photograph
was the memory not only of its repre-

261   262

sented subject but also of being present at the moment of its
imprint. This is to say that his returned gaze (fig. 263) produced the very expression on her face. And it is an expression
seen proleptically by him at this moment of willed recovery
as if it were already faintly encircled by the oval of the
framed portrait (fig. 264). Accompanying this effect, a
shot/reverse shot pattern of exchanged looks serves further
to narrativize and ground the present-day optical contin-
gency that has earlier merged, by reflection, her glassed
image and his superimposed look. As emphasized by this
blending of temporal "frames," she has all along been looking through time not just at him but at his own erotic past.
His contemporary voyeurism is thus justified in retrospect
along with its faint narcissistic overlay.

263

Now, after one night of love, he is flung back into the
present by the discovery, in the pockets of his rented Victorian costume, of coins dating from the 1970s. Time has
called in its debt. Triggered like so much other contemporary media eroticism by the fetishizing of a photographically based image, the closure of *Somewhere in Time* also involves both a gender inversion and a genre slippage. The
film's sentimental and conservative appeal attaches not simply, that is, to the fantasy of an inextinguishably single-
minded male passion in an era of licensed promiscuity. That
passion must in turn be feminized. Back in the present, the
hero is stricken with an unappeasable erotic nostalgia for the
Edwardian love of his life, whom he rejoins in a final transcendental vision that wallows in the contemporary cinema's special effects. In his all-consuming grief, the obsessive hero resembles nothing so much as the hysterical
heroine of earlier Victorian stereotypes. Pining away and fi-

264

nally starving in an anorectic *Liebestod*, he embraces death less like Brontë's
Heathcliff than like Dumas Fils's Camille.[6] And having been torn from his fixation on the mechanically reproduced body, itself fixated in the glance of desire

across time, his own image disappears into the technical flair—and flare-up—of a sci fi fantasy. The heritage film collapses into its own antithesis, that is, at the point of the body's ecstatic disintegration.

At the opposite extreme from this adult (if also infantalizing) sexual obsession—but on an underlying cultural continuum regarding the circulating power of the eroticized image—is the kind of inescapable sexual pedagogy associated with photographs in the adolescent imagination. Such sexual naïveté is, in its own right of course, often a figurative stand-in for Victorian society's wholesale relation to its own maturation forward toward modernity. Hence the use of a "children's film" in helping to situate the photographic moment of Victorian heritage films. Not yet released by the time of Salman Rushdie's critique of Raj nostalgia both on film and in such TV epics as *The Jewel in the Crown,* with their soft spot for the imperialist mission in India, the Agnieszka Holland version of Frances Hodgson Burnett's 1911 adolescent classic *The Secret Garden* (1993) would have been vulnerable to the same critique.[7] Holland's film not only highlights the imperialist aspect of the text but also inserts into the story (as did Harold Pinter's screenplay for *The French Lieutenant's Woman*) a photographic subtext not found in the novel, one that directly sexualizes the frustrated yearnings of the characters in a manner that both "updates" the book and complicates the narrative's sense of a lost past, now as much erotic as colonial.

On first returning to England after her parents' death in India, the heroine, Mary, comes upon a gilt-framed photograph of her mother on a garden swing with her own double, the long-dead twin sister (fig. 265). Later Mary and her cousin discover a stash of pictures of his dead mother (her aunt) together with a younger version of his father in various smiling embraces on the same swing (fig. 266), an erotic sport that momentarily discomfits the children as they shuffle through the photos on Colin's bed. Since the viewer is aware by now that the boy's mother died in a fall from that very swing, the camera's ability to fix the swing's potentially fatal arc in position lends an eerie (death-defying) privilege to these moments frozen in time. Further, in immediate conjunction with the episode of embarrassed recognition before the photographs, the one later moment when sexuality intrudes explicitly into the children's secret garden is when, retrieving the camera that has (presumably) taken the original pictures, Colin tries photographing Mary and the fieldhand Dickon on that fateful swing. He seems half hoping to bring the parental photograph back to life as the outward symbol of his own regeneration. Almost unconsciously, though, the recorded boy and girl begin tentatively trying on some of the intimate and giddy poses of the photographically embalmed couple (fig. 267). Behind the camera, but looking up suddenly from the lens, Colin is flustered, unnerved (fig. 268)—and not just by the cross-class liaison. Some photographs dare not be restaged, must know their place, their time. Beyond its general role in the aesthetics of retrospect—as the textual regress of an already archived (or visually simulated) past—the primal scene of photography figures a repressed that dares not return.

And beyond this, such an exacerbated moment of libidinal ricochet underscores

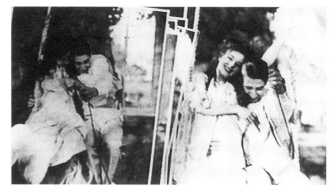

265

266

a yet more general implication of photography, one that aligns its visible technology in film narrative with the sexual ethos so often under examination in recent Victorian and Edwardian screen plots. Independent of immediate subject matter, there is a quasi-erotic tension in the camera's very manner of regard. This is a tension that narrative film inherits whenever it claims kin for its enactments with the documentary moment of the photographic image. That the photographed subject can never return any look subsequent to the camera's own recording gaze lends a voyeuristic taint to all later inspection. Film narratives that embed a photograph— or a photographic session, either of taking pictures or of looking at them—thus often instill this troublesome reminder. And a case like *Somewhere in Time* only further narrativizes, without overturning, such a paradigm of the gaze. Its plot revolves around a photographic fixation that seems entirely voyeuristic, almost a masturbatory obsession, until the image in question turns out, against all odds, to be the document of a once reciprocal erotic look. And yet what is this in turn but the illusion come true of any photograph, its lure and its disquiet both: the way it makes you feel you were there?

Where the Edwardian sequence of *Somewhere in Time* is directly precipitated by a photograph, however, the interpolation of photography into the film version of *The Secret Garden* operates at a level redundant to plot—even as it seems to saturate the familiar visual ethos of this and other heritage films from the period. The study and subsequent execution of a photographic record in this one plot remind us that what might be characterized as the photographic effect, rather than the photographic moment, is present even in those recent cinematic representations of the Victorian period where neither the labor nor the products of photography are given prominence. Time and again, in these films of a lost time made available again, the contemporaneous ma-

267, 268

chine of record operates as the structuring absence not so much of plot as of the viewer's own fictionally removed, and thereby doubly fetishized, access to the past. It is because we owe to early photography our confidence in the general look of the screen fiction that allusions to it can take the form, as suggested, of a nostalgia for the medium rather than the milieu.

The aristocratic context of *The Secret Garden,* however, helps bring out the other, sociological, side of this point. In associating the nineteenth-century past with the early days of photography, one usually associates such photography in turn either with the upper-class luxury of the studio portrait or at least with the pastimes of bourgeois family leisure. One links the commercial aspect of the new technology, in other words, to certain class-based exclusions of visual material: unseen social strata outside the purview of the new representation. This is of course directly comparable to that circumscription of narrative matter within which the comfort zone of domestic melodrama does its generic work.

More, too, is broadly implied by Holland's film. Given the historical tunnel vision of contemporary filmmaking, *The Secret Garden* recommends itself as a screen topic in part because its bildungsroman of maturation, once given a sexual spin, serves yet again to dramatize the gestation of a modern and expressive self-confidence out of the anemic depletion of our forebears. In this typical rearview mirror of cinematic Victoriana, we watch the period struggling to live up to its—primarily sexual—destiny in becoming our own. This is why films so often gravitate either toward the cusp moment of Edwardian turmoil on the brink of the modern (*Room with a View, Howards End*) or toward a kind of layered vision that structures into plot one or more intermediate plateaus of already dramatized retrospect (*Orlando, The Age of Innocence*). Edith Wharton, writing in 1920 about two strata of her own culture's prehistory, the early 1870s and the late 1890s, provides in *The Age of Innocence* a perfect example of the latter, and Virginia Woolf offers what we can only call its mythic parody in *Orlando.* The interest of most contemporary films set in the nineteenth century or its immediate aftermath does indeed rest in part with the psychosexual mapping that goes on between the former "period" (bounded) and our own "time" (in process). Victorians are repeatedly redefined on-screen, in a word, as the premoderns, with all the erotic inferences—and narrative mandates—this definition involves, including the supplemental infiltration of message by its medium. For between them and us, in both senses, stands cinema.

LAST STAGE OF INNOCENCE

Even historical narratives that do not directly invoke the photographic prehistory of cinema may manipulate the cinematic—and its filmic basis—into a kind of reflexive discourse on the limits of visual representation. In *Howards End* (James Ivory, 1992), a momentary specular crisis is thematized into moral symptom as follows. Confronting Henry after learning of his adulterous past, Margaret insists on her forgiveness across three short segments of dialogue in which Henry's guilty recoil—marked by Anthony Hopkins's gesture of hiding behind his hands—seems transferred to the cinematic mechanism itself. The screen literally blacks out for seconds at a time, leaving the two characters their intermittent privacy by seeming to close the camera's prying eye. When we return from these raw blanks to the hesitant conversation, it is not clear how much time has passed—split seconds or whole unendurable minutes. The effect is as searing as it is muted. The ordinary technology of photogrammatic difference, aided by the regular pass of the shutter, is stretched out into a radical disjunction bridged only by spectatorial will. Continuity regularly (but effortlessly) depends on gaps and their overleaping—just as does spiritual renovation in E. M. Forster. It does so, here, more blatantly than in any other scene of the film, which otherwise forgoes the novel's famous opening motto, "Only connect . . . " Editing alone seems to be giving the motto now in a visual emblem: a stylistic quirk that, doing more than figure the need for intuitive connection within plot, tracks that imperative—in something of a modernist rather than Edwardian mode—to the basis of the medium itself.[8]

Unlike *Howards End,* the self-conscious technical mannerisms of *The Age of Innocence* (Martin Scorsese, 1993) are steeped in the fin-de-siècle culture of the image and its photographic accoutrements. In the film's straitjacketed marital context, even photography seems leveled from indexical representation to one among a series of empty signifiers, as expressed in general by a voice-over borrowed directly from the novel: "In reality they all lived in a kind of hieroglyphic world, where the real thing was never said or done or even thought, but only represented by a set of arbitrary signs."[9] This is highlighted in a transition from reading to photomechanical sighting. There is an ineluctable swift fade, and spiritual fade-out, from Archer crushing a note addressed from May to Countess Ellen about the upcoming wedding to an inverted full-screen image of May in her bridal gown (figs. 269-71). Across this disjunctive transition, the supplanting of one self by the other suggests—along the associational links of our specular unconscious—that all Archer's dreams have been turned upside down by the new triangulation figured for a moment here in its abstract geometric instability. So that it will not remain abstract for long, however, a reverse dolly shot immediately discovers that this skewed image of May is registered in the viewfinder of a camera at the moment of recording (fig. 272), an image then "corrected," via a subsequent dissolve, when appearing right side up as a mere reflection in the lens of that camera when seen from the outside (fig. 273). In the process, we can also recognize that it is the director himself taking the wedding pictures in this scene (fig. 274): at once a cameo miniature and a photochemical *mise en abyme* of the film's double origin in ironic authorship and bravura visual technology.

The point is next pushed to—and beyond—a far limit of visual credibility when, just after spying the photographer, the film cuts to a reverse shot of the posed bride in the middle distance, seen between black curtains rapidly parting in the foreground (fig. 275). There is no way to interpret these curtains but to think we have taken up a POV behind the draped camera box, and yet, as the curtains are somehow pulled open (and revealed to have no diegetic status or justification), we see the photographer and his camera stationed behind them to the left of the screen. The curtaining we took to assist in the management of photochemical reg-

269, 270, 271, 272, 273, 274, 275

istration within the scene of a photographic session can now only be read as figuring instead the theatricalized cinematic site as a whole. It does so through a mobile reframing that alternately blocks and discloses mere images, keepsakes, but in this case images already boxed in by ironic retrospect.

In the immediate manifestation of this irony, the discrepancy between the film's saturated eroticism of the gaze and the clinical chill of this bridal portrait session is as striking as the tricky correspondences between photographic and cinematic media. A similar tonal discrepancy is introduced by the scene of nuptial photography in *The Piano* (Jane Campion, 1993). In that earlier film, the memorial photo is as trumped up as the marriage itself. Under the leaking roof of a dilapidated lean-to, in order to maximize the day's

276

277

dreary light, a traveling photographer snaps a picture of the New Zealand farmer and his bought bride in the false front of a formal wedding, the heroine draped with a cutaway mock-up of a lace gown. "If you can't have a ceremony," says one of the matrons on hand, "at least you'll have a photograph." Here too the photograph is another mode of ritual rather than another modality of desire. As it has certainly seemed in its final appearance in *The Age of Innocence*: the posthumous image of the now dead wife as Diana the "archer" (a visual emblem of the couple's semantically as well as socially overdetermined match).[10] Viewed on his desk in the two-decade voice-over transition through the elapsing years of Archer's life until the coda, this memorial photo (fig. 276) embalms an image of a lost past, past which the camera slowly pans. Included in the slow sweep of this photopan is, next to the framed picture, a marble sculpture of May's hands, which we have briefly seen her model in a Paris studio on the couple's honeymoon: a related index of the body's former presence, another variety of life mask. Caught together by the camera are both the photographic and the plastic "mold" in a mortuary trope used before in Truffaut's *The Green Room* to erase the gap between imaging and embalming in the hero's morbid shrine to his dead wife (fig. 277). In *The Age of Innocence*—as with the earlier wedding picture, if only for a split second—we may even remember having seen this now posthumous photo being taken during the scene at the Newport Archery Club just after the honeymoon, staged by an unseen photographer (Scorsese again?) behind a camera on the lawn.

CINEMA'S TELEPATHY MACHINE

The question remains how the amber-washed glamour of recent dressy retrospects is put into cultural play against the technophilia (despite explicit cyberphobia) of the sci fi action pictures that have shared the cineplexes with them. One period film whose fin-de-siècle evocations happen to coincide with the latest word in electronic special effects invites extended attention with just this question in mind. In the process, it will also bind more tightly the photographic insert with the photogrammatic moment of filmic self-exposure as twin registers of the cinematic basis—and heritage—of screen Victoriana. Most popular of all recent period

278

279

280

adaptations, this gothic amalgam is the disingenuously titled *Bram Stoker's Dracula* (Francis Ford Coppola, 1992). At the narrative's instant disposal are bodies as the photographic mechanism first knew them versus bodies as image technology can now willfully construe them. In the age of the digitalized generation rather than the chemical registration of images, there is, as we saw in the previous chapter, a growing nostalgia for the real itself—and for the way the real once gave itself up to film, first to photography and then to cinema. In scene after scene of Coppola's film, this nostalgia is figured by the fetishizing of a photographic portrait and its extravagantly engrained associations with montage itself, the cinematic coming thing.

A flamboyant photographic moment occurs early on, interpolated into Stoker's narrative in preparation for associated cinematic disclosures to come. In the plot's first change of international scene, the very rudiments of parallel editing are spelled out, under the spell of vampiric intervention, as a matter of photographic interchange—and its libidinal investments. As Harker speeds by train to Transylvania, his glimpse of his own features reflected upon the frame of Mina's portrait, which he clutches (fig. 278), dissolves to her yearning look at a photograph of those very features in her own keeping back home (fig. 279). The whole (disjoint) time, each alternating image—of body and its distant duplication—is under surveillance by the omniscient eyes of the Count superimposed over the locomotive vehiculation of his own plot design (fig. 280). That Dracula claims not only oversight but tacit control of the very motion of the plot's first change of scene is only the earliest of his links to the industrial mechanization—and white magic—of screen narrative. Once the photographic portrait of the heroine has been inserted into Coppola's story (in the novel, Harker is carrying only Kodak views of the English real estate in which the Count is interested), the image takes on a life—or, better, a death—of its own. Assuming that he has somehow lost the photograph, Harker suddenly spies it on Dracula's desk at their first meeting. Again, as in *Some-*

281

where in Time, a single framed image recalls for the protagonist a past erotic scenario sprung from the eerie resemblance between Mina and his lost medieval bride (a detail new to the film version). This is only the beginning, for the intrusion of the photo seems to open a vein of further inference. Almost at once the image is also overlain, and seemingly invaded, by signs not only of former passion but of present depravity in the Count's hinted bloodlust. In the throes of candlelit recognition, Dracula nervously spills ink on the glass of the frame. The medium of textual inscription thus partially defaces the imprint of light in such a way that, with the ink bleeding across the neck of the black-and-white photo (fig. 281), this blot—this shadow of blight—becomes not only the index of Dracula's recalled desire for Mina's precursor but the proleptic moving image of his subsequent bloodletting.

We are still at an early phase of the interpolated photograph's weird career in Coppola's plot. On the opening train journey, as we have seen, it has provided the backdrop for the hero's own framed self-imaging. Now it seems animated by the very death at work in its delectation. "Oh, I see you found Mina. I thought I had lost her," Harker has blurted out when spying the Count with the stolen image. The shorthand personification of the icon is reciprocated by its virtual animation under the Count's gaze. What would typically have been a "negative regress" marked by a single fixed image, coveted and portable, especially an image stamped into fixity within a film of such manic kinesis, will get perversely dynamized instead. Mina's photograph, we find, is eventually to be siphoned off by the photogrammatic track, stolen away by laboratory process itself. As prelude to the closing chase sequence, that is, Mina's framed picture is returned only after Dracula has vampirized the woman herself and brought her partially under his spell. The image comes back into plot both as photographic icon and as (now cinematic) marker of the Count's demonic power to commute between image and flesh. Turning up in the smoldering rubble of Dracula's mansion, the photograph is lit this time not by a single candle but by the pyre of his British base of operations. Here,

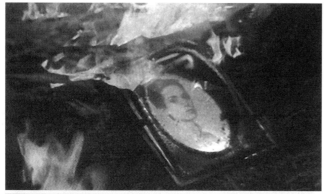

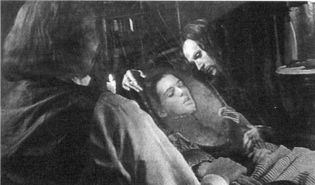

282, 283, 284

through a graduated series of edited spatial elisions, the bond between photochemical preservation across time and space and the telepathic sensorium of the Count is made manifest. The scene change fades over in layered stages from Mina's abandoned image (no longer necessary given the vampire's mesmeric access to his victim) to her interrogation in the flesh by Van Helsing (where he impresses her into service for the experiment in hypnotic double cross, so that she becomes a psychic antenna to trace the retreat of the Count). The con-catenated dissolves of this lingering transition (figs. 282-84) display the vampire looming spectrally now over Mina's mere image, now over her person. Narrative momentum, as if presided over by the spirit of the vampire himself, is thus suspended in an ontological limbo of converging absences—image and phantom, image as phantom—until it resolves it-self into a domestic interior where the forces of the here and now, visually restabilized, can regroup against the vampire's spatiotemporal promiscuity. Yet by insinuating itself into the seams and folds of narrative transition per se, supernatural agency has also lent its authority to the filmic mechanism.

The effect of this collusion between form and content spreads wide. That overdetermined segue becomes in itself a consequential metaphor for a preternatural shuttling across time and space. Between the apprehended "likeness" of Harker's fiancée, with its startling likeness to Dracula's lost love, and the final enlisting of Mina's own services in track-ing down the Count by hypnosis—between these poles there lurks suspended, I want to say, the ghostly image of vampiric or preternatural agency as the very medium of visual mani-festation and scenic exchange in Coppola's narrative. We now appreciate in retrospect the full force of Dracula's first appearance, by apparition, in the film—though not yet in the plot. For his huge eyes were superimposed, as mentioned, over the train coach in which Mina's photograph was ini-tially seen—seen by a character, glimpsed by the viewer, and spied upon by the title figure: the figure of ubiquity (omniscience) itself (fig. 280 again). Corroborated locally by the moments in which the camera's POV is marked by skid editing to coincide with the vampire's-eye view in his own pre-ternatural locomotion, as well as by the scenes in which the film looks away from his carnage by cutting, as it were, on the cut, what I want to get at is this more suf-fused and amorphous sense in which the vampire *is* cinema.

The point has already been dwelled on well in advance of the late lap dissolve, discussed above, by which Dracula seems to have invaded the interstices of filmic mediation itself. Before this final return of Mina's photograph, the elusive bonds between desire and visual imprint have surfaced, displaced onto public spectacle, just after Count Dracula first sees her in London. The Count in fact accosts her by telepathy across a crowded London square, issuing from a distance his inaudible command, "See me—see me now." We have already begun hearing in the background a hawker's voice calling out in a simultaneous imperative, "See the amazing cinematograph, the wonder of the modern world, the greatest attraction of the century." What exactly motivates the twinned calls to attention? What links Dracula's advent in London to such an updated sideshow attraction? Details accumulate toward a complicated response. For one thing, just as the image in this sequence is suddenly bled (I choose the metaphor of drainage advisedly) of some of its high-tech color, it appears differently cranked from the rest of the film also, evoking the visual flutter of silent projection as well as the clicking whir of sprocket noise.

The subsequent scene inside the cinematographic arcade extends such media-historical suggestions. It is a scene that has already spawned what appears to be a teasing homage in more recent Hollywood filmmaking: a parallel rerouting of vampiric desire through a metacinematic detour that sums up the diverted energies that bring us to the cinema in the first place. Departing from the Anne Rice novel and taking Coppola's film as intertext, Neil Jordan's film version of *Interview with the Vampire* (1994) intrudes a bridge passage from the Victorian to the modern period by sequestering its vampire hero, Louis, in a New Orleans movie theater. There, through technological mediation (which is to say through artificial preservation and reanimation), the undead himself can look without flinching upon the recorded glow of innumerable sunrises, the first he has seen in a century. What flashes before him as he waits out the decades of modernity down to his roaming the streets of a present blood-sick San Francisco is, as it happens, a telescoped film history running from F. W. Murnau's 1927 *Sunrise* (followed by a brief clip of Murnau's own 1922 *Nosferatu*) through *Gone with the Wind* (1939) to the sun rising over the entire globe in *Superman* (1978). Accompanied by Louis's voice-over about the coming and gradual perfection of color on film, the sequence ends with him exiting a theater from under a marquee advertising the 1988 *Tequila Sunrise*. What transpires in this sequence, in other words, is a montage of filmic visibility itself as manifested, in dawn after dawn, by the spreading beam of its own founding light source. But the episode is more pointedly reflexive than this might suggest. No less than we do in the film audience (reconfigured by this *mise en abyme*), the protagonist makes psychotherapeutic use of cinema precisely by indulging his desire for the very sights from which in reality he would have to avert his gaze.

Coppola's version of vampire as film fan presses a different point. After entering the phantasmagoric space of that early cinema arcade, the Count makes his first balked advances against the exposed throat of Mina while milling patrons gawk at double-screen images of a cinematic sex farce (fig. 285), including the ultimate media attraction of a bare-breasted woman. This carnivalesque revel of spectatorship turns to riot when the Count's alter ego in the wolf is let loose in the exhibition space, to be caught in frame with the Count in front of an image recalling the most famous—because most shocking—of cinema's debut effects, the

285

286

287

288

notorious footage of a train rushing straight toward the audience (fig. 286). Not only do we have compressed within this scene the pioneering efforts of cinema's inchoate institution as shock attraction (its violence and its sex together upstaged by the Count and his lupine double), but we detect its prehistory as well—in the orchestrated mechanics of a silhouette show. Within this chaotic pleasure palace of visual simulation, that is, we catch a glimpse of a miniature theater where a set of warring puppets (fig. 287)—closely resembling the film's early, artificially silhouetted battle scenes of the Count's medieval debacle (fig. 288)—cast their shadows on a screenlike sheet. The sophisticated audio and visual montage of contemporary film technique is referred back to a pretechnological diversion. Then, too, beyond this embedded media history there is the inferred relation of film itself to history, to time passing and past—to generation and regeneration. Though the new illusionist wonder of the cinematograph strikes Mina as rather tawdry and trivial, it immediately fascinates Dracula—and for reasons not far to seek. "Astounding," he says in watching past action renewed from second to second on the multiple screens, "There are no limits to science!" For him the scene begins to compete with the supernatural—an anything but disinterested reaction from the man who would live forever.

But we know better by now than to accept this as the whole affiliation between cinema and vampirism. The latest evidence of a more tainted kinship comes in the transitional scene that offers a contrapuntal bridge from the Count's sighting Mina on the London street to their ensuing encounter in the darkened film emporium. Inserted between is what can only be called a metatextual diagnosis of Mina's friend, Lucy Westenra, recent victim of the *nosferatu*. Dollying in on the twin puncture wounds of Dracula's canine teeth visible on her throat (fig. 289), the screen image then dissolves (fur replacing lace) to the eyes of the wolf (fig. 290) roaming in and out of visibility within the subsequent panic at the cinematographic arcade. The visual pun on the "eye-teeth" of vampiric incision (as well as on the scene's meta-morphic rather than abrupt form of "cutting") thus distills an entire thematic to a single spliced instance of visual condensation and displacement (as in Christian Metz's rethinking of film syntax in terms of a psychodynamic succession in the cinematic chain).[11] The plot's governing nexus of surveillance and penetration materializes in transit as the pervasive scopic regime against which the comforting two-dimensionality of the cinematograph, and its reduced essence in the puppet theater's cast of shadows, is inserted as welcome relief, yes, but also as extended metaphor. In an aggravated microcosm, that is, of the medium at large (to be matched later by the Count's rather than the wolf's intrusion into the narrative infrastructure of montage [see again figs. 282-84]), we find the self-devouring file of photogrammatic signifiers. Performing their transitional dissolve (and human dissolution) from pierced flesh to piercing eyes, they have already foregrounded the mutable cinematic flow as a vampiric defilement. Even more than with the last demonic image of Kurtz in his torn Cambodian photograph, hovering between

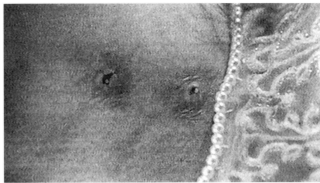
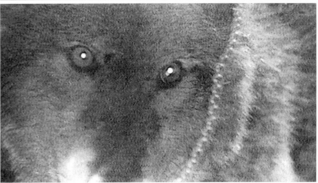

289, 290

frames as the motor of their plotted advance and the specter of their destination in Coppola's *Apocalypse Now* (fig. 74), the insatiably mutable force of the Dracula, death within life, is configured before us as the secret demon and genie, the emblematic technical genius, of an inescapably vampiric medium. This is a cinema vampiric not only in the parasitism of its empathies but in the quick-change artistry of its edited teleportations.[12] Here too is a title figure who embodies, in his own recycled person, the cinematic phantom of the past made present—and embodies it twice over, both as film character and as *nosferatu*. On film, all heroes *are* the undead.

Here is where—in yet another contemporary (modernist) turn of Victorian material—the modality of narrative form is once more the structural fulfillment of its own content: where the spectatorial apparatus of cinema is a function of film plot rather than just the other way around. This is to say that if Mina, in the normalized Victorian role of Mrs. Jonathan Harker in later life, were still to find herself craving the preternatural intensities of desire once ignited in her, about 1897, by the *nosferatu*'s obsession, she would be licensed to sate such desires—her passion for erotic visitations—only through encounters with deathless but entirely two-dimensional specters. Having been forced to decapitate her demon lover, to exorcise the demon of *that* kind of eroticism, she might well find herself needing recourse to the new century's reigning form of paid pleasure, learning after all to be fascinated by movies as Dracula was—movies like *Dracula*. If so, she would fulfill a decisive post-Victorian legacy—channeled in advance through the cinematographic moment of this one period plot—by numbering herself among the first-generation clientele of a modern culture machine, submitting herself willingly to the vicarious erotics of industrial spectacle. "See me—see me now."

I would like to take such convolutions of visual technology—where characters seek their destiny in something like the material conditions of their own medium and its spectation—as an overarching fable. To the larger question about how contemporary culture can flirt with the elegiac mood in heritage films even while celebrating the supremacy of the present, Coppola answers at the level of the cinematic machination itself. Cinema promotes its own representational agenda by recovering the naive raptures that greeted its arrival on the scene of mere photography. And what we have been noting as this laminated perspective on cinema and its photographically based (pre)history applies here, as elsewhere, to the aesthetic and social as well as the technological level of the narrative. This is because the erotic plotlines of Coppola's film, and the Victorian domestic ideology they derive from (even in deviating from the novel), coalesce around the necromantic shadows and figurative vampirism—living perpetually off the spectator's fascination—of the primitive screen image itself. The maneuver is typical. In film after film over the past decade or so, we look back by seeing how. The technological form of retrospect infiltrates its content, just as a contemporary social or psychosexual vantage invades and revises the past. The modernist "make it new" has become a postmodernist revamping: the resuscitating of history in an image of the present—and of the present's own image systems. To borrow a term from the photochemical medium itself, this is the true double exposure of Victorian culture in contemporary film. This is, in other words, how cinema's telepathy machine puts us into communication with the undead across the disjunctive spaces and disparate cognitive zones of its own privileged machination.

HISTORIES OF THE IMAGE IN THE IMAGE OF HISTORY

Well before *Bram Stoker's Dracula*, another ambitious Victorian gothic (or biopic) closed by summing up the mortal charge of photography's *mise en abyme* in the system of cinema's telepathic presencing: an audiovisual system that projects consciousness into spaces where we are not present. In David Lynch's 1980 *The Elephant Man*, in what amounts to a more explicitly Oedipal recasting of the trope from *Somewhere in Time,* the deformed title character dies alone, yearning for his dead mother, amid the cinematic intervention of a transcendental light show following his last look at the photograph of the actress who has become his patroness and eroticized maternal substitute—as if he were looking back into the recesses of his deviant origination. All modes of absentation collaborate in this moment of compound loss. A last celluloid image of a man dying away in the represented Victorian past—and yet passing away before our eyes only in the mode of all images on-screen—is placed over against a photograph lifted out of time to begin with, an index of the already gone past. Technological history overtakes historical recreation, that is, as the always undead status of the cinematic character rejoins his own origins not so much in the image of sensuous maternal affection as in the illusory body of imprint itself.

But technological history, we must remember, is easier to mention knowingly than to summarize, even in regard to the evolution within print media of photography into motion pictures. As we saw early on, this very notion of cinematic genealogy is currently in international dispute. Because this chapter will continue to find such technological parameters tacitly inscribed, both as historical telos and as narrative impetus, within films of Victorian retrospect even in the years since *Dracula*, it needs to reenter just this dispute. Despite the screen's temporary flight from the premodern technology of Victorian image culture into the prephotographic drawing rooms of Jane Austen—for *Sense and Sensibility* (Ang Lee, 1995), *Persuasion* (Roger Mitchell, 1995), and *Emma* (Douglas McGrath, 1996)—production has returned to the latter end of the nineteenth century with a trio of far more tortuous literary adaptations, of James, Hardy, and Conrad, that each pivot—or slam shut—on what comes to seem a knowing technological anachronism: a modernist filmic device imposed not upon the era of precinematic representation, exactly, but upon the usual zero-degree cinematography of heritage film style. Given such stress (and stress points) in these later screen adaptations, this chapter's persisting question arises once more. To what effect is the photographic moment of Victorian culture plotted out by a given screen narrative—and I do mean *out*, right to the borders of the screen frame, warping the image plane with those marks of disclosed filmic mediation characteristic of the second modernist turn?

When I say modernist here, I refer again to cross-fertilized developments of the 1960s through the early 1970s in American and European film production. But there is, of course, also a modernism, and a modernity, that precedes and conditions the institution of cinema altogether. And this industrial and urban modernity develops a visual culture in which (recalling Crary and Aumont) the photograph's place is by no means primary, even en route to cinema's industrial automation of the gaze. We would need to take warning, not just heed, if this were a book whose claims for the photographic wellsprings—and mainsprings—of cinema were detached from film's own demonstrations of the photogrammatic presence *within* cinema. Still, why should so many films, even heritage films having nothing do on the face of it with their own technological lineage as cinematic artifacts, link their own materialization to the presence of photography within the diegesis? Why attempt this if photography has in fact less to do with the direct lineage of cinema than we have previously been comfortable in assuming under the sign of a narrow technological rather than broader cultural and psychophysiological account? Maybe a material more than a historical argument is being insinuated. Think back to chapter 1 and to that most masterly of all nineteenth-century period pieces, *Letter from an Unknown Woman.* There train temporality and panoramic perception, as well as ghostly projections ultimately indebted to the mirror tricks of the diorama (I am recalling here the final superimposition of the dead heroine), connive to evince the manifold optic intertexts, if you will, of cinema's historical hybrid. Yet in a central scene they are all related—I want to say

all related back—to photography in its mortuary associations with the lifeless finality of graphic representation per se, in images and written inscription both.

To be sure, a film like this, this and others, *could* be wrong about the material
priority it accords to photography. Is it? Are they? I think not. One misplaced complaint about my whole line of argument could well crystallize around the retinal
frenzy of *Dracula*'s postmodern phantasmagoria, not only the hectic multimedia
emporium within it but the touted commercial dazzle (and computer-edited enhancements) of the film itself. Given that cinema's evolution from photography is
neither monolithic nor even a predominant line of descent in terms of the spectatorial position of the modern ocular subject, why should the photograph offer
unique abyssal leverage in any specific film, especially a vertiginous pastiche like
Dracula? One does not need to misrepresent a given cinematic experience to get
at this aspect of its constitution. With *Dracula* we are indeed far removed from
those heritage films that may have a tacit stake in their medium's historical out-
growth from the photographic print—as a way of naturalizing the fabrication of
their montage, elevating it to transparent pseudodocument rather than mechanical construct. For isn't the whole point of *Dracula*'s photographic inflection that
the objectified fixed image of the absent Mina is an image tossed into deliberate
contrast to the panoptic and invasive, the polymorphous and self-resuscitating nature of a racy postmodern cinema not only vampiric but mediumistic through and
through? Such a cinema can only be a technology of preternatural vantage and inhabitation, subjective to the point of nightmare, rather than a moving photograph
of the objective world.

It should be apparent that we need another way to appreciate the constititive
force of the photographic moment on film. Here it is essential to reiterate that the
difference between still photographs and even the most manic, fractured montage
has already been synthesized in advance by the photogrammatic differential of the
strip itself. Once this is acknowledged, a sense of film's true relation to a contributory (rather than exclusive) photographic origin can survive any number of conflicting revisionist claims about paradigm shifts in the expectations of the modern
beholder, survive and engage them, simply by passing through the concept of negative regress. This seems to me particularly well evinced in the films that make for
the recent resurgence of screen Victoriana. Though sometimes incorporating the
framed photographic portrait inlaid into the *mise en scène*, these are films, sur-
prisingly, in which the photographic—become photogrammatic—moment is
more often elicited by indirection in the reflexive recoil of the freeze-frame.

And in the least predictable places. Recalling Jonathan Crary's stress on the
stereographic break from stable organic sighting, as it leads to the dissociated cinematic gaze, one gets a curious vantage on this technological "heritage" from the
IMAX 3-D production *Across the Sea of Time* (Stephen Low, 1995). The plot concerns a contemporary Russian immigrant boy retracing the Manhattan footsteps of
his dead ancestor through stereocard photographs shipped a century before to the
family in Europe. The film's textual surface (become eerie depth) enfolds impecca-
ble blowups of original stereographic plates as the prompting of its plot and the prehistory of its own presentation, interlarding them in full-screen recess in the way

traditional film may deposit, for instance, if plot permits, the Victorian daguerreo-type. Going further, the narrative closes upon a present-day freeze-frame of the re-united family on the West Village stoop. The shot is caught on the photographer's snap in an implausible 3-D update of cinematic cliché: the stop-action photo finish, with the whole image plane now having become a posthumous high-tech relic of itself—willed to posterity by analogy with the film's own "found" images.

My continuing sense is that any advanced optical science of narrative repre-sentation is likely to embed its technical predecessor, if at all, in just this way: as checkpoint, outdistanced benchmark, and reductive *mise en abyme*. But the cor-relations called out thereby are not always the obvious ones—or, let us say, not al-ways as reductive as they may seem (the seed medium entirely outdone and for-gotten, on strictly technical grounds, by its own evolution). In this respect, the empowering nostalgia of a glimpsed ancestral past in *Across the Sea of Time* can be contrasted with the one other, and brief, allusion to popular stereography in re-cent film Victoriana. In the shop of "shady wares" run by Verloc in *Joseph Con-rad's "The Secret Agent"* (Christopher Hampton, 1996), a narrative set in the 1880s, the chief police interrogator awaits his chance for an interview with Verloc's wife by distracting himself with a glance into the floor-model pornographic viewer. Though we see nothing of what he sees, the so-called Inspector is, in so looking, given an intimate, quasi-tactile access to the kind of erotic poses that the film audience catches only in passing, and from an illegible distance, in the shop window. If only for a moment, official surveillance is carried into the recesses of commercialized desire. At the same time, according to Crary's revisionist teleol-ogy, we may recognize, by latent contrast, almost the historical necessity of cin-ema in such a scene. We sense it, that is, in the welcome removal (in which we of course participate by the very act of viewing the film) of voyeuristic impulse away from closeted titillation to the sanitized public space—the narrative space—of more mobile and automatized, less willfully obsessive, beholding.

In contrast, the IMAX film (with, among other devices of immediacy, a 360-degree audio sensor in the headset) openly champions a postmodern cinematic technology edging toward the full sensorium of virtual reality—and does so by rhapsodizing the radiant technology of the dated stereograph and its further up-grading by cutting-edge cinematic production. There is no narratively troubling anachronism in the cinematic one-upmanship here, even with the freeze-frame, only the trumpeted diachrony of a teleological dream come true: the perfection of representational fullness. But the more ambitious narrative exercises that await us, like *The Secret Agent* itself in its closing moments, dissever their own continuity through devices of a modernist cinematic dispensation meant to jar with, even to transcend, the historical deadlocks recounted by plot. Let us grant that *Across the Sea of Time*, for all its sentimentality about emigration, is really about media history. The remaining films that claim our notice, however, are found subordinating media history to their local historical ironies, converting the medium to its own metaphor by reverting or regressing, as we will find, to its se-rial basis on the strip (or to the exigencies of its multiple registration there in the fixated image).

FISSURED PICTURING

The most widely seen case is Jane Campion's miscast, stiffly scripted, but visually ambitious *The Portrait of a Lady* (1966), where the Victorian heroine, early in the film, has an extended dream in mostly silent cinematic images (before they were even invented): an incongruous flux of black-and-white shots anticipating both primitive travelogue and surrealist experiment.[13] This inset footage reads as a technological throwback in the contemporary film's own terms but as a distracting media forecast within the 1870s plot. It is in the very nature of the heroine's fantasy life for it to be ahead of her time and behind ours, lost in a hinterland—a libidinal limbo—of mostly voiceless because historically unspeakable desire.[14] All the while, the film must sustain that premium placed in period filmmaking on the contemplated frocked body of the woman. Film Victoriana has a way of maximizing the continuing currency of this pleasure in the gaze by blaming it on the sublimations of a past cultural moment or, in this case, on the misogynist kinks of the festering aesthete, Gilbert Osmond.

In Campion's densely filmic film, we follow the heroine through three stages of optical entrapment or impasse, each slyly associated with cinema's material and specular basis on the racing strip. After Isabel has already begun to fall under Os-

291

292

mond's sickly spell, we see him framing his view of her by the delicate shutter effect of her idly spun parasol, now in his hands. The manipulative voyeur produces her image as a stroboscopic flicker effect between spokes of a wheeling device (fig. 291) whose fluttering sprocketlike whir on the sound track further calls to the mind's ear the primitive click of the cinematic reel—until the parasol image returns via superimposition as a specific hypnotic prompt in the surrealist film within the film, like a vortex drawing Isabel's body into Osmond's gaze (fig. 292).

Stage two of her optical disempowerment—her veritable dismemberment—follows much later, where the technology of image reproduction has all the more obviously imploded upon content. At times Isabel's self-division, in her literalized split from Osmond, is contained within narrative space as a telling accident of normal optics, as for instance in the splintering of her image by a beveled train window during her sudden return to England (fig. 293). At other times narration itself is made to register the fissuring more exorbitantly. At the nadir of her marriage, walking away at last, Isabel's face is blatantly double-exposed on-screen. The whole image plane seems disintegrating (fig. 294), with the riven subject hinged about the phantasmatic mind's eye of self-recognition (fig. 295 especially). This apparent overlap of separately tracked photograms (resembling the dysfunction of a old-fashioned range finder struggling for focus) is an internal rift of the image that is finally—stage three in the heroine's specular curtailment—strung out along the serial axis of movement itself. Fleeing in recoil from Goodwood's too insistent kiss at the end, Isabel floats away in a syncopated slow motion that elides a frame or two in each station of retreat. As she reaches finally for the locked doors of Gardencourt, in a steady kinetic decrescendo of blurred gesture, she realizes there is no going back. As she turns outward in an stepprinted attenuation of all vital force, there is no going forward either. This cul-de-sac of plot is rubbed in on track by the stalled photogram in a virtually inevitable freeze-frame, the punitive return of the filmic from within the cinematic. The last shot is the film's true title scene: a portrait of the lady as posed image.

As we began to see in *Dracula*, however, and as we may suspect as a lurking principle at work in *The Portrait of a Lady* as well, there is a curi-

293

294

295

ously meliorist dimension to the reflexive media devices in such recent films. To smoke this out, let me clarify an assumption that bonds this chapter with the last. Dystopian narratives of the future tend to figure, as we have seen, the future of moving-image technology, extrapolating the present state of media art into the apparatus of some projected innovation. Idylls of the Victorian past, in contrast,

tend to be about the prehistory of their own mediation—about the derivation of
movies, for instance, from the optical toy and the portrait daguerreotype. Against
the cautionary drift of the sci fi prolepsis, the elegiac leanings of Victorian period
film suggest a compensatory role for cinema on the historical side of the equation.
By a structure akin to that of self-fulfilling prophecy, the cinematic institution
builds in its own aesthetic compensation for the human losses tallied by technique.[15] In *Dracula,* to put it as bluntly as possible, cinema on its own terms sates
and hence sanitizes our desire for the undead. In a not dissimilar fashion, however,
there is the suggestion in *The Portrait of a Lady* (triggered first by its film within
the film) that the experience of movies like this one (or, say, of Campion's *The
Piano* before it), with their feminist diagnosis of gender's dated hierarchies and
constraints, might have schooled its own heroine in a mix of erotic speculation and
emotional wariness more in line with her desires.

But we leave Campion's film behind too soon if we do not let it send us back to
the James novel for a loaded moment of quotation. The image of Isabel cut loose
from any specific emotional gravity, her body as if swimming across the grounds of
Gardencourt (distantly evoking the underwater images of death and resurrection in
The Piano as well), derives a certain authority from the novel's own metaphoric
language. Goodwood's kiss, at first like "white lightning," is soon an undulation of
warmth that "spread, and spread again, and stayed" (55:482). And in this rippling
intensity, Isabel feels herself submerged: "So had she heard of those wrecked and
under water following a train of images before they sink." If we want to assume
that Campion borrowed this trope in order to transfer it to the elided "train"—and
gently jagged track—of her own micro-optic (microptic) jump cuts in the resultant
slowed dance of entranced flight, we would not be far wrong.

And if we wished, further, to find a prose equivalent in the novel, a lexical syncopation that matches the film's close-coupled train of decelerated images, we
would need go no farther than the sentence just before. In the grip of Goodwood's
kiss, Isabel "felt each thing in his hard manhood that had least pleased her, each aggressive fact of his face, his figure, his presence, justified of its intense identity and
made one with the act of possession." Taking that last noun in both senses, we find
a self-possessed masculine aspect fully realized in the attempted possession of its
erotic object. But what really anticipates the screen narrative's closing transactions
from frame to frame of the filmic "defile"—and hence anticipates the lexical analogues for photogrammatic advance in our next and closing chapter—is what we
might call the montage by collision (within the empiricist precision) of "aggressive fact." Abutting phonograms are hazed by their tautological shadow within the
paradigmatic axis of word choice. As if by a chain reaction, the phrasing then
seems verbally to precipitate—along the route of the horizontal or syntactic
axis—the elided "act" of possessive transgression.[16] So with any such erotic fact,
always manifesting itself in the heat of act.

The remaining two films that return us to late Victorian settings after the
prephotographic culture of Jane Austen's world may also be taken to valorize their
own media aftermath through the most roundabout technological figuration—albeit in the least celebratory of terms. With *Jude* (Michael Winterbottom, 1966), the

hero's last howling denunciation of the
marriage laws, rather than his
deathbed's mock graduation ceremony
in Hardy, politicizes and updates the
novel by its singular sociological emphasis. Whence, again, the self-ratifying
cinematic drift. In our greater clarity
about matters of flesh and cohabitation
(the film seems asking us to say to ourselves), modern society is the plot's one
eschatological hope: history's eventual
rectification by a change to which the

296

sexual mores and representational models of cinema itself have contributed. But it
is no surprise that the scene focusing this point would come as a surprise to Hardy's
readers, just as Coppola's film emporium would to readers of Bram Stoker's own
Dracula. Indeed Coppola's idea may well be the source of *Jude*'s implanted episode.

Just before the story's turning point in the murder of the other children and
himself by Jude's returned son, there is a fairground scene that unmistakably anticipates the coming of cinema as technology and as institution—as well as the subsequent public discourse of its emotional risks. Drawing on the prehistory of the
medium in traveling optical amusements and their sideshow marketing, the scene
takes our dysfunctional family into a makeshift tent for a low-budget magic-
lantern phantasmagoria. What we see with them are translucent spectral graphics
(not photographs) of hovering skeletal ghosts, abetted in their spookiness not only
by crude flash-powder bursts—as if distantly associated with the magnesium flares
of early photomechanical registration—but by the precursor of cinematic superimposition in the diaphanous overlay of one image upon the next (fig. 296). The
spectacle thus amounts to a kind of animated though nonfilmic version of that spirit
imaging that was so popular in the photographic kitsch of the period, all glossed by
the master of ceremonies as "terrors that come at you out of nowhere."[17] It is clear
that the artificial scare tactics do not just prefigure the boy's grotesque violence but
precipitate it. In the film rather than the novel, Little Jude thus emerges as an im-
pressionable victim of precinematic screen thrills. But, again, the tacit coun-
terthrust: along with other social alleviations to be chronicled by the next century's
film narrative, only our assurance that the mass institution of cinema will one day
devise fitter amusements for children could begin to allay this vision of spectatorial vulnerability. Here again is the feel-good teleology of all such films, no matter
how unrelievedly dreary. But where is photography's place in this left-handed testament to the film medium?

In another and earlier episode new to the plot, the departure of Jude's school-
master Phillotson is ceremonialized by a photograph taken of the whole class near
the end of a black-and-white prologue—whose whole stark palette is now associated by synecdoche with the photochemical process of this climactic event. Jude,
by the way, is first from the right in this shot, told "to hold still" in a life going
nowhere (fig. 297). Thereafter, the often noted prevalence of photographic keep-

297

298

sakes (as erotic surrogates) in Hardy's novel is centered upon a single image in the film, actually given screen credit as "Sue Bridehead photograph."[18] This is the portrait of his cousin that is said by Hardy to have "haunted" Jude. Lifting it from its place on his aunt's mantel, Jude later enshrines the photo on his desk against the statue of an angel and alongside his fortress of books: the secular muse as blatant metonym of his frustrated lust for the theological life (fig. 298). But how does this photograph do what we might want to call filmic as well as filmed service? What does it connect with?

The answer lies in an aberrant but heavily motivated disruption in the period realism of the film's narrative treatment. I refer again, as with *The Portrait of a Lady,* to an anachronistic intrusion of modernist device (specifically discontinuous editing and the freeze-frame). That such effects should be apparent, even prominent, in three of the films released since the first round of late twentieth-century screen Victoriana seems to suggest a new and more reflexive stage, an almost mannerist phase, in our fin-de-siècle subgenre, however short-lived it may already have been. As Hardy's phobic version of the New Woman, Sue Bridehead is framed in isolation during an early conversation with Jude in which he flatters her in voice-off about her stunning noncomformity. Under this barrage of compliments, the image of Sue responds with a disruptive brief freeze that dams the stream of phenomenological continuity that is usually a prerequisite for the ordinary protocols of period filmmaking as much as for its alternative genre in futurist sci fi. Anticipated here are such photogenetically modernist film gestures as the ironic jump-cut anatomy of Jean Seberg's charms under the optic scalpel of Belmondo's dismembering appreciation in Godard's *Breathless* or the midstream freeze on Jeanne Moreau's face in the eyes of her suitors in Truffaut's *Jules and Jim* (see Cavell on the latter).[19] But with a difference. By a logic associated in part with the diegetic photograph of Sue, this reflexive objectification of the image plane rebounds upon the subjectivity of the imaged person herself. At the height of Jude's passionate encomium, Sue's paralyzing self-consciousness freezes her into a semblance of her own photograph, an image struck from time and continuity. Not so much through the fixating power of the male gaze

as through the disempowering arrest of a nervous self-image broken from all flow, the medium offers another portrait of a lady poised in the emotional foreclosure of the ongoing. Yet once again, as with Campion's film, the filmic modernity of technique postdates—and thereby tacitly appeases—the cultural impasse of the cornered female inside the cinematic plot. Device itself carries with it, by metafilmic association, the knowing irony but also the liberatory break with received views—and viewing—that media history, in its role as flash point of cultural evolution, will gradually bring to bear on such typing of the feminine and the deadlocks it can cause.

In the meantime Sue, the would-be female iconoclast, has been transfixed as a self-icon, and no good can come of it. What remains to the hero in the end is only the "haunting" of *himself* as a living obituary image. On the sleet-gray day of their final separation, we see Jude's emaciated figure in an overhead shot that recalls the chromatic wastes of the black-and-white prologue. The held view is now gradually hazed over by an extradiegetic fog, producing a muted halo effect like the iris masking of an old photograph (fig. 299). The effect resembles an aureole of departed vital aura rimming him like a phantom noose. In summation of the film's prolonged photomechanical subtext, the hero is once again standing still to have his picture taken, become the mere image of his obscured defeat in the eye of fate.

CINEMA'S SECRET AGENCY: THE DETONATED PHOTOGRAM

The end of Christopher Hampton's *The Secret Agent* (1996) is wrenched even one notch further into the dead-ended, literally ratcheted down by the step printing of its last apocalyptic retard. In Hitchcock's version of *The Secret Agent*, retitled *Sabotage* (1936), the anarchist Verloc runs a seedy movie theater—and sends off his stepbrother, Stevie, with a bomb concealed as a projector part along with a set of film canisters. Movies too, we are to gather, have their anarchic charge.[20] In Hampton's version, once we have returned in three separate narrative loops, and in increasing slow motion, to the bomb death of Stevie, disintegrating the track at the moment of detonation, turning montage itself into a trope for the explosive, we are ready for the internal pulverizing of the image. We are ready, in short, for the skid editing in the staggered optics that yield to the last freeze-frame.

What induces the abrogation of all further movement is that living time bomb of a radical nihilist known only as the Professor, his body strapped with dynamite and waiting to self-destruct. Having toasted with his last drink "the de-

300, 301

struction of what is," the anonymous nemesis (played anonymously—without screen credit—by Robin Williams) moves from the anarchist tavern (a change from the novel) to the metropolitan street, where he will press an explosive release mechanism to obliterate the crowd. In the novel's last sentence the threat remains latent, almost anagrammatic: "He *passed* on unsu*spected* and *dead*ly, like a *pest* in the street full of m*en*." On film, the anagrammatic turns photogrammatic. The nihilist doesn't pull a trigger or depress a plunger. Rather, in his collapse of all eros upon the death drive, he closes his masturbatory hand upon the "india-rubber ball" yanked from his bulging pocket, a device explained in the novel as operating on none other than "the principle of the pneumatic instantaneous shutter for a camera lens" (4:66). Roland Barthes might have dictated that line. All photography is a kind of death; all instantaneous annihilation on film owes a debt to photography.

A debt that is called in, called up, by the photogram's incursion into the cinematic track, here in a pronounced convulsion of the screen image. This once again I can only barely cite, not really illustrate, with a stilled frame. The roar of the crowd has built steadily on the sound track as the Professor plows his way through it, but when the detonator is activated (fig. 300), all sound stops a few seconds before the lurching freeze, as if the world were holding its last breath. At this point film as a putative world viewed must either undergo death in the membrane of its own representational presence or brake against it in an arrest of such destruction, either explode or hold the line. In the latter case, as elected here, cinematic procedure embalms rather than activates the moment of historical crisis, peels away its image from all consequence. That this last frozen moment of hermetically sealed duration (fig. 301) can be read to quarantine violence as well as to suffer violence is, once again, the way cinematic self-consciousness can defuse the most catastrophic historical turns in the fiction a given film is based on. The future itself may seem to be winning out in the deus ex machina of its own foregrounded modes of mediation. The more anachronistic (hence proleptic) the texture of the cinematic device, the better. As it happens, there is a famous theoretical emphasis against which to measure this last optic gasp of *The Secret Agent*. For Walter Benjamin, in the Artwork essay, film breaks the deadlock of nineteenth-century urbanism, deflecting any threat, we might add, of revolutionary sabotage by the explosive but restorative violence of montage. The metaphor is Benjamin's own: "Our taverns and our metropolitan streets"—like the film's own divided (and revised) public locales at the end—"Our taverns and our metropolitan streets, our offices and furnished rooms, our railroad stations and our factories appeared to have us locked up hopelessly. Then came the film and burst this prison-world asunder by the *dynamite of the tenth of a second.*"[21] It all of course derives from what Benjamin elsewhere calls the "optical unconscious" to which mechanical imaging frees up our access, a liberation into the quotidian unseen. Translating this logic to film, what I have been arguing into the open in *The Secret Agent* amounts once again to the specular unconscious of received projection in the track itself, the undulant run of photograms, with all their suppressions and their weird returns.

To say that cinema thrives on the denial of the photogram—now you see it, now you don't—is only to be reminded that my question throughout these examples has been directed at the mortuary underside of artificial animation, at the filmic beneath the filmed. Victorian event on-screen, if you're with me, measures its mediated resuscitation of the past against the receded past of the period's own photographic mementos, but this distance reduces toward equivalence in the differential imprints of the strip. And that reduction can at times erupt back into plot, obliterating the lifelike in the very mode of its constitution. James's portrayed lady, draped in mourning for herself as well as her cousin, dies to time present in her decelerated flight from the past. In the last shot of *Jude,* the hero seems lapsing back toward the carnal nullity of the photographic still. In Hampton's film, the secreted agency of death is there under erasure in the petrified last frame. What we have been seeing is that, within plot, figurative death passes over to literal death by a more and more direct seizure of film's material base in the slide—or jam—of photograms.

HISTORICAL RESURRECTION

The opposite trope can also be installed by the same process, so that a freeze-frame may fly in the face of death. This book goes to press just as a 1998 British film has been distributed in the United States that reinscribes with new clarity the connection between this chapter and the previous one. It locates again the photographic touchstone of both cinematically and electronically achieved science fantasy inside a quaint historical narrative instinct with a never more than latent anticipation of cinematic modernity. *Photographing Fairies* (Nick Willing), with its Merchant/Ivory-style trans-European settings and its literate dialogue, achieves far more sedately than *Bram Stoker's Dracula*—and with its cinematic references entirely submerged—the crossing of heritage luxury with digital enhancement in its narrative quest for a photographically confirmed supernaturalism.

Mass death in World War I has rendered a culture desperate for proof of an embodied afterlife, and the Victorian fairy craze is revived in the belief that these creatures might be "messengers from across the border." The plot is advanced by one photographic moment after another in search of these hovering presences in an always elusive still image. Only a definitive fixed shot would offer the redemptive proof of another world. And as it turns out, only cinema's ingenuity can finally arrange this. Though the plot depends explicitly on the difference, in the

302

303

304

305

mouth of one believer, between "the miracle of photography" and the "photograph of a miracle," it is cinema's machinated magic that arrives, at the point of not only narrative but textual closure, as the missing third term. Here is another period melodrama, then, for which the genealogical history of image media affords a kind of last-ditch metanarrative rescue.

A professional photographer in 1912 shoots his own wedding party with a timer camera, racing into frame (for a photo we later see on his studio wall as well) just too late to keep from blurring his own image beyond recognition when the entire screen freezes on the flash (fig. 302). On the first day of his honeymoon in the Alps, by contrast, his wife gives him a commemorative locket watch containing a fully focused studio photograph of herself (fig. 303). But their time together is up. Just moments later, she slips out of sight and life into the snowy chasm of an ice fissure. Still in deep mourning, and having rejected all the consolations of religion, the widower goes to the European front as a battlefield photographer of corpses, returning after the war to a private practice specializing in "trick photography," including paste-up illusions of dead soldiers as living sons in posthumous family portraits (fig. 304). "I am the life and the resurrection," he mumbles ironically to himself, playing god with the touch-up brush. He is thus keenly alert, indeed allergic, to unacknowledged photographic fakery. In debunking a notorious fairy photo at a theosophy symposium (in Arthur Conan Doyle's credulous presence), the hero's own silhouette blocks the immediate grip of the fantastic photo in the very act of exposing its patent artifice (fig. 305).[22]

On the strength of his authoritative performance, however, the photographer is subsequently asked by one of the audience to authenticate the more credibly blurred photographic images of a putative fairy on her daughter's fingertip. At first attributing the smear of light to a "defect in the lens" or a "glitch in the emulsion," he later notes it reflected in miniature on the negative in the girl's eye (fig. 306). An homage to *Blow-Up* ensues, where the image is obsessively enlarged and multiplied until it fills the screen frame with evidence of an "untrickable" duplicate in the confirming lens not of the camera but of the retina itself (fig. 307). From this evidentiary document in close-up, we cut to an overhead shot of his studio—where unlikely multiples of the photo chime with the parquet pattern of the floor as the new ground of his belief (fig. 308).

Relentless efforts follow to photograph the fairies on the rural site. Efforts include the use of twenty-four-hour time-set cameras and elaborate flash contraptions. Here and elsewhere, no one thinks of using a motion-picture camera. It is as if the evidentiary status of the photograph (rather than the inherent *trucage* of film) still far outweighs the advantage of the newer medium (already in its third decade by now) in being able to catch the shimmering fairies in flight. No one thinks of motion pictures, that is, except this film as a whole, whose combination of slow-motion and reverse-action footage, in league with computer graphics, increasingly tampers with screen temporality as the plot pushes its hero nearer to the brink of supernatural contact.

Reprising the *Liebestod* of *Somewhere in Time,* the inconsolable widower

306

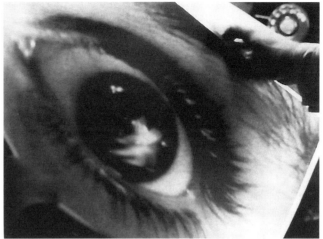

307

pleads guilty to a murder he didn't commit so as to rejoin his wife "on the other side." Just as the snow-weighted trap of the gallows opens beneath him, he is plummeted through a burst of digital effects—and a last apparition of the harbinger fairy—into the snow cleft of his tragic past, this time retrieving his wife from the frozen abyss. At which point the earlier blur of the wedding photo, the effaced groom of the ceremonial kiss, is "corrected" by a further power of cinematic mechanism, beyond slowed and reversed time: a close-up freeze-frame on their embrace, fixed and irreversible, in the film's long-held last shot. The frame does not, this time, cut to a black-and-white image of imprint. It is not a photograph that way, but a photogrammatic metaphor for a transcendental prolongation of desire: a paradoxical freezing to life in the eternal snow. It is in this manner that cinema itself, as the structuring absence of this

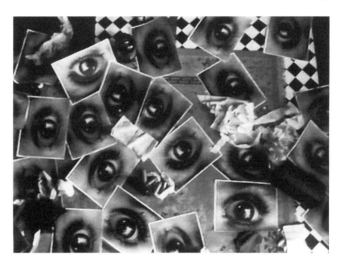

308

Edwardian venture in photochemical registration, comes into sharp focus for the first time. We are left, in textual as well as narrative closure, with the following conclusion. Whether as photograph or repeated photogram, standard ocular mechanics cannot, of course, be counted on to capture (that is, represent) the otherworld of immortality. As many a film has reminded us, photochemistry can only instantiate death's flight from time. Hence the freeze-frame: the near side of forever. If cinema per se, unmentioned by this one film, is modern culture's new immortality machine, it relives time only in its transience. Historical spectacle, history as specular rerun, comes forward as the wholesale model of this opportunity. Within such spectacle, then, the stop-action frame offers a yet more pointed trope for the single image won from flux—in this case, for erotic fixation vindicated.

The inference of digital form within narratives concerned only with the photographic, rather than the cinematic, detection of the otherworld emerges just this year, too, from the alter-genre of the 1990s heritage film, sci fi melodrama. Addiction to photography is tied again to the mastered terror of death's advent. This may be imagined as the smartest suspected borrowing from *The Asphyx* (shortly after its 1998 DVD issue as an occult collector's item) in the tamed-down script for an *X-Files* episode aired on 24 January 1999. The weary, deathless protagonist (born in 1849) is a freelance photographer who has for over a century been taking pictures of the dying, hoping to capture Death himself—even as his own ID photographs have come down through various police records mostly unchanged and entirely ageless. The closest he gets to the record of death rather than dying is an odd blur or glare near certain photographed corpses, explained away by the heroine Scully as a "lens flare." In fact, the whole perennial labor of photography is something of a detour in the plot, which is more concerned, as is the *Asphyx* by the end, with overcoming the fear of death than with fixing its imprint.

Though unexplored in dialogue, the historical timeline says it all. Any man born in the first decade of widespread photographic production in the 1840s numbers himself among the original generation of human beings offered a new but decidedly insufficient way of allaying death's threat: namely, through photography's fully intact image of life. History's technological scapegoat in this *X-Files* segment, who once closed his eyes to his own slated death in a yellow fever ward so that the nurse tending him died instead, needs now to confront his doom unmediated by the tools of his trade. He must break the deadlock in which he finds himself, so averted from life in his obsession with death that he has become in fact the undead. In the climactic moment he must be shot down by an FBI agent straight through the lens of his camera, all technical intervention blasted away. To save Scully, who is hit by the same bullet—in other words to accept death wholly—the mortally wounded photographer is more than willing at last to look death (unseen by us of course) straight in the face in a final open-eyed stare. All we in the audience ever see by way of ocular astonishment is not death but the ongoing temporal process of death at work, the closing-in of fatality—and this only through a technology that exceeds photochemistry altogether. In several POV shots from the photographer's perspective spaced across the episode, computerized manipulation of the image carves out from normal color footage of the shot the black-and-white specter of the one about to die. Whereas photography and cinema put death and life into dialectical tension, including the limit case of the neither/nor, this one video episode suggests that only video technology can break with representational norms for the preternatural immanence of the uncanny.

In sci fi's companion genre of the heritage retrospect, the technique of *Photographing Fairies*, though partly digital, retains, as we have seen, some sense of cinema's own uncanny in the bargain. But to what real rather than fictionalized historical conditions of media technology do such heritage films return us, finally? This question requires a word more about the putatively falsifying emphasis on

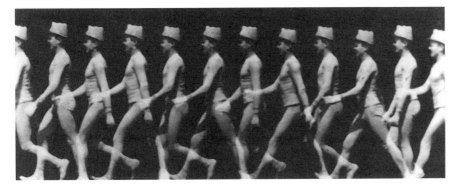

309

film's narrowly photographic prehistory that such technical obtrusion might be seen to lend. If the newer archaeologies of the moving image—often prosecuted in Benjamin's name as well as in Foucault's—wish to eschew all notion of a linear descent from static photochemical print to photomechanical projection, then they have a further task. They need to account directly—if not precisely—for the strategic forgetting of the fixed imprint beneath the newly privileged dynamism, on-screen as elsewhere, of the assailed and flexibly observant eye. What I mean is that even the most sweepingly culturalist and cross-media account of cinema, one that would mostly dismiss the photogram from consideration before the motion picture even comes up (on-screen) for discussion, could not deny, even though ignoring, the material source of projection, the slivers of image spun out as motion on the silver screen. Taken seriously—that is, structurally—the very notion of a historically specified *suppression* would indeed constitute one potential strength of any such nonlinear account of cinema. As other dispositions of the observer's gaze take hold, the naturalist grip of the fixed and examinable photograph must be weakened to make cinema possible, dissolved at least into the filmic stratum of the scopic process. Unless the first motion-picture audiences could have kept from mind what they knew, more vividly than we, about the "natural" limits of the predecessor medium of photography, that is, they could never have relaxed into the deep aptness of cinema's cultural moment within pervasive new paradigms and managements of the gaze.

A recent case of media-historical precision serves to confirm such a proposed adjustment to the archaeological overview. Tom Gunning has demonstrated a newly specific technical debt of the Lumières' cinematograph to the immediately preceding developments in so-called amateur photography. Improved by the dry-plate rather than collodion process, "instantaneous photography" (of the sort laboriously perfected by Marey and Muybridge for their serial strips) had become, in the decade just before cinema, commercially available to "a culture voracious for the seizing of reality"—not just for the seeing (Crary, Aumont) but for the seizing of the world, a capture of the view as much as a distracted captivation through the gaze.[23] When the cinematograph debuted in 1895, despite its intended design for private use (as both recorder and projector), it became instead the instrument of paid public spectacle, turning the Lumière clientele from active producers to passive receivers overnight. In this way the invention's initial astonishment for an immobilized audience would have been quite palpably measured against the hands-on, split-second technology of the instantaneous frozen pose (in candid or amateur rather than portrait photography), a fixity the cinematograph built upon even while transforming it to increment. Here was an evolutionary leap, to be sure, yet almost a contrary one. If the discrete photographic imprint must be automatized into invisibility, canceled and forgotten, to permit full credence in receipt of the motorized cinematic image, all the more so must the early cinematograph's immediate predecessor in the instantaneous midgesture snapshot have needed to be driven from mind as well as spun from view. There was no denying it, only the automated trick of overcoming it.

Overcoming not only the amateur snapshot but the scientific exactitude of alternative and more specialized techniques. Consider Marey's "chronophotography," for instance, given here in the example printed by Bazin in the French edition of *What Is Cinema?* to accompany his essay on the ontology of the photograph and its teleological fulfillment in the moving image (fig. 309). In nineteenth-century ocular experience, this was the closest any filmic mechanism had ever come to recording motion—or, rather, to delineating motion's essence in difference (if not in continuity). The stages of a regimented movement were displayed, splayed apart, as marked intervals rather than achieved traverse, exaggerated rather than naturalized. When in the new cinematograph, then, photographic fixity broke from itself to create motion, rather than merely to multiply itself over space (as if over time), the retained but invisible dynamic of such multiplication, such instantaneous sequencing, was more likely than now to be part of the active cultural intertext for the reception of such ocular technology. We are reminded again that the outer limits of photographic science would have been much on the mind's eye of audiences astonished to see those limits ingeniously overleaped by cinema's new technology. This points to one of the best reasons for having begun the earliest cinematographic screenings, as Gunning mentions, with a dilatory projection of a first stilled frame (aided by water filters to cool the lamp). The image was held for as long as possible, like a stalled magic lantern slide, until it visibly burst into motion—or, in the words of an early rapt spectator quoted by Gunning, until "all at once the image stirred itself and came alive." Again, as invited by the metaphoric animism of this very remark: cinematic ontogeny recapitulating filmic (i.e., once solely photographic) phylogeny, here in the deferred first lurch of the differential strip. Cinema, then, whether as breakthrough technology or as one more technique of a disembodied modern vision or (of course) as both, arrived as a perceived mechanical descendant as well as a present derivative of the photograph. It came forth as precisely that medium whose operation is mounted upon the suppressed or elided evidence in progress of the single filmic imprint: the photogram in motion. Once this point is granted, everything in this book, as well as in this chapter, follows from it. For suppression, like repression, knows its returns.

But where, exactly? We have repeatedly located this turmoil in the photogrammatic *undertext* of cinema. On just this score, a further clarification needs to be borne home as we pass to a final consideration of filmic textuality under the aegis and exigencies of a modernist poetics. On the way there, this chapter on film's historical mediation as an inferential media history has prompted a justified balancing act. If we no longer dispatch our most searching histories of the cinema by a connect-the-dots trail of technological landmarks, this does not mean we need to obscure the material basis of the medium itself in a hunt for the force fields of its preconditioning. Even if cinema history is no longer the genealogy of optic invention but has become the archaeology of ocular convention, still nothing requires us to close our eyes to the object. A comparison may clarify. To insist on seeing more in literary textuality, for instance, than the stages of mechanical dissemination in the centuries between the house of Gutenberg and Random House does not mean averting one's gaze forever from the legibly printed page. As the next chapter will further explore, the impressed page stands to the invisible textual system of literature, the decipherable object to the underlying rules of writing that permit its operation, as the cinematic spectacle stands to the photogrammatic underlay. The motion picture is, in short, the phenotext to the photogram's genotext.

One provocative line of connection between this chapter and the remaining discussion is sketched out in the unlikeliest corner, perhaps, of the history of vision school of media theory. In *War and Cinema,* with his emphasis on the spatiotemporal interval destabilized by long-range optic and ballistic mediation, Paul Virilio develops, early on, a comparison between the marked rather than disguised sequencing of Marey's chronophotography and the openly discontinuous print culture of "silent reading," a comparison that highlights the numerous "affinities . . . between the instantaneities of writing and photography, both being inserted in time which is 'exposed' rather than simply passing."[24] In a point coincident with Bergson, Virilio implies that cinema's subsequent invention and proliferation falsifies this inevitably time-bound "exposure" by imposing an automated continuity with no remaining sign(s) of its stage-by-stage advance. In an engineering subterfuge dear to cinematic phenomenology, the motion picture thereby reembodies ocular decoding in the supposedly natural mechanism of human anatomy. Summing up the ethnological overtones of this automatism in connection with the international aftermath of World War I, Virilio writes cryptically: "The exposure time of silent reading vanishes in the anatomical eye of the camera, releasing a flood of illiteracy in the developed countries" (37-38). Against this mass illusion of unmediated access (the next chapter will go to show), the lettered reading of modernist writing—silent, but gripped still by the syncopation of phonemes and the serial jots that indicate them in the unmasked "exposure time" of differential inscription—makes its stand. In so doing, it joins forces with the deanthropomorphized eye of modernist montage, or in other words the recursion of the filmic within the cinematic, to recover the textual candor of mark rather than flow. But my own elaboration of this argument needs to install a clarification precisely where Virilio slides between the serial exposure of print per se and its apparent cognitive equivalent in the very act of silent reading. However much it records a sequential imprint, an inscribed page is all spatial array without temporal process. Only inspection reactivates the specks as a temporal series, and there the exposure, in the play between graphic and phonemic trace within and across separate word units, may be retimed, under modernist pressure, as a momentary oscillation or skid. With cinema's filmic equivalent of this we are by now familiar.

The solicited anthropomorphic gaze of mainstream cinematic practice, by contrast (and here I return to the surface/depth model in all such superficial masking of the imprint's original exposure time), is a gaze that sees rather than reads. In reception, any projected narrative surface is cast before us, therefore, only by riding upon—or overriding—the specular unconscious (or preconscious, or both) of its own processing by the viewer. On this point we must be relentlessly clear. Not unlike the operations of the unthought in psychic life, nonconscious material (or, better, suppressed materiality) does not return into full expressive presence. Instead, it leaks back in dreamlike associations and elisions, slips of the track rather than of the tongue, the unbidden risks of impulsion itself. When in *The Secret Agent*, the onetime camera-shutter bulb, now bomb detonator, is squeezed in the fist of the apocalyptic nihilist (after Virilio again, the mediated violence of terrorist warfare suicidally erasing the difference between agent and other), we do not suddenly recognize the single photograms splattered forth on-screen. Narrative retains its fractured hold on visualization. It is instead the specular underside of conscious spectation, in sudden goading, that nags at us beneath the seen snags in continuity, whispering of the elemental sundering beneath the ultimate abrogated thunder of the triggered explosives. Which is only to say that in film viewing we regularly conceptualize *through* photograms rather than thinking of or through *to* them. They remain the cinematic unthought, tapped only by photosynthetic rupture, accidentally on purpose. Insofar as they can be shown in the next chapter to operate in this way like the perturbations of wording under stress from the preconscious fluctuations of ambiguous lexical juncture in literary practice, these photograms locate the level at which even our specular attachment to the screen image is structured like a writing, if not like a language. But it is so structured, one must add again, only by a continuous undoing that necessitates no conceptual recourse to overthrown linguistic models for the normative codes of cinematic "syntax." I keep trying to get this just right: In their deepest analogy with the slide of verbal formation under the operations of intentional utterance, photograms in screen cognition are not what we perceive, but how.

In sum, when photograms fail us, fail to self-erase fast enough for us, the default is registered over against our mostly unconscious sense of their normative overlay in the first place, now buckling under duress. Though the strip is always geared for motion, it does sometimes appear to strip its own gears. But I repeat: Ruptural moments of this sort do not call the photograph or photogram to full mind so much as they cede representation to the marked evanescence of trace. Modernism is one name for the institution, across media, of just such ceding. And if this is only one among myriad characterizations of the modernist venture, it brings an unexpected number of others along in tow. Such, at least, is the assumption of the next and final chapter.

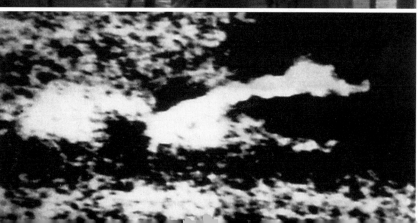

SEVEN

Modernism and the Flicker Effect

CINEMA AS FILM FULFILLS THE GENEALOGY
NOT OF MIMESIS BUT OF TEXT.

Whereas the previous two chapters were ventures in genre criticism taking the film medium's own materiality as pretext, this chapter seeks a wider context for just that materiality. The very matter under inspection is now conceived as a more intermedial substrate: a differential plasticity crossing between filmic module and morphophonemic segment. And the historical and cultural context has been ventilated to include theoretical and industrial science, aesthetics, and everything in between, from locomotive engineering through Fordist manufacture to military technology to radical linguistic production. This chapter travels back and forth, that is, between mechanics and textuality, between the technological ferment of industrial modernity, on the one hand, and the exploratory technique of literary modernism on the other. Under pressure of modernity, modernism becomes a name for what the electric cluster of the screen image has in common with the unsung glisten of the subvocal signifier.

But cinema's modernity, like literature's, turns modernist only in postures of reception I am inclined to call *attention surfeit disorder*. On the linguistic side, unheard determinants quaver everywhere in modernist writing, waver there, crowding its textual surfaces, flooding its utterance with excess enunciation, drifting across its wording in the unsounded racket of stray signification. And despite its estranging zing, this scud of lettered speech remains the very stuff of the everyday. We all have our Joycean accidents. In saving on computer disk a list of the film clips from *Apocalypse Now* that I planned to screen for a class, I once resorted to my available eight-letter WordPerfect shorthand for file names, with the usual ad hoc decisions and elisions, coming up, I noticed only upon later retrieval, with the all but letter-perfect overlapping portmanteau APOCLIPS. Abbreviation's lucky break? The fractal symmetry of a self-replicating scale model? In any case, the left hand often knows better than the right brain what the wrong spelling can get right.

Not rigidly periodizable, literary modernism begins, is always beginning again, with such incursions of linguistic eccentricity into our habituation to lexical and syntactic code. Rather than thinking to listen in on such textual phenomena in their contextualized literary manifestations, as if writing somehow contained its sonic (or even phonetic) matter, one has only to listen up, to alert oneself—not so much giving voice as giving thought to voice. The rough equivalent in film is a surrender, induced by the text itself, to the optically unthought of the moving image. That equivalence—dependent, in fact, on a roughening of the representational surface in both media—is the subject of this chapter. Such roughening is, first of all, an affront to the phenomenological model. Our eyes don't see the world *that* way. Words don't make it through to you from a strictly communicating consciousness *that* way. In each case the message circuit is attenuated in proportion to the thickening of the signifier. Modernism favors a programmatic elevation of that ratio.

More than Victorianism, the very concept of the modern tends, of course, to straddle a pervasive social ethos and a cross-media aesthetic movement. But so does cinema, a new way of seeing and a new mode of making. Bringing cinema to bear on modernity and modernism alike can help specify these notoriously porous terms. Bringing modernism (in its aspect as literary experimentation) to bear on cinema helps clarify the special kind of newness that accrues to photographic imprint in its deliberately unrecognizable form of motorized disappearance. Under consideration to follow, then, is the shared modernist strain, in every sense, of literary and filmic textuality. Cinematic spectation and read writing: these are the very different results of two less different, because each strictly differential, causes. If, beneath the shows of representation, the oscillating materiality of the cinematic mirage generates what can be entertained as modernism's exemplary filmic register, this is because, at a comparable depth, modernist writing also vibrates with the undulant undoing of continuous signification. Narrative cinema as film, literature as denaturalized language: these then are the modernist reductions that affiliate textualities beneath the contest of media.

Six chapters leading toward a study of this filiation should have made at least one thing hard to miss. This is, as it happens, the one thing we need to build on now in the lateral move to literary modernism and to a broader textualist theory of the adjacent inscriptive media of film and literature. Whereas the terra firma of traditional film theory is the screen frame, with all its variable extensions and flexions, the terra incognita of the same theory is often the photogrammatic track. In this respect, some far-reaching historical schemata may help break down the barriers between separate aesthetic lineages so completely that new space will be made for comparison between the occasionally intractable photogram and the insurgent phonemic trace of alphabetic writing. When cinema's technological advent is cast in terms so broad that its specific photographic heritage is reconceived altogether rather than discounted, a notion of the literary *phonogram* may more readily shift into conceptual proximity to its cinematic counterpart. In the extreme historical long views soon to be sampled and examined, where whole centuries are swallowed on the run without the least sign of indigestible anomaly, cinema becomes not only a mere blip on the screen of media history but an evolved function of inscriptive practice per se from the Paleolithic era forward.

Taking the previous chapter as lead, we know that certain narrative films may themselves engage some phase of this media-historical sweep. Retrofitting the decadent splendors of film's postmodern excess to the eerie spirit of the cinematograph's first screenings as well as to its mediumistic associations with the preternatural overtones of Victorian photography, a film like *Bram Stoker's Dracula* allegorizes its own specular immanence to a gothic fare-thee-well. There seems nowhere left to go in this vein. Yet half a decade later *Joseph Conrad's "The Secret Agent"* ends with a clenched stab at an alternative mode of filmic reflex, matching Victorian anarchy's fantasized end of social history to the blasting open of the cinematic illusion itself. By commenting on the fracturing role of cinema in an articulation of the modern polis in crisis, the technical device of the film's frame-jamming deviance, its ocular skid and final blockage, may be associated with the articulatory overload of another medium as well. For Hampton's insistently discontinuous editing throughout *The Secret Agent*, with its flouting of linear temporality, calls to mind the rapid fin-de-siècle evolution of prose fiction from, say, Stoker to Conrad, where the spirit of fragmentation has been carried from the level of plotting to the level of the phrasing. In arguably evoking Conrad's migratory linguistic signifiers (soon to be tracked in more detail) as well as his structural experiments with narrative form—in a move from the totalizing coherence of high Victorian realism toward the touted vigor of modernist discontinuity—the film's last shattered images also reach back to something near the core of each of our chapters so far.

In an exaggerated extrapolation from the novel's own ironic tonality in closure, the squeeze of the bulb and the skid of the image toward the freeze-frame in Hampton's *Secret Agent* return us to the revealed photo-engravement of moving presence on-screen (chapter 1), offering not merely a one-man demonic Armageddon but a thematized apocalypse of the medium's own basis (chapter 2), with the image track suddenly thrown off, laid bare, flayed apart. As such, this maddened foreclosure of continuity, historical as well as representational, highlights the freeze as inherent frame of reference for the whole relation of regimented chaos to screen picture in the cinematic institution, the regulated multiplicity of the track to the manifested stable image (chapter 3). Through the paradoxically approached visibility of an absentational death in process (chapter 4), *The Secret Agent*'s artificial disarticulation (just before presumed disintegration) of the moving human image on-screen also diagnoses the artificial ontology of all such images as constructed duplicates of the human form. This last is a condition, in and beyond screen mediation, which one genre among others, namely science fiction, repeatedly exploits in its cautionary futurism (chapter 5). By contrast, and according to the prevalent "double exposure" of film Victoriana (chapter 6), the backdated metacinematic irony of a film like Hampton's *The Secret Agent* stalls on the imminent decimation of all immanence and of all historical self-presence. Only the styleme of the jagged, then stilled screen frame—in other words, the return *toward* spectatorial consciousness of the suppressed single photogram—is left to cue the viewer (borrowing Bordwell's definition again) in reconstructing from the truncated *syuzhet* the elided finality of an explosive *fabula*.[1]

As this refracted set of essays moves toward conclusion, each offering a facet of what I hope is approaching a rounded view, it is important to emphasize again what it is a view of. Of film as object? Of cinema as event? Neither. Of their inextricability? Not exactly, because many writers, let alone viewers, find it effortless to separate them. Let us say of their simultaneity in projection, the event and the object at once and at one, whatever the spectator or theorist makes of it. Let us again call any marked sign of this simultaneous manifestation within narrative cinema, as developed so far in these chapters, a thematerialization of the medium's filmic basis. To do so is also to lay stress on what this book has not been. It has not been a history of film as emerging from photography. It therefore has no immediate quarrel with the various efforts to locate film within far broader cultural discourses and social practices of spectation, observation, gazing. My point has never been that the filmic moment within the cinematic is primarily a site where cinema comes bearing genetic scars, like birthmarks, of its definitive historical origin. I have emphasized instead how, in the photogrammatic moment, filmic operation registers, by lifting to view, the *present* genesis of cinema—its generativity—in the variable image on the track.

One should therefore be perfectly glad to agree with a gamut of widely different commentators (from Stanley Cavell through Jacques Aumont to Jonathan Crary) that film, quite apart from its technical photographic aspects, enters modernity already enmeshed in its more culturally pervasive "conditions of possibility" (Aumont) or "world view" (Cavell). In Crary's case especially, as we explored in the first chapter, a Foucauldian archaeology of the media—in a shift from the immediate look to the dissociated gaze—moves to situate film, one might say, in a more general cultural exhibitionism. In any such account, cinema could not help but take its place at the end of the nineteenth century amid a spectatorial disposition whose coordinates of ocular reception had been transformed, according to Aumont's emphasis again, by everything from railroad travel through mountain climbing to the artistic practice of the spontaneous *étude* sketch (in its rejection of art as the more studious decoding of nature's text). We then add to these factors, via Crary's argument, the more particular specular technologies of such devices as the stereopticon, with its self-defusing and ultimately dead-ended ruse of near presence. Neither, as more generally in Cavell, could cinema fail to gather cultural definition from a world view in which the receiving subject, subject to numerous solicitations of the image media, is variously placed at a mechanized and *suspicious* distance from the real.

One can be quite ready to grant these things, take an interest in them, as long as one reserves the right to suggest that when film is too directly assimilated to certain of these "conditions," trouble begins. Whether or not new modes of vision are found succumbing primarily to the adjusted natural optics of the framed train window, say, to the painterly spread of the panorama, to a flood of imagery in advertising print in both public and private space, or to that underlying spectatorial remove from the real to which these epiphenomena separately attest—even to an entire zeitgeist of epistemological anxiety—there is a further fact from which the diversions of the look in this history-of-vision approach should not avert our gaze. For cinema is first if not foremost the photographically based *simulation* of such kinetized gazing elsewhere available—and increasingly through the nineteenth century—in cognitive experience. In its graphically segmented and electro-mechanically paced signals, therefore, cinema is in one respect as close to the magic lantern, to phonography, or even to typewriting, as it is to an urban tram journey past commercial billboards.

Let me make this as plain as I can. To see cinema entering the scopic regimes of modernity is one thing. Not to bear in mind that it mechanizes that new scopic dispensation through a masking of its photographic *basis* (rather than its origin) is another—and a mistake. To recognize that cinema emerges, through its own automatisms, from a detextualizing of nature as the world's legible book (Aumont again) is one thing. Not to stress that it retextualizes the world (however imperceptibly) on its own photomechanical and constructivist terms is another. To allow for the former insistences while avoiding the latter confusions is the reason I wish now to shift the terms from modernity to a more admittedly textualist modern*ism*, by no means period bound. To do so opens film back, in turn, to a number of longer-span developmental accounts of exactly the sort Aumont, among others, writes either to resist or to specify more precisely. Yet it is very much in the spirit of a nonlinear story of cinema's invention—as elemented in cultural and aesthetic conditions other than sheer technological refinement—that one is drawn to those more sweeping overviews (cinema, say, as the fulfillment of Plato's myth of the cave) lately downplayed in media studies by the weight of a more closely historicized cultural evidence.

A quick survey of the numerous conflicting but often imbricated claims for the historical necessity of cinema's emergence—in commentators as diverse as André Bazin and Jean-Louis Baudry, André Malraux and Gilles Deleuze—makes one salient tendency inescapable. Teleology seems fiendishly difficult to resist, even if one veers from the narrow lineage of lens and print technology. Looking back on the forked and reforked pathways of aesthetic and industrial evolution, cinema often seems the one road that could never have failed to be taken. Film, we may say, is foreseen in retrospect as the dream come true. Not just the fated manifestation of a whole new regime of viewing, cinema is, among other proposals, a decisive turn in the histories of both the mechanical tool and the plastic arts, an evolutionary leap in the function of the sign, and the fulfillment of a millennial development in a theoretical physics of the interval. Before we can add microlinguistics to these templates derived from mechanics, aesthetics, semiotics, and physics, as well as to claims (elsewhere) for the anticipation of cinema in everything from Egyptian mummification to the specific space/time ratios of industrial locomotion, we will need an additional brief scan of this crowded historical terrain. The importance of these separate histories for our ongoing discussion has in part to do with the way certain films rehearse a sense of such elongated lineages specifically in relation to their photographic point of departure. How then can cinema be found to resituate its local parentage within a larger family history of mimesis and mechanization that roots more intricately, rather than overrules, the primary optic basis of the filmic text?

"FILM IN THE HOUSE OF THE WORD"

Himself an accomplished photographer as well as a piercingly articulate film-maker, the late Hollis Frampton was perhaps the least likely of all film theorists after Eisenstein to downplay the photogram. But before encountering the fore-word to his collected essays, nothing could have led me to anticipate that *Circles of Confusion—Film, Photography, Video* would share a common point of historical entry with my own work on literary language. Indeed, I borrow for this section the title of Frampton's paper on Eisenstein to focus his sense of the filmic heritage, which takes its bearings, as did my book on the literary phonotext, from early experiments in silent reading tried out by Saint Ambrose and spied upon (eavesdropping no longer possible) by the young monk Augustine, as later recounted in his *Confessions*. Frampton's fuller discussion of this cultural turn to unsounded reading crosses paths, therefore, with Paul Virilio's brief allusions to it, as taken up at the end of the previous chapter. Subordinated to an emphasis on print textuality, Virilio's concern with silent (private) reading (rather than oral recitation) is primarily a concern shared by Friedrich Kittler, in his emphasis on mediality, with the visible "exposure time" of serial imprint. For Frampton, who has the morphophonemic structure of language more directly in mind, silent reading takes, in a sense different from Virilio's, an implicit step in the direction of cinema's automatism: a suppression of a phonic signals laden, in Frampton's view, with atavistic ties to the codified marks of a pictogram, a kind of halfway house of the image.[2] Whereas Virilio stresses the persistence of instantaneous and discrete marking, for Frampton silent reading may be said to liberate the mental picture once and for all from the sense of an arbitrary sensory mediation (voice)—and thus to open the possibility (centuries later) for a directly imagistic representation of reality.[3] By an alternative route leading on from this Augustinian anecdote, my own use of Ambrose's innovation as point of departure for the evolution of a phonemically conceived silent reading has been to note the way such a reading practice eventually necessitated the insertion of word breaks into the previously continuous lineation of scribal Latin: a flagging of juncture meant to mitigate the slippages that a slow-paced oral voicing could no longer disambiguate.[4] One view of literary language in the centuries since would therefore be to see its phonemic saturation tending to erode the reader's relaxed confidence in the policed borders of regimented script.

This is quite aside from Frampton's claims for the emergence of cinema out of written imprint, however. As he sees it, writing, processed as text rather than as vocal score, "superannuates the registration of phonemes by an arrangement of degenerate images" (8) and in so doing makes way for an eventual photographic (and finally photogrammatic) regeneration of the image in full autonomy from abstract signifiers of any sort. What Ambrose discovered before Augustine was that consciousness could leap from the arbitrary graphic mark to the conjured image without, in effect, passing through the redundant stage of oral phonation. Centuries later the mechanics of photography, once further mechanized by film, narrowed the lag time of such passage (from mark to picturing) to the point of simultaneity. At the dawn of silent text production, the stream of representational notations grew cognitively indistinguishable (at least in the instant) from the meanings they spurred into image—in other words, brought to mind. On Frampton's long view, reading thus went silent, bypassing the oral dimension, to make space for the *illusion* of immediate impressions, a process whose subjective component it took several centuries more for photography, and then film, to reduce gradually toward a true zero. Photography automatized in pure objecthood what silent reading yearned for: the independence of the image in full freedom from the perceiver. "It is only with the intervention of photography, along with its evolutionary progeny, film and video, that a reproducible and verifiable stream of images begins, just as the historic stream of words begins, for us, not with the articulating voice but with print, the sociable image of language" (9). For all this transformative potential in Frampton, a question persists: the extent to which film, having transcended the written, still shelters within itself the shadow of differential inscription. If so, its flicker effect, even when reduced to the negligible, would still bear comparison with those ambiguous ripples of differential phonation that are never entirely suppressed by silence in the deciphering act.

To suspect as much may still imply a sense of cinema's serialized imprint as remote as possible from the cineaste tradition of a *camera-stylo,* as if distantly indebted to Fox Talbot's famous trope for photography as the "pencil of nature," and hence from the consequent valorization of *auteur* as term for a penmanlike director.[5] Cinema may have its stylistics, personal and otherwise, but film in process has its *textuality.* The assignment of this chapter is therefore to go as far as previous examples will permit, backed by a few more here, in seconding—and specifying—Roland Barthes's rhetorical question, "Why not forgo the plurality of the 'arts' in order to affirm more powerfully the plurality of 'texts'?"[6] To do so we will need to carry a dialectical understanding of textual differentiation, leagued with Eisenstein's theory, into the creases of representation itself.

What would this mean? On the literary front, it would mean remaining alert to the continual—not quite continuous—winning out of the lexeme, and then (ultimately) the mental image, over the phonemes that generate it. This winning out is, of course, a victory always still in process, incurring its own setbacks, counterforays, border raids. With just their aid, we seem to hear words overreading themselves, encroaching across the graphic blanks. This proposal means, in addition, attending to a "plurality" (Barthes's word again) distributed within as well as among texts, not only their multiplicity of kind but their multi-ply nature in production. Such is the lure of the plural within the apparent monologism of the scriptive sign as well as the filmic signal. To lift and vary the example extracted from the protomodernism of Henry James's thickened prose at the end of the previous chapter: the successive (f)act of the phoneme is part of the act of reading.

Before I take up other aspects of Frampton's writing on film more obviously concerned with the photogram's relation to the screen frame, his own recourse to the linguistic analogy prompts some additional clarification from the different perspective of this chapter. Literary readers have, as a rule (the rule called language), as little time to notice the letter in their reading of words as do viewers the photogram on-screen. That is also, one might insist, the beginning and the end of the analogy, since readers could if they chose slow over an alphabetic (or phonemic) cluster or its bordering gaps, whereas film viewers never have such time at their disposal. But we cannot afford to leave the matter there. Pushing harder: Though the analogy must remain partial, there is indeed a two-stage process in the generation of the screen image out of the spinning strip that is in some measure comparable, as I noted in earlier discussion, to the linguistic regime of "double articulation." The latter term names the hierarchical process whereby the graphic (alphabetic) integers or bunchings that "represent" (stand in for) phonemic patterns must in turn cluster, one level up, into that lexical assemblage of words in grammatical motion that we ordinarily know as representation. These words are dependent on blanks, the interstices of Virilio's "exposure time." So, of course, are film images. But the barred blank between photograms—barred in both senses, delineated as a band on the strip and blocked in process (by the shutter mechanism) on the racing track—is invisibly returned to the primary level of inscription or imprint, masked entirely in the screen event. Unlike the word breaks one must see in order to minimize the subvocal equivocation of juncture and so maximize reading speed, the space between photograms must be *unseen* from the start (Arnheim's "imperceptible montage" again) to sustain the view. Wording is, rather, a perceptible collage. Yet even there the edges of signification may be hedged or fudged as well.[7]

In the ordinary shunting of word toward word, each warding off the other long enough to have its say, reading too has its own (variable) shutter speeds. Whenever the gaps flare to recognition—just as, on-screen, whenever a photogrammatic impaction betrays the cinematic norm through some untoward rush or concussion of the filmic cell—the system has reverted to the increments it stems from. Their calibration and timimg, too, have a history outside textuality. We have seen Paul Virilio compare serial photography to linguistic inscription. In the 1989 preface to the English edition of *War and Cinema*, he reviews his larger argument by tracing a connection between the "industrial production of repeating guns and automatic weapons" and "the innovation of repeating images, with the *photogram providing the occasion*" (emphasis added). Through self-erasure, the photogram takes its place in what Virilio elsewhere calls an *esthétique de la disparition*.[8]

The linguistic equivalent of such rapid-fire filmic seriality is evinced repeatedly in that heightened, tightened linkage of subvocal filaments known as modernist *écriture*, where traditional literary diction, at loose ends with itself, forges new lateral ties in the disappearing flash of its own exposure time. Letters that have flocked together in wording may be unlocked and redistributed by the random adhesions of sequence itself. In this way the phonemic stray brings to view the internal succession of an alphabetic order subsumed to a lexical one, precisely the controlled subordination that stands as norm to the instanced deviance. This is because, as I have been saying, letters generally disappear into the words they constitute as do photograms into the motion they impel, one after the other even though seemingly all at once. It is only under undue duress, however, that a letter may be prematurely released to the next word in line, reshuffled into an overlapping phrasal alternative. Photograms always work this way. Their automation is at base a persistent lamination. This, once again, is the real difference within a fundamental linkage of the two media. The film track is a total machination to begin with, at the level of its own "primary" articulation; to slow or detain the photogram is an overt and intentional disruption. In the discontinuous nature of writing, however, the automatism includes in its operative structure a variable format of breaks. This is a format whose constitutive necessity may thus be found exaggerated and displaced by those collaborative accidents of eye and ear that span— as well as snap open—more gaps than mandated by the dictates of syntactic sense.

The supposed integral structure of the word, like the supposed integral structure of the screen image, is thus deconstructed from within by its own habitual functioning, which typically masks the work of supplementation as mere succession. To put it this way is to prepare for this chapter's step beyond the strict logic of difference toward a cross-media dialectics of the temporal interval, where the collisions incident to normal reading speed will be reconceived in line with disjunctive effects staged by invariant filmic velocity. For now, we think of the frayed lexeme rearrayed by the reader's subvocal scan as an indwelling weld of phonemic matter, internal and annexational at once.[9] For what is surely clear about filmic as well as lexical succession is that the integrity of the signifier in its smallest molecules cannot be ensured in the immanent functioning of either medium of imprint. Phonemic play and photogrammatic disclosure have this much in common, then, after all: They can both goad us to notice the unstable successivity of their mechanism by skipping a beat or two, exposing overlay itself as the undertext of the consecutive. The phoneme, transcribed by one or more graphemes, remains even in silent reading an undertow in the instantaneous flow of diction and syntax toward the summoned mental referent. Such a *phonogram*, operating on that rapid treadmill of the read, is therefore a revealing counterpart to the unsegregable increment of film's self-agitated image, which only a specialized pedagogy of filmic (within cinematic) practice can lift to notice.

What we can "learn" through cinema about its constituent frame, what Frampton calls "our white rectangle" (196), can be fully appreciated only in sight of another history Frampton himself has to tell. This concerns more than the climactic place of the filmic image in a streamlining of the sign function. It also accounts for cinema's emergence within technology as the final instrumentation not just of war machinery but of the machine age all told—and hence the first motorized art thereof. In "For a Metahistory of Film," Frampton writes with capitalized hyperbole: "Cinema is the Last Machine. It is probably the last art that will reach the mind through the senses" (113). He generalizes from this claims as follows. Art arises when *techne* is no longer necessary for the preservation of the species—and can now be artificially maintained for its edification. Scapegoat ritual became drama, as, say, music grew out of the warning call or signal. Frampton's examples: cave paintings as dossiers of external threat transformed to fetishes of its transcendence.

We can sum up the argument this way: Art is the aftermath of necessity in the realm of survival tactics. It is an argument strikingly parallel to that developed not only by Virilio but by Kittler for the modern era of technology, in which military intelligence devices preceded and necessitated the steady escalation of modern media science. Kittler reviews everything from the frequencies of radio transmission and its ramified alternatives for escaping countersurveillance to the propeller–machine gun synchronization borrowed, on the subsequent home front, to refine the operation of the cinematic projector and reduce its jarring flicker.[10] Frampton too takes his bearings from advances in military technology. For him the machine age ends not in video but in radar's replacement of reconnaissance flights (113): the traced presence of what we would have to call a clear and absent danger.[11] After this, with the Machine itself largely outmoded, mechanism could for the first time become re-presentational art—namely, through the cinematic apparatus, an art in the wake of the technological utility of its own constituent devices. One has only to add to this version of apparatus theory, and very much in Frampton's spirit, the thought that if one forgets the photogram that spins through the coils of this aestheticized device, then the apparatus is no longer the kind of machine it is, no longer producing the kind of aesthetic construct it does.

To bring that other telos of Frampton's semiotic (rather than technological) history into the picture at this point does not seem impossible, despite Frampton's own separate attention to these issues. Only when oral reading became no longer necessary for the accessible preservation of records, and so no longer necessary to the cultural preservation of the species, only when silence had been normalized as the genuine ether of textual imaging, could the phonic element return to attention not as mandatory decipherment but in the vestigial form of art. Here is where Frampton's separate speculations converge upon the task of this chapter. Such a history of inscription, whereby the biomotor mechanics of phonatory decoding get revalorized in the mode of aesthetics, is the same kind of history that rescues for aesthetic force the automated photogrammatic "rectangle" otherwise lost to recognition in what Frampton calls the disembodied (printed, no longer vocally mediated) image system born of silent reading and fulfilled in mechanized screen picturation.

Ars ex machina: this notion in Frampton gains support from a rather distant quarter, the magisterial art history of André Malraux. By the title of his influential chapter "Museum without Walls," Malraux refers to the photographic reproduction of paintings that alone makes art widely available for study, its history for the first time a credible enterprise.[12] Scholars could now compare not just visited masterworks but whole oeuvres, and the concept of "style" emerges more productively. From the Renaissance forward, it was primarily a style of rendering. The first nineteenth-century stirrings of modernism, however, overturned the values of transparent rendering by those of marked execution. And at just this point, the photographic facilitation of art history that allowed for a newly definitive view of this transformation—in other words, the archival instrumentation of comparative taxonomy through photo imprint—has emerged as a competitive (and compensatory) art form in its own technological right. In painting, that is, even as the pictorial came forward from represented space to a disclosed act performed upon the canvas surface, photography was automatizing the former aesthetic of the faithfully rendered scene.

The very fact of cinema, according to Malraux, would dawn upon these early modern developments as a yet more complete revalorization of rendering over execution. It was only later that the art (or style) of cinema would gradually assert itself by striking a balance between the two, between representation and making, that would exceed the complacent confines of the fixed-frame shot, the sheer uninflected record, the mere photography of motion. In short, the filmic (i.e., photographic) technology that allowed for the archival mechanization of art history matures into a new mechanical medium in the history of art. Half a century after Manet suspended the mimetic telos of realism, then, cinema arrives to complete its mission. But it does so by recovering an earlier and deeper motive (rather than superficial motifs) in the history of art. For Malraux, the photographically based art of cinematic kinesis is the true fulfillment of the baroque period's dynamization of the image. Once film passed from the static shot's indebtedness to the very theater of the world (or to actual vaudeville sketches), as patiently recorded by the stationary camera, the art of cinema, strictly speaking, emerges for Malraux with the "cut," with the shifting of ocular planes, where the fixed view of photography has become a dynamism *of views* rather than the mobilization of objects or bodies. "The means of reproduction in the cinema is the moving photograph, but its means of expression is the sequence of planes" (123). It hardly needs saying at this point that such cutting, such sequencing of "planes," not only depends on the cellular photogram but summons up its discreteness in a for once visible disjuncture. In its enhanced "expression," therefore, cinema is all the more poised to recover the very basis of its mechanical "reproduction."

"OUR WHITE RECTANGLE": FROM PHOTOGRAM TO SCREEN FRAME

Call Malraux's "planes" the avatars of a persistent rectangle, their "sequence" a serial succession, and the homology between track and strip stands forth more clearly than ever. That's just where Frampton wants it, out in the open. The true work of cinema is to keep the photographological basis of the screen's play of images recognizably *in play*. This is of course his Brechtian modernist streak, his urge to alienate motion's easy receipt by the eye, his favored estrangement of the screen image by the return, at several levels, of what it screens out. Frampton speaks here as an experimental pedagogue—and perpetual student—of the photogram: "We *learned* long ago to see our rectangle, to hold all of it in focus simultaneously. If films consist of consecutive frames, we can learn to see *them* also."[13] Avant-garde cinema can teach us this second sight, this access to our specular unconscious, in "flicker films" and elsewhere. In complementing such experimental pedagogy, the chief concern of this book has been with the way even certain main-

stream narrative films can never entirely *unlearn* this fact of the photogram, however unable the spectator may be to hold it either in mind or in view for too long at a time. In this sense I take what I had to say in chapter 5 about the matte implacable rectangles constituting the space of withheld disclosure in the briefing room of *2001* to be one of narrative film's true object lessons in its own celluloid objecthood. As we will see in a moment, this rigorous self-meditative film of Kubrick's has extensively prepared the context for such a negative *mise en abyme.*

Screening produces in essence, writes Frampton, "only a rectangle of white light. But it is all films. We can never see *more* within our rectangle, only *less*" (194). He means that the human image, for instance, appears on-screen only by removing various amounts of the original beam. The screen image "subtracts" from what we might call the ur-blur of light, "makes a vacancy," one that "looks to us like, say, Lana Turner" (196). Confusion sets in only when he suggests ("it is all films") that every such vacancy taken together, rather than their universal latency in the pure beam, would return us to that primal gleam of the rectangle's scouring luminosity. In fact, all the subtractions that make for all the shadow play on all the cinema's screens would be an absolute blackness—not searing clear the image but surcharging the photogram, each in overlain serial projection, with an unreadable repletion rather than reduction. In this light, this nonlight, I return one last time to Kubrick's masterwork as its own "metahistory of film." The central plot mystery of *2001* might be posited as if to trump the notion that all films together would visibly concentrate all the light of all the world's projectors. Substitute black for white (as follows) in Frampton's characterization and you are closer at once to the technical case and to Kubrick's insinuated subtext: "Our rectangle of black light is eternal. Only *we* come and go; we say: that is where I came in. The rectangle was here before we came, and it will be here after we have gone" (184).

This takes us, in Kubrick's film, to that definitive final conjunction of primal geometry—rectangle and circle in their hovering three-dimensional avatars as slab and sphere—and then takes us further back, in turn, to the rectangular photogram on the track. As motivated by and materialized within the screen-engulfing "plane" of the black monolith in the film's last stunning cut (detailed below), the evenly weighted convergence of earth's globe and the amniotic sac of the newborn starchild (see fig. 316) fulfills, for one thing, Eisenstein's dream of a pure dialectic even within the frame, where discrepancies of volume, mass, and scale collide upon each other in a poised but shattering ambiguity.[14] How big is this undreamed-of new life form? In what sense does its wheeling mass, or at least its spiritual density, displace the earth as we know it? But how in fact do we know the earth in this way, decentered, seen from outside itself, like a gargantuan marble? Only from the photographic technology of early space probes. This leads to the second aspect of the shot in question. Men were not on the moon until the year after the 1968 premiere of *2001: A Space Odyssey.* And yet the conjunction of these two previously unseen dimensions of existence, of human enterprise—on the one side, the embryonic possibility in emergence like a moon in the ascendant; on the other, the parent world actually seen, rather than imagined, in the round— place the true historical moment of Kubrick's vision at a technological crossroads

in the development not only of cinema but of photography per se. Whence the intertextual resonance of the starchild's enlarged fetus.

Lennart Nilsson's Hasselblad camera, with which he first photographed the gestation of life in the womb for *Life* magazine in 1965, is an adaptation of the same Swedish camera technology that would later, just after the release of *2001*, be used by the first astronauts on the moon (as it had previously been used in preliminary orbital missions). The museum exhibit in Stockholm that called this coincidence to my attention, with no reference to *2001*'s intervening graphic convergence, nevertheless puts my point about it as succinctly as I can imagine. Showing a fetus on one side, the moon landing on the other (with earth in the distance), the paired photographs were captioned, respectively, "mikro" and "makro."[15] In a single antithesis, we find distilled the Eisensteinian dialectic of Kubrick's finale.

I reiterate, then, Frampton's lyric absolutism—with Kubrick's illustration of my own disclaimer: "That rectangle was here before we came, and it will be here after we have gone." Name it a monolith, and you have a mythic plot. But the preexistence of this rectangle, and its posthumous survival of our spectation, can only take the form of a frame thick to occlusion with the numberless shadows it has imprinted. It cannot be a frame of light, but only of midnight black. This transhistorical rectangle is Kubrick's galactic interloper, the monolithic nature of directional temporality itself. And in a moment of sublime—exactly because subliminal—transition, the monolith becomes, by filling, the very screen for which it has been serving as synecdoche. The camera's last dollying motion, that is, leaves behind the human bier as birthbed (fig. 310) to edge in upon the slab's blank surface like a POV displaced into an out-of-body shot (fig. 311). Just as humanity's last vestige is for a moment relayed by the eye of the camera alone, so now is the prompting monolithic source subsumed to the ephemera of montage across an indeterminate and invisible cut. In the lunge/lap/plunge of that last tracking glide, smoothly tossing us into the bottomless levitation of a sublunar orbit, the numinous (precisely because lumenless) rectangle's approached—seemingly approaching—verticality is engorged by the suddenly isomorphic horizontality of the Cinerama screen format (figs. 312-14).

This takes place in a shift across a momentary black blank—equivalent to a run of indecipherably overloaded photograms—that brings before us, as if suddenly released and realized within the parameters of the monolithic surface itself, the cinematographic *fiat lux*. Precipitated out from a planar surface hollowed and overbrimmed at once, there is, first, earth's subservient moon lifting into frame (fig. 315). This image is backed by a dusting of pinpoint stars illegible in a reproduced still, needing

310

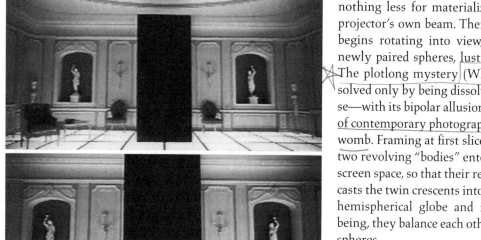

nothing less for materialization than the intensity of the projector's own beam. There follows, next and last, as earth begins rotating into view, the materialized slow duet of newly paired spheres, lustral globe and fetal sac (fig. 316). The plotlong mystery (What is motivating the whole?) is solved only by being dissolved into screen manifestation per se—with its bipolar allusion to the outer and inner envelopes of contemporary photographic penetration, stratosphere and womb. Framing at first slices off a comparable section of the two revolving "bodies" entering from opposite wings of off-screen space, so that their reciprocal jockeying for dominance casts the twin crescents into graphic equilibrium. Pared from hemispherical globe and from orbiting lobe of incipient being, they balance each other in a literalized harmony of the spheres.

In all this, the puzzle of a cosmic agenda succeeds to the dazzle of technology's own projections. In terms of narrative enigma and resolution in this apocalyptic jump cut (as epochal as the earlier famous match cut between primeval bone and oblong spacecraft), historical evolution is translated to a metanarrative phenomenon. Cosmic process amounts to the editorial ingenuity of an unseen technical mastermind, a harmonizing artisan of specular discrepancy. Imperceptible in the minutiae of its transitions, nevertheless genuine filmic disclosure is an always visible magic and machination. Here, further, its pivotal effect is intertextually ratified by allusion to a media-historical convergence (Hasselblad camera or otherwise) between the micro and the macro: their convergence, that is, in a felt space of metaphysical adequation.

But think Eisenstein even an instant sooner than the famous last shot of orbiting biospheres. In being ushered to a discrepancy within the frame, we have entered upon a dialectical collision *between* frames: always the precedent filmic moment within cinema. Just before the disorienting flotation of englobed worlds, that is, we have seen the slicing intersection of now stable, now vectorized forms. Here rests

311, 312, 313, 314, 315, 316

in evanescence the true apotheosis of Kubrick's masterly rectangle, less a religious epiphany than a technological one. Across a single photogram lost to view somewhere in that black cavern or avenue between the approached monolith on end and the spread arms of the screen is the film's deepest bid for *self*-transfiguration. An uprush of primal difference—impenetrable black plane versus infinite deep space—marks the cusp of absentation itself as an immeasurable temporal chasm. Knotted up—or folded over, hymenlike—in that node of transition between the retention of the vertical image (black) and the protention of the horizontal (the momentarily prolonged full-screen blank) is the crux and crossing (the crucifi-cial—and posttheological—afterimage) of filmic incarnation itself. From which all is risen to view. In Kubrick's metacinematic squaring of the cosmic circles, his rec-tangulation of the spheres, the vacated black interval of spaced sequence, especially if it calls to mind the instantaneous metamorphic power of photogrammatic advance, is translated to a temporal quantum leap.

IN VIEW OF THE INTERVAL

Putting aside for now the immediate 1960s photographic subtext of Kubrick's micro/macro finale, we can watch the technology of photomechanical imprint take up its varying place in a lengthier history of scientific speculation as well as experiment, a lineage not just of the Machine but of classical optics, mechanics, physics, and finally relativity. Many of the most ambitious theorists of the medium are drawn to such world-stage claims, and Jean-Louis Baudry dispatches his straight off in an influential essay that moves on to quite different matters.[16] For Baudry it is no accident that the birth of modern science is precisely coincident with the birth of optics, so that the breakthroughs of Galileo are the direct fore-runners of the cinematic lens. The stakes are metaphysical—but the game is a los-ing one, for what film completes in the heliocentric discourse of Galileo is the final decentering of the terrestrial human subject, now satellite (as spectator) to a radi-ant and autonomous world in view. Here too is where Gilles Deleuze returns to our purpose, with another version of the modernist telos different from Malraux's on the one hand, Baudry's on the other. Guided once again by Bergson, Deleuze understands cinema to be derived not just from a photochemical and ocular tech-nology running back from the photogravure through the optical toy to the cam-era obscura and the first telescope. Rather, he traces cinema's descent from a broader technological and theoretical prehistory entwined with the evolution of physics at large rather than optics per se, with theoretical studies of the kinetic in-terval rather than the techniques of movement's visual capture.

Deleuze follows Bergson again in seeing the history of what was once called natural philosophy mutating into the history of modernist art. Kepler, Galileo, Descartes, Newton, Leibniz: "Everywhere the mechanical succession of instants replaced the dialectical order of poses,"[17] with time dissevered from movement through space as "an independent variable." (We will want shortly to attach this notion to the calculus of the "delta function.") Toward the climax of such devel-opments in cognitive paradigms, so also "dance, ballet and mime were abandoning

figures and poses to release values which were not posed, not measured, which related movement to the any-instant-whatever" (6). Over against the fixed instant—or call it the definitive position, the instance, the stance—one important object of theory had become instead the interval. Thomas Pynchon joins Bergson and Deleuze in tracing this lineage back to the invention of calculus as a predecessor of cinema. In *Gravity's Rainbow,* German rocket scientists watch the daily rushes of high-speed photography during flight tests, fulfilling a "strange connection between the German mind and the rapid flashing of successive stills to counterfeit movement, for a least two centuries—since Leibniz."[18] In cinema, Deleuze sees Astaire and Chaplin capitalizing on such models, but this is more or less incidental. *As* film, the mechanized image is, in wholesale terms, a postscientific fulfillment of this routinization of the arbitrary interval, linked across media with the apotheosis of the differential *phase* rather than the *pose* in the synthesized fragmentations of cubist art. Deleuze once more: "Everywhere the mechanical succession of instants replaced the dialectical order of poses." Along these lines, modernity waits for both Einstein and Eisenstein, each in his own way, to discover the inherent dialectics of the interval itself, where time and space strain toward a sublation beyond either. Frampton's paradigm comes to the fore again in a new form. While modernity rides on physical theory and its technological implementation, that is, modernism gathers up the backwash of innovative science for revaluation as aesthetic experience.

Aesthetic experience, yes—as well as the estimate of such experience in materialist-formalist theory, including even linguistic phonology. For film's place, according to Bergson and Deleuze, in the ascendancy of the interval within scientific paradigms is in fact matched with a definitive historical move in linguistic science. What we find there issues permission to this chapter's whole attempted link between the operations of the cinematic image track and the verbal activation of literary textuality. I quote, to this end, a suggestive road sign planted by Roman Jakobson in his late work on *The Sound Shape of Language,* dating his interest in these matters to the epoch of experimental modernism: "The autonomization of minimal formal units, a characteristic procedure of the arts and sciences around World War I, was saliently manifested in the growing inquiry into the sound shapes of language."[19] Hold on to that term: *autonomization.* It will be the keynote of what follows on the breakdown of the modular into the molecular in verbal as well as visual inscription. To the lineage stretching from Galileo to Einstein, Duchamp, Balanchine, and beyond, one should add, in other words, the name of another scientist of protocubist op/positionality: Ferdinand de Saussure, the founder of modern linguistics as an autonomized synchrony of pertinent difference. The discussion that comes next, concerning a related plateau of conjunction between cinema and modernist literary language, will bring us round in a few pages to the Saussurean fundament once more.

In his role now as literary historian rather than film critic (a part he will play later in this chapter), Fredric Jameson nonetheless finds an elucidating intersection between cinematic framing and the new modes of literary cognition at the turn of the century. And this intersection has to do in large part with new valences of the space-time interval in perceptual life. Jameson's work thus comes to invoke yet another technological paradigm (familiar lately from other sources as well) for the origins and orientation of early cinema: its affinity with the processes of commercial locomotion. For Jameson, this industrial armature of capitalism is made to subserve the diffuse colonialist subtext of E. M. Forster's *Howards End*—as manifested in a valorized new form of equivocated stylistic effect, even as such early modernist writing is distinguished from the supposedly *astylistic* verbal machinery of James Joyce.[20] Jameson's cinematic analogy for such effects should help direct us toward a deeper-going poetics of the differential *styleme* in filmic machination as well as in cinematic representation.

Jameson begins, near where the action proper of *Howards End* begins, with a typically evocative passage of Forsterian reflective prose. This description of a train journey has Aunt Munt leaving London, and all that its metropolitan enterprise has foisted upon the spreading clutter of the outlying landscape, to rescue a niece from a precipitous engagement. Viaducts, roadways, tunnels come and go, while the half-distracted mind is elsewhere, bent on its social purpose. Yet Forster's comedy of manners is less single-minded than its immediate comic character, making mental space instead for the ideologically fraught undecidabilities of space itself. Jameson rightly characterizes the paragraph led off by such a narrative thrust as "an amiable simplicity filled with traps and false leads" (52). Such prose conduces to what is for him the ultimate modernist disjunction: the gap between the evocations of descriptive style and the spatial (and spatiotemporal) references to which they are no longer quite tethered.

What Forster's Mrs. Munt submits to, says Jameson, "is of course a cinematographic kind of space, with its Einsteinian observer on a train moving through a landscape whose observation it alters at the very moment that it makes it possible" (53). This is not so much a historical as a theoretical point, since "what is most significant is not some possible influence of nascent cinema on Forster or on the modernist novel in general, but rather the confluence of the two distinct formal developments, of movie technology on the one hand, and of a certain type of modernist or protomodernist language on the other, both of which seem to offer some space, some third term, between the subject and the object alike" (53). For Jameson that term is in effect the apparatus, the disembodiment of perception by technique—or in Cavell's language for film, the automatisms. Literary writing is for the first time, from Conrad (elsewhere Jameson's example) and Forster on, more a concerted medium than a representational means, an overt textuality as well as a conspicuous rhetoric of narrative persuasion. Modernist writing is neither predominantly impressionist nor expressive (since both imply the intervening subjectivity of an author) but in some new way strictly technical, a prosthesis of observation in the mode of inscription.[21] By the time of Forster, and of Conrad before him, style has become one of the suddenly reified specialties of fiction. It is now a "category" of effect rather than a tool of rhetorical production, so that it appears "urgent to disjoin" such style "from conventional notions of psychology and subjectivity: whence the therapeutic usefulness of the cinematographic parallel, where an apparatus takes the place of human psychology and perception" (53).

This is where Jameson leaves the matter of cinema in relation to a slowly crystallizing modernist aesthetic. Yet it is only a start. To pursue it further with full clarity, however, we need first to fend off certain objections his previous work on film has met with. When I join Jameson in speaking, here and throughout this book, about the early modernist dispensation of cinema (signaled by French surrealism or Russian constructivism, say), I mean neither to dismiss nor to contest the definitive recent work on early cinema that sees its opening decade or so as fundamentally more experimental, and more disruptive to spectatorial attention, than the consolidated narrative codes of the immediately succeeding years. A certain ironic dissonance within the new histories of cinema, between the archivists and the theorists if you will, is much to the point here. Only in the routinization of visual options (after 1910, roughly speaking) do the corporealized mobile "gaze" (Crary) and the "variable eye" (Aumont)—currently advanced as the leading *pre*conditions of cinema—come fully into their own with the systematic multiplication of shots through editing. In this light it seems that early cinema scrambled to adjust its ways to the cultural context prepared for it, so that it might become part of a spectatorial discourse rather than remain an optical aberration, might become a fully tooled distraction factory rather than an arresting "cinema of attractions."[22] In the very beginning, however, all effects were special, all shots astonishing. The *art* of kinesis, as Malraux would say, came later—with the mobilization of the plane itself.

None of this, although it is often taken to do so, need compromise one's sense of a later phase in experimental cinema associated with international high modernism and emerging two or three decades into the history of the new medium. After all, the aesthetic animus of such modernism was directed precisely against the rapidly standardized narrative codes of the medium rather than its ocular conditions. We do not have to agree, then, on the necessary "reversal" of Jameson's classic-modernist periodization in film history to appreciate the shock effect of early cinema—as one of the things 1920s modernism sought to retrieve from its rapid normalization.[23] Jameson's stress on the cognitive allegiance between Forster's writing as early as 1910 and the railroad's links to a cinematic automatism thus appears to enter the very territory he is sometimes seen to ignore: the unstabilized advent of cinematic fascination in its inaugural phase. His work both credits the upheavals of cinema's first decade *and* detects the main path of an aesthetic dissociation, a valuation of cognitive disjuncture itself, leading on to high modernism.

We can now rejoin the power of Jameson's suggestions at the point where he himself lets them rest. He urges, we have seen, a thorough disarticulation between the notion of style and the "conventional" notion of literature's subjective inflection. Once the shibboleth of expressive intentionality in writing is thrown over, we might begin to add, the dawning sense of a divisive, incremental, disjunctive subject, split, multiplied, and incommensurable with its objects, always fractionally out of phase, may take us back to the filmic track at a level of more precise "confluence" between modernist writing and the filmic imprint. For the utility of the "cinematographic parallel" in Jameson's modernist stylistics is, again, that it introduces an "apparatus" to account for the undisguised *technical* mediation of even proto-modernist prose. This is what we can sketchily detect in the passage from Forster that Jameson starts with. The first sentence is all we need for now: "The train sped northward, under innumerable tunnels." Nothing could be crisper, less encumbered. The writing is as gracefully transparent as the railway glass through which its summoned prospect is glimpsed—and as swift in its strokes as the passing landscape. But if Jameson is even half right, no prose could be more tightly attuned to the cinematic effect as well as to the apparatus of its projection.

In this essay, Jameson does not relate his claims for the studied obscurantism of modernist spatial description to the break into *écriture* with Conrad, which, as we will see below, he has elsewhere stipulated as one founding moment in modernist narrative. But we will soon be in position to do so—and by returning, in fact, to the verbal rather than visual impaction and overlay of Conrad's 1907 *The Secret Agent*. Even in the genial lilt of Forster's cadenced diction, however, one can see at work this writing beneath the written. It offers the near equivalent in prose for the filmic beneath the cinematic. Forster's train makes its way, again, "under innumerable tunnels." One doesn't ordinarily pass *under* tunnels, one goes *through* them, unless of course one is looking for a prepositional echo in the disyllable of "under" for the ultimately unsaid "numberless." Prose seems caught in the very process of deciding against a too studied assonance of this sort. Avoiding it, Forster's writing instead stretches the epithetical effect out across the five syllables of "innumerable" toward the uptake of "tunnels"—involving the perfect graphemes for them, two pictograms each of their carved arches: *nn* and then again *nn*. It is as if, following Frampton, morphophonemic writing has come full circle back to the only gradually aestheticized glyph. In routing itself back toward this faintest trace of the pictogram, modernist writing has also engaged again the undertext of writing's own forward motion, a motion whose disturbances can indeed be said to tunnel beneath the bedrock of script.

In its immediate critical context, such descriptive insinuations can all be absorbed by Jameson's argument about the tug of the Forsterian "unseen" (a version of "the infinite") on a metropolitan modernism that figures the colonial outreach and underpinnings of its own socioeconomy as an unfathomable totality available to cognition only through the mystified gestures of hazy evocation (associated here with railroad lines trailing off to infinity). The global circuit of imperial exchange is thus at the same time serviced and dispersed by a postmetaphysical rhetoric of visionary inclusion. But in the larger context yet of literary language and its evolutionary mutations, Jameson has struck an entangled and even richer vein. For what the depersonalized cinematic mechanism may actually provide is more than evidence for a politics of obscuration and dispersal within an aesthetics of epiphany. On offer, in addition, may be a model for linguistic free play as not only an "autonomization" (Jakobson) but an *automatism* of language beneath the intentionalities of inscription, a writing always in flux beneath the written, undoing what it funds in utterance, unraveling the lexical discreteness it both requires and provides. What the "critical flicker fusion" of the cinematic apparatus (again, the technical term in projection for the shutter's role in the masking of disjuncture) has in common with the lexical transfusions of modernist literary excess would thus run deeper than otherwise imagined. Across a comparable thickness of notation in each medium, we find unreeling the still active signifier (or signal) beneath the marshaled blocks of representation. In this sense the filmic stands to the cinematic, once again, as *écriture* does to classic narrative. And in this sense too we must indeed complement the relation of cinema to the intervallic science of Leibniz through Einstein, of differential calculus through relativity, with film's own quasi-Saussurean (or Eisensteinian) automatisms, its dialectics of pertinent collision borrowed from the paradigmatic axis and arrayed across the horizontal span of representation. In pursuit of such a complementary perspective, we may call in some further evidence.

But let me be unambiguous about my point of departure in Jameson. What has been suggested already about the Forsterian passage's oscillatory internal echo and fugitive iconicity, its arched phrasing on the run, is an effect generated in the depiction of a rotary motion (the train's) always out of sight (like cinema's) from the spectatorial point of view. By the engines of wheeled motion, as elsewhere by the spin of projection, the engineered and constrained vision produced by train travel—the stroboscopic now you see it, now you don't of the rectangularly framed and glassed-off landscape—is only exaggerated, in the further direction of cinema's perceptual blank between photograms, by the intermittent prolonged occlusion of any one among numerous tunnels. But stressing this railway analogy could put from consideration a broader point. Nor do I wish for a moment to lay primary emphasis on "under innumerable tunnels" as phonetically or metrically, let alone graphically, hypermimetic. What I do mean to highlight, moving beyond Jameson on the very path he clears, is the apparatus-like automatism of the *verbal* as well as the inferred perceptual effect: somewhere between syllabic accident and rhetorical intention, between linguistics and poesis, motored by a verbal drive unleashed in the technological (scriptive) hinterland between subjective and objective notation. So with the following example from Conrad's revolutionary instrumentation of *écriture* (Jameson gives none, even in lodging a claim for it).[24] Here too mimesis does not merely redouble itself in verbal self-enactment; it permeates from representation to linguistic execution, from signified to signifier. And it does so in a passage every bit as concerned as any in *Howards End* to elevate obscure colonial dependency to tragic epiphany.

I refer to a phonemically congealed moment in Conrad's most inescapably "impressionist" set piece, the mutating chiaroscuro of "gloom . . . brooding" at the opening of *Heart of Darkness*. The cleanly delimited effect of a romantic landscape painting in prose undergoes its own protomodernist sfumato. In the process, it seems to validate Conrad's whole theory of literary significance in this same opening passage: the kind of narrative whose vague aura of suggestion is suffused with meaning in the way that a haze is brought out by a glow. This hazing seems transferred from the level of significance to that of the signifier itself, now rimmed with its own phonic blur. One stretch of wording should do for illustration, a description that reduces to inscription by catching word formation on the very cusp of its constitutive difference: "And at last, in its curved and imperceptible fall, the sun sank low, and from glowing white changed to a dull red without rays and without heat." The imperceptible is captured by the phonemic afterimage itself. Dissolving the integrity of separate lexemes in the phrase "sank low," one word seems immersed in the next, the glottal *k* blending with *low* to anticipate the already disappearing *glow* of the next phrase, whose ruddiness "withou*t r*ays" is, on the way to effacement, a red without any trace but the phonetic.

I offer, for immediate comparison, an example from Joyce as openly cinematic as I could find. Pace Jameson, it also seems "stylistic" in just his revisionary sense, decoupled from the ordinary registers of rhetoric in a manner tested out far more faintly and fitfully in the conservative and transitional writing of Forster. Style in this case is more like an "apparatus" of mediating imprint than a captured human tone. As far as imaginable from the authorial management of "voice" parodied in *Ulysses* as an evolution of obvious and imitable devices, here is a detachment that carries its freedom from "personality" into the internal detachments of wording itself as the smallest expressive unit of an outmoded rhetorical motive. Certainly the locus classicus of the anticlassical regime of the signifier, the clearinghouse of all such self-rotational phrasing, such spun punning, is *Finnegans Wake*. What follows is one of those moments, in the very teeth of a dated apostrophe (crisis point of subjectivity in literary writing, according to Jonathan Culler's widely accepted view), in which voice has vanished into *écriture* without a trace—or should we say with only a trace?[25] The famous section of the *Wake* that begins "O / tell me all about / Anna Livia" (196) quickly reiterates the command with "Tell me all. Tell me now" (196). It closes twenty pages later, after the speaker's identification with the insentient environs ("I feel as old as yonder elm" [215]), with the exploded pathetic fallacy of "Tell me, tell me, tell me, elm!" (216), where the vocative syllable ("elm") seems released from the belling repetition ("[t]ell m[e]") of the imperative form.[26] A principle akin to filmic succession has penetrated to the "imperceptible montage" of word formation itself. Three identical repetitions of the same blocked-out alphabetic matter along the syntactic strip finally dispel the lexical autonomy of each unit by spelling out the dialectical third term (beyond word and its spacing blank) of their automatic overlap in the *phonogram.* Joyce's true wake, like his true cinematographic modernism, is that of inscription itself, always dragging in tow a phantom element (or elm meant).

That one might wish to call such effects, from the undertexts of books as different as *Heart of Darkness* and *Finnegans Wake,* the lap dissolves of morphology and grammar together is a way of coming at the largest emphasis of this chapter. In their ominous superimpositions, the spectral overlays of Coppola's Conrad (in chapter 2) find something of a prose equivalent in the synthesized relation between, for instance, "without rays" on the one hand, "without trace" on the other—and, in between, their very difference in action, in the verbal event. We are moving far from Jameson's argument, but in a direction pointed by his own sketch of the cultural commonality between automated image projection and the depersonalized verbal techniques of a modernist stylistic "apparatus." We may now be able to reconceive the very notion of modernist "technique" in relation to the differential play of language, both grapheme and phonogram together.

DELTA FUNCTIONS

What thus glimmers into possibility is a decisively new view of the convergence between the filmic apparatus and a whole stratum of literary writing tapped and maximized by modernism: namely, a technology not just of inscription or writing but of "style" itself. Between strip and image, the track: so much has been established about cinema. So, too, in the case of literary writing: between visible script and representation, the text in production. Along with the political obfuscations that Jameson shows it is prey to, the reified category of modernist style tends toward the detached mechanism of a signifying over and above the signified, a drift, skid, and elision of verbal notation on which the serial aggregate of meaning both depends and may momentarily founder. The overwrought style of epiphany (with its necessary phenomenological engagement) disappears at least part of the way into sheer linguistic phenomenality. Never wholly masked in Forster, never far from view in Joyce, the mechanisms of linguistic articulation—its differential linkages—are brought forward, in other words, as the suppressed material basis (phonemic even when not phonic or oral) of all lexical processing. Whatever mystificatory business it may also be about by way of imperialist evocation or metaphysical inflection in either Forster or Conrad, the newly dissociated and hence partly automatized "apparatus" of modernist style emerges as the very sign of writing's access to its own undertext.

On this score, and beyond Coppola's filmic evocation of Conradian *écriture*, there remains for consideration that Conrad adaptation even closer at hand in these pages, the one that closed the last chapter with the step printing of an even more immanent apocalypse n-n-n-n-nowwwww. In the work that really deserves to be called Joseph Conrad's *The Secret Agent*, the novel by that name, much that is at issue in this chapter can be found thematized in the defective articulatory gestures of a single character. And not only thematized there, but condensed elsewhere into a single grapheme that is both geometric alias and Greek letter—and something more as well. In the film, the code name of the double agent Verloc is never given, let alone said by transliteration. In the novel, however, he is known prominently, if undercover, as Δ. The cross-wired double agent as human cipher? The triangulation of two inimical powers (Russia and England) in a secret go-between? The sign of an empty synthesis in a dialectic between radicalism and reactionism? All these and, more to our point, the so-called delta function of calculus: most succinctly explained as the "increment of a variable"—the differential measure of change itself. Or in the words of a mathematical dictionary contemporaneous with Conrad: "The symbol Δ is employed to designate a finite difference."[27]

On-screen, as we know, this calculable function of change in *The Secret Agent*, long immobilized within the plot by counterrevolutionary espionage, is finally devolved, after the murder of Δ himself, upon the last image of the nihilist Professor lurching forward in decelerated intervals toward the stopgap of historical catastrophe. All that is left of the delta function is the place where, as film, it all began: in the finite increments of the photogram. In the novel, instead, the equivalent delta function of intervallic progression must be given in the overtonalities of script itself. The linked passages I am thinking of are as follows. Various incremental meshes of Conrad's lexical sequencing seem attached to the sensorium, verbal as well as visual, of Verloc's mentally defective brother-in-law, Stevie, eventual victim of the disintegrating bomb blast. Recall Conradian narration's most famous chiaroscuro densities—and the lexical smudging that often accompanies them—when reading about Stevie "muttering half words, and even words that would have been whole if they had not been made up of halves that did not belong to each other" (8.139-40).[28] Think, in a word, and then another, of "sank (g)low." When the boy's tongue-tied lexical imagination finds its counterpart in images, he appears yet again as the impaired artist of both concentric and permeable suggestion, "drawing circles, circles, circles; innumerable circles, concentric, eccentric" (3.76).[29] By the sibilant liaison of the repetition, the tripled plural ("circle s/circle s/circles") ends up eliding with the singular in this bewildering and echoically captured "uniformity of form," where another self-exampling verbal stem ("centric") becomes insistently redoubled in order to steady the flux of lexemes. All of Stevie's involute scribbling suggests, by way of a primal oxymoron, "a rendering of cosmic chaos" resembling nothing so much as "the symbolism of a mad art attempting the inconceivable"—and making that attempt across the tangency and abrasion of englobed but porous words.[30] Where the chief objection to the anarchists, from within their cynical midst, is the Professor's charge that "you talk, print, plot, and do nothing" (4.96)—exactly like a charge leveled against narrative utterance in published form—Stevie's overlapping stammers and the tirelessly revolved and intersecting forms of his disinterested shaping are in the root sense revolutionary.[31]

In the advance of the cinematic track, the delta function is strictly cumulative. In wording, it is (re)distributional. *Cinécriture*, then, as neologism, is an internal "deltaction" of textual sequence, subtracting the increment of a morphemic variable from one word in order to permit its attraction to another. In light of poststructuralist theory, it seems a happy accident that mathematics has another name for the delta function as well: the "difference operator." On-screen, that operator is the photographic counterplay across the raced trace of frames. On the page, what operates the difference internal to meaning, hence to representation, but also the shifting differend unleashed or discharged in stray fluctuations, is the junctural phoneme. This is hardly to suggest that Conrad set out to illustrate in prose the Δ function of calculus or physics across the calibrations of wavering phonographemic play, even in a novel that makes much of the ascendancy of science over religion and art in the contemporaneous public imagination (more specifically, the science of space/time intervals in the symbolic bombing of Greenwich). The point is rather that, if scientific modernity is defined in part as an episteme of the interval, then Conrad's writing effects may be conditioned by such a cultural moment along with the flicker fusions of the cinematic apparatus.

Lest this linguistic inflection of technological modernity suggest any rigid periodizing of literary modernism, however, there is always Dickens, half a century before Conrad: a Dickens protofilmic in a way never fully evoked by Eisenstein's stress on his Griffith-like narrative "editing." When Dickens gives us the nineteenth-century novel's first great description of urban locomotion in *Dombey and Son*, he in fact closely anticipates the automatisms ascribed by Jameson to a locomotive and quasi-filmic modernism. A single bifocal sentence from *Dombey* will do for example, where the train's alliterative "shrill yell of exultation" seems to descend the scale of vowels (*il-el-ul*) as it sweeps past: a kind of phonemic Doppler effect. Seen from the reverse angle (from inside the carriage with Mr. Dombey), the new space/time ratios involve "sometimes pausing for a minute where a crowd of faces are, that in a minute more are not."[32] The eccentric verb number for the collective crowd serves to pluralize the window-framed bodiless faces even as they rush by in a single composite blur, while the expected grammar of full predication ("are seen on the platform," say) is truncated by sudden nonpresence: no sooner are they (there), than they no longer are.[33]

Or to choose, for the sake of example, another mid-nineteenth-century "modernist" of the interval, in verse rather than prose, take Dickinson rather than Dickens. Appropriately enough, the incremental differentiae of her verse have helped occasion a major theoretical position paper on the junctural interval of literary writing, but one whose implications for film remain unexplored. Pressurized gaps and sutured lacunae are one of Geoffrey Hartman's great subjects as well as Emily Dickinson's. "Human life, like a poetical figure, is an indeterminate middle between overspecified poles always threatening to collapse it," Hartman writes in his landmark essay "The Voice of the Shuttle."[34] Put differently, a metaphor is only a tautology held at bay. Hartman's most extended reading (349-51) is in fact of Emily Dickinson's "Our Journey had advanced," a journey he maps straight through to its equilibration of the death moment. When the pace slows in "awe," there is, however, an effect that escapes even Hartman's scrutiny: "Before—were Cities—but Between— / The Forest of the Dead." Exemplifying more precisely than Hartman himself notes the junctural "zero values" (347) of his own theory, the catachresis of *forest* (in metonymical relation to the lumber of death's coffins, no doubt, but still a metaphor for which there is no literal substitute) seems generated not only from the cross-lexical hint of "forward" in "be*fore were*" but from the apocalyptic promise of death as merely the "fore rest" of resurrection. Beyond Hartman's claims, this thicket of knotted lexicality, this protomodernist bothering of the signifier as well as the signified, also contributes to an account of the photogrammatic interval and its own approach to zero value. For like the iridescent ripple of the phonogram in modernist phonemic byplay, the filmic photogram passes before us like "the ghost of departed quantities" (Hartman's borrowing from Bishop Berkeley to describe his own favored elisions [347]). As such, this sheer differentiation in the spatiotemporal intervals of the read or viewed chain—or train—of signals.

IMAGE STRAIN

Before leaving behind our technological and industrial measures of the delta function in nineteenth-century instrumentations of the interval, one might recall Dickinson's own protocinematic figure for the racing locomotive: "I like to see it lap the miles" (no. 585). I say protocinematic because of her figural turn on incremental segmentation and its consumed stages. Dickinson's personifying diction captures at once the railway's mechanic licking up of distance and the overtaken phases (or "laps") of that distance.[35] This double verb form suggests a devouring momentum of traverse as well as the intervals it greedily subsumes, so that only the swift, disjunctive structure of Dickinson's hyhpenated verse seems to meet the speeding mechanism on its own terms. We have reached an apt moment, therefore, to shift once again from the linguistic field of modernism to the technological scene of modernity. Seeking a contextualized sense of cinema as film and of literature as letters, such transit helps to describe once more a cultural and discursive circuit between conditions of production and conditions of reception, material both. Jameson, we have seen, carries the recognized impact of railway transit on modernity into the realm of subsequent literary modernism with his sense of a detached or disembodied stylistic perception, independently generated somewhere between object and subject. But this invites now a closer and more fully historicized look. Dialectically conceived, the built-in commercial compensations for the drawbacks of railway travel may have sprung the modernist literary option not only through automatistic modeling but also by way of cognitive backlash.

When the early *Hale's Tours*, as precursors of the contemporary ride films, approximated the rumble of train motion while directing the gaze of its compartment of spectators *forward* toward a screen, they simulated one aspect of locomotion's ocular experience while shifting the axis of the others.[36] Three salient others, in particular. Though his classic study of locomotion is unconcerned with railroad vision as a specifically cinematic prototype, Wolfgang Schivelbusch does bring out certain ocular aspects of railway transit that presage cinema's serial automatizing of photographic frames.[37] These are, in brief, the mechanization of point of view that allowed for armchair tourism; the cultural connection of locomotive vision to the contemporaneous decline of panoramas and dioramas on the one hand, the rise of photography on the other; and the effect of iron-and-glass construction (for train windows as well as in stations) as a distancing of the immediately visible by an "unnatural" transparency. In regard to the outer world beyond this invisible buffer zone, there were two other pervasive aspects of the new locomotion that, though not ocular in themselves, affected the channeling of a traveler's gaze. The result was almost paradoxical. For the nervous anxiety connected with the risks of derailment or collision was matched with the boredom induced by having nothing to look at in a focused or concentrated way. We will come eventually to reading's low-cost, mass-marketed way of solving both problems at once—and to the modernist overthrow of this "cheap" solution.

Schivelbusch emphasizes, first, how the lateral breadth of the railway's "panoramic vision" eclipsed the appeal of urban visual spectacles with a new access to the exotic vistas of real locales. Looking ahead to cinema, we can say that all views were suddenly traveling shots. The gain carried with it an inherent loss. Despite the new ocular sweep, the most disturbing result of such locomotive optics, much discussed at the time, was that nearby images—in anything like their former sensory immediacy—were now blurred and illegible in their rapid passing. So for Schivelbusch, second, the "intensive experience of the sensuous world,

terminated by the industrial revolution, underwent a resurrection in the new institution of photography" (63). In railroad travel, the eye had to retrain its flexi-
bility and range, avoiding foreground images, scanning the horizon instead. Photography made its mark on visual culture at just this historical moment, therefore,
in part by recovering both from the "optical unconscious" (one might say, following Benjamin) and from a widespread surrender to a new spatiotemperal regime
(more Schivelbusch's point) precisely those aspects of the visual that remained inaccessible to normal sight. These included not only the scrutinizable close-up but
the registered phases or intervals (rather than the imperceptible rush) of motion.
In a history of the image approach to industrialized transport, such were the two
leading curtailments incident to "panoramic" vision. Third, for Schivelbusch, railway viewing was further denatured by the effects of what we should call the iron-
and-glass horse, harbinger of the modern turn toward "ferro-vitreous" architectural engineering. This third innovation, I would add, completes the precinematic
picture by sealing off the sounds of the visible world from those of the spinning
mechanism: first from the clackety-clack of wheels on the track, later from the
clicking whir of the projector (before it too was muted).

Along the technological trajectory (rather than causal chain) I am sketching,
cinema arrives to combine previously antithetical engineering developments in a
cultural logic more compensatory than "resurrectional" (Schivelbusch's sense
above). On this model, each phase of industrial advance gives back with one hand
what it takes with the other. Building on the photomechanical recovery of a foreground from the ocular losses of locomotion, and indeed on photography's enhanced possibility for prolonged contemplation of an entire vista, cinematic projection introduces another sort of high-speed rotary mechanism. It does so in
order to produce a visual synthesis whose link to the previous industrial transformation in human optics was not likely to have been lost on early film spectators,
whether their chairs swayed or not. Especially in a period before the perfection of
synchronized shutter speed and the fine-tuning of "flicker fusion," audiences
would have come to the moving image with a more nearly photogrammatic conception, if not perception, of motion pictures as (so the ads boasted) "animated
photographs." In early cinema, that is, the known but now unseen speed of a motorized apparatus would have recalled the railway experience not only through its
technological miracle of instantaneous tourism but, more technically yet, through
its artificial generation—from within a calibrated apparatus of motion—of the
previously natural and now mechanically restored continuity of near and far distance in the once organic view. On-screen, this remains a view melded and held at
a framed distance from reception (a view silent at first as well as unedited) by the
rigid transparent partition that renders it visible and that cushions the spectator
from bodily shock (of whose risks early train travelers were keenly aware).[38] In
sum, the iron-framed industrial glass window becomes an industrial screen, behind which things soundlessly but legibly come and go because of the mostly inaudible speed of the segmented mechanical "track" racing unseen beneath it all.

As regards this window of opportunity for a new kind of high-speed gazing,
one of the greatest of all train films, not from the silent heyday of the mode but

on the eve of the gradual eclipse of locomotive travel itself in the fifties, is also one of the greatest of all B films, *The Narrow Margin* (Richard Fleischer, 1952). In the prolonged hermetic setting of a single train journey, hit men try to stop the eventual testimony of a gangster's widow en route to a Los Angeles court. Their efforts are foiled only at the last minute when the detective accompanying her, by turning off the light in his compartment, is able to detect and prevent the assassin's final move next door. A plotlong claustrophia has been rectified by ocular mechanics. In this last fortuitous turn for the narrative within the framed purview of its own film screen, the hero stares through three internal layers of visual reframing: out from his own carriage window and back into the lit rectangle of the adjacent compartment via the fluttering file of reflections in the serial windows of a suddenly adjacent train. The title's slim margin has become exactly the saving (because now mimetic) space between parallel but differently paced vectors of automated transit. I return to the larger discussion by noting how all that is left of this brilliant metacinematic twist in the lackluster 1990 remake, *Narrow Margin* (Peter Hyams), is the telltale throwing of the hit man's huge undulating shadow on mountain rocks flanking the train during a stunt-heavy showdown on top of the racing cars.

In the context of industrial modernity, we are now prepared to see how the history of vision approach to cinema, often prosecuted with Schivelbusch as friendly witness, connects with an evolutionary account of textual cognition and its discontents. But in this respect, according to a compensatory or dialectical history of mediated reception, one last stage in the journey toward modernism, literary and filmic alike, needs filling in. It has to do with that last highlighted aspect of railway transit in Schivelbusch: the overlay of boredom upon nervous tension, which seeks "correction" in a new technique not of observation but of redirected textual attention—namely, the mass-marketed "railway novel" and its own eclipse by the newspaper and tabloid. Schivelbusch uses contemporary testimony to demonstrate that, in response to "dissolution and panoramization of the outside landscape due to velocity" (67), a "process of deconcentration, or dispersal of attention, took place in reading as well as in the traveler's perception of the landscape" (69). This tendency saw, over time, the eclipse even of streamlined narrative fictions by the ephemera of journalistic print. To note this impact of both industrial excitation and enforced leisure on reading habits is to return us, if indirectly, to Jameson's literary claims with a fuller sense of the parallel with locomotive prototypes of cinemachination. For modernist practice across media, faced with the proliferation of formulaic narrative cinema and easily consumable fiction, may be said to reintroduce a technical deficiency (disturbing oscillation) in the converted form of a motivated cognitive challenge. This is the place within imprint media of resurgent photograms and phonograms alike, spoilers of transparency, goads to textual notice. In the double negations to which media history is prone, modernism arrives to concentrate again the "deconcentrated" gaze of reading and viewing.

In respect to cinema, we can quickly review the previous stages of naturalization that led in turn to a realienating emergence of film's constituent segmentation.

As soon as cinema discovered and mastered its narrative (editing) capacities and began to compete more fully, on its own terms, with the deceptively seamless mimesis of the railway novel, for instance, modernist experiment in film arrived to "resurrect" not the reflective stasis of the contemplative view (once recovered by photography) but precisely the unsettling perceptual discontinuities that beset early train spectators when their eyes strayed from the calculated distractions afforded by the popular page, distractions from ocular disorientation, from anxiety, and from boredom alike. Train travel, Schivelbusch explains, had once provided the "annihilation of space and time," as the contemporaneous truism had it, by subordinating the feel for topographic immediacy to a new "geographic" perspective (33). It thereby downgraded real space to the compressed temporal intervals of unnatural transit and unprecedented access. By its second decade, cinema had carried this "annihilation" (only to rescind it) into the very chinks of perceived motion in and across scenes. In avowed popular association with the locomotive engine of industrial modernity, then, and in covert league with those slippages of the letter in the unconscious to be ever more persistently exposed by modernist writing, cinema's manifest fabrication retemporalizes the photographic image in order to normalize the world's s/pace once more. It does so, however, by an almost paradoxical return to the centered gaze, mechanically induced at high speed to begin with, later openly mobile and automatized. The distraction that *is* cinema overcomes the distractions—and more—that it shelters us from, train travel among them.

Here we enter upon that elusive double valence of Frankfurt school distraction theory where such a social phenomenon seems both cause and effect of cinema as modern medium: the environing whirl of ocular bombardment and the machine that reorchestrates it for a newly focused if hyperkinetic attention, a rapt concentration rescued from the midst of specular overload. As always, one needs to bear in mind the modernity of cinema apart from, and before, its modernist phase. Yet again, too, the technical mutations of literary language and its dynamics of reception crisscross the path of technological advance in the realm of visual mediation. Cinema's modernity, involving its own evolution from the fixed-frame view to the edited sequence, induced a return from ocular stability to the unmanageably rapid and discrepant sighting that had troubled the eye in railway transit. Not for long. On-screen, even radical disjuncture was channeled into a system of narrative transition. As soon as this new discontinuity had been routinized (coded) in the ascendancy of cinema as a modern narrative form, however, filmic modernism interceded to shake things up again. But this is also what literary modernism was doing, on its own front, to a print culture by now long attuned to the easily digestible print fare associated in part with the circumscribed leisure of train travel: the mile-a-minute quick read.

Here we also connect with a textual paradigm to be developed further in my closing pages. For if light reading in the hurtling train car was not just a solacing diversion from tedium but an active repression of both ocular disturbance and high-speed vehicular anxiety, cinema may well have been felt by its first spectators to have emerged from the wonders of technological invention with a built-in repressive mechanism all its own. Even before flicker was fully subdued, cinema aspired to erase the signs of merely mechanical speed—and its shuttling past of discrete imprints—in favor of the steadied and pacifying view. To vary a tacit dichotomy in Dickinson, film turned the nervous interval and its gaps into a clockwork lapping. Made possible by such an automatically achieved suppression of discontinuity was a protected zone of benign shock attractions (among the earliest of them, not accidentally, a train barreling straight at the camera) that were for the first time transparently shielded from all potential for literal impact. But this melodramatic return of the holistic view was itself a manifest technical ruse. As such, its single instants—now speeding segmental increments—were always liable to recognition as fragments rather than moments in a discontinuous and arbitrary totality. In the compensatory logic of the psychoneural economy I am proposing for cinematic spectation, then, the world's restructured virtuality was the price paid for the viewer's invulnerability to it. Confronted with such trade-offs of modernity in several media, modernism responds by making us nervous all over again, unsettling the narrative and descriptive codes by which we had come to manage our compartmentalized (hence by nature escapist) representations of the impinging world beyond. In a literary practice pitted against the mass consumption of railway fiction and journalism, the flicker effect associated with locomotion, beaten back by photography and tamed by cinematic projection, makes its return on the underside of words themselves—and in the new hyperconcentration they fleetingly induce.

PHONEMIC MONTAGE

In the comparable practices of writerly writing and filmic cinema, the mechanism is clear enough: signifiers s/crawling by, text t/racing on. I am concerned in the rest of this chapter (until a return to Chaplin) with the second modernist phase of cinematic development. This involves not the revival of locomotive energy and imagery in 1920s international modernism but rather the medium's distressed photographic increments in the modernist valedictions of the 1960s. In comparison with the flickering filmic signal, the main point is, has always been, this: Just as the photograms that we register as continuous film images are in fact incremental textual imprints stripping over themselves from projected frame to frame, so too is the apparent ribbon of syntax a continual overlap of lexigrams and functional blanks. These are, and must be, spliced by conventions that exert no absolute control over the disruptive overrun of one word upon the next in the inevitable slippage of subvocal response. Gaps happen—and overlaps. Reading's efficiency is purchased at the cost of their overlooking. The greater speed of cinema merely holds a comparable gaping more tightly in check. But even in literature such syncopation must be kept, so to say, in syntactic line, resisting dismemberment. As with the filmic chain, however, this resistance cannot always be ensured. High modernism is one name for a more than ordinary letting down of the guard. Pursuant to this slackening of linguistic vigilance, we have by now rethought certain distinctive features of an opaque and resistant modernist style in their relation to the twin mechanisms (in part locomotively conceived) of cinematic transcription and differential projection—as well as, within the rule of writing itself, in relation to the slippage of script in textual enunciation. This we have seen, too, as an aleatory automatism of the reader's linguistic preconscious, brought back into play via the unruly returns of "exposure time."

In pursuing further this parallel between inscriptive subvocalization and filmic difference, I am about to single out an epitomizing—if by no means typical—moment of sheer homophonic wordplay from the title of a legendary late modernist film text, *La jetée,* a multiple slippage of lexical intervals that in its own way serves to rehearse the layered rather than animated stills of the narrative's own enunciation. Indeed, for the lexical splaying of Marker's title there may be a notable high modernist prototype in cinema's own avant-garde canon. In his silent, anagrammatically titled *Anemic cinéma* (1927), Marcel Duchamp inscribes a series of homophonic puns—"esquimaux au mots esquise" and the like—on a set of spiraling disks. Simulating the spooling of the cinematic reel in its own silent visual slippage from one celluloid frame to another, frames that blur like Duchamp's high-speed wordplay into various signifying permutations, these spirals bespeak a moment of alliance between the linguistics of literature and the mechanics of a recently arrived and rival medium. From here to the punning title of another nondialogue film half a century later, *La jetée,* is a shorter step than it may seem in the history of modernist experiment in verbal and visual succession. Moreover, this step is effectively halved by a direct link recently demonstrated between another of Duchamp's kinetic investigations, this time on canvas (*Nude Descending a Staircase* [1912]), and the late nineteenth-century protocinematic studies of the biomotor "trace" conducted via the chronophotography of Etienne-Jules Marey.[39] These last are experiments that went so far in the direction of my present thesis as to include—but always without full success in the cinemalike resynthesizing of its analytic breakdowns—a "phonoscope" designed to reinscribe the precise facial and lip movements necessary for the execution of speech patterns.[40] At the center of its narrative almost a full century later, *La jetée* embeds an exercise in such analysis-cum-synthesis—the woman waking under the eye of desire—that may be found to replay the technological origins of both pictorial and literary modernism, each in its own way cubist and polysemous, diffracted and multivalent.

Given the psychoanalytic topic (and subject) of Marker's film—a self vanished into his own artificially induced and self-displacing memory traces as visual fixations—the thematizing of the medium as the carrier of consciousness (and its repressions) seems inevitable. For Lacan, the *aphanisis* of self-consciousness, its phased fading in and out, constitutes the subject only as "flickering in eclipses" within the metonymic slide of its own enunciation.[41] Comparably, in Marker's "photoroman"—composed all but exclusively of still photographs edited together—we are made uniquely aware of kinetic representation in cinema as the flickering-in-eclipses of the single photogram on the image track. This fact is brought out most forcefully by that cinematically "realized" moment when the flow of discrete images of the hero's dream woman asleep in bed is sped up to the point where it begins to resemble, and then actually becomes, a moving-image shot of her waking face in close-up. Just before the photographic encroaches in this way upon the cinematic, the separate images have grown so nearly coincident with each other that they narrow to that differential spread—the delta factor or "difference operator," if we wish—necessary to the process of "animation." Even before the filmic achieves its own cinematicity in a brief stretch of "moving pictures," then, its mechanisms have been rehearsed and asserted in what we might call again a pressure toward cinema. (Something like the obverse effect transpires when the syncopated, frame-deleted slow motion that closes Campion's *The Portrait of a Lady* serves mostly to remind us of the hidden gulfs between *any* two consecutive photograms even in the normal course of screen motion, a constitutive lack in all filmic representation.)

Brought forward at such a moment according to traditional accounts would be not the delta function, but (also in Greek) the "phi effect" at the basis of filmic projection. This is dependent in some part on that "persistence of vision" long thought to bridge the dis/juncture between separate photograms in order to help produce the illusion of continuous motion across the succession of single frames.[42] In the sequence (woman waking) where an all but animated montage of hairbreadth deflections builds toward a fugitive engagement with the full cinematic process, Marker's point is perhaps best captured by precisely the impossibility of seizing this moment through frame enlargements. Once they are blocked out in sequence, one cannot be expected to read the feathery difference between those stills that remain within the thematic logic of perpetually fading fixations and those that accelerate toward the enhanced cognitive (and emotional) dimension of the moving image (cf. figs. 142-43, indistinguishable in their sequencing on the page from any other stills in the film). My own point has been that the mechanical rudiments of the apparatus may well evoke at such a moment, as if standing in for all filmic projection, that flickering representation that film shares, while literalizing, with the file of the signifier in writing. This is all the more tempting a connection in the case of Marker's film because, again, it is a connection staged—if only in lexical pantomime—by the ambiguities of its very name.

In approaching this contorted lexical performance, a methodological clarification is not only in order but perhaps overdue. It concerns the difference between my sense of the filmic delta function and the permutations of cinematic "writ" in the work of Marie-Claire Ropars-Wuilleumier. For John Mowitt in *Text*, the interest of her procedures rests with the way Ropars theorizes the film image "by first showing how its effacement of the spacing (the enunciative ordering) that conditions the image (as a recognizable visual phenomenon) makes film complicit with . . . the ideological system that, among other things, reduces writing to a seamless representation of speech."[43] Instead of acquiescing in this plenary representation, Ropars unstitches the seams. "From this perspective," Mowitt's summary continues, "filmic writing qualifies as 'writing,' not because it generates aesthetic effects (like literary writing), but because it is, in many ways, a consummately 'modern' articulation of the heterogeneous spacing that comprises writing *in general*" (171). It is just such a constitutive *modernist* enterprise, of course, that this chapter has set out to specify. But not in the way Ropars herself tends to do. When her method is applied, for instance, as mine will shortly be, to the homophonically loaded title of a single film, in her case Godard's *Breathless*, what she means by a disruptive spacing of its "cinescripture" becomes clear in its difference from this chapter's emphasis on the corrugated junctures of internal lexical slippage.[44] On Ropars's hearing, the cinematic composite of the film's French title, *A bout de souffle*, reveals how a "single graphic tracing ('*souffle*') ... generates elements ('*sous*') which are figurable or phonetically combinable into such (absent, phantom) collocations as '*souvenirs brisés*' (broken memories)" (151).[45]

What Ropars thus stresses is the dismemberment rather than the supplement of signification, fracture rather than internal juncture. The drawback of this approach to the common textuality of both cinematic and literary writ remains, at least from the perspective of this book, that her tactics of "reediting" are too much focused on the subsidiary sites of oral or scriptive wording on-screen (and the free associations thereby induced) rather than keeping attention trained on the medium's sighted images as an automatism of filmic inscription in its own right. I will be laboring to avoid this "secondariness" even in bringing together the collaged lexicality of Marker's title with the deconstructed montage of his overlapping stills. I will be working, in other words, to motivate the title from within the filmic chain as an almost accidental, even though exemplary, complement to the spun strip as image track. This is why, in contrast with Ropars's sense of "cinescripture," I have coined instead the dialectical portmanteau *cinécriture*, meant more nearly to catch the intrinsic "deltaction" of the filmic integer and its phonotextual parallels. By this term I have tried to emphasize the mechanized differential imprints of the tracked image itself rather than the scriptive dispersals and overlaps that are either imaged on track or found somehow to emblematize the discontinuous and accretive function of montage. Only in this "thingness" of the imprint at the base of its signaled world views do we find a real equivalent to the eruption of the signifier from beneath the signified in an account of literary modernism like Foucault's: the dissipating return of language within and against discourse.[46]

Ropars's "hieroglyphic interpretation of cinema"—characterizing as it does the film's textuality as a rebus of discrete signifying ingredients not unlike free-form and extrasyntactic punning—of course calls to mind the more famous "ideogram hypothesis" of half a century before.[47] By a different route, however, it is indeed Sergei Eisenstein who may lead us once again to a closer tie between the flicker fusion of the filmic apparatus and the ripple effect of cinematic *écriture*. For it was Eisenstein who defiantly minimized the element of succession itself in the film strip, subsuming sequence instead to a perceptual dialectic. Despite the rolling past of images, film *reads* not as a textual scrolling but rather as a reciprocal displacement and mutual exclusion of image flashes. This is the base level of Eisenstein's claims for the destabilizing essence of the montage principle apart from—and before—an actual montage sequence. Cinema is at base a continuously unsettled palimpsest. To repeat: "For, in fact, each sequential element is perceived not *next* to the other, but on *top* of the other"—in a perceptual "conflict"[48] that generates not so much the moving image (images are already speeding by) but the held image of another and *represented* motion, one autonomous rather than automated. Whence the conflictual as the dialectical. Whence, too, the parallel with the latent graphic/phonic (graphonic) syncopation of modernist style. Like continuous visibility on-screen, continuous referentiality on the page is thus generated by a process that grammatology itself would recognize as a "'dialectic' of protention and retention"—the ongoing and overlain alter(n)ation of phonemes and constitutive *blancs*.[49]

We are now primed to consider how the dialectical tension of the photogrammatic sequence takes what might be sensed as its homologous lexical toll on the title as well as the narrative logic of *La jetée*. In ways almost uncannily matched to the ironies of Marker's tacit psychoanalytic plotting, the film's self-mutating title is a gestalt all its own, now alternative noun phrases, now wavering full clauses. Framing the story's post-Proustian allegory of psychic time travel, in a narrative pitched between science fiction thriller and existential reverie, the at first uninvolving phrase *La jetée* refers most obviously (and trivially) to the jetty (or outdoor passenger platform) at Orly airport. This is the walkway—and psychological transit zone—that locates the story's primal scene of eroticism and death, twice visited, twice evacuated. It is according to something like the plot's double pattern of anticipation and retrospection—or in an extrapolation from Derridean trace to the track of plot, of protention versus retention as a narrative double cross—that the title begins to unfurl its layers of imbricated syntactic pertinence. This we might have been prepared for from our earlier discussion of the film in the second chapter. What is mostly to be added here is a sense of the blocked delta function of postnuclear history collapsed upon the jammed signals of a single lexical span.[50] As with the phonemic contractions of Geoffrey Hartman's literary poetics, the fatal collapse of end upon beginning in Marker's plot also permeates to the microlevel through the unstable dissolve of single filmic imprints in the elision of their lifelike cinematic intervals.

How, then, is this line of thought entitled by the unprepossessing designation of Marker's film? The first break with lexical borders begins with the elision that would permit *Là j'etais* (the imperfect mode of a continuous past: "There I was") to emerge by exact echo with the inscribed *La jetée*, pointing on the sly to the hero's original presence on the jetty of his memory. But no sooner has the title displaced the naming of its in/augural (because ominous) dramatic site than the emergent elegiac clause begins stripping its own linguistic gears. It slips or drifts, in other words, toward an ironically overlapped temporality in its slide from imperfect to perfect mode: to the homophonic (and further elided) overtone of *Là j'ai été* ("There I have been")—as if to say once and always, inescapably.[51] If clausal alternatives of this sort occur to or accurse our ears, bedeviling the linearity of this particular signification, then we are all the more likely to allow Marker's overcrowded title a last sem/antic latitude. This slippage would insinuate a less than strictly grammatical figure for the dreamed season of an at once unrecoverable and inescapable past: *L'âge été*, that phantasmatic summer before the fall. All told, like the enchained photogram giving way to the fractionally discrepant double in Eisenstein's sense of dialectical superimposition, the lexical phonogram is also mobilized to put one over on us, one of the same-but-different. To sum it up for both media under comparison: *L'/la/à/âge/je/j'/e/ai/été/ée/ais* offers the self-jetti-soned signifier in extremis.[52]

In all of this greased significatory slippage along the gathering creases of ad-verb, pronoun, and verb in their various contractions and decontractions (enunci-atable on the run as a slur of sheer lingual urgency), text can be felt to "turn struc-ture into event."[53] It thereby generates its own lexical equivalent to the filmic "afterimage"—in what we might call a persistence of (subvocal) audition. Such is the enunciated (even when unspoken) fluxion, both form and overflow at once, that sustains the filaments of ambiguity across the gaping integument of script. Cinema masks the gap, the splice, that reading must honor and at the same time sur-mount—and not only overleap but unsettle, vexing the junctural interval in the self-regrouping drive of lettered sense. At the same time, according to a different teleological destiny than is usually sketched for either medium, we may say that cinema maximizes everything in literature that it fails to outmode as mimetic sys-tem. It does so by rendering almost tangible, albeit invisible, the underlying textual dynamism of inscription at large. Of course, photogram as much as phonogram must disappear into the processed unit of signification as its inner lining and its negative imprint, at one and the same time the rudiment and the exclusion of its linear effect. It is in this way that cinema lends itself to the ethos of modernism in part to make materially available not so much the strict binarism of the linguistic system as the more mobile and fluid counterplays upon which the flicker effect—and flicker fusion—of literary writing is also, and always, mounted. These are the sensed tremors that penetrate the sound barrier of standard inscription. Here is the sprocket noise of textual machination as the very engine of reading's second sense: a whir that is every so often urged toward wording by the listening eye. To borrow again from the abutted automatisms and resultant homophony of Conrad's *écrit-ure,* we may say that in film too the projected "rays" of luminous movement de-pend on the *aphanisis,* the intermittent eclipse, of the phased, the self-faded "trace."

PHOTOGRAPHY'S STOLEN MOMENTS

An emphasis now needs reclaiming from the book as a whole. To place *cinécriture* more firmly yet in the context of all that has preceded (and in fact necessitated) this last chapter, we need to monitor its filmic operations across an entire cinematic plot: a last exemplary metanarrative about photographic mediation. I take aim at a deceptively easy target. Need it be said that Antonioni's 1966 fable of alienated consciousness, *Blow-Up,* is *the* film about photography that leaps to everyone's mind when the topic arises? The infrequency with which it is assumed to be about photography's *relation to film* measures its potential use here.

Antonioni's film track kicks into aberrant action with the first scene of the hero's perfunctory fashion shoot. Jump cuts of Thomas the photographer, his cam-era, and his models reproduce at the level of filmic form the piecemeal seizure of the image that is the narrative content of the scene. As usual, editing editorial-izes—but here on the photomechanism's own terms, with the hero submitted by the film as a whole to the blunt discontinuities he deals in. The film that is here reduced toward the fragmentation of a photo shoot will, in other words, later try to turn a photo shoot back toward a film, to narrativize a roll of discrete images, to piece out a (com)plot. In the process, a turning point in media history, the passage from photographic print to filmic image, transpires symbolically in the eventual fate of these fugitive few views.

How so? How is this film famously about photography also a film about film, let alone about film history and its modernist valences? Leaving aside its overriding epistemological thematic, how is *Blow-Up* a film about its own medium at the very point when it is also most preoccupied with the aching stillness of the photograph—namely, in that minutely calibrated display of laboratory technique that occupies the great title episode, with its segmented blow-up of individual still images into the forensic tracks and traces of a crime in (past) progress? Our most prolific theorist of the modernist aspiration and the postmodernist condition has opened a certain teleological route toward an answer. One possible answer, at least, though somewhat different from mine. Jameson's view of *Blow-Up* within the long view of mutating cinematic styles beckons to us at this point for the way it follows out lines laid down in my previous review of film's place, variously theorized, within the history of technology and its scientific paradigms.

Jameson's careerlong engagement with questions of literary and cinematic modernism shows its technological side most obviously, perhaps, in the way modernism comes increasingly to be viewed in the retrospective light of the postmodern simulacrum, flash point for a whole array of electronic virtualities. (This is one of the chief reasons to regret that Jameson's extensive writing on literary science fiction has never carried him over into any prolonged consideration of the genre on film.) In his riveting four pages on *Blow-Up*, one of his most condensed and resolute allegorical readings of any modernist text, the camera's place (still and moving-picture camera alike) in the evolution of optical technology, and film's own internal evolution from black and white to color, are together refigured—in their deepest ontological implications—by the narrative of an existential ennui nodalized around a murder plot. It is a plot (and epistemological metaplot) where the eventual encounter with the actual dead body may well seem, as Jameson suggests, a signal flaw in the film. With all the epistemological mystery that collects around the photographer's accidental snapshots of what might be a murder site— is that a gun in the bushes? the features of an assassin streaked by foliage? a body stretched out under the tree? or just a shadow? and how much can you enlarge the picture before losing it?—Jameson is right to be startled by proof positive: the dead mass itself lying supine after a long night's onset of rigor mortis.[54]

The "formal doubt" (195) induced by this narrative turn has to do with whether, to borrow the title of Jameson's collection, the "signatures of the visible" should not have been kept in doubt as an undecidable sign, left without a determined "referent" (195), open to the mind's forgery. Attributing the appearance of the actual cadaver to a narrative and thematic misstep, Jameson is nevertheless quick to infer the excessive facticity of the corpse as functioning within the film's own metahistory of its medium. He drops just a hint, which needs to be spelled out here. For the cold waxen body ("far and away the most unreal object in the film,"

195), touched by the suddenly cameraless photographer, offers up one of film history's earliest prospects (outside of science fiction, we may presume) of human remains passing over toward "image—or simulacrum—status" (195). This is the organic form approximating a mannequin of itself—and not by accident, I should add, in a story about a glamour photographer who converts his so-called fashion plates into photographic ones, posed dummies for ocular consumption. Under the sign of the simulacrum—or the corpse—everyone ends up as only a model, mold, or trace of themselves, vacant and glassy-eyed.

This alienation effect of self-removal, suffusing the film as it does in less immobile forms than the corpse, is the debt Antonioni pays to his own second-period work in Italian cinema, where he became the indelible maestro of anomie and urban psychic deracination. For Jameson, the black-and-white photographs of the park, by contrast, pay a more wrenching homage yet to Antonioni's previous—and ontologically unrecoverable—work in neorealism. I take a double lead from this passing suggestion. For one thing, the hero's photo models, like the film

317

around them, are shot in saturated and schematic color; black and white is used only for the photographer's planned volume of "art" shots, among which he hopes to include his freewheeling takes of the park. By way of a *mise en abyme* that recalls what Lucien Dällenbach terms the "Doppelroman" within a fictional text, these alternative photos—the supposed restorative underside of the superficial fashion world—are being pieced together into a quasi-narrative album for publication as an art-book documentation of contemporary life, from graffiti to hoodlum violence to homeless destitution.[55] By his own admission, Thomas needs a contrasting shot for closure, one that will be "quite beautiful, quite still." It isn't that easy. On that roll of film shot in the park, he gets, instead, only one more scene of violence in a public space: the inescapable synecdoche for, rather than antidote to, the whole sequence of his book's stark documents.

And the synecdoche for something else as well: part object, in negative regress, of the film's whole photogrammatic automatism, both in this sequence and beyond. As the photographer scans the work he has pinned in huge enlargements to his studio walls (fig. 317), that is, over a dozen full-screen matches between his blow-ups and the cinema screen serve in evenly paced sequence to cross and penetrate the space of the crime, from the apparently oblivious couple (fig. 318) brought into telephoto enlargement (fig. 319) to the woman's cautious glance (fig. 320) at a man hiding in the bushes (captured within the same print via the motion-picture camera's panning across a single image [figs. 321 and 322]), followed by an incremental close-up on this lurking figure and his gun (figs. 323-24). From which we cut back to the woman (Vanessa Redgrave) suddenly made aware of the photographer (fig. 325), her mounting nervousness intercut with a shot of the lover still unaware of his danger (figs. 326-28). After her frantic effort to interrupt the shoot of the shooting (fig. 329), we are left with the apparently empty

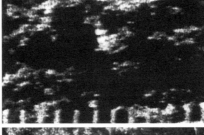

318, 319, 320, 321, 322, 323, 324, 325, 326, 327, 328, 329, 330, 331, 332

park (fig. 330), then a closer shot of the woman in the far background looking down next to the tree (fig. 331), then another long shot of the fully deserted (or is it?) scene (fig. 332). By the traversable sight lines of his now energized gaze and the camera movements that further schematize it, the photographer grows into his role as detective by becoming, through mental montage, a protocinematic manipulator of an ocular gestalt.

So much for the lovely stillness upon which he hoped his volume would close. Only the film of *Blow-Up* itself—in its underlying function as one image tossed (and lost) upon another in sequence—will end on a serene note. This is possible only when a trick jump cut removes the hero's figure from the last overhead shot of the park—leaving merely, by a kind of scenic pun, a ground without a figure. But there is more here, or less: a redoubled absence. And it may help return us to Jameson's complaint about the appearance of a "real corpse" in the film, rather than just its putative image, in a way that might understand differently the symbolic utility of the lifeless body, above and beyond its prolepsis of the postmodern simulacrum. In returning eventually to the corpse (as the hero tries to do), we must also keep our eyes on the film's trick ending, which functions as the structural opposite of a freeze-frame, offering in its own way the revelation and the effacement of normative cinematic succession.

In this slippery ellipsis of presence, the hero's vanished body closes off something like a time-lapse image of the self's own existential disappearing act. All film process, of course, must in a different sense be able to remove an imaged figure from view while retaining its variable backing in a visualized space. So in another manner does all film, like all photography before it, both kill off and steal away bodies. The specific *narrative* ingenuity of *Blow-Up* is that it pries wide the temporal space between the two actions—murder and removal, the twin effects of cinematic "shooting"—in order to wedge open the latitude for an allegory more technological yet than the one Jameson's draws out: an allegory, as complete as any on film, of film's own photogrammatic undertext. With the narrative understood in this way, the corpse cannot long remain gratuitous in its lifeless fixity—or merely be contained (and finally secreted from sight) as the peripheral encroachment of the contemporary simulacrum, inert and waiting. The body's living features s/lain into stasis, it is swept from view in the film's pivotal moment as the swivel point of plot's most encompassing technological trope.

Jameson's argument, however, needs to dispose of the corpse more summarily on the way to his own historical claim. The movie whose plot climaxes with stolen photographs is, on his account, about the confiscation of something like the documentary tradition itself—and with it the absconding of an even more encompassing aesthetic. "With their disappearance, the 'realist' vocation of Bazin and Kracauer, the mission of film to redeem physical reality, or rather to reinvent the photographic libido that was its lost origin and starting point, its nostalgia and its secret death wish or eros all at once, comes to an end and something else (which is no longer modernism either) takes its place."[56] That "no longer modernism either" is the oblique key to the largest historical arc of his claim. Thus Jameson's conclusion about a film that barely holds at bay the looming dead weight of post-

modernism. (To the probable allusion to Benjamin in his phrase "photographic libido" I will return in a moment.)

But there is another way of talking about plot's ultimate suppression of photographic evidence. To appreciate the eventual difference from Jameson's results,
however, we need the fuller context for his paragraphs on *Blow-Up*, the media
philosophy they spring from. Indeed, the discussion of Antonioni follows from
Jameson's most thoroughgoing reflection on film's difference from photography.
For him, in the "interpretation of still photography," the qualities of "time and
death, the very death of the image in question" are regularly "added in as content
and as message" (192), a sense of things he shares with Roland Barthes. By contrast, in film this dimension of the image is "drawn back into the formal process"
(192). This is the way Jameson's tacit phenomenological emphasis on film as "the
deconcealment of Being" (193), its unveiling in and across time, coincides rather
closely with Bergson's emphasis on becoming (a quality regretted by Bergson,
however, in its patent absence from the filmic mechanism). The passage from
Jameson bears quoting in full measure for its alignment with the ontological view
of film from Bazin to Cavell, a view he finds thematized—even, we might say,
mourned in its passing—by Antonioni. As an ontological phenomenon, film becomes an event rather than an icon; film *occurs*. "No consumable image—of the
type of the still photograph—survives this process as an object: and the great moments of some Bazinian 'epiphany' are not salvageable as simple 'freeze frames'
reproduced from the negative." The epiphanic moment has little, therefore, in
common with that "third meaning" of photostatic contemplation explored by
Barthes. These moments of disclosed ontological resonance "cannot, in other
words, be *translated* back into photography, but constitutively presuppose the inevitability of time and change and loss as the price they must pay to become
events rather than things" (192).

Nothing could be truer, with the lone (though perhaps demolishing) proviso
that the accession to event, the coming into as well as the passing from being, is
a projected "becoming" that is—well before time's own melancholy enters the
field of representation—built upon one thing's losing place to another's taking
hold. And those things, exchanged in succession, are the photograms, pieces of the
illusional continuum, units that neutralize, as units, the motion they fuel. These
subepiphanic disclosures of film's material base do not so much "*presuppose* the
inevitability of time and change and loss" (my emphasis) as they willfully mech-
anize the specter of absentation in the name of transition. This axis of shared imprint between the stasis of the photograph and the race of the photograms gives
us our different—less evolutionist, more materialist (and narratively cued)—
sense of *Blow-Up* as allegory. And this sense would include, more nearly at its
center, the Jamesonian crux of the supererogatory corpse. In terms of media history, the film may well look back—up to and *including* the emergent corpse—on
the documentary origins of a neorealism that fulfilled the Bazinian imperative toward ontological realization. If so, it looks back on its own lost illusions. Rather
than a proleptic postmodern simulacrum, the body struck from time and already
losing its flesh tones on color stock, turning blue (if not black and white) as if

333

334

335

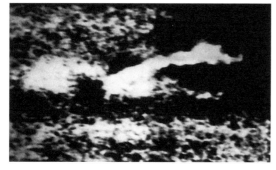

336

right before the camera's gaze, represents more than its own neutered subjectivity and inertia. It represents as well the fixity that any attempted animation—like and including that performed laboratory magnification and the subsequent editing of POV shots in the hero's studio—must overlook or mask.

All the while, in my reading, a wholesale dramatic irony accompanies this revelation of the photogrammatic undertext. I refer to that theft of photos—all but the one overlooked enlargement—the very timing of which seems to refigure the steps of the revelation whose evidence it sweeps away. These steps need to be closely remarked. As the hero's trained eye and visual imagination go to work on the still images—the film now editing them together along the grooves of constructed reaction shots and eye-line matches, even simulating zoom shots by the progression of incremental close-ups—what the hero comes to believe is that, through his arbitrary gesture of record and preservation, intervening in the cruelty of the real, he has in fact *saved a life:* the personified form of the realist "redemption of reality." Instead, as he later discovers by a fuller "cinematizing" of the scene, he has merely captured a death in action.[57] When his decisive recognition of this depends on rephotographing the area of the suspected body after examining it under a magnifying glass (figs. 333-34), and then rephotographing it (fig. 335) so that the already maximum blow-up can be redoubled (fig. 336), the point is sealed. The resulting photograph of a photograph yields the confirmatory image of an already corpsed image, decomposing before our eyes into the almost illegible second-generation graininess of some postpointillist abstraction.

This extreme blow-up, as if inevitably, is the only print that remains in the photographer's keep, having slipped out of sight when the others were confiscated. It remains not only because, in its illegible blotches, it mocks its own cogency as proof. In the wake of all those other photos that would contextualize it within a set of credible testimony (the plot twist), this last blow-up stays behind as the essence and emblem of them all (the synecdochic irony). This latter turn is perverse and complete. Doubting Thomas (his last name is never given) has gone to see the body without (inexplicably) his otherwise ubiquitous camera (fig. 337). What results is the structural chiasmus (the double cross) of the whole plot sequence, with its x-ing out of evidence. Discovering the theft of his reproductions, Thomas returns again, this time with his camera, to find and fix their original in the flesh, as if the corpse were not in its own right only an indexical sign of evacuated being, of absence. By now this evidence too, reciprocally, has disappeared. All that is left after ransack and removal, blown out of all proportion so to speak, is the granular trace of a trace. Outside the photographer's studio, all we see is a corpse there one minute, gone the next, like the hero's own body lost at the last in a shallow depth of field. Inside, all we see are the photographs here now, edited into narrative sequence, then gone.

Such is my alternative—or complement—to Jameson's allegory. The film's climax figures, on this account, less the historical loss of photographic realism on film and its ontological privilege than the undone fundament of the realist illusion itself, the illusion of screen presence. The crisscrosses of plot would thus snare the very site of the filmic per se: not just the never visibly removed picture(s) of a scene (of a crime or otherwise) but, more fundamentally, the *already having vanished* of one ingrained image after another—all of these afterimages interchangeable together with the materialized but itself vanishing *absence* of life in the corpse. For only in such a rapid removal of the imaged static form (body or photo imprint) where once there was life—only in and along the photogrammatic track—does a spectral flux of images ever rematerialize as a moving ghost on-screen, presiding host to all ontological credence, hospitable to any identification. Again, then: For Jameson's "photographic libido" (compounded of eros and death wish, and with Benjamin's "optical unconscious" feasibly in mind) substitute (one level down) the incremental photogram as the always vanished preconscious of the received screen scene. For this reading of the film, where blow-ups could name the relation of frame on track to enlarged screen-scaled image as well as the process from negative to magnified print, one strange touch stands out as a symptomatic glitch in dialogue, a Freudian slip or a metafilmic gaffe, in any case an abyssal key. When Thomas refuses to turn over the photos to the nameless woman whom he has caught off guard in the park, he explains more than he means, or means to, when he misspeaks as follows: "There are other things I want on that reel." So designating the "roll" of exposed negatives, the screen character (inadvertently?) anticipates the way just those retained and blown-up images, *photograph by photogram*, will become the climax of the present film in its crucial last reel, its detective plot tantalizing the viewer's own narrative "want" as well as the hero's.

337

MODERN TIMING

Having tracked the fate of the photogram by proxy through the photomontage of *Blow-Up,* I round out this chapter by returning from that film's precipice of the postmodern to an early modern classicism so transparently cinematic that it doesn't look filmic at all. Again, however, the vulnerable (if surviving) human body is the chief clue to this narrative's localized encoding of photogrammatic indexicality. We have thought of such moments, so far, as cathartic breakdowns in the naturalized stream of cinematic motion. They are bracketed disclosures from which normative action must pull itself together again. To this purgative orphic crisis of the rerisen image, often a metamorphic return from the photograven moment of embalmed finality, the viewer must at times submit in more or less shaken transit. I am quick to recognize that any such appeal to the therapeutic metam/orphism of

338 (Courtesy of the Museum of Modern Art Film Stills Archive)

339

340

the track, as a death and dismemberment that fulfills and defines the moving image even while violating it, might sound like a solemnly inflated account of cinema's plenary image and its intermittent deflation into film. It might sound silly, if its truth weren't serious enough to be made funny.

But it is, and has been. A close look at our most gifted physical actor's greatest moment of orphic recuperation, the death and rebirth of Charlie in the bowels of the machine in Chaplin's *Modern Times* (1936), offers up the icon of a more underlying and mechanized mobility yet. It does so with no allusion to photography and no tampering whatever (at least at first) with the image track. It does so, instead, by set design's own invocation of the motion picture apparatus: as a last stage in the denaturing—ultimately disembodying—machination of industrial modernity. Out of all dramatic context, a famous production still from this episode (fig. 338) shows Charlie straddling the factory cogwheel like an equestrian acrobat in the many-ringed circus of modernity's clockwork mechanism, taking industrialization itself for a ride. For those who remember the episode, however, the very insouciance of the shot's comic brio blunts the larger specular parable. Borrowing as their image does from the opening reflexive montage of self-generative filmic manufactory in Fritz Lang's *Metropolis* a decade before (fig. 339), these rotary engines of progress—never visible in the factory set until now, and looking like nothing so much as giant projector reels—first swallow Charlie up in a long shot of their incessant advance (fig. 340). When camera position shifts to the medium shot on which the production still is based, we see from the frenetic narrative context (stepped through below, figs. 341-43, and then in the composite of fig. 344) that the squashed Tramp is just hanging in there, barely holding on, even as he feels obliged to wrench tight in progress the mechanism of his own sacrificial submission.

Walter Kerr sees Charlie as a maddened "Pan" in the hallucinated "Elysian Fields" of industrial progress.[58] To call him instead a deranged Orpheus is not to aggrandize the crisis but rather to rachet the point a notch or two deeper into the hidden gears of the filmic illusion.[59] I have said enough in chapter 5, I trust, to suggest the place of this film—with its closed-circuit screens within screens—in a history of near-futurist science fiction, a mode of narrative given to taking the contemporaneous cinema as its benchmark of historical (as well as scopic) projection. At that level of narrative, *Modern Times* could scarcely be more self-referential. But Chaplin's text is now pressed to refer further to itself, less as silent film spectacle than as rudimentary filmic process. Beyond genre, that is, what happens deep within the gnashing innards of the factory apparatus is a more medium-encompassing gesture yet. As if sprocket by sprocket, rocketed forward as spun image as well as stunned agent, Charlie's mechanistic reduction becomes the very picture of cinematic picturation, an icon of frame advance in heavy-industrial disguise. Flattened out and rolled over in instantaneously layered succession, the world's most famous screen image becomes, in short, his own photogram: raw material of all specular awe.

Two further and related aspects of this sequence bear stress at the culmination of this book. First, these images from *Modern Times* do not directly reveal—or even "illustrate"—frame advance; rather, they serve (as instanced by the opening, closing, and intermediate points in the rotational series I reprint) to refigure such advance as a scenographic joke. They do not just call out the photogrammatic progression of the filmic undertext; instead they emblematize it in the mode—and on the model—of a different mechanism altogether: on the spools of a different, if you will, assemblage line. This is why the perfect final touch in this episode, probable enough on reflection but unthinkable in the grips of the comic ritual, does finally involve a tricking of the image track. For when the foreman shifts gears and regurgitates Charlie backward out of the chute, we see the hero reverse direction by none other than reverse-action footage, his rescue identical to his descent.

Second, what the mechanized succession of the star image also does, as if by happenstance, is to bring into theoretical conjunction two separate realms of Bergsonian thought (one already discussed at length, one new to these pages): the perceptual illusion of successive positionality, on

341, 342, 343

344

the one hand, which falsifies the very becoming of movement as a modality of lived duration, and on the other, the
role of such falsity, such denaturing artifice, in the whole
genre of comedy, physical and otherwise—comedy being
elsewhere defined by Bergson as the dehumanizing mechanization of natural life.[60] Chaplin's tour de force locates a
point where the comic and apocalyptic coincide: a slapstick
apotheosis in which the juggernaut of the routinized is
trumped by the comedian's *routine*. Here too, as we have
seen, is a threatened death by dismemberment that puts us
in memory of the screen's fragile presence to begin with.
Eaten alive by the maw and teeth of the machine, Charlie is
tooled back into view by a mechanism analogous to the one,
never otherwise glimpsed by us in screen engagement, that
he both services as director and subserves as fugitive human
image. The contrastive disclosure could hardly be more extreme. From amid the
staid framings of Chaplin's characteristic long takes and the pellucid classicism of
his *mise en scène,* the work of the shifting strip breaks through.

Two quite different critical perspectives on mechanistic modernity intersect
the technological satire of *Modern Times* at just this point, in ways that invite return to our own axis of comparison between the photogrammatic integer of the
filmic circuit and the phonogrammatic substructure of literary inscription. From
the orientation of media critique and literary history, respectively, Peter Wollen
and Hugh Kenner each seize upon the industrial intertext (as well as overt thematic) in *Modern Times,* though without probing the materiality of the film's own
mechanized image system. Concerning the mechanistic quantifications of human
labor under industrial capitalism, Wollen writes that when Charlie "runs amok"
in and beyond the factory, he "proves unable to acquire the new psycho-physical
habits required under Fordism" and is thus "unable to stop performing his segmented mechanical action even when away from the assembly line" (37-38).[61]
The machine has been internalized, just as Charlie will be engorged by the machine. Moreover, in the overthrown semiotics of so-called meaningful work, labor
has been broken down into separate units that fall short of the comprehensible.
Following Gramsci, Wollen speaks of this assembly-line leveling in explicitly linguistic terms: "Fordism introduced an industrial regime—for the worker—of pure
signifiers, stripped of meaning" (52). In the realm of text production itself, historical precedent confirms that strict mechanical segmentation prevents distraction.
"Medieval copyists, Gramsci observed, became interested in the text they were
copying and consequently made mistakes" (52). But as Wollen generalizes for industrial production at large, the subsequent "mechanization of copying through
printing led to a mechanization of the labour process, a suppression of the signified, an end to the creative rewriting of the copyist" (52).

Before considering Kenner's approach to the oblique impact of print technology upon Chaplin's screen persona in *Modern Times* (rather than upon his filmic

mechanism), we need again, for clarification's sake, to narrow the linguistic (within the historical) focus. What Gramsci passes over in the suggestion borrowed by Wollen is that the copyist's imaginatively engaged and thus slipshod "rewriting" could also happen far beneath the level of invested interest in the larger signified. Having precisely to do with the undecidabilities of segmentation, such mistakes were often caused by the accidents of phonation (both before and after the breaking up of scripted lexemes into separate word blocks). Scholarship on manuscript emendation is full of examples in which word boundaries and internal juncture were rendered ambiguous to the subvocalizing ear, against (at slower speed) the intended increments of script.[62] In this sense even scribal copying had a quasi-automatic risk built in to the very mechanism of double articulation, a risk manifested (to shift Virilio's emphasis again) in the "exposure time" of reading rather than writing. I bring this aspect forward here, one last time, only because it suggests an underlying level of significatory slippage that might allow for just the connections Wollen himself does not draw out between Chaplin's anti-Fordist irony (as invisibly deepened by his filmic textuality) and the praxis of literary modernism that derives in part, as shown by Kenner, from routinizing the compositor's marks in the technologies of mass-produced typesetting.

What we might call this technological "prototype" for the compositorial eccentricities of modernist language is Kenner's leading point in *The Mechanic Muse*, where the innovative machination of the linotype process, as a technological armature for word production, influenced a wide variety of lexical reconfigurations in Joyce, Pound, and other modernists.[63] In drawing his parallel to Chaplin, Kenner concentrates, within the factory sequence of *Modern Times*, on the famous feeding-machine episode, in which corn on the cob is forced through the teeth of the unsuspecting hero, who thereby submits to a motorized—and quintessentially modern—action derived from that of a "typewriter carriage" (7). But this comes only halfway toward a filmic apprehension of this cinematic joke. Whereas, in connection with linotype processes, Kenner flags with scare quotes the late nineteenth-century production of "reading matter" (7) by the industrial press, he doesn't ponder the difference it could have made to the reception of cinema as industrial product if the idiom "viewing matter" had ever caught on. Of course, it didn't. At least in the vulgate, the film experience remains more disembodied, less *plastic* and technological, more immanent. As no one has shown more resolutely than Kenner himself, modernist literature arises to take the *matter* of reading with unprecedented seriousness. So does Chaplin take the technical basis of film—and in just those moments of technological satire that prompt Kenner's allusion to *Modern Times*. For if the feeding machine calls to mind the automated revolution and return of the typewriter carriage in modernity's preeminent text machine, the subsequent immolation of Charlie on the turbine wheels replays this latent image of *serial imprinting* to highlight its filmic equivalent in the rotational basis of photogrammatic frame advance.

Kenner asserted in 1987 that it was "time to sketch" not just the literary precedents of modernism but the way its practitioners were conditioned by the "most salient feature" of their modern environment: namely, for Kenner, "intelligence questing after what can be achieved by a patterned moving of elements in space: the mats of a linotype, the words of a poem" (15). Add to this the photograms of a projected screen frame—and the time is now. Nonetheless, Kenner's contextualist proposal by no means halts his recourse to literary-historical determinants in order to shore up the same point from a different vantage. In an appendix to *The Mechanic Muse*, he finds Victorian symbolist practice serving to release the signifier from centuries of post-Enlightenment confusion about the proper wedding (or at least cousining) of word and thing. In his most Foucauldian moment, Kenner seems to imply that the detachment of the signifier from the signified, and the consequent return of ornamental language into the resultant semiotic gap, was the resuscitation of the word itself *as thing*, rather than the "mercantile" (118) quid pro quo of one word for every thing. If so, Kenner has returned in a different key to the materialist textuality underlying the linotype apparatus as modernist touchstone, with its manipulable integers of an aggregate linguistic construct. Foucauldian on one face, this would also be an argument not unlike Jameson's for the autonomous segmentations of a new "stylistic" regime, the ornamental instrumentality of a specifically modernist *écriture*.

Here, then, is where Kenner's technographic and Wollen's Fordist muses—with Jameson's locomotive muse in the background—may meet on the oscillating *plane* of literary and filmic signification. Despite precision tooling, the splutter of the spooled image may assert itself from beneath the mechanized screen action. Despite the calibration of alphabetic imprint, the permutations of reading may shake loose lateral regroupings in those slats across lettering that usually give words a breather from each other. In a general culture of mechanism and modular segmentation, the flutter of lexical utterance and the continuous clustering of projected images do more, therefore, than manifest what each owes to the second industrial revolution in the quantified breakdown of technologized output. They also comment on each other's share in the modernist disposition of *textuality*, resisting their assigned roles as instrumental media from within the materiality of each medium in turn.

Both film and literature make their modernist bids by becoming, if by different routes, less "scenic"—and each in view of the other's popular norms. For one way that modernist literature could resist the mass visual media was to reverse its own subordination to visual culture, via the obligation to word pictures. Rather than providing a secondary summons to the seen, writing learned to turn the impressed letter per se not only into a visibly permutable mark along the self-reset line but into the covert escape valve for its own phonemic alternatives. By contrast, cinema as world picture could resist its birthright as instantaneous record only by now and again turning its operative motion into a discrete array of traces stitching over the inscriptive rips of imprint. If literature resists its derivative mimetic status by making the sign function rather than its reference freshly visible, and not only visible but revocalized in the unsounded belling of its letters, cinema cancels or defers its mimesis only by recurring to the filmic marks that underlie all kinetic gesture. Photography emerges from beneath cinema as film, in short, the way phonographesis (with its twin, homophony) sneaks surfaceward from beneath writing as text. This is the point most worth stressing, across our selectively paired media, about the modernist assertion within the modern expectation. Beyond competition, cinema and "reading matter" become most like each other by becoming most themselves, now filmic, now linguistic: in short, textual. Hence the common denominator between the lexical flick and the filmic fleck suggested by the very term *cinécriture.*

In comparing Wollen and Kenner, media theory and contextualized literary history, we have moved to the doorstep of interdisciplinary resolution and the threshold of further overview. Whereas social modernity is segregated, discrepant, routinized, aesthetic modernism is openly fractured and refractive. Where modernity is automated, modernism (Jameson's point again in this new technological context) grows detached and automatized. Given our examples, accelerated print technique is answered by the collisions and derailments of *écriture,* the Fordist modernity of industrial cinematic production by the precubist modernism of the revealed filmic gestalt. Whereas the industrial signified of cinematic assemblage is modern, the glimpsed return to its racing signifier as motorized signal is modernist. Modernity is modular, modernism molecular. Modernity is mechanical and composite, modernism is atomistic but textured, manifestly differential. When the fabricated and synthetic elements of modernity seek their new syntheses in modernism, the component yields place to the supplement. From the private appliance of reading to the public apparatus of screen spectacle, industrial imprint across media is modern, whereas modernism is text.

I have said it before in other terms. The cinematic is modern; the filmic is modernist. In their composite work on-screen, they make manifest what for good reason, under the historical aegis of the Freudian problematic, we call the "psychic mechanism." In this performative repetition, as we have seen, modernism's filmic register joins literature's linguistic register to address (not redress) the loss of another totality: the self-presence of human perception, which can no longer be fully cognizant of the very thing that makes it what it is, an *un*conscious zone of fragments and segments, irreconcilable impulses and their displaced combinations. Perceptual attention, consciousness per se, must be *defined as* a diverting of energy from all else that accompanies it. In this way does the human psyche find its place (if not its home) in a modernity strangely homologous to the mind's own discrepant operations. And aesthetic modernism unsettles that place, the better to recapture its founding tensions. Here is cinema's true and double foothold in the culture of industrial modernity. By mass mechanization, and its basis in arbitrary segmentation, totality can be lost (sight of) in, as it were, a whole new way. The worker mechanically distracted from any sense of overall "meaning" by the piecemeal concentration of his work, like the train traveler buffeted by impressions, is given in compensation a new art born from mechanical distraction itself. Cinema requires no close attention, in fact militates against it by its potential for automatic absorption. (Except, for Benjamin, in those moments when it brings back from the "optical unconscious" the unattended increments of human gesture itself.[64]) In any case, from within the compensatory logic of technological modernity, filmic modernism takes upon itself the obligation to turn the aestheticized distraction of moviegoing back into a work.

Such, we might say in sum, is Chaplin's "allegory of film" from within his satiric fable of cinema. In arguing for Chaplin's cinematographic (ultimately intervallic) modernism in view of literature's oscillating lexical texture, serendipity dictates a glance at the 1926 poem by Hart Crane called "Chaplinesque," written a decade before *Modern Times* but celebrating even then Chaplin's genius for transcending the "rushing, humdrum, mechanical scramble of today."[65] As an instance of what Crane may have meant when feeling that he "captured the arrested climaxes and evasive victories of [Chaplin's] gestures in words," I give only the flickering slapstick diction attached to the "random consolations" of experience that "the wind deposits" in the tramp's pockets, where the segmental conflation "windy" rushes upon us by random liaison before it can be properly parsed by the thinking eye. If such moments transcend the mechanical, they do so from within the linguistic register of such mechanism. So with our chosen sequence from *Modern Times*, and so with a brilliant comment upon it by Walter Benjamin that never mentions the film once.

For Benjamin, Chaplin seems quite literally to *incarnate*, as actor as well as screen image, the cinematic option of modernity, performing the very dance of filmic intermittence. In a remarkable note to "The Work of Art in the Age of Mechanical Reproduction" not given in the English translation, Benjamin writes: "Every single one of [Chaplin's] movements is put together from a series of hacked-up pieces of motion. Whether one focuses on his walk, on the way [he] handles his cane, or tips his hat [or, we might add, submits to the machines of industrial production]—it is always the same jerky sequence of the smallest motions which raises the law of the filmic sequence of images to that of human motor action."[66] This is, of course, exactly the reversal of Bergson's complaint about the sensorimotor continuum of the immanent world getting reduced to and betrayed by both filmic analogy and cinema's dismembering analog technology. Instead, for Benjamin, in Chaplin's aesthetic embrace of mechanization the modality of photogrammatic sequence ("the law of the filmic sequence of images") is elevated to an analysis—and redemption—of modernity's discontinuous and routinized doing. Embodying the medium itself as a model of modernity, Chaplin's very image on film enacts the unread tread of the skittish photogram beneath all screen motion.

This championing of Chaplin's silent comedy is certainly no minor digression in Benjamin's thought. Nor, on the tacitly literary side of the modernist equation, is Benjamin's association of the "optical unconscious" with a linguistically attuned psychoanalysis. In the main text of the Artwork essay, just before he transposes his notion of the stilled image as the unconscious underlay of quotidian vision (from his earlier writing on photography) into the quintessentially modern cinematic domain, where the shot rather than the photogram would take on the burden of intercepting the otherwise routinely seen, the transition is telling. For he gets there by way of remarks on Freud's modern contribution to the age-old but long analytically ignored prevalence of slips of the tongue in ordinary language use.[67] This is the same Benjamin who elsewhere resorts to cross-lexical wordplay of his own, when he deconstructs the very chronotope of a commodified bourgeois culture as a time-space exposed as time-dream: *Zeitraum* broken down, under analysis as it were, to *Zeit-traum*.[68] To draw such a flicker effect of junctural ambiguity into English, transposing it into this book's own terms for the mechanization of the specular unconscious in the time/space ratios on the commercial screen, we may say that the time-dream of representation submits in filmic modernity to the calibrated mechanism of *timed dream* beneath the mirage of a waking present. Complementing such ghostly slips of the tongue, a whole modernist zeit-geist seems betokened as well by the spectrality of filmic juncture in the chimerical séance of cinematic apparition.

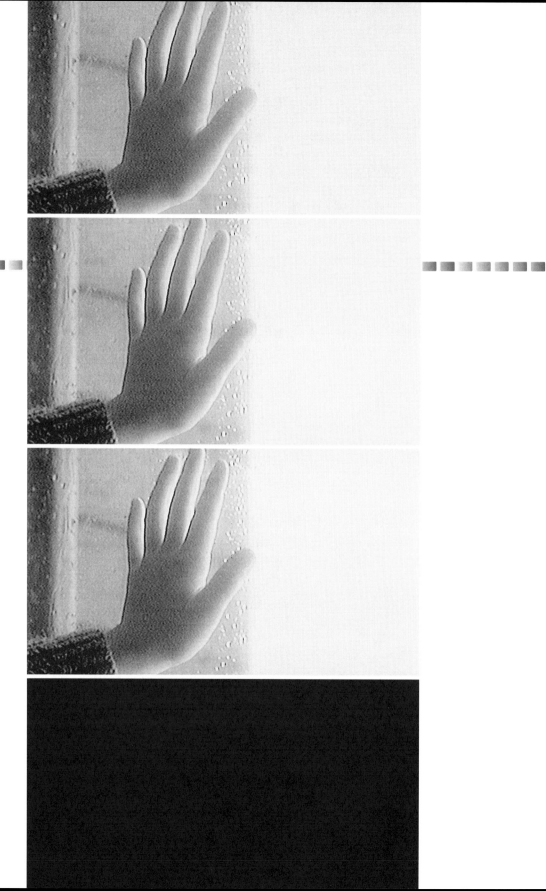

End Title/Exeunt

I choose the Latin plural advisedly. Before we file out, they do: the images that, filing past, have riveted us with their peculiar mix of imprint and nonfixity. We have been sitting still in rows to be carried away by another rushing row, a strip of ribboned pictures all just a little different from each other, until the tiny differences spread themselves out over time to an entire world in view. But as we gaze, the imprinted pictures continue invisibly to gape. If we are every once in a while cued by certain overdetermined automatisms of narrative style—technique in reversion to technology—to apprehend the skewed trace of such gaping, such gapping, what we see is never of course the strip, nor entirely the screened world any longer, but instead, unsteadily, a sudden evidence of the underlying means: plastic velocity in action, the return of the incremental suppressed. Be this as it may en route, at some later point in any film such motoring suppression is entirely suspended. All at once the continuously overlapped gap prolongs its stay to absolute lapse. Constitutive limit or verge—the single frame's sped edge—becomes, after all is seen and done, seen undone, THE end.

But what, exactly, does closure testify to on its own material terms? A conclusive example of the filmic moment within cinema will soon help us gauge, even by its deliberate exaggeration, the true level of such inquiry. By what must the cinematic finis always be underwritten on the suddenly abrogated track? There's the start of an answer just there—in the very notion of a canceled track. With the photogram no longer ramming up against another almost like it, overtaking it by taking it over, whatever has been visible is severed, over. The screen viewer is strung along by photograms only so long as they are still wheeling past. Every merger into screen motion is therefore seeded with its own latent end in the blended lending of one imprint to a next in line, since such scrolling annexation may be x-ed out at any appropriate moment by the final truncating cut. In literary writing, every period may seem proleptic; in film syntax, every quick cut cuts to the quick of the motion it propels, thus anticipating the final blank. Cinema must overcome this stab, this tabulation of the increment, only by coming over it with another one fast, a little different, edging on. Eventually there is nowhere left to go. Having seen through photograms, we see them through at the last, the framed imprint finally uncoupled from its near double in uptake. All of cinema's narrative aggregation gets shrunk to an edit without destination: the isolated and suddenly disallowed difference internal to all screen motion, all time on-screen. As is the case in narrative literature with the last but not least rip from inscription in the white silence following "The End," although without the possibility of immediate rescanning, the final snippet of screen image spins to invisibility, over and out. In the absence of film's photogrammatic ground, black leader leads nowhere. What goes around ultimately comes aground.

Think of it this way—since for once, in closure, you have time to. Cinema persists as institution; movies end; narratives drive for finish; exposed film just stops—stops on the spot. Retrospectively, film isolates the photogram's necessity in the very act of its effacement. Decisive proof of photogrammatic constitution, in other words, awaits us at the tail end of closure's dissolve—or sudden lunge—to negation. The filmic image, after frame upon frame of split-second celluloid loitering, is gone on the instant. Whatever your attachment to it, *it* must in the end tear itself away from *you*. Film's final differential is all rent, cheated of succession by the wrench of cancellation. This, as we saw in chapter 2, is part of what *Proof* attests to in its last plangent cut to black. Long marking the very structure of the interval, the absentation of the photogram converts from impetus to end-stop, the germinal gone terminal.

On exit, and on just this score, we will be holding our attention, as we are forced to do by the dynamics of the shot in question, on a lingering last frame of a classic narrative, *Grand Hotel*, designed to highlight (precisely by its melodramatic dimming down) the rectangular field of film's graphic basis. We will do so in full view (and review) of the terrain these chapters have attempted to cover. On the matter of film and its photo synthesis, their cumulative thesis has been this: that the photogram on-screen is the (mostly) missing perceptual link as well as one obvious historical link—via the filmic per se—between the age of photography and the age of cinema; that the photogram is not solely a function in cinematic manifestation but a potential factor in its narrative momentum as well; that film theory evades film practice in this regard when it factors out the photogram, in the name either of a visual ideology assumed to depend on its utter suppression or of an aesthetics that finds no use for medium-specific determinations at this level; and that an attention to the counterplay of motion and fixity often at tension in narrative cinema provides one means toward the necessary triple historicizing of film's relation to the twentieth century.

So seen, cinema comes into being, first of all, as the scion of nineteenth-century literary realism—as well as the product of any number of other conditioning epistemic shifts from Renaissance science forward. Second, cinema arrives as the prescient instrumentation of a differentially geared high modernism: the whole *ballet mécanique* of the interval. Such is the rule of the interval whose peculiar aesthetics of ocular discontinuity on film would, third, lie fallow in the culture of cinema for almost half a century after the medium's first onslaught of formalist experiment before resurfacing in spurts, not just as structuring condition but as programmatic device, in commercial cinema's own evolution into a deferred and soon vanished late modernist phase. After which point the motion picture's undertext in photogrammatic advance returns to a prevailing latency and an all but continuous elision for a decade or so until the escalating encroachments of computer-driven "visuals." Whether amplified or damped down, however, the filmic underside of cinema's world sightings might at any point sustain comparison not only with Bergson's critique of mechanistic thinking but with the automatized sliding signifier of a literary practice carried beyond the conventional domain of style as rhetoric. When such *écriture* finds its most fully wrought manifestation in sublexical montage, it does so by releasing a feature I have thus taken to calling the phonogram of the syntactic track. What the phonogram does for, or to, literary writing is comparable to the advent of the photogram in the effect of cinema as film, vexing that usual course of things wherein the strictly contiguous is made seemingly continuous. Form will out even when the norm wins out.

All told, a compound thesis, a multiple set of consequences—together suggesting, among other things, that cinema knows better than most commentary its own varying relations to the photographic imprint. But there is another form of review that comes readily to mind and to hand, since these broad claims have been further specified and separately tested in progress. Seven chapters unfolding seven related declarations now converge in straightforward replay simply by collecting those launching sentences that have urged them forward. Cinema, to begin with, can engrave its own relation to the still image from within the flow of motion. In such a materialist apocalypse, narrated Last Things in cinema may revert to filmic first things. In the most extreme case of the freeze-frame, movement's exception reproves (chastens even while reconfirming) its screen rule. In this and other ways, death in cinema regularly takes the form of photographic form itself. Often under the sign of such dying, the media turn in futurist film fiction addresses the postphotographic science of cinema's own dubious future. By contrast, recent period cinema turns a rearview mirror upon the whole course of mutating filmic technology. In all these ways, then, cinema as film fulfills the modernist genealogy not of mimesis but of text. This *is* its modernism.

No amount of double vision, no cognitive squinting, will bring this filmic matter to the fore of the projected picture in ordinary circumstances. That is why it becomes a true *theoretical issue,* so abstract as to remain for the most part altogether "off the screen" of narrative consciousness. Why, then, doesn't any such consideration of the filmic object, of the strip in action as track, lead to the most banal of medium-specific rumination, as tangential as it is tendentious? Even as theory, what can rescue such considerations from an exile that goes even beyond the peripheral? Simply this: that for the undertext of the filmic mirage to be localized on-screen, even if not exactly made visible, to be cited if not sighted, requires in narrative cinema a perceptual discharge sufficient for the bracing estrangement of the entire screen illusion. I have called this discharge, in narrative instances, a moment of thematerialization.

In preview of all this, I needed early on to clarify for photography, then to deploy at a new level for cinema, Walter Benjamin's notion of the optical unconscious. In so doing I soon came face-to-face, if not eye-to-eye, with Rosalind Krauss's own adaptation of Benjamin, where discussion found cause to demur from her sense—and further dissemination—of his famous term. Once more, and in short, the visible world is neither conscious nor unconscious about anything we see in it. It is we who know what we see, and who see more than we always know or recognize. Photography is our prosthesis, not the world's. What it reveals to us has been latent in our seeing, not in the world's constitution. So, too, when that world comes to film. Only we in an audience, not the world's objects, look on with new eyes for what cinema draws forth and recasts from the scopic field of our regularly envisaged space. But even at that, since cinema is also film, so much per second, we look on without looking too closely into how this new view of things comes to be there before us: machine art's new form of suspended disbelief. In this technological suppression, as I have been calling it, something like a specular preconscious seems to know—at least on occasion to show—its place.

Those clarifications of Benjamin behind us, with many examples to secure them, it should now further come clear how this book diverges from the mainstream approach to material demystification in cinema studies—from, that is, the blanket political stress of apparatus theory. I suppose my irreducible point of difference from Baudry's influential position paper,[1] whose emphasis on the spectator's normative denial of the relational nature of photographic animation is otherwise close to my own, has to do with the level at which ideology is found to intercede. For Baudry, as his revealing footnote on the relation of linguistic to cinematic signification brings out (as discussed in chapter 2), it is the relation *among* rather than the fractional (and potentially frictional) difference *between* the separate sublexical signifiers of the verbal sign that offers the closest analogy from linguistics for the filmic apparition—and hence the closest tie of each field separately to a broader cognitive paradigm of the interval. In normative reception, the denial of difference, the myth of ocular plenitude, becomes, according to his account, an englobing fact about the filmic apparatus. Call it, as almost everyone does now, an ideology.

On this theoretical view of the viewing situation, the trouble is that one is inclined to ignore the transitional stress points where a risked disengagement from the moving image, even in the occasional materialist flourish of classical cinema, flattens the cinematic space to the obvious condition of an oscillating trace. Call it, as I have been doing, a node of impacted textuality. The moments thus ignored by theory cannot be termed subversive. But neither do they sustain denial en masse. The same constitutive fact—the fact of the photogram—can thereby be understood as either institutional or textual. In the former case we sign off on the lie up front, buy into the denial at the box office. In the latter *event* we renegotiate the terms of the specular contract from shot to racing frame and back again, the intervals fused as a rule, their recognized disjunctures few and far between. But always possible—as if flying in wait. In short, the ideology of the apparatus is never quite so smothering as in the imputations of its critique.

Having established this difference from the theory of "negation" and its disavowal in Baudry (and by extension in Metz), I saw more clearly the large and lingering question that might burden these pages with the weight of the inconclusive. In the spirit of supposition, one has to live with some of this, I guess. But more can be pinned down in exit than has been so far. Correct me if I'm wrong, but what remains to be asked is what stands to be gained, in detail as well as at large, from any notion of a specular subconscious (whether non-, pre-, or un-)—and particularly in a textualist response to the film medium committed to more cinematographic specificity than one finds in the ideological critique of the apparatus per se. How does the concept of specularity and its constitutive deflections usefully diverge from, if only to underpin, the "imaginary signifier" of Metz's Lacanian picture, where images come before us on-screen not only as signs with meanings but as a presymbolic plenum of phantasmatic presence?

To think this out, as the spectator seldom inclines to do in front of the screen, we are sent back further than Metz to the most famous figurative claim in probably the most famous essay on photographic representation, the funerary gambit of Bazin's "The Ontology of the Photographic Image."[2] For all the renown of his essay, his opening hypothesis has remained too little investigated. It might fairly be said that twenty years' worth of institutional film study, from semiotics through psychoanalytic linguistics, was spawned by the hat-trick flourish of his closing remark, coming at the reader out of nowhere in a last cliff-hanging paragraph all its own: "On the other hand, of course, cinema is also a language" (16). But no such legacy attends his breezy first sentence, however famous the soon reiterated point. The what-if structure of Bazin's tantalizing gambit is in fact a shade too hypothetical to have much immediate force: "*If* the plastic arts were put under psychoanalysis, the practice of embalming the dead might turn out to be a fundamental factor in their creation" (9; emphasis added). There follows the more often quoted pithiness of the next formulation, where "at the origin of painting and sculpture there lies a mummy complex" (9). What might come off as an egregious joke in English—the "mother complex" involved in the media's search for origins, a kind of "mummy envy"—is in the original French not just a serious and fertile speculation but, in the disarming conditional of its initial phrasing, a powerfully unfollowed lead.[3]

For when are the plastic arts—and numbering among them film as an art of sequential photography—when are they ever *not* "under psychoanalysis" in (perceptual) effect: that is, in the event of reception? By which I mean simply to offer a synonym for the—always transactional—reading (i.e., viewing) event. Once the textual unthought of our relation to cinema is implicitly delved in the full array of its automatized elisions and strategic lacunae, what is further psychoanalyzed, in the act of engagement with such representation, is the viewer myself. Emphasis falls on precisely the investments and transferences—and repressions—that bring plastic form to cognitive impact. This too remains implicit. About the various levels of my fascination, I am kept, yes, mostly in the dark. But how, and how often, does an ingrained reflexive analysis of my spectatorial position actually take registered place in film? If, for instance, mummification and its discontents can ever be dredged up by the viewer (the transferentially engaged subject) as an immemorial impetus beneath the sublimated process of time's own chemical preservation in cinema, one site of such retrieval must be the sequential effigy of the single frame. This is the frame ordinarily staved off, deferred and forgotten, in its deathlike fixity from disavowed instant to instant. But, even when exposed, what does such a defection from the reality effect effect? In the deepest of all screen disavowals, we accept automatically the photogram's elided and hence elusive relationship to time and change, even its illusory manipulation of them—accept its continuously lost *elusions* of presence. But not always. So?

Let me approach my answer by following on more directly from Bazin. What the cinema spectator must defend against in order to placate a neurosis (a primordial "complex" behind the mimetic urge) that finds intermittent gratification or relief in the aura of immortality attaching to the film spectacle, what the viewer must wish away in the cathexis of "embalmed time," is always at root the photogram: returning symptom of the plastic (before kinetic) mummy complex. The same with writing in its different set of differences. We suppress the fixating letter and its sound cues for the law of the activated lexeme. Words must slough off and attempt to forget the phonemic cocoon that releases their brief flight of meaning. Literacy renders the process automatic, whatever literature may then do to impede it with the return of the phoneme. With the comparable textuality of the screen image, the filmic track further automatizes all such suppression. Film's success rests, that is, with the speed of succession: the mechanical inhibition of the recognized single frame within the perceived motion of the picture. In this sense cinema's immortality machine cranks out its fantasy as a kind of reaction formation in the spectator, an unconscious conversion of the manifestly vanishing into the evidently forever available.

But are we being, as one might object, overspecific? To see through cinema's illusion of the holistic image—or at least to recognize that a flurry of photograms is the source of all such screen sightings—would be only one of the spoilages of screen appeal against which we in the audience immunize ourselves. So that if, as film viewers, our quite conscious banking on the ideology of the plenary image, replete in itself and completing us as situated subjects—willing, receptive, and rewarded—entails a necessary repression or disavowal of many different things we know to forget (like plugs, wires, celluloid, bulb, and the rest, let alone the constructedness of character and the mythology of social roles) what, then, is the theoretical yield from a more localized paradigm (a photogrammatic model) of the returned repressed—or suppressed? As a trope for irruptive technique beneath the mystique of presence (or even the mystique of thematized evanescence, as with the dissolutions of the frame in *La jetée*), it does well enough—but for what exactly? If the specular preconscious is little more than a metaphor for the cinematic essence, if it is so long lost to view as to condition mostly nothing in our immediate screen experience, but only the advance possibility of such experience, then of what real use is the psychoanalytic figure of speech? What form of return, I am asking again, might justify even the term "suppression"?

The answer is as simple as it is huge. This is why multiple examples have seemed in order. En masse, their common fact grows hard to obscure, whether by their own separate complexities or otherwise. Even sophisticating the tacit spectatorial contract to include the transferential dynamics of the analytic viewing act is not likely to lose our focus. If we say, for instance, that our unconscious recognition of cinema's photogrammatic basis (and all this implies about the made object rather than the received world) seems displaced onto, rather than generated by, a given film's own insistence on the filmic within the cinematic, even a convolution of that order cannot blunt the force of the larger point. This is the simple part. To let film recognize for us the specular unthought of our own attachment to it, without severing its seductive sight lines, is in short a therapeutic event. Certain films dare to exorcise in reception the disjunctive ghostliness of their own empty show. Such films renew themselves—with our elicited complicity—from the piecemeal debris of credence. The transference is so complete that they may scramble to remobilize their own systems in full view, so to speak, of our readiness to receive them.

At which point a psychoanalytic template for cinematic subjection may be resituated within a larger cultural evolution for which modernism is a kind of metadiscourse. This is the huge part. Older than the physics of relativity, older than the mass visual media, older than the Fordist assembly line, older than automatic weaponry, older than stereography, phonography, or mechanized typography, older than the locomotive transformation of landscape vistas, older than photography, older than cognitive shifts in the sketchbook tradition, older than automata research, older than a calculus of intervals, older than experimental optics, older than the invention of silent reading, older than the Machine itself, older that the world view attached to Plato's cave and even of the pictographic montage of the first cave draftsmen—antedating all is the birth of art out of ritual practice, art as a sublimation of primal violence. To this the photogram in its own way reverts. For the therapeutic exchange of recognition it precipitates—instilled at times by that sudden stilling of the image that converts on the very spot the moviegoer into a *film* watcher—partakes in this primitive aesthetic function as well. On film, the displacement of violence to the sign function of symbolic ritual is, of course, further disembodied by technology. Yet the logic persists—thinned, even rarefied, but culturally in place. No longer carrying representational force, such moments of cinematographic obtrusion drive out ready illusion in order to carry the very principle of catharsis beyond the dramaturgy of the view to the material conditions of the seen. Cinema dies, dies back into film, for our sincerities of conviction in it. We might say, as I have been at various points tempted to say, that such moments thus carry—in a way modernism makes over into a wholesale poetics—the former negativity of the tragic vision into the crevices of textuality itself, where expressive subjectivity is dethroned by an unruly automatism of the signifier.

But this therapeutic prototype is more complicated (or multiple) yet—and yields to an unexpected historical placement across discourses. Modernist literary inscription arises (as international movement rather than long-standing stylistic undercurrent) alongside the dawn of cinema, I may now propose, in a way that serves collaboratively to midwife (out of philosophy, if we follow Cavell) the very birth of the modern psyche. What can this mean? And even if plausible, what would it mean for cinema's intersection with the viewer's own psychic attachments to the screen? Early on, we needed to distinguish the tumultuous logic of the unconscious in Freud from the routinized censorship and suppression (in the preconscious, rather) that keeps the photogram from notice on-screen. Since then we have plumbed certain literary parallels in a field where the linguistic construct has been far more stringently theorized in terms of psychic processes, as, for instance, via Lacan's famous slippage of the letter in the unconscious. This will encourage another form of appeal (in a moment) to the topographic model of psychoanalysis—at least to the heuristic place of the model, however metaphoric still, in an account of screen reception.

It may justify the chapters behind us to realize that one can successfully make this appeal only by recalling photography's central place in any account of cinema's paradigm shift in the history of vision. Cinema arrives on the historical scene to redefine the history of images, to be sure, if for no other reason than that it is only after film that idiom comes to terms with what would have been the former tautology of "still photography." Teleologies miss the very boat on which they seem launched if they fail to note that photography hasn't from the beginning itched to become film. Its technology was a wonder sufficient unto the day. Its limitations are noted only in retrospect. The logic of cinema, that is, retroactively brackets fixity and atemporality as resistant conditions of the new medium, thereby marking its own overridden dependence on them. By similar means, cinema often finds a place for the limits of photography inside its plots, so as to make its own *use* of the photograph, liminal and imperceptible, look good—if still mysterious. This mystery can never be overestimated. Only with cinema, last and least obviously mediated of the arts, could I say of a produced object not just that I don't know what I am seeing (as with an obscure surrealist painting, say), but that I don't know *how*. Even thoroughly informed about sprocket holes, shutter mechanisms, and focal lengths, as film spectator I am no longer quite sure I fully realize how the image is realized, in other words exactly how it is constituted for and before me, or just how it differs from the things I normally take for seen. Which is to say that movies enter the history of visual art by way of questioning art's ocular as much as its aesthetic assumptions. Cinema is a quizzing of vision itself. Even so, the object (if not the process) of our gaze in the everyday world is usually material in itself, an objective thing, like a tree or a canister of celluloid. Cinema is more strangely material*ized.*

In adjacent visual forms, we can and do see *where* paint would have struck the canvas, a chisel the stone. Through a dancer's flesh, we glimpse outer signs of the muscles that spring the leap, *la jetée*. On-screen, only the thrown light: *la projetée.* As always, one important way to think about this begins with photography. Whereas in the previous plastic and performing arts the material or tactile basis of the art is mostly visible to us, whether as a bodily marked surface or as a skilled body, photography changes all this in two main ways, both of which, of course, delay its recognized status as art. It is, first, automatic rather than bodily in origin and, second, invisibly so. With photography alone, as the first mechanical art, and hence the first art "compromised" (or compounded) from within by mechanics, technique withdraws altogether from result. The automatism of photography passes through the laboratory, reversed in the negative stage, chemically treated and matured, before it becomes the object photograph, wherein none of this process is visible, only the initial choice of framing. One step (or more) further along in the history of enhanced technological resemblance, and hence one step further removed from the "frame" on strip to that on-screen, cinema comes to existence precisely in the split seconds, one after the other, of its multiply disappeared material base. Gone is the negative into the positive, the positive into the celluloid transparency, the transparent frame into the projected pattern of light and dark, and each separately into the current of presentness, the *currency*, of the immanent moving image.

Cinema, then, is a skein of effects shorn of origin. So with read writing. Only part of literature's materiality, almost none of its artistry, is visible to us. We see where the words hit the page, in script or print, but rather in the way we notice where inscribed notes dot the staff on a sheet of music. When the black on white of verbal text is "performed" in silent reading, the (trans)formative reader produces signification—and its literary slippages—only by the sudden disappearance of the given into the instantaneously remade. The latent sensorium of material cause—morphophonemic structure in production—is as removed from plain sight in the inked increments on the page as is the photochemical negative from the photograph or, in closer correlation with the temporal textuality of continuous imprint, as is the oscillated photogram from the mirage of motion in plain view on-screen. When modernist *écriture* is said to reinject the thingness of the linguistic into the otherwise transparent work of language, it must dredge up phoneme as well as morpheme from beneath the complacent availability of a transcribed message. In the same way, the *cinécriture* of movies is the return of the filmic within (and against) the grain, the supervening reign, of the cinematic. This means the return at once of the mechanical absentation of photography and the mechanical segmentation of photogrammaticality.

Cinema is the quintessential modern art because it so fully recruits technology—the quintessential modern condition—in the service of representation. But filmic cinema, as we have amply seen, is modernist rather than just modern when it troubles the automatism with its own atomism. Here is where *techne* encroaches upon psyche. One could certainly say that film introduces into the history of fabricated imaging a genuinely new order of mimesis, so immediate and automatized that it seems more like "living" record than representation. One could also say that film introduces into the history of consciousness a radical new order of imaging—distanced from both event and reception at once. But one could further say that film introduces into culture a whole new level of anxiety: not only a new mode of being gone from appearances, of absence and disappearance each, but, on the side of reception, an entirely new way of being brought face-to-face with the fragility of impressions and with the unknowability of their constitution in the moment of perception. In this sense cinema only maximizes its modernist contribution to the history of vision when it vexes, by strange flexions, its own filmic substrate—and not so much, via formalist modernism, in order to bare the device as, more transactively, to *figure* the unknowable depths of perception beneath the surface of the seen. When we are no longer simply receiving messages from the printed page or screen, when we are reading words or images not only for what they invent but for what makes them up, the doubleness of the procedure reflects inevitably upon the double nature of our own receptive apparatus. In this sense film's debut collides with the modernist bent of letters precisely when it is taken to enter not only the history of visual art, or even the history of vision, but—in collision with psychoanalysis as well—the history of subjectivity.

This routes us back to the potential place of photogrammatic disclosure in Stanley Cavell's problematic of skepticism, a disclosure entertained somewhat against Cavell's own inclination in chapter 3, and further back to the "optical unconscious" brought out (in Benjamin) both by photography and, in an adjusted sense, by film. In Cavell's more recent formulations about psychoanalysis and philosophy, occasioned in fact by his latest essays on narrative cinema, he suspects that for Freud psychoanalysis seemed born *from* philosophy—rather than over against it—as the answer to philosophy's own perennial question about the constitution of the human subject.[4] Framed as always by his critique of skepticism, Cavell's inferences seem to run as follows. If personal existence, as the locus of self-presence, depends so absolutely and paradoxically on the unconscious, and if it is so difficult to station oneself in any confident relation toward that unconscious, how surprising can it be that one lives in and upon an uncertainty verging on skepticism? If we know our own existence only as based on all that we can never know of ourselves, how can we be sure of what we know of others or the world?

Strangely enough, perhaps, this is where the stray letter of the literary phonogram and the motivated glitch of the recursive photogram both come in. I thus move aside once more from Cavell's main path of thought (while well in mind of those moments concerning photographic insets and films within films upon which our interests converge) to the undertext of automated world movement. Here art's therapeutic function would not be entirely compassed by the anxieties worked through in Shakespearean tragedy, say, or in Hollywood remarriage comedies and their generic complement in female melodramas, in all of which skepticism becomes primarily a *dramatic* (hence thematic) problem—often called out, of course, by the problematizing of formal mediation per se. The dilemmas of skepticism may also have a more radical psychic residue, cast into unusual illumination across media. In this sense art's function would indeed emerge, beyond catharsis, as more *textually* transferential. Literary language and cinematic perception, articulating various modes of consciousness for us, also *act as if* they have something like a sub-conscious of their own as well, as if structures of otherness are involuntarily enunciated by and through them, sometimes wearing away at the grain of intent, erosive and definitive at once, contributory and disintegrating.

This may be a figurative conceit, but it is theirs, not mine, part of the way literary writing and, if I may, filmic filmmaking *come across to us*.

Syntactic sense and motion-picture image each exist, as we have seen, by exclusion. As signifying procedures based on the sequestering of phonogram and photogram alike, they distract in action from their own mechanics. Grammatically and cinematically, both proceed by suppression. They are built up and sustained at a certain perceptual speed, that is, upon what composes—but could at any moment also depose—their coherence. Other protective exclusions attend each, of course, especially in the case of film. We are invited (if not impelled) to forget not only, as in reading, the bill collector at the writer's door or the Nobel Prize in wait, but in the cinematic instance the whole technical crew encumbering the set, to say nothing of the budget office, the eventual distribution deals, or the ideological field in which the film is meant to circulate. This is only to acknowledge that any suppression in film, connected to all the others, may bear all the more weight. But I have been stressing the peculiar internal leverage of the photogram—and its induced recoil in response—rather than ulterior ideological motives under seamless (even when contradictory) narrative implementation. This is what I have meant by the therapeutic modality of aesthetic *experience* rather than the co-optive force of its interpellating preconceptions. Where propaganda programs recognition, art demands response.

That response is what we call analysis. When, in those familiar forms of articulation known as wording and picturing, the founding suppression of the naturalized increment is lifted or gives, then we in our role as involuntary analysts (if also potential hermeneuts) of the literary or screen scene, receiving its suddenly uncensored raw matter through the chinks of its representational medium, find ourselves oddly—eccentrically—positioned. Though we are there to read the artifact, it seems to analyze us. While holding out untoward patterns of perception, it also throws us back on new ways of perceiving our own definitive—and entirely functional—*un*awareness as cognitive agents. This is because the textually sprung uprush of an otherwise leashed and disciplined photogram, or of an unwritten phonemic possibility normally kept down by script, is contagiously transferred to us in reception—to us who, as analysands, must suddenly "rewrite" our relation to a comfortably presumed textual coherence our minds have eagerly met halfway. At such moments the obtruded increment arrives with the slap of unwanted release, release from an experience more libidinally invested and defended than merely technological and involuntary. In the case of film, as soon as we are spurred by its very interruption to recognize our willing (however automatic) complicity in the normative screen flow, we *identify*, that is, with the technical superstructure by which its usual erasures have until now been dictated. We, in a word, project. As they are suddenly thrust into view, we see something like our own unconscious at work in the fugitive and unruly functions of the constitutive filmic span. We don't see an image of the unconscious, of course; we see the trace of its work: the trouble it can cause from being kept mostly in check. What I am getting at isn't, as they say, strictly theoretical. My guess is that most viewers feel this way when the illusion snaps. Every shock tactic of this sort delivers the shock of recognition.

So when I suggested that film introduces a new anxiety into visual culture and cognitive life, I had in mind that this anxiety deserves the name only because it strikes at the heart of film's simultaneous new dispensation. For the first time in visual culture, the experience of cinema is the experience of fantasy wedded credibly to its object. Cinema thus comes to us, or we come to it, without the discomfort otherwise posed by the unconscious. Cinema allows us to enjoy what we cannot have without having to repress what we desire. One level of anxiety, the skeptic's, is thus abolished because we need no proof of the existence of the screen image (as fantasy). This is why, for Cavell, to take cinema as a model for the illusions of reality would be to travesty the crisis of skepticism. But whereas the unconscious is in one sense placated by the fantasy quotient of the screen view, the same unconscious—or some such stratum of a cognitive topography—may now and then appear (into the text) to revolt against the coherence of the proffered image. When applied to film rather than photography, therefore, Benjamin's model of the "optical unconscious" seems, after all, both hasty and right. The specular suppressed in screen automatism, though not necessarily resulting from a psychic process per se, but merely a mechanical and perceptual one, is sometimes forced back upon us in such direct defiance of mimesis and its wish fulfillments that it has the *feel* of something repressed, after all, by the very mechanisms of desire itself.

If for Deleuze cinema is a mode of philosophy, I have built upon Cavell to suggest that cinema, with its transparent world pictures, is at the same time, or at least some of the time, the textually opaque interface of philosophy and psychology. In this sense we return also to Münsterburg and his mentalist paradigm.[5] On-screen, we see not only the associative and mutable operations of the mind's eye, its bizarre byways and gestalts, but more specifically the difference between the mind's cognitive primacy and its normally (normatively) invisible psychic depths, between consciousness and its continuously transformed and deferred undertext. The philosophic mind may teach us how to think cinema, but cinema reminds us how we think—or, better, how we keep thinking going across the discontinuities that structure it from beneath and between. The literary parallel within modernist textualities again commends itself to attention. If reading is the silent talking cure of writing's supposed (and vocally derived) wholeness and self-presence, then the elusive phonotext of the literary page "enacts" (without in any way directly representing) the structuring unconscious of the reader. So, by analogy, with filmic perception. Screen art, bracketing its own world pictures as it may, can stave off not just the epistemological but the psychoanalytic anxiety of a skeptical modernity, the unknowability of the self's own determining form. This is the deep unease that results from an understanding of human consciousness, even from within, as positioned against—and defined by—all that it is not. Cinema calms this anxiety by aestheticizing, and so in a way domesticating, it: in other words, by staging it (repeatedly, manageably) through the histrionic flicker of photograms.

This is what I want finally to characterize by the double interchange of filmic transference. By sliding its most basic operations beneath conscious perception to one depth or another (sub-, pre-, un-), cinema as film thereby *performs* the operative doubleness of the non/conscious before our eyes, an enactment visible only when it bursts its own seams. As the analyzed object in reception, film at such moments brings up from the immediate prehistory of its construction ("transfers" forward, temporally, in the first of Freud's senses, or as if "up" from memory) what its very projection, to say nothing of its filming, has excluded from view: photographicity per se. It then transfers laterally (or synchronically, in the second valence of this Freudian term) by displacing this prevarication (or prefabrication) back onto the viewing audience as the belated acknowledgment of a suddenly uneasy pleasure. That audience, in a flash of (re)cognition, returns the favor in what psychoanalysis calls countertransference, attributing to the analyzed film a device-baring candor—a return of the suppressed—that allows the audience nevertheless to retain the film as a mobile image (a *textual* model) of its own deepest cognitive negotiations with the real.

   We have arrived again at the modern (and modernist) crossroads where aesthetic phenomenology may best get rethought by just this twofold concept of transference (*from* a previous state; *between* psyches). Literature gives access to formulated conceptions not our own. Cinema gives access to linked perceptions not our own. In that access these phrasings and sightings become ours, or so it seems. But that access gives way in turn. In reading a certain kind of writing, inscription will not sustain an unruffled flow of enunciation. In receiving a certain kind of screen event, projection will not quite sustain the world view. Where wording disintegrates around the edges to its own lettering, picturing may be disarticulated to a chain of pictures. To the extent that wording and picturing have been borrowed as ours in reception, the trouble seems ours as well, even as we blame it on, transfer it back onto, the text. The suppressed has returned as a cognitive surplus, as if we should or might or could have been attending to it all along. What the text seemed unconscious of for us, we now know we could never have gotten by or gone forward with—or without. The paradox is constitutive. Syntax and screen picturing, as temporal phenomena, like consciousness as a temporal phenomenon, must for the most part subordinate, subsuming the gaps and aggregations they build on to the continuities they need, in every sense, to *assume.* Such phenomenological conviction must always fade away when the technical phasings of its effects are brought forward. But communicated cognition, if you will, does not just dissipate into static (or stasis) at such crisis points. It regroups as a figure for all the psychic friction and interplay that conscious attention normally suspends. Hegel characterized language as "self-consciousness existing for others."[6] Once transcribed, written language is thus a mechanism of that transferred consciousness. We may define cinema, though already transcribed, as "seeing for other eyes." But each medium, writing and film, is a technology as well as a prosthetic extension of the mind. In this, each may block the processes it externalizes and simulates precisely in order to examine them.

   In the recursive and dislocating moments that have concerned this book, then, to submit to the uncanny lure of reversible transference (taking the screen apparition as itself a quasi-psychic apparatus) is to grant film the chance of picturing for us, aslant, our own perceptual constitution. If the modernist inflection of writing can put us through the paces of an unconscious structured like a language, film can *put us in mind* of a mental perception structured like an image track—fabricated and layered, oppositional and ever deferred in its stabilities, dialectical rather than direct, synthetic. This is the chief or at least deepest respect in which the photogrammatic moment in film, passing antidote to the photo-synthetic continuum, like the differential rather than referential moment in literature, can be taken as therapeutic. Its perceptual regimen operates, again, formally rather than (or as well as) thematically. It operates in the face, we may say, of precisely Freud's greatest epistemological crisis according to Cavell: the empirical unknowability of those processes that underlie and ground consciousness. Less as fictions than as textual functions, therefore, and in their moments of severest formal extremity, literature and film phrase for us, picture for us, a fundamental doubleness that they too could never test for and prove, let alone directly record.

Film's philosophical use in performing for the collective not only the individual mind's slippery hold on the world but that mind's (rather than that world's) subjective constitution in the unconscious—all this directs us back in closing to the cultural writings of Siegfried Kracauer. For it is a founding impulse of his work (less in his later film theory, important in different ways for Cavell's ontology, than in his early social critique) that we should confront the use of mass art (cinema only by inference) in displaying to society, through a denatured replica, the fabricated assemblage of its own cultural reality. In closing this book, as I am now to do, with a fixed-frame closural fade-out, I wish to review as concisely as possible the transfer from material form to social content that can result from photogrammatic reading as a *textual* attention, in this case a final acclimation to the intrinsic passing of the filmic frame. For this is exactly the methodological (as well as material) synthesis to be derived from the photofusion under scrutiny across these chapters: the synthesis of rudimentary textual demystifications and a broader critique. Such an analytic synthesis may arise from even the most streamlined studio product. In a final modernist fillip won from the clutches of classic Hollywood "realism" and its machinated glamour, the 1932 MGM production of *Grand Hotel* (Edmund Goulding), with the Barrymore character now dead and Garbo in every sense swept away, closes with a multiple disclosure of the filmic works. The entire screen experience becomes the cinematic parable of a sociological microcosm: the haut bourgeois hotel as centered in a public space of anonymous specular circulation like the movie palace itself.

Vicious (because meaningless) circularity and recurrence is only the most vocal of the ironies at the tail end of *Grand Hotel.* The world within this film is glossed by its closing choric voice (the bystander figure, Lewis Stone) as no more real than the film work that generates it, where action and repetition never attain the status of a certifiable event, only a specular distraction. Stone, who has missed most of the intrigue and melodrama to which the camera has made us privy, groans out in sepulchral monotone the film's last and least throwaway line, its allegorical giveaway: "The Grand Hotel. Always the same. People come, people go. Nothing ever happens." Nothing happens in *Grand Hotel* either—except a narrative, but one for which only the film by such a title, not the portrayed establishment itself, has use. Stone speaks with the complicit glum neutrality of management, as Siegfried Kracauer might have put it in an early essay called "The Hotel Lobby," an essay that nowhere mentions film but that bears in uncanny ways on the logic and the closing visual logistics of *Grand Hotel*.[7] This is not the Kracauer famous in film studies (in some circles, notorious) for the subtitle to his *Theory of Film:* namely, *The Redemption of Physical Reality*.[8] Rather, this is the earlier Kracauer who stressed instead the blatant constructedness of social reality—and in a way that allows the manifest fabrication of film (even when unmentioned) an immediate deconstructive purchase, whatever its subsequent redemptive potential.

In this most Lukácsian of Kracauer's investigations from the early twenties, the hotel lobby delimits the allegorical site of a wholly false and fallen world, an artificially configured social ambience distanced irredeemably from the real, a "space of unrelatedness" that is the "negative church" of an absconded theology.[9] Compared with Chaplin's factory, it is the place of alienated leisure rather than labor. Like the social order from which it pretends to seek respite, the lobby too is a space without meaning, groundless and routinized. In a language that comes revealingly close to evoking the mechanisms of cinema, Kracauer makes his largest point about the intervention of art, even popular art (like detective stories), in culture's distance from "totality" (Lukács's key phrase, taken up as the lapsed "reality" in Kracauer). Society cannot see the existential limbo to which it consigns itself, any more than lobby itinerants wish to see beyond the contractual anonymity of their transit. Or any more, we would want to add, than film viewers can afford to see beyond the artificial view before them, whether to recognize in its full intrusion the architecture that houses, the institution that structures, or the machinery that projects such a consumerist construct. In regard to the mixed spectrum of cultural experience, such an enforced seeing-beyond would be art's particular and primary role in Kracauer's negative aesthetics: to embody (hence diagnose) the artifice of a fallen and refabricated reality in art's own internal and true form—namely, artificial.

As this book should by now have put us in position to insist, however, filmic representation embodies its own constructedness at two strata of apprehension: by the artificial (because mechanized) piecing together of an already artificial (because staged) human scene. This is what happens when the set design (of a hotel lobby, say) gets dismembered into photograms and then reassembled as a world in little. The subsidiary articulation on the strip might therefore have provided Kracauer with filmic materiality's unique contribution to the distancing service of cinematic art. The rudiments of form estrange the already artificially formulated, put the fabricated at a further distance. Filmic plasticity becomes in this way a special impacted case of the general principle. In Kracauer's chosen terms for any medium, art's work seems to expose the cinema-like artifice of even our three-dimensionally constructed public spaces, our temples and transit stations of an ersatz community. This is because, in his phrasing (and here we find his implicitly cinematic vocabulary), it is "the aesthetic construct" alone "whose form renders the *manifold* as a *projection*" (175; emphasis added). It is a case not of form following the functions of representation but of form figuring the content of that representation in the specified mediation of its own manifold medium—in film's case, artificial, constructed, ephemeral, backlit, immaterially projected, synthetic, and illusory. Certain films can, as it were, literalize the manifold by a projection of the strip itself, even as it unwinds off the spool in conclusion. As if to emblazon this point, the last shot of *Grand Hotel*, movie and commercial mansion alike, reverts to a manifest painted set that drops further into recess the lifeless fixity of a motionless movie projection on one of the lobby's supposed walls: the single suspended image of "The End," complete with MGM logo. This in(set) joke is so inspired it almost passes unnoticed, mistaken for the status quo of closure. This is exactly its point, for it approaches the norm in order to expose it.

To get us there, the camera has implied its own passage through the wheeling glass panels of the hotel's main entrance (fig. 345), with its glinting, transparent carousel as emblem of photogrammatic rotation itself. In the ensuing final shot of the lobby's pictured (painted) emptiness, the trompe l'oeil flat thus displays across most of one wall a kind of metacinematic mural composed of nonnarrative footage detained beyond plot to sign off on that plot in closure. In the institution of cinema, yes, as well as of haut bourgeois hostelry, the lobby is our anonymous place of closure and exit as well. But this is the least of the self-engulfing ironies that attend this fantasmatic fade-out after the artificial merry-go-round of paid cinematic fascination. The image spread before the absent spectators in this one lobby, or before us in their place, is none other than a nugatory acknowledgment of cinematic production *as sheer projection*. From our first glimpse of this screen within the screen and the fake backdrop upon which it is purportedly mounted, the camera has pulled back (as if across the nonexistent floor space of the lobby) to a medium shot (fig. 346) that, once held upon, is now protracted in the vanishing of its own backlit visibility (below and finally, figs. 347-49). In that long-held laboratory shot, there is certainly no way to credit "The End" as projected from within the lobby itself. This is because our picture of the whole fictitious space darkens in steady closural gradations along with the internally beamed last two words. The whole effect of visual diminuendo is the work of photogrammatic duplication (and fading out) in the optical printer. In this way has the cinematic undertext pressed itself, from within a stop-action finale, back beyond the strip to evoke the implacable lamp that produces both stasis and motion with equal and transitory indifference. The same projector casts the abyssal shadow of this two-word script and the film it finishes off from within. The same multiplied frame on track (picturing the lighted lobby embedding the lit screen that centers it) surrenders its self-emitted brightness, photogram by photogram, until extinguished altogether. The film called *Grand Hotel*, inseparable all along from the three-dimensional space so named, a space of sheer display, has now been contained—and foreclosed—within that same confected space, projected at last for what it is: a mere two-dimensional imprint. The modernist convolution is complete in a deep sociological irony. The supplemental form of screen narration is evacuated into its own content in the illustratively lifeless form of form itself. All that is left is the manifold in projection for a final dimming glimpse of its sheer specular status.

In bringing a lengthy argument like mine to conclusion, any such frame analysis had better be exemplary—even if (or exactly because) the frozen frame of reference in this case defers by slow effacement to another fundamental aspect of the apparatus in the lit strip. What I have wanted to draw out, one last time, is that such reading attempts a commutation in two senses—a direct transport and an indirect transposition—between textual analysis and cultural emplacement: again, if we must, between film studies and cinema studies. We may call such a theoretical crossing the commute from undertext to superstructure. Once again, that is, I see no reason to resist the suspicion that such textual analysis gets access to a political as much as a formal dimension of film narrative—and the one because the other. Such reading, rather than interpretation, drives analysis into the furrows of representation per se, where the artifice that characterizes our general perceptual experience is more foundational yet in its frailty and groundlessness as well as in its largely unshakable cognitive consensus. Avowed "projection" is thus the potential exception to a workaday acceptance of the given.

For Kracauer again, as for Lukács before him in different terms, the contingent reality effect of artistic construction holds up to our supposed social "nature" the mirror of its own artificiality. In going to the movies—just as, for instance, in reading detective fiction—life is divulged in the very forms of its representation as a thing of pervasively empty forms. Characterize it, one step further back, as an exposed phantasm of continuity within a disjunct and fabricated stream of deferred existential validity—and you have set the photogrammatic parable of certain overdetermined filmic artifacts alongside the generalized formal estrangement they effect. Here we reach to the flip side of a bracketed philosophical skepticism quarantined in its debilitating effects (Cavell's heuristic use of film) and enter upon the tonic skepticism of social critique. For the outbreak of the photogram often amounts to the powerful lower limit of cinema's inquiry into a constructed environment of programmed drives and hollowed or fragmented agency.

Like all film narrative, *Grand Hotel* throws its doors open to paying guests, the visits calibrated in advance according to predetermined temporal intervals. *Citizen Kane* will extend its invitation more ironically, when the opening shot of the No Trespassing sign at Xanadu returns at the end converted from imperative to tacit declarative, negating the very notion of illicit access on metacinematic grounds. But in our welcome watching, we remain just a little on edge. This seems to me the perfect affective fit between the cinematic spectacle and the engaged psychic apparatus of the viewer: that the medium, too, is tensed in its material essence, conflicted, conflict-dedicated. Eisenstein said it best, and first: screen vision is collisional. Because of that lightning-fast strife with which the riven track is rife—and upon which the usual image path thrives in series—photograms in the cinematic system cannot always be counted on to release us to representation by their dialectical fusion. When they do not, the breach in film's naturalizing drive opens a whole new transaction with the viewer. So much for the screen meeting of my sensorium with the world's coherent body in existential unfolding. Out goes the phenomenological warrant of the world's becoming (again) before my eyes. The loss is real. It is the death of a certain level of borrowed reality. This deprivation is plenty to suppress in order to sustain the pleasure of the scene—until text itself becomes part of the pleasure. Including the elusive granular basis of such text. And including the obverse of such pleasure in its unsettling of extrafilmic assumptions—with cinematic spectacle becoming, in the negative sense, a reality *check,* both a curb on the world's received views and a reminder of mind's unconscious mutation of them. The photogram has been our changeling agent in this story of internal resistance, since by its mediation the former hustle of so-called reality is reduced to the sheer rustle of what Kracauer stressed as art's manifold projections: the screen's spectralized serial imprints reaching the first stage of their dematerialization on the way to the constructed subjectivity of the spectator's gaze.

If cinema's vaunted lifelikeness cannot help but question the world on which it stakes its trembling resemblance, the place of the photogram in fostering such semblance has been crucial to isolate in these chapters. While cousin to death, the photogram, surviving itself on the filmic track, bursts to multiplied posthumous animation on the cinema screen. About the textual transfusions that result, I hope I may best summarize as follows, with one last syllabic composite: Only through this tension in essence of the filmic within the cinematic, only through the passage, as slippage, from strip through track to screen, can the specular work of cinema move to forge, out of photos-in-the-system, its photo synthesis.

I have spoken repeatedly about the photogrammatic moment in cinema, meaning the filmic eruption from within mimetic movement, the instant of revealed instantaneity at the level of advancing frames. At the back of my mind, the term "moment" (from mechanics as well as common parlance) has always carried the sense of a textual leveraging as well as of a temporal node. It is not too late to explain why.

345

Partly, this sense of a critical balancing point has to do exactly with what is further yet in back of my mind during screen viewing: the site of projection itself, whose distance from the screen my body roughly bisects. When I am not just the focalized center of perception (directed upon a projection of the withheld world) but a cognitive sensor of cinema's material texturation as film, the focal can become fulcral as well. Here, then, the topographical *figure* from psychoanalysis, that uneasy shearing force between surface and depth, gives way to a more material thing yet: the felt and unconceptual *fact* of filmic aggregation. Whether we come to grips with it or not, what kind of materiality is it that grips us? If the answer turns out to be that this materiality is in part our own, then the process may run parallel, after all, to the screen's ocular enactment of psychic mechanisms.

Not just a wrench to succession on the track but a realignment in the axis of reception itself, the photogrammatic "moment" balances between screen view thrown before me and automated image behind, between cinematic immanence at the receiving end and plastic strip, reels, lamp, and aperture at the projected source. Certain filmic events in cinema seem, in other words, to close the distance between booth and view by inviting a pivotal reversion from the motion picture toward its constituent and immobile pictures. When the strip itself seems to burn up under the lamp in the diegetic surcharge of Bergman's *Persona*, for example, one natural response would be to turn our gaze back toward the site of projection, as if to spot the cause of the trouble. So with certain forms of slow motion, abrasive jump cuts, unexpected freeze-frames, even the exaggerated fading of an image. (That's not the look of a movie, we might well think; there must be something wrong with the film.) If we didn't know *Grand Hotel* was over, for instance, we might look

round toward the projector to see why the screen was going dark, our attention swiveling from mimesis to apparatus, from representation to material base.

The photogrammatic moment levers just such a turn at the conceptual level, tilting us away from realized world projections toward our no longer suppressed specular consciousness of their machinated, fragmentary origin in the projection booth. This is the materialist recognition that in normal viewing we do indeed, in every sense, put behind us. In those pivotal or fulcral turns that revert—by way of an on-screen recursion—to the generative energies of the speeding track, all lines of cognitive force may be felt to intersect. They converge, with sudden undeniability, upon my cognitive body as it mediates between textual productivity and represented space. When the undertext breaks out from suppression, in short, my heightened senses channel its return. Rear projection (from the far rather than near side of the screen) wouldn't change the paradigm; it would merely emphasize the resemblance to the imprinted page of literary textuality. Comprehension operates in the circuit between racing marks and their understood representation in either medium of intermittence, whether writing or cinema. In the lag time of reception, that is, if not in any measurable space traversed, stands the cognitive process of reading or spectation. When such reception—knowingly, under transferred instruction from the undertext—fails to accept the mimesis whole and inseparable, materiality has exerted its intransigent pull. Against the overarching flow of motion, the screen image's aggregated fragments may therefore begin to dismantle totality even as they generally simulate its continuum.

Cinema puts the world on view. Film knows better. Through our triggered acknowledgment, film knows better than it normally shows the atomism of cinema's

345

automated and supposedly autonomous reality. The transferential dynamic of filmic reception, with its unconscious mix of visual fascination and visual anxiety, thus marks at the same time a tactical (if entirely tacit) critique and a tactile acceptance, both a stand taken and a giving way. To mention the latter sensuous submission is to move beyond Kracauer's point to a yet more textualist, though no more formalist, perspective. It is also to receive the screen picture at a level more immediate than Cavell's in using cinema—as he often does, and as he elsewhere and differently might—to intervene in the problematic of skepticism. The world projected by cinematic images may be distant from me in its completeness without me (Cavell's axiom), even while the sheer image units that automate and project that world may be reclaimed, now and again, as intimate to me. Their disclosed tangibility can recall me to my own. In this manner, and for all the sensuous thrall of the screen spectacle, it is the filmic element of cinema that brings me to my senses.

To say so is to close in upon this book's ultimate question about the textuality of representation across media—and about the modernist promise of that textuality. Regardless of what cinema asks of the viewer by the cross-grained investigation of its own undertextual tremors, with their dubious further take on the world's continuum, what's in it for the viewer? What's in it for me that I should be so willingly taken out of it, released from the spell of world projection? For the letdown, just a wising up? What could possibly compensate for the realist plenitude surrendered, however distanced from me that viewed world has been? And in what new transferential economy would this compensation be put into play?

Here our ongoing comparison with the microtextuality of literary engagement suggests an important remaining facet of the answer, having to do once more

345

with the return of the body to the scene of reception. Not the disciplined and policed body of cultural studies, constructed in the image of Kracauer's socially fabricated reality—even though such a body certainly does exist, to be found under
any number of descriptions and constraints. Rather, the sensory body of eyes and
ears—cohabiting with its socially inscribed double but not reducible to it. From
amid the materialized scenes of received representation, a countering textuality
serves to materialize that sensorial (rather than censored) body. When I find myself reading sublexically, even ideology must momentarily hold its breath. The
very event of wording (rather than scriptive intention) is present to me, and I (its
sounding board) to it. When I find myself seeing a film photogrammatically, there
also I find myself, something left of myself—not my integrated subjectivity as
free agent but my particular constellation of subject senses. When I am made in
this way to help unmake the screen's representational edifice, cinema may momentarily vanish, but I am all there. Not all there is, in some englobing and delusional subjectivity, and not consolidated there in some briefly stabilized *propria
persona*. But all there, nonetheless: a nervous cognitive body immersed in the
working upon me of the film work, unalienated for a change from the stuff of the
given. Keyed to the filmic photo synthesis behind the narrative flow, I sense that I
am both taking and leaving the image at once.

Motion pictures, cinema screens, film frames, and I there, making up my
mind both with and about their passing apparitions. Motion pictures a world.
Cinema screens it. Film frames and advances it. That is why, finally, besides shutter, lens, and a certain distance, both nothing and everything must come between
film and screen.

NOTES

INTRODUCTION

1. Such a comparison between the differential seriality of the film strip and the sequential dynamics of verbal inscription, a comparison ultimately between the photogram as filmic integer and the phonemic building blocks of (even) written language, must be distinguished at the outset from the "inner speech" through which Eikhenbaum and other early theorists saw the cinema assimilated to meaning in the mind. This more familiar principle in film discussion depends on a logic of tacit translation, where the image chain makes sense, makes meaning, only by being reconceptualized in an unexpressed language of systemic coherence. My entirely different emphasis on the more material inner lining of the projected image in the flickering photogram, rather than its mental readout, has therefore less to do with that unverbalized inner utterance posited for all screen images in reception than with a parallel between the mostly unseen oscillation of such images and the close-grained linguistic increments of specifically written textuality: wording not as mental conception but as sequential inscription. On the more traditional sense of film's verbal correlation, including its psychoanalytic valences, see Paul Willemen, "Cinematic Discourse: the Problem of Inner Speech," in *Looks and Frictions: Essays in Cultural Studies and Film Theory* (Bloomington: Indiana University Press, 1994), 27-55. "Although endophony, the calling to mind of the phonetic signifier, can occur in inner speech, the latter cannot be reduced to the former," writes Willemen (43). In other words, we do not regularly "voice" our sense of cinematic meaning to ourselves. This is indisputable. My quite different point, however, is that filmic process can erode what we tell ourselves we see on-screen much as the heterogeneous potential of linguistic (morphophonemic) structure may jostle the written signifier within the textual aggregate. My claims for subtextual parallels between the flitting of the photogram and the binary oscillation of the linguistic segment are also to be distinguished from the mostly grammatical or syntactical models for cinematic operations initially elaborated by Christian Metz in *Film Language: A Semiotics of the Cinema,* trans. Michael Taylor (New York: Oxford University Press, 1974) and in *Language and Cinema,* trans. Donna Jean Umiker-Sebeok (The Hague: Mouton, 1974).

2. For an influential engagement with this distinction in view of Siegfried Kracauer and Walter Benjamin, see Thomas Elsaesser, "Cinema—the Irresponsible Signifier or 'The

Gamble with History': Film Theory or Cinema Theory," *New German Critique* 40 (winter 1987): 65-89.

3. Walter Benjamin, "The Work of Art in the Age of Mechanical Reproduction," in *Illuminations*, ed. Hannah Arendt, trans. Harry Zohn (New York: Schocken, 1969), 249 n. 17. Jonathan Crary's emphasis on the stereoscope, in *Techniques of the Observer: On Vision and Modernity in the Nineteenth Century* (Cambridge: MIT Press, 1990), will be taken up in chapter 1.

4. The term "photogram" is universal in film studies and is not to be confused with the identical nineteenth-century nomenclature for those light-sensitive plates that took the immediate indexical impression—in negative image—of an object contiguous to them, turning, for instance, the look of a leaf into the seeming trace of a ghostly fossil. See Helmut Gernsheim, *The History of Photography, from the Camera Obscura to the Beginning of the Modern Era* (New York: McGraw-Hill, 1969), 96-97. Despite the idiomatic acceptance of "photogram" in film terminology, it has next to no currency in analysis. Note its exemplary absence from the index of terms in a recent methodological overview of the field, Robert Stam, Robert Burgoyne, and Sandy Flitterman-Lewis, eds., *New Vocabularies in Film Semiotics* (New York: Routledge, 1992).

5. There is a momentary confirmation of this in the opening scene of Buster Keaton's majestic film "essay" *Sherlock, Jr.* (1924), where the would-be detective hero and present film projectionist, reading in an empty movie theater his how-to book on detective work, tries out the fingerprint process on the cover of the instruction manual. He is briefly baffled when, without an ink pad, he seems to have left no mark. But we know better. He has, and he does: the impress of a medium without basis in anything but surface and light. The identifying imprint of the actor is, in short, there before us all the while.

6. See Garrett Stewart, *Reading Voices: Literature and the Phonotext* (Berkeley: University of California Press, 1990).

7. Tom Gunning, "New Thresholds of Vision: Instantaneous Photography and the Early Cinema of Lumière," in *Impossible Presence: Surface and Screen in the Photogenic Era*, ed. Terry Smith, Power Institute Series 2 (Sydney: Power Institute of Art, University of Sydney, forthcoming), an argument based on a lecture given at the University of Iowa in December 1997 titled "A Mischievous and Knowing Gaze: The Lumière Company and the Culture of Amateur Photography."

8. See Marta Braun, *Picturing Time: The Work of Etienne-Jules Marey (1830-1904)* (Chicago: University of Chicago Press, 1992), and François Dagognet, *Etienne-Jules Marey: A Passion for the Trace*, trans. Robert Galeta and Jeanine Herman (New York: Zone, 1992).

9. The process is succinctly explained in David Bordwell and Kristin Thompson, *Film Art: An Introduction* (New York: McGraw-Hill, 1990), 6, as the "fusion" induced when the projector's shutter interrupts the beam often enough (two or three times per frame at twenty-four frames per second) to mute or smooth the flickering disjunction between nearly identical frames.

10. In the extensive and uncredited "Fan's Notes" in an interactive addendum to the Criterion laser-disc version of *Blade Runner*, my own lingering suspicion about the close-up of this photograph is matter-of-factly confirmed: the sense that shadows (credibly cast only from the patterns of light in Deckard's present room) play over the image as if a flutter of leaves within the past (and suddenly cinematized) scene were speckling the faces on the summer porch.

11. Philip K. Dick, *Do Androids Dream of Electric Sheep?* (1968; New York: Ballantine, 1992).

12. Quotations from Rudolf Arnheim, *Film as Art* (Berkeley: University of California Press, 1957), 118, as cited from the German edition (1932) by Siegfried Kracauer, *Theory of Film: The Redemption of Physical Reality* (New York: Oxford University Press, 1960), 44,

under the rubric "nascent motion," where Kracauer repeats Arnheim's curious emphasis on the "insertion" of the photographic still, resulting in the "whirlpool of the motionless" (44). On Kracauer's retelling of the sequence, "snapshots of the photographer's, taken of the bathers on the spot, are inserted in different places" (44). One might better say that these ten "inserts," which are visibly stop-action film footage rather than refilmed photographic prints with a different lighting and grain, are displaced on the track to produce a slight margin of spatial discrepancy that may well be intended to mark the temporal disjuncture between scene and its subsequent printed record. Nonetheless they figure this lag time by the work of the strip per se, not the refilming of a portable photograph (a figuration similarly effected by *Under Fire* in chapter 1, for instance, through the instantaneous shift on the track from color image in the viewfinder to black-and-white freeze). From the same year as *People on Sunday* (*Menschen am Sonntag*), in Vertov's *Man with a Movie Camera* (1929) there is also—in the famous editing-room sequence discussed in the introduction—the photogrammatic variant of such photographic self-reflex. My thanks to Janet Bergstrom for helping me gain access to *Menschen am Sonntag,* held at the UCLA film archives.

13. As with *People on Sunday,* the slippage from narrative arrest to future print dissemination is to be understood in the next chapter as a transit between the reflex action of the freeze and the inset photochemistry of the narratively reframed still image. See, in other terms, Stanley Cavell's discussion of Cukor's stop-action closure in "What Photography Calls Thinking," *Raritan* 4 (spring 1985): 7-8, where he expands upon the scene originally discussed in *Pursuits of Happiness: The Hollywood Comedy of Remarriage* (Cambridge: Harvard University Press, 1981).

14. I thank Charles Wolfe for alerting me to this genre prehistory. The media historian's usual debts to his published work, as to that of Rick Altman and Tom Gunning, are compounded in my case by gratitude for private conversations with each about the spotty early career of the photomechanical fixed frame after the development of the optical printer in the early 1920s, as well as about later Hollywood deployments and variants of this freeze on action (or its reverse in gradual photographic animation). Subsequently, I find that I am yet further indebted to Tom Gunning's expertise in his extraordinarily thoughtful reading of my manuscript for the University of Chicago Press. Thanks also, at that stage, go to William Galperin, whose expert Press report helped align the weight of my cinematic evidence with its intended linguistic parallels. And from beginning to end of this project I owe thanks to the skill and patience of Linda Edge-Dunlap in helping capture and reproduce the illustrations.

15. David Bordwell, *Narration in the Fiction Film* (Madison: University of Wisconsin Press, 1985), 53.

16. Such attention need not decline into the predictable thematic of self-reflexivity chastised by David Bordwell as one of the rhetorical strategies massaged in the "reading"—by which he means, as I do not (more below), merely the interpretation—of films, a supposedly reductive approach that smacks of the "medium specificity talk" against which Bordwell shares Noël Carroll's animus. See Bordwell, *Making Meaning: Inference and Rhetoric in the Interpretation of Cinema* (Cambridge: Harvard University Press, 1989), 111-15. In regard to the photogrammatic undertext of film, to pursue its rippling implications at the surface of a text, as occasioned by the technique of given film narrative, cannot, it seems to me, be written off as some meaning-generating institutional heuristic on the assembly line of interpretative commentary (Bordwell's gripe) until, at the very least, given films found engaged in this way can be shown *failing to contradict* much of the reigning institutional theory that persists around and despite them. Until then, they bring theoretical news—in a word, news worth *reading.* (For Noël Carroll's more extended critique of the claims for "medium specificity," see chapter 3 below.)

17. This manifestation may not always happen—or not always be attended even in connection with a noticed photograph on-screen. In most senses comparable to the treat-

ment of painting in film (see chapter 1 note 22), photography as cinematic topic can easily be consigned to the diegesis (or mimetic level) alone. In a special issue of *La Recherche Photographique* titled "Le çinéma, la photographie" (December 1987), Isabelle Delsus and Christine Petiteau compile an extensive dossier of film titles on the variously refracted topic of photography and photographic images in cinema (41-47), with such subheadings as "the professional photographer and the amateur photographer," "the photographic reporter," "the photo as object" (further subdivided into "paper," "slides," "mircrofilm," and "photo-roman"), and among further discriminations, "the fantastic of the photo" (as in *The Shining*). Such a spread may seem thoroughgoing without being necessarily foundational. Carefully surveyed is photography *in* cinema; even photography as highlighted visual *object* (rather than plot device) in cinema; even photography as element in a certain mode of photomontage—but not yet photography *as* cinema or, in other words, cinema as film. Many of the films in this extensive bibliography do have this latter (or constitutive) concern, but a taxonomy could never be expected to reveal it.

18. They may even have critical precedent. Despite the relative paucity of such commentary, I do not mean to suggest that when films put into narrative play their own photogrammatic underlay, they do so in a complete theoretical vacuum. Anticipating my own use of the specifically semiotic category of "double negation" in chapter 3, used to locate the freeze-frame within the very *logic* of motion pictures, the article by Phillipe Dubois in the special issue of *La Recherche Photographique* (note 17), "Photo tremblée et le cinéma suspendu" (19-27), does give the photogram its due, its place within a rolling displacement. Building upon earlier work by Raymond Bellour on cinema's "unfindable text," Dubois argues (translation mine) that "the photogram reveals itself . . . as a double negation of cinema" as well as its "living heart" (26) because it cancels the "defile" of movement as well as founding it in those separate fixed impressions that cinema, properly speaking, "doesn't permit us to apprehend" (27). Hence the photogrammatic frame as the essay's closing (and clinching) emphasis: "The photogram is a photo trembling and cinema suspended" (27). Or, we might want to say, it is cinema shaken to its roots. Other writers who have factored in the photogram to their theories of the medium, even if only to factor it out again, will emerge as discussion proceeds.

19. Though with none of this book's emphasis on the material synthesis of the track or its constituent photograms, the sense of an Anglo-European modernism running roughly from Michelangelo Antonioni's *L'avventura* (1959) through Alain Resnais's *Providence* (1977), and including the early work of Altman, Coppola, Scorsese, and others in America, is given its fullest treatment in John Orr's *Cinema and Modernity* (Cambridge: Polity Press, 1993). See p. 18 for the bracketing texts of what Orr has begun by designating as the second phase of modernism, the "neo-modern" (2). In Orr's view, the legacy of Bergman's prototypical modernist text, *Persona*, also extends into the decades since, across a spectrum of international production treated with fresh insight in his sequel *Contemporary Cinema* (Edinburgh: Edinburgh University Press, 1998).

20. Rosalind Krauss, *The Optical Unconscious* (Cambridge: MIT Press, 1993); see discussion in chapter 2.

CHAPTER ONE

1. Published with selected proceedings of the 1985 Athens (Ohio) conference in Garrett Stewart, "Photo-gravure: Death, Photography, and Film Narrative," *Wide Angle* 9, no. 1 (1987): 11-40.

2. For the circulation and uptake of this formal category, see Peter Gidal, "Theory and Definition of Structuralist/Materialist Film," and Stephen Heath, "Repetition Time: Notes around 'Structural/Materialist Film,'" both in *The British Avant-Garde Film, 1926-1995*, ed. Michael O'Pray (Luton, Eng.: University of Luton Press, 1996), 145-70, 171-80. This

category of subcultural cinema is related to what P. Adams Sitney called "structural film" in the last chapter of *Visionary Film: The American Avant-Garde* (New York: Oxford University Press, 1974).

3. David E. James, *Allegories of Cinema: American Film in the Sixties* (Princeton: Princeton University Press, 1989), lays emphasis on what is otherwise called structural film in his chapter "Pure Film" (237-79), where a "minimalist aesthetic" (242) concentrates, hypertrophically, on a restricted number of cinema codes.

4. In this notion of the "visionary" film, I allude to the title—and central claims—of P. Adams Sitney's study of American experimental practice, *Visionary Film.*

5. See Paul Sharits, "A Cinematics Model for Film Studies in Higher Education," *Film Culture* 65-66 (1978): 43-68.

6. This moment in the voice-over is cited by Corey K. Creekmur to support his claim for the film as a kind of prolonged mourning work, where images disappear before coinciding with meaning. Such a claim may thus be differentiated from my emphasis in the rest of this chapter on photography's intrusive stasis in commercial narrative film as a preemptive arrest of the cinematic continuum in the name (the figuration) of death per se. See Creekmur, "The Cinematic Photograph and the Possibility of Mourning," *Wide Angle* 9, no. 1 (1987): 41-49.

7. See the landmark intertext of this effect in Bergman's 1966 *Persona,* discussed in chapter 2.

8. All the while, flanking the growing stack of single-shot notations, are on the one hand (the left) the prickly otherness of an indigestible reality (a potted cactus) and on the right a partly empty coffee cup. If enough time were to pass in the accumulation of pages, of course, one might see the cactus grow, the coffee evaporate. Evoking by avoidance the time-lapse cinematography of bursting blooms and the like, only in this case at degree zero, these stationary organic and inorganic anchors, these real things, instead testify more directly to the fixity of photography in its occasional near convergence with the uneventful duration of real time.

9. André Bazin, "The Ontology of the Photographic Image," in *What Is Cinema?* trans. Hugh Gray (Berkeley: University of California Press, 1967), 1:14.

10. James, *Allegories of Cinema,* 275.

11. Bazin mentions the "mummy complex" in the first paragraph of his opening essay, "The Ontology of the Photographic Image," in *What Is Cinema?* For the way time creeps back into this concept of plastic fixation, time in its anything but petty pace for Bazin— time, rather, as the very feel of an almost hieratic quotidian—see his less-discussed views on "change mummified" later in this same essay (treated below in chapter 3).

12. Stanley Cavell, "What Photography Calls Thinking," *Raritan* 4 (spring 1985): 11.

13. When Barthes turns to the motion-picture medium for commentary, he notoriously resists its movement. Though in passing conversation about my interest in the photogram I have often noticed people assuming an affinity between this interest and Barthes's notion of cinema's "third" meaning, the connection would in fact mislead. His thirdness is a meaning located beyond both celluloid frame and screen image, somewhere closer to a diacritical inflexion of the isolated photographic still or frame enlargement. Such thirdness cannot inhere in a mere production still, because it needs one foot in the flow of diegesis. But it is a meaning never generated in screen viewing. See Roland Barthes, "The Third Meaning: Research Notes on Some Eisenstein Stills," in *Image/Music/Text,* trans. Stephen Heath (New York: Hill and Wang, 1977), 52-68. There is, as a result, no real affinity between our positions on this score, merely a faint overlap as we move in opposite directions. Anticipating, perhaps, his own later sense, in *Camera Lucida,* of a private semiosis in the *punctum* of the photograph, Barthes dreams of film's utopian resistance to the hegemony of movement. In the process, the terms of his "theoretical fumblings" (65) are precisely—

hence instructively—not mine. The perceived still is unique to cinema, for him, and different from photography and painting, because of cinema's "diegetic horizon" (66). The erupted photogram, as it preoccupies these pages, is the microsecond-long occlusion of that horizon. It has to do *not* with a "permutational unfolding" (97) of image material, where the third meaning emerges, but rather with the automatized succession of those images as speeding frames. For Barthes the site of tertiary semiosis is a "quotation," not a "sample." The photogram is the opposite, a subliminal section. The third or "obtuse meaning" of the still is achieved from an oblique angle that "offers us the *inside* of the fragment." The photogram is, by contrast, the fragment itself, unmeant, mechanized. The Barthesian still has to do with the vertical (synchronic) organization of meaning in its imaginative redistributions, the photogram with the horizontal (diachronic) stream, for Barthes a sheer "technical constraint" (68) to be overridden in response. The third meaning stilled into visibility "scorns logical time (which is only an operational time)" (68), whereas the photogram—as subsignifier—is the very *operator* of all screen time. Barthes's distinctions make the point in his own terms that "the filmic is not the same as the film." What I want instead from that adjective, again, is as follows: The photogram as a subsignifying unit, full of no meaning in its own invisible right, is what becomes of the iconic sign, the image, on the celluloid strip—what has always and already become of it—when the single print cell is stirred forward from the photographic into the filmic on the way toward the cinematic. For a study of Eisenstein's frames closer to Barthes's emphasis than to mine, see Sylvie Pierre, "Eléments pour une théorie du photogramme," *Cahiers du Cinéma* 226-27 (1970-71): 75-83.

14. Roland Barthes, *Camera Lucida: Reflections on Photography,* trans. Richard Howard (New York: Hill and Wang, 1981), 92.

15. Quoted from Philippe Dubois, *L'acte photographique* (Paris: Nathan and Labor, 1983), by Christian Metz, "Photography and Fetish," *October* 34 (fall 1985): 83, a paper originally delivered at a symposium on the theory of film and photography at the University of California, Santa Barbara, May 1985.

16. Raymond Bellour, "Le spectateur pensif," an unpaginated commentary in *Photogénies: La photo fait du cinéma,* ed. René Burri, Francesco Maselli, and Thierry Girard (Paris: Ministère de la Culture, 1984), the illustrated catalog for an exhibition on photography and film at the Centre National de la Photographie (Paris, spring 1984). See the translation by Lynne Kirby in *Wide Angle* 9, no. 1 (1987): 6-10. Bellour suggests that by the reframing of photographs within a stilled camera shot, even when not full-screen, we "are led toward the still frame (the photogram)," the film shot thereby approximating "a freeze-frame within a freeze-frame [un arrêt dans l'arrêt]" (10).

17. Barthes, *Camera Lucida,* 96.

18. In the first of these shots, it is also apparent that the letter to which the protagonist has given his attention is placed over sheet music on his desk, thus displacing the score of his ordinary virtuoso performances with his present imaginative enactment (through flashback) of the letter's annotated past. Recall the comparable overlay of photographs upon sheet music in *Blade Runner*—and the subsequent digital reinterpretation of a single evidentiary image.

19. In a tacit connection with this photograph not pursued in his discussion, we can listen to Cavell again on the deathwork of the image in what remains of this one plot. The issue of film's as well as photography's "participation in death" (see note 12 above) comes round again in Cavell's *Contesting Tears: The Hollywood Melodrama of the Unknown Woman* (Chicago: University of Chicago Press, 1996), where he distinguishes the swirling gallery of flashbacks, summoned up before Stefan's averted gaze after he finishes the letter (and sees the picture that grounds it in the mind's eye), from the last image of Lisa at his door as he moves off toward the duel (cf. Cavell's frame enlargements 174-75 and 176-77, respectively). Calling the former images "death-dealing," he reserves for the latter the cat-

egory of "death-enhancing" (171)—that is, one assumes, enriching loss with comprehension. It follows that "both modes of returning images raise the question of how desires, and their images, are of death; of the relation of film as such, always coming after, immortalizing events, to death" (171). The very last image of Lisa has its own way of confirming this. According to Cavell, it "differs notably from the earlier sequence of images in being located in the same space with Stefan, as if he is taking some present part in this quasi-hallucinatory image" (170). The other difference, for our purposes, is that this image does not just arrive and depart but *appears* in superimposition, never more than a ghostly overlay (which is what Cavell no doubt means by "quasi-hallucinatory"). And if the image of Lisa shares a (partly disembodied) space with Stefan, it is not even a psychic space grasped by the camera all at once. She only gradually materializes before us through his point of view (POV), and hence as an isolated screen figment available across a regress of spectation from ours to Stefan's own—and then, which is my main point, only as a translucent (i.e., filmy) image linked perforce to that other sheer image (rather than memory or fantasy) he has had of her: the balloon photo, opaque and portable where the later illusion is bodiless and ephemeral. (On the persistent loading of such POV shots with thematic weight in Ophuls's narrational strategies, see the film's use as theoretical test case in Edward Branigan's *Narrative Comprehension and Film* [New York: Routledge, 1992], 177-91.) This last manifestation of Lisa, never quite there—the palpably vanishing one, if you will—is taken from us like all images in the photogrammatic chain, only more so, gone ghostly as its own afterimage to begin with. One casts back here to Cavell's discussion of the "ugly duckling" photograph in *Now, Voyager*, which, he adds in parentheses, "longingly invites the question of the photographic basis of cinema, barely touched on in the present pages. Does, for example, the moving picture do its work by fixation or by metamorphosis?" (141). Both, as Lisa's last inscription within the *Letter* might suggest—her superimposed apparition being an exaggerated case of pure cinematographic *transition*, always on the way out.

20. I originally tried, in "Photo-gravure: Death, Photography, and Film Narrative," to clarify the systemic correlation between a freeze-frame (as screen seizure) and a refilmed photograph (in momentarily full-frame equivalence with the screen) according to the linguistic analogy of reflexive versus cognate grammar. I had in mind the difference, say, between a film "picturing itself" (verb taking a reflexive object) and "picturing a picture" (verb taking a so-called cognate object, as in "to dream a dream"). In the interests of the broader band of examples to follow in this book (where the second category includes the whole spectrum from a distantly glimpsed to a screen-engulfing photograph), I wish now—and more than ever in the service of systemic correlation—to subsume both instances under a common heading. The inset photograph (however much set back into the filmed scene) and the iterated single photogram set off from normal filmic advance will be found to operate comparably within the more semiotic than grammatical category of internal "regress."

21. Such a distinction may recall Michael Fried's organizing dichotomy between the theatrics of overt rhetorical posturing in late baroque painting and the absorptive scene (often of characters reading) that heralded the rise of realism. See Fried, *Absorption and Theatricality: Painting and Beholder in the Age of Diderot*, rev. ed. (Chicago: University of Chicago Press, 1988), a study that penetrates so deeply into a founding dialectic of the realist disposition, implicitly across various media and historical periods, that his art-historical model in fact offers a template for the structural logic, synchronic as well as diachronic, of a whole representational mode. Cognate photo stands to freeze-frame, then, as an absorptive site of attention to the theatricalized display of cinema itself as image system. In a study drawing on Fried's distinction to highlight continuities, elsewhere minimized in film scholarship, between nineteenth-century stage drama and early narrative cinema, Ben Brewster and Lea Jacobs, in *Theater to Cinema: Stage Pictorialism and the Early Feature*

Film (London: Oxford University Press, 1997), conclude that the stop-action, friezelike emphasis of the theatrical tableau finds its way into not only the acting but the editing technique of the 1910s (perhaps most notably in the inclusive framing of closural shots), even in "the absence of a long-held freezing of all actors in attitudes" (213). We may speculate further that, with the development of the laboratory freeze-frame in the next decade, via optical printing rather than diegetic "attitude," editing continued to innovate ways of breaking the spell of absorption with the manufactured (and again often closural) theatrics of the pose. Yet by being automated from within the mechanism, resuming itself from frame to frame even while offering a static résumé or epitome of the scenic action, this new mode of theatricality opened the door to the opposite of Victorian stagecraft: the modernist irruption of technical device onto the scene of represented event.

22. In this regard, compare the inset photo as recessed planar field with the cinematic topos to which was devoted an entire issue ("The Painted Portrait in Film") of *Iris* 14-15 (autumn 1992), with essays drawn from a colloquium at the Louvre the year before. Marc Vernet finds cinema's painted portrait, as I do the photographic insert, glossing the famous Bazinian trope of mummification: "It would thus realize the fantasm of André Bazin about an embalming image that would forever forbid aging or at least disappearance" ("Irrepressible Gaze," 9). Dominique Paini, in "A Detour for the Gaze," finds a similarly arresting effect even in the histrionic stasis of the painted picture plane, which "awakens the notion that the film could stop, end, break, get stuck" (5). In this way the "painted portrait plays on our fear that the spectacle might vanish as a fluid movement, as a fictive cocoon" (5). This is the peril to movement linked, in Thomas Elsaesser's account, to cinema's fondness for fixating, in particular, the image of woman—and for then motivating around her image a plot ("Mirror, Muse, Medusa: *Experiment Perilous*," 147-60). In the frequent kitsch realism of the female portrait in Hollywood film, the painted surface "sucks up all energy and movement, and to that extent, it is the painting that mocks cinema" (148). So it is, for Elsaesser, that cinema must take its "revenge" on painting by dwelling upon it, "but at quite a risk to itself," since "the horror provoked by a painted portrait in a film is the horror of the insipid, the merely descriptive, the cinema haunted by its own origins in photography, the view, the pictorial, the naturalistic, and at the limit: the mechanically reproductive" (158). In other words, the tendency toward failed classicism in the usual Hollywood portrait, a mediocre and saccharine hyperrealism, is not stationed to devalue art in cinema's favor on strictly pictorial grounds. The problem of the portrait is, rather, "less a matter of aesthetics and more a question of ontology" (149). Like the stalled and emptied female figure such portraits predominantly represent, the ontological void of this art makes cinema *necessary* both as fuller illusionistic system and, most of all, as temporal narrative. Also in this issue of *Iris,* Reda Bensmaia continues to develop his psychoanalytic perspective on the lap dissolve in cinema (see chapter 2 below, note 26), by contrasting the cinematic transition of facial image to the fixity of the painted portrait ("La figure d'inconnu, ou L'inconscient épingle: *Le Portrait de Dorian Gray* d'Albert Lewin," 177-86). This is an argument closely related to Janet Bergstrom's concern in the same issue with expressionist facial framing and superimposition in conjunction with explicit expressionist portraiture in Lang's *Mabuse* films. See "Expressionism and Mabuse," 85-98 in this same issue.

23. Since my own commentary on this film, Fredric Jameson has mentioned it in passing in *The Geopolitical Aesthetic: Cinema and Space in the World System* (Bloomington: Indiana University Press, 1992) with severely mixed reactions, admiring its "very real aesthetic and political merits" but objecting to "the ingenious episode of the death of this particular fictional leader" as it "utterly misrepresents the revolutionary process in Nicaragua by attributing to it the structural need for a charismatic figure which it was precisely the originality of the Nicaraguan revolution, with its collective dynamics and leadership, to have been able to do without" (40-41). Highlighted by the photographs of Rafael, this mis-

representation is therefore the price paid for the critique of photographic representation elsewhere in the film, with its parable of the murderous neutrality of journalistic intervention.

24. Barthes, *Camera Lucida*, 84.

25. Anticipating the next chapter, these details suggest a quite specific metaphysical bond between Holly's stereocards and the "apocalyptic" fourth dimension, the temporal long view, of their 3-D manifestation to her alone.

26. Sheerly by accident, I came upon the resulting stereocard print at the Kristianstad Filmmuseum in Sweden, in an exhibition that included the usual array of precinematic gadgets.

27. Jonathan Crary, *Techniques of the Observer: On Vision and Modernity in the Nineteenth Century* (Cambridge: MIT Press, 1990), 8.

28. Jacques Aumont, "The Variable Eye, or The Mobilization of the Gaze," trans. Charles O'Brien and Sally Shafto, in *The Image in Dispute: Art and Cinema in the Age of Photography*, ed. Dudley Andrew (Austin: University of Texas Press, 1997), 231-58.

29. In Noël Burch's *Life to Those Shadows*, trans. and ed. Ben Brewster (Berkeley: University of California Press, 1990), his lead essay, "Charles Baudelaire vs. Doctor Frankenstein" (a loaded way to bill the contest, to say the very least), sums up its main point at the outset. Camera movement is what gives film more of a claim than photography on an occupied three-dimensional space, so that for Burch "it was this aspiration to three-dimensionality that was satisfied by the blossoming of the Institutional Mode of Representation from around 1910, and . . . the latter continues to satisfy it more than all the ephemeral reappearances of red-and-green or polarising spectacles, raster screens, etc." (6-7). I presume one can take Burch's point about film's Frankenstein-like urge for simulated life (versus Baudelaire's contempt for realist representation) without denying that Malick's stereoptic episode still inscribes a strictly ocular "deficiency" in normal screen projection. Cinema is more like resurrected reality than the stereograph is, yes, but so is the stereograph more like reality than is that mere photographic imprint that it not only becomes when projected on the cinema screen but is to begin with on the strip.

30. Burch ends his chapter in a critique of bourgeois cinema's "supreme fantasy: the suppression of death" (21). He is thus as resistant to this aspect of the Bazinian legacy, as cathected around the mummy complex of photography and its reanimation by film, as are the present chapters, with their attention to precisely that analytic interval of the strip that can work to attach even institutional cinema back to the filmic rudiments of chronophotography.

31. For this reason—as with the marginalization of holography elsewhere—developments in 3-D film have been notoriously hard to assimilate into the cinematic institution (Crary, *Techniques of the Observer*, 127, n. 45), encumbered as they are with ancillary devices (like glasses or headsets) and resultant distortions. Stereography was, in short, exacerbated in its prosthetics of observation, a case of enhanced visuality heightened toward its own frustrated limit. Cinema's dispersed and dynamized gaze follows historically from the stereopticon, in other words, by circumventing its dead end—and has as a medium no easy way of recuperating such exhausted options in the specialized mode of 3-D projection.

32. A comparison offers itself from another among the optical toys that are widely understood to presage the cinema. If the thaumatrope (separate images on each side of a revolving disk, fused in rotation) is a predecessor of montage by virtue of its sequential separation of images—horse plus rider plus horse plus rider equals horserider, bird plus birdcage equals caged bird (see Crary's illustrated examples, 105)—then the stereograph in its own right—*within* the simultaneous gestalt of composite image rather than across the thaumatrope's first isolated, then slurred, components—is also (as suggested above) a precursor of montage: one angle plus another slightly different angle triangulating the cone of

depth perception itself. The discrepancy of separate flipped images in the thaumatrope is lateralized to slight photographic shift (and full ocular overlap) in the twinned imprint of the stereograph—or, to enact the effect in an apt verbal portmanteau, of the stereopticon. To say this is a way of noting that the stereocard image inlaid within a moving-image technology is not simply set back to set off the mobile powers of the lineal technological advance constituted by the cinematic machine that re-presents such an antique image. Not simply—and not exclusively. Beyond this, stereography (simulated and one-upped on the 3-D screen, or held in abeyance by two-dimensionality as in *Badlands*) may also be cited to recall the dispersal and subjectivity of vision that led in the first place, by a more circuitous and crowded historical route than the single path of photomechanical advance, to the heterogeneity of the cinematic composite.

33. These freezes-on-action permit Lang some hyperbolic visual rhetoric denied to his earlier, more straightforward footage of the same scene. The freeze device has an unexpected afterlife in Lang's career. A decade later, in his 1946 noir espionage thriller *Cloak and Dagger*, a film punctated with photographs, a German spy is blackmailed using a forgeable signature obtained from her room-service bill. The camera is concealed in an Allied agent's fountain pen, and when the shot is taken the screen's own image, strangely enough, freezes at the moment of registration before dissolving into the reprocessed signature in the darkroom's developing pan.

34. The most recent retro instance of the genre, *L.A. Confidential* (Curtis Hanson, 1997), plays among pornographic, forensic, and blackmail photographs in a narrative that frequently arrests its color action with black-and-white freeze-frames that cut to headlines in the *Hush-Hush* crime journal or the *L.A. Times*.

35. On the variable play between diegetic and extradiegetic audiences in trial films, see Carol J. Glover, "'God Bless Juries!'" in *Refiguring American Film Genres*, ed. Nick Browne (Berkeley: University of California Press, 1998), 255-77. Though she begins with D. W. Griffith's 1907 version of a film within the film used as courtroom evidence in *Falsely Accused!* (257), she makes no comparison with Lang's *Fury*.

36. See "Decoding Film Noir" in Tom Conley, *Film Hieroglyphs: Ruptures in Classical Cinema* (Minneapolis: University of Minnesota Press, 1991), where the supposed rebuslike character of certain inscriptions anticipates a high modernist aesthetic play on the graphological signifier. Typical of Conley's relentlessly overingenious reading is the woman's occluding profile that puts the "bust" back in Bus Stop in *High Sierra* (174-76) or the anagram of King Lear in Roy (Roi) Earle (172).

37. Roland Barthes, "Myth Today" (1957), in *Mythologies*, trans. Annette Lavers (New York: Hill and Wang, 1972), 111.

38. Lotte Eisner, *Fritz Lang* (New York: Da Capo, 1986), 173.

39. Louis Schwartz, "Mechanical Witness, Moving Testimony: Film and Video Evidence in United States Courts" (Ph.D. diss., University of Iowa, 1999).

40. In Michael Riffaterre's terms, an aphoristic cliché—here the classical "intertext" *tempus fugit*, if you will—would provide the avoided "matrix" (or seed phrase) whose materialization must occur by a certain indirection to preserve the originality of the text, to deflect its status as mere citationality. These terms are developed at length in Riffaterre's *Semiotics of Poetry* (Bloomington: Indiana University Press, 1978), *Text Production*, trans. Terese Lyons (New York: Columbia University Press, 1983), and *Fictional Truth* (Baltimore: Johns Hopkins University Press, 1990). See note 43 below for a further filmic example, where the given verbalism is removed one level from cliché—again, toward visual metaphor or pun— by the inherent distance between conceptualization in film versus writing. See also the visually literalized verbal figures accompanying the death scene of *Citizen Kane* in chapter 4.

41. See Raymond Williams, *Marxism and Literature* (London: Oxford University Press, 1977), 121-27, where these categories are in the service of what Williams calls the

"'epochal' analysis" of cultural forms. This is the spirit in which they have been employed by Fredric Jameson in the account of genre developments in both literature and film. My own application of them to a particular styleme of filmic rhetoric is meant to connect with the larger patterns of such historical mutation.

42. On the violent doublings of this confrontation, in light of René Girard's theories about the negative face of triangular desire in primitive scapegoat rituals, see my "Coppola's Conrad: The Repetitions of Complicity," *Critical Inquiry* 7 (spring 1981): 455-74.

43. In varying as I do the terms of subtext and intertext repeatedly mobilized in the semiotics of Michael Riffaterre, I should add that *Apocalypse Now* boasts what can well be seen as an activated "matrix" dead at its center. This is the Riffaterrean matrix in its purest form of an intertextual allusion (see the classical prototype above, note 40) to the sponsor text that generates the whole by repression and conversion. For when Willard (just after his long look at the last pirated photo of Kurtz) has completed, with brutal logic, the slaughter of the young girl in the sampan and taken up a seat in isolation at the stern of his boat, the screen fades to black leader—unexposed photograms—for a full fifteen seconds. Narration is resumed only with a slow return fade to the boat's progress and to Willard's voice-over about now knowing "one or two things about Kurtz that weren't in the dossier"—one for each of them or two together in the ruthless clarity of their shared violence. Blackness itself—as a rite of invisible passage at the heart of the film—thus comes as close as possible to inscribing the name of the novel it derives from, Conrad's *Heart of Darkness*.

44. With thanks to Nancy L. West for the occasion, the next chapter is adapted from my contribution to the special issue ("Picturing the End of Things: Photography and Apocalypse") of *Genre* 29, nos. 1-2 (1996): 193-242.

CHAPTER TWO

1. Recent books touching on photography's relation to death include Barbara P. Norfleet, *Looking at Death* (Boston: David R. Godine, 1993); Jay Ruby, *Secure the Shadow: Death and Photography in America* (Cambridge: MIT Press, 1995); Joel-Peter Witkin, ed., *Harm's Way: Lust and Madness, Murder and Mayhem* (Santa Fe, N.Mex.: Twin Palms, 1994); and Rupert Jenkins, ed. *Nagasaki Journey: The Photographs of Yosuke Yamahat* (San Francisco: Pomegranate Artbooks, 1995). They have been reviewed together by David L. Jacobs under the title "The Art of Mourning: Death and Photography," *Afterimage*, summer 1996, 8-11.

2. See Raymond Bellour's suggestive paragraphs on Bergman's film in "L'interruption, l'instant," in the special issue on photography and cinema of *La Recherche Photographique* titled "Le cinéma, la photographie" (December 1987), where he compares it to Chris Marker's *La jetée*, among other films, as an epitomizing text of cinema "après-guerre," in which "movement is no more guaranteed than speech" and may at any moment be "condemned" to arrest (57). Of all major theorists of cinema, perhaps, Bellour is the one most consistently interested in the various manifestations of its photographic basis. (Cf. his treatment of the photo "arrest" of *Letter from an Unknown Woman* in the previous chapter.)

3. Bellour, "L'interruption, l'instant," reads this effect to illustrate Baudry's concept of film as "dream screen," hovering in its oscillating instability between "hallucination and perception" (56). This is convincing enough, but I take it to be a somewhat *more* metaphorical conception than my own sense of the scene as activating the specular "unconscious" (the photogrammatic moment) of normal screen viewing, as it will be developed later in this chapter.

4. Paul Virilio, *Guerre et cinéma I: Logistique de la perception* (Paris: Cahiers du Cinéma/Editions de l'Etoile, 1984), given in translation only with the English terms "Scan. Freeze." *War and Cinema: The Logistics of Perception,* trans. Patrick Camiller (London: Verso, 1989).

5. *Fail-Safe* opens before the credits, in fact, with a SAC pilot's nightmare of death in the ritual slaughter of the bullring, saturated with premonitions of its atomic equivalent through the irradiated sickly glow of negative printing.

6. Deleuze awaits us in a moment and at length. He is in good company on this question. Following on from Bazin, Metz, Cavell, and Barthes, as discussed in the preceding chapter, Fredric Jameson too sees the film image, even of actors long dead, as coming before us "with the lively energy of radical difference, rather than with the melancholy of mortality." See Jameson, *Signatures of the Visible* (New York: Routledge, 1990), 193. It is no accident that the association of the isolated single imprint with death would come into a less single-minded contrast to filmic succession in the rare (because consistently) deconstructive reading—in the sense promulgated by Paul de Man—carried out on Otto Preminger's *Laura* (1944) by Lee Edelman in *Homographesis: Essays in Gay Literary and Cultural Theory* (New York: Routledge, 1994). Suppression of difference is the political thematic that leads back to the track. There the monitoring of homosexual *différance* is pursued to the level of the film's own constructedness both in the spectrality of lap-dissolve superimpositions (figs. 2-4, 216-27) and in the constitutive relation of photographic absence to film's (heterosexist) ideology of presence, the former dependent on "the enabling but repressed technology at the origin of the moving picture" (240). In a displacement of pyschoanalytic gaze theory to the microlevel of the elementing strip, refigured through a de Manian emphasis on the giving face of all figuration (including now the sexed kinetic body on film), Edelman suggests that sexual difference can be found equivocated at the level of the photogrammatic same but different. Elaborating this notion within the terms of Preminger's film, Edelman filters a point of received wisdom in media studies (to be questioned from various perspectives across my chapters) through a revisionist gender grid when allowing that the photograph, here in association with homoerotic deviance, "calls forth the stasis and fixity of death while cinema insists on its fidelity to life by bestowing motion, vitality, animation on the photographic still" (240).

7. Jean-Louis Baudry, "Ideological Effects of the Basic Cinematographic Apparatus," in *Narrative, Apparatus, Ideology: A Film Theory Reader,* ed. Phil Rosen (New York: Columbia University Press, 1986), 290.

8. Peter Brunette and David Wills, *Screen/Play: Derrida and Film Theory* (Princeton: Princeton University Press, 1989), 78. Appropriately enough, the foregrounding of film's scriptive signifiers in the work of Marie-Claire Ropars-Wuilleumier and Tom Conley is taken up and debated in this study, as later in mine, as representing an anagrammatic resistance to film's analogic fit with the world (86-94). Beyond this, of course, I am trying to extend the application of a grammatological rather than a strictly linguistic model to the image track itself. At that level the self-disclosures of the strip, in light of 1970s ideological critique, may suggest a new slant on the Althusserian "interpellation" of the subject into the social network and its aesthetic forms. In normative process there is a kind of workaday "counterapocalypse" that provides the deceptive naturalization of all ends.

9. Henri Bergson, *Creative Evolution*, trans. Arthur Mitchell (Westport, Conn.: Greenwood, 1975); Gilles Deleuze, *The Movement-Image*, vol. 1. of *Cinema*, trans. Hugh Tomlinson and Barbara Habberjam (Minneapolis: University of Minnesota Press, 1986-89), 3.

10. In this objection I am not alone. D. N. Rodowick, in *Gilles Deleuze's Time Machine* (Durham, N.C.: Duke University Press, 1997), admits that "Deleuze's reasoning is certainly weak here" (22), noting that instead of "photograms or the individual frames on the film strip . . . what counts for Deleuze is the brute empiricism of an image in movement," which has supposedly "corrected" any artificial discontinuity in ordinary perception. It is a point Rodowick returns to later, suggesting that a "more skeptical view would continue to take seriously Bergson's critique of the 'cinematographic illusion'" (216 n. 2).

11. This empiricist emphasis is not what we might have expected from Deleuze's previous philosophical work. The Deleuze alluded to by Phillipe Dubois, for instance, is not so much the historian of the movement-image as the poststructuralist theorist, closer to Derrida, of the *pli* or "fold." When Dubois suggests in "Photography *Mise-en-Film:* Autobiographical (Hi)stories and Psychic Apparatuses," trans. Lynne Kirby, in *Fugitive Images: From Photography to Video,* ed. Patrice Petro (Bloomington: Indiana University Press, 1995), that "we must insert ourselves into the *fold* (in Deleuze's sense), the intersection that relates these two media [photography and cinema] so often deemed antagonistic" (153), he refers to the hinge point of the *photogramme,* what we might characterize as the tucking-under of the still by the moving image. But this is an emphasis foreign to Deleuze's stress on the latter in his work on film, where the single imprint is not appreciably folded into the movement-image so much as forgone by it. Is anything "more central," Dubois asks rhetorically about a film soon to be discussed in this chapter, "than Chris Marker's *La jetée* for understanding photographically the nature of cinema (and vice versa)?" (153). Probably not, but symptomatically the film is never once mentioned in either of Deleuze's volumes. "And in theoretical and aesthetic terms, is the film frame (*photogramme*) not somewhere near the heart of the fold, in other words simultaneously beyond photography and before cinema, more than the one and less than the other, while being a little of both at the same time?" (153). Not for Deleuze either, except for his remarks on the exceptional practice of Vertov.

12. Sergei Eisenstein, "A Dialectic Approach to Film Form," in *Film Theory and Criticism: Introductory Readings,* 2d ed., ed. Gerald Mast and Marshall Cohen (New York: Oxford University Press, 1979), 105. The claim, originating in a 1929 Stuttgart lecture and little appreciated since, is the starting point for François Albera's essay "Eisenstein and the Theory of the Photogram," in *Eisenstein Rediscovered,* ed. Ian Christie and Richard Taylor (New York: Routledge, 1993). For David Bordwell in *The Cinema of Eisenstein* (Cambridge: Harvard University Press, 1993), the whole dialectic principle appears "wildly implausible above the level of the shot" (130), yet he seems to grant some credence to a molecular dialectic in the procession of the strip. Here is his paraphrase of the same often revised and retitled position paper that concerns Albera, and from which I have quoted above: "When the visual system registers the quantitative disparity between two frames there is a leap to a new quality—movement" (129). For Albera, the maintenance of this subnarrative dialectic is in keeping with Eisenstein's whole program "to make a movement or gesture something *filmic* rather than *filmed*" (203), a structure rather than an event composed of photograms or *kadriki,* "little frames" (206). Remembering these frames is a way of finding in film a model for an experience of reality that Eisenstein himself, long before Deleuze, explicitly meant to place over against Bergson's insistence on a homogeneous continuity betrayed by the mechanisms of perception (202). Albera's case is made by example. The turn from narrative emblem to material allegory or "analogue" in his analysis of a famous loop shot in *October,* Kerensky ascending the stairs, summarizes Albera's sense of the primacy of the photogram in Eisenstein's aesthetic. Rejecting Adrian Piotrovsky's reading of the staggered image as "metaphor," Albera sees it dispelling at once "the diegetic illusion of a Kerensky rising to full power and the purely optical illusion of a continuous rising movement" (208). What it discloses instead: "The staircase, by virtue of its regular division, equidistant steps, and unidirectionality, offers a kind of analogue of the film strip, with its material base and structure of successive photograms" (208).

13. The Muybridge-like six-second freeze-frame on a hurdle-leaping horse is not even the most photogrammatically self-conscious moment in Vertov. Shots from a speeding tram in *Man with a Movie Camera* instantaneously transform the rows of windows swept past its traveling camera into a celluloid-like blur of horizontal rectangles. (See a similar ef-

fect in the film *Proof* below.) Moreover, this same footage is later prominently featured on the screen within the screen of the movie theater that provides a kind of narrative frame for Vertov's ocular pyrotechnics—as if these in particular, the stroboscopic window frames, were the reduced essence of cinematic animation. From such oscillations of the projected image we then revert to the track itself in the editing room as discussed in the introduction: Vertov's equivalent of the portrait photographer's freeze-frames in *People on Sunday* from the same year (introduction, note 12), with the seized imprint of a held pose hereby reversed in the shift from cellular analysis to synthetic motion.

14. Without (typically) making the direct photographic connection, but instead evoking the encasing "crystal of time," this is the one specific shot Deleuze alludes to in connection with his few sentences on "Truffaut's fine film," where the "glaucous existence" of the hero's image under glass makes it "impossible to tell whether he is living or dead" (Gilles Deleuze, *The Time-Image*, vol. 2 of *Cinema*, trans. Hugh Tomlinson and Barbara Habberjam [Minneapolis: University of Minnesota, 1986-89], 74).

15. Half in allusion, no doubt, to her previous *succès d'éstime*, half to implement straight off the code of familial nostalgia, Jocelyn Moorhouse's more conventional next film, *How-to-Make-an-American-Quilt* (1995), begins with the heroine's retrospective voice-over describing photographs in a family album scanned by her younger self as she sits under the table where the so far unseen subjects are holding a quilting bee. Nothing in the plot to come returns us, however, at either narrative or textual level, to this opening suggestion of film—or memory—as a patchwork of restitched photos.

16. Not since Michael Powell's notorious *Peeping Tom* (1966) has a photographer's story been so laden with emphasis on the image's fetishistic displacement of an Oedipally blocked sexuality. The unapproachable mother in Moorhouse's film is in Powell's the cold, scientific father, whose psychological experiments, after the mother's death, involve filming the male child during every hour of his waking and sleeping life, checking all erotic privacy in a way that leads to a homicidal psychosis fully revealed only at the end of the film. The son, Mark, now a B-film cinematographer who takes "girlie" photos on the side, finds a way to combine the moving image with the pornographic fixity of the still by taking moving-image footage of women as he is murdering them. The director on the set who badgered an inept starlet with the punning line "Forget that you're stunning and just try to look stunned" seems the model for Mark's effort to capture beauty in the recoil of panic. In the final contrivance of a cinematic rather than photographic apocalypse in Powell's film, we discover that Mark's only erotic release is to record the ultimate horror on the face of his model when, at the moment of a trick tripod's phallic knife thrust to her throat, a mirror is mechanically produced to show her the fear of fears: the very face of her own terror. What the police snapshots of such doubly petrified faces reveal on post mortem examination—an unprecedented terror in the moment of death—has been sustained across the agony of time itself by the movie camera's all but caricatural version of *death at work*.

17. In the symbolic reconciliation with the mother's memory that this image assists, the validating photo also points back to the hint of a patriarchal lineage photographically preserved as well. The very nature of Oedipal configurations—and their repair—is that they may go mostly unsaid. Hence a mere trace. In the earliest flashback, next to the mother's eventual slow deathbed, we could glimpse the photographic portrait of a man about her age—quite possibly the hero's absent origin proved (for us rather than him) by photochemical imprint. Now the garden photo, with its unseen benign male gardener (as described by Andy), is the only originary icon, long postponed, that remains.

18. Not only the origin of cinema in high-speed precision technology but its early links to excursion travel and to the new ocular privilege of framed motion for the train (or tram) spectator (as in Vertov, note 13 above)—all these historical associations of cinema and the train as machines of synchronicity and visual syncopation—erupt in the rush of this one

film's first cinematographic move. On the relation of early cinema to railroad technology and its new visual epistemology, see Lynne Kirby's *Parallel Tracks: The Railroad and Silent Cinema* (Durham, N.C.: Duke University Press, 1997), as well as Fredric Jameson's sense of this in relation to modernist style (chapter 7 below). For the most recent film to engage the logic of locomotion in this way, see Terence Davies's *The Neon Bible* (1995), where nondiegetic—or metaphoric—insets of a growing boy's train transit are used to figure diminished rites of passage in his stalled life: fixed lateral views in medium close-up of a train carriage chugging in place to nowhere. When plot catches up with this figural device in the end, the film closes with an actual booked passage (destination unknown) in flight from the charge of murder. The sheer abstracted vector of chronological narrative has become literalized (though no more realistic in treatment) as the hero's only way out from the narrative.

19. *Proof* offers recent cinema's most interesting version of this classic narrative device in its compromised objectivity. On the general problem of the flashback in this regard, see especially the fourth chapter, "The Subjectivity of History in Hollywood Sound Films," in Maureen Turim, *Flashbacks in Film: Memory and History* (New York: Routledge, 1989), 103-42.

20. A prototype does come to mind from mainstream Hollywood cinema, however, with blackness thematized as death rather than blindness. The is the abrupt blackout for the murder of the Warren Beatty character at the end of *The Parallax View* (Alan Pakula, 1974), which plays in the process (in the very filmic process) into the postmodern conspiracy thriller template developed by Fredric Jameson in *The Geopolitical Aesthetic* (Bloomington: University of Indiana Press, 1992), in the section titled "Totality as Conspiracy" (9-86). Jameson himself does not mention the closural violence of this narrative at the level of the track, but it could only support his argument. Now implicated in the political assassination he has tried to prevent, the hero's only hope for escape from the auditorium catwalk is through an exit door, on the other side of which the government hit men await him. Instead of the inescapable finish, we get the film's own inevitable foreclosure: blank finality. The panoptic circuit of surveillance that has caught him in its web not only is all-seeing but controls even the medium of our own vicarious sight. The cinematic totality, covering its own tracks, thus erases all evidence of its plot's climactic murder by occluding projection itself with black leader rather than holding on the hero's last moment in a more predictable photo finish closure. The gaze of the other, in short, asserts final veto power over our own.

21. As apparent from the screenplay by Paul Auster, *"Smoke" and "Blue in the Face": Two Films* (New York: Hyperion, 1995), and as discussed by Auster in the interview published with it, this footage was originally to be intercut with the monologue to "illustrate what Auggie was saying" (12). Its displacement to a coda cuts it free from such a clear evidentiary tether into a zone of greater epistemological uncertainty that complicates its inevitable association with Auggie's black-and-white stills.

22. This too, one finds, is a change from the screenplay, a device—call it an inspiration—of the editing table. Mere cuts seem indicated in the initial conception: "One by one, a single picture occupies the entire screen. One picture follows another. . . . Dozens of stills" (45). But when script becomes film *text*, the mode of this following up/on becomes the lamination of temporal collage—in other words, photomontage. At which point the differences (never quite cinematic in the spread of their intervals) grow all but visible *as difference* in the trace and blur of transition. One result is that the accompanying dialogue discussed below, taken directly from a script that made no indication of lap dissolves at this point, ends up fortuitously redoubled in its application—to filmic succession as well as to a photographic series.

23. On the racial utopia of this coda, I have profited from discussion with Kurt Rahmlow.

24. Paul Auster, *The Invention of Solitude* (New York: Penguin, 1982), 139.

25. It is a testament to the ephemeral force of the film's textuality as cinematic (if not quite cinematographic) narrative that the recent lavishly produced "text" of the film, *La jetée: Ciné-roman* (New York: Zone, 1992), with scores of impeccably restored frame enlargements, welcome as the volume is, misses almost entirely the narrative's aesthetic and philosophical effect as screen event.

26. This sense of the lap dissolves as carrying the actual meaning, rather than conveying us from one fixed signifier to the next, is also pursued from a psychoanalytic perspective in an untranslated article by Reda Bensmaia, whose inference is that death inhabits the very interval of deliquescence. Carefully illustrated by frame enlargements of the superimposed images, "Du photogramme au pictogramme: A propos de *La jetée* de Chis Marker," *Iris* 8 (1988): 9-31, suggests that the prolonged dissolve of Marker's shot transitions evokes the Lacanian "fading" (given in English) of subjectivity itself (27)—an operation of *la bande* (or film strip) that, in Bensmaia's wordplay, is at the same time *contrebande* (27). In the words of the essay's brief English abstract, the passage from held photogram to phantasmal "pictogram" (a concept drawn from a psychoanalytic study by Piera Aulagnier) replays the "repressed representation of an affect present in the psyche at a very early stage of development, closely linked to the unceasing struggle between the desires for fusion and for destruction" (31). For the fuller textual implications of the photogram's own repression by movement in connection with the slippage of the signifier in literary writing, and for a consideration of the brief seconds of actual moving-image footage in the narrative, I will return to Marker's film in the closing chapter.

27. Vivian Sobchack, *The Address of the Eye: A Phenomenology of Film Experience* (Princeton: Princeton University Press, 1992), 59. See my further debate with Sobchack's position in the next chapter and then again in a fuller discussion of science fiction film (chapter 5), where I in fact press for testing her phenomenological axioms against the ironies of a genre on which she has also written at length from a different perspective.

28. See chapter 7 for a further gloss on the monolith's own image plane as standing in for the transitional blanked screen that leads to final revelation. In such an approach, as well as in an intermediate treatment of the film in chapter 5, I am in part attempting to draw back to the frame, whether on track or on-screen, and hence to the level of textuality, the generalized intuition about Kubrick's film—about the work as *objet*—voiced early on, after nine ecstatic viewings, by Annette Michelson in a wry parable about critical incomprehension. Like the film, the black monolith is an "unheralded materialization" carrying the "disquieting function of Epiphany," emitting "signals" that are "received by a bewildered and apprehensive community (tribe? species?) of critics. . . . And still the 'object' lures us on. Another level or 'universe' of discourse awaits us." See Michelson, "Bodies in Space: Film as Carnal Knowledge," *Artforum*, February 1969, 56-63, where she adds in this same vein: "In that oscillating movement between confirmation and transformation, the film as a whole performs the function of a Primary Structure, forcing the spectator back, in a reflexive gesture, upon the analytic rehearsal of his experience, impelling, as it does so, the conviction that here is a film like any other, like all others, only more so—which is to say, a paradigm, unique" (56).

29. Robert Burgoyne, "Narrative Overture and Closure in *2001: A Space Odyssey*." *Enclitic* 5-6 (1981): 172-80.

30. Linking Kubrick and Resnais as masters of a "cinema of the brain" (204), Deleuze sees *2001* as one of those Kubrick films that epitomize a directorial vision in which "the world itself is a brain" (*Time-Image*, 205). The overarching issue in this second volume, "the time-image," is stressed here without recourse to Deleuze's recurrent notion of "sheets of time"—even as they might well be found competing, with rare clarity, in the penultimate editing sequence, with its simultaneous staging of the very ages of man. "At the end of *Space Odyssey*," writes Deleuze, "it is in consequence of a fourth dimension that

the sphere of the foetus and the sphere of the earth have a chance of entering into a new, incommensurable, unknown relation, which would convert death into new life" (206). But this is only, I venture to add, because what he calls the "membrane" of temporality has been "pierced" (206) from two directions at once within the cerebral englobement of the image. I like to think—though there is no authority for it in *this* volume of Deleuze—that the puncture wound in this temporal membrane, as refigured by the film strip itself, has left its lesion precisely in the fourfold freeze-frames of the preceding sequence, where sectioned mobility has been riven in an instant of arrest as a sheet of revealed duration (or call it the world-brain's memory) peeled away from the free fall of succession.

31. This suspension of photographic checkpoints takes the remarkable form in Kubrick's film of a double intertextual allusion to 1960s photographic technology, as I discuss in chapter 7.

32. Half a decade after "A Short History of Photography," in the famous essay "The Work of Art in the Age of Mechanical Reproduction" (1936), Benjamin closely echoes his own 1931 observation about the photographic intervention in normal movement: "Even if one has a general knowledge of the way people walk, one knows nothing of a person's posture during the fractional second of a stride" (in *Illuminations*, trans. Harry Zohn, ed. Hannah Arendt [New York: Schocken, 1969], 237). Having spoken of the camera's "lowerings and liftings, its interruptions and isolations, its extensions and accelerations, its enlargements and reductions" (237), Benjamin by this point clearly means to include movie as well as still cameras in his summarizing sentence, based on a model already familiar from the earlier treatise on photography: "The camera introduces us to unconscious optics as does psychoanalysis to unconscious impulses" (237). Lumped together as offering the underside of normal perception, cinema and photography may be accepted in this conjoint role without dismissing the need for a further hierarchical distinction—the one at which this book is continually aimed—concerning the former's suppressive mobilization of the latter.

33. Rosalind E. Krauss, *The Optical Unconscious* (Cambridge: MIT Press, 1993), 179.

34. Walter Benjamin, "A Short History of Photography," in *Classic Essays on Photography*, ed. Alan Trachtenberg (New Haven, Conn.: Leete's Island Books, 1980), 202-3.

35. In "The Work of Art in the Age of Mechanical Reproduction," Walter Benjamin notes that in cinema the "equipment-free aspect of reality . . . has become the height of artifice; the sight of immediate reality has become an orchid in the land of technology" (233).

36. David E. James, *Allegories of Cinema: American Film in the Sixties* (Princeton: Princeton University Press, 1989), 275.

CHAPTER THREE

1. Vivian Sobchack, *The Address of the Eye: A Phenomenology of Film Experience* (Princeton: Princeton University Press, 1992), 63 n. 14.

2. James Dudley Andrew, *The Major Film Theories* (New York: Oxford University Press, 1976).

3. Rudolf Arnheim, *Film as Art* (Berkeley: University of California Press, 1968), 2. These are essays written in the 1930s and first reprinted in 1957.

4. See François Albera, "Eisenstein and the Theory of the Photogram," in *Eisenstein Rediscovered*, ed. Ian Christie and Richard Taylor (New York: Routledge, 1993).

5. At which point some further pictorial theory may be called in. In terms circulated by Jacques Derrida, the "parergon" or frame in painting is less an external verge than an internal margin, one of his signal points of sheer difference. In view of this emphasis, we might say that the screen border—the cinematic parergon—becomes an internal supplement to the image field as well as marking its exclusions. But the double valence of the "frame" that composes that image, filmic as well as cinematic, is generally elided in discussion. What results is a kind of displaced parergon: not the internalization of the image's own

limits on the track but the extroversion of the picture surface itself—as photochemistry—to the mere parameters of its beamed manifestation as scene: the world space held on display between and behind the four edges of the lit screen frame. It is as if magnification explodes the printed surface (this sense of "frame") into the expanded boundaries of its own projected field of view. For the complications attendant on the frame in painting, see Jacques Derrida, *Truth in Painting,* trans. Geoff Bennington and Ian McLeod (Chicago: University of Chicago Press, 1987), 37-83.

6. Arnheim, *Film as Art.* Arnheim's whiplash equivocations characterize the entire volume. The writer who means to surprise us by declaring that "stationary photography is not as fundamentally remote from film as might be supposed" (117) is the same critic who insists elsewhere, and with the same ostensibly foundationalist adverb, that film is "more than a variation of the immobile image, obtained by multiplication: it is *fundamentally* new and different" (180; emphasis added). Discrepancies of this sort proliferate until they accrue to their own kind of clarity, defining a conceptual space between alternating (and otherwise contradictory) claims: those of strip and screen. The theorist who, in surveying a certain technological impetus in the history of representation (namely the always elusive mimesis of "motion by motion in such a way as to obtain a faithful and readily available reproduction" [169]), remarks that "even film does not meet this specification: it does not render motion by motion but gives an illusion of it by means of immobile images shown in sequence" (162)—this is the very writer who will say elsewhere, at the close of the same essay in this case, that "the motion picture is not a synthetic agglomeration of individual images but [is] based on a recording process that is as continuous and unitary as the movement of the photographed objects" (169). Unitary? Continuous? "Film—the animated image—comes midway between the theater and the still picture" (25). Has "animated" lost all its force as a past participle? If film is not the inherently "animate" image, then indeed the mechanical intervention that distances it from the "still photograph" must also be seen to depend on the still (if transparent) photographic frame. To avoid admitting as much with any disabling consistency is the reason Arnheim so often, though not always, seems to downgrade the animation effect as a definitive aspect of film's conceptual profile. Yet this same critic, vigilantly defending the motion-picture image against the sense of "illusion" he elsewhere insists on, will in 1957 introduce the republication of this commentary from the 1930s by still calling film an "animated photograph" (2), only to rephrase (revise?) this notion at the end of the prefatory remarks with the characterization "undisturbed animated images"—as if the adjective "undisturbed" smuggles back in his frequent emphasis on the continuity rather than fundamental discontinuity of the movement effect.

7. The essays in question are from Noël Carroll, *Theorizing the Moving Image* (Cambridge: Cambridge University Press, 1996): "Medium Specificity Arguments and the Self-Consciously Invented Arts: Film, Video and Photography" (3-24); "The Specificity of Media in the Arts" (25-36); and "Concerning Uniqueness Claims for Photographic and Cinematographic Representation" (37-48).

8. See two coauthered articles in *The Cinematic Apparatus,* ed. Teresa de Lauretis and Stephen Heath (New York: St. Martin's, 1980): Joseph Anderson and Barbara Anderson, "Motion Perception in Motion Pictures" (76-95), and Bill Nichols and Susan J. Lederman, "Flicker and Motion in Film" (96-105).

9. Sobchack, *Address of the Eye,* 63.

10. Hugo Münsterberg, *The Film: A Psychological Study* (New York: Dover, 1970), 26; reprint of edition cited in note 11 below.

11. Hugo Münsterberg, *The Photoplay: A Psychological Study* (New York: Appleton, 1916), 70.

12. For Kracauer's more critically edged views on the distancing service provided by film in recasting reality in the form of a subjectively invested (and scarcely coherent) dream

projection, see "Photography," in Siegfried Kracauer, *The Mass Ornament: Weimar Essays,* trans. and ed. Thomas Y. Levin (Cambridge: Harvard University Press, 1995), 47-63. Whereas memory establishes an image holistic and unreductive, called by Kracauer the "monogram" (55) of remembered life, photography "is the sediment which has settled from the monogram" (55). But when such sedimented entities, in the form of photograms, are reelemented as fragments of the cinematic track, they collect toward an illusion that aspires again to the monogrammatic fullness of time passing—but not of a time wed indelibly to the real. Rather, filmic photograms, bunched into discontinuous stretches of moving action, generate images more oneiric than realistic. At which point the montage of sequence is processed as an unconscious disjuncture and a game—or gamble—of productive aesthetic alienation. Hence, in Kracauer's closing emphasis, the critical advance of cinema over the equally discrepant spread (and widespread popularity) of journalistic photography: "If the disarray of the illustrated newspapers is simply confusion, the game that film plays with the pieces of disjointed nature is reminiscent of *dreams* in which the fragments of daily life become jumbled" (63). I return to this aspect of Kracauer's thought in the coda, "End Title/Exeunt."

13. Stanley Cavell, *The World Viewed: Reflections on the Ontology of Film,* enlarged ed. (Cambridge: Harvard University Press, 1979).

14. See the specifications of some of these ways in the work of Jacques Aumont and Jonathan Crary, among others, discussed in chapters 6 and 7.

15. A striking point of uncited convergence with Cavell's thinking appears, in connection with the films of Philippe Garrel and inflected by Deleuze's own particular slant toward the schizophrenic reapprehension of the world, when he writes that "if the world has become a bad cinema, in which we no longer believe, surely a true cinema can contribute to giving us back reasons to believe in the world and in vanished bodies? The price to be paid, in cinema as elsewhere, was always a confrontation with madness" (Gilles Deleuze, *The Time-Image,* vol. 2 of *Cinema,* trans. Hugh Tomlinson and Barbara Habberjam [Minneapolis: University of Minnesota, 1986-89], 201).

16. See chapter 7, where the likelihood emerges of a specifically photographic intertext for the closing moment, as well as a self-consciously photogrammatic pivot for its realization.

17. To attempt this reformulation is perhaps also to see why, for Cavell, "movies" can afford so little resemblance to that cartoon "animation" with which it seems to him perverse, on other and good grounds, to confuse them (168). Arnheim's own equivocation on the question of "animation" is, of course, part of this deep phenomenological sore spot—both for "material theory" and for those modernist "acknowledgments" of the medium that bear witness to the medium's kinetic materiality.

18. Stanley Cavell, "What Photography Calls Thinking," *Raritan* 4, no. 4 (1985): 8, in a discussion that reviews his original treatment of these freeze-frames in Cavell, *Pursuits of Happiness: The Hollywood Comedy of Remarriage* (Cambridge: Harvard University Press, 1976).

19. Vachel Lindsay, *The Art of the Motion Picture* (New York: Macmillan, 1915).

20. As will shortly emerge, I mean by this something more specific to the time of the film track itself than what Bazin generally implies by the straining of baroque art, with its fulfillment in film, toward the "psychic fourth dimension" of movement in time. See André Bazin, "The Ontology of the Photogragphic Image," in *What Is Cinema?* trans. Hugh Gray (Berkeley: University of California Press, 1967), 1:11.

21. This camera movement is mentioned by Richard Neupert in *The End: Narration and Closure in the Cinema* (New York: Wayne State University Press, 1995) as evidence for the "open story film" (as direct obverse of the open discourse film). In discursive closure, Truffaut's "optical zoom approaches, turning him [Antoine] into a static spectacle," all

looking dissociated finally from narrative (discursive) advance, all story suspended (unfinished) in a gaze (the spectator's) no longer containable by it.

22. One doesn't, of course, wish to throw over the traditional terminology—with its stress on an apparent icing over rather than a sculpting of motion. We will be coming in the next chapter to the celluloid frieze as specifically *narrative*—that is, temporal—seizure in *The Shining*'s labyrinthine avoidance of the "frozen" shot (rather than corpse) in closure.

23. See Ana Lopez, "An Elegant Spiral: Truffaut's *The 400 Blows*," *Wide Angle* 7, nos. 1-2 (1985): 147, where she notes that the child's view of the world from within this zoetrope-like spinning drum is the first POV shot in the film, thus marking a new stage in our subjective participation in the narrative. My own stress would fall upon what we see him seeing there: an already cinematized whirl of a world.

24. Gilles Deleuze, *The Movement-Image*, vol. 1. of *Cinema*, trans. Hugh Tomlinson and Barbara Habberjam (Minneapolis: University of Minnesota Press, 1986-89), 3.

25. I draw here on an important distinction developed out of Peircean semiotics by Dominique Chateau, who stresses the inevitable iconic element, conjoined to the indexical sign function, not only in the photographic image but in film's rendering of movement. Cinema offers not an index or imprint of real movement but a reconstituted picturing of it. Though Chateau does not discuss the stop-action image in this regard, it seems to me the definitive limit case for his point: the advent of a pure iconicity from within the illusory index of an autonomous action. See Chateau, *Le bouclier d'Achille: Théorie de l'iconicité* (Paris: Harmattan, 1997).

26. In this explicitly feminist remake of the Garland version, what we see in closure may well be an effort to wrest female stardom from the paralytic categories of screen culture's gendered glance. Such is the logic by which the female under scrutiny is the always compromised object of the look-bearing male: the woman scoped out (as idiom might suggest) of all narrative function except to sustain the gaze. Streisand's attempt is to trump voyeurism by heroic exhibitionism. To this end even the track is recruited, with the freeze-frame coming to the rescue of the screen image itself at a further level of performative (now filmic) self-consciousness. In the "castrating" absence of the dead male, women's exclusion from narrative time in submitting to mere objectification by the gaze would become here—or strain to become—woman's momentary and recuperative vanquishing of narrative time by the filmic equivalent of sheer stage *presence*, an image inscribing the terms of our own attention.

27. That this final image might borrow some of its effect, by way of irony, from the clicks and flashes of the paparazzi throughout, as well as from the outsize publicity photos of Esther that appear in the background of several scenes, illustrates again this book's interest in the collisions of diegetic photography with cinematic photogrammaticality. In this regard an earlier Streisand film, *Hello Dolly!* (Gene Kelly, 1969) might be said to begin where *A Star Is Born* ends: in photographic stasis. It opens upon a black-and-white, then sepia, then color photograph (seemingly) of an 1890s New York street scene that is eventually revealed as, instead, a temporary freeze-frame when, with the first sounds of mechanical motion, an iris on a moving elevated train traversing an upper fraction of the screen widens out to animate the entire image plane. This is Kelly's obvious homage to such MGM musicals as *Meet Me in St. Louis* that often evoked postcardlike stills, deceptive freeze-frames teased into kinesis after an initial nostalgic glimpse into the *optically recorded* past. (In *Meet Me in St. Louis* there is one sepia-tinted photograph for each of the four seasons that block out the plot, seen first in a decorated family album, then closed in on by the camera until the shot snaps to animation as a narrative scene.) In *Hello Dolly!* the opening still device is extended into the first musical number by a half dozen midstream freeze-frames on flabbergasted bystanders reading Dolly Levi's marriage-brokering business card: the textualization of the image plane at the moment of stunned encounter with another form of text.

28. Referring back to François Albera's discussion in "Eisenstein and the Theory of the Photogram," this is his qualified sense of "'lived' duration." It is a time of encountered footage rather than represented action, a temporality induced upon us rather than produced before us in representation.

29. See Roland Barthes, *Camera Lucida: Reflections on Photography*, trans. Richard Howard (New York: Hill and Wang, 1981), 27.

30. Henri Bergson, *Creative Evolution*, trans. Arthur Mitchell (Westport, Conn.: Greenwood, 1975), 331.

31. André Bazin, "The Concept of Presence," in *What Is Cinema?* trans. Hugh Gray (Berkeley: University of California Press, 1967), 96-98.

32. Bazin, "Ontology of the Photogragraphic Image," 14.

33. André Malraux, *The Voices of Silence*, trans. Stuart Gilbert (Garden City, N.Y.: Doubleday, 1953), 10.

34. Bazin, "Ontology of the Photogragraphic Image," 15.

35. Deleuze, *Movement-Image*, 3.

36. Mary Ann Doane, "Temporality, Storage, Legibility: Freud, Marey, and the Cinema," *Critical Inquiry* 22, no. 2 (1996): 313-43, introducing the comparison with Bergson on 323. This is an argument influenced throughout by the work of Friedrich Kittler (see below, chapter 7, n. 10). In its focus not only on the hyperindexicality of cinematic representation, however, but on the flip side of its storage mechanism in pure subjectivity, Doane ends on a Freudian note for which the freeze-frame might be found to offer a perfect gloss. If representation, mental or mechanical, is not entirely a recording mechanism, then it declares itself engaged—such is the modern anxiety and the modernist vaunt—in "the production of temporalities with no referent other than that of the representational system itself (the psyche, the cinema)" (343). As time-image, then, the freeze is referred back to the time of the track itself. By the same token, as this chapter has been hoping to show, it is also referred outward to the time of the spectator's own attention, where psychic operations converge with as well as merely parallel the machinations of cinema.

37. Deleuze, *Movement-Image*, 59.

38. Deleuze, *Movement-Image*, 23, 2, 3.

39. Cavell, *World Viewed*, 24.

CHAPTER FOUR

1. There is a fuller context yet, across more representational practices than just film and photography, for the focus of this chapter. Apart from a general theoretical account of literary writing's flexed access to the gapped lineation of script, death's arrest of the cognitive subject is a narrative moment I have elsewhere had reason to find crucial to the structure of prose fiction, modernist as well as classic, both in the linguistic limit case of its textual signification and in the closural logic of its plotting. See Garrett Stewart, *Death Sentences: Styles of Dying in British Fiction* (Cambridge: Harvard University Press, 1984).

2. Rudolf Arnheim, "Death in Film," in *Film Essays and Criticism*, trans. Brenda Benthien (Madison: University of Wisconsin Press, 1997), 74.

3. This is the phrase used for "the turning point of death" in connection with the end of Gentleman Brown in Conrad's *Lord Jim* (chap. 41), as discussed in Stewart, *Death Sentences*, 152-53.

4. This incineration marks something like the opposite of the doctored but supposedly exonerating photographs burned up by accident in Fritz Lang's last American film, *Beyond a Reasonable Doubt* (1956). Catherine Russell's *Narrative Mortality: Death, Closure, and New Wave Cinemas* (Minneapolis: University of Minnesota Press, 1995) opens with an extended reading of this narrative in establishing a link, important throughout her study, between photographic fixity and cinema's own mortal closure. Exploring what she calls "the

discourse of photography in film" (41), she takes off from Raymond Bellour's brief comments on Lang's film in finding it haunted by the burned Polaroid evidence for which there are no negative master images. The loss of these prints results, for Russell, in a "mortification of cinematic presence" (41-42) by the abjection of its own basis in the evidentiary imprint. Russell's analysis returns to American cinema for a brief discussion of slow-motion and freeze-frame deaths in her chapter "American Apocalypticism" (173-208).

5. Roland Barthes, "Diderot, Brecht, Eisenstein," in *Image/Music/Text*, trans. Stephen Heath (New York: Hill and Wang, 1977), 77.

6. André Bazin, "Mort tous les après-midi," in *Qu'est-ce que le cinéma?* vol. 1, *Ontologie et langage* (Paris: Editions de Cerf, 1958), 68.

7. M. M. Bakhtin, *Art and Answerability: Early Philosophical Essays*, trans. Vadim Liapunov (Austin: University of Texas Press, 1990), 166.

8. Gilles Deleuze, *The Time-Image*, vol. 2 of *Cinema*, trans. Hugh Tomlinson and Barbara Habberjam (Minneapolis: University of Minnesota, 1986-89), 105.

9. One of the more intriguing production details unearthed by Robert L. Carringer in *The Making of "Citizen Kane"* (Berkeley: University of California Press, 1985) involves the ad hoc nature of this superimposition, thus explaining its absence from the shooting script at least, if not from the cutting continuity. Welles decided at the last minute that a blanket of snow might help mask the otherwise telltale graininess of the toy scene, which had been many times magnified rather than merely photographed in close-up. I nevertheless cling to my point by suggesting that Welles recognized something about the spatial fluidity and psychic porosity of this deathbed moment that would harness his poetic license to thematic effect. In any case, Welles's happy accident has passed into film history as a locus classicus, cited in Robert Benton's *Nobody's Fool* (1994) when the Jessica Tandy character, suffering a heart attack while sitting at a window looking out at the snow, knocks a teacup to the floor in a parlor suddenly overlain with the exterior snowfall.

10. My intermittent emphasis in this chapter on such unspoken but visualized clichés is informed by Michael Riffaterre's work on the signifying avoidances that produce literary semiosis. See Riffaterre, *Semiotics of Poetry* (Bloomington: Indiana University Press, 1978). But whereas a buried verbal cliché (as generative "matrix") must be more obliquely manifested, and hence more elaborately transcoded, in written texts, film can find visual correlatives for a given verbal stereotype without falling directly into cliché on its own cinematic terms. The literal fact of letting go, for instance, keeps its metaphoric equivalent somewhat at bay.

11. The mutual interplay of actual and virtual in the "crystal image" is briefly exemplified by this impossible snow scene in Deleuze's fourth chapter (*Time-Image*, 74).

12. My sense of this brief shot is thus related to the way James Naremore singles it out as "the most confusing shot of all" in the opening sequence, "creating an elaborate fish-eye effect which is virtually a parody of the lens Toland will use to photograph the movie." See Naremore, *The Magic World of Orson Welles* (New York: Oxford University Press, 1978), 72. To his observation I would add that such a "parody" can only remind us that there is nothing behind this evacuated POV shot but the camera apparatus itself, its lens refigured within the scene. Putting it this way conforms also with one's sense that only "narration," the storytelling apparatus, "hears" the word "Rosebud."

13. The shooting script would have had it as follows instead, with the trope of fragmentation carried by disruptive lighting effects rather than by discrepant reflection: "The ball falls off the last step on to the marble floor where it breaks, the fragments glittering in the first ray of the morning sun. This ray cuts an angular pattern across the floor, suddenly crossed with a thousand bars of light as the blinds are pulled across the window" (97). See the story board for this transition, without the distorted, low-angle shot of the nurse, reprinted in Carringer, *Making of "Citizen Kane,"* 41.

14. Carringer, *Making of "Citizen Kane,"* happens to include a frame enlargement of this shot, without comment, at the top of a page where his discussion is laying stress on how many images in the film are the result of "special effects" (99).

15. Continuous with an argument about the poetics of death in British fiction in Stewart, *Death Sentences,* is my comparison between fictional and filmic representations of death in "Thresholds of the Visible: The Death Scene of Film," *Mosaic* 16, nos. 1-2 (1983): 33-54, as well as in "'This Vertiginous Film': Signifying Death in *Citizen Kane,"* in *Perspectives on "Citizen Kane,"* ed. Ronald Gottesman (New York: Hall, 1996), 430-48. That essay involves a fuller discussion than reprinted here of the hermeneutic circle fenced off by the film's opening and closing imperative, "No Trespassing," when transformed to the declarative "no trespassing [here]" of film's fictive invitation.

16. Slavoj Žižek, *Looking Awry: An Introduction to Jacques Lacan through Popular Culture* (Cambridge: MIT Press, 1991), 90.

17. Such a Bakhtinian "author" needs to be distinguished, at least in this application, from anything like the omniscient interpretive authority that is one of the targets of a polemical essay on *Kane* by Marie-Claire Ropars-Wuilleumier. As we move toward the film's denouement, with its virtual parable of the filmic signifier, I should note that she is the one previous critic who has insistently privileged, as I do, the *textual* link between the processes of cinematic articulation in the opening and closing sequences—though without linking them in turn, as this chapter will go on to do, with the intervening place of the inset photograph and the photogrammatic freeze in the transit between death and referential disintegration. See Ropars-Wuilleumier, "Narration and Signification: A Filmic Example," trans. Michael C. Pounds, in *Perspectives on "Citizen Kane,"* ed. Ronald Gottesman (New York: Hall, 1996). Beginning with the camera angles that compose the death scene, Ropars approaches *Kane* by way of its narrative enunciation—what she calls its "cinematographic writ"—in order to counter two opposing approaches to the film that she finds based on a nonetheless comparable "reduction" (449). On the one hand, there is Bazin's "sentimental interpretation" (450) in which realism (including deep focus) is put in the service of an "unbiased intellect" (449) arranging and assessing the events. (Here is where we need to keep such a view apart from the Bakhtinian "excess" of authorial—more like narrational—perspective.) On the other hand, there is the ideological critique that sees the film as one of those deceptive conventional narratives that "disguise the production process to render the cinematographic apparatus 'invisible'" (449). Each reading is found to flatten the film's narrational complexity to a coherent level of articulated intentionality. Ropars is drawn instead to those moments that defy such claims by their overt and even contradictory manipulations of the narrational process. In the shot sequence I have just discussed, moving from the overlain snowscape to the shattered reflection, all camera positions demarcate a "supplemental emanation" from the original omniscient "voice" (456) or enunciation, present before Kane's own lone word. They do so even as they are also extrapolated from "Kane's glance—the glance of his death" in a ramified POV that "will not be identified as such by the spectator until after it has disappeared" (457). One might want to single out, more rigorously than Ropars does, the superimposed snowfall as the *single* instance of demonstrable subjectivity in the scene, displaced to a kind of mind's-eye view of Kane's own failing body. One would then want to find in the floor-level shot that follows something like a subsidiary "supplemental emanation" of the subjective shot itself. In this way the ambiguous senses of Ropars's phrase "the glance of his death" can be ratified as playing between objective and subjective genitive (glance *at* vs. glance *from*) in a pivot between inert corpse and the posthumous continuance of the look.

18. André Malraux, *Lazarus,* trans. Terence Kilmartin (New York: Grove, 1971), 67.

19. Walter Benjamin, "The Work of Art in the Age of Mechanical Reproduction," in *Illuminations,* ed. Hannah Arendt, trans. Harry Zohn (New York: Schocken, 1969), 249 n.

17. In *Picturing Ourselves: Photography and Autobiography* (Chicago: University of Chicago Press, 1997), Linda Haverty Rugg notes a canceled passage in Benjamin's autobiography, *Berlin Childhood*, that happens to recycle this particular bit of remembered apparatus: "I imagine that the 'whole life' that is supposed to pass before the eyes of the dying is made up of the kind of pictures that . . . flash quickly past like the leaves of those stiffly bound books that were once the forerunners of our cinema" (172). He continues with a clear evocation of just that photogrammatic discontinuity that Rugg is concerned to explore in her own terms, as a figure for the interruptions of retrospect: "Thumbs pressed slowly along the edges of the pages, and second-by-second pictures appeared, scarcely differing from one another. In their fleeting course they would reveal the boxer at work and the swimmer fighting his waves" (172-73).

20. Deleuze, *Time-Image*, 35. The classic film prototype for this sense of life replayed in death as omniscient film narrative is Fritz Lang's *Liliom* (1934). This from the director of *Fury* two years later (see chapter 1) and *Beyond a Reasonable Doubt* (above, note 4); decades apart, photographic evanescence underwrites, in all its vanishing assurance, the filmic (or photogrammatic) narrative. This also from the director of *Metropolis* (see chapter 5), in which the panoptic surveillance of an industrial overlord, cinematically accommodated by a closed-circuit screening device, takes on an aura of godlike omniscience. In *Liliom* the dead hero is confronted at the threshold of purgatory with a filmic review of a turning point in his life, a life projected now on a metaphysical screen within the screen. This involves incriminating footage of his unfinished business in this world (time and place marked on the very corner of the image plane as the replay begins). Anticipating as well the angel's-eye view of George Bailey's history at the start of *It's a Wonderful Life* (as discussed in the introduction), where a freeze-frame is the mark of divine intervention, the temporality of the human image is displaced in *Liliom* to an extraterrestrial vantage point. Only the discrete index of absence remains behind on earth in the form of a framed photograph of the hero (along with a framed pressed flower, another index of the organic), to which the camera more than once recurs after Liliom's murder. With death's bodily arrest, you give way to your own photograph. From the perspective of eternity, you become the cinema-like compendium of your lived days—all as if rerun in a last split second of panoptic self-consciousness.

21. Georges Poulet, "Bergson: La thème de la vision panoramique des mourants et la juxtaposition," appendix to *L'espace proustien* (Paris: Gallimard, 1963), 137-77.

22. "It will probably turn out to be a very simple thing" (325). As the film presses forward, this idiomatic "very simple thing" becomes literalized and unmistakable, in pyschoanalytic terms, as *das Ding*, the fixated Thing of desire awaiting its demolition at narrative's end—in other words, preparing its own deconstruction as a supposed piece of the real already constituted in the symbolic. Žižek describes "the Thing," the "Freudian *das Ding*," as "the impossible-unattainable substance of enjoyment" (*Looking Awry*, 83). Earlier: "Why must the symbolic mechanism be hooked onto a 'thing,' some piece of the real?" (33). The Lacanian answer is that the "function of the 'little piece of the real' is precisely to fill out the place of this void that gapes in the very heart of the symbolic" (33). When the sled is remembered by name, and taken up by that name as significant signifier, its role has been entirely co-opted by the apparatus of meaning—indeed as privileged signifier for the symbolic's own void—and must eventually be exposed in this light by the film's climactic shot.

23. This penultimate shot involves another special effect detailed by Carringer, *Making of "Citizen Kane"*: "The final move up to the decal on the burning sled was accomplished by placing footage of the sled in the optical printer and moving the projector toward the recording camera as the footage ran through, thereby creating an optical zoom effect" (94). Cinema as complex technological apparatus, that is, gets not only closer than the human eye, but closer than a mere recording mechanism could get to the voided presence of the long-absent referent.

24. Jameson's tantalizing allegory thus helps make sense of the time-loop trick ending as more than an autoreferential noose about photographical immortalization as corpse. To this end, there is even more evidence than Jameson brings to court. If the hotel is the site of wealth's former complacency, then it seems much to the point that Jack insists on staying there (even before he discovers that all drinks are "on the house") so that he doesn't have to lapse back from his dream of being a professional writer to the demeaning odd jobs waiting for him in Boulder: shoveling snow by the hour, as he says, rather than being productively holed up in it for the season. Slipping into the proletariat is the middle-class fear that fuels his empty self-employment. Also harking back to a bygone era of flaunted class security is an ironic vestige of turn-of-the century colonialist jingoism, reduced on the modern American home front to the private onus of chronic inebriation. As Jack suggests to the ghostly bartender in the hotel lounge, alcohol itself is a mission—the "white man's burden." This political irony of delusional empowerment, drink's artificial elevation and outreach, connects up with two other details even more notably (though still confirmingly) absent from Jameson's account. First, the closing preternatural photograph of Nicholson taken before he was born is identified by date (so we discover in the film's last shot) as if it were imprinted with one of the narrative's own temporal intertitles attached now to an embedded photograph. As such, the date recurs not just in general to the heyday of deco glamour in the first year of the Roaring Twenties but to none other than the Fourth of July ball of that year. Independence Day, in this film, comes carrying its full murderous, indeed genocidal, connotations as well, since we have heard in seeming filler dialogue during the initial job interview that the hotel was originally built in the first decade of this century upon sacred Indian land. In a local frontier mythology superimposed upon twenties internationalism (in a way that would perfectly suit Jameson's claims), the monument to transient pleasures was erected only by "repelling" violent efforts to prevent it by some straggling Native American resistance. Imperial power, murder, freedom: these, as well as easy living and sleek high style, are the collective unconscious of Jack's American dream come true.

25. In the decade and a half between *Blow-Up* and *The Shining,* the corpse as simulacrum has come forward as an explicit cinematic prop. As in Jameson's account of Antonioni's corpse in chapter 7, this is the postmodernist site of displaced organic life par excellence, one that precipitates in Kubrick's film, in the flight to photography, what we might call a fantasized escape from the posthistorical—in preference for the dead and gone.

26. As the camera moves forward into the image plane of a single photograph, the intertext in Michael Snow's *Wavelength,* as discussed in the chapter 1, has grown unmistakable. In Snow's film the same asymptotic destination in the two-dimensional space of photography (a picture of ocean waves) deconstructs the previous half-hour's edging forward of the camera in a supposed depth of real space (a New York loft, with windows once visible on a far wall where now, at the end, there is only the engulfing frame of a photograph).

27. Siegfried Kracauer, "Photography," in *The Mass Ornament: Weimar Essays,* trans. and ed. Thomas Y. Levin (Cambridge: Harvard University Press, 1995), 57. The relation of photography to Freud's account of doubling and the uncanny is discussed by Catherine Russell, *Narrative Mortality,* 43.

CHAPTER FIVE

1. Along with *The Address of the Eye: A Phenomenology of Film Experience* (Princeton: Princeton University Press, 1992), the other books by Vivian Sobchack under discussion here are *The Limits of Infinity: The American Science Fiction Film, 1950-1975* (Cranbury, N.J.: A. S. Barnes, 1980) and its revised edition, *Screening Space: The American Science Fiction Film* (New York: Ungar, 1987), no longer so openly acknowledging by title its lack of prewar genre coverage.

2. On this subject, as centered upon the recurrence of mediating screens within the screen in the genre, see Garrett Stewart, "The 'Videology' of Science Fiction Film," in *Shadows of the Magic Lamp,* ed. George Slusser and Eric S. Rabkin (Carbondale: Southern Illinois University Press, 1985), 159-207. An important complementary argument is advanced by Brooks Landon in *The Aesthetics of Ambivalence: Rethinking Science Fiction Film in the Age of Electronic (Re)Production* (Westport, Conn.: Greenwood, 1992). Finding "the *spectacle of production technology* deserving and rewarding our attention just as surely as do narratives about the *impact of technology"* (xiv), he follows out the various consequences, in and beyond the sci fi genre, of this pervasive claim. "Hence my contention that simulation technology has become a narrative in itself, that computer-generated virtual images serve as science fiction regardless of the verbal narrative with which they may be associated" (151).

3. More than in most of her writing on the immanent life world projected by film, Sobchack does seem to acknowledge here the mechanically mediated photographic nature of ordinary cinema—on the road to the entirely virtual. "Electronic battles," writes Sobchack, "are easy to watch," since they are "*nonphotographic* and thus not existentially indexical," transforming "mortality" itself "into the astronomical abstraction of a truly new metaphysics" (261; emphasis added). For my fuller discussion of Sobchack's approach, see the article from which part of this chapter has been drawn, Garrett Stewart, "The Photographic Ontology of Science Fiction Film," *Iris* 25 (spring 1998): 101-6.

4. Lucien Dällenbach, *Le récit spéculaire: Essai sur la mise en abyme* (Paris: Editions de Seuil, 1977), rpt. as *The Mirror in the Text,* trans. Jeremy Whitely with Emma Hughes (Chicago: University of Chicago Press, 1989).

5. This "wipe" as marvel, this enunciative device as plot phenomenon, illustrates in strategic reverse Christian Metz's compelling argument about the gradual "de-diegetization" of trick effects in the evolution of cinematic syntax. What was once a fantastic materialization, like superimposition, fades diachronically into a mere editing device of scene change, moving from a diegetic signified to an inflection or "taxeme" of transition, from fiction to its enunciation. I build on Metz to suggest that certain films of the fantastic, including such sci fi variants as *The Invisible Ray,* depend upon inverting the historical process, so that a grammar of transition is catapulted back into plot as a miracle, a visitation, a spectral intervention: form remotivated as content. See Christian Metz, *"Trucage* and Film," *Critical Inquiry* 3 (summer 1977): 657-75.

6. In "Tracing the Individual Body: Photography, Detectives, and Early Cinema," in *Cinema and the Invention of Modern Life,* ed. Leo Charney and Vanessa R. Schwartz (Berkeley: University of California Press, 1995), Tom Gunning pursues Philippe Dubois's interest in the once reputable science of the *optogramme.* Under the auspices of the Paris Society for Legal Medicine, a belief in this hypothetical image trace led to experimental procedures whereby murder victims had their retinas surgically removed to produce "an imprint of the victims' last sight—an image of their murderers" (37).

7. To effect this result—or rather merely to indicate it—Trumbull devised for the film's initial release a unique gimmick: widening the visual field of the theater screen to full panavision ratio (with anamorphic wraparound) from its narrower normal rectangle, but only when the headset is engaged by an experimental subject. The POV shot becomes the POV frame.

8. I refer to the paradigm of the past recaptured as fuel for renewed desire in the classic comedies discussed by Stanley Cavell in *Pursuits of Happiness: The Hollywood Comedy of Remarriage* (Cambridge: Harvard University Press, 1981).

9. Georges Poulet, "Phenomenology of Reading," *New Literary History* 1 (October 1969): 56.

10. Jean Baudrillard, *Simulacra and Simulation,* trans. Sheila Faria Glaser (Ann Arbor: University of Michigan Press, 1994), 2. In my essay "The Photographic Ontology of Sci-

ence Fiction Film," I further elaborate (by means of Greimassian semiotics) the relation of photography and its filmic activation to varieties of the simulacrum (118-22).

11. Gilles Deleuze, *The Time-Image,* vol. 2 of *Cinema,* trans. Hugh Tomlinson and Barbara Habberjam (Minneapolis: University of Minnesota, 1986-89); also 263, 265, drawing on Jean-Louis Schefer, *L'homme ordinaire du cinéma* (Paris: Cahiers du Cinéma/Gallimard, 1980).

12. This incineration of the human image has been figured just before in the underground resistance shelter. We first see two ragged children staring into a TV set that, when viewed from the front, turns out to have been gutted of its electronic works and used instead as a makeshift fireplace.

13. The film's vision of altered biological status thus approaches to the double valence of Scott Bukatman's title *Terminal Identity: The Virtual Subject in Postmodern Science Fiction* (Durham, N.C.: Duke University Press, 1993). An expendable scene of comic shock, turning on a kind of heavy-handed visual pun, may be said to pinpoint the film's anxieties about the outworn nature of human, as against computerized, genetics. In an otherwise digressive interlude, the hero attends the concert of a piano virtuoso who throws his Glenn Gould–style white gloves into the audience during the ovation, gloves that the camera discovers have space for six adept fingers each. Filmmakers, one supposes, are among the first to notice that aesthetic technique and its execution have been mutated as well as expanded by the epoch of the *digital.*

14. The evidentiary use of such photo portraiture is rendered obsolete in an even more recent dystopian sci fi film, *Dark City* (Alex Proyas, 1998), eclipsed by the digital manipulations of a panoptic master race. In an updating of the stop-the-world premise from *Paris qui dort,* the plot concerns a future metropolis where each midnight all motion, both organic and mechanical, is suspended so that certain wholesale adjustments to the spatial arrangement of the urban space can be carried out in order to test the cognitive resilience of the human mind. What results is a mélange of architectural transformations whose logic is only that of postmodernism itself, its spatial distortions offering the objective correlative, as one of the alien operatives explains, of "stolen memories, different eras, all rolled into one." The computer visuals that permit such metamorphoses are then placed in direct opposition to an older photomechanical technology. With their obvious evocation of the cyborg's faked photographic prehistory in *Blade Runner,* the several scenes of family photos and slides that punctuate the hero's slow realization of his own concocted subjectivity in *Dark City* emblematize more than the superannuation of human consciousness by the invasive mediation of the Strangers. They mark further, by a double technical estrangement, the outmoding not just of photography by the simulacral mock-up, but of cinema, from within itself, by computerized encroachments of every description.

15. Steven Spielberg, *Close Encounters of the Third Kind* (New York: Delacorte, 1977), 251.

16. Distribution history records an accident of technological accommodation that results in an almost equally modernist "alienation effect" of the human body in death. As filmed by Wise for the Panavision screen, the right half of the image, as we see, resembles the opening credits of *Proof* (chapter 2). When reedited for video release in nonletterboxed TV format, shots of the reconnaissance team are intercut with full-screen versions of the photographed corpses as if they were freeze-frames, comparably stark and denaturalized.

CHAPTER SIX

1. Even with a trend, it's never over till it's over. About half a decade ago I was commissioned by an interdisciplinary journal to think about the recent flurry of Victorian studies on-screen. See Garrett Stewart, "Film's Victorian Retrofit," *Victorian Studies* 38, no. 2 (1995): 153-98, which involves a fuller discussion of several films treated here. Since

then, the Austen boom. And in the wake of that concerted literary raid, a return to late nineteenth-century topics in three novelistic adaptations released late in 1996—under titles by turns truncated (*Jude*), ponderously overexplicit (*Joseph Conrad's "The Secret Agent"*), or more gracefully canonical (*The Portrait of a Lady*). What might it all (still) mean? The time has come to think again, since both the thematics and the mechanics of photography have leaped to minor technological prominence once more by the return to the latter end of the nineteenth century. Since then, too, the tail end of the James revival. *Washington Square* (Agnieszka Holland, 1997), by being in the first place a novel of the recent past, is set before the age of photography, so it is only a painted rather than a daguerreotype portrait of Dr. Sloper's dead wife that remains to "give her presence" in his world. By contrast, *The Wings of the Dove* (Iain Softley, 1997) is updated further beyond the first decade of cinema with no effort to capture, any more than in James himself, this new technological spirit of the age. Steeped in cinema's photographic prehistory, however, the most recent of the retro films, *The Governess* (Sandra Goldbacher, 1999), imagines a mid-Victorian Jewish woman assisting a British lord in beating "Monsieur Daguerre" to the punch with a fixative capable of retaining light's graphic traces after their first impression on paper. But against the Anglo male inventor's staid sense of the new medium's neutral recording capacities, the heroine's own flair for eroticism and melodrama leads her to a separate commercial practice in portraits and staged scenes. That this should be taken to anticipate the later cinematic institution seems emphasized by the film's deployment, for its penultimate shot and at intervals throughout, not of a freeze-frame at the moment of mechanical capture but of a prolonged moving-image closeup meant to register, over the course of primitive exposure time, the reined-in play of emotions across the performative surface of the human face.

2. For the mostly pejorative sense of this genre designation, though with no particular emphasis on its mediating technology, see Andrew Higdon, "The Heritage Film and British Cinema," in *Dissolving Views: Key Writings on British Cinema*, ed. Andrew Higdon (London: Cassell, 1996), 232-48.

3. Thomas Hardy, *Tess of the D'Urbervilles*, ed. Scott Elledge (New York: Norton, 1979), 105, Hardy's phrase in 1891 for the "feelings . . . of the age."

4. See Sergei Eisenstein, "Dickens, Griffith, and the Film Today," in Eisenstein, *Film Form: Essays in Film Theory*, ed. Jay Leyda (New York: Harcourt Brace, 1949), 198-99.

5. There could scarcely be a clearer instance of what Peter Brooks examines throughout *Body Work: Objects of Desire in Narrative* (Cambridge: Harvard University Press, 1994) as the conversion of the scopophilic into the epistemophilic impulse, inscribing the erotic gaze into a whole plotline of disclosed carnal knowledge.

6. We may now sense a larger point to an otherwise distracting bit of business earlier in the plot: the fact that his dress suit (his rented costume) seems to one of the fashionable Edwardian hotel guests "at least ten years out of date." As if wearing the retrograde nature of his more than monogamous, his deathless, passion on his sleeve, the atavistic romantic hero is, in short, even more Victorian than the world it kills him to leave.

7. See "Outside the Whale" in Salman Rushdie's *Imaginary Homelands: Essays and Criticism, 1981-1991* (London: Granta, 1991), 87-106, where he discusses such films as *A Passage to India* and *Gandhi* along with TV productions like *The Jewel in the Crown* and *The Far Pavilions* as "Raj fiction" characterized by "the zombie-like revival of the defunct Empire" (101). Toward a similar end, the sentimental cover story of *The Secret Garden* returns an orphaned child from her upbringing in colonial India to the crumbling British castle of her aristocratic uncle, where she sets about weeding and seeding its garden even as she helps restore her withered stripling cousin, Colin, languishing in bed for years under the shadow of death, who is ready for his first steps by the film's climax. The colonial apologetic is unmistakable. Mary's imperium-schooled imperiousness prepares her for the barely disguised na-

tionalist task at hand: to restore the degenerated status quo. The tone of command she has learned in dealing haughtily with subalterns, that is, allows her both to hector her cousin into shape and to encourage aristocratic command in his own dealings with servants (to turn him into "a little Raj"). By such learned techniques of subordination, the heroine thus aids in rehabilitating the native patrilinear continuities of British lord and legatee.

8. The effect cuts as close to the allusive bone as does the black leader at the center of *Apocalypse Now* (chapter 1, note 40) as an intertextual operator of darkness's own heart. About the place of Forster's own prose in a "closet modernism" of quasi-cinematic disjunctures and forced connections, I will have more to say, via Jameson, in the coming chapter.

9. Edith Wharton, *The Age of Innocence* (New York: Collier, 1986), 6:44.

10. In the novel it is instead "his first photograph of May . . . in the Mission garden" (4:347-48) that offers in itself an icon of her fixity, her invulnerability to change: "And as he had seen her that day, so she had remained" (348).

11. See especially his emphasis on the lap dissolve as a "figuration" derived from the Freudian processes of "condensation and displacement" in Christian Metz, *The Imaginary Signifier: Psychoanalysis and the Cinema,* trans. Celia Britton, Annwyl Williams, Ben Brewster, and Alfred Guzzetti (Bloomington: Indiana University Press, 1982), 274-80. In "Specularity and Engulfment: Francis Ford Coppola and *Bram Stoker's Dracula,*" in *Contemporary Hollywood Cinema,* ed. Steve Neale and Murray Smith (New York: Routledge, 1998): 191-208, Thomas Elsaesser has come at the question of the film's rampant superimposition from a perspective that also historicizes its production, as I do, from a double fin-de-siècle perspective (then and now), locating the film's optic layerings as the "key technical means or figural trope" use to evoke "the pictorialism and representational codes that are the precursors of abstract art, namely symbolist painting, expressionist colour schemes, art nouveau ornament" (202). But Elsaesser also suggests the overlain image as a kind of allegory of the film's own relation to cinema history, the layered and congested scene offering no longer a distanced spectacle but an aesthetics of "engulfment" (203-6). Though Elsaesser places no emphasis on the local photogrammatic substrate of these overlays, superimposition remains for him the chief symptom of that deliberate mix of primitivism and decadence that resists as far as possible—"if we believe the publicity department's assertion" (204)—the substitution of digital for photographic effects. Cinematic to the core, superimposition thus creates, on the "classical/post-classical divide" (196) that his essay sets out to investigate, "an 'authentic pastiche' of the thrusting enthusiasm and craftsmanlike pride associated with the cinema's inventor-bricoleur-pioneers" (204).

12. It is the former aspect, the empathetic transference figured by supernatural agency, that applies in similar ways to the literary metatext of vampire fiction, where the phenomenological engagement with otherness through reading—being more willed and mysterious, less mechanized, than in film viewing—would trope even more fully the weird penetrations of vampiric telepathy. See my discussion of Bram Stoker's novel in Garrett Stewart, *Dear Reader: The Conscripted Audience in Nineteenth-Century British Fiction* (Baltimore: Johns Hopkins University Press, 1996), 377-84. In "Specularity and Engulfment," Thomas Elsaesser's equally reflexive stress on Coppola's vampiric text falls less on its mutable photographic materiality and promiscuously inhabited POV and more on its blend of shock associations and hypnotic fascination ("'contamination' . . . involuntary attraction . . . addiction" [204-5]), all connected to its parasitic plundering of film history and its prolongation of the cinephile craving—"because," as he closes, "who does not want the cinema to be the love that never dies?" (206).

13. For a general account of the types of laminated images that characterize Campion's film within the film, see Marc Vernet's chapter on superimpositions, which he calls "surimpressions" as if to suggest their links with surrealism, in *Figures of Absence* (Paris: Editions de l'Etoile, 1988), 59-88.

14. In a second consideration of this film in his regular column, Stuart Klawans is struck by the blocked erotic possibilities of the same double anachronism in the film within the film. See *"The Portrait of a Lady," Nation,* 3 February 1997, 36.

15. This indirectly self-ratifying drift in the technology of cinematic backcast reaches its reductionist apogee in *Across the Sea of Time,* where the merchandise mart in the Lincoln Square lobby only confirms our sense that when the young boy's stereo pictures are stolen from him by Central Park vandals and his viewer smashed beyond repair—a truly shocking plot turn by any measure of empathy—we have Sony alone to thank for the preservation of these treasures, before us now on-screen and well into the fiscal future.

16. I allude here to Roman Jakobson's famous definition of the poetic function, as taken up in chapter 5, a function that "projects the principle of equivalence from the axis of selection into the axis of combination." See Jakobson, "Linguistics and Poetics," in *Essays on the Language of Literature,* ed. Seymour Chatman and Samuel R. Levin (Boston: Houghton Mifflin, 1967), 303. In the James example, the oppressive poetry of the lexical overlay is a momentary disturbance in selection that gets sorted out by the subsequent logic of syntactic combination.

17. On early cinema's relation to such predecessor thrills as carnival trickery and spiritualist photography, see Tom Gunning, "The Cinema of Attractions: Early Cinema, Its Spectator and the Avant-Garde," in *Early Cinema: Space, Frame, Narrative,* ed. Thomas Elsaesser (London: BFI, 1990), 56-62, as well as Gunning, "Phantom Images and Modern Manifestations: Spirit Photography, Magic Theater, Trick Films, and Photography's Uncanny," in *Fugitive Images: From Photography to Video,* ed. Patrice Petro (Bloomington: Indiana University Press, 1995), 42-71. See also Joss Lutz Marsh, "In a Glass Darkly: Photography, the Pre-modern, and Victorian Horror," in *Prehistories of the Future: The Primitivist Project and the Culture of Modernism,* ed. Elazar Barkan and Ronald Bush (Stanford: Stanford University Press, 1995).

18. This is a dimension of the novel recently surveyed by Jennifer Green-Lewis in *Framing the Victorians: Photography and the Culture of Realism* (Ithaca: Cornell University Press, 1996), 85-88. In brief preparation for the marked ocular deviances of the film, what I would add to her tabulation of the novel's exchanged photographs is their consistent role in the transferences and effacements of self-image. The syndrome begins when Jude burns the wedding-day photograph of himself once he discovers that his wife, Arabella, has left it behind in its auctioned-off frame after their separation. Jude happens upon it in a broker's shop as the last enumerated item in a random miscellany, preceded in this ad hoc inventory by a "swing looking-glass." The framed plane of his own image has a reverse face as well: "On the back was still be read, '*Jude to Arabella,*' with the date" (Thomas Hardy, *Jude the Obscure,* ed. Norman Page [New York: Norton, 1978], 1, 2:61). This is the mirror image of a self no longer the object of any "tender sentiment," for the nuptial identity it portrays has suffered, like Arabella's feelings for him, an "utter death" (61). All that is required is cremation, so he "paid the shilling, took the photograph away with him, and burnt it, frame and all" (61). But with this self-image and its stabilizing frame removed, a paragraph later he finds that he "could not realize himself" (61)—either recognize or effectuate a cogent being in the aftermath of the relationship. Much later, after an inconclusive interview with Sue, Jude passes by her room to discover that she has not drawn the curtains. He is therefore able to see her looking at an image lifted from her workbox: "Whose photograph was she looking at? . . . He had once given her his; but she had others, he knew. Yet it was his surely?" (4, 1:164). As if indistinct to himself except in the eyes of the other at this point, he wants confirmation of her sympathy. Such is the dependent relay of his displaced self-scrutiny, and it replays his own retroactive urge in an earlier scene, without photographic prompting, when he "looked back at himself along the vista of his past years" (2, 6:94). After his looking on at Sue's indeter-

minate looking, there is no further mention of his photographic image until Arabella's return at the Agricultural Fair, and her recognition of Jude there, is marked by the reduction of his recorded image to mere evidentiary document in her goading of her husband Cartlett: "Don't you recognize the man. . . .Not from the photos I have showed you" (5, 5:230). Despite the auctioned wedding picture, she has apparently stashed away some images after all. But they do Jude no good now. With self-realization no longer possible, all recognition is that of others—or of himself as his own other, as captured in its own way by the film's last shot.

19. Stanley Cavell, *The World Viewed: Reflections on the Ontology of Film,* enlarged ed. (Cambridge: Harvard University Press, 1979), 38.

20. On the relation of Hitchcock's explosive cinematographic technique to the underlying aesthetic of his early period, see Mark Wollaeger's "Killing Stevie: Modernity, Modernism, and Mastery in Conrad and Hitchcock," *Modern Language Quarterly* 58, no. 3 (1997): 323-50, where the montage treatment of Stevie's death (340-47) is aligned in passing with the same year's *Modern Times* (346, 347) and the mechanistic modernism of the very scene (Chaplin in the cogs of cinematographic as well as industrial progress) I discuss in my coda below. (Wollaeger's essay was written before Hampton's film version of the Conrad novel had appeared.)

21. Walter Benjamin, "The Work of Art in the Age of Mechanical Reproduction," in *Illuminations,* ed. Hannah Arendt, trans. Harry Zohn (New York: Schocken, 1969), 238.

22. The same hoax photograph forms the centerpiece as well of the recent *Fairy Tale: A True Story* (Charles Sturridge, 1997), where its authenticity is debated by Doyle (who loves any form of detection) and his friend Harry Houdini (who hates any competition for an astonishment that would not accrue strictly to human ingenuity). Unlike *Photographing Fairies,* however, this film never calls the history of cinema to mind through its own foregrounded screen devices.

23. I quote from Tom Gunning's "New Thresholds of Vision: Instantaneous Photography and the Early Cinema of Lumière," in *Impossible Presence: Surface and Screen in the Photogenic Era,* ed. Terry Smith, Power Institute Series 2 (Sydney: Power Institute of Art, University of Sydney, forthcoming), an argument based on a lecture given at the University of Iowa in December 1997, titled "A Mischievous and Knowing Gaze: The Lumière Company and the Culture of Amateur Photography."

24. Paul Virilio, *War and Cinema: The Logistics of Perception,* trans. Patrick Camiller (London: Verso, 1989), 36.

CHAPTER SEVEN

1. For Bordwell's definition, see introduction, note 9. Note also how completely, in that spluttering, all but splattered, close-up, the correlated aspects of Deleuze's movement-image—perception, action, and affection—cave in upon each other in overload and cancellation, extruding as a result the instantaneous negative imprint of a time-image.

2. Hollis Frampton, *Circles of Confusion—Film, Photography, Video: Texts, 1968-1980* (Rochester, N.Y.: Visual Studies Workshop Press, 1983), 8. Shedding vocalization, the historical advance of writing was in fact, for Frampton, a return to its specular roots. This is because all writing, long after its pictographic phase, must still "be understood to harbor as its progenitor the dark repletion of the image" (9), what Frampton further terms "the opening montage of our own ancestral alphabet" (9)—as given in the title to his foreword: "Ox House Camel Rivermouth" (7). To recall that the opening word of *Finnegans Wake* is the fluxional elision of "riverrun" should be a way of hearing Joyce tap the primitive hieroglyphics of the sign function in a new phase of mimesis as textual self-mime, where the riving and the running on are syllabic rather than cartographic alternatives. (More to come on this Joycean channel; stay tuned.)

3. Frampton's argument is to find historical qualification in the later thinking of Friedrich Kittler, *Discourse Networks 1800/1900*, trans. Michael Metteer with Chris Cullens (Stanford: Stanford University Press, 1990), for whom silent reading once anchored the signified image in the myth of a transcendent vocal origin. Kittler's point is that cinema and other technologies of discursive storage and dissemination—as media rather than communication—arrive to break the stranglehold of an alphabetized orality in Western culture. This was the regime of a mystified organic picturing where "poetry could let its film roll"—in a continuous "leap into pure signifieds" (166). For Kittler, phonography later mechanizes the formerly privileged vocal register of writing, while photographs in motion automatize the referent of description, severing it irreversibly from all dependence on a sounded mark. Borrowing terms from Lacan and Metz, Kittler finds that cinema as medium thus arose to separate off the former "imaginary" of symbolic writing from the immanence of a now segmentally analyzed voice (the rise of empirical phonetics over phonology). "The real of speaking took place in the gramophone; the imaginary produced in speaking or writing belonged to film" (246). Kittler goes on to note that literature responded to this "triumphant competition" (247) in part by retreating into the graphic insistence of a no longer voiced utterance in the new typographic prominence of modernist "letters." But what his analysis underplays is exactly what this chapter is meant to put forward: the equivalent mobilization of film's materiality, both constitutive of its function and maximized by its own modernism. This is a segmental seriality that not only sustains cinema's visual data but returns against the discursive grain as the filmic "noise" Kittler elsewhere finds inherent in the channels of any medium (always subtending its message). To this extent, whereas phonography denatures the former signifier of alphabetic language, photographic media denature the signified.

4. See Garrett Stewart, *Reading Voices: Literature and the Phonotext* (Berkeley: University of California Press, 1990), 19-20, as well as the frontispiece illustrating a medieval manuscript before the custom of word breaks had been introduced. Some of the articles of medieval textual research by Paul Saenger that I was drawing on in my 1990 book have since been collected in Saenger, *Space between Words: The Origins of Silent Reading* (Stanford: Stanford University Press, 1997), where his "paradoxical" historical point that "*scriptura continua*" (10) persisted in Roman practice even while the introduction of vowels was assisting lexical discrimination has a parallel in the modernist phonemic "continuum" sometimes released beneath the fully established system of word breaks.

5. Fox Talbot's essay "A Brief Historical Sketch of the Invention of the Art," the original introduction to the 1844-46 portfolio of his prints published in London under the title *The Pencil of Nature,* is reprinted in Alan Trachtenberg, ed., *Classic Essays on Photography* (New Haven, Conn.: Leet's Island Books, 1980), 27-36. Without evoking the actual inscriptive impression on the celluloid strip, Alexandre Astruc provided the seminal metaphor for the New Wave's scripture of the image in his essay "The Birth of a New Avant-Garde: La Camera-Stylo," *Ecran Français* 144 (30 March 1948): 5, rpt. in Peter Graham, ed., *The New Wave* (New York: Doubleday, 1969).

6. Roland Barthes, *S/Z: An Essay,* trans. Richard Miller (New York: Hill and Wang, 1974), 56.

7. This is a constitutive possibility of their phonemic accretion at the primary level. Take a flamboyant example from the folksy courtroom wit of John Ford's *Young Mr. Lincoln* (1939). As reiterated punningly by Honest Abe, unless the name of the witness "Jack Cass" could be misheard (misread) as "jackass," even on paper, by the inner ear of silent (as much as oral) processing, it would never have been possible to construct in the first place, upon the flexible combinatory principles of alphabetic writing, the names of man or beast.

8. Paul Virilio, *War and Cinema: The Logistics of Perception,* trans. Patrick Camiller (1983; London: Verso, 1989), 4. In his book of three years before, we see the theoretical origins for his combined mechanics and aesthetics of speed (*The Aesthetics of Disappearance,*

trans. Philip Beitchman [1980; New York: Semiotext(e), 1991]). Beginning with the biological "lapse" or syncope, where "conscious time," briefly interrupted, "comes together again automatically" (9), Virilio calls this "'picnolepsy' (from the Greek, *picnos:* frequency)" (10). He later relates this subsuming of the dead spot, the lost interval, to the development of "the cinematic accelerator" (53) out of Marey's chronophotography, since in each medium "the aesthetics of disappearance renews the enterprise of appearance" (52).

9. This supplemental process calls up Derrida's notion of the *hymen* or "double fold" of meaning, the breaking crease between words that is also a flange, a contingent hinge. The hymeneal ligature between lexemes, ordinarily marked by the white space as *blanc,* draws its power for Derrida from its etymological paradox of both prevention and wedding, membrane and embrace, edge and merger, veil and penetration. See Jacques Derrida, "The Double Session," in *Disseminations,* trans. Barbara Johnson (Chicago: University of Chicago Press, 1981), 173-285, where he speaks of "the blank as a blank *between* the valences, a hymen that unites and differentiates them in the series" (252).

10. Though many of Kittler's remarks in this vein remain unpublished in translation and are cited from a series of seminars he gave at the University of California, Santa Barbara, in 1987, his sense that the "general digitalization of information and channels erases the difference between individual media" (102) is historically fleshed out in "Gramophone, Film, Typewriter," *October* 41 (summer 1987): 101-18.

11. As we saw with Paul Virilio's closing trope of scan-and-freeze ballistics in chapter 3, the sense of war as a modern *medium*—a high-speed and long-distance imaging system—obtains all the more in an electronic epoch, which permits a closing of the gap between sighted and obliterated target through the supersonic "projection" of a retaliatory missile. Detonation as well as surveillance is now a postocular technology of digitally controlled mediation.

12. André Malraux, *The Voices of Silence,* trans. Stuart Gilbert (Garden City, N.Y.: Doubleday, 1953), 13-130.

13. Frampton, *Circles of Confusion,* 196.

14. See the various modalities of collision in Sergei Eisenstein, "A Dialectic Approach to Film Form," in *Film Theory and Criticism: Introductory Readings,* 2d ed., ed. Gerald Mast and Marshall Cohen (New York: Oxford University Press, 1979), 101-22.

15. They thus measure the definitive phenomenological arc of screen scale according to Stanley Cavell's view of film's viewed world, with camera access "limited by the smallness of the object it can grasp only by the state of its technology, and in largeness only by the span of the world." See Cavell, *The World Viewed: Reflections on the Ontology of Film* (New York: Viking, 1971), 25. In connection with microphotography rather than film, Nilsson's name is evoked in passing by Donna Haraway in developing her thesis about the cybernetic colonization of the organic body. In *Simians, Cyborgs, and Women: The Reinvention of Nature* (New York: Routledge, 1991), she notes as postmodern symptom of high-tech imaging the attempted "fraternal relation of inner and outer space" (222), mentioning the link in the 1987 centenary volume of *National Geographic* between high-gloss photographs of astronauts in orbit and the last chapter in that volume, called "Inner Space," which includes Nilsson's luminous biomedical images (222).

16. Jean-Louis Baudry, "Ideological Effects of the Basic Cinematographic Apparatus," in *Narrative, Apparatus, Ideology: A Film Theory Reader,* ed. Phil Rosen (New York: Columbia University Press, 1986).

17. Gilles Deleuze, *The Movement-Image,* vol. 1. of *Cinema,* trans. Hugh Tomlinson and Barbara Habberjam (Minneapolis: University of Minnesota Press, 1986-89), 4.

18. Thomas Pynchon, *Gravity's Rainbow* (New York: Viking, 1973), 407. This notion is borne out in closure when a movie theater's suddenly blank screen, just after a single last frame "too immediate for any eye to register," coincides with a falling rocket's "last im-

measurable gap above the roof of this old theater, the last delta-t" (760). To keep the record straight on cinema's intervallic prototypes, however, it bears noting that there is what we might call a different axis of the perceptual "interval" eventually given more prominence in Deleuze: not the periodic difference between separate positionalities of matter in motion but the gap opened in consciousness, often at right angles to the trajectory of motion, by the necessity of its registration. The interval under this description has become more a subjective apprehension than an objective period, has come indeed to delimit "affection" as the third avatar of subjectivity (along with "perception" and "action") in Deleuze's triad. It is to this sense of interval that D. N. Rodowick, *Gilles Deleuze's Time Machine* (Durham, N.C.: Duke University Press, 1997), gives primary attention when he writes about the passage from pure perception to the perception-image. Such a passage marks the divergence "between absolute movement and the interval as movement in relation to a center of indetermination" (57)—in other words, to a center of unstabilized perception for which movement "is always constituted as an interval opened on one side as movement received and closed on the other as a movement executed" (57).

19. Roman Jakobson and Linda R. Waugh, *The Sound Shape of Language*, 2d ed. (Berlin: Mouton de Gruyter, 1987), 181.

20. Jameson's remarks on Forster are followed by a quite different treatment of Joyce's *Ulysses* in "Modernism and Imperialism," in *Nationalism, Colonialism, and Literature*, ed. Terry Eagleton (Minneapolis: University of Minnesota Press, 1990), 43-66. Jameson altogether exempts the combinatory linguistic apparatus of Joycean writing after *Portrait* from the precincts of style, which had become "an absolute category of the modern canon" (61). He thus finds Joyce leaping "over the stage of modernism into full postmodernism" (62). Style in this outmoded sense—the sense chronologically parodied by Joyce in *Ulysses*—is a "category of some absolute subject" (61), so that it can in fact be historically situated and demystified. But this seems to contradict Jameson's earlier emphasis, to be discussed below, on the disjoining of high modernist style, as tentatively deployed by Forster, from "conventional notions . . . of subjectivity" (53). Without caviling over the term "style," what exceeds the normal range of authorial voicing in the machinations of Forsterian syllabic play, we will find, makes connection with Joyce at the level of an *écriture* that can never be successfully folded back into absolute expressivity. For an account of Joycean writing as it more nearly straddles the modern/postmodern divide, see my "'An Earsighted View': Joyce's Modality of the Audible," in Stewart, *Reading Voices*, 232-58.

21. Another metatechnological history of modernism, advanced by Hugh Kenner, aligns various stylistic devices of the major modernists with correlative developments in recording, transmission, transport, and computational technology. Eliot and the telephone, Pound and the typewriter, Joyce and the commuter tram, Beckett and the arithmetical permutations of the primitive calculator/computer: these are the extraliterary cultural affiliations at the root of modernist verbal praxis in Kenner's *The Mechanic Muse* (New York: Oxford University Press, 1987). Add to these, as Kenner doesn't, a conjunction like Proust and photography to instance a fixational sublime and subsume them all to cinema as a communicative link between separate perceptual and temporal loci, and you have cinema emerging (as it does not for Kenner) as the master trope of modernism's new regime of cognitive orchestration and displacement.

22. This is the term put into circulation by the influential work of Tom Gunning. See, for instance, "An Unseen Energy Swallows Space: The Space in Early Film and Its Relation to American Avant-Garde Film," in *Film before Griffith*, ed. John Fell (Berkeley: University of California Press, 1983), 355-66.

23. I refer to the critique of Jameson in Michael Walsh, "Jameson and Global Aesthetics," in *Post-theory: Reconstructing Film Studies*, ed. David Bordwell and Noël Carroll (Madison: University of Wisconsin Press, 1996), 492-93.

24. Fredric Jameson, *The Political Unconscious: Narrative as a Socially Symbolic Act* (Ithaca: Cornell University Press, 1981), 206, where Conrad's unclassifiable genius depends on his "reclaiming great areas of diversion and distraction by the most demanding practices of style and *écriture* alike, floating uncertainly in between Proust and Robert Louis Stevenson." My own sense of Conrad's writing effects would find them operating deliberately to press style *over into* the logic of *écriture*, confounding at this level as well the difference between subjective and objective text production.

25. On the verse tradition of apostrophic invocation and the vexed subjectivity it tends to index, see Jonathan Culler, "Apostrophe," in *The Pursuit of Signs: Semiotics, Literature, Deconstruction* (Ithaca: Cornell University Press, 1981), 135-54.

26. Quotations are from James Joyce, *Finnegans Wake* (Harmondsworth, Eng.: Penguin, 1976).

27. Charles Davies and William G. Peck, *Mathematical Dictionary and Cyclopedia of Mathematical Science* (New York: Barnes, 1983), 81.

28. This and subsequent quotations by chapter and page are from the Penguin edition (Harmondsworth, Eng., 1984).

29. Terry Eagleton places more emphasis on Stevie's drawing than on his stammering (whose precise lexical confusion is not explored). The defective speech is seen thematized as the modern self silenced by ideological contradiction, whereas the drawing is seen textualized as evincing the boy's role as "mad artist" of the novel, transmitting its irresolvable status as text. See "Form, Ideology, and *The Secret Agent*," in *Against the Grain: Essays, 1975-1985* (London: Verso, 1986), 23-32.

30. I take this level of graphonic (graph/phonic) emphasis to corroborate Michael Fried's views of graphic and lexigraphic patterning in *The Secret Agent*—as evidence of the novel's radically materialist account of the world as well as its representations. (I refer here to an unpublished lecture given in March 1997 at the University of Iowa, to be included in his book in progress on literary impressionism, *Almayer's Face*.) For the materiality of language, I would add, inheres as much in its phonic provocations as in its anagrammatic permutations. More specifically, my sense of Stevie's verbal and graphic habits as collaborating in unsettled relation to Conrad's craft may be found to complement Fried's emphasis, following Leavis, on Decoud as an authorial surrogate in *Nostromo*. See Fried, "Almayer's Face: On 'Impressionism' in Conrad, Crane, and Norris," *Critical Inquiry* 17, no. 1 (1990): 229. Decoud's fixation just before death on the synesthetic reification of silence as a visible "cord" (rather than chord) that he yearns to hear snap before he dies finds its scriptive equivalent in the taut pull of words against one another in the disrupted lineation of internal echo. This happens when the negated recurrence of Decoud's mental state ("he felt no remorse") takes anatomical form a page later, his legs obeying his last wish before suicide in the flickering elision of "without *t*remor." Thus, in the very execution of *écriture*, can silence not only become visible in scriptive rifts but snap under pressure of reading's own intensifications. As regards *The Secret Agent*, I have mentioned elsewhere the "roulette spin of contingent syllabification" in the sentence that marks Winnie Verloc's successful knife thrust between her husband's ribs: "Hazard has such accuracies" (Stewart, *Reading Voices*, 220). At such a moment, too, the undecidable tension between necessity and volition so powerfully adduced by Fried's sense of this materialist novel seems driven to the internal limit of a single compacted echoism.

31. This too would be related to Conrad's sense in the "Author's Note" that in his concentrated imaginative investment while writing the novel he was "an extreme revolutionist" (Penguin ed., 42), more purposefully radical than any of the anarchists whose aimless schemings he detailed.

32. Charles Dickens, *Dombey and Son* (Harmondsworth, Eng.: Penguin, 1970), 20:354.

33. For comparison of a Dickensian passage explicitly about sonic oscillation in *Little Dorrit* to Emily Dickinson's great poem of the forlorn interval, "To Fill a Gap," see the more

extended treatment of nineteenth-century stylistic differentials in connection with the flutter of film projection in Garrett Stewart, "Cinécriture: Modernism's Flicker Effect," *New Literary History* 29, no. 4 (1998): 750.

34. Geoffrey Hartman, "The Voice of the Shuttle: Language form the Point of View of Literature," in *Beyond Formalism: Literary Essays, 1958-1970* (New Haven: Yale University Press, 1970), 348.

35. Thomas H. Johnson, ed., *The Poems of Emily Dickinson* (Cambridge: Harvard University Press, 1955), 2:447-48. If, given the dead metaphor of "lap," a hint of "lick" is detected in "like," it is confirmed by the second line's "And lick the Valleys up—." Further on, in a metaphoric predicate meant to mark the railroad's aggressive denaturalization of forest sounds (owls hoot, not trains), we hear of the locomotive's "horrid—hooting stanza." There, Dickinson's signature dash is deliberately unable to wedge the utterance open far enough to prevent its cross-lexical reversion (via the displaced dental sound) to the clichéd "d/tooting" that the phrase, at first *sight*, seemed animistically to evade. Instead, the exposure time of reading has yet again licked the lexical valley up.

36. See Lauren Rabinovitz, "From *Hale's Tours* to *Star Tours*: Virtual Voyages and the Delirium of the Hyper-Real," *Iris* 25 (spring 1998): 133-52.

37. Wolfgang Schivelbusch, *The Railway Journey: The Industrialization of Time and Space in the Nineteenth Century* (Berkeley: University of California Press, 1977).

38. Within Lynne Kirby's two paradigms, cultural and perceptual, for the railroad as historical precondition of cinematic acceptance—having to do with social (and gendered) legitimation and ocular cognition respectively (see Kirby, *Parallel Tracks: The Railroad and Silent Cinema* [Durham, N.C.: Duke University Press, 1997], 6-10)—I have been expanding here on the aspect of "shock" as well as of temporal reorientation in the second. Such is the destabilizing force of cinema naturalized by early narrative production and then released again in the 1920s by such directors as Gance, Clair, and Vertov, for whom the racing locomotive—as tool of modernity but emblem of modernism—was deployed as "a terrifying vehicle of speed and a dynamic technology capable of representing film's own power" (8).

39. François Dagognet, *Etienne-Jules Marey: A Passion for the Trace*, trans. Robert Galeta with Jeanine Herman (New York: Zone, 1992), 140-51.

40. Dagognet, *Etienne-Jules Marey*, 60-62. See a fuller discussion of the phonoscope in Marta Braun, *Picturing Time: the Work of Etienne-Jules Marey (1830-1904)* (Chicago: University of Chicago Press, 1992), where the *London Globe* of 1892 is cited for its fantasy of inscribed optical enunciation: "How nice to be able to send your enemy your photograph, on which he may be able to read, without bringing an action for libel, your opinion of his conduct and personal appearance" (182). My own point is that the motion picture, and long before sound synchronization, achieved this inventive leap by its own different but related brand of sequential (and imperceptible) *articulation*.

41. Jacques-Alain Miller, "Suture (Elements of the Logic of the Signifier)," trans. Colin MacCabe, *Screen* 18 (winter 1977-78): 34.

42. This continuity is also made possible by the "critical flicker fusion" as explained by David Bordwell and Kristin Thompson, *Film Art: An Introduction* (New York: McGraw-Hill, 1990). Persistence of vision is a phenomenon also aligned by Jonathan Crary—in full view of the debates around it—with the studies of retinal afterimages that help inflect the discourse of subjective vision in the prehistory of cinema (Crary, *Techniques of the Observer: On Vision and Modernity in the Nineteenth Century* [Cambridge: MIT Press, 1990], 102-7).

43. John Mowitt, *Text: The Genealogy of an Antidisciplinary Object* (Durham, N.C.: Duke University Press, 1992), 170.

44. For this term, see Marie-Claire Ropars-Wuilleumier, "The Graphic in Filmic Writing: *A Bout de Souffle,* or The Erratic Alphabet," *Enclitic* 5-6 (1982): 147, 158.

45. See also Marie-Claire Ropars-Wuilleumier, "Film Reader of the Text," *Diacritics* 15 (1985): 18-36, where the concern of her analyses is with "multiple circuits, both heterogeneous and simultaneous" (26). In a parallel reading of a novel by Maurice Blanchot and a film by Alain Resnais, Ropars claims to have "pushed the deconstruction of the sign by the overlapping of letters to its most vertiginous point" (26). She does so, for instance, through the byplay latent in Blanchot's *L'arrêt du mort* on the proper noun "Louise" (with its hidden "oui") and the pronoun smuggled into the enunciation "ote elle" (26). When Ropars takes up a similar impaction of syllabic matter in "Nevers," a town in the remembered past of the heroine in *Hiroshima mon amour,* the place-name is found overlain in context with, among other monosyllabic infratexts, *verre* (glass), *vers* (toward) and *vert* (green). Her analytic "process of unbinding" is thereby directed upon "the intertangling and reciprocal disintegration of the elements where meaning is undone" (30).

46. What breaks into language or discourse from sheer verbality, according to Foucault, corresponds in part to what disperses the cinematic image in its tactical reversion to the differential track, the return of cinema toward film. We can make this observation a good deal more specific merely by quoting, albeit from a difficult passage in the closing section of *The Order of Things.* What Foucault sees as the fourfold assault against humanist subjectivity mounted by the modernist return of the letter within the sign, of the verbal signifier within the signified, would find direct cinematic equivalence in the uncertain suppression of the mechanized fragment behind the sustained image. Once modernist literature "posited itself as experience," an event in itself rather than a tool of representation, it did so four times over: "as experience of death (and in the element of death), of unthinkable thought (and in its inaccessible presence), of repetition (of original innocence, always there at the earliest and yet always the most distant limit of language); as experience of finitude (trapped in the opening and the tyranny of that finitude)." At this late point in our discussion, and despite the daunting abstraction of Foucault's summary, correlation comes easily. We can readily replay Foucault's quartet of proposals in our own terms for the plasticity and differential fixities of the filmic strip. *Death* is materialized in the element of the lifeless. *Thought* (imaging) emerges from the otherness of the "unthinkable" (in the sense of the strictly material as well as the unconscious). *Repetition* is disclosed as both foundation and limit case of enchained signification in the "innocence" and candor of its plastic form. *Finitude* of the bounded unit (the photogram) becomes an opening out that is also an end point. So, respectively, might we picture the graduated segment on the track, in concert with its machinated next in line, as it (1) overcomes death, (2) generates cognizable action, (3) resists the sudden return of the strict duplicate (or succumbs to it in frozen motion), and hence (4) finesses its repetitive finitude by the play of difference. I cannot forbear to add, in view of my cross-media extension of Foucault's emphasis on the pulverized signifier, that in one of those inspiriting accidents of computer spell-checking, "finitude" comes up queried on my program as "phonated" (?) The answer is yes.

47. The phrase "hieroglyphic interpretation of cinema" is quoted in English by Mowitt, *Text,* 171, from Marie-Claire Ropars-Wuilleumier, *Le texte divisé* (Paris: Presses Universitaires de France, 1981), 73.

48. Eisenstein, "Dialectic Approach to Film Form, ," 105.

49. Jacques Derrida, *Of Grammatology,* trans. Gayatri Chakravorty Spivak (Baltimore: Johns Hopkins University Press, 1974), 117.

50. At issue here is of course not the instance but the principle. It doesn't matter for my argument that any given film text (whether by Marker or Godard) indulges in lexically erosive wordplay, but it is central that all films perform something like the cinematic coun-

terpart of this frictional byplay in the confounding (as well as foundational) overlap of simultaneity upon succession. Other sorts of wordplay, etymological rather than phonological, can thus be extracted for other thematic purposes from Marker's—or any—scriptive node. For Joan Copjec's psychoanalytic reading of *La jetée*, included in "Vampires, Breast-Feeding, and Anxiety," *October* 58 (fall 1991): 36-38, in which the plot turns on the hero's psychotic incapacity to disengage from the libidinal cathexis of an obsessional childhood image, the title thus ironically evokes that throwing-off, that "ejection," that has failed to release him. In my reading, however, the lexical dynamic of the phrasing sustains a multiple self-ejection that removes all priority and therefore all possible exile. What it sustains is exactly that paradox of simultaneous alternatives that, in terms of the plot's time-loop narrative, presents for its spatiotemporal agent an impossible double bind.

51. My thanks to Nataša Ďurovičová for first calling to my mind's ear this instance of the French perfect tense.

52. Such necessarily sequential typography is not meant to falsify, only to clarify. To object that my composite wording is, in vocal effect, mostly one big lumbering and simultaneous pun, rather than a cascade of spaced difference, and thus resistant to cinematic analogy, is to minimize precisely the all but indistinguishable incremental differentiations that the apparently holistic screen image also depends on.

53. This was a phrase Michael Holquist used to characterize my investigation when this essay was read as a conference paper at the University of Aarhus, Denmark, in 1994.

54. Fredric Jameson, *Signatures of the Visible* (New York: Routledge, 1990), 194-97.

55. Lucien Dällenbach, *Le récit spéculaire: Essai sur la mise en abyme* (Paris: Editions de Seuil, 1977), rpt. as *The Mirror in the Text*, trans. Jeremy Whitely with Emma Hughes (Chicago: University of Chicago Press, 1989).

56. Jameson, *Signatures of the Visible*, 197.

57. It is this unforgettable central segment of the film, as the camera watches the hero's eyes rove and flick from one pinioned oversized snapshot to another (anticipating his darting eye moments in close-up at the end as he attempts to follow the imaginary tennis ball of the traveling mimes) that inspires the only inspired moment in Brian de Palma's labored homage to Antonioni. In *Blow Out* (1981) the hero is an "artist" of sound montage working on the cheap for a maker of slasher films. He has accidentally recorded the sounds of a gunshot blowing out the tire of the front-running presidential hopeful and sending him to his death, and he needs to reconstruct the accompanying optical track of the crime. This is made possible when a photographer comes forward who has "accidentally" filmed the crash (a photographer specializing in blackmailing adulterous spouses who is actually in on the assassination plot) and sold his pictures to a national glossy, which reproduces them in sequential frame enlargements. The hero first scissors them up and staples them together into a flip-book, which produces a trial animation effect of the car plunging into the river. He then painstakingly rephotographs each cut frame on a roll of film and has it processed as a film reel. At this point he is able to synchronize his recorded double burst of sound with the split-second lag between a small burst of light from the bushes at roadside and the resultant skid of the tires.

58. Walter Kerr, *The Silent Clowns* (New York: Knopf, 1979), 358. Chaplin as risen demiurge of the organic body has been transmogrified, in Kerr's perfect pun, into "a disoriented but deliriously happy *deus ex machina*" (358). I draw on Kerr for a fuller treatment of Chaplin's modernism in Garrett Stewart, "Modern Hard Times: Chaplin and the Cinema of Self-Reflection," *Critical Inquiry* 3, no. 2 (1976), 295-314.

59. Even the main factory set has been recognized as schematic before Charlie's precipitous descent into the literalized *grind* of the cogwheels. As with that still from Frankenstein's laboratory a few years before Chaplin's film (fig. 217), the main floor of the factory set has been arranged as an unmistakable *mise en abyme* of the industrial construct called

projection, its looming wheels as reels, including the one centered behind the foreman's head as he takes video (in enacted fact, film) instructions from the presidential overseer (fig. 222). But this effect is redoubled—in a way no viewer could have been prepared for—by the generative abyss into which Charlie is suddenly fed headlong.

60. See Henri Bergson's "Laughter," published with George Meredith's "Essay on Comedy," in *Comedy*, ed. Wylie Sypher (Garden City, N.Y.: Doubleday, 1956). *"The attitudes, gestures and movements of the human body are laughable in exact proportion as that body reminds us of a mere machine"* (79), writes Bergson in italics, where his own "in exact proportion" seems deliberately to partake of the rigidity it analyzes. All comedy derives from this principle, to whose variant phrasing Bergson returns with more italics later: "To sum up, then, we have one and the same effect, which assumes ever subtler forms as it passes from the idea of an artificial *mechanization* of the human body, if such an expression is possible, to that of any substitution whatsoever of the artificial for the natural" (90). Not only is the expression "mechanization" doubly permissible in film, but it passes in Chaplin's hands into a kind of tautological reduction of screen comedy to its processional essence in the scene we are considering.

61. Peter Wollen, "Modern Times: Cinema/Americanism/the Robot," in *Raiding the Icebox: Reflections on Twentieth-Century Culture* (Bloomington: Indiana University Press, 1993), 35-71.

62. See my *Reading Voices*, 20-21, on the pitfalls of such "assimilative" misreading.

63. Kenner, *Mechanic Muse*.

64. "Shades of Taylor and his chronophotography of work gestures!" writes Wollen in "Modern Times," suggesting that Benjamin seems "unaware of the fatal concession he was making to 'scientific management' in the Taylorist sense" (53).

65. Quotations here and below from Crane's correspondence about Chaplin appear in Richard Ellmann and Robert O'Clair, eds., *The Norton Anthology of Modern Poetry* (New York: Norton, 1973), 582. With the lexical decentering of "wind deposits," sequential textuality is edging toward what Crane celebrated as early as Chaplin's *The Kid* as the actor's "eccentric, homely" power. Carried over from this minimal syntactic double take in the evocation of the Tramp's signature tatters and gaping pockets, the effect surfaces again in the skewed or slant wording of the next stanza's "warm torn elbow coverts." Just as a self-exampling randomness of phonemic contiguity—as its own quirky solace—has sprung a momentary transformation of "wind de" into "windy," here a subvocal dialectic flashes into earshot by generating a third term born on the run by the conflation of "warm" and "torn" into their probable narrative cause: the almost unavoidable "worn." In a third instance of verse's silent but subvocalized mime, there is the transfigurative image of the last stanza, where we are all asked to remember seeing "The moon in lonely alleys make / A *grail of laughter of* an empty ash can." Converting the redoubled thud of the *ofs* from awkwardness to levity, we hear the earliest ripple and swell of *"laugh*ter" in the off-rhyme "grail *of*." First a slippage, then a fusion, now a hiccup in the wavering phonemic flow: all gestures toward the words that aren't there, or there yet, in this jaunty balletic spree of phrasing.

66. Given in translation by Susan Buck-Morss, *The Dialectics of Seeing: Walter Benjamin and the Arcades Project* (Cambridge: MIT Press, 1989), 268-69. In an essay that makes more of the centrality of these effects to Benjamin's sense of language, Werner Hamacher, "The Word *Wolke*—If It Is One," *STCL* 11, no. 1 (1986): 133-61, cites such translexical effects as *Blume-Zoof/Blumeshof* (143) and *Kupferstichen/Kof-ver-stich* (161), among many other "paronomasies" (146), as instances of the "traumatic" nature of reading (143), which "takes place on a level of linguistic receptivity inaccessible to intended meaning" (143)—and where the "physiognomic effect" of the word confounds its semantic function. It is, however, precisely because one might also wish to lay stress on the phonemic underface of both writing and silent reading that one is readier than otherwise to ac-

cept Hamacher's epitomizing example, where a childhood verbal amalgam on Benjamin's part—in a misreading of *Muhme Rehlen* as *Mummerehlen* (146)—enacts in the mummery of carnivalesque transformation "the ironic allegory of the linguistic essence of the world and of the dumbfounded interior of language" (146). Founded in writing's dumbness, yes, but silently vocalized, I would add, into various subversions of a fixed (physiognomic) script. Read this way, for the pantomime of its own surrendered oral warrant, writing thus comes into comparison with the viewer's potentially "traumatic" reception of the cinematic image as disruptive film track.

67. Walter Benjamin, "The Work of Art in the Age of Mechanical Reproduction," in *Illuminations*, ed. Hannah Arendt, trans. Harry Zohn (New York: Schocken, 1969), 235.

68. Buck-Morss, *Dialectics of Seeing*, 272.

END TITLE/EXEUNT

1. Jean-Louis Baudry, "Ideological Effects of the Basic Cinematographic Apparatus," in *Narrative, Apparatus, Ideology: A Film Theory Reader*, ed. Phil Rosen (New York: Columbia University Press, 1986).

2. André Bazin, "The Ontology of the Photographic Image," in *What Is Cinema?* trans. Hugh Gray (Berkeley: University of California Press, 1967).

3. Indeed, the accidental joke of the English vernacular makes its way into Phil Rosen's own pun, "Mummy Dearest," in titling the subdivision of his corrective commentary on this canonized ontological moment in Bazinian theory. See Rosen, "History of Image, Image of History: Subject and Ontology in Bazin," *Wide Angle* 9, no. 4 (1987): 11. With no emphasis on the essay's opening move—"If the plastic arts were put under psychoanalysis"—nevertheless Rosen seems to me altogether right in stressing the psychoanalytic allusion in "complex," and hence the subjective element in the vesting of the film image with a deathless presence. "So what is usually regarded as Bazin's ontology describes a subjective intentionality for automatically produced images based on a preservative obsession" (16). As much a diagnosed wish fulfillment as an unqualified ontological claim, then, Bazin's sense of the preservation neurosis at the root of mimesis is every bit as much the stuff of obsessional investment as of perceptual surety—and hence (I would add) dependent on a necessary repression.

4. Stanley Cavell, *Contesting Tears: The Hollywood Melodrama of the Unknown Woman* (Chicago: University of Chicago Press, 1996), 94-95. I am indebted, as always in connection with Cavell's work, to discussion with Timothy Gould, a privilege now extended to a broader audience through the publication of *Hearing Things: Voice and Method in the Writing of Stanley Cavell* (Chicago: University of Chicago Press, 1998).

5. Münsterburg's influence on the work of Bruce Kawin in *Mindscreen: Bergman, Godard, and First-Person Cinema* (Princeton: Princeton University Press, 1978) needs, however, to be distinguished from my emphasis here. Kawin wants us to entertain the possibility that film is its own dream of itself, detached from the subjectivities of either director or character. This figuration makes certain films, as it were, entirely unconscious (however reflexively knowing they may be). My concentration is, rather, on the tension between an apparent mimetic surface and its quasi-unconscious material underlay.

6. Georg Wilhelm Friedrich Hegel, *Phenomenology of Spirit*, trans. A. V. Miller (New York: Oxford University Press, 1977), 395.

7. Siegfried Kracauer, "The Hotel Lobby," in *The Mass Ornament: Weimar Essays*, trans. and ed. Thomas Y. Levin (Cambridge: Harvard University Press, 1995), 173-89, the only piece from his study of detective fiction (written from 1922 to 1925) that was published during his lifetime. The faceless hotel management looms as a tacit metaphor for something like ideological hegemony, where facts must be held back to ensure interpellation into the bland flux of paid convenience. "Were the mystery to come out of its shell"—

NOTES TO PAGE 329 377

the plot secrets, in this case, of a novel Kracauer is discussing called *Death Enters the Hotel*—these details would violate the social contract of all such impersonal spaces, the cultural leveling and vacated subjectivity symbolized by their public rooms, especially their lobby. "Were the mystery to come out of its shell," that is, "mere possibility would disappear in the fact: . . . the Something would have appeared. The hotel management therefore thoughtfully conceals from its guests the real event which could put an end to the false aesthetic situation shrouding [its] nothing" (184). So too with passion, murder, and discreet police arrest in the MGM Grand Hotel, Berlin rather than Las Vegas.

8. Siegfried Kracauer, *Theory of Film: The Redemption of Physical Reality* (London: Oxford University Press, 1960).

9. Kracauer, "Hotel Lobby," 179, 175.

INDEX

MEDICAL SPANISH FOR NURSES

Soledad Traverso, PhD, is a professor of Spanish at Penn State Behrend, located in Erie, Pennsylvania, where she has taught since 1996. She is also the program chair for foreign languages. Dr. Traverso instructs students at all levels, from introductory to advanced courses. A native of Chile, she has written extensively about South American literature and has published books and articles about authors from her home country. In 2013, Dr. Traverso and Laurie Urraro cotaught a medical Spanish continuing-education course for health care providers at St. Vincent Hospital in Erie, Pennsylvania, which became the foundation for this work. As a result of her commitment to providing health care professionals in the Erie community with the ability to speak medical Spanish and the tremendous success of this course, Dr. Traverso received the Distinguished Award for Excellence in Outreach by the School of Humanities and Social Sciences at Penn State Behrend. Dr. Traverso and Dr. Patty Pasky McMahon teach "Conversational Spanish for Future Health Care Providers" at Penn State Behrend's nursing program, which has become a highly sought-after course among students.

Laurie Urraro, PhD, is a full-time lecturer of Spanish at Penn State Behrend, Erie, Pennsylvania. Her areas of interest include contemporary female-authored Spanish drama, specifically through the lens of sex and sexuality, as well as feminist and LGBTQ issues in contemporary Spanish drama. Current projects include a coauthored bilingual children's book about a trans individual, and a bilingual collection and analysis of contemporary female-authored Spanish plays.

Patty Pasky McMahon, PhD, CRNP, has been in active practice as a family nurse practitioner for over 30 years and has experience in rural health, occupational medicine, women's health, primary care, and college health. She is the director and certified family nurse practitioner at the Health and Wellness Center at Penn State Behrend. She also instructs the doctor of nursing progam at Gannon University, Erie, Pennsylvania. She teaches "Conversational Spanish for Future Health Care Providers" at Penn State Behrend College's nursing program with Dr. Traverso. She holds multiple professional licenses and certifications. Dr. McMahon has been awarded several government grants and has received multiple honors and awards. She has been a primary reviewer of a forensic textbook and has authored several articles. Dr. McMahon has been an invited presenter at many national and regional professional conferences.

MEDICAL SPANISH FOR NURSES

A Self-Teaching Guide

Soledad Traverso, PhD

Laurie Urraro, PhD

Patty Pasky McMahon, PhD, CRNP

Illustrations: Sergio Traverso and Soledad Traverso

SPRINGER PUBLISHING COMPANY

NEW YORK

Springer Publishing Company, LLC
11 West 42nd Street
New York, NY 10036
www.springerpub.com

Acquisitions Editor: Joseph Morita
Senior Production Editor: Kris Parrish
Composition: diacriTech, Chennai

ISBN: 978-0-8261-3294-9
e-book ISBN: 978-0-8261-3295-6

Audio files to accompany this text may be accessed at springerpub.com/traverso.

16 17 18 19 20 / 5 4 3 2 1

The author and the publisher of this Work have made every effort to use sources believed to be reliable to provide information that is accurate and compatible with the standards generally accepted at the time of publication. Because medical science is continually advancing, our knowledge base continues to expand. Therefore, as new information becomes available, changes in procedures become necessary. We recommend that the reader always consult current research and specific institutional policies before performing any clinical procedure. The author and publisher shall not be liable for any special, consequential, or exemplary damages resulting, in whole or in part, from the readers' use of, or reliance on, the information contained in this book. The publisher has no responsibility for the persistence or accuracy of URLs for external or third-party Internet websites referred to in this publication and does not guarantee that any content on such websites is, or will remain, accurate or appropriate.

Library of Congress Cataloging-in-Publication Data
Names: Traverso-Rueda, Soledad, author. | Urraro, Laurie, author. | McMahon, Patty Pasky, author.
Title: Medical Spanish for nurses : a self-teaching guide / Soledad Traverso,
    Laurie Urraro, Patty Pasky McMahon.
Description: New York, NY : Springer Publishing Company, LLC, [2017] |
    Includes bibliographical references and index. | English and Spanish.
Identifiers: LCCN 2016028645| ISBN 9780826132949 | ISBN 9780826132956 (ebook)
Subjects: | MESH: Nursing | Dictionary | Terminology
Classification: LCC RT21 | NLM WY 13 | DDC 610.7303--dc23 LC record available at
https://lccn.loc.gov/2016028645

Special discounts on bulk quantities of our books are available to corporations, professional associations, pharmaceutical companies, health care organizations, and other qualifying groups. If you are interested in a custom book, including chapters from more than one of our titles, we can provide that service as well.
For details, please contact:
Special Sales Department, Springer Publishing Company, LLC
11 West 42nd Street, 15th Floor, New York, NY 10036-8002
Phone: 877-687-7476 or 212-431-4370; Fax: 212-941-7842
E-mail: sales@springerpub.com

Printed in the United States of America by LSC Communications.

*To all those working in
the health care field*

CONTENTS

SECTION III   REVIEW EXERCISES   255

FOREWORD

As a physician who has practiced primary care internal medicine for almost 40 years in various settings, whose only Spanish training occurred in high school, I see this book potentially as valuable as my stethoscope or blood pressure cuff.

Despite all the great technical advances in modern medicine, effective care still requires good communication and trust between patients and caregivers if it is to succeed. In the United States, there are now 40 million primary Spanish speakers, some with little or no English. Many of us in the medical professions who speak only English or rudimentary Spanish need a practical tool to be able to communicate with those patients and their families, even if only in the most basic ways. Although translators are sometimes available, often they are not. Used properly, this book can change frustrating, unsatisfying encounters into meaningful, worthwhile exchanges. Even when communication is very basic, the effort to try to understand sends a powerful message to the patient that "I care enough to try." That effort can help to ameliorate some of the isolation, mistrust, and fear that the Spanish-speaking patient, already vulnerable because of illness, can experience in the English-speaking world of medicine.

Robert Magrisso, MD

Senior Attending
Department of Medicine
NorthShore University HealthSystem
Evanston, Illinois

Senior Clinician Educator
Department of Medicine
University of Chicago Pritzker School of Medicine
Chicago, Illinois

PREFACE

THE STORY BEHIND THIS BOOK

The inspiration for this book began in a hospital setting. Soledad Traverso experienced some health issues that caused her to be admitted. While in the hospital, Laurie Urraro visited with Soledad. The nurses related how much they wished that they understood and could communicate in basic Spanish with their Spanish-speaking patients. The weeks following Soledad's discharge from the hospital, Soledad felt the strong need to reciprocate for all the dedicated care she had received while in the hospital.

At this point, Soledad invited Laurie to participate in the creation of a medical Spanish course. When first hearing of this course, I knew that this would be essential to enhancing the medical care for my Spanish-speaking patients. I attended the course at the hospital where Soledad had been a patient. For the course, Soledad and Laurie prepared a reader and accompanying CDs. This reader became the foundation for this medical Spanish textbook.

The reader was basically a book of Spanish with medical vocabulary. When the idea of a book came about, the authors of the reader asked me to participate in the writing of this textbook in order to extend the medical knowledge within the book.

I have always been aware of a gap in my knowledge that neither my doctoral nor my nurse practitioner education filled: my inability to communicate with my Spanish-speaking patients in basic medical Spanish. This book is unlike any other Spanish-language textbook in that it imparts to the health care provider the basic tools of Spanish linguistics needed to provide care for the Spanish-speaking patient. Exclusively in this text, the reader is provided with a variety of options to incorporate into his or her language goals. It includes basic to advanced grammar, basic to advanced history and physical examination scenarios, and hospital-specialty-based patient encounters. In addition, an entire chapter is dedicated to enhancing the transcultural awareness of the health care provider caring for patients in the various countries that comprise Latin America.

This textbook is unique because you do not need to have any previous knowledge of Spanish to use it. This text provides the reader with all the essential elements and translations (with accompanying audio) needed to communicate about everyday care with his or her Spanish-speaking patients in a variety of health care settings. *The accompanying audio files may be accessed from springerpub.com/traverso.*

—*Patty Pasky McMahon*

ABOUT THE AUDIO

Each chapter includes a range of 8 to 36 audio segments that have been recorded by Dr. Soledad Traverso, a native Spanish speaker, in the Spanish language, and Dr. Patty Pasky McMahon in the English language. The purpose of these segments is to enable the student to hear the pronunciation of the words, phrases, and sentences designed to enhance the interactions between the nurse and the Spanish-speaking patient. These audio files are designed with a pause following the translation that allows the student to repeat the Spanish version. Symbols located within the text are provided to alert the student to the audio accompaniment. The audio enumeration corresponds to the numbered sections within each chapter. This provides the student with the ability to easily locate the particular section of interest. **These audio segments may be accessed from springerpub.com/traverso.**

KEY

inf. = informal

F. = formal

sing. = singular

pl. = plural

Sp. = Spain (Used only in Spain)

m. = masculine

f. = feminine

= Audio

SECTION I

THE BASICS OF SPANISH

1

THE ALPHABET, SALUTATIONS, AND BASIC MEDICAL PHRASES

CONTENTS

Referring to patients and patient items / Cómo referirse a los pacientes y artículos relacionados a los pacientes

Essential verbs for patient care / Verbos esenciales para el cuidado del paciente

Forming medical questions in Spanish / Cómo formular preguntas en español en el ámbito de la medicina

Summary exercise / Ejercicio a modo de resumen

Reading: Florence Nightingale, founder of modern nursing / Lectura: Florence Nightingale, fundadora de la enfermería moderna

Idiomatic expressions / Expresiones idiomáticas

SPANISH ALPHABET, GREETINGS, AND FORMING BASIC MEDICAL PHRASES / EL ALFABETO ESPAÑOL, LOS SALUDOS, Y LA FORMACIÓN BÁSICA DE FRASES EN EL ÁMBITO DE LA MEDICINA

In this chapter, the material presented introduces the nursing and medical provider to the basics of the Spanish language. Learning to correctly pronounce the Spanish alphabet is central to communication with the patient. For example, each vowel in Spanish maintains its own individual sound even when two vowels are combined. The use of the infinitive "to be" is presented with indications as to when to use the appropriate form of one of the two ways in which "to be" is translated. The chapter concludes with essential question words central to assessing the needs of the patient, which includes formulating basic medical questions, phrases, and responses. The summary exercise at the end of the chapter reinforces the essential points of the chapter. To strengthen medical Spanish applications presented in this chapter, refer to Chapter 11: Summary Review Exercises.

SPANISH ALPHABET / EL ALFABETO ESPAÑOL

- The Spanish alphabet contains 27 letters. Pronounce the letters using the adjacent examples.

Pronunciation of letters of the alphabet / Pronunciación de las letras del alfabeto

- "A" has an [AH] sound as in "father."
- "B" has a [B] sound, not as strong as in English, as in "bay."
- "C" can either be a hard [C] as in "cut" or a soft [S], as in "silk."
- "D" is a hard [D] sound, but not as strong in English, as in "doctor."
- "E" has an [A] sound, as in the word "eight."
- "F" has an [F] sound just like English, such as the word "final."
- "G" has either a hard [G] sound, as in "goat," or a soft [H] sound, as in "horse."
- "H," when starting a word, is silent; the first pronounced sound of the word would be the next letter; however, when accompanied by a "c," it carries a [CH].
- "I" is an [E] sound as in "either."
- "J" is an [H] sound, as in "holler."

- "K" is a hard [K] sound, as in "kite."

- "L" is the same [L] sound as in English, such as in "little"; when doubled, the "ll" carries a [Y] sound, as in "yellow."

- "M" is the same [M] sound as in English, such as in "mother."

- "N" is the same [N] sound as in English, such as in "note."

- "Ñ" is like the [NY] sound in English, as in "canyon."

- "O" is like the [O] sound in English, as in "organ."

- "P" sounds the same [P] as in English, but not as strong, as in "person"; sometimes, when initiating a word followed by an "s," the "p" is silent, as in "psychiatry."

- "Q" is a [K] sound as in English, such as in the word "kite."

- "R" has a slight trill sound, unlike an English "r" (hernia); when doubled, the "rr" is very trilled (carro).

- "S" has the same [S] sound as in English: "silk."

- "T" has the same [T] sound as in English, but is not as pronounced, as in "tongue."

- "U" has an [OO] sound as in English: "rule."

- "V" has a similar sound to that of "B" ([B]), but is not as pronounced as in English, as in "bay."

- "W" is an imported letter and is only used to pronounce foreign words, as in "Washington."

- "X" has a [KS] sound as in the English word "extension."

- "Y" has the same [Y] sound as does English, as in "yes"; when it is alone, "y" (and), it sounds like [E].

- "Z" is the same as the [S] sound in English, as in "speak."

FACTS ABOUT THE SPANISH ALPHABET

- The letter names are feminine.
- Until mid-1994 the Spanish alphabet had three additional letters: **ch, ll, and rr.**
- The letters **b/v** are pronounced exactly alike, as a **b.**
- The letters **k/w** are not common in Spanish.
- At the beginning of a word **r** is always pronounced as a trilled **rr**: Ramón, Rosa.

(continued / continuado)

(*continued* / *continuado*)

FACTS ABOUT THE SPANISH ALPHABET

- Depending on its position, the letter **y** can be semivowel, as in **Paraguay**, **voy**, or a consonant like the Spanish **ll**: yo, maya.

- The letter **c** before **e and i** sounds like an "s": cero, cinta.

- The letter **g** is pronounced as a **j** before **e and i**: Germán, gitano. The combination **ga, go, gu** are pronounced like the English **g** in "gate": gato, Gómez, Gutiérrez.

- When a letter carries a written accent, say **"con acento"** after saying the name of the letter: María: **i con acento**.

- The combination **qu** is pronounced as a **k**: que, quiero, queso.

AUDIO 1.1

LETTER / LETRA	NAME / NOMBRE	EXAMPLES / EJEMPLOS
a	a	Ana, asma
b	be	Bárbara, bacteria
c	ce	Carlos, Cecilia, cáncer, cistitis
d	de	Pedro, demencia, diabetes
e	e	Ernesto, edema, éter
f	efe	Fernando, fibroma, fractura
g	ge	Germán, gas, genético
h	hache	Hernán, hola, hormona
i	i	Inés, impaciente, inmune
j	jota	José, jalea
k	ka	kilo, Kegel
l	ele	Luis, láser, leucocito
m	eme	María, medicina, microbio
n	ene	Nora, nasal, nódulo
ñ	eñe	niño
o	o	ocho, ovario, operación

(*continued* / *continuado*)

(*continued* / *continuado*)

LETTER / LETRA	NAME / NOMBRE	EXAMPLES / EJEMPLOS
p	pe	Pepe, palpitación, privado
q	cu	queso, quirófano
r	ere	Roberto, radiografía, recipiente
s	ese	Sara, sangre, sigmoide
t	te	Tomás, tétano, tumor
u	u	Úrsula, urólogo
v	ve chica/uve	Vena, virus
w	doble ve	Washington
x	equis	México, excelente, oxígeno
y	i griega	Yolanda, yogurt
z	zeta	Zóster, zinc

PRONUNCIATION OF MEDICAL ACRONYMS / PRONUNCIACIÓN DE SIGLAS MÉDICAS

AUDIO 1.2

Pronounce the following aloud:

For example,　A fib = a-efe-i-be

A fib	Atrial fibrilation
BMI	Body mass index
BP	Blood pressure
CBC	Complete blood count
ED	Emergency department
EKG	Electrocardiogram
FDA	Food and Drug Administration
GERD	Gastroesophogeal reflux disease
HDL	High-density lipoprotein
HIV	Human immunodeficiency virus

HR	Heart rate
IBS	Irritable bowel syndrome
LDL	Low-density lipoprotein
NKDA	No known drug allergies
OD	Overdose
PMH	Past medical history
QD	Every day
RBC	Red blood cells
Rx	Prescription
TB	Tuberculosis
TID	Three times/day
URI	Upper respiratory infection
UTI	Urinary tract infection
VIH	Virus de la inmunodeficiencia adquirida
VS	Vital signs
WBC	White blood cells
WHO	World Health Organization

ACRONYM IN ENGLISH	MEANING	ACRONYM IN SPANISH	MEANING IN SPANISH
BMI	Body mass index	IMC	Índice de Masa Corporal
EKG	Electrocardiogram	ECG	Electrocardiograma
GERD	Gastroesophageal reflux disease	ERGE	Reflujo Gastroesofágico
MRI	Magnetic resonance imaging	IRM	Imagen por Resonancia Magnética
HIV	Human immunodeficiency virus	VIH	Virus de la inmunodeficiencia adquirida
WHO	World Health Organization	OMS	Organización mundial de la salud

SPECIFIC SOUNDS / SONIDOS ESPECÍFICOS: "C," "G," "J," "H," "Y"

Pronunciation of specific letters of the Spanish alphabet

- In Spanish "C" has two different sounds: [S] and [K]. The [S] sound occurs in **ce** and **ci**, the [K] sound in **ca, co, cu, cl**, and **cr**. Read the following words aloud:

  - célula
  - ciencias
  - cáncer
  - cirrosis
  - clínica
  - gracias
  - condición
  - crónico
  - control
  - corazón
  - cicatriz
  - cervical
  - cesárea
  - contagioso
  - calambre
  - suicidio

- The "G" is either hard [G, gue, gui] or soft [H, ge, gi]:

  - vagina   gripe   glándula   laringitis   gas   gastritis

- The "J" is an [H] sound:

  - vejiga   jarabe   juntura   jeringa

- The "Qu" sound is a hard [K] sound:

  - quemadura   queja   quitar   bronquitis   quirófano
  - quiste   quimioterapia

- The "H" sound is silent when initiating a word. The "CH" sound is the same in Spanish and English.

  - hola   hemorroides   hambre   hígado
  - pinchar   chico   pecho   chocolate

- The "Y" is a [Y] sound as in English:

  - yeso   yogur   yo

When standing alone, it is an [E] sound: y (and).

MEDICAL SPANISH–ENGLISH WORD EQUIVALENTS / PALABRAS SIMILARES EN ESPAÑOL Y EN INGLÉS EN EL ÁMBITO DE LA MEDICINA

- There are medical words in English and Spanish that resemble each other.
- These are called "cognates." A "cognate" is a word that resembles a word in appearance and meaning from one language to the next.

- There are many cognates in Spanish. Take note of the following rules to determine cognates.
- Some cognates are very obvious, such as the following:

el aborto	el accidente	la ambulancia	la anemia
el antibiótico	el colon	examinar	el hospital
las náuseas	nervioso/a	normal	el trauma

- Words ending in -itis are almost always cognates:

la apendicitis	la bronquitis	la flebitis
la hepatitis	la laringitis	la sinusitis

- Words ending in -ista are usually cognates and are -ist words in English:

el/la dentista	el/la especialista	el/la terapista

- Words ending in -ción or -sión relate to words ending in -tion in English, and they are generally feminine nouns:

la comunicación	la convulsión	la institución	la operación	la respiración

- Words ending in -tad or -dad often end in -ty in English, and they are generally feminine nouns:

la comunidad	la dificultad	la maternidad

- Words ending in -ía often end in -y in English:

la radiografía	la vasectomía

- Nonetheless, be aware of false cognates:

the net = la red	congested = constipado/a
soup = la sopa	pregnant = embarazada

Pronounce the following cognates aloud:

animal	chocolate	colon	cruel	doctor	factor
fatal	fecal	hernia	horrible	hospital	hotel
humor	idea	mosquito	musical	natural	real
religión	saliva	sentimental	televisión	tendón	terrible

www.springerpub.com/traverso
AUDIO 1.5

PATIENT GREETINGS / CÓMO SALUDAR AL PACIENTE

Pronounce the following greetings in Spanish aloud:

Good morning	Buenos días
Good afternoon	Buenas tardes
Good night	Buenas noches*
Good-bye	Adiós
See you later	Hasta luego
See you tomorrow	Hasta mañana
Hello; Hi	Hola
Do you speak English?	¿Hablas inglés?
How is it going?	¿Qué tal?
Bye, *inf*	Chao
How are you? to one person, *inf*	¿Cómo estás?
How are you? to one person, *F*	¿Cómo está usted/Ud.?**
How are you? to more than one person	¿Cómo están ustedes/Uds.?
Well	Bien
Bad	Mal
So so	Regular
My name is	Me llamo
What is your name?	¿Cómo se llama usted?

* Whereas in the United States, "Good evening" may occur from 6 p.m. on, in Spanish-speaking countries, the phrase "Buenas noches" is used frequently after 8 p.m. From noon until 8 p.m., "Buenas tardes" is used.

** In Spanish, the pronoun "usted," often used as the abbreviation "Ud." (formal "you") is used when addressing an adult patient or someone to whom you desire to show respect.

REFERRING TO PATIENTS AND PATIENT ITEMS / CÓMO REFERIRSE A LOS PACIENTES Y ARTÍCULOS RELACIONADOS A LOS PACIENTES

Gender / El género

- Keep in mind that nouns are persons, places, and things. All nouns in Spanish have gender. Most nouns ending in **-o** are masculine; those ending in **-a** are generally feminine. When learning a noun, practice it with the appropriate article (described in the following text).

- In romance languages the gender of nouns is arbitrary.

- The ways to say "the" in Spanish are: *el, la, los, las*.

- "El," "La," "Los," "Las" are "definite articles."

  Use "el" when preceding a masculine, singular noun (the hair = el pelo).

  Use "la" when preceding a feminine, singular noun (the leg = la pierna).

  Use "los" when preceding a masculine, plural noun (the fingers = los dedos).

  Use "las" when preceding a feminine, plural noun (the ears = las orejas).

- To demonstrate gender in words ending in "e," use the article:

  For example,   The (male) patient = El paciente

  The (female) patient = La paciente

- The ways to say "a" or "an" in Spanish are: *un, una*.

- The ways to say "some" in Spanish are *unos, unas*.

- "Un," "Una," "Unos," "Unas" are "indefinite articles."

  Use "un" when preceding a masculine, singular noun (a thermometer = un termómetro).

  Use "una" when preceding a feminine, singular noun (a syringe = una jeringa).

  Use "unos" when preceding a masculine, plural noun (some antibiotics = unos antibióticos).

  Use "unas" when preceding a feminine, plural noun (some capsules = unas cápsulas).

  - Some words end in "a" but have a masculine gender.

  For example,   day = el día

  map = el mapa

  problem = el problema

- Some words end in "o" but have feminine gender.

  For example,   hand = la mano

Patients and patient items: Pluralization in Spanish / Pacientes y artículos relacionados al paciente: La pluralización en español

- Nouns that end in a vowel form the plural by adding **-s**:

  For example,   the table = la mesa ➜ the tables = las mesas

  the finger = el dedo ➜ the fingers = los dedos

  the accident = el accidente ➜ the accidents = los accidentes

- Nouns that end in a consonant form the plural by adding **-es**:

  For example,   the woman = la mujer ➜ the women = las mujeres

  the injection = la inyección ➜ the injections = las inyecciones

  the bean = el frijol ➜ the beans = los frijoles

- To make plural nouns that end in a **-z**, change the **z** to **c**, and add **-es**:

  For example,   the pencil = el lápiz ➜ the pencils = los lápices

  the nose = la nariz ➜ the noses = las narices

AUDIO 1.6

Addressing and referring to patients / Cómo dirigirse y referirse a los pacientes

- Pronouns are words that take the place of nouns to avoid repetition. In English, they are: "I," "you," "he," "she," 'it," "we," "they."

Pronounce the following pronouns aloud in Spanish:

- I   Yo

  You (*inf*)   tú

  He   Él

  She   Ella

  You (*F*)   Usted/Ud.

  We   Nosotros/Nosotras

  You (*pl*) (*Sp*)   Vosotros/Vosotras

  You (*pl*)   Ustedes/Uds.

  They (all male or mixed group)   Ellos

  They (all female)   Ellas

www.springerpub.com/traverso
AUDIO 1.7

ESSENTIAL VERBS FOR PATIENT CARE / VERBOS ESENCIALES PARA EL CUIDADO DEL PACIENTE

Patient descriptors, identifiers, location, and condition / Descripción, identificación, ubicación y condición del paciente

In Spanish, to describe, identify, locate, and note the condition of the patient(s), the infinitives for "to be"/"ser" and "estar" are used.

- The English infinitive "to be" has two Spanish equivalents, "ser" and "estar," which have distinct uses and are not interchangeable.

Uses of "to be"/"ser" / Usos de "ser"

- "Ser" describes the basic nature or inherent characteristics of a person or thing.

  For example, Fernando is young and tall. = Fernando es joven y es alto. (characteristic)

  Fernando is from Colombia. = Fernando es de Colombia. (origin)

  I am the nurse. = Yo soy la enfermera. (occupation)

Uses of "to be"/"estar" / Usos de "estar"

- "Estar" is used to express more transitory states than "ser," and often implies the possibility of change.

  For example, Alicia is in the hospital because she is sick. = Alicia está en el hospital (place or location) porque está enferma (condition at a given moment in time).

- In Spanish, subject pronouns may precede verbs. For example, "Yo soy la doctora" and "Soy la doctora" both mean "I am the doctor" and are both correct.

- In third person (meaning "he," "she," or "Ud." in singular and "ellos," "ellas," and "Uds." in plural), it is helpful to place the subject pronoun before the verb.

- The subject pronoun when used in third-person singular or plural specifies to whom one is referring.

  For example, "Ella es"   "She is" indicates the subject, she, to be female.

  "Él es"   "He is" indicates the subject, he, to be male.

  "Ud. Es"   "You are" indicates the subject, you, to be formal and singular.

"Ellos son"	"They are" indicates the subject to be female and plural.	
"Ellos son"	"They are" indicates the plural subject to be male or male and female.	
"Uds. Son"	"You (*pl*) are" indicates the subject, you, to be plural.	

Pronounce the forms of each verb aloud:

ENGLISH SUBJECT PRONOUNS	VERB TO BE	SPANISH SUBJECT PRONOUNS	SER	ESTAR
I	am	yo	soy	estoy
You (*inf*)	are	tú	eres	estás
He/she	is	él/ella	es	está
You (*F*)	are	Ud.	es	está
We	are	nosotros/as	somos	estamos
You (*Sp*)	are	vosotros/as	sois	estáis
They	are	ellos/ellas	son	están
You (*pl*)	are	Uds.	son	están

Conjugation of "Ser" and "Estar"

- The following are acronyms that will help you determine when to use "ser" and "estar."

- Helpful acronyms for "ser" and "estar" are the following:

SER = DO IT:

Description

Origin

Identification

Time

ESTAR = HELP:

Health

Emotion

Location

Present Progressive (e.g., I "am studying"; we "are reading")

Practice the following questions and answers aloud:

USES OF "SER"	QUESTION	PREGUNTA	ANSWER	RESPUESTA
Description	Is your father tall?	¿Es alto tu padre?	Yes, my father is tall.	Sí, mi padre es alto.
Origin	Where are you from?	¿De dónde es usted?	I am from Mexico.	Soy de México.
Identification	Who is your doctor?	¿Quién es su doctor/a?	He is Dr. Gómez.	Él es el Dr. Gómez.*
Time	At what time is the operation?	¿A qué hora es la operación?	The operation is at 8.	La operación es a las ocho.

* The definite article is used before most titles of people about whom one is speaking; the article is omitted when directly addressing the person---
For example,   Hello, Dr. Gómez. = Hola, doctor Gómez. (article omitted); Who is the nurse? = ¿Quién es el enfermero? (article not omitted)

USES OF "ESTAR"	QUESTION	PREGUNTA	ANSWER	RESPUESTA
Health	How are you?	¿Cómo está Ud.?	I am sick.	Estoy enfermo.
Emotion	How are you?	¿Cómo está Ud.?	I am sad.	Estoy triste.
Location	Why is Mrs. Rodríguez in the hospital?	¿Por qué está en el hospital la Sra. Rodríguez?	Mrs. Rodríguez is in maternity.	La Sra. Rodríguez está en la maternidad.
Present Progressive	What is the doctor looking at?	¿Qué está mirando el doctor?	The doctor is looking at the X-ray.	El doctor está mirando la radiografía.

www.springerpub.com/traverso
AUDIO 1.8

FORMING MEDICAL QUESTIONS IN SPANISH / CÓMO FORMULAR PREGUNTAS EN ESPAÑOL EN EL ÁMBITO DE LA MEDICINA

Pronounce the following question words and phrases aloud.
Please note the Spanish punctuation marks required when asking questions.

ENGLISH	ESPAÑOL	EXAMPLES	EJEMPLOS
What	¿Qué?	What symptoms do you have?	¿Qué síntomas tiene?
Where	¿Dónde?	Where are you?	¿Dónde está Ud.?
To where?	¿Adónde?	Where are you going?	¿Adónde va?
From where?	¿De dónde?	Where are you from?	¿De dónde es usted?
When?	¿Cuándo?	When is your birthday?	¿Cuándo es su cumpleaños?
How many?	¿Cuántas?	How many pillows do you have?	¿Cuántas almohadas tiene?
How many?	¿Cuántos?	How many bones do we have in the body?	¿Cuántos huesos tenemos en el cuerpo?
How much?	¿Cuánta?	How much water do you need?	¿Cuánta agua necesita?
How much?	¿Cuánto?	How much do you weigh?	¿Cuánto pesa?
Which one?	¿Cuál?	Which one is better?	¿Cuál es mejor?
Which ones?	¿Cuáles?	Which ones are your nurses?	¿Cuáles son tus enfermeros?
Who?	¿Quién?	Who is your doctor?	¿Quién es su doctor?
Who?	¿Quiénes?	Who are they?	¿Quiénes son?
How?	¿Cómo?	How are you?	¿Cómo está (Ud.)?
Why?	¿Por qué?	Why are you worried?	¿Por qué está (Ud.) preocupado/a?*

* In Spanish, adjectives agree in gender (masculine/feminine) and number (singular/plural) with the noun. When questioning a female patient, "preocupado" becomes "preocupada."

Practice saying the following questions and answers aloud:

Where are you?   ¿Dónde está Ud.?
I am in the hospital.   (Yo) Estoy en el hospital.

Forming Medical Questions in Spanish

Where are you from?   ¿De dónde es (usted)?
I am from Honduras.   (Yo) Soy de Honduras.

When is your birthday?	¿Cuándo es su cumpleaños?
My birthday is March 2.	Mi cumpleaños es el dos de marzo.
What medicines do you take?	¿Qué medicinas toma (Ud.)?
I take medicine for my heart.	(Yo) Tomo medicina para el corazón.
How much water do you have?	¿Cuánta agua tiene (Ud.)?
I have one bottle of water.	(Yo) Tengo una botella de agua.
Which one is your nurse?	¿Cuál es tu enfermera?
My nurse is Susana.	Mi enfermera es Susana.
Who is Pedro?	¿Quién es Pedro?
Pedro is the father.	Pedro es el padre.
How are you?	¿Cómo está (usted)?
I am nervous.	(Yo) Estoy nerviosa.
Why are you in the hospital?	¿Por qué está (Ud.) en el hospital?
I am sick.	(Yo) Estoy enfermo/a.
Where are you going?	¿Adónde va (Ud.)?
I am going home.	(Yo) voy a la casa.

Culture/Cultura: **Social Greetings.** Among South American people, the greeting that can be observed between friends and someone new being introduced is different than what the traditional greeting is between two people in the United States. For example, in South America, friends will usually greet each other with a kiss on the cheek; this includes females greeting females as well as females and males greeting each other. When a person is introduced to a group, it is not unusual for the friends in that group to greet the new person with a kiss on the cheek. Men often will shake hands as is done in the United States, but it is also acceptable for men to greet each other with a hug and/or a kiss on the cheek.

SUMMARY EXERCISE / EJERCICIO A MODO DE RESUMEN

What would you say in the following situations? What might the other person say?

For example,   Mrs. García is your patient. How would you ask her how she is?

Yo: Hola, señora García. ¿Cómo está usted?

Sra. García: Bien, gracias.

1. Jorge is a 12-year-old patient. Say hello to him.
2. It is night and you wish one of your patients "good night."
3. Ask a family member whether the patient is sick.
4. Ask your patient where she is from.
5. Ask the patient how old he is.
6. Ask your patient who his doctor is.
7. Ask your patient to spell her last name (apellido).
8. Ask your patient who is with her (with you = con Ud.).
9. Ask your patient why he is worried.
10. Ask the patient how much he/she weighs.

READING: FLORENCE NIGHTINGALE, FOUNDER OF MODERN NURSING / LECTURA: FLORENCE NIGHTINGALE, FUNDADORA DE LA ENFERMERÍA MODERNA

Reading

Florence Nightingale (1820–1910, b. Florence, Italy), the founder of modern nursing, is best known for her work attending wounded soldiers during the Crimean War, when she carried a lamp around as she attended to the soldiers at night. In 1860, Florence Nightingale created a nursing school in London at St. Thomas Hospital, the first ever secular school for nursing. She is credited with social reforms, such as improvements to health care for all sectors of British society, increased hunger relief in India, and expansion of the female workforce. The International Day of Nursing is celebrated yearly on her birthday.

Lectura

Florence Nightingale (1820–1910, n. Florencia, Italia), fundadora de la enfermería moderna, se reconoce por su trabajo y esfuerzos en la asistencia a los soldados heridos durante la guerra de Crimea, en donde portaba un farol para poder atenderlos durante la noche. En 1860, Florence Nightingale creó una escuela de enfermería en Londres, en St. Thomas Hospital, la primera escuela secular de enfermería. Se le atribuyen muchas reformas sociales, como, por ejemplo, las mejoras en la atención médica para todos sectores de la sociedad británica, el auxilio contra el hambre en India, y la expansión de la población activa para la mujer. Se celebra el Día Internacional de la Enfermería cada año en el día de su cumpleaños.

IDIOMATIC EXPRESSIONS / EXPRESIONES IDIOMÁTICAS

To pull one's leg   English expression
Tomar el pelo   Spanish expression
To pull one's hair   Literal translation

I got up on the wrong side of the bed.   English expression
Me levanté con el pie izquierdo.   Spanish expression
I got up with my left foot.   Literal translation

2

BASIC ANATOMY

CONTENTS

APPLYING BASIC ANATOMY TO MEDICAL SCENARIOS / ANATOMÍA APLICADA A ESCENARIOS EN EL ÁMBITO DE LA MEDICINA

Anatomy, assessment of pain, and essential medical phrases are the focus of this chapter. The intent is to offer the nursing and medical provider patient scenarios that incorporate medical terminology that the provider is able to use without the need for an in-depth comprehension of the Spanish language. Demonstrating an understanding of the patient's pain, the type of pain, and the location of the pain enables a treatment plan to evolve. Because the Spanish language differs in how pain is expressed by the patient, charts to be used by the provider for reference when communicating with the patient are supplied. The chapter concludes with a summary exercise with the objective to enable the health care provider to assess comprehension of the presented materials found in this chapter. To strengthen medical Spanish applications presented in this chapter, refer to Chapter 11: Summary Review Exercises.

Clarification of the use of the subject pronoun "you" in Spanish

ENGLISH SUBJECT PRONOUNS	USE OF THE SUBJECT PRONOUN "YOU" IN SPANISH	SPANISH SUBJECT PRONOUNS
I		yo
You	Informal singular	tú
He/she		él/ella
You	Formal singular	Ud.
We		nosotros/as
You	Used in Spain plural (all of you)	vosotros/as
They		ellos/ellas
You	Plural formal or informal (all of you)	Uds.

VOCABULARY: ANATOMY OF THE BODY / VOCABULARIO: ANATOMÍA DEL CUERPO

Head and neck / La cabeza y el cuello

Brain	el cerebro
Cheek	la mejilla
Chin	la barbilla
Ears	las orejas
Esophagus	el esófago
Eyebrow	la ceja
Eyes	los ojos
Face	la cara
Forehead	la frente
Hair	el pelo
Inner ear	el oído
Jaw	la mandíbula
Lips	los labios
Mouth	la boca
Neck	el cuello
Nose	la nariz
Sinus	los senos
Teeth	los dientes
Temple	la sien
Throat	la garganta
Tongue	la lengua
Tonsils	las amígdalas
Trachea	la tráquea

Senses / Los sentidos

Hearing	el oído
Sight	la vista
Smell	el olfato
Taste	el gusto
Touch	el tacto

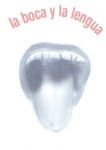

la boca y la lengua

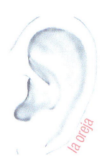

la oreja

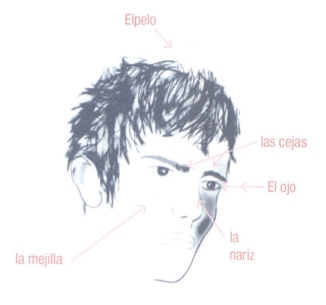

Elpelo

las cejas

El ojo

la mejilla

la nariz

www.springerpub.com/travels

AUDIO 2.2

The body / El cuerpo

Ankle	el tobillo
Arm	el brazo
Back	la espalda
Calf	la pantorrilla
Chest	el pecho
Fingers	los dedos
Foot	el pie
Hand	la mano
Knee	la rodilla
Leg	la pierna
Nails	las uñas
Shoulder	el hombro
Stomach	el estómago
Toes	los dedos del pie
Umbilicus	el ombligo
Waist	la cintura
Wrist	la muñeca

El Cuerpo

la cabeza

el hombro izquierdo

el brazo izquierdo

los dedos de la mano derecha

la mano izquierda

la rodilla

la pantorrilla

el tobillo

el pie izquierdo

los dedos del pie derecho

Left	izquierdo/a
Right	derecho/a

Internal organs / Los órganos internos

AUDIO 2.3

Anus	el ano
Appendix	el apéndice
Bladder	la vejiga
Colon	el colon
Gall bladder	la vesícula
Heart	el corazón
Intestines	los intestinos
Kidneys	los riñones
Large intestine	el intestino grueso
Liver	el hígado
Lungs	los pulmones
Pancreas	el páncreas
Rectum	el recto
Small intestine	el intestino delgado
Spleen	el bazo
Stomach	el estómago

el cerebro

el corazón

el hígado

la vesícula

el estómago

el páncreas

intestinos

el colon

los riñones

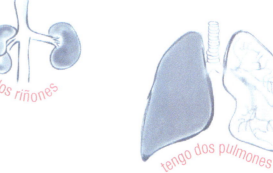

tengo dos pulmones

www.springerpub.com/traverso
AUDIO 2.4

Skeletal structures / La estructura ósea

Skull	el cráneo
Orbit	la órbita
Nasal bone	el hueso nasal
Maxilla	el hueso maxilar superior
Mandible	la mandíbula
Spine	la espina dorsal
Scapula	la escápula
Clavicle	la clavícula
Humerus	el húmero
Radius	el radio
Ulna	el cúbito
Carpals	los carpianos
Phalanges	las falanges
Ribs	las costillas
Pelvis	la pelvis
Sacrum	el sacro
Coccyx	el cóccix
Femur	el fémur
Patella	la rótula
Fibula	el peroné
Tibia	la tibia
Ankle	el tobillo
Calcaneus	el calcáneo
Tarsals	los tarsianos
Metatarsals	los metatarsianos

www.springerpub.com/traverso
AUDIO 2.5

Reproductive Anatomy / Anatomía de la reproducción

Groin	la ingle
Labia	los labios vaginales
Ovaries	los ovarios
Penis	el pene

Prostate	la próstata
Testicles	los testículos
Urethra	la uretra
Uterus	el útero
Vagina	la vagina

AUDIO 2.6

Basic Anatomy of the Body / Anatomía básica del cuerpo

1. Skull	el cráneo
2. Orbit	la órbita
3. Mandible	la mandíbula
4. Humerus	el húmero
5. Rib	la costilla
6. Vertebra	la vértebra
7. Pelvis	la pelvis
8. Ulna	el cúbito
9. Radius	el radio
10. Femur	el fémur
11. Tibia	la tibia
12. Fibula	la fibula
13. Tarsals	los tarsianos
14. Metatarsals	los metatarsianos
15. Toe	el dedo del pie

A. Head	la cabeza	I. Wrist	la muñeca
B. Nose	la nariz	J. Abdomen	el abdomen
C. Teeth	los dientes	K. Leg	la pierna
D. Neck	el cuello	L. Knee	la rodilla
E. Shoulder	el hombro	M. Calf	la pantorrilla
F. Arm	el brazo	N. Ankle	el tobillo
G. Finger	el dedo	O. Toes	los dedos del pie
H. Hand	la mano		

INTERPRETATION OF PATIENTS' HEALTH STATUS AND PAIN RESPONSE / INTERPRETACIÓN DE LA CONDICIÓN DE SALUD DEL PACIENTE Y DE SU DOLOR

Conjugation of the verb "to have" / Conjugación del verbo "tener"

Conjugation of "Tener"

ENGLISH SUBJECT PRONOUNS	VERB "TO HAVE"	SPANISH SUBJECT PRONOUNS	VERB IN SPANISH TENER
I	have	yo	tengo
You	have	tú	tienes
He/she	has	él/ella	tiene
You	have	Ud.	tiene
We	have	nosotros/as	tenemos
You	have	vosotros/as	tenéis
They	have	ellos/ellas	tienen
You	have	Uds.	tienen

Dialogue/Diálogo: A student goes to the school nurse because he has a stomachache. Pronounce the following dialogue aloud.

Nurse: Hello, how are you? What is your name?
Enfermera: Hola, ¿cómo estás? ¿Cómo te llamas?
Student: I am Pedro Bustamante. I have a stomach ache.
Estudiante: Soy Pedro Bustamante. Tengo dolor de estómago.
Nurse: I am Nurse Carmen. Do you have nausea?
Enfermera: Soy la enfermera Carmen. ¿Tienes náuseas?
Pedro: Yes, I have nausea and I am dizzy.
Pedro: Sí, tengo náuseas y estoy mareado.
Nurse: What is going on?
Enfermera: ¿Qué te pasa?
Pedro: I am worried. I have an exam in the afternoon.
Pedro: Estoy preocupado. Tengo un examen en la tarde.

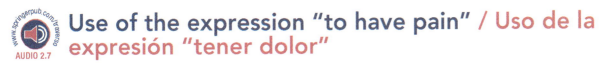

Use of the expression "to have pain" / Uso de la expresión "tener dolor"

AUDIO 2.7
www.springerpub.com/traverso

Conjugation of "Tener Dolor"

ENGLISH SUBJECT PRONOUNS	VERB TO HAVE PAIN	SPANISH SUBJECT PRONOUNS	VERB IN SPANISH TENER DOLOR
I	have pain	yo	tengo dolor
You	have pain	tú	tienes dolor
He/she	has pain	él/ella	tiene dolor
You	have pain	Ud.	tiene dolor
We	have pain	nosotros/as	tenemos dolor
You	have pain	vosotros/as	tenéis dolor
They	have pain	ellos/ellas	tienen dolor
You	have pain	Uds.	tienen dolor

- To use the expression "to have pain," "tener dolor," conjugate the verb "tener" and follow with the noun "dolor."

- This expression is used to indicate a general sense of having pain.

la espalda
los glúteos
tengo la mano en la rodilla
¡me duele el pie!

Pronounce the following aloud using the expression "tener dolor:"

- To identify the location of pain, the preposition "in/on" = "en" follows the expression "tener dolor."

For example,	I have pain.	Tengo dolor.
	I have pain in my feet.	Tengo dolor en los pies.
	I have pain in my back.	Tengo dolor en la espalda.
	I have pain at the incision site.	Tengo dolor en el sitio de la incisión.
	I have pain in my knees.	Tengo dolor en las rodillas.

- To use the expression "tener un dolor," conjugate the verb "tener" and follow with "un dolor" plus an adjective to indicate a specific type of pain.

For example,   I have a sharp pain.   Tengo un dolor fuerte.

Types of pain / Tipos de dolor

- In Spanish, adjectives, words that describe nouns or pronouns, follow the noun.

For example,	The tall man	el hombre alto
	A dull pain/ache	un dolor sordo
	A sharp pain	un dolor fuerte
	A stabbing pain	un dolor punzante
	A piercing pain	un dolor penetrante
	A burning pain	un dolor quemante
	A mild pain	un dolor leve
	A severe pain	un dolor severo
	A constant pain	un dolor constante
	A referred pain	un dolor referido
	A radiating pain	un dolor que se irradia
	A localized pain	un dolor localizado
	A phantom pain	un dolor fantasma
	A strange pain	un dolor raro
	Pain when I breathe	un dolor cuando respiro
	Pain when I cough	un dolor cuando toso
	Pain when I move	un dolor cuando me muevo
	Pain with certain positions	un dolor en ciertas posiciones

Pronounce the following aloud using the expression "tener un dolor:"

I have a dull pain.	Yo tengo un dolor sordo.
You have a sharp pain.	Tú tienes un dolor fuerte.
He/she/you has/have a mild pain.	Él/ella/Ud. tiene un dolor leve.
We do not have pain.	Nosotros/as no tenemos dolor.
You have a phantom pain.	Vosotros/as tenéis un dolor fantasma.
They/you have pain in certain positions.	Ellos/ellas/Uds. tienen un dolor en ciertas posiciones.

Pronounce the following sentences using "tener dolor":

Where do you have pain?	¿Dónde tiene dolor Ud.?
I have pain in my kidneys.	Yo tengo dolor en los riñones.
Do you have pain in your forehead?	¿Tiene Ud. dolor en la frente?
I have pain in my bones throughout my body.	Yo tengo dolor en los huesos por todo el cuerpo.
Where does Carmen have pain?	¿Dónde tiene dolor Carmen?
She has a radiating pain to her back.	Ella tiene un dolor que se irradia a la espalda.

USING SPANISH MEDICAL PHRASES TO COMPREHEND PATIENTS' PAIN / FRASES PARA INTERPRETAR EL NIVEL DE DOLOR DE LOS PACIENTES

www.springerpub.com/traverso

AUDIO 2.9

- The verb "to hurt" = *doler* is another way to express pain.

When interacting with Spanish-speaking patients who are reporting pain to you, these phrases are commonly used.

Conjugation of "Doler"

ENGLISH	SPANISH	ENGLISH	SPANISH
Something is hurting me.	Me duele.	Some things are hurting me.	Me duelen.
Something is hurting you.	Te duele.	Some things are hurting you.	Te duelen.
Something is hurting him/her/you.	Le duele.	Some things are hurting him/her/you.	Le duelen.
Something is hurting us.	Nos duele.	Some things are hurting us.	Nos duelen.
Something is hurting you.	Os duele.	Some things are hurting you.	Os duelen.
Something is hurting them/you.	Les duele.	Some things are hurting them/you.	Les duelen.

- When obtaining information from your patient regarding his/her pain, use the following:

Where?	¿Dónde?	What?	¿Qué?
When?	¿Cuándo?	How much?	¿Cuánto?

Where does it hurt you, Mrs. Pérez?	¿Dónde le duele, señora Pérez?
When does it hurt you?	¿Cuándo le duele?
Does it hurt you when you breathe, Anita?	¿Te duele cuando respiras, Anita?
What hurts you, Mr. Rodríguez?	¿Qué le duele, señor Rodríguez?
What hurts you, Pedrito?	¿Qué te duele, Pedrito?
How much does your knee hurt, Mr. Gómez?	¿Cuánto le duele la rodilla, señor Gómez?

The chart in Figure 2.1 explains how to formulate phrases using "doler."

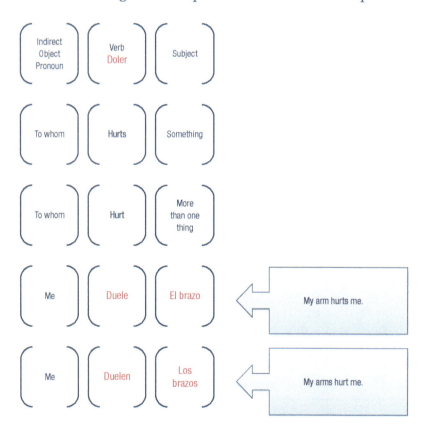

FIGURE 2.1 Formulating phrases with "doler"

Figure 2.2 shows questions and answers used when conversing with patients in Spanish.

On the left side of the figure are possible questions the health care provider may ask a patient. On the right side of the figure are possible responses from a patient.

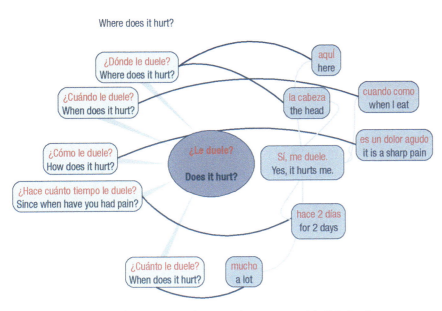

FIGURE 2.2 Formulating questions and answers with "doler."

¡AY! Me duele…..

El estómago   La garganta

Numeric Pain Scale	
0	It does not hurt me.
1	It hurts me very little.
2	
3	It hurts me a little.
4	
5	It hurts me.
6	
7	It hurts me a lot.
8	
9	It hurts me a great deal.
10	The pain is unbearable!

SUMMARY EXERCISE / EJERCICIO A MODO DE RESUMEN

The following are questions in Spanish that the health care provider may ask the patient. Challenge yourself to generate a few more.

> María Elena, a 16-year-old girl, presents to the clinic with a headache and abdominal pain. When asked where the pain is, she points to her head and to her abdomen on the right. When asked to describe the pain, she says that the pain in her head is severe. She says when she moves, the pain in her abdomen is sharp.

1. What is your name?   ¿Cómo te llamas?
2. Do you have pain?   ¿Tienes dolor?
3. Where do you have pain?   ¿Dónde tienes dolor?
4.
5.
6.

READING: BARUJ BENACERRAF, IMMUNOLOGIST / LECTURA: BARUJ BENACERRAF, INMUNÓLOGO

Reading

Baruj Benacerraf (1920–2011, b. Caracas, Venezuela) is an immunologist who works in the United States and France studying the relationship between genetics and immunological reactions. While studying medicine, he participates in World War II, in 1943 he becomes a U.S. citizen, and in 1945 he finishes his medical studies. He receives the first Nobel Prize in Physiology in Medicine in 1980. He dies of pneumonia at age 90.

Lectura

Baruj Benacerraf es un inmunólogo que estudia en los Estados Unidos y en Francia la relación entre la genética y las reacciones inmunológicas. Cuando estudia medicina, participa en la II Guerra Mundial, en 1943 se convierte en ciudadano estadounidense y en 1945 termina los estudios de medicina. Recibe el Premio Nobel de Medicina en 1980. Muere a los 90 años de neumonia.

IDIOMATIC EXPRESSIONS / EXPRESIONES IDIOMÁTICAS

In the blink of an eye   English expression
En un dos por tres   Spanish expression
In a two for three   Literal translation

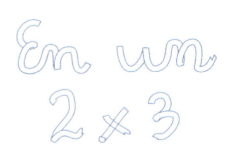

To eavesdrop   English expression
Parar la oreja   Spanish expression
To have one's ear stand up   Literal translation

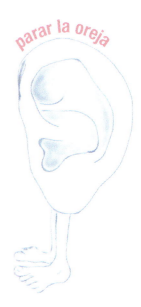

ESSENTIAL VERBS

CONTENTS

Verbs that express patient capabilities / Verbos que expresan lo que el paciente puede no puede hacer

Verbs that express patient knowledge of people, places, and information / Verbos que expresan lo que el paciente "sabe" o "conoce" respecto a gente, lugares, e información

Summary exercise / Ejercicio a modo de resumen

Reading: Bernardo Houssay, studies related to treatment of diabetes / Lectura: Berrnardo Houssay, sus estudios relacionados con el tratamiento de la diabetes

Idiomatic expressions / Expresiones idiomáticas

ESSENTIAL VERBS FREQUENTLY USED IN HEALTH CARE / VERBOS ESENCIALES USADOS FRECUENTEMENTE EN EL ÁREA DE LA MEDICINA

To extend the health care provider's ability to communicate with the patient in basic Spanish, verbs are the focus of this chapter. The verbs presented are those most commonly needed when providing care for the patient. Vocabulary and phrases also are presented that enable the provider to communicate with the patient about the future and the immediate past without the need to learn the verb tenses. Verbs related to patient needs; knowledge of people, places and information; and patient capabilities are offered in chart and pictorial formats to make this information easy to refer to in the future. The summary exercise at the conclusion of this chapter reinforces the parameters presented here. To strengthen medical Spanish applications presented in this chapter, refer to Chapter 11: Summary Review Exercises.

Clarification of the use of the subject pronoun "you" in Spanish

ENGLISH SUBJECT PRONOUNS	USE OF THE SUBJECT PRONOUN "YOU" IN SPANISH	SPANISH SUBJECT PRONOUNS
I		yo
You	Informal singular	tú
He/she		él/ella
You	Formal singular	Ud.
We		nosotros/as
You	Used in Spain plural (all of you)	vosotros/as
They		ellos/ellas
You	Plural formal or informal (all of you)	Uds.

VERBS USED TO ADDRESS PATIENT NEEDS (-AR, -ER, -IR VERBS) / VERBOS USADOS EN EL CUIDADO DEL PACIENTE (VERBOS -AR, -ER, -IR)

- All Spanish verbs end in one of three letter combinations, -ar, -er, or -ir.
- Words that appear in this form are known as "infinitives" and mean "to + verb," for example, "hablar" (to speak), "comer" (to eat), "escribir" (to write).

-AR verbs and medically related vocabulary / Verbos -AR y vocabulario relacionado al ámbito de la medicina

- To put -ar verbs into a usable form (what we call "conjugation"), you drop the -ar and add one of the appropriate verb endings below:

-AR verb endings (used only for -AR verbs):

yo:	**o**	nosotros/as:*	**amos**
tú:	**as**	vosotros/as:**	**áis**
él/ella/Ud.:	**a**	ellos/ellas/ Uds.:	**an**

*Remember that "os" in nosotros and vosotros indicates an all male or mixed-gender group, whereas the "as" indicates an all female group.
**Remember that "vosotros" indicates "you" (plural) for an all male or mixed-gender group.

- In Spanish, the ending of the verb indicates the subject pronoun and the tense; for example, verbs ending in "o" can only mean the subject is "I" and the tense is the present. Verbs ending in "amos" can only mean the subject is "we."

The verb "to need" / El verbo "necesitar"

AUDIO 3.1

Pronounce the following conjugation of the verb "to need"/"necesitar" aloud:

ENGLISH SUBJECT PRONOUNS	VERB TO NEED	SPANISH SUBJECT PRONOUNS	VERB IN SPANISH NECESITAR
I	need	yo	necesito
You	need	tú	necesitas
He/she	needs	él/ella	necesita
You	need	Ud.	necesita
We	need	nosotros/as	necesitamos
You	need	vosotros/as	necesitáis
They	need	ellos/ellas	necesitan
You	need	Uds.	necesitan

- In order to ask someone what he/she needs ("What do you need?"), use the following form:

For example,	What do you need?	¿Qué necesitas?
	I need…	Necesito…
	What do you need?	¿Qué necesita (Ud.)?
	I need…	Necesito…

- In English, the function of "do" is to indicate that there is a question in present tense. (Do you need…? = Necesitas…?). In Spanish the "do" is implied in the way verbs are conjugated: What do you need? =¿Qué necesitas?

This diagram explains how to formulate phrases using "necesitar."

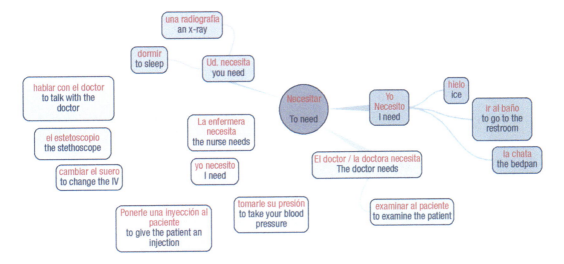

The verb "to speak" / El verbo "hablar"

Pronounce the following conjugation of the verb "to speak"/"hablar" aloud:

ENGLISH SUBJECT PRONOUNS	VERB TO SPEAK	SPANISH SUBJECT PRONOUNS	VERB IN SPANISH HABLAR
I	speak	yo	hablo
You	speak	tú	hablas
He/she	speaks	él/ella	habla
You	speak	Ud.	habla
We	speak	nosotros/as	hablamos
You	speak	vosotros/as	habláis
They	speak	ellos/ellas	hablan
You	speak	Uds.	hablan

- In Spanish, when a verb is negated (is not…/does not…/do not…), the "no" is placed before the verb:

  For example,   I do not speak English. = No hablo inglés.

- When forming questions in Spanish, the verb frequently comes before the subject pronoun.

  For example,   Do you speak English?   ¿Habla (Ud.) inglés?

  Yes, I speak English.   Sí, hablo inglés.

- When a question is answered in the negative, the word "no" is used twice, once to answer the question "no" and another to negate the verb:

  For example,   Do you speak English?   ¿Hablas inglés?

  No, I do not speak English.   No, no hablo inglés.

  No, I do not speak English.   No, yo no hablo inglés.

- Prepositions commonly used with the verb "to talk"/"hablar" in Spanish are "with" = con, and "about" = de.

  To talk with   Hablar con (with = "con")

  To talk about   Hablar de (of/ about = "de")

- When using "de" (of/from/about) with "el" (the), they form a contraction, "del."

  For example,   We are talking about the excellent Doctor Jiménez. = Hablamos del excelente doctor Jiménez.

- When using "a" (to/at) with "el" (the), they form a contraction, "al."

  For example,   I am going to the hospital. = Voy al hospital.

  The following are examples using "hablar de" and "hablar con."

  For example,   Are you speaking with the   ¿Habla con la doctora?
                 doctor?

                 Yes, I am speaking with the   Sí, hablo con la doctora.
                 doctor.

                 Are they speaking about the   ¿Hablan de la operación?
                 operation?

                 No, they are not speaking   No, no hablan de la operación.
                 about the operation.

                 Are you speaking   ¿Habla con la doctora del dolor?
                 with the doctor about the pain?

                 Yes, I am speaking   Sí, hablo con la doctora del dolor.
                 with the doctor about the pain.

More -ar verbs and medically related vocabulary/Más verbos -ar y vocabulario relacionado al ámbito de la medicina

More -ar verbs/Más verbos -ar:

To ask a question	preguntar
To breathe	respirar
To call	llamar
To consult	consultar
To defecate	defecar
To faint	desmayarse
To go to the bathroom	ir al baño
To listen to	escuchar
To look at	mirar
To operate	operar
To point to	señalar
To prepare	preparar
To remove/take out	sacar
To take your blood pressure	tomar su presión
To take your temperature	tomar su temperatura
To touch	tocar
To try/to treat	tratar
To urinate	orinar
To wait/to wait for	esperar

For example,   I need to listen to her heart.   Necesito escuchar su corazón.

He/she needs to point to the pain.   Él/Ella necesita señalar el dolor.

We need to look at the x-ray.   Necesitamos mirar la radiografía.

Medically related vocabulary/Vocabulario relacionado al ámbito de la medicina

Antibiotic	el antibiótico
Aspirin	una aspirina
Doctor	un doctor/una doctora
Fracture	una fractura
Medicine	la medicina

Nurse	un enfermero/una enfermera
Sprain	un desgarro
Strain	una torcedura
Symptoms	los síntomas
Therapist	el/la terapeuta
Therapist	el/la terapista
Water	el agua

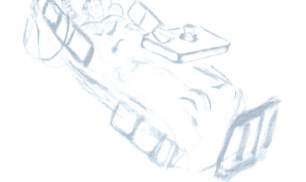

-ER verbs / Verbos -ER:

- To conjugate -er verbs, drop the -er and add one of the appropriate verb endings as follows.

-ER verb endings (used only for -ER verbs):			
yo:	**o**	nosotros/as:	**emos**
tú:	**es**	vosotros/as:	**éis**
él/ella/Ud.:	**e**	ellos/ellas/Uds.:	**en**

The verb "to eat" / El verbo "comer"

Pronounce the following conjugation of the verb "to eat"/"comer" aloud:

ENGLISH SUBJECT PRONOUNS	VERB "TO EAT"	SPANISH SUBJECT PRONOUNS	VERB IN SPANISH COMER
I	eat	yo	como
You	eat	tú	comes
He/she	eats	él/ella	come
You	eat	Ud.	come
We	eat	nosotros/as	comemos
You	eat	vosotros/as	coméis
They	eat	ellos/ellas	comen
You	eat	Uds.	comen

AUDIO 3.4
www.springerpub.com/traverso

The verb "to drink" / El verbo "beber"

Pronounce the following conjugation of the verb "to drink"/"beber" aloud:

ENGLISH SUBJECT PRONOUNS	INFINITIVE "TO DRINK"	SPANISH SUBJECT PRONOUNS	VERB IN SPANISH BEBER
I	drink	yo	bebo
You	drink	tú	bebes
He/she	drinks	él/ella	bebe
You	drink	Ud.	bebe
We	drink	nosotros/as	bebemos
You	drink	vosotros/as	bebéis
They	drink	ellos/ellas	beben
You	drink	Uds.	beben

The verb "to want" / El verbo "querer"

- Note the difference in spelling in some of the verb forms below. This is called a "stem change."

Pronounce the following conjugation of the verb "to want"/"querer" aloud:

ENGLISH SUBJECT PRONOUNS	VERB "TO WANT"	SPANISH SUBJECT PRONOUNS	VERB IN SPANISH QUERER
I	want	yo	quiero
You	want	tú	quieres
He/she	wants	él/ella	quiere
You	want	Ud.	quiere
We	want	nosotros/as	queremos
You	want	vosotros/as	queréis
They	want	ellos/ellas	quieren
You	want	Uds.	quieren

- The infinitive "querer" is often followed by an infinitive indicating someone wants "to" do something.

For example,	I want to eat.	Quiero comer.
	What do you want to eat?	¿Qué quieres comer?
	What do you want to eat?	¿Qué quiere comer?
	I want to eat now.	Quiero comer ahora.
	Gustavo wants to sleep.	Gustavo quiere dormir.
	What do you want to drink?	¿Qué quieren beber?
	We want to drink water.	Queremos beber agua.

This diagram explains how to formulate phrases using "querer."

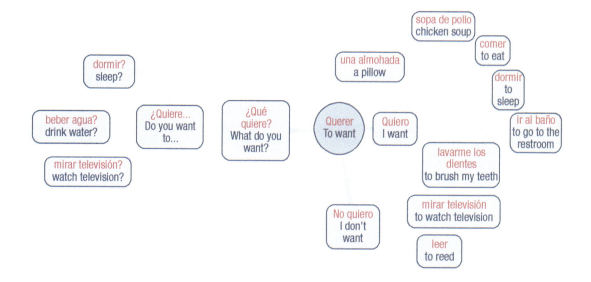

More -ER verbs / Más verbos -ER

AUDIO 3.7

Pronounce the following -er verbs aloud:

To believe (that)	creer [que]
To drink	beber
To eat	comer
To learn	aprender
To respond	responder
To run	correr
To understand	comprender

Pronounce the following aloud:

Do you understand?	¿Comprende?
Yes, I do understand.	Sí, comprendo.
No, I do not understand.	No, no comprendo.
Do you drink alcohol?	¿Bebe alcohol?
No, I do not drink alcohol.	No, no bebo alcohol.
When do you want to eat?	¿Cuándo quiere comer?
I want to eat now.	Quiero comer ahora.
Do you run a lot?	¿Corre mucho?
Yes, I run every day.	Sí, corro todos los días.
Are you learning Spanish?	¿Aprende español?
Yes, I am learning Spanish.	Sí, aprendo español.
Do you believe that the child has the flu?	¿Uds. creen que el niño tiene gripe?
Yes, we believe that the child has the flu.	Sí, creemos que el niño tiene gripe.
Is the patient responding to the treatment?	¿Responde la paciente al tratamiento?
Yes, the patient is responding to the treatment.	Sí, la paciente responde al tratamiento.

-IR verbs / Verbos -IR

To conjugate -ir verbs, drop the -ir and add the appropriate verb endings as follows.

-IR verb endings (used only for -IR verbs):

yo:	**o**	nosotros/as:	**imos**
tú:	**es**	vosotros/as:	**ís**
él/ella/Ud.:	**e**	ellos/ellas/Uds.:	**en**

www.springerpub.com/traverso
AUDIO 3.8

The verb "to write" / El verbo "escribir"

Pronounce the following conjugation of the verb "to write"/"escribir" aloud:

ENGLISH SUBJECT PRONOUNS	VERB TO WRITE	SPANISH SUBJECT PRONOUNS	VERB IN SPANISH ESCRIBIR
I	write	yo	escribo
You	write	tú	escribes
He/she	writes	él/ella	escribe
You	write	Ud.	escribe
We	write	nosotros/as	escribimos
You	write	vosotros/as	escribís
They	write	ellos/ellas	escriben
You	write	Uds.	escriben

Pronounce the following conjugation of the verb "to prefer"/"preferir" aloud:

• Note the difference in spelling in some of the verb forms of "preferir" as previously demonstrated with the conjugation of the verb "to want"/"querer."

ENGLISH SUBJECT PRONOUNS	VERB TO PREFER	SPANISH SUBJECT PRONOUNS	VERB IN SPANISH PREFERIR
I	prefer	yo	prefiero
You	prefer	tú	prefieres
He/she	prefers	él/ella	prefiere
You	prefer	Ud.	prefiere
We	prefer	nosotros/as	preferimos
You	prefer	vosotros/as	preferís
They	prefer	ellos/ellas	prefieren
You	prefer	Uds.	prefieren

For example,

What do you prefer to eat?	¿Qué prefiere comer?
Do I write my name here?	¿Escribo mi nombre aquí?
The doctor prefers to look at the x-ray now.	El doctor prefiere mirar la radiografía ahora.
I prefer to write in Spanish.	Prefiero escribir en español.

The infinitive "to sleep" / El verbo "dormir"

Pronounce the following conjugation of the infinitive "to sleep"/"dormir" aloud:

• Note the difference in spelling in some of the verb forms of "dormir."

ENGLISH SUBJECT PRONOUNS	VERB TO SLEEP	SPANISH SUBJECT PRONOUNS	VERB IN SPANISH DORMIR
I	sleep	yo	duermo
You	sleep	tú	duermes
He/she	sleeps	él/ella	duerme
You	sleep	Ud.	duerme
We	sleep	nosotros/as	dormimos
You	sleep	vosotros/as	dormís
They	sleep	ellos/ellas	duermen
You	sleep	Uds.	duermen

More –IR verbs / Más verbos –IR

Pronounce the following -ir verbs aloud:

To admit	admitir
To attend	asistir a

To decide	decidir
To describe	describir
To lift/raise	subir
To live	vivir
To open	abrir
To receive	recibir
To suffer	sufrir

For example,

The doctor decides to admit the patient.	El doctor decide admitir al paciente
Are you attending anatomy class today?	¿Asiste a la clase de anatomía hoy?
The patient describes the symptoms of the flu.	El paciente describe los síntomas de la gripe.
The nurse raises the bed of the patient.	La enfermera sube la cama del paciente.
The patients receive the forms today.	Los pacientes reciben los formularios hoy.

www.springerpub.com/traverso
AUDIO 3.11

VERBS USED TO DESCRIBE THE PATIENT'S DAILY ROUTINE AND RELATED VOCABULARY: REFLEXIVE VERBS / VERBOS PARA DESCRIBIR LA RUTINA DIARIA DEL PACIENTE Y EL VOCABULARIO RELACIONADO: VERBOS REFLEXIVOS

- The use of reflexive verbs in the health care field primarily describes personal care and daily habits.

- Reflexive verbs take a reflexive pronoun if the same person performs and receives the action.

- Any verbs ending in the pronoun "se" in the infinitive are reflexive verbs, and must be conjugated with the reflexive pronouns.

- Reflexive pronouns are placed immediately before the conjugated verb.

For example,

Me levanto.	I get myself up. = I get up.
Ella se cepilla los dientes.	She brushes her own teeth. / She brushes her teeth.
Nos despertamos temprano.	We wake ourselves up early. / We wake up early.

- The reflexive pronoun "se" applies to both él/ella/Ud. (third-person singular) as well as ellos/ellas/Uds. (third-person plural).

  For example,   Carmen takes a bath.   = Carmen se baña.

  The children take a bath. = Los niños se bañan.

ENGLISH SUBJECT PRONOUNS	REFLEXIVE PRONOUN	SPANISH SUBJECT PRONOUNS	REFLEXIVE PRONOUN
I	Myself	yo	Me
You	Yourself	tú	Te
He/she	Himself/herself	él/ella	Se
You	Yourself	Ud.	Se
We	Ourselves	nosotros/as	Nos
You	Yourselves	vosotros/as	Os
They	Themselves	ellos/ellas	Se
You	Yourselves	Uds.	Se

- The use of reflexive verbs in the health care field primarily describes personal care and daily habits, as demonstrated in the reflexive verbs that follow:

To apply makeup	maquillarse
To bathe	bañarse
To brush one's hair	cepillarse el pelo
To brush one's teeth	cepillarse los dientes
To comb	peinarse
To dress	vestirse
To get up	levantarse
To go to bed	acostarse
To look at oneself	mirarse
To put on	ponerse
To relax	relajarse
To remove	quitarse
To shave	afeitarse
To sit down	sentarse

To stand up	pararse
To wake up	despertarse
To wash	lavarse

AUDIO 3.12

The verb "to feel" / El verbo "sentirse"

- The verb "sentirse" (to feel) is a stem-changing verb and a reflexive verb.

Pronounce the following conjugation of the verb "to feel"/"sentirse" aloud:

ENGLISH SUBJECT PRONOUNS	VERB TO FEEL	SPANISH SUBJECT PRONOUNS	REFLEXIVE PRONOUN	VERB IN SPANISH SENTIRSE
I	feel	Yo	me	siento
You	feel	Tú	te	sientes
He/she	feels	él/ella	se	siente
You	feel	Ud.	se	siente
We	feel	nosotros/as	nos	sentimos
You	feel	vosotros/as	os	sentís
They	feel	ellos/ellas	se	sienten
You	feel	Uds.	se	sienten

AUDIO 3.13

Related vocabulary / Vocabulario relacionado

- The following vocabulary words can be used by patients to describe their feelings.
- These vocabulary words are often used with "to feel"/"sentirse."
- The majority of these vocabulary words are gender specific.

Pronounce the following aloud:

Angry	enojado/a	Excellent	excelente
Anxious	ansioso/a	Exhausted	agotado/a
Bad	mal	Fantastic	fantástico/a
Confused	confundido/a	General unwell feeling	descompuesto/a
Depressed	deprimido/a		
Embarrassed	avergonzado/a	Great	regio/a

Happy	contento/a	So so	regular
Hurt	herido/a	Terrible	fatal
Nauseated	mareado/a	Terrified	aterrado/a
Nervous	nervioso/a	Tired	cansado/a
Sad	triste	Very well/great	muy bien
Sick	enfermo/a	Well	bien

Examples:

How do you feel?	¿Cómo te sientes?
How do you feel?	¿Cómo se siente Ud.?
I feel nauseated.	Me siento mareado/a.
How does the patient feel?	¿Cómo se siente el/la paciente?
He/she feels depressed.	Se siente deprimido/a.
The student feels exhausted.	El estudiante se siente agotado.
Lidia feels sick.	Lidia se siente enferma.

This diagram explains how to formulate phrases using "sentirse."

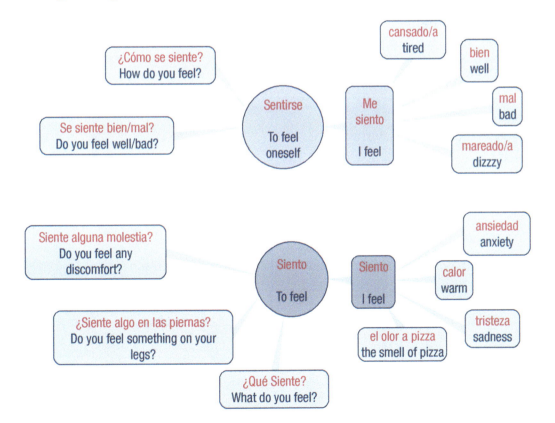

The infinitive "to take a bath" / El verbo "bañarse"

- Another reflexive verb is the -ar verb to bathe oneself/to take a bath ("bañarse").

Pronounce the following conjugation of "to take a bath"/"bañarse" aloud:

ENGLISH SUBJECT PRONOUNS	VERB "TO TAKE A BATH"	SPANISH SUBJECT PRONOUNS	REFLEXIVE PRONOUN	VERB IN SPANISH BAÑARSE
I	take a bath	Yo	me	baño
You	take a bath	Tú	te	bañas
He/she	takes a bath	él/ella	se	baña
You	take a bath	Ud.	se	baña
We	take a bath	nosotros/as	nos	bañamos
You	take a bath	vosotros/as	os	bañáis
They	take a bath	ellos/ellas	se	bañan
You	take a bath	Uds.	se	bañan

- Some verbs can be reflexive or non reflexive. For example, "bañar" = to bathe someone else, whereas "bañarse" is reflexive, meaning that one bathes oneself/takes a bath.

For example,   Reflexive: I feel well. = Me siento bien.

Nonreflexive: I feel the cold stethoscope on my chest.

Yo siento el estetoscopio frío en mi pecho.

Reflexive: He talks to himself.

Él se habla.

Nonreflexive: He talks to the doctor.

Él habla con el doctor.

Reflexive: Carmen takes a bath.

Carmen se baña.

Nonreflexive: Carmen bathes the dog.

Carmen baña el perro.

Reflexive: The nurse washes his hands.

El enfermero se lava las manos.

Nonreflexive: The nurse washes the table.

El enfermero lava la mesa.

IRREGULAR VERBS: "TO GO" AND "TO GIVE" / VERBOS IRREGULARES: "IR" Y "DAR"

- Below is the conjugation of both verbs. Note the similarity in conjugation.

Pronounce the following conjugation of the infinitives "to go" / "ir" and "to give" / "dar" aloud:

TO GIVE	WHO?	DAR	TO GO	IR
I give	Yo	doy	I go	voy
You give	Tú	das	You go	vas
She/he gives	Él, Ella	da	She/he goes	va
You give	Ud.	da	You go	va
We give	Nosotros/as	damos	We go	vamos
You give	Vosotros/as	dais	You go	vais
They give	Ellos, Ellas	dan	They go	van
You give	Uds.	dan	You go	van

For example,

Where does the family go during the operation?	¿Adónde va la familia durante la operación?
The family goes to the waiting room.	La familia va a la sala de espera.
Where do I go before the operation?	¿Adónde voy antes de la operación?
You go to the waiting room.	Va a la sala de espera.
Where is the patient going?	¿Adónde va el paciente?
The patient is going to the lab to give a specimen.	El paciente va al laboratorio para dar una muestra.

SPANISH VERBS USED TO INDICATE PATIENT ACTIONS IN THE FUTURE AND THE RECENT PAST / VERBOS UTILIZADOS EN ESPAÑOL PARA INDICAR ACCIONES DEL PACIENTE EN EL FUTURO Y EL PASADO RECIENTE

Expressing future plans of the patient / Cómo expresar los planes futuros del paciente

- To express that someone is "going to do something," use a conjugated form of "ir" + "a" + an infinitive.

For example,	I am going to speak with the doctor tomorrow.	Voy a hablar con el doctor mañana.
	Are you going to go to the bathroom?	¿Va a ir al baño?
	The child is going to sleep at 7 p.m.	El niño va a dormir a las siete de la tarde.
	We are going to rest in the evening.	Vamos a descansar en la noche.

Expressing immediate past patient actions / Cómo expresar acciones del pasado reciente del paciente

- To express that someone has "just done something," use a conjugated form of "acabar" (to have just…) + "de" + an infinitive.

Pronounce the following conjugation of "to have just done something"/"acabar de" aloud:

ENGLISH SUBJECT PRONOUNS	VERB TO HAVE JUST	SPANISH SUBJECT PRONOUNS	VERB IN SPANISH ACABAR DE
I	Have just	yo	acabo de
You	Have just	tú	acabas de
He/she	Has just	él/ella	acaba de
You	Have just	Ud.	acaba de
We	Have just	nosotros/as	acabamos de
You	Have just	vosotros/as	acabáis de
They	Have just	ellos/ellas	acaban de
You	Have just	Uds.	acaban de

For example,	I have just spoken with the doctor.	Acabo de hablar con el doctor.
	Have you just gone to the bathroom?	¿Ud. acaba de ir al baño?
	The child has just slept.	El niño acaba de dormir.
	We have just eaten.	Acabamos de comer.

Using the present tense to express how long something has been going on with the patient / Cómo usar el presente para expresar "hace cuánto tiempo" algo le ocurre al paciente

- Structures with "hace" allow the speaker to indicate ongoing past activities without having to use the past tense.

- There are specific structures used with "hacer" that allow the speaker to ask and answer in order to express how long something has been going on, meaning that the event began at some point in the past and continues on into the present time.

- To ask the question how long has something been going on, use:

| ¿Hace | + | cuánto tiempo | + | que | + | verb in the present? |
| It has been | + | how long | + | that | + | something has been going on? |

For example,	How long has it been that you have had a cough?	¿Hace cuánto tiempo que tiene tos?
	How long have you had a cough?	¿Hace cuánto tiempo que tiene tos?
	Since when have you had a cough?	¿Hace cuánto tiempo que tiene tos?

- In Spanish there are three ways to ask a question using "hace cuánto tiempo."

- To answer the question, use:

| Hace | + | period of time | + | que | + | verb in present |
| Hace | + | una semana | + | que | + | tengo tos. |

- It has been + one week + that + I have had a cough.

For example,	It has been a week that I have had a cough.	=	Hace una semana que tengo tos.
	I have had a cough for a week.	=	Hace una semana que tengo tos.
For example,	How long have you not been eating?	=	¿Hace cuánto tiempo que no come?
	(translates in English to: When was the last time you ate?)		
For example,	How long have you had a sharp pain in your abdomen?		¿Hace cuánto tiempo que tiene un dolor punzante en el abdomen?

Since when have you had a sharp pain in your abdomen?	¿Hace cuánto tiempo que tiene un dolor punzante en el abdomen?
It has been four hours that I have had a sharp pain in my abdomen.	Hace cuatro horas que tengo un dolor punzante en el abdomen.
I have had a sharp pain in my abdomen for four hours.	Hace cuatro horas que tengo un dolor punzante en el abdomen.

VERBS TO INDICATE PATIENT NEEDS / VERBOS PARA INDICAR LAS NECESIDADES DE LOS PACIENTES

The use of "tener" to determine patient conditions / El uso de "tener" para determinar las condiciones del paciente

- Recall that "to have" translates as "tener." Asking "What is wrong with me?" translates in Spanish as "What do I have?" = ¿Qué tengo?

- The response would be "You have…" = Ud. tiene…

Logical sentences using "tener" may be created combining elements from the following columns.

For example,	Nosotros tenemos miedo de ir al hospital.	We are afraid/have a fear of going to the hospital.

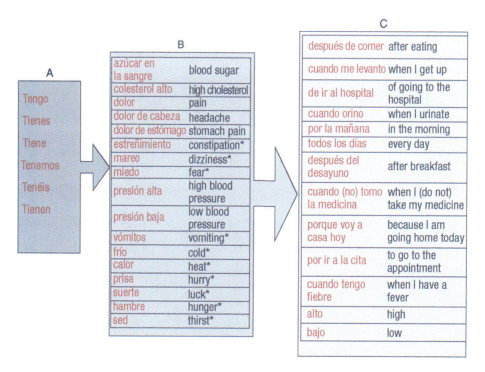

A

Tengo
Tienes
Tiene
Tenemos
Tenéis
Tienen

B

azúcar en la sangre	blood sugar
colesterol alto	high cholesterol
dolor	pain
dolor de cabeza	headache
dolor de estómago	stomach pain
estreñimiento	constipation*
mareo	dizziness*
miedo	fear*
presión alta	high blood pressure
presión baja	low blood pressure
vómitos	vomiting*
frío	cold*
calor	heat*
prisa	hurry*
suerte	luck*
hambre	hunger*
sed	thirst*

C

después de comer	after eating
cuando me levanto	when I get up
de ir al hospital	of going to the hospital
cuando orino	when I urinate
por la mañana	in the morning
todos los días	every day
después del desayuno	after breakfast
cuando (no) tomo la medicina	when I (do not) take my medicine
porque voy a casa hoy	because I am going home today
por ir a la cita	to go to the appointment
cuando tengo fiebre	when I have a fever
alto	high
bajo	low

* Recall that in Spanish "I have hunger" (yo tengo hambre) translates in English to "I am hungry." The same applies to *constipation, dizziness, fear, vomiting, cold, heat, hurry, fear, luck,* and *thirst.*

The use of "tener + que + infinitive" and "ir + a + infinitive" to describe what patients have to do and are going to do / El uso de "tener + que + infinitive" e 'ir + a + infinitivo" para describir lo que tienen que hacer y lo que van a hacer los pacientes

- To express obligation, having to do something, use the following structure:

  Form of "tener" + que + an infinitive

- The "que" does not translate but is part of the structure in Spanish.

  For example,   I have to fast.   Tengo que ayunar.

                     He has to walk.   Tiene que caminar.

                     They have to take a bath.   Tienen que bañarse.

- To express future plans, going to be doing something, use the following structure:

  Form of "ir" + a + infinitive

- The "a" does not translate but is part of the structure in Spanish.

  For example,   I am going to take the medicine.   Voy a tomar la medicina

                     We are going to stand up.   Vamos a pararnos.

                     You are going to wait for the doctor here.   Uds. van a esperar a la doctora aquí.

This diagram explains how to formulate phrases using "tener" and "tener + que + infinitive."

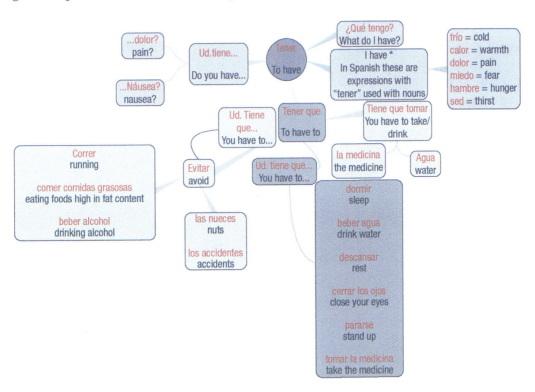

Logical sentences using "tener + que + infinitive" may be created combining elements from the following columns.

For example,   You have to get up at 8./(Ud.) tiene que levantarse a las ocho.

Tengo Tienes Tiene Tenemos Tenéis Tienen	que		

ayunar	To fast
bajar	To lower
caminar	To walk
decir algo	To say something
evitar	To avoid
levantar	To lift
levantarse	To stand up
mover a la derecha/a la izquierda	To move to the right/left
sacar la lengua	To stick out your tongue
sentarse	To sit down
tomar la medicina	To take the medicine
tragar el líquido	To swallow the liquid
volver en 5 días/en una semana	To return in 5 days/in a week

The use of "tener + ganas de" to comprehend what patients feel like doing / Uso de la expresión "tener ganas de" para entender lo que el paciente quisiera hacer

- Use a form of "tener" + ganas de + an infinitive to indicate that someone "feels like" doing something.

For example,   Do you feel like sleeping?   ¿Tiene Ud.ganas de dormir?

I feel like watching television.   Tengo ganas de mirar la televisión.

What do you feel like doing?   ¿Qué tiene Ud. ganas de hacer?

I feel like eating something.   Tengo ganas de comer algo.

VERBS THAT EXPRESS PATIENT CAPABILITIES / VERBOS QUE EXPRESAN LO QUE EL PACIENTE PUEDE NO PUEDE HACER

- "To be able to"/"Poder" is a "stem-changing" verb.

Pronounce the following conjugation of the verb "to be able to"/"poder" aloud:

TO BE ABLE TO/"CAN"	WHO?	PODER
I am able to/I can	Yo	puedo
You are able to/You can	Tú	puedes
She/he is able to/She/he can	Él, Ella	puede
You are able to/You can	Ud.	puede
We are able to/We can	Nosotros/as	podemos
You are able to/You can	Vosotros/as	podéis
They are able to/They can	Ellos, Ellas	pueden
You are able to/You can	Uds.	pueden

- The verb "poder" is frequently followed by an infinitive.

  For example,

Mr. Lopez, can you eat popcorn?	Sr. López, ¿puede Ud. comer palomitas de maíz?
Yes, I can eat popcorn.	Sí, puedo comer palomitas de maíz.
No, I cannot.	No, yo no puedo.
Carlos cannot drink water because his throat hurts.	Carlos no puede beber agua porque le duele la garganta.
Can we speak to the doctor now?	¿Podemos hablar con el doctor ahora?
Is she able to walk?	¿Ella puede caminar?
Can you eat pineapple?	¿Pueden Uds. comer piña?
No, we cannot because we are allergic to pineapple.	No, no podemos porque tenemos alergia a la piña.

This diagram explains how to formulate phrases using "poder."

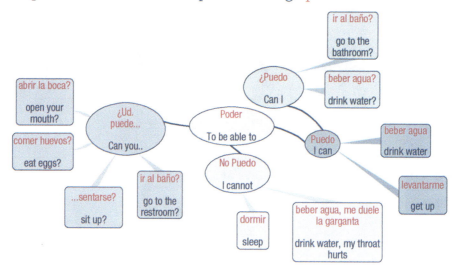

Expressions using "poder" may be created combining elements from the following:

For example,   Is he able to open his eyes?   =   ¿Puede él abrir los ojos?

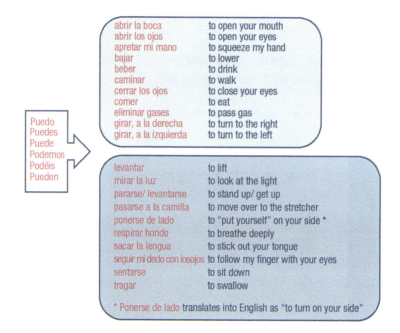

VERBS THAT EXPRESS PATIENT KNOWLEDGE OF PEOPLE, PLACES, AND INFORMATION / VERBOS QUE EXPRESAN LO QUE EL PACIENTE "SABE" O "CONOCE" RESPECTO A GENTE, LUGARES, E INFORMACIÓN

- In Spanish, two verbs indicate "to know" (saber and conocer).

- Each verb is used in specific circumstances and they are not interchangeable.

The verb "saber" / to know / El verbo "saber"

- The verb "saber" is used to know facts, information, or how to do something.

- In the conjugation of "saber," note that only the "yo" form is irregular.

- To express whether someone "knows that" something occurs, has occurred, or will occur, the structure of "saber" + que is used.

Pronounce the following conjugation of the verb "to know"/"saber" aloud:

ENGLISH SUBJECT PRONOUNS	VERB "TO KNOW"	SPANISH SUBJECT PRONOUNS	SABER
I	know	yo	sé
You	know	tú	sabes
He/she	knows	él/ella	sabe
You	know	Ud.	sabe
We	know	nosotros/as	sabemos
You	know	vosotros/as	sabéis
They	know	ellos/ellas	saben
You	know	Uds.	saben

To know that (fact)	Saber + que
To know how to do something (skill)	Saber + infinitive
To know something (fact)	Saber + algo
To know who someone is (information)	Saber + quién
To know where, when, how (information)	Saber + dónde, cuándo, cómo
To know if... (fact)	Saber + si
To know about (fact)	Saber + de

Knowing a fact: The doctor knows that the patient has an embolism.	El doctor sabe que el paciente tiene una embolia.
Knowing whether/a fact: Do you know whether I need an x-ray?	¿Sabe (Ud.) si necesito una radiografía?
Knowing about/fact: I know about the accident.	Sé del accidente.
Knowing something/ fact: They know the days of the week in Spanish.	Ellos saben los días de la semana en español.
Knowing information: We do not know the name of the patient.	No sabemos el nombre del paciente.
Knowing who someone is/information: Do you know who is on call?	¿Uds. saben quién está de turno?
Knowing about/ information: Do you know anything about cardiology?	¿Sabes algo de cardiología?
Knowing information: Do you know where the patient's son is?	¿Sabes dónde está el hijo de la paciente?
Knowing information: Do you know when they are going to discharge the patient?	¿Sabe Ud. cuándo van a dar de alta a la paciente?
Knowing how to do something/skill: I know how to give an injection.	Yo sé poner una inyección.
Knowing how to do something: Do you know how to start an IV?	¿Sabe cómo ponerle el suero?

The infinitive "conocer" means "to know" / El verbo "conocer"

- The verb "conocer" is used to know people, places, or being familiar with something.
- In the conjugation of "conocer," note that only the "yo" form is irregular.
- When using the verb "conocer" to indicate knowing a person, the "personal a" must be inserted immediately after the form of "conocer," and does not translate to English.
- When combined with the "el" of phrases such as "el paciente" or "el doctor," the "a" and "el" form one of only two contractions in Spanish, *al*.
- "Conocer" is not used with an infinitive after its form.

Pronounce the following conjugation of the verb "to know"/"conocer" aloud:

ENGLISH SUBJECT PRONOUNS	VERB "TO KNOW"	SPANISH SUBJECT PRONOUNS	CONOCER
I	know	yo	conozco
You	know	tú	conoces
He/she	knows	él/ella	conoce
You	know	Ud.	conoce
We	know	nosotros/as	conocemos
You	know	vosotros/as	conocéis
They	know	ellos/ellas	conocen
You	know	Uds.	conocen

To (not) know someone	(No) Conocer + a alguien
To (not) know a place/To (not) be familiar with a place/thing/topic	(No) Conocer + algo (lugar, a thing, a topic)

For example,

Knowing a person: I know Dr. Rodríguez.
Conozco a la doctora Rodríguez.

Not knowing a person: We do not know the husband of Mrs. Pérez
No conocemos al esposo de la Sra. Pérez

Knowing/Not knowing a place: The new nurse is (not) familiar with Chicago.
La enfermera nueva (no) conoce Chicago.

Being familiar with a topic: They are familiar with the history of neurosurgeon Alfredo Quiñones.
Ellos conocen la historia del neurocirujano Alfredo Quiñones.

Knowing a thing: Are you familiar with the anatomy book?
¿Conoces el libro de anatomía?

The following sentences demonstrate differences in the use of "saber" and "conocer" within the same sentence.

I do not know Dr. Ramírez (knowing a person), but I know that he is an excellent surgeon. (knowing information)	No *conozco* al doctor Ramírez, pero *sé que* es un excelente cirujano.
We are not familiar with the vegetarian restaurant (knowing a place), but we know that it is on Central Street. (knowing a fact /piece of information)	*No conocemos* el restaurante vegetariano, pero *sabemos que* está en la calle Central.
Paulina, are you familiar with the low-fat diet (Being familiar with a topic)?	Paulina, ¿*Conoces* la dieta baja en grasas?
No, Alicia. I do not know whether we are going to have an appointment with the dietician. (knowing information)	No, Alicia. *No sé si* vamos a tener una cita con la dietista.

Culture/Cultura: What is his name? He is Dr. Yamamoto. (¿Cómo se llama? Es el Dr. Yamamoto.)
Keep in mind that there have been many Asian immigrants who have settled in Spanish-speaking countries. For example, Peru has a large number of Japanese immigrants, whereas Chile has many immigrants from Korea, and many Chinese immigrants live in Venezuela.

SUMMARY EXERCISE / EJERCICIO A MODO DE RESUMEN

Hector visits his father, Pablo, who just came back from the dietitian. Translate the following conversation to Spanish.

Hector: Hello, Dad. How are you?
Pablo: Fine, son. Do you know Mrs. Vásquez? She is my dietitian.
Hector: No, I do not know her. Do you know now what you need to eat?
Pablo: Yes. Can we go to the supermarket?
Hector: Yes. Where it is?
Pablo: Do you know Peach Street?
Hector: Yes.

READING: BERNARDO HOUSSAY, STUDIES RELATED TO TREATMENT OF DIABETES / LECTURA: BERNARDO HOUSSAY, SUS ESTUDIOS RELACIONADOS CON EL TRATAMIENTO DE LA DIABETES

Reading

Bernardo Houssay (1887–1971, b. Buenos Aires, Argentina) is the first Latin American to receive the Nobel Prize in science, in 1947, for the discovery of the role that the hypophysis has in the metabolism of sugar in an organism, and the function of insulin in the treatment of diabetes.

Lectura

Bernardo Houssay (1887–1971, n. Buenos Aires, Argentina) es el primer latinoamericano que recibe el Premio Nobel en ciencias, en 1947, por el descubrimiento del rol que tiene la hipófisis en el metabolismo del azúcar en el organismo y la función de la insulina en el tratamiento de la diabetes.

IDIOMATIC EXPRESSIONS / EXPRESIONES IDIOMÁTICAS

Costs an arm and a leg — English expression

Cuesta un ojo de la cara — Spanish expression

It costs an eye from your face — Literal translation

It is ancient — English expression

Tiene el año de la pera — Spanish equivalent

It has the year of the pear — Literal translation

4

TIME AND NUMBERS

CONTENTS

Patient orientation to time and numerical expressions related to patient care / Orientación del paciente respecto al tiempo y expresiones numéricas relacionadas al cuidado del paciente

Numbers in Spanish / Los números en español

Use of "hay" (there is/there are) in descriptions of quantity related to patient needs / Uso de "hay" en descripciones de cantidad relacionadas a la necesidad del paciente

Number one and indefinite articles / El número uno y los artículos indefinidos

What time is it? / ¿Qué hora es?

Calendar / El calendario

Using colors in descriptions / Uso de los colores en las descripciones

Summary exercise / Ejercicio a modo de resumen

Reading: Clara Barton, a female pioneer who believed in the rights of women and in humanitarian causes / Lectura: Clara Barton, Una mujer pionera que cree en los derechos de la mujer y en las causas humanitarias

Idiomatic expressions / Expresiones idiomáticas

PATIENT ORIENTATION TO TIME AND NUMERICAL EXPRESSIONS RELATED TO PATIENT CARE / ORIENTACIÓN DEL PACIENTE RESPECTO AL TIEMPO Y EXPRESIONES NUMÉRICAS RELACIONADAS AL CUIDADO DEL PACIENTE

This chapter enables the nurse and physician to communicate with the patient about important topics in health care that require knowledge of numbers, time, and dates. Expanding on these topics so as to include descriptors of quantity and colors complete the information presented. A summary exercise that reviews this necessary knowledge for patient care concludes this chapter. To strengthen medical Spanish applications presented in this chapter, refer to Chapter 11: Summary Review Exercises.

Clarification of the use of the subject pronoun "you" in Spanish

ENGLISH SUBJECT PRONOUNS	USE OF THE SUBJECT PRONOUN "YOU" IN SPANISH	SPANISH SUBJECT PRONOUNS
I		yo
You	Informal singular	tú
He/she		él/ella
You	Formal singular	Ud.
We		nosotros/as
You	Used in Spain plural (all of you)	vosotros/as
They		ellos/ellas
You	Plural formal or informal (all of you)	Uds.

www.springerpub.com/traverso
AUDIO 4.1

NUMBERS IN SPANISH / LOS NÚMEROS EN ESPAÑOL

Pronounce the following aloud:

1	uno	(oo-noo)
2	dos	(dose)
3	tres	(trace)

4	cuatro	(kwat-ro)
5	cinco	(sink-o)
6	seis	(saze)
7	siete	(see-yet-eh)
8	ocho	(och-o)
9	nueve	(new-eh-veh)
10	diez	(dee-ace)
11	once	(ohn-say)
12	doce	(dos-say)
13	trece	(treh-seh)
14	catorce	(ca-TOR-say)
15	quince	(KEEN-say)
16	dieciséis	(dee-AY-see-saze)
17	diecisiete	(dee-AY-see-see-AY-tay)
18	dieciocho	(dee-AY-see-och-o)
19	diecinueve	(dee-AY-see-new-EH-veh)
20	veinte	(veh-een-tee)
21	veintiuno	(veh-een-tee-oo-no)
22	veintidós	(veh-een-tee-DOS)
23	veintitrés	(veh-een-tee-TRACE)
24	veinticuatro	(veh-een-tee-KWAT-ro)
25	veinticinco	(veh-een-tee-SINK-o)
26	veintiséis	(veh-een-tee-saze)
27	veintisiete	(veh-een-tee-see-ay-tay)
28	veintiocho	(veh-een-tee-OCH-o)
29	veintinueve	(veh-een-tee-new-EH-veh)
30	treinta	(treh-een-tah)

31	treinta y uno	(treh-een-tah ee oo-no)
32	treinta y dos	(treh-een-tah ee DOS)
33	treinta y tres	(treh-een-tah ee tres)
34	treinta y cuatro	(treh-een-tah ee KWAT-ro)
35	treinta y cinco	(treh-een-tah ee SINK-o)
36	treinta y seis	(treh-een-tah ee saze)
37	treinta y siete	(treh-een-tah ee see-ay-tay)
38	treinta y ocho	(treh-een-tah ee OCH-o)
39	treinta y nueve	(treh-een-tah ee new-EH-veh)
40	cuarenta	(kwar-EN-tah)
41	cuarenta y uno	(kwar-EN-tah ee oo-no)
42	cuarenta y dos	(kwar-EN-tah ee DOS)
43	cuarenta y tres	(kwar-EN-tah ee tres)
44	cuarenta y cuatro	(kwar-EN-tah ee KWAT-ro)
45	cuarenta y cinco	(kwar-EN-tah ee SINK-o)
46	cuarenta y seis	(kwar-EN-tah ee saze)
47	cuarenta y siete	(kwar-EN-tah ee see-ay-tay)
48	cuarenta y ocho	(kwar-EN-tah ee OCH-o)
49	cuarenta y nueve	(kwar-EN-tah ee new-EH-veh)
50	cincuenta	(sink-KWEN-tah)
51	cincuenta y uno	(sink-KWEN-tah ee oo-no)
52	cincuenta y dos	(sink-KWEN-tah ee DOS)
53	cincuenta y tres	(sink-KWEN-tah ee tres)
54	cincuenta y cuatro	(sink-KWEN-tah ee KWAT-ro)
55	cincuenta y cinco	(sink-KWEN-tah ee SINK-o)
56	cincuenta y seis	(sink-KWEN-tah ee saze)
57	cincuenta y siete	(sink-KWEN-tah ee see-ay-tay)

58	cincuenta y ocho	(sink-KWEN-tah ee OCH-o)
59	cincuenta y nueve	(sink-KWEN-tah ee new-EH-veh)
60	sesenta	(seh-SEHN-tah)
61	sesenta y uno	(seh-SEHN-tah ee oo-no)
62	sesenta y dos	(seh-SEHN-tah ee DOS)
63	sesenta y tres	(seh-SEHN-tah ee tres)
64	sesenta y cuatro	(seh-SEHN-tah ee KWAT-ro)
65	sesenta y cinco	(seh-SEHN-tah ee SINK-o)
66	sesenta y seis	(seh-SEHN-tah ee saze)
67	sesenta y siete	(seh-SEHN-tah ee see-ay-tay)
68	sesenta y ocho	(seh-SEHN-tah ee OCH-o)
69	sesenta y nueve	(seh-SEHN-tah ee new-EH-veh)
70	setenta	(seh-TEHN-tah)
71	setenta y uno	(seh-TEHN-tah ee oo-no)
72	setenta y dos	(seh-TEHN-tah ee DOS)
73	setenta y tres	(seh-TEHN-tah ee tres)
74	setenta y cuatro	(seh-TEHN-tah ee KWAT-ro)
75	setenta y cinco	(seh-TEHN-tah ee SINK-o)
76	setenta y seis	(seh-TEHN-tah ee saze)
77	setenta y siete	(seh-TEHN-tah ee see-ay-tay)
78	setenta y ocho	(seh-TEHN-tah ee OCH-o)
79	setenta y nueve	(seh-TEHN-tah ee new-EH-veh)
80	ochenta	(och-EHN-tah)
81	ochenta y uno	(och-EHN-tah ee oo-no)
82	ochenta y dos	(och-EHN-tah ee DOS)
83	ochenta y tres	(och-EHN-tah ee tres)

84	ochenta y cuatro	(och-EHN-tah ee KWAT-ro)
85	ochenta y cinco	(och-EHN-tah ee SINK-o)
86	ochenta y seis	(och-EHN-tah ee saze)
87	ochenta y siete	(och-EHN-tah ee see-ay-tay)
88	ochenta y ocho	(och-EHN-tah ee OCH-o)
89	ochenta y nueve	(och-EHN-tah ee new-EH-veh)
90	noventa	(no-VEHN-tah)
91	noventa y uno	(no-VEHN-tah ee oo-no)
92	noventa y dos	(no-VEHN-tah ee DOS)
93	noventa y tres	(no-VEHN-tah ee tres)
94	noventa y cuatro	(no-VEHN-tah ee KWAT-ro)
95	noventa y cinco	(no-VEHN-tah ee SINK-o)
96	noventa y seis	(no-VEHN-tah ee saze)
97	noventa y siete	(no-VEHN-tah ee see-ay-tay)
98	noventa y ocho	(no-VEHN-tah ee OCH-o)
99	noventa y nueve	(no-VEHN-tah ee new-EH-veh)
100	cien	(see-EHN)

From 101 to 199, use "ciento": ciento uno (101), ciento dos (102), ciento tres (103), ciento sesenta (160), etc.

120	ciento veinte
130	ciento treinta
140	ciento cuarenta
150	ciento cincuenta
160	ciento sesenta
170	ciento setenta
180	ciento ochenta
190	ciento noventa
200	doscientos

Ordinal numbers / Los números ordinales

Pronounce the following aloud:

First	Primero/a
Second	Segundo/a
Third	Tercero/a
Fourth	Cuarto/a
Fifth	Quinto/a
Sixth	Sexto/a
Seventh	Séptimo/a
Eighth	Octavo/a
Ninth	Noveno/a
Tenth	Décimo/a
Eleventh	Décimo primero/a
Twelfth	Décimo segundo/a
Thirteenth	Décimo tercero/a
Fourteenth	Décimo cuarto/a
Fifteenth	Décimo quinto/a
Sixteenth	Décimo sexto/a
Seventeenth	Décimo séptimo/a
Eighteenth	Décimo octavo/a
Nineteenth	Décimo noveno/a
Twentieth	Vigésimo/a

Practice the following examples that use ordinal numbers:

For example, Where is
Dr. Ramírez?

She is on the
fifteenth floor.

You are the first
patient today.

¿Dónde está la
doctora Ramírez?

Ella está en el
décimo quinto piso.

Ud. es la primera
paciente hoy.

Tengo fiebre. Tengo 37.5 grados.

USE OF "HAY" (THERE IS/THERE ARE) IN DESCRIPTIONS OF QUANTITY RELATED TO PATIENT NEEDS / USO DE "HAY" EN DESCRIPCIONES DE CANTIDAD RELACIONADAS A LA NECESIDAD DEL PACIENTE

- In order to quantify objects and people, use the verb "hay."

- The correct pronunciation of "hay" is "I."

- The verb "hay" means both "there is/there are" in a statement and "is there/are there" in a question.

Pronounce the following aloud:

Are there three gowns?	*¿Hay* tres uniformes?
No, there are twelve gowns.	No, *hay* doce uniformes.
Is there an operation today?	*¿Hay* una operación hoy?
Yes, there is an operation today.	Sí, *hay* una operación hoy.

The use of "to be": "hay" versus "ser" versus "estar" / El uso de "hay" versus "ser" versus "estar"

- The verbs "hay," "ser," and "estar" use a form of "to be" when translated to English.

- These verbs are not interchangeable.

- "Hay," "ser," and "estar" are used in distinct scenarios.

See the following for examples of how to use each one.

- Existence = Hay

Is there a doctor in the hospital?	*¿Hay* un doctor en el hospital?
Yes, there is a doctor in the hospital.	Sí, *hay* un doctor en el hospital.

- Identification = Ser

Who is the therapist at the hospital?	¿Quién *es* el terapeuta del hospital?
Mr. Ramos is the therapist at the hospital.	El señor Ramos *es* el terapeuta del hospital.

- Location = Estar

  | Where is the doctor? | ¿Dónde *está* el doctor? |
  | The doctor is on the ninth floor. | El doctor *está* en el noveno piso. |

- "Hay," "estar," and "ser" may be used in the same sentence.

  On the fourth floor, there is an ill person who is in the operating room and he is the patient of Dr. Quiroga.

  En el cuarto piso, *hay* un enfermo que *está* en la sala de operación, y él *es* paciente del doctor Quiroga.

AUDIO 4.4

Expressions of quantity / Expresiones de cantidad

Pronounce the following aloud:

A lot	Mucho
A little	Poco
Very little	Poquito

For example,	How much does it hurt you?	¿Cuánto le duele?
	It hurts a lot.	Me duele mucho.
	Do you run?	¿Corre Ud.?
	Yes, I run a little.	Sí, corro un poco.
	Do you want to eat?	¿Quiere comer?
	I want to eat very little.	Quiero comer un poquito.

NUMBER ONE AND INDEFINITE ARTICLES / EL NÚMERO UNO Y LOS ARTÍCULOS INDEFINIDOS

- In Spanish there are definite articles and indefinite articles.
- Definite articles translate as "the."
- Indefinite articles translate as "a," "an," "some."

DEFINITE ARTICLES: "THE"		INDEFINITE ARTICLES: "A," "AN,", "SOME"	
El (m. sing.)	La (f. sing.)	Un (m. sing.)	Una (f. sing.)
Los (m. pl.)	Las (f. pl.)	Unos (m. pl.)	Unas (f. pl.)

For example,   A boy   un niño

A girl   una niña

An animal   un animal

- "Un" is also the form used in counting.

For example,   How many children are there?   ¿Cuántos niños hay?

There is one child.   Hay un niño.

- Use "un" when preceding a singular, masculine noun.

For example,   There is one child. = Hay "un" niño.

- Use "uno" if you omit the masculine noun.

For example.,   There is one. = Hay "uno."

- With numbers ending in "uno," the "uno" changes to "un" before masculine, singular nouns.

For example,   There are twenty-one boys. = Hay veintiún niños.

- With numbers ending in "uno," the "uno" changes to "una" before feminine, singular nouns.

For example,   There are thirty-one girls. = Hay treinta y una niñas.

- "Y" ("and") is not used after "ciento"

For example,   110 = ciento diez

- When saying or writing numbers in Spanish, use "and" (y) between the placement of the tens and the ones.

For example,   2,386. (See the table that follows.)

THOUSANDS	HUNDREDS	TENS	"AND"	ONES
2	3	8		6
Dos mil (2,000)	Trescientos (300)	Ochenta (80)	"y"	Seis (6)

- In Spanish-speaking countries, decimal points are used in numbers in the thousands and higher. Commas are used for decimal points.

ENGLISH	SPANISH
1,000	1.000
3,049.12	3.049,12
1,000,000	1.000.000

WHAT TIME IS IT? / ¿QUÉ HORA ES?

- The verb "to be"/"ser" is used to express the time of day in Spanish.

- Use **es** + **la** with **una** to indicate "it is one o'clock."

- Use **son** +**las** + the number to indicate all times other than "it is one o'clock."

- The feminine word "hora" (hour) is omitted and replaced by the article "la"/"las."

Pronounce the following aloud:

It is one o'clock: 1:00.	**Es** la una.
It is two o'clock in the afternoon: 2:00 p.m.	**Son** las dos de la tarde.
It is four o'clock: 4:00.	**Son** las cuatro.
It is five after three: 3:05.	**Son** las tres y cinco.
In the morning	De la mañana
In the afternoon	De la tarde
In the evening	De la noche

- The equivalent of "past" or "after" is "y."

  For example, It is 1:20 p.m. = Es la una y veinte de la tarde.

- The equivalent of "to" or "til" is "menos."

  For example, It is 11:50 a.m. = Son las doce menos diez de la mañana.

  It is 11:50 a.m. = Son las once y cincuenta de la mañana.

- "El mediodía" is the equivalent of "noon."

  For example, It is noon. = Es mediodía.

  It is 12 p.m. = Son las doce de la tarde.

- "La medianoche" is the equivalent of "midnight."

  For example, It is midnight. = Es medianoche.

  It is 12 a.m. = Son las doce de la mañana.

- The term "cuarto" translates as "quarter" (15 minutes).

- The term "media" translates to "half" (30 minutes).

- As in English, numbers can be used in place of the expressions "cuarto" and "media."

For example, It is 15 minutes to 5.	Son las cinco menos quince.
It is 4:45.	Son las cinco menos cuarto.

It is 4:45.	Son las cuatro y cuarenta y cinco.
It is 4:30.	Son las cuatro y treinta.
It is half past four.	Son las cuatro y media.

Pronounce the following aloud:

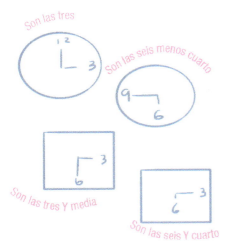

1:40	Es la una y cuarenta./Son las dos menos veinte.
3:00	Son las tres.
5:45	Son las seis menos cuarto./Son las cinco y cuarenta y cinco.
3:30	Son las tres y media./Son las tres y treinta.
6:15	Son las seis y cuarto./Son las seis y quince.

AUDIO 4.6

At what time? / ¿A qué hora?

- To ask at what time an event is, use the construction:

  ¿A qué hora es + (name of the event)?

- To respond with what time an event occurs, use the construction:

  (name of the event) + es + a + la(s) + time

For example,

At what time is the operation?	¿A qué hora es la operación?
The operation is at noon.	La operación es al mediodía.*
At what time is the MRI?	¿A qué hora es el IRM?
The MRI is at three p.m.	El IRM es a las tres de la tarde.

*Remember "a" + "el" = al

Culture/Cultura: The Mayan culture (Mexico, Yucatán Peninsula) is credited with the creation of a complex calendar system that demonstrated an in-depth knowledge of astronomy and mathematics. Unknown by many is that there are millions of Mayan people still in existence who are living their traditions. What remains a mystery is

(continued / continuado)

(continued / continuado)

why the ancient Mayan civilization collapsed. Of interest is the discovery that the ancient Mayan physicians were skilled medical providers. They sutured wounds with human hair, set fractured bones, repaired dental cavities, and made dental prostheses from jade and turquoise. The Mayans also loved sports and there is evidence that they knew how to make rubber and created balls to use in their sports.

Time expressions / Expresiones de tiempo

- Time expressions include "in a minute, " "in an hour, " "two hours, " "in the afternoon, " and so on

  Pronounce the following time expressions aloud:

In a minute	En un minuto
In an hour/in one hour	En una hora
In two hours	En dos horas

- De la mañana/tarde/noche are used when an exact time is present.

  In the morning = De la mañana

  For example,   It is 6 a.m./in the morning. = Son las seis *de la mañana*.

  In the afternoon = De la tarde

  For example,   It is 4:15 p.m./in the afternoon. = Son las cuatro y cuarto *de la tarde*.

  In the evening = De la noche

  For example,   It is 11:35 pm./ in the evening. = Son las once y treinta y cinco *de la noche*.

- En la mañana/tarde/noche are used when the exact time is not indicated.

  In the morning = En la mañana

  For example,   The operation is in the morning. = La operación es *en la mañana*.

  In the afternoon = En la tarde

  For example,   The blood test is in the afternoon. = La prueba de sangre es *en la tarde*.

  At night = En la noche

  For example,   I have pain at night. = Tengo dolor *en la noche*.

- Additional expressions with time include:

  Every six hours = cada seis horas

For example,   When do I need to take the medication? = ¿Cuándo necesito tomar la medicina?

You need to take the medication every six hours. = Ud. necesita tomar el remedio cada seis horas.

Every day = todos los días

For example,   When do we need to exercise? = ¿Cuándo necesitamos hacer ejercicio?

You need to exercise every day. = Uds. necesitan hacer ejercicio todos los días.

CALENDAR / EL CALENDARIO

● In Spanish, the months of the year, the days of the week, and the seasons are not capitalized.

The months of the year	Los meses del año
The days of the week	Los días de la semana
The seasons	Las estaciones
The date	La fecha

AUDIO 4.8

The months of the year / Los meses del año

Pronounce the following aloud:

January	enero
February	febrero
March	marzo
April	abril
May	mayo
June	junio
July	julio
August	agosto
September	septiembre
October	octubre
November	noviembre
December	diciembre

For example,   What is the month = ¿Cuál es el mes?

It is August. = Es agosto.

The days of the week / Los días de la semana

The gender of the days of the week is masculine.

Pronounce the following aloud:
The following are examples of expressions with days of the week:
For example,   What day is today? = ¿Qué día es hoy?

Today is Monday. = Hoy es lunes.

Monday	lunes
Tuesday	martes
Wednesday	miércoles
Thursday	jueves
Friday	viernes
Saturday	sábado
Sunday	domingo

To express "on (day)," use "El" + day of the week.

For example,   The operation is **on** Wednesday. = La operación es **el** miércoles.

To express "on (days)," use "Los" + days of the week.

For example,   The doctor is here **on** Thursdays. = El doctor está aquí **los** jueves.

The seasons / Las estaciones del año

Pronounce the following aloud:

Spring	la primavera
Summer	el verano
Fall	el otoño
Winter	el invierno

For example,   What is the season? = ¿Cuál es la estación?

It is summer. = Es verano.

Note: When the northern hemisphere is in summer, the southern hemisphere is in winter. This is true for all four seasons.

Date / La fecha

Pronounce the following expressions with examples of date aloud:

For example,   Independence Day is July 4, 1776. = El Día de la Independencia es el cuatro de julio de 1776 (mil setecientos setenta y seis).

The number is followed by the preposition **de** (of) and then the month

For example,   The 15th of May = el quince de ma

The 4th of July = el cuatro de julio

To inquire about the date, use the following structure:

What is the date today? = ¿Qué fecha es hoy?

Today is the X (number) of Y (month). = Hoy es el (número) de (mes).

The ordinal number **primero** (first) is used when referring to the first day of the month.

For example,   The first of October = el primero de octubre

Today is the first of January. = Hoy es el primero de enero.

In Spanish-speaking countries, the date is written with the day/month/ year, whereas in the United States, it is written with the month/day/year.

For example,   July 4, 1776 = 07/04/1776 (U.S.)

el 4 de julio de 1776 = 04/07/1776 (Spanish-speaking countries)

Date of birth (DOB) / La fecha de nacimiento (F. de N.)

To ask someone what is his or her date of birth use "cuál."

For example,	When is your date of birth?	¿Cuál es su fecha de nacimiento?
	My date of birth is October 20, 1999.	Mi fecha de nacimiento es el veinte de octubre de mil novecientos noventa y nueve.
	What is Jorge's date of birth?	¿Cuál es la fecha de nacimiento de Jorge?
	Jorge's date of birth is March 26, 2008.	La fecha de nacimiento de Jorge es el veintiséis de marzo de dos mil ocho.

To ask someone when his or her birthday is use "cuándo."

When is your birthday?	¿Cuándo es tu cumpleaños?
My birthday is January 6.	Mi cumpleaños es el seis de enero.
When is Mrs. Gómez's birthday?	¿Cuándo es el cumpleaños de la Sra. Gómez?
Mrs. Gómez's birthday is December 17.	El cumpleaños de la Sra. Gómez es el diecisiete de diciembre.

USING COLORS IN DESCRIPTIONS / USO DE LOS COLORES EN LAS DESCRIPCIONES

Pronounce the following aloud:

ENGLISH	SPANISH
White	Blanco
Yellow	Amarillo
Orange	Naranja
Pink	Rosado
Red	Rojo
Brown	Marrón, Café
Purple	Morado
Blue	Azul
Light blue	Celeste
Green	Verde
Black	Negro
Gray	Gris

A full-color version of this chart appears on the inside back cover of this book.

Colors agree with the noun in gender and number, except for colors ending in "e," which also form the plural by adding "s."

Colors ending in "s" as gris (gray) form the plural by adding "es."

For example, The urine is yellow.	La orina es amarilla.
The taxi is yellow.	El taxi es amarillo.
The buttons are red.	Los botones son rojos.

The pupils are black.	Las pupilas son negr**as**.
The uniform is light blue.	El uniforme es celest**e**.
There are three light blue uniforms.	Hay tres uniformes celest**es**.
The sofas are gray.	Los sofás son gris**es**.

SUMMARY EXERCISE / EJERCICIO A MODO DE RESUMEN

Diego is talking with his mother (Dora) and the admissions clerk (Cindy) in the admitting office of the hospital where they are completing admission forms for Diego. Translate the following scenario.

Dora: Today is Tuesday, and the date is what?

Cindy: Today is Wednesday, September 23.

Dora: Yes, today is Wednesday, it is not Tuesday! It is the first day of fall!

Cindy: When is your birthday, Diego?

Diego: My birthday is August 15.

Dora: You are going to be 15!

Cindy: Why are you here?

Diego: It has been one month since I have had a sore throat and now the doctor needs to remove my tonsils.

Cindy: I have just talked to the nurse and the operation is tomorrow.

READING: CLARA BARTON, A FEMALE PIONEER WHO BELIEVED IN THE RIGHTS OF WOMEN AND IN HUMANITARIAN CAUSES / LECTURA: CLARA BARTON, UNA MUJER PIONERA QUE CREE EN LOS DERECHOS DE LA MUJER Y EN LAS CAUSAS HUMANITARIAS

Reading

Clara Barton, a female pioneer who believes in the rights of women and in humanitarian causes (1821–1912, b. Massachusetts, United States): Clara Barton first works as an educator and later as a nurse. Since childhood she demonstrates an interest and vocation in helping sick individuals. When the Civil War begins in the United States, she offers herself as a volunteer in order to help the wounded soldiers. In 1869, she goes to live in Europe for a few years and during this period she becomes associated with the Society of the Red Cross and when she returns to the United States she founds the U.S. Red Cross.

Lectura

Clara Barton, una mujer pionera que cree en los derechos de la mujer y en las causas humanitarias (1821–1912, n. Massachusetts, Estados Unidos): Clara Barton trabaja primero como una educadora y luego como enfermera. Desde niña demuestra interés y vocación para ayudar a personas enfermas. Cuando comienza la Guerra Civil en los Estados Unidos se presenta como voluntaria para ayudar a los soldados heridos. En 1869 va a vivir a Europa por unos pocos años y durante este tiempo se relaciona con la Sociedad de la Cruz Roja y cuando regresa a los Estados Unidos funda la Cruz Roja estadounidense.

IDIOMATIC EXPRESSIONS / EXPRESIONES IDIOMÁTICAS

Healthy as an ox   English expression

Tener salud de fierro   Spanish expression

To have the health of iron   Literal translation

tener salud de fierro

Like father, like son   English expression

De tal palo, tal astilla   Spanish expression

From such a block of wood, such   Literal translation
a splinter

5

GETTING TO KNOW THE PATIENT: FAMILY, DIET, PREFERENCES, AND MORE

CONTENTS

Spanish expressions related to the patient's family, diet, commands, and preferences used in patient care / Expresiones en español relacionadas con la familia, la dieta, mandatos y preferencias utilizadas en el cuidado del paciente

Patients and their relationship to the family / Los pacientes y la relación con su familia

Essential Spanish expressions used to address patient nutritional needs / Expresiones esenciales usadas para tratar las necesidades de nutrición del paciente

Spanish expressions for instructing the patient / Expresiones en español para darle indicaciones al paciente

Summary exercise / Ejercicio a modo de resumen

Reading: Jean Henri Dunant, humanitarian / Lectura: Jean Henri Dunant, humanitario

Idiomatic expressions / Expresiones idiomáticas

SPANISH EXPRESSIONS RELATED TO THE PATIENT'S FAMILY, DIET, COMMANDS, AND PREFERENCES USED IN PATIENT CARE / EXPRESIONES EN ESPAÑOL RELACIONADAS CON LA FAMILIA, LA DIETA, MANDATOS Y PREFERENCIAS UTILIZADAS EN EL CUIDADO DEL PACIENTE

The ability for the health care provider to have a basic understanding of terminology related to the family and the health history within the family introduces this chapter. Nutritional assessment is critical to the health and healing of the patient. Several areas are addressed in this section of the chapter that include basic food items, the ability to discuss with the patient healthy food choices, and the patient's preferences in food choices. The chapter concludes with an extensive list of what may be called "commands for patient care." The commands provided enable the health care provider to instruct the patient in what the patient needs to do when the patient is an inpatient or is in an outpatient setting. The summary exercise reviews these important areas. To strengthen medical Spanish applications presented in this chapter, refer to Chapter 11: Summary Review Exercises.

Clarification of the use of the subject pronoun "you" in Spanish.

ENGLISH SUBJECT PRONOUNS	USE OF THE SUBJECT PRONOUN "YOU" IN SPANISH	SPANISH SUBJECT PRONOUNS
I		yo
You	Informal singular	tú
He/she		él/ella
You	Formal singular	Ud.
We		nosotros/as
You	Used in Spain plural (all of you)	vosotros/as
They		ellos/ellas
You	Plural formal or informal (all of you)	Uds.

PATIENTS AND THEIR RELATIONSHIP TO THE FAMILY / LOS PACIENTES Y LA RELACIÓN CON SU FAMILIA

 Pronounce the following aloud:

Boy/girl	el chico, el niño/la chica, la niña
Boyfriend/girlfriend	el novio/la novia
Brother/sister	el hermano/la hermana
Brother-in-law	el cuñado
Children	los hijos
Cousins	los primos
Daughter-in-law	la nuera
Father	el padre
Father-in-law	el suegro
Mother-in-law	la suegra
Goddaughter	la ahijada
Godson	el ahijado
Godfather/godmother	el padrino/la madrina
Godparents	los padrinos
Grandfather/grandmother	el abuelo/la abuela
Grandparents	los abuelos
Grandson/granddaughter	el nieto/la nieta
Male/female cousin	el primo/la prima
Mother	la madre
My partner	mi pareja
Parents	los padres
Siblings	los hermanos
Sister-in-law	la cuñada
Spouse/husband	el esposo/el marido
Spouse/wife	la esposa/la mujer
The couple	la pareja
Uncle/aunt	el tío/la tía

Uncles and aunts	los tíos
Family pets	mascotas
Bird	el pájaro
Cat	el gato
Dog	el perro
Fish	el pez
Guinea pig	el conejillo de Indias
Hamster	el hámster
Horse	el caballo
Kitten	el gatito
Puppy	el cachorro
Rabbit	el conejo

Civil or marital state	estado civil
Divorced	divorciado/a
Married	casado/a
Separated	separado/a
Single	soltero/a
Widow	viuda
Widower	viudo
Maternal	materno/a
Paternal	paterno/a

La familia

Additional medically related vocabulary /
Más vocabulario relacionado al ámbito de la medicina

Bill (to pay)	la cuenta
Bills (money)	los billetes
Book	el libro
Bus	el autobús

Car	el coche
Coins	las monedas
Door	la puerta
Form	el formulario
Magazine	la revista
Medical record	récord médico
Microwave	el horno microondas
Money	el dinero
Newspaper	el periódico
Nurse's station	la unidad de enfermería
Paper	el papel
Pen	el bolígrafo
Pencil	el lápiz
Sticker	la calcomanía
Stove	la cocina
Taxi	el taxi
Window	la ventana

Culture/Cultura: Godparents/Los Padrinos

The "compadres" are an important cultural element in Spanish-speaking countries. "Compadre," loosely translated as "co-parent," is a term that describes the relationship that arises between biological parents of a child and the godparents of that child when he/she is baptized. At the time of baptism, the godparents and natural parents thus become each other's "compadres." Thus, the child's father will be the "compadre" of the child's godmother, and the child's mother will be the "comadre" of the child's god-father and vice versa. All will be "compadres" of each other, demonstrating the necessity of sharing the role in collectively helping to parent the child, and indicating the strong family bonds that exist in the Spanish-speaking world. With time, the practice of establishing "compadres," or, as it is sometimes referred to "compradazgo," has ceased to be solely a Catholic act, but is now a general facet of all Spanish-speaking cultures. Compadres can also translate as "close friends" or "buddies."

Use of possessive adjectives in family relationships / Uso de adjetivos posesivos en las relaciones familiares

- Possessive adjectives are words that indicate possession or ownership, such as "my," "your," "his/her," "our," and "their."

- Possessive adjectives in Spanish agree with who/what is "owned," not who is in possession of something. If the noun possessed is singular, the possessive adjective is singular; if the noun possessed is plural, the adjective is plural.

Pronounce the following aloud:

ENGLISH POSSESSIVE ADJECTIVES	SPANISH POSSESSIVE ADJECTIVES
My	Mi/ Mis
Your	Tu*/Tus
His/her/your	Su/Sus
Our	Nuestro/ nuestra/ nuestros/ nuestras
Your	Vuestro/ vuestra/ vuestros/vuestras
Their/your	Su/Sus

* Tú = you (with an accent); tu = your (without an accent).

For example, My child   Mi hijo (one person; one child)

My children   Mis hijos (one person; more than one child)

Our child   Nuestro hijo (more than one person; one child)

Our children   Nuestros hijos (more than one person; more than one child)

- "Our" (nuestro/a/os/as) and "your" (vuestro/a/os/as) also agree in gender with the noun they modify, so each possessive adjective/noun combination has four forms.

For example, Our son/child   Nuestro hijo (more than one person; one child)

Our daughter/child   Nuestra hija (more than one person; one child)

Our children/sons   Nuestros hijos (more than one person; more than one child)

Our daughters/children Nuestras hijas (more than one person; more than one child)

Questions used to identify patient's family members / Preguntas utilizadas para identificar a los familiares del paciente

- To ask who someone is, the verb "ser" (to be) is used with question words.

Pronounce the following aloud:

Who is he/she?	¿Quién es?
Who are they?	¿Quiénes son?
Who is he?	¿Quién es él?
He is my son.	Él es mi hijo.
Who is she?	¿Quién es ella?
She is the grandaughter.	Ella es la nieta.
Who are they?	¿Quiénes son ellos?
They are my parents.	Ellos son mis padres.

- To ask someone's name use the question word "Cómo."

What is his/her name?	¿Cómo se llama él/ella?
Her name is Ana.	Ella se llama Ana.
His name is Gerardo.	Él se llama Gerardo.

- To determine the specific of the patient's family tree the verb "to have" (tener) is used as well as "how many" (cuántos').

Do you have brothers and sisters?	¿Tiene Ud. hermanos?
Do you have children?	¿Tiene Ud. hijos?
How many children do you have?	¿Cuántos hijos tiene Ud.?
How many siblings do you have?	¿Cuántos hermanos tiene Ud.?
I have three siblings.	Tengo tres hermanos.
I have five children.	Tengo cinco hijos.

- To establish whether family members are alive or deceased use the infinitive "estar" (to be) and the terms "vivo/a" (alive) or "muerto/a" (deceased).

Is your wife alive?	¿Está viva su esposa?
No, my wife is deceased.	No, mi esposa está muerta.
No, I am a widower.	No, soy viudo.

Culture/Cultura: In some Spanish countries, the immediate family includes the parents, brothers and sisters, as well as the grandparents, uncles, aunts, and cousins.

Las flores son para la Sra. María Teresa Serrano que está enferma.
Habitación 22.
The flowers are for Mrs. María Teresa Serrano who is sick.
Room 22.

las flores

ESSENTIAL SPANISH EXPRESSIONS USED TO ADDRESS PATIENT NUTRITIONAL NEEDS / EXPRESIONES ESENCIALES USADAS PARA TRATAR LAS NECESIDADES DE NUTRICIÓN DEL PACIENTE

www.springerpub.com/traverso
AUDIO 5.3

Pronounce the following food-related vocabulary aloud:

Food	La comida
A slice	una tajada
Beans	los frijoles
Bread	el pan
Caramel custard	el flan
Cereal	el cereal
Cheese	el queso
Chicken	el pollo
Dessert	el postre
Eggs	los huevos

Fiber	la fibra
Fish	el pescado
French fries	las papas fritas
Fruit	la fruta
Ham	el jamón
Hamburger	la hamburguesa
Ice cream	el helado
Lamb	el cordero
Meat (beef)	la carne
Pizza	la pizza
Popcorn	las palomitas de maíz
Potato	la papa
Shellfish	los mariscos
Shrimp	los camarones
Soup	la sopa
Steak	el bistec
Toast	las tostadas
Tuna	el atún
Turkey	el pavo

*In Spanish, you "drink" soup: use "tomar."

Vegetables   **Las verduras**

Bell pepper	el pimentón
Broccoli	el brócoli
Carrot	la zanahoria
Cauliflower	la coliflor
Corn	el maíz
Cucumber	el pepino
Garlic	el ajo
Green beans	los porotos verdes

Lettuce	la lechuga
Onion	la cebolla
Mushrooms	los champiñones
Peas	las arvejas
Potato	la papa
Sweet potato	la papa dulce/el camote
Tomato	el tomate

Fruit   La fruta

AUDIO 5.5

Apple	la manzana
Avocado	el aguacate/la palta
Banana	la banana
Cantaloupe	el melón
Grapefruit	la toronja
Grapes	las uvas
Orange	la naranja
Peach	el durazno
Pear	la pera
Pineapple	la piña
Watermelon	la sandía

Dressing, etc.   El aderezo, etc.

AUDIO 5.6

Butter	la mantequilla
Dressing	el aliño/el aderezo
Honey	la miel
Ice	el hielo
Ice chips	el hielo picado
Jelly	la mermelada

Mayonnaise	la mayonesa
Mustard	la mostaza
Nuts	las nueces
Oil	el aceite
Peanut	el maní, el cacahuate
Peanut butter	la mantequilla de maní
Pepper	la pimiento
Salt	la sal
Seeds	las semillas
Sugar	el azúcar
Sugar substitute	el sustituto de azúcar
Vinegar	el vinagre

Beverages

AUDIO 5.7

Bebidas

Alcohol	el alcohol
Apple juice	el jugo de manzana
Beer	la cerveza
Coffee	el café
Decaffeinated coffee	el café descafeinado
Diet soft drink	el refresco dietético
Herbal tea	el té de hierbas
Hot chocolate	el chocolate caliente
Juice	el jugo
Lactose-free milk	la leche sin lactosa
Lemonade	la limonada
Milk	la leche
Orange juice	el jugo de naranja
Red wine	el vino tinto
Skim milk	la leche sin grasa
Soft drink	el refresco

Tea	el té
Water	el agua
White wine	el vino blanco
Wine	el vino

 **Utensils**

Utensilios

Bowl	un cuenco/un tazón
Cup	una taza
Fork	el tenedor
Glass	un vaso
Knife	cuchillo
Menu	el menú
Napkin	la servilleta
Plate	un plato
Saucer	un platillo
Spoon	la cuchara
Tray	la bandeja
Wine glass	una copa

 **Meals**

Las comidas

Aperitif	el aperitivo
Breakfast	el desayuno
Diet	la dieta
Digestive liqueur	el bajativo
Dinner	la cena
Fast food	la comida chatarra

| Lunch | el almuerzo |
| Snack | la merienda |

 ## Measurements

Medidas

Cup	una taza
Liter	un litro
Serving of	una medida de
Tablespoon	una cucharada
Teaspoon	una cucharadita

 ## Verbs

Verbos

To be able to	poder
To fast	ayunar
To have breakfast	desayunar
To have dinner	cenar
To have lunch	almorzar
To order	pedir
To prepare	preparer
To recommend	recomendar

 ## Adjectives

Adjetivos

Acidic/sour	ácido/a
Bad	malo/a
Bitter	amargo/a
Cold	frío/a

Dry	seco/a
Good	bueno/a
Hot	caliente
Raw	crudo/a
Salty	salado/a
Spicy	picante
Sweet	dulce
Tasty	sabroso/a

Culture/Cultura: Many of the crops we eat today originated in the Americas and were cultivated by the indigenous people long before Columbus arrived in the Americas. For example, corn, tomatoes, avocados, bell peppers, chili peppers, peanut, and cacao (chocolate) were cultivated by the Mayans and the Aztecs. The words "tomato" and "chocolate," among others, come from Nahuatl, the indigenous language spoken by the Aztecs: "tomatle," "xocoatl." The Incas cultivated different types of potatoes, sweet potatoes, quinoa, corn, and other grains.

AUDIO 5.13

Patient food preferences / Preferencias de comida del paciente

To like / Gustar

- In Spanish, we do not say "I like something," "you like something," but rather "something is pleasing to me" or "something is pleasing to you."
- "Gustar" conjugates in two forms ("gusta" and "gustan") and is accompanied by an indirect object pronoun:

to me = me	to us = nos
to you = te	to you = os
to him/her/you = le	to them/you = les

- The same type of conjugation for "doler" is used for "gustar."
- When what is liked is one thing, an action, or a series of actions, use "gusta."

For example,   I like Jell-O. = Me gusta la jalea.

I like to sleep. = Me gusta dormir.

I like to eat, to drink, and to sleep. = Me gusta comer, beber, y dormir.

- When what is liked is more than one thing, use "gustan."

For example,   I like apples. = Me gustan las manzanas.

- It is important to note that when translating "I like it" to Spanish, the "it" is not translated.

For example,   Do you like water = ¿Te gusta el agua?

Yes, I like it. = Sí, me gusta.

The structure of "gustar" ("to like") / La estructura de "gustar"

Pronounce the following aloud:

LIKE	GUSTAR	NOT TO LIKE	NO GUSTAR
I like	Me gusta(n)	I do not like	No me gusta(n)
You like	Te gusta(n)	You do not like	No te gusta(n)
She/he likes	Le gusta(n)	S/he does not like	No le gusta(n)
You like	Le gusta(n)	You do not like	No le gusta(n)
We like	Nos gusta(n)	We do not like	No nos gusta(n)
You like	Os gusta(n)	You do not like	No os gusta(n)
They like	Les gusta(n)	They do not like	No les gusta(n)
You like	Les gusta(n)	You do not like	No les gusta(n)

Do you like sweet Jell-O?	¿Le gusta la jalea dulce?
No, I do not like Jell-O.	No, no me gusta la jalea.
Do you like the hospital?	¿Le gusta el hospital?
Yes, I like it.	Sí, me gusta.
Pepito, do you like ice cream?	Pepito, ¿te gusta el helado?
Yes, I like it a lot.	Sí, me gusta mucho.
Do you like to exercise?	¿Les gusta hacer ejercicio.
Yes, we like to exercise.	Sí, nos gusta hacer ejercicio.
Do you like green beans?	¿Les gustan los porotos verdes?
No, we like peas.	No, nos gustan las arvejas.

Culture/Cultura: To fast = ayunar; fasting = el ayuno

The verb "desayunar" ("to eat breakfast") translates as "to break the fast" from not eating since the previous night.

> Do I have to fast for the blood test? = ¿Tengo que ayunar para la prueba de sangre?
>
> Yes, you have to fast. = Sí, Ud. tiene que ayunar.

The noun "el ayuno" translates as "fasting." Some religions and traditions fast before certain celebrations.

> Fasting is part of our tradition. = El ayuno es parte de nuestra tradición.

Use of "hacerle bien / hacerle mal": Something is good / bad for me / Uso de "hacerle bien / hacerle mal"

- The expression "me hace bien" or "me hace mal" translates as something "makes me feel good"/"is good for me" or "makes me feel bad"/"is bad for me."
- The chart on the next page demonstrates the use of the structure "hacerle bien/ hacerle mal."
- The chart uses an indirect object pronoun (me, te, le, nos, os, les) + hace/hacen + bien/mal to indicate that something is good/bad for someone.

Pronounce the following aloud:

Fruit is good for me.	La fruta me hace bien.
Milk is bad for you (pl.) because you (pl.) have a lactose intolerance.	La leche les hace mal porque (Uds.) tienen intolerancia a la lactosa.
Shrimp are bad for you because you have an allergy.	Los camarones te hacen mal porque tienes alergia.
How does the medication make you feel?	¿Cómo le hace sentir la medicina?
The medication makes me feel dizzy.	La medicina me hace sentir mareado.
Nuts are bad for us because we have an allergy.	Las nueces nos hacen mal porque tenemos alergia.

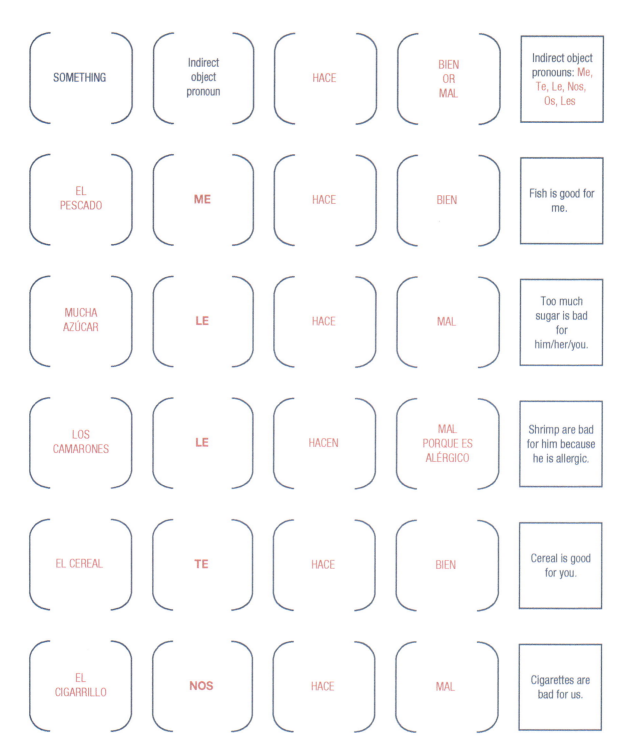

SOMETHING	Indirect object pronoun	HACE	BIEN OR MAL	Indirect object pronouns: Me, Te, Le, Nos, Os, Les
EL PESCADO	ME	HACE	BIEN	Fish is good for me.
MUCHA AZÚCAR	LE	HACE	MAL	Too much sugar is bad for him/her/you.
LOS CAMARONES	LE	HACEN	MAL PORQUE ES ALÉRGICO	Shrimp are bad for him because he is allergic.
EL CEREAL	TE	HACE	BIEN	Cereal is good for you.
EL CIGARRILLO	NOS	HACE	MAL	Cigarettes are bad for us.

Culture/Cultura: Propolis is made from the work of the bees that collect resins from a variety of trees and plants and then use these combined materials to support the beehive. Uses in the beehive

¡yo hablo español!

(continued / continuado)

(continued / continuado)

include structural stability, sealant, inhibit bacterial and fungal growth, and mummification of any intruder that is too large for the bees to remove.

Because of the variety of sources the bees use to form the resin, the composition will vary according to the location of the beehive from which it is collected and even the season of the collection period. The medicinal properties also will vary from hive to hive and region to region.

Propolis originates from the times of the Ancient Greeks, who used this resin-like material to treat abscesses. Later others used it to support wound healing and to treat tumors. It is thought that the Egyptians used it as an integral ingredient for mummification.

Today propolis is used worldwide for a variety of health issues as well as an ingredient in some cosmetics. Proponents of propolis use this material to treat burns, cold sores, as an antioxidant, as an antimicrobial for wound healing, and as a treatment for an assortment of other health-related issues.

AUDIO 5.15

SPANISH EXPRESSIONS FOR INSTRUCTING THE PATIENT / EXPRESIONES EN ESPAÑOL PARA DARLE INDICACIONES AL PACIENTE

- Command forms of a verb are used to tell someone to do/not to do something.

- Spanish has two types of commands: formal (Ud. and Uds.) and informal (tú). The focus will be on learning the formal commands.

- To instruct someone to do (or not to do) something, observe the following:

  For regular -ar verbs, remove the -ar from the infinitive and add -e (for Ud.) or -en (for Uds.).

  For regular -er and -ir verbs, remove the -er or -ir from the infinitive and add -a (for Ud.) or -an (for Uds.).

INFINITIVE	UD.	UDS.
Descansar (To rest)	Descanse Rest (to one person)	Descansen Rest (to more than one person)
Comer (To eat)	Coma Eat (to one person)	Coman Eat (to more than one person)
Subir (To raise)	Suba el brazo Raise your arm (to one person)	Suban el brazo Raise your arm (to more than one person)

This diagram explains how to formulate commands using regular verbs.

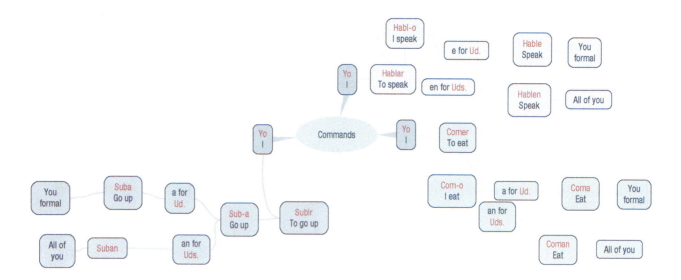

- To form commands with irregular verbs, use the "yo" form of the present tense, drop the "-o" ending, and replace it with -e/-en for -ar verbs, and -a/-an for -er and -ir verbs.

INFINITIVE	UD.	UDS.
Cerrar* los ojos (To close one's eyes) "cierro"	Cierre los ojos Close your eyes (to one person)	Cierren los ojos Close your eyes (to more than one person)
Mover* (To move) "muevo"	Mueva los dedos Move your fingers (to one person)	Muevan los dedos Move your fingers (to more than one person)
Decir* (To say) "digo"	Diga "adiós" Say "good-bye" (to one person)	Digan "adiós" Say "good-bye" (to more than one person)

*"Cerrar," "mover," and "decir" are stem-changing verbs like "poder."

- To form negative commands, place the "no" before the verb:

Do not open your mouth	No abra la boca.
Do not drink the water.	No beban el agua.
Do not be afraid.	No tenga miedo.

- There are some irregular verb commands. (Refer to the following table.)

IR (TO GO)	VAYA A LA SALA DE EMERGEN- CIA GO TO THE EMERGENCY ROOM	VAYAN A LA SALA DE EMERGENCIA GO TO THE EMERGENCY ROOM
Ser (to be)	Sea amable Be kind	Sean amables Be kind
Estar (to be)	Esté a tiempo Be on time	Estén a tiempo Be on time
Dar (to give)	Dé una muestra de Give a sample of	Den una muestra de Give a sample of
Ver (to see)	Vea al* doctor See the doctor	Vean al doctor See the doctor

*When there is an action verb, and the recipient of that action verb is a person, an "a" is placed before the noun. This is called the "personal a." The "a" does not translate but is part of the structure.

For example,

Carlos, visit the nurse.

Carlos, visite a la enfermera.

Maria and Javier, call the doctor.

María y Javier llamen al doctor. (Ojo: a + el = al)

Maria, look at the patient.

María, mire a la paciente.

Maria and Javier look at the patients.

María y Javier Miren a los pacientes.

Pronounce the following commands commonly used in patient care aloud:

ENGLISH INFINITIVE	SPANISH INFINITIVE	ENGLISH	COMMAND (TO ONE PERSON)
To open	Abrir	Open your mouth.	Abra la boca.
To lower	Bajar	Lower the bed.	Baje la cama.
To drink	Beber	Drink./Do not drink.	Beba./No beba.
To walk	Caminar	Walk carefully.	Camine con cuidado.
To close	Cerrar	Close your eyes.	Cierre los ojos.
To eat	Comer	Eat./Do not eat.	Coma./No coma.
To give	Dar	Take a step.	Dé un paso.*

(continued / continuado)

(continued / continuado)

ENGLISH INFINITIVE	SPANISH INFINITIVE	ENGLISH	COMMAND (TO ONE PERSON)
To say / tell	Decir	Say "ah."	Diga "ah."
To allow	Dejar	Let me take your blood pressure.	Déjeme tomarle la presión.
To rest	Descansar	Rest.	Descanse.
To bend	Doblar	Bend your knee.	Doble la rodilla.
To sleep	Dormir	Go to sleep.	Duerma.
To make a fist	Empuñar	Make a fist.	Empuñe la mano.
To speak	Hablar	Speak./Do not speak.	Hable./No hable.
To look at	Mirar	Look at me.	Míreme.
To show	Mostrar	Show me the paper.	Muéstreme el papel.
To move	Mover	Move your foot.	Mueva el pie.
To ask for	Pedir	Ask for help.	Pida ayuda.
To press	Presionar	Press the red button.	Presione el botón rojo.
To remove	Quitar	Take off the dressing.	Quítese el vendaje.
To breathe	Respirar	Breathe deeply.	Respire profundamente,
To point to	Señalar	Point to where it hurts.	Señale dónde le duele.
To raise	Subir/Levantar	Raise your arm.	Suba el brazo./Levante el brazo.
To have	Tener	Do not be afraid.	No tenga miedo.
To take	Tomar	Take/Do not take the medication.	Tome la medicina./No tome la medicina.
To cough	Toser	Cough.	Tosa.
To bring	Traer	Bring./Do not bring the book.	Traiga./No traiga el libro.
To come	Venir	Come to the hospital.	Venga al hospital.

*"Dar un paso" is an idiomatic expression meaning "to take a step."

- The following are examples of reflexive construction in which the subject is both the performer and the receiver of the action expressed by the verb.

- When a reflexive verb is used in a formal command the reflexive pronoun ("se") agrees with the subject pronoun (Ud. or Uds.).

- When instructing someone not to do something, the pronoun ("se") goes before the command.

    For example,   To get up   Levantarse

                    Get up.   Levántese.

                    Do not get up.   No se levante.

- Reflexive verbs in infinitive form will always end in the pronoun "se."

AUDIO 5.16

Pronounce the following reflexive verb commands aloud:

ENGLISH INFINITIVE	SPANISH INFINITIVE	ENGLISH	COMMAND (TO ONE PERSON)
To go to bed	Acostarse	Go to bed. or Lie down./Do not go to bed. or Do not lie down.	Acuéstese./No se acueste.
To roll up one's sleeve	Arremangarse	Roll up your sleeve.	Arremánguese la manga.
To take a bath	Bañarse	Take a bath.	Báñese.
To calm down	Calmarse	Calm down please.	Cálmese por favor.
To brush	Cepillarse	Brush your teeth/hair.	Cepíllese los dientes/el pelo.
To wash	Lavarse	Wash your hands.	Lávese las manos.
To get up	Levantarse	Get up./Do not get up.	Levántese./No se levante.
To move	Moverse	Move to the stretcher.	Muévase a la camilla.
To stand up	Pararse	Stand up./Do not stand up.	Párese./No se pare.
To comb	Peinarse	Comb your hair.	Péinese.
To put on	Ponerse	Put on/Do not put on the shoes.	Póngase/No se ponga los zapatos.
To turn on one's side	Ponerse de lado	Turn on your side.	Póngase de lado.
To become nervous	Ponerse nervioso/a	Do not become nervous.	No se ponga nervioso/a.

(continued / continuado)

(*continued* / *continuado*)

ENGLISH INFINITIVE	SPANISH INFINITIVE	ENGLISH	COMMAND (TO ONE PERSON)
To remove/ take off	Quitarse	Take off/Do not take off the bandage.	Quítese/No se quite el vendaje.
To relax	Relajarse	Relax.	Relájese.
To sit down	Sentarse	Sit down./Do not sit down.	Siéntese./No se siente.
To sit up	Sentarse derecho/a	Sit up.	Siéntese derecho/a.
To cover	Taparse	Cover your mouth.	Tápese la boca.

- To form commands with verbs that end in -car, change the -c to -qu.

- To form commands with verbs that end in -gar, change the -g to -gu.

- To form commands with verbs that end in -zar, change the -z to -c.

Pronounce the following commands whose infinitives end in -car, -gar, -zar aloud:

ENGLISH INFINITIVE	SPANISH INFINITIVE	ENGLISH	COMMAND (TO ONE PERSON)
Not to touch	No tocar	Do not touch the dressing.	No toque el vendaje.
To add	Agregar	Add fiber to your diet.	Agregue fibra a la dieta.
To analyze	Analizar	Analyze the data.	Analice los datos.
To arrive	Llegar	Arrive at eight.	Llegue a las ocho.
To begin	Empezar	Begin the test.	Empiece la prueba.
To cross	Cruzar	Cross your fingers.	Cruce los dedos.
To eat lunch	Almorzar	Eat your lunch.	Almuerce.
To explain	Explicar	Explain the test.	Explique la prueba.
To look for	Buscar	Look for the shoes.	Busque los zapatos.
To play	Jugar	Play quietly.	Juegue en silencio.
To practice	Practicar	Practice the exercises.	Practique los ejercicios.

(*continued* / *continuado*)

(continued / continuado)

ENGLISH INFINITIVE	SPANISH INFINITIVE	ENGLISH	COMMAND (TO ONE PERSON)
To stick out one's tongue	Sacar la lengua	Stick out your tongue.	Saque la lengua.
To swallow	Tragar	Swallow the liquid.	Trague el líquido.
To take out	Sacar	Take out his/her IV.	Sáquele el suero.

SUMMARY EXERCISE / EJERCICIO A MODO DE RESUMEN

The dietician is meeting with your patient, Mr. Cortés, and his wife, Mrs. Cortés. Mr. Cortés is recovering from open-heart surgery. He needs to be instructed on healthy food choices and will start with the dietician helping him with the food menu available for tomorrow. Mr. Cortés informed the dietician that he likes fried foods, sweets, and beer. The dietician smiles and begins to help Mr. Cortés with his menu.

Translate the following scenario:

Dietician: What do you like to eat for breakfast?

Mr. Cortés: I like 3 eggs, 2 pieces of bacon, 3 pieces of sausage, toast and coffee with milk, and 2 teaspoons of sugar.

Dietician: Mr. Cortés, you need to eat more fruits and vegetables.

Mrs. Cortés: And add fiber to your diet.

Mr. Cortés: OK, for breakfast I want fiber cereal and a banana and coffee with milk.

Dietician: Very good, what do you want for lunch?

Mr. Cortés: I want to eat 2 hamburgers with cheese on bread, French fries with ketchup and a soft drink with ice cream for dessert!

Mrs. Cortés: You have to listen to the dietician.

Dietician: Mr. Cortés, do you want to eat a salad with tuna and cucumbers for lunch and have water to drink?

Mr. Cortés: Yes, I like salad and tuna but am I able to have dressing with the salad?

Dietician: Yes, Mr. Cortés, you can put vinegar and oil on the salad. What do you want to eat for dinner?

Mr. Cortés: I want a big steak, a potato with a lot of butter, beans with cheese, and caramel custard!

Dietician: Mr. Cortés, do you like vegetables?

Mr. Cortés: Yes, I like vegetables with butter!

Mrs. Cortés: Eat vegetables, but not with butter.

Mr. Cortés: Yes, I want a small steak with a potato, carrots with no butter and two beers.

Mrs. Cortés:	Beer is bad for (para) your diet.
Mr. Cortés:	OK, I want to have water with dinner.
Dietician:	Do you want a snack?
Mr. Cortés:	I want tres leches, thank you.
Mrs. Cortés:	You have to listen to the dietician. You eat too much (demasiado) sugar.
Dietician:	For a snack eat an apple or orange or three cups of popcorn with no butter or salt.
Mr. Cortés:	Thank you!
Dietician:	Thank you Mr. Cortés!

READING: JEAN HENRI DUNANT, HUMANITARIAN / LECTURA: JEAN HENRI DUNANT, HUMANITARIO

Reading

Jean Henri Dunant, humanitarian (1828–1910, b. Geneva, Switzerland): Humanity credits Jean Henri Dunant with the creation of very important institutions. Dunant is originally a business man but when he observes the outcome of the battle of Solerino (1859), during the Italian unification, he completely changes his life and creates a volunteer corps that helps to gather the wounded soldiers, regardless of whether they are part of the Austrian army or of the Piedmont–French army. In 1863, he founds the International Red Cross and in 1864 he influences the creation of the Geneva Convention, which protects those wounded in the war. In 1901, he receives the first Nobel Peace Prize.

Lectura

Jean Henri Dunant, humanitario (1828–1910, n. Ginebra, Suiza): La humanidad le debe a Jean Henri Dunant la creación de instituciones muy importantes. Dunant es primero un hombre de negocios pero cuando observa las consecuencias de la batalla de Solferino (1859), durante la unificación italiana, cambia totalmente su vida y crea un cuerpo de voluntarios que ayudan a recoger los cuerpos de los soldados heridos, sin importar si pertenecen al ejército austriaco o al ejército franco-piamontés. En 1863 funda la Cruz Roja Internacional y en 1864 influye en la creación de la "Convención de Ginebra" que protege a los heridos en la guerra. En 1901 recibe el primer Premio Nobel de la Paz.

IDIOMATIC EXPRESSIONS / EXPRESIONES IDIOMÁTICAS

To turn red as a tomato   English expression

Ponerse como un tomate   Spanish expression

To become like a tomato   Literal translation

A piece of cake   English expression

Pan comido   Spanish expression

Eaten bread   Literal translation

6

SPANISH PHRASES COMMONLY USED IN PATIENT CARE

CONTENTS

Idioms: Basic Spanish grammatical expressions used in patient care / Modismos: Expresiones básicas de gramática en español utilizadas en el cuidado del paciente

Using the past tense to determine the patient's current health status / Uso del pasado para determinar el estado de salud actual del paciente

To whom or for whom things are done: Use of indirect object pronouns in conversation with Spanish-speaking patients / Para quién es algo o a quién se le hace algo: El uso del complemento indirecto en conversaciones con pacientes hispanohablantes

The use of demonstratives ("this," "that," "these," "those") and adverbs of location ("here," "there") / El uso de demostrativos ("este," etc.) y adverbios de lugar ("aquí," "ahí," "allí")

The Spanish use of the double negative / El uso de la doble negación en español

Use of the prepositions "por" and "para" ("for" and "in order to") in patient care / Uso de las preposiciones "por" y "para" en el cuidado del paciente

Expressing subjective opinions, desires, emotions, doubts, necessities in Spanish: The subjunctive mood / Cómo expresar opiniones subjetivas, deseos, emociones, dudas, necesidades en español: El subjuntivo

Summary exercise / Ejercicio a modo de resumen

Reading: Severo Ochoa, Spanish physician and biochemist / Lectura: Severo Ochoa, médico y bioquímico español

Idiomatic expressions / Expresiones idiomáticas

IDIOMS: BASIC SPANISH GRAMMATICAL EXPRESSIONS USED IN PATIENT CARE / MODISMOS: EXPRESIONES BÁSICAS DE GRAMÁTICA EN ESPAÑOL UTILIZADAS EN EL CUIDADO DEL PACIENTE

This chapter is designed to enhance the linguistic abilities of the health care provider to communicate with the patient. Advanced topics provided include the past tense, use of the indirect object and demonstrative pronouns, Spanish use of the double negative, the challenges of the correct use of "por" and "para," and the subjunctive mood. Summary exercises review these advanced topics as each relates to the care of the patient. To strengthen the medical Spanish applications presented in this chapter, refer to Section II.

Clarification of the use of the subject pronoun "you" in Spanish

ENGLISH SUBJECT PRONOUNS	USE OF THE SUBJECT PRONOUN "YOU" IN SPANISH	SPANISH SUBJECT PRONOUNS
I		yo
You	Informal singular	Tú
He/she		él/ella
You	Formal singular	Ud.
We		nosotros/as
You	Used in Spain plural (all of you)	vosotros/as
They		ellos/ellas
You	Plural formal or informal (all of you)	Uds.

USING THE PAST TENSE TO DETERMINE THE PATIENT'S CURRENT HEALTH STATUS / USO DEL PASADO PARA DETERMINAR EL ESTADO DE SALUD ACTUAL DEL PACIENTE

- To form the simple past (preterit) in Spanish, drop the infinitive ending and add one of the verb endings indicated in the chart that follows.
- The **-ar** verbs have one set of endings; the endings for **-er** and **-ir** verbs are identical.

SUBJECT PRONOUNS		AR VERBS		ER VERBS		IR VERBS	
		To take	Tomar	To eat	Comer	To write	Escribir
I	yo	took	tomé	ate	comí	wrote	escribí
You	tú	took	tomaste	ate	comiste	wrote	escribiste
He/she	él/ella	took	tomó	ate	comió	wrote	escribió
You	Ud.	took	tomó	ate	comió	wrote	escribió
We	nosotros/as	took	tomamos	ate	comimos	wrote	escribimos
You	vosotros/as	took	tomasteis	ate	comisteis	wrote	escribisteis
They	ellos/ellas	took	tomaron	ate	comieron	wrote	escribieron
You	Uds.	took	tomaron	ate	comieron	wrote	escribieron

Past tense/preterit verbs commonly used in health care / Verbos en el pretérito utilizados en el cuidado del paciente

To take	Tomar
Did you drink the soup?	¿Tomó Ud. la sopa?
How long did the operation take?	¿Cuánto tiempo tomó la operación?
The operation took one hour.	La operación tomó una hora.
The patient took an overdose of pills.	La paciente tomó una sobredosis de pastillas.

To cut oneself	Cortarse*
How did you cut yourself?	¿Cómo se cortó?
I cut myself with the knife by accident.	Me corté con el cuchillo por accidente.

*   The verb "cortarse" is used for an accidental cut to oneself as well as to indicate self-harm.

To happen	Pasar
What happened?	¿Qué pasó?
When did it happen?	¿Cuándo pasó?

To occur	Ocurrir
Where did the accident occur?	¿Dónde ocurrió el accidente?
The accident occurred at home.	El accidente ocurrió en casa.

To eat	Comer
What did the patient eat?	¿Qué comió el/la paciente?
She ate the fruit.	Ella comió la fruta.

To swallow	Tragarse
Did the patient swallow the barium?	¿El paciente se tragó el bario?
Did the child swallow the coins?	¿El niño se tragó las monedas?

This diagram demonstrates how to use the expression "what happens" in the present and in the past tense/preterit.

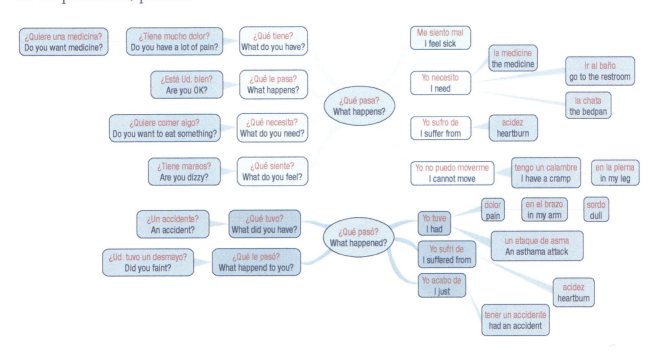

Preterit of verbs whose infinitives end in -car, -gar, -zar / El pretérito de verbos cuyos infinitivos terminan en -car, -gar, -zar

- With verbs whose infinitives end in –car, -gar, and –zar, the "I" ("yo") form in the past is irregular.

  For example,　I touched the button. = Yo toqué el botón.

  (Tocar: "c" changes to "qu" in "yo" form.)

  I arrived at the hospital at 8 p.m. = Yo llegué al hospital a las ocho de la noche.

  (Llegar: "g" changes to "gu" in "yo" form.)

  I began the diet on Friday. = Yo empecé la dieta el viernes.

  (Empezar: "z" changes to "c" in "yo" form.)

Irregular preterit verbs commonly used in health care / Frecuentes verbos irregulares usados en el pretérito en el cuidado del paciente

- Hacer in the preterit is irregular.

ENGLISH SUBJECT PRONOUNS	VERB TO MAKE/DO	SPANISH SUBJECT PRONOUNS	VERB IN SPANISH HACER
I	made/did	Yo	hice
You	made/did	Tú	hiciste
He/she	made/did	él/ella	hizo
You	made/did	Ud.	hizo
We	made/did	nosotros/as	hicimos
You	made/did	vosotros/ as	hicisteis
They	made/did	ellos/ellas	hicieron
You	made/did	Uds.	hicieron

- Tener in the preterite is also irregular.

ENGLISH SUBJECT PRONOUNS	VERB TO HAVE	SPANISH SUBJECT PRONOUNS	VERB IN SPANISH TENER
I	had	Yo	tuve
You	had	Tú	tuviste
He/she	had	él/ella	tuvo
You	had	Ud.	tuvo
We	had	nosotros/as	tuvimos
You	had	vosotros/as	tuvisteis
They	had	ellos/ellas	tuvieron
You	had	Uds.	tuvieron

AUDIO 6.4

Adverbs of time: "Yesterday," "last night," "last week," and other helpful expressions with the past tense / *Adverbios de tiempo: Ayer, anoche, la semana pasada, y otras expresiones útiles en el pasado*

- Some helpful words/phrases that can accompany past-tense verb expressions in Spanish are the following:

ENGLISH	SPANISH
Yesterday	Ayer
The day before yesterday	Anteayer
Last night	Anoche
Last week	La semana pasada
Last month	El mes pasado
Last year	El año pasado
Suddenly	De golpe/De repente
This morning	Esta mañana

Ud. tiene tos, por favor, tápese la boca

For example,	When did Pepe's nose bleed start?	¿Cuándo le empezó la hemorragia nasal a Pepe?
	It began yesterday.	Le empezó ayer.
	When did the accident occur?	¿Cuándo ocurrió el accidente?
	The accident occurred last night.	El accidente ocurrió anoche.
	When did you eat the peanut?	¿Cuándo comió Ud. maní?
	I ate the peanut twenty minutes ago.	Comí maní hace veinte minutos.
	When did you cut your hand?	¿Cuándo se cortó la mano?
	I cut my hand last night.	Me corté la mano anoche.

AUDIO 6.5

TO WHOM OR FOR WHOM THINGS ARE DONE: USE OF INDIRECT OBJECT PRONOUNS IN CONVERSATION WITH SPANISH-SPEAKING PATIENTS / PARA QUIÉN ES ALGO O A QUIÉN SE LE HACE ALGO: EL USO DEL COMPLEMENTO INDIRECTO EN CONVERSACIONES CON PACIENTES HISPANOHABLANTES

- The indirect object pronoun replaces the person "to whom" or "for whom" something is done.

- The indirect object pronoun may be placed either before the conjugated verb when there is only one verb in the sentence, or it may be attached to the infinitive when there are two verbs in the sentence.

    For example, My mother prepares the food *for me.* = Mi madre *me* prepara la comida.

- The indirect object pronoun would be "me," meaning that the action was done "to/ for me."

    For example, Our friend is going to buy *us* the pencils. = Nuestro amigo *nos* va a comprar los lápices. = Nuestro amigo va a comprar*nos* los lápices.

- Some verbs always take indirect object pronouns because, by definition, they express actions "to" or "for" someone else: "to give" = "dar," "to send" = "enviar," "to prescribe" = "recetar," "to ask" = "preguntar."

    For example, The nurse sends *me* the forms./The nurse sends the forms *to me* = La enfermera *me* envía los formularios.

- Indirect object pronouns are used when an action is done "to" or "for" *another,* but reflexive verbs are used when the performer and receiver of the action are the *same person.*

For example,   The doctor gives *you* the injection. = El doctor *le* pone a Ud. la inyección (indirect object pronoun).

For example,   You give *yourself* an injection of vitamin B$_{12}$ every month. = (Ud.) *se* pone una inyección de la vitamina B$_{12}$ cada mes. (reflexive verb)

*   Use "poner" in Spanish to indicate "to give" an injection.

Indirect Object Pronouns

For/to me	Me
For/to you	Te
For/to him/her	Le
For/to you	Le
For/to us	Nos
For/to all of you	Os
For/to them	Les
For/to all of you	Les

Examples using indirect object pronouns / Ejemplos del uso de los complementos de pronombre indirecto

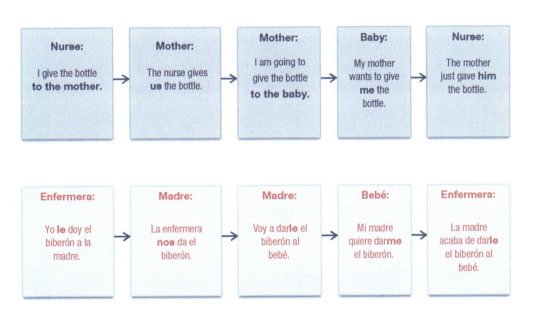

Nurse: I give the bottle **to the mother.** → **Mother:** The nurse gives **us** the bottle. → **Mother:** I am going to give the bottle **to the baby.** → **Baby:** My mother wants to give **me** the bottle. → **Nurse:** The mother just gave **him** the bottle.

Enfermera: Yo **le** doy el biberón a la madre. → **Madre:** La enfermera **nos** da el biberón. → **Madre:** Voy a dar**le** el biberón al bebé. → **Bebé:** Mi madre quiere dar**me** el biberón. → **Enfermera:** La madre acaba de dar**le** el biberón al bebé.

THE USE OF DEMONSTRATIVES ("THIS," "THAT," "THESE," "THOSE") AND ADVERBS OF LOCATION ("HERE," "THERE") / EL USO DE DEMOSTRATIVOS ("ESTE," ETC.) Y ADVERBIOS DE LUGAR ("AQUÍ," "AHÍ," "ALLÍ")

 ## Adverbs of location: "here," "there," and "over there": / Adverbios de lugar: "aquí," "ahí," y "allí"

- In English, we express the location of things as "here" or "there," but, in Spanish, location is distinguished by proximity, using the adverbs of location: **aquí** (here)* close to the speaker, **ahí** (there) close to the listener, and **allí** (over there)** far from both the speaker and the listener. This same concept is applied when using demonstrative adjectives.

 ## Demonstrative adjectives: "this," "that," "these," "those" / Los adjetivos demostrativos: este / esta / estos / estas, ese / esa / esos / esas, aquel / aquella / aquellos / aquellas

- In Spanish there are three sets of demonstrative adjectives.

| SINGULAR | | PLURAL | |
MASCULINE	FEMININE	MASCULINE	FEMININE
este (this)	esta* (this)	estos (these)	estas (these)
ese (that)	esa (that)	esos (those)	esas (those)
aquel (that) [over there]	aquella (that) [over there]	aquellos (those) [over there]	aquellas (those) [over there]

*"Esta" = "this"; "está" = "is" (from "estar"/"to be")

- The demonstrative adjectives **este**, **esta**, **estos**, and **estas** are used to point out nouns that are close to the speaker and the listener.

---

* "Aquí" and "acá" both mean "here" and are interchangeable.
** "Allí" and "allá" both mean "there" and are interchangeable.

- The demonstrative adjectives ese, esa, esos, and esas are used to point out nouns that are close to the listener.
- The demonstrative adjectives aquel, aquella, aquellos, and aquellas are used to point out nouns that are far away from the speaker and the listener.

Here = Aquí

This nurse (before a masculine, singular noun)	Este enfermero
This nurse (before a feminine, singular noun)	Esta enfermera
These nurses (before a masculine, plural noun)	Estos enfermeros
These nurses (before a feminine, plural noun)	Estas enfermeras

There = Ahí

That nurse (before a masculine, singular noun)	Ese enfermero
That nurse (before a feminine, singular noun)	Esa enfermera
Those nurses (before a masculine, plural noun)	Esos enfermeros
Those nurses (before a feminine, plural noun)	Esas enfermeras

Over there = Allí

That nurse (before a masculine, singular noun)	Aquel enfermero
That nurse (before a feminine, singular noun)	Aquella enfermera
Those nurses (before a masculine, plural noun)	Aquellos enfermeros
Those nurses (before a feminine, plural noun)	Aquellas enfermeras

For example,	I need to go to **that** clinic *over there*.	Necesito ir a **aquella** clínica *allí*.
	The child of **that** mother, Mrs. Escobar, is *here* in the hospital.	El niño de **esa** madre, la señora Escobar, está *aquí* en el hospital.
	The parents of **this** girl live in **that** city *over there*.	Los padres de **esta** niña viven en **aquella** ciudad *allí*.
	Here is the doctor who is going to help **this** child.	*Aquí* está el doctor que va a ayudar a **esta** chica.

THE SPANISH USE OF THE DOUBLE NEGATIVE / EL USO DE LA DOBLE NEGACIÓN EN ESPAÑOL

- The double negative is a grammatically correct structure in Spanish.

The structure of the double negative / La estructura de la doble negación

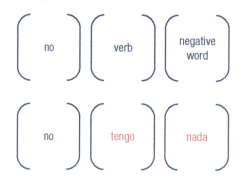

I do not have anything.

- When you have a positive word like "alguien" (someone) in a sentence, there is no double negative.

- When the sentence is negative, then "alguien" is replaced by the corresponding negative word "nadie" after the verb:

For example,   Is there someone in the bathroom?   ¿Hay **alguien** en el baño?
               Yes, there is someone in the bathroom.   Sí, hay **alguien** en el baño.
               No, there is nobody in the bathroom.   No, **no** hay **nadie** en el baño.

- All positive words have a corresponding negative:

   Do you have something to eat? = ¿Tiene **algo** para comer?

   Yes, I have something to eat. = Sí, tengo **algo** para comer.

Do you not have anything to eat? = ¿**No** tiene **nada** para comer?

No, I do not have anything to eat. = No, **no** tengo **nada** para comer.

List of affirmative and negative words / Lista de palabras afirmativas y negativas

AFFIRMATIVE WORDS		NEGATIVE WORDS	
Something, anything, everything	algo	nothing	nada
Everything, all	todo		nada
Everybody, all	todos, todas	nobody	nadie
Someone, somebody	alguien	no one, nobody	nadie
A, an, some, any	algún, alguno*, algunos, alguna, algunas	none, not any	ningún*, ninguno ninguna
either, or	o	neither, nor	ni...ni
always, every day	siempre todos los días	never	nunca, jamás
sometimes	a veces	never	nunca, jamás
also, too	también	neither, either, nor	tampoco

*   The adjectives **alguno** and **ninguno** shorten to **algún** and **ningún**, respectively, before a masculine singular noun—just as "uno" shortens to "un." **Ninguno** or **ningún** is always used in the singular.

For example,

Do you have any pain?	¿Tiene **algún** dolor?
I do not have any pain.	No tengo **ningún** dolor.
I do not have any.	No tengo **ninguno**.
Do you have any allergies?	¿Ud. tiene **alguna** alergia?
No, I do not have any allergies.	No, no tengo **ninguna** alergia.
No, I do not have any.	No, no tengo **ninguna**.
Did you have any problems with the medication?	¿Ud. tuvo **algún** problema con la medicina?
No, I did not have any.	No, no tuve **ninguno**.

- In Spanish, when using "algún" or "alguna" in a question, the singular is used because it refers to an indefinite quantity.

- When "algunos" or "algunas" is used in an answer, the translation is "some."

For example,	Do you have **any** pencils?	¿Tiene **algún** *lápiz*?
	Yes, I have **some** pencils.	Sí, tengo **algunos** *lápices*.
	No, I do not have **any** pencils.	No, no tengo **ningún** *lápiz*. / No, no tengo **ninguno**.

AUDIO 6.10

How to use the double negative when obtaining information from the patient / Cómo usar la doble negación cuando se obtiene información del paciente

- To establish family history, the questions, "Did anyone/someone in your family have…" are used.

- The words "someone/somebody" (**alguien**) as well as "no one/nobody" (**nadie**) are incorporated into questions and responses.

- When "nobody" (nadie) is used as a subject, it can be placed before the verb, and there is no double negation.

- When "nadie" is used after the verb, it is part of the double-negative structure.

For example,	In your family did anyone have tuberculosis?	¿En su familia **alguien** tuvo tuberculosis?
	Yes, my father had tuberculosis.	Sí, mi padre tuvo tuberculosis.
	In your family did anyone have chicken pox?	¿En su familia **alguien** tuvo varicela?
	No, nobody had chicken pox.	No, **nadie** tuvo varicela.

- The words "**nunca**" and "**jamás**" mean "never." In a question, "jamás" translates to "ever."

For example,	Did you ever have blood in your urine?	¿Alguna vez tuvo sangre en la orina?
	I never had blood in my urine.	**Jamás** tuve sangre en la orina.
	Did you ever have the measles?	¿**Jamás** tuvo sarampión?

For example,	Did you always have that mole on your calf?	¿**Siempre** tuvo ese lunar en la pantorrilla?
	No, I never look at my calves.	No, **nunca** me miro las pantorrillas.
For example,	Do you want to eat meat or fish?	¿Quieres comer carne **o** pescado?
	I do not want to eat either meat or fish.	No quiero comer ni carne, ni pescado.
	Nor do I want to eat chicken.	**Tampoco** quiero comer pollo.
For example,	Is there something for the patient?	¿Hay **algo** para el paciente?
	No, there is nothing for the patient.	No, no hay **nada** para el paciente.
For example,	Do you have pain when you urinate?	¿Tiene dolor cuando orina?
	Yes, sometimes I have pain when I urinate.	Sí, **a veces** tengo dolor cuando orino.
For example,	Do you always need to use an inhaler when you run?	¿**Siempre** necesita usar un inhalador cuando corre?
	Yes, I always need to use an inhaler when I run.	Sí, **siempre** necesito usar un inhalador cuando corro.

USE OF THE PREPOSITIONS "POR" AND "PARA" ("FOR" AND "IN ORDER TO") IN PATIENT CARE / USO DE LAS PREPOSICIONES "POR" Y "PARA" EN EL CUIDADO DEL PACIENTE

Distinguishing the usage of "por" from "para" / Cómo distinguir "por" y "para"

- These prepositions can both translate to "for" in English but they are not interchangeable.
- "Para" is more precise/targeted, whereas "por" is less direct, and can point in various directions.
  "Para"
- Use the following acronym to help you remember the uses of "para": PERFECT

P urpose
E ffect
R ecipient
F uture dates/events
E mployment
C omparison
T oward

Purpose: We use the scalpel in order to make an incision.

Usamos el bisturí **para** hacer una incisión.

Effect: I study in order to become a doctor.

Yo estudio **para** ser doctora.

Recipient: The elastic bandage is for the patient.

La venda elástica es **para** el paciente.

Future dates/events: The x-ray has to be ready for tomorrow.

La radiografía tiene que estar lista **para** mañana.

Employment: The midwife works for this hospital.

La matrona trabaja **para** este hospital.

Comparison: For a 5-month-old baby, he is very big.

Para un bebé de cinco meses, es muy grande.

Toward: The family of the patient leaves for Mexico tomorrow.

La familia de la paciente sale **para** México mañana.

AUDIO 6.12

"Por"

• Use the following acronym to help you remember the uses of "por": ATTRACTED

A round a place
T hrough a place
T ime of the day
R eason for errand
A ccount of/behalf of
C ost
T hanks
E xchange
D uration

Around a place: The children walk around the park.

Los niños caminan **por** el parque.

Through a place: We have to pass through security before entering the airport.

Tenemos que pasar **por** la seguridad antes de entrar al aeropuerto.

Time of day: It is important to take the pills in the morning.

Es importante tomar las pastillas **por** la mañana.

Reason for errand: I am going to go to the pharmacy for the antibiotic.

Voy a ir a la farmacia **por** el antibiótico.

Account of/behalf of: Ana has to work for Victoria because she is sick.

Ana tiene que trabajar **por** Victoria porque ella está enferma.

Cost: I have just paid a lot of money for the uniform.

Acabo de pagar mucho dinero **por** el uniforme.

Thanks: Thanks a lot for the help.

Muchas gracias **por** la ayuda.

Exchange: The dietician exchanges the soda for water.

La dietista cambia la soda **por** agua.

Duration: Do not move for one minute please.

No se mueva **por** un minuto, por favor.

EXPRESSING SUBJECTIVE OPINIONS, DESIRES, EMOTIONS, DOUBTS, NECESSITIES IN SPANISH: THE SUBJUNCTIVE MOOD / CÓMO EXPRESAR OPINIONES SUBJETIVAS, DESEOS, EMOCIONES, DUDAS, NECESIDADES EN ESPAÑOL: EL SUBJUNTIVO

AUDIO 6.13

Explanation of the subjunctive / Explicación del subjuntivo

- The subjunctive is not a tense but rather a mood in Spanish, and is used to express moods such as a desire, emotion, want, wish, need, doubt, permission, prohibition, or fear.

- This text will highlight a few uses of the subjunctive that are pertinent to the health care provider.

Forming the present subjunctive / Cómo formar el presente del subjuntivo

- To form the subjunctive, start with the "yo" ("I") form in the present tense:

I take = tomo (tomar)	I eat = como (comer)	I live = vivo (vivir)

- Remove the final "o" off the "yo" form.
- Add the opposite endings: For –ar verbs, add –er/-ir endings; for –er/-ir verbs, add –ar endings.

Tomar - tom+e
Comer - com+a
Vivir - viv+a

TO TAKE = TOMAR	TO EAT = COMER	TO LIVE = VIVIR
tome	coma	viva
tomes	comas	vivas
tome	coma	viva
tomemos	comamos	vivamos
toméis	comáis	viváis
tomen	coman	vivan

Hint/OJO: Note that first-and third-person singular forms are identical.

Irregular subjunctive forms / Formas irregulares con el subjuntivo

- Note the forms of the following irregular verbs:

ENGLISH INFINITIVE	SPANISH INFINITIVE	"YO" FORM = FORMA "YO"	SUBJUNCTIVE = SUBJUNTIVO
To have	tener	Tengo	tenga, tengas, tenga, tengamos, tengáis, tengan
To say or tell	decir	Digo	diga, digas, diga, digamos, digáis, digan
To order	pedir	Pido	pida, pidas, pida, pidamos, pidáis, pidan
To sleep	dormir	Duermo	duerma, duermas, duerma, durmamos, durmáis, duerman

(continued / continuado)

(continued / continuado)

ENGLISH INFINITIVE	SPANISH INFINITIVE	"YO" FORM = FORMA "YO"	SUBJUNCTIVE = SUBJUNTIVO
To make or do	hacer	Hago	haga, hagas, haga, hagamos, hagáis, hagan
To bring	traer	Traigo	traiga, traigas, traiga, traigamos, traigáis, traigan
To swallow	tragar	Trago	trague, tragues, trague, traguemos, traguéis, traguen
To touch	tocar	Toco	toque, toques, toque, toquemos, toquéis, toquen
To begin	empezar	Empiezo	empiece, empieces, empiece, empecemos, empecéis, empiecen
To be able to	poder	Puedo	pueda, puedas, pueda, podamos, podáis, puedan
To rest	descansar	Descanso	descanse, descanses, descanse, descansemos, descanséis, descansen
To put	poner	Pongo	ponga, pongas, ponga, pongamos, pongáis, pongan
To follow	seguir	Sigo	siga, sigas, siga, sigamos, sigáis, sigan
To try	probar	Pruebo	pruebe, pruebes, pruebe, probemos, probéis, prueben

AUDIO
6.31–6.35

• The following verbs are irregular and form the subjunctive in the following manner:

To go	ir	vaya, vayas, vaya, vayamos, vayáis, vayan
To give	dar	dé, des, dé, demos, deis, den
To be	ser	sea, seas, sea, seamos, seáis, sean
To be	estar	esté, estés, esté, estemos, estéis, estén
To know	saber	sepa, sepas, sepa, sepamos, sepáis, sepan

Use of basic structures of the subjunctive / Uso de estructuras básicas del subjuntivo

• The subjunctive occurs in the dependent clause of a sentence. The word "that"/"que" usually precedes the subjunctive phrase. The independent clause usually has a different subject and verb than the dependent clause.

• In order to have the subjunctive case, there must be two different subjects. These two subjects are generally separated by the word "that" ("que"). The verb that accompanies the first subject is not in the subjunctive and becomes a trigger verb if it implies a want, emotion, doubt, fear, or desire. If the first verb is a "trigger verb," the verb accompanying the second subject would be in the subjunctive.

For example,   The child wants his mother to bring him ice cream. = The child wants that the mother bring him ice cream. = El niño quiere que su madre le *traiga* el helado.

| SUBJECT 1 + | INDICATIVE VERB + | THAT + | SUBJECT 2 + | SUBJUNCTIVE |
SUJETO 1 +	VERBO INDICATIVO +	QUE +	SUJETO 2 +	SUBJUNTIVO
The nurse	wants	that	the patient	does not smoke.
La enfermera	quiere	que	el paciente	no fume.
I	fear	that	the dog	is sick.
Yo	temo	que	el perro	esté enfermo.
I	hope	that	you	do the exercises.
Yo	espero	que	Ud.	haga los ejercicios.
George	needs	that	I	bring the newspaper.
Jorge	necesita	que	yo	traiga el periódico.

The subjunctive with impersonal expressions: It is important / necessary / urgent that / El subjuntivo con expresiones impersonales: Es importante / Es necesario / Es urgente que...

• The following are examples of impersonal expressions that use the subjunctive because there is no clear first subject. These expressions are generally used in opinions or recommendations.

For example,   **It is important** that you go to bed now. = **Es importante** que Ud. se acueste ahora.

IT IS +	ADJECTIVE +	THAT +	SUBJECT +	SUBJUNCTIVE
ES +	ADJETIVO +	QUE +	SUJETO 2 +	SUBJUNTIVO
It is	urgent	that	the family	come to the hospital.
Es	urgente	que	la familia	venga al hospital.
It is	necessary	that	we	talk with the doctor.
Es	necesario	que	nosotros	hablemos con el doctor.
It is	good	that	you	feel better.
Es	bueno	que	Ud.	se sienta mejor.
It is	possible	that	she	goes home today.
Es	posible	que	ella	vaya a casa hoy.
It is	advisable	that	you	follow the diet.
Es	aconsejable	que	Ud.	siga la dieta.

SUMMARY EXERCISE / EJERCICIO A MODO DE RESUMEN

A 28-year-old female (Javiera) is talking with her health care provider about starting birth control pills. Translate the following conversation from English to Spanish.

HCP:	Javiera, does anyone in your family have a history of breast cancer (cáncer de seno)?
Javiera:	Yes, my grandmother and aunt.
HCP:	On which side of the family? (Del lado de la madre o del lado del padre?)
Javiera:	My paternal grandmother and her sister had breast cancer.
HCP:	Are your grandmother and aunt alive?
Javiera:	Yes, they both (las dos) are alive.
HCP:	Does anyone in your family have migraine headaches?
Javiera:	No, no one in my family has migraine headaches, but I have migraine headaches.
HCP:	Do you have an aura with the migraine headache?
Javiera:	Yes.
HCP:	When do you have migraine headaches?
Javiera:	I have migraine headaches before (antes de) my period (la regla).
HCP:	Does anyone in your family have a bleeding disorder?
Javiera:	Yes, I have Factor V Leiden (el factor V Leiden).
HCP:	I am going to give you a prescription for progestin-only birth control pills, pills without estrogen (la píldora con progesterona sin estrógeno).

READING: SEVERO OCHOA, SPANISH PHYSICIAN AND BIOCHEMIST / LECTURA: SEVERO OCHOA, MÉDICO Y BIOQUÍMICO ESPAÑOL

Reading

Severo Ochoa (1905–1993, b. Asturias, Spain) is a Spanish physician and biochemist who received (with Arthur Kornberg) the first Nobel Prize in Physiology and Medicine in 1959. In 1923, Ochoa studied at the University of Madrid medical school, where he and a colleague developed a method to estimate creatinine in the muscles. In 1945, at the University of New York, he investigated the fields of pharmacology and biochemistry, and, in 1954, he discovered an enzyme capable of synthesizing RNA (ribonucleic acid) in vitro.

Lectura

Severo Ochoa (1905–1993, n. Asturias, Spain), médico y bioquímico español, recibió (junto con Arthur Kornberg) el Premio Nobel de Fisiología y Medicina en 1959. En 1923, Ochoa estudió en la Universidad de Madrid, donde él y un colega desarrollaron un método para calcular la creatinina en los músculos. En 1945, en la Universidad de Nueva York, investigó en el campo farmacológico y bioquímico, y, en 1954, descubrió una enzima capaz de sintetizar ARN (ácido ribonucleico) in vitro.

IDIOMATIC EXPRESSIONS / EXPRESIONES IDIOMÁTICAS

To sleep like a log	English expression
Dormir a pierna suelta	Spanish expression
To sleep with a free leg	Literal translation

To be born with a silver spoon in your mouth	English expression
Nacer con la marraqueta bajo el brazo	Spanish expression
To be born with bread under the arm	Literal translation

SECTION II

MEDICAL SPANISH IN CLINICAL PRACTICE

7

PATIENT ASSESSMENT

CONTENTS

Attending to patients in urgent situations / Cómo atender a pacientes en situaciones de emergencia

Attending to noncritical patients / Cómo atender a pacientes en situaciones no críticas

Reading: Alfredo Quiñones, neurosurgeon / Lectura: Alfredo Quiñones, neurocirujano

Idiomatic expressions / Expresiones idiomáticas

PATIENT HISTORY AND NURSING ASSESSMENT / HISTORIAL DEL PACIENTE Y VALORACIÓN DEL PACIENTE

The information in this chapter guides the nurse in the assessment of the patient who presents to the hospital in a variety of situations. An overview of terminology needed to obtain the current patient history and basic assessment is provided. Terminology that is essential to providing care for the patient in various circumstances is presented in specific sections related to the particular hospital scenario. Urgent situations that include a general intake of a patient in the emergency department (ED), presenting to the ED after an automobile accident, having a drug-related issue, and altered states of consciousness are translated from English to basic Spanish. Essential phrases for inpatient care are also provided. This includes the assessment of patients in pain, dietary concerns for the post operative patient, fall-risk assessment and assistance with activities of daily living (ADL), care of the diabetic patient, frequently used statements and questions for hospitalized patients, as well as those in need of wound and catheter care. It is assumed that a translating device is available to explore the more serious issues of patients presenting for urgent care.

NURSING HISTORY AND ASSESSMENT OF THE SPANISH-SPEAKING PATIENT / HISTORIAL Y VALORACIÓN DEL PACIENTE HISPANOHABLANTE

AUDIO 7.1

Patient history / Historial del paciente

PERSONAL HISTORY	HISTORIA PERSONAL
What is your name?	¿Cuál es su nombre?/¿Cómo se llama Ud.?
How old are you?	¿Cuántos años tiene Ud.?
Where are you from?	¿De dónde es Ud.?

(continued / continuado)

(continued / continuado)

PERSONAL HISTORY	HISTORIA PERSONAL
Are you . . .?	¿Es Ud.?
Single	soltero/a
Married	casado/a
Divorced	divorciado/a
Widower/widow	viudo/a
Separated	separado/a
Do you have children?	¿Tiene Ud. hijos?

MEDICATIONS	MEDICINAS
What medication do you take?	¿Qué medicinas toma Ud.?
Do you take vitamins?	¿Toma Ud. vitaminas?
Do you take herbal supplements?	¿Toma Ud. suplementos homeopáticos?

ALLERGIES	ALERGIAS
Are you allergic to any medications?	¿Es Ud. alérgico a alguna medicina?
Are you allergic to any substances such as latex?	¿Es Ud. alérgico a alguna substancia como al latex?
What type of reaction do you have?	¿Qué tipo de reacción tiene?

HABITS	HÁBITOS
Do you smoke cigarettes?	¿Fuma Ud. cigarrillos?
Do you drink alcohol?	¿Bebe Ud. alcohol?
Do you use drugs?	¿Usa Ud. drogas?

CHIEF COMPLAINT	PROBLEMA PRINCIPAL DE SALUD
What type of health problem do you have today?	¿Qué tipo de problema de salud tiene Ud. hoy?

Vital signs / Signos vitales

BLOOD PRESSURE	PRESIÓN ARTERIAL
Hello Mr./Mrs., my name is _____.	Hola, Sr./Sra., mi nombre es _____.
I need to take your blood pressure.	Necesito tomarle la presión.

(continued / continuado)

(continued / continuado)

BLOOD PRESSURE	PRESIÓN ARTERIAL
Please give me your arm.	Me da su brazo, por favor.
I need to place the cuff on the arm.	Necesito ponerle el brazalete en el brazo.
Please do not move the arm.	Por favor no mueva el brazo.
The blood pressure is good.	La presión está bien.
Thank you!	¡Gracias!

TEMPERATURE AND PULSE	TEMPERATURA Y PULSO
I need to take your temperature and pulse.	Necesito tomarle la temperatura y el pulso.
Please open your mouth so I can place the thermometer under your tongue.	Por favor, abra la boca para colocarle el termómetro bajo la lengua.
The temperature is normal.	La temperatura está normal.
I need to take your pulse. I need to hold your wrist.	Necesito tomarle el pulso. Necesito sujetarle la muñeca.
Your pulse is good.	¡El pulso está bien!
Thank you!	¡Gracias!

HEIGHT AND WEIGHT	ALTURA Y PESO
I need to take your weight and height.	Necesito pesarlo/a y medirlo/a.
Please stand on the scale.	Por favor suba en la pesa.
Now please turn around on the scale. I need to take your height.	Ahora, por favor gire. Necesito medirlo/a.
Your weight is . . . kilos.	El peso es . . . kilos.
Your height is	La altura es . . ..
Thank you!	¡Gracias!

Assessment / Valoración

AUDIO 7.2

I need to listen to your lungs.	Necesito escuchar sus pulmones.
I need to listen to your heart.	Necesito escuchar su corazón.
I need to listen to your abdomen.	Necesito escuchar su abdomen.
I need to press on your abdomen. Does it hurt when I press?	Necesito presionar su abdomen. ¿Le duele esto cuando presiono?

(continued / continuado)

(continued / continuado)

I need to look at the skin on your feet and legs.	Necesito mirarle la piel de sus pies y piernas.
I need to check the pulses on your feet.	Necesito tomarle el pulso en los pies.
I need to talk to the doctor.	Necesito hablar con el doctor.

Discharging the patient / Dar de alta a un paciente

AUDIO 7.3

Today you are going home.	Hoy se va a casa.
Do you have any questions about your medicines?	¿Tiene preguntas relacionadas con sus medicinas?
Do you know when you need to see your practitioner after you are home?	¿Sabe Ud. cuándo necesita ver a su proveedor de salud cuándo ya está en casa?
Do you have your prescriptions?	¿Tiene sus recetas?
When is your family coming to take you home?	¿Cuándo viene su familia para llevarlo/a a casa?
Can I help you pack your clothes?	¿Puedo ayudarle a empacar su ropa?
Do you want to eat before you go home?	¿Quiere comer antes de irse a casa?
You need to sit in the wheelchair and I will take you to where your family is waiting for you.	Necesita sentarse en la silla de ruedas y le voy a llevar donde su familia lo/la está esperando.
Good bye! Take care of yourself!	¡Hasta luego! ¡Cuídese!

MEDICAL SUPPLIES AND EQUIPMENT / MATERIAL MÉDICO Y EQUIPO MÉDICO

AUDIO 7.4

Medical supplies / Material médico

Adhesive bandage	la curita
Alcohol swab	la toallita desinfectante
Blood test tube	el frasco de análisis de sangre
Brace	la abrazadera/el soporte
Catheter	el catéter/la sonda
Cotton balls	las motas de algodón
Cotton swabs	los palillos de algodón
Culture tube	el cultivo para el exudado faríngeo
Disinfectant	el desinfectante
Disposable gloves	los guantes desechables
Elastic bandage	la venda elástica

Facial tissue	el pañuelo de papel
Gauze	la gasa
Gauze bandage	la venda de gasa
Ice bag	la bolsa de hielo
Needle	la aguja
Pen light	la linterna de diagnóstico
Scale	la pesa
Sling	el cabestrillo
Suture kit	el material para suturar
Tape	la cinta
Tongue depresor	el depresor de lengua
Tourniquet	el torniquete

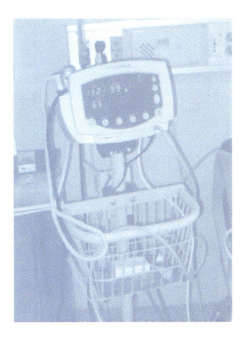

Medical equipment and related vocabulary / Equipo médico y vocabulario relacionado

AUDIO 7.5

Bandage scissors	las tijeras de vendaje
Blood pressure cuff	el tensiómetro/el esfigmomanómetro
EKG (electrocardiogram)	el electrocardiograma (ECG)
Glucometer	el glucómetro
Injection	la inyección
IV	el suero
Microscope	el microscopio
MRI	IRM (la imagen por resonancia magnética)
Opthalmoscope	el oftalmoscopio
Otoscope	el otoscopio
Oxymeter	el oxímetro
Pacemaker	el marcapasos
Probe	la sonda
Pulsimeter	el pulsómetro/el pulsímetro
Reflex hammer	el martillo de reflejo
Spirometer	el espirómetro

Stethoscope	el estetoscopio
Syringe	la jeringa
Thermometer	el termómetro
Tuning fork	el tenedor de sintonía
Tweezers	las pinzas
With contrast	con contraste
Without contrast	sin contraste
X-rays	los rayos equis

tomando la presión

Medical equipment and medical supplies

gasa

motas de algodón

palillos de algodón

tijeras de vendaje

curitas

cultivo para el exudado faríngeo y tubo de cultivo

linterna de diagnóstico

depresor de lengua

El otoscopio

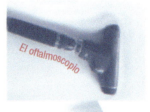
El oftalmoscopio

El Estetoscopio

El martillo de reflejo

El tenedor de sintonía

prueba cutánea de tuberculosis
regla

COMMON MEDICAL CONDITIONS AND RELATED VOCABULARY / LISTA DE CONDICIONES MÉDICAS FRECUENTES Y VOCABULARIO RELACIONADO

Acid reflux	la acidez
AIDS	el síndrome de inmunodeficiencia adquirida/SIDA
Arthritis	la artritis
Bleeding disorder	la hemorragia
Bronchitis	la bronquitis
Cancer	el cáncer
Cataracts	las cataratas
Chicken pox	la varicela
Cirrhosis	la cirrosis
A cold	un catarro/un resfriado
Conjuntivitis	la conjuntivitis
Cough/to cough	la tos/toser
Diabetes	la diabetes
Diarrhea	la diarrea
Diverticulitis	la diverticulitis
Ear infection	la infección de oído
Fatigue	la fatiga
The flu	la gripe
Gastritis	la gastritis
GERD (gastric esophageal reflux disorder)	ERGE (enfermedad por reflujo de ácido)
German measles	la rubeola
Goiter	el bocio
Gout	la gota
Headache	el dolor de cabeza
Heart attack	el ataque al corazón
Heart disease	la enfermedad del corazón
Hemorrhoids	las hemorroides
Hepatitis	la hepatitis

Hernia	la hernia
High blood pressure	la presión alta
Hyperthyroidism	el hipertiroidismo
Hypothyroidism	el hipotiroidismo
Irritable bowel syndrome/IBS	el síndrome del colon irritable/SCI
Kidney stones	los cálculos renales
Laryngitis	la laringitis
Leukemia	la leucemia
Measles	el sarampión
Meningitis	la meningitis
Migraine headache	la migraña/la jaqueca
Migrane headache with aura	la migraña con aura
Mononucleosis	la mononucleosis
MRSA (Methicillin-resistent *Staphlococus aureus*)	Estafilococo Dorado Resistente a la Meticilina (EDRM)
Nausea	la náusea
Pain	el dolor
Pharyngitis	la faringitis
Pneumonia	la neumonía
Productive cough	la tos con flema
Rash	el sarpullido
Rheumatoid arthritis	la artritis reumatoide
Sexually transmitted infection	la enfermedad transmitida sexualmente
Shingles	el herpes zóster/la culebrilla
Strep throat	la faringitis estreptocócica
Stroke	el infarto cerebral
Tonsilitis	la amigdalitis
A tumor	un tumor
Ulcer	la úlcera
Urinary tract infection	la infección urinaria
Viral pharyngitis	la faringitis viral

USEFUL PATIENT CARE EXPRESSIONS / EXPRESIONES ÚTILES PARA EL CUIDADO DEL PACIENTE

TRANSLATION	INFINITIVE	TRANSLATION	USAGE
To read the x-ray	Analizar la radiografía	I need to read the x-ray.	Necesito analizar la radiografía.
To check your reflexes	Chequearle los reflejos	I need to check your reflexes.	Necesito chequearle los reflejos.
To cut the gauze bandage	Cortarle la venda de gasa	I need to cut your gauze bandage.	Necesito cortarle la venda de gasa.
To give you . . .	Darle . . .	I need to give you a sling.	Necesito darle el cabestrillo.
To disinfect	Desinfectar	I need to disinfect the table.	Necesito desinfectar la mesa.
To listen to your heart	Escucharle el corazón	I need to listen to your heart.	Necesito escucharle el corazón.
To examine you	Examinarle	I need to examine your wound.	Necesito examinarle la herida.
To do a neurologic test	Hacer una prueba neurológica	I need to do a neurologic test with the tuning fork.	Necesito hacer una prueba neurológica con el tenedor de sintonía.
To do . . .	Hacer . . .	I need to do physical therapy.	Necesito hacer la terapia física.
To give you an injection	Inyectarle	I need to give you an injection.	Necesito inyectarle.
To measure the oxygen level	Medirle el nivel de oxígeno	I need to measure your oxygen level.	Necesito medirle el nivel de oxígeno.
To look under the microscope	Mirar bajo el microscopio	I need to look under the microscope.	Necesito mirar bajo el microscopio.
To look at you . . .	Mirarle . . .	I need to look at your sutures.	Necesito mirarle las suturas.
To order an MRI	Pedir una IRM	I need to order an MRI.	Necesito pedir una IRM.
To start an IV	Ponerle el suero intravenoso	I need to start your IV.	Necesito ponerle el suero intravenoso.

(*continued / continuado*)

(continued / continuado)

TRANSLATION	INFINITIVE	TRANSLATION	USAGE
To breathe deeply	Respirar profundo	Breathe deeply.	Respire profundo.
To remove . . .	Sacarle . . .	I need to remove your IV.	Necesito sacarle el suero.
To take your temperature	Tomarle la temperatura	I need to take your temperature.	Necesito tomarle la temperatura.
To take a sample of you . . .	Tomarle una muestra de . . .	I need to take a blood sample.	Necesito tomarle una muestra de sangre.

ESSENTIAL SPANISH VOCABULARY FOR PATIENT CARE / VOCABULARIO IMPORTANTE EN ESPAÑOL EN EL CUIDADO DEL PACIENTE

AUDIO 7.8

Medication delivery system / Sistemas de suministro de medicinas

Antibiotic	el antibiótico
Capsule	la cápsula
Compress	la compresa
Cream	la crema
Drops	las gotas
Inhaler	el inhalador
Medication	la medicación
Medicine	la medicina
Nasal spray	el aerosol nasal
Ointment	el ungüento
Pain pill	el calmante para el dolor
Pill(s)	la(s) pastilla(s)/la(s) píldora(s)
Prescription	la receta
Sublingual	sublingual
Syrup	el jarabe
Tablet	la tableta

The patient room / La habitación del paciente
AUDIO 7.9

Bed	la cama
Bedpan	la chata
Blanket	la frazada
Call bell	el timbre
Pillow	la almohada
Sheets	las sábanas
Siderails	la baranda
Urinal	el orinal

Ambulatory care / El cuidado ambulatorio
AUDIO 7.10

Cane	el bastón
Crutches	las muletas
Walker	el andador
Wheelchair	la silla de ruedas

The patient bathroom / El baño de paciente
AUDIO 7.11

Cup	la taza
Deodorant	el desodorante
Lights	las luces
Mirror	el espejo
Shampoo	el champú
Shower	la ducha
Sink	el lavamanos
Soap	el jabón
Toilet	el inodoro
Toilet paper	el papel higiénico
Toothbrush	el cepillo de dientes
Toothpaste	la pasta de dientes
Towel	la toalla
Washcloth	la toalla para jabonarse
Waste basket	el basurero

Clothing / Ropa

Bra	el sostén
Cap/hat	el gorro
Coat	el abrigo
Dress	el vestido
Jacket	la chaqueta
Ladies' underwear	los calzones
Men's underwear	los calzoncillos
Pajamas	el pijama
Pants	los pantalones
Robe	la bata
Shirt	la camisa
Shoes	los zapatos
The sleeve	la manga
Slippers	las pantuflas
Socks	los calcetines
Underwear	la ropa interior

Personal effects / Efectos personales

Body piercings	los aros para el cuerpo
Brush	el cepillo
Cellular phone	el teléfono celular
Changing/dressing room	el vestidor
Comb	el peine
Contact lenses	los lentes de contacto
Credit/debit card	la tarjeta de crédito/débito
Dentures	la dentadura/prótesis dental
Driver license	la licencia de conducir
Earrings	los aretes
Glasses	las gafas
Hearing aid	el aparato auditivo

Identification	la identificación
Jewelry	las joyas
Money	el dinero
Passport	el pasaporte
The restroom	el baño
Ring	el anillo
Tattoo	el tatuaje
Umbrella	el paraguas
Wallet	la billetera
Watch/Clock	el reloj

ATTENDING TO PATIENTS IN URGENT SITUATIONS / CÓMO ATENDER A PACIENTES EN SITUACIONES DE EMERGENCIA

Obtaining the history of a patient presenting to the emergency department / Cómo obtener el historial del paciente en la sala de emergencia

AUDIO 7.14

General emergency intake / Recepción del paciente en emergencias

What is your name?	¿Cuál es su nombre?
What is the name of your nearest relative?	¿Cuál es el nombre de su pariente más cercano?
Can I call someone to tell them you are in the hospital?	¿Puedo llamar a alguien para decirle que Ud. está en el hospital?
How old are you?	¿Cuántos años tiene usted?
What is your birthdate?	¿Cuál es la fecha de su nacimiento?
What is your marital status?	¿Cuál es su estado civil?
What type of medical insurance do you have?	¿Qué tipo de seguro médico tiene usted?
I need you to fill out this form. Do you need help to fill out this form?	Necesito que llene este formulario. ¿Necesita ayuda para llenarlo?
This is a form for permission for us to treat you. Please sign here.	Este es un formulario que nos autoriza para iniciar el tratamiento. Por favor, firme aquí.
What medicines are you taking?	¿Qué medicinas está usted tomando ahora?

(continued / continuado)

(continued / continuado)

Do you have health problems like heart disease, high blood pressure, or diabetes?	¿Tiene problemas de salud, como enfermedad al corazón, presión alta o diabetes?
Are you allergic to any medicines?	¿Tiene alergias a algunas medicinas?
When were you injured?	¿Cuándo se lastimó?
What happened?	¿Qué pasó?
Do you have pain?	¿Tiene dolor?
Where is the pain?	¿Dónde tiene dolor?
How long have you had the pain?	¿Hace cuánto tiempo ha tenido el dolor?
Does it hurt when I press here?	¿Le duele cuando le aprieto aquí?

Car accidents / Accidentes de automóviles

AUDIO 7.15

What is your name?	¿Cómo se llama?
You are in the emergency room. You were in a car accident. Do you remember anything about the accident?	Ud. está en la sala de emergencia. Ud. tuvo un accidente de auto. ¿Recuerda algo del accidente?
Who can I call to tell them that you are in the emergency department?	¿A quién puedo llamar para decirle que Ud. está en la sala de emergencia?
Do you have any drug allergies?	¿Tiene alergia a alguna medicina?
Are you taking any medications?	¿Está Ud. tomando alguna medicina?
Were you drinking alcohol?	¿Había bebido alcohol?
Do you have any health problems such as heart disease, high blood pressure, or diabetes?	¿Tiene problemas de salud, como enfermedad al corazón, presión alta o diabetes?
When was your last tetanus shot?	¿Cuándo recibió la última vacuna contra el tétano?
Do you have any pain?	¿Le duele algo?
Does your head hurt?	¿Le duele la cabeza?
Does your neck hurt?	¿Le duele el cuello?
Please lie still and do not move your neck.	Por favor no se mueva y no mueva el cuello.
Is your vision blurry?	¿Tiene la visión borrosa?
Do you have any problems breathing?	¿Tiene problemas para respirar?
Does your chest hurt you?	¿Le duele el pecho?
Do you have pain when you move your arms or legs?	¿Le duele cuando mueve los brazos o las piernas?
I need to start an IV, please hold your arm still.	Necesito ponerle el suero, por favor no mueva el brazo.

(continued / continuado)

(continued / continuado)

I need to take blood from your arm, please hold your arm still.	Necesito sacarle sangre, por favor no mueva el brazo.
Your arm is bleeding. I need to put a bandage on your arm.	Su brazo está sangrando. Necesito ponerle una venda en el brazo.
You need to have sutures in your arm.	Necesita puntos en el brazo.
You need to have a tetanus shot.	Necesita una vacuna contra el tétano.
You need to have an x-ray of your leg.	Necesita una radiografía de su pierna.

Drug-related emergencies / Emergencias relacionadas a las drogas

What is your name?	¿Cómo se llama?
Do you know what drug/s you took?	¿Sabe qué drogas tomó?
Do you know when you took the drug/s?	¿Sabe cuándo tomó las drogas?
What drugs do you usually use?	¿Qué drogas consume generalmente?
Have you vomited?	¿Ha vomitado?
Were you drinking alcohol?	¿Estaba tomando alcohol?
I need to take blood from your arm, please hold still.	Necesito sacarle sangre, por favor no mueva el brazo.
I need to start an IV.	Necesito ponerle el suero.
Please hold your arm still.	Por favor no mueva el brazo.
Do you know what drug/s the patient took?	¿Sabe Ud. qué drogas tomó el paciente?
Do you know when the patient took the drug/s?	¿Sabe Ud. cuándo tomó las drogas?
What drugs does the patient use?	¿Qué drogas usa el paciente?

Loss of consciousness / Pérdida de conciencia

What is your name?	¿Cómo se llama?
Do you know where you are?	¿Sabe dónde está Ud.?
Do you know what the date is?	¿Sabe qué día es hoy?
What is the last thing that you remember?	¿Qué es lo último que recuerda?
Do you have a family member or friend whom I can call?	¿Hay algún miembro de su familia o amigo a quien yo pueda llamar?
Do you remember what you were doing before you lost consciousness?	¿Recuerda qué estaba haciendo antes de perder la conciencia?

(continued / continuado)

(*continued* / *continuado*)

Was anyone with you when you lost consciousness?	¿Había alguien con Ud. cuando perdió la conciencia?
Has this ever happened to you before?	¿Le había pasado esto antes?
Are you taking any medicines for any type of health problems?	¿Está tomando alguna medicina para algún problema de salud?
Does your head hurt?	¿Le duele la cabeza?
Do you have any pain?	¿Le duele algo?
Where do you have pain?	¿Dónde le duele?
Are you able to move your arms and legs?	¿Puede mover sus brazos y piernas?
Did you see the patient lose consciousness?	¿Ud. pudo ver cuando el paciente perdió la conciencia?
What was the patient doing when he/she lost consciousness?	¿Qué estaba haciendo el paciente cuando perdió la conciencia?
How long was the patient unconscious?	¿Cuánto tiempo estuvo inconsciente el paciente?
Did the patient have any seizure-like movements when he/she was unconscious?	¿Tuvo algún tipo de convulsión el paciente cuando perdió la conciencia?
Did the patient take any medications or drugs today?	¿Tomó alguna medicina o drogas el paciente hoy?

www.springerpub.com/travieso
AUDIO 7.18

Essential terms related to emergency care / Vocabulario relacionado a las situaciones de emergencia

Abuse	el abuso
Accident	el accidente
Allergic reaction	la reacción alérgica
Ambulance	la ambulancia
An attack of	el ataque de
Bleeding	la hemorragia
Blunt-force trauma	el traumatismo
Bruise/contusion	el moretón
Burn	la quemadura
Car accident	el accidente de coche/auto
Coma	el coma

Complete blood count	el hemograma completo
Concussion	la conmoción cerebral
Cut	una cortada
Deep	profundo/a
Diagnostic	el diagnóstico
Difficulty breathing	la dificultad al respirar
Dislocation	la dislocación
Donor	el/la donante
Embolism	la embolia
Emergencies	emergencias/urgencias
Emergency department	la sala de emergencia
Fall	una caída
Foreign body	un cuerpo extraño
Forensic nurse	el/la enfermero/a forense
Knife	el cuchillo
Muscle strain/pulled muscle	un desgarro muscular
Nosebleed	la sangre de nariz
Obstruction	la obstrucción
Occult blood	la sangre oculta
On call	de turno
Open heart surgery	la operación a corazón abierto
Paramedics	los paramédicos
Procedure	el procedimiento
Puncture	la punción
Punctured	punzado/a
Rape	la violación
Ruptured	roto/a
Sexual assault	el asalto sexual
Shooting	el asalto con disparos/tiroteos
Shortness of breath	la falta de aire
Slow	despacio
Spasm	un espasmo

Stabbing (attack)	la puñalada
Stitches	los puntos
Stretcher	la camilla
Surgeon	el cirujano/la cirujana
Tetanus	el tétano
Unconscious	inconsciente
Victim	la víctima
Wound	la herida

AUDIO 7.19

Communicating with the patient in the emergency department / Comunicación con el paciente en la sala de emergencia

Are you able to sit up?	¿Puede sentarse?
Are you able to walk?	¿Puede caminar?
Are you allergic to anything?	¿Es alérgico/a a algo?
Breathe slowly.	Respire despacio.
Can I call someone for you?	¿Quiere que llame a alguien?
Do not move from the stretcher.	No se mueva de la camilla.
Do you feel dizzy?	¿Está mareado/a?
Do you need a blanket?	¿Necesita una frazada?
Do you need the urinal?	¿Necesita un orinal?
Hold your arm still.	No mueva el brazo.
Is there someone with you?	¿Hay alguien con Ud.?
Lie still.	Recuéstese sin moverse.
Please relax.	Por favor cálmese.
Press the button if you need something.	Presione el botón si necesita ayuda.
Wait here.	Espere aquí.
We will help you.	Le vamos a ayudar.
We will take care of you.	Vamos a atenderle bien.
Where are your belongings?	¿Dónde están sus pertenencias?
Who is your doctor?	¿Quién es su doctor?
You must wait in the waiting room.	Ud. tiene que esperar en la sala de espera.

www.springerpub.com/traverso
AUDIO 7.20

Useful phrases for the health care provider in the emergency department / Frases de utilidad para *health care provider* en la sala emergencia

To amputate = amputar	When was your leg amputated?	¿Cuándo le amputaron la pierna?
To apply = aplicar	I need to apply pressure to the wound.	Necesito poner presión en la herida.
To attack = atacar	When were you attacked?	¿Cuándo lo/la atacaron?
To be admitted = ser admitido/a	You need to be admitted to the hospital.	Necesita ser admitido/a en el hospital.
To be discharged = dar de alta	You are discharged to go home now.	Le vamos a dar de alta para que se vaya a casa.
To be in a coma = estar en coma	Your father is in a coma.	Su padre está en coma.
To bleed = sangrar	You are bleeding.	Está sangrando.
To break something = quebrarse	You broke your arm.	Ud. se quebró el brazo.
To choke (on something) = atorarse/atragantarse	The boy is choking on a peanut.	El niño está atorado/atragantado con maní.
To clean = limpiar	I need to clean your wound.	Necesito limpiarle la herida.
To cut oneself = cortarse	How did you cut yourself?	¿Cómo se cortó?
To dislocate = dislocarse	You dislocated your shoulder.	Ud. se dislocó un hombro.
To donate = donar	People who donate an organ save a life.	Las personas que donan un órgano, salvan una vida.
To drown = ahogarse	Wear a life preserver so you do not drown.	Use un salvavida si no quiere ahogarse.
To faint = desmayarse	Did you faint?	¿Se desmayó?
To fall = caerse	Where did you fall?	¿Dónde se cayó?
To fracture something = fracturarse	Did you fracture your pelvis?	¿Se fracturó la pelvis?
To injure oneself = lastimarse	How did you injure yourself?	¿Cómo se lastimó?
To insert = insertar	I need to insert this catheter.	Necesito insertarle el catéter.
To intubate = intubar	We had to intubate your father.	Tuvimos que intubar a su padre.
To puncture oneself = punzarse	How did you puncture your hand?	¿Cómo se punzó la mano?

(*continued / continuado*)

(continued / continuado)

To put in a cast = enyesar	The doctor needs to put a cast on your leg.	El doctor necesita enyesarle la pierna.
To remove = quitar	We need to remove the glass from your cut.	Necesitamos sacarle el vidrio de la cortadura.
To run into = golpearse	What did you run into?	¿Contra qué se golpeó?
To stop = parar	We need to stop the bleeding.	Tenemos que parar el sangramiento.
To strain = desgarrarse	How did you strain your back?	¿Cómo se desgarró la espalda?
To stretch = estirar	You need to stretch your back every day.	Necesita estirar su espalda diariamente.
To suture = suturar	I need to suture your wound.	Necesito suturarle la herida.
To take an x-ray = sacar una radiografía	I need to take an x-ray of your leg.	Necesito sacarle una radiografía de la pierna.
To wheeze = respirar con silbidos	When did you start to wheeze?	¿Cuándo comenzó a respirar con silbidos?

Mental health related terminology / Términos relacionados a la salud mental

AUDIO 7.21

Addiction = la adicción	Do you have an addiction to drugs?	¿Tiene adicción a alguna droga?
Anxiety = la ansiedad	Do you have a history of anxiety?	¿Tiene un historial de ansiedad?
Depression = la depresión	Does your son have a history of depression?	¿Su hijo tiene un historial de depresión?
Hallucination = alucinación	Do you experience hallucinations?	¿Experimenta alucinaciones?
Intoxicated = intoxicado/a	Were you intoxicated when you were driving?	¿Estaba Ud. intoxicado/a cuando manejaba?
Poison = el veneno	Did you call the poison control center?	¿Llamó al Centro de Control de Venenos?
To attempt suicide = intentar suicidarse	Your sister attempted suicide.	Su hermana intentó suicidarse.

(continued / continuado)

(continued / continuado)

To harm oneself = hacerse daño	Why did you harm yourself?	¿Por qué se hizo daño?
To overdose = tomar sobredosis	Your friend overdosed on drugs.	Su amigo tomó una sobredosis.
To take drugs = tomar drogas	Do you take drugs?	¿Toma drogas?

ATTENDING TO NONCRITICAL PATIENTS / CÓMO ATENDER A PACIENTES EN SITUACIONES NO CRÍTICAS

Intake questions / Preguntas frecuentes en la recepción de emergencias

AUDIO 7.22

Do you have any past medical history of health conditions/surgeries?	¿Tiene un historial médico con problemas de salud u operaciones?
What medications (prescription/over the counter) are you taking?	¿Qué medicinas toma Ud.?
Are you on a special diet?	¿Sigue una dieta especial?
Are you current on your immunizations?	¿Está al día en sus vacunas?
What immunizations have you had?	¿Qué vacunas ha recibido?
When was your last tetanus shot?	¿Cuándo fue la última vez que le pusieron una inyección para el tétano?
Do you have any allergies to medications/materials?	¿Tiene alguna alergia a medicinas/materiales?
When was your last menstrual period?	¿Cuándo tuvo su último período?
Do you have any open sores/cuts?	¿Tiene algunos cortes o llagas?
Do you have any special religious/cultural needs?	¿Tiene alguna preferencia religiosa o espiritual?

Assessing patient pain / Cómo evaluar el nivel de dolor del paciente

AUDIO 7.23

On a scale of 1–10 could you rate your current level of pain?	En la escala de uno a diez, ¿Dónde ubica Ud. su dolor?
Can you describe your pain?	¿Puede describir su dolor?
Where is your pain?	¿Dónde tiene el dolor?
When did your pain start?	¿Cuándo le empezó el dolor?

(continued / continuado)

(continued / continuado)

| Do you need anything/medication for pain? | ¿Necesita algo o alguna medicina para el dolor? |
| I have your pain medication for you. | Tengo la medicina para el dolor para Ud. |

Advancing diet for the postoperative patient / Fases en la dieta postoperatoria del paciente

AUDIO 7.24

Have you passed any flatus/gas?	¿Ha eliminado gases?
Are you experiencing any nausea?	¿Tiene náuseas?
(If yes) Would you like medication to help with the nausea?	(Si la respuesta es sí) ¿Quiere una medicina para la náusea?
Are you tolerating ice chips/clear liquids/regular diet?	¿Tolera bien el hielo picado/líquidos claros/una dieta normal?
Do you need any assistance ordering meals?	¿Necesita alguna ayuda para pedir comida?

Fall-risk patients and patients needing assistance with ADL / Pacientes con riesgo de caídas y pacientes necesitados de ayuda con actividades de la vida diaria

AUDIO 7.25

Please do not get out of bed on your own.	Por favor, no se levante de la cama sin ayuda.
Ring your call bell for assistance.	Presione el timbre cuando necesite ayuda.
Here is your call bell.	Aquí está el timbre.
Do you feel steady on your feet?	¿Se siente seguro cuando está parado/a?
Do you feel dizzy?	¿Se siente mareado/a?
Do you need a walker? Wheelchair?	¿Necesita un andador? ¿Una silla de ruedas?
Here is the hand rail.	Aquí está la baranda.
This is a gait belt to help keep you safe while we walk.	Éste es el arnés para que esté seguro/a cuando caminemos.
Do you need to use the bathroom?	¿Necesita ir al baño?
I can help you to the bathroom. Ring the call bell when you are done.	Puedo ayudarlo/la a caminar al baño. Presione el timbre cuando termine.
I will help you get on/off the bedpan.	Voy a ayudarlo/la para que use la chata.
I am going to change your soiled Attends®.	Voy a cambiarle los calzones desechables.

(continued / continuado)

(continued / continuado)

Roll your body to the right/left.	Dése vuelta hacia la derecha/la izquierda.
Please cross your arms/give yourself a hug.	Por favor, cruce los brazos y abrácese.
Lay still, do not help.	Quédese tranquilo/a, no ayude.
We are going to slide you up in bed.	Vamos a moverlo/la hacia arriba en la cama.
We are going to slide you onto the stretcher.	Vamos a pasarlo/la a la camilla.
On the count of three: one, two, and three.	Voy a contar hasta tres: a la una, a las dos, y a las tres.
This may feel cool/warm/wet.	Esto va a sentirlo fresco/cálido/mojado.
Can I help you get repositioned?	¿Puedo ayudarlo/la a cambiar de posición?
It is time to get repositioned.	Hay que cambiar de posición.
It is time to get washed up.	Hay que lavarse ahora.
Can I help you get washed up?	¿Puedo ayudarle a lavarse?
I am going to wash your perineal area.	Voy a lavarle el área perineal.
I am going to lift your left/right leg.	Voy a levantarle la pierna derecha/izquierda.
Bend your left/right knee.	Doble la rodilla izquierda/derecha.
I will dry you off.	Voy a secarlo/la.
Would you like me to apply lotion?	¿Quiere que le aplique crema?
Put your arm through the sleeve.	Ponga su brazo en la manga.
I am going to put slippers on you.	Voy a ponerle las pantuflas.
I will tie your gown.	Voy a atarle la bata de hospital.
I am going to raise/lower your bed.	Voy a subirle/bajarle la cama.
I am going to raise the head of your bed.	Voy a subirle la parte superior de la cama.
I am going to help you sit up.	Voy a ayudarlo/la a sentarse.

Care of the diabetic patient / El cuidado del paciente diabético

AUDIO 7.26

Hello Mr./Mrs._____. It is time to check your blood glucose/sugar.	Hola señor/señora _____. Ahora voy a revisarle el nivel de glucosa en la sangre.
Which hand/finger do you prefer I use?	¿Qué mano/dedo prefiere que use?
It is time for your insulin injection.	Le toca la inyección de insulina ahora.
Where would you like me to give your injection?	¿Dónde prefiere que le ponga la inyección?
What would you like for your evening snack?	¿Qué prefiere para su merienda esta noche?

Frequently used statements and questions for hospitalized patients / Preguntas y respuestas frecuentes relacionadas al paciente hospitalizado

Please ring your call bell if you need anything.	Por favor, presione el timbre si necesita algo.
Is there anything I can get for you?	¿Puedo traerle algo?
Are you comfortable?	¿Está cómodo/a?
It is time to take your vital signs.	Hay revisarle los signos vitales.
I need to check your IV site.	Necesito revisarle el lugar donde tiene el suero.
I need to flush your IV site to keep it open.	Necesito limpiar el suero para que esté abierto.
I need to start an IV.	Necesito ponerle el suero.
It is time to change your IV site.	Es el momento de cambiarle donde le ponemos el suero.
I need to change your IV fluids.	Necesito cambiarle los líquidos que van en el suero.
I have to reset your IV pump.	Tengo que reajustar la bomba del suero.
I have your medication(s).	Tengo sus medicinas.
I have your injection.	Tengo su inyección.
Where would you like me to give your injection?	¿Dónde prefiere que le ponga la inyección?
Good morning/afternoon/evening, my name is . . . and I will be your nurse for this shift.	Buenos días/buenas tardes/buenas noches, mi nombre es . . . , y soy su enfermero/a durante las próximas horas de turno.
Your room number is . . .	El número de su habitación es . . .
Visiting hours are from . . . to . . .	Las horas de visita son de . . . a . . .
Can you tell me your birthdate?	¿Puede decirme su fecha de nacimiento?
It is time for physical therapy.	Ahora viene la terapia física.
It is time for your test.	Ahora le haremos la prueba médica.
Do you have any questions?	¿Tiene alguna pregunta?
Do you understand my instructions?	¿Entiende mis instrucciones?
Do you understand what the doctor said?	¿Entiende lo que dijo el doctor/la doctora?
You will be discharged . . .	Lo/La van a dar de alta . . .
Would you like to speak with the chaplain?	¿Quiere hablar con el capellán?
I have a clean gown and linens for you.	Tengo una bata y ropa limpia para Ud.
Do you need another blanket?	¿Necesita otra frazada?
Are you cold/hot?	¿Tiene calor/frío?

(continued / continuado)

(*continued* / *continuado*)

Do you need any toiletries? (toothbrush/ toothpaste/deodorant/ shampoo/conditioner/ feminine pad)	¿Necesita algunos artículos de tocador? (cepillo de dientes/pasta de dientes/desodorante/ champú/acondicionador/toallas sanitarias)
Are you hungry/thirsty?	¿Tiene hambre/sed?
The doctor/surgeon will be here . . .	El doctor/La doctora/El cirujano/La cirujana va a estar aquí . . .
Would you like me to call your family?	¿Quiere que llame a su familia?
This is an oxygen mask/nasal cannula.	Ésta es una máscara de oxígeno/cánula nasal.
The doctor ordered . . . (tests/medications).	El doctor/La doctora ordenó . . . (pruebas médicas/ medicinas)
Would you like to speak to the case manager?	¿Quiere hablar con el trabajador social?
Is there someone to help you at home?	¿Hay alguien en casa que pueda ayudarlo/la?
Are you safe at home/do you feel safe at home?	¿Se siente seguro/a en casa?
Do you know where you are? Do you know what year it is?	¿Sabe dónde está? ¿Sabe en qué año estamos?
You are doing great.	Vamos bien.
Everything is alright.	Todo va bien.
I need to do an assessment/exam on you, is that OK?	Necesito hacerle un examen médico/una evaluación médica ¿está bien?
I am going to listen to your lungs.	Voy a escucharle los pulmones.
I am going to listen to your heart.	Voy a escucharle el corazón.
I need to listen to your abdomen to check the bowel sounds.	Necesito escucharle el abdomen para chequear los sonidos del colon.
I am going to feel/palpate for a pulse.	Voy a palparle para ver cómo está su pulso.
I am going to check your heart rate.	Voy a evaluarle el ritmo del corazón.
I am going to check your oxygen level.	Voy a evaluarle el nivel de oxígeno.

AUDIO 7.28

Care of patients with wounds and incisions / Cuidado de pacientes con heridas e incisiones

It is time to change your dressing.	Ahora hay que cambiarle el vendaje.
It is time to remove your staples/sutures.	Ahora hay que quitarle las suturas.
Would you like pain medicine before I change your dressing?	¿Quiere medicina para el dolor antes de que yo le cambie el vendaje?
It is healing well.	Se está curando bien.

(*continued* / *continuado*)

(continued / continuado)

It looks like it is getting infected.	Parece que se está infectando.
Gently cleanse the incision with soap and water.	Limpie suavemente la incisión con agua y jabón.
Keep the incision clean and dry.	Mantenga la incisión limpia y seca.
This might be uncomfortable for you.	Puede ser incómodo para Ud.

AUDIO 7.29

Attending to the patient with urinary catheters and other drains / Cómo atender a pacientes con catéteres y otros tipos de drenajes

I need to insert a urinary catheter.	Necesito insertarle un catéter urinario.
I need to empty your catheter.	Necesito vaciarle el catéter.
It is time to clean your catheter.	Ahora hay que limpiarle el catéter.
It is time to empty your drain.	Ahora hay que vaciarle el drenaje.
It is time to take your catheter out.	Ahora hay que quitarle el catéter.

READING: ALFREDO QUIÑONES, NEUROSURGEON / LECTURA: ALFREDO QUIÑONES, NEUROCIRUJANO

Reading

Alfredo Quiñones (1968–, b. Mexicali, Mexico), a neurosurgeon at Johns Hopkins Bayview Medical Center in Baltimore, Maryland, began life in America as an illegal Mexican immigrant with his family. From a young age he worked at various jobs and eventually he studied at Harvard Medical School. Now he directs the Brain Tumor Surgery Program. He also directs the Laboratory for Brain Tumors and Stem Cells. His life and work serve as testament to the fact that even with humble beginnings, it is possible to achieve your objectives.

Lectura

Alfredo Quiñones, neurocirujano (1968–, n. Mexicali, México), neurocirujano en el Centro Médico Johns Hopkins Bayview en Baltimore, Maryland, comenzó su vida en America como inmigrante ilegal desde México con su familia. Desde joven trabajó en diversos oficios y, eventualmente, estudió en la Escuela de Medicina de Harvard. Ahora es director del Programa Quirúrgico de Tumores Cerebrales. También dirige el Laboratorio de Tumores Cerebrales y Células Madre. Su vida y trabajo dan testimonio al hecho de que, incluso con orígenes modestos, es posible alcanzar tus objetivos.

IDIOMATIC EXPRESSIONS / EXPRESIONES IDIOMÁTICAS

My hair stands on end
Se me paran los pelos
My hairs stand up

English expression
Spanish equivalent
Literal translation

I have goosebumps
Se me pone la piel de gallina
I am getting chicken skin

English expression
Spanish equivalent
Literal translation

8

PREGNANCY, CHILDBIRTH, AND CONTRACEPTION

CONTENTS

The nurse's guide to pregnancy, babies, and children / Guía para la atención de mujeres embarazadas, bebés, y niños

Vocabulary related to pregnancy, babies, and children / Vocabulario relacionado al nacimiento, a los bebés y a los niños

Intake questions for the expectant mother / Preguntas preliminares para la mujer embarazada

Attending to the woman in labor / Cómo asistir a la mujer embarazada

Childbirth education for the expectant mother / Educación para la mujer embarazada

Basics of conception and contraception / Aspectos básicos de la concepción y contraconcepción

Diminutives and related expressions / Los diminutivos y expresiones relacionadas

Reading: Jonas Edward Salk, physician and virologist / Lectura: Jonas Edward Salk, médico y virólogo

Idiomatic expressions / Expresiones idiomáticas

THE NURSE'S GUIDE TO PREGNANCY, BABIES, AND CHILDREN / GUÍA PARA LA ATENCIÓN DE MUJERES EMBARAZADAS, BEBÉS, Y NIÑOS

This chapter translates essential interactions of the health care provider with the female gynecological patient. Included is vocabulary related to women's health care before, during and after pregnancy. Specific intake questions are included to assess the expectant mother before and during labor. A section is included that provides the health care provider with educational information to share with the woman when she is pregnant. This includes ways to have a healthy pregnancy, the growth and development of the fetus, and the physical changes the mother's body will undergo during pregnancy. To support the woman's understanding of reproduction, a discussion for the health care provider to have with the patient on the menstrual cycle is offered. This then leads into specifics for the health care provider to discuss with the patient concerning the various methods of contraception.

VOCABULARY RELATED TO PREGNANCY, BABIES, AND CHILDREN / VOCABULARIO RELACIONADO AL NACIMIENTO, A LOS BEBÉS Y A LOS NIÑOS

 ## From birth to childhood / Del nacimiento a la niñez

AUDIO 8.1

The following is a list of commonly used words and expressions related to childbirth and children.

Childbirth / Parto

Amniotic sac	la bolsa de agua
Cervix	el cuello uterino
Cesarean	la cesárea
Childbirth	el parto
Contractions	las contracciones
Cramps	los calambres
Delivery room	la sala de partos
Dilated	dilatado/a
Dilitation and curettage (D and C)	la dilatación y curetaje (D y C)
Ectopic pregnancy	el embarazo ectópico

Egg	el huevo
Epidural	la epidural
Fallopian tubes	las trompas de Falopio
Fetus	el feto
Gynecologist	el ginecólogo/la ginecóloga
Maternity	la maternidad
Menstruation	la menstruación
Midwife	la matrona/la partera
Miscarriage	el aborto natural/la pérdida
Months, how many months?	los meses/cuántos meses
Obstetrician	el/la obstetra
Ovaries	los ovarios
Ovum	el óvulo
Period	el período/la regla
Pregnancy	el embarazo
Pregnancy test	la prueba del embarazo
Pregnant	encinta/embarazada
Sanitary pads	las toallas higiénicas
Sperm	el esperma
Tampons	los tampones
To be born	nacer
To be pregnant	estar embarazada
To give birth to	dar a luz
To ovulate	ovular
To push	empujar, pujar
Umbilical cord	el cordón umbilical
Vagina	la vagina

Babies / Bebés

A boy/A girl	un niño/una niña	To hold in your arms	tomar en brazos
Baby	el/la bebé	To nurse	dar pecho
Baby bottle	el biberón	To roll over	girar sobre
Baby bottle top	el pezón del biberón	To take care of	cuidar
		To teethe	salirle dientes
Breast	el pecho	To test the milk	probar la leche
Care	el cuidado		
Crib	la cuna	To wash	lavar
Development	el desarrollo	To weigh	pesar
Disposable diaper	el pañal desechable	Triplets	los trillizos
		Vegetable purée	el puré de vegetales
Fraternal twins	los mellizos		
Identical twins	los gemelos		
Incubator	la incubadora		
Kilograms	Kilos		
Nipple	el pezón		
Ounces	Onzas		
Pounds	libras		
Solids	los sólidos		
To bathe	bañar		
To burp	eructar		
To change	cambiar		
To clean	limpiar		
To cry	llorar		
To feed	alimentar		
To give drops or syrup	dar gotas o jarabe		

La madre y el bebé

Children / Niños

A boy/a girl	un/una niño/a
Carry	portar
Cough	la tos
The clinic	la clínica
Doll	la muñeca
Put him/her	póngalo/la
on his/her side	de lado
on his/her back	de espalda
on his/her stomach	sobre su estómago
Rash	el sarpullido
Teddy bear	el osito de peluche
To crawl	gatear
To scratch	rascarse
To sit	sentar
To walk	caminar
Toys	los juguetes

el bebé está enfermo

el bebé usa pañales
la mamá le cambia
los pañales
el padre cuida al bebé
el bebé es mi nieto
la señora es mi abuela
¿para quién es el biberón?
la mamá le da pecho al bebé
el bebé o la bebé

Birth control options / Opciones para el control de natalidad

Birth control pill	la píldora anticonceptiva
Cervical cap	el capuchón cervical
Condoms	los condones
Diaphragm	el diafragma
Hormone shot	la inyección de hormonas
Implant	la implantación
IUD (intra uterine device)	DIU (dispositivos intra-uterinos)
Natural family planning	la planificación familiar
Patch	el parche
Spermicide	el espermicida
Sponge	la esponja anticonceptiva
Sterilization	la esterilización
Sterilize	esterilizar
Vaginal ring	el anillo vaginal
Vasectomy	la vasectomía

Gynecological Tests / Exámenes ginecológicos

Amniocentesis	la amniocentesis
Annual exam	el examen anual
Chorianic villi sampling	la biopsia coriónica
Mammogram	el mamograma
Pap smear	la prueba de Pap/el Papanicolaou
Pregnancy test	la prueba de embarazo
Sexually transmitted infection (STI)	la enfermedad de transmisión sexual (ETS)
Speculum	el espéculo
Ultrasound	el ultrasonido

www.springerpub.com/traverso
AUDIO 8.4

Hospital locales for the expecting family / Sitios en el hospital para la familia de la mujer embarazada

Bathrooms	los baños
The cafeteria	la cafetería
Clinic	la clínica
Delivery room	la sala de parto
The doctor's/health care provider's office	el consultorio
Elevator	el ascensor
Emergency room	la sala de emergencias
Gift shop	la tienda de regalos
House/Home	la casa
ICU (Intensive Care Unit)	la unidad de cuidados intensivos (UCI)
Nursery	la guardería
Office	la oficina
Operating room	la sala de operaciones
Pediatric unit	la unidad de pediatría
Pharmacy	la farmacia
Social service department	el departamento de servicios sociales
Stairway	la escalera
Waiting room	la sala de espera

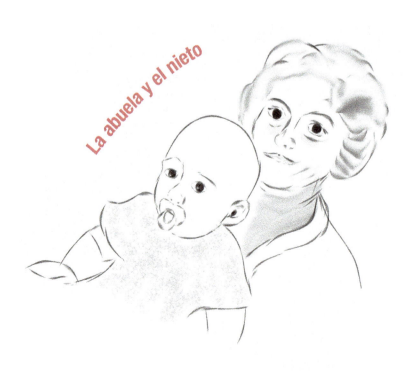

La abuela y el nieto

INTAKE QUESTIONS FOR THE EXPECTANT MOTHER / PREGUNTAS PRELIMINARES PARA LA MUJER EMBARAZADA

Hello. What is your name?	Hola. ¿Cómo se llama?
When is your baby due?	¿Cuándo nace el bebé?
How often are your contractions?	¿Cuán a menudo tiene las contracciones?
Is your water leaking?	¿Está perdiendo agua?
What time did your water break?	¿A qué hora se le rompió la bolsa de agua?
Do you have any bleeding? Is it dark or bright red?	¿Está sangrando? ¿Es de color rojo oscuro o rojo claro?
Do you have any pain? Where?	¿Tiene dolor? ¿Dónde le duele?
Show me where the pain is.	Enséñeme dónde le duele.
Please remove all your clothes and put on the hospital gown.	Por favor, desvístase completamente y póngase la bata de hospital.
How old are you?	¿Cuántos años tiene?
Do you have any allergies?	¿Tiene alergias?
What diseases have you had?	¿Qué enfermedades ha tenido?
How long have your hands and feet been swollen?	¿Cuánto tiempo hace que se le hinchan las manos y los pies?
Do you have high blood pressure?	¿Tiene presión arterial alta?
Are you nauseated?	¿Tiene náuseas?
Do you feel dizzy?	¿Tiene mareos?
Do you feel any pressure in your lower abdomen?	¿Siente alguna presión en la parte de abajo del abdomen?
I do not understand.	No entiendo.
One minute, please.	Un momento por favor.
Yes./No.	Sí./No.
Please	Por favor
Thank you.	Gracias.

ATTENDING TO THE WOMAN IN LABOR / CÓMO ASISTIR A LA MUJER EMBARAZADA

How often are your contractions?	¿Cuán a menudo tiene las contracciones?
Is your water leaking?	¿Está perdiendo agua?
What time did your water break?	¿A qué hora se le rompió la bolsa de agua?
Do you have any pain? Where?	¿Tiene dolor? ¿Dónde le duele?
Show me where the pain is.	Enséñeme dónde le duele.
Are you afraid?	¿Tiene miedo?
Do you have family with you?	¿Tiene familia con usted?
I will be right back. Press this button for help.	Vuelvo enseguida. Presione este botón si necesita ayuda.
I do not understand.	No entiendo.
One minute, please.	Un momento por favor.
The doctor wants to check your cervix.	El médico quiere revisarle el cuello uterino.
Turn on your side, please.	Póngase de lado, por favor.
Do you want any water or ice?	¿Quiere agua o hielo?
Do you need some medicine for pain?	¿Necesita una medicina para el dolor?
Do you want to push?	¿Quiere pujar?
Do not push.	No puje.
Breathe. Again.	Respire. Otra vez.
I am going to clean you off.	Voy a limpiarla.
Are you going to breast or bottle-feed?	¿Va a darle pecho o biberón?
Lift your legs.	Levante las piernas.
Do you want to shower?	¿Quiere tomar una ducha?
Hot/cold	Caliente/Frío
Arm/hand/legs	Brazo/mano/piernas
Better	Mejor
Yes/no	Sí/No
Please	Por favor
Thank you.	Gracias.
Are you hungry?	¿Tiene hambre?
How far apart are your contractions?	¿Cuán separadas tiene las contracciones?
Your contractions are 2 minutes apart.	Tiene contracciones separadas por dos minutos.

(continued / continuado)

(continued / continuado)

Your cervix is fully dilated; your baby is ready to come!	Tiene el cuello uterino totalmente dilatado; ¡su bebé está listo para nacer!
With the next contraction, take a deep breath in through your nose and now breathe out through your mouth as you push.	Con la próxima contracción, respire profundo por la nariz y ahora bote el aire por la boca mientras puja.
Take slow deep breaths.	Respire profundo y lentamente.
You are doing very good!	¡Todo va muy bien!

CHILDBIRTH EDUCATION FOR THE EXPECTANT MOTHER / EDUCACIÓN PARA LA MUJER EMBARAZADA

Dos and Don'ts of pregnancy / Lo que se debe hacer y no hacer durante el embarazo

Women need to be made aware of some important facts about how to achieve a healthy pregnancy and support the healthy development of their baby. Listed below are some essential yet basic information translated into Spanish for nurses to share with their Spanish-speaking pregnant patients.

AUDIO 8.7

Dos of pregnancy / Lo que se debe hacer durante el embarazo:

Prenatal care is important for you and your baby.	El cuidado prenatal es importante para Ud. y para su bebé.
It is important that you go to all of your appointments.	Es importante asistir a todas las citas.
You need to take a prenatal vitamin every day.	Se debe tomar una vitamina prenatal todos los días.
Are you able to take your prenatal vitamin every day?	¿Puede tomar las vitaminas prenatales todos los días?
Do the prenatal vitamins make you feel sick?	¿Las vitaminas prenatales le hacen sentir mal?
The vitamins help you and your baby to stay healthy.	Las vitaminas les ayudan a usted y a su bebé a mantenerse sanos.
Do you have any questions about what you should eat while you are pregnant?	¿Tiene preguntas sobre lo que se debe comer durante el embarazo?
How much water do you drink every day?	¿Cuánta agua bebe cada día?
You need to drink extra water.	Necesita beber más agua.
It is normal to gain weight during your pregnancy, but gaining too much weight can cause problems when you are pregnant.	Es normal subir de peso durante el embarazo, pero demasiado peso puede causar problemas durante el embarazo.

(continued / continuado)

(continued / continuado)

You need to listen to your practitioner about how much weight is good for you to gain.	Necesita hacerle caso a su doctor/a o matrona acerca de cuánto peso es bueno subir.
Sleep is important.	Es importante dormir.
It is good for you to sleep on your left side when you are pregnant.	Es bueno dormir en el lado izquierdo durante el embarazo.
You can use pillows between your legs and under your abdomen to help you sleep better.	Puede usar almohadas entre las piernas y bajo el abdomen para ayudarle a dormir mejor.
Before you take any medication, ask your practitioner if it is ok to take that medication.	Antes de tomar una medicina, se debe consultar con su doctor/a o matrona para ver si puede tomar la medicina.
It is good to get a flu shot when you are pregnant.	Es bueno vacunarse contra la gripe cuando está embarazada.
When you are in a car, always wear a seatbelt.	Al ir en un auto, siempre use un cinturón de seguridad.
Are you taking childbirth education classes?	¿Usted toma clases de parto?
Eat healthy foods.	Coma comidas sanas.
Rinse fresh vegetables well before you eat them.	Enjuague bien los vegetales frescos antes de comerlos.

Pregnancy don'ts / Lo que no se debe hacer durante el embarazo

Do not smoke cigarettes when you are pregnant.	No fume cigarrillos cuando está embarazada.
Do not drink alcohol when you are pregnant. Drinking alcohol when you are pregnant can harm your baby.	No beba alcohol durante el embarazo. Consumir alcohol durante el embarazo puede hacerle daño al bebé.
Do not take illegal drugs, such as marijuana and cocaine.	No tome drogas ilegales, como la marihuana o la cocaína.
Do not change the cat litter when you are pregnant as you can get an infection that can harm the baby.	No cambie la arena higiénica para gatos durante el embarazo, porque puede causarle una infección que dañe al bebé.
Do not use hot tubs or saunas when you are pregnant as the high temperatures can harm your baby and also cause you to faint.	No tome baños de tina calientes ni saunas durante el embarazo, porque las temperaturas altas pueden hacerle daño al bebé, y pueden hacer que usted se desmaye.
If you need to get an x-ray when you are pregnant, tell the person ordering the x-ray that you are pregnant.	Si necesita una radiografía durante el embarazo, dígale a la persona que pide la radiografía que usted está embarazada.

(continued / continuado)

(continued / continuado)

Do not use scented sprays or bubble baths when you are pregnant that can irritate the vaginal area and cause vaginal infections.	No use esprays perfumados ni baños de burbujas durante el embarazo, porque pueden causarle irritación al área vaginal, y pueden causar infecciones vaginales.
Do not come in contact with urine, droppings, or nest material from hamsters and guinea pigs. These animals carry a virus that can be harmful to your baby.	No tenga contacto con la orina, materia fecal, o materia de los nidos de hámsteres ni cuyes. Estos animales tienen un virus que le puede causar daño a su bebé.

Fetal growth and development / Crecimiento y desarrollo del feto

Women often are unaware of the early development that occurs when they are pregnant. Knowing about the critical developmental stages that occur throughout the period of the baby's development can support the education that it is essential for the mother to make safe and healthy decisions during this time. These healthy choices positively impact the normal growth and development of the baby. Listed here are some of the significant developmental milestones that the baby is experiencing throughout the three trimesters of pregnancy, along with the Spanish translation. The nurse can choose any of the following to help expand the patient's understanding of the development of her baby.

AUDIO 8.8

First Trimester / Primer trimestre

By 4 weeks, the baby begins to develop the brain and spinal cord. The heart begins to form.	A las cuatro semanas, el cerebro y la columna vertebral empiezan a formarse en el bebé. El corazón comienza a formarse.
By 8 weeks all major organs begin to form.	A las ocho semanas, los órganos principales se comienzan a formar.
The heart beats a regular rhythm.	El corazón late a un ritmo regular.
The fingers and toes begin to form.	Los dedos de la mano y del pie empiezan a formarse.
At 12 weeks the baby is able to make a fist.	A las doce semanas, el bebé puede empuñar su mano.
The heart and brain continue to grow. The internal organs continue to grow.	El corazón y el cerebro siguen creciendo. Los órganos internos siguen creciendo.
The baby has eyelids and the eyelids close to protect the development of the eyes.	El bebé tiene párpados, y éstos se cierran para proteger el desarrollo de los ojos.

Second Trimester / Segundo trimestre

At 16 weeks, the skin is forming.	A las dieciséis semanas, la piel empieza a formarse.
Muscle and bone continue to form.	Los músculos y los huesos siguen formándose.
The baby makes sucking motions with the mouth.	El bebé empieza a mover la boca como si estuviera chupando.
The baby is 4 to 5 inches long and weighs 3 ounces.	El bebé mide de cuatro a cinco pulgadas de largo y pesa tres onzas.
At 20 weeks, the baby is active and the mother begins to feel slight fluttering in her abdomen.	A las veinte semanas, el bebé está activo y la madre empieza a sentir una leve agitación en el abdomen.
Eyebrows, eyelashes, fingernails, and toenails are present.	Ya están formadas las cejas, las pestañas, y las uñas de las manos y pies.
This is now half-way through the pregnancy and the baby is about 6 inches long.	Éste es el punto medio del embarazo, y el bebé mide aproximadamente seis pulgadas de largo.
At 24 weeks footprints and fingerprints are present.	A las veinticuatro semanas, las huellas de los pies y las huellas digitales están presentes.
Hair begins to grow on the baby's head.	El pelo empieza a crecer en la cabeza del bebé.
The lungs are formed.	Se forman los pulmones.
The baby sleeps and wakes on a regular basis.	El bebé duerme y se despierta con regularidad.
If the baby is a boy, the testicles begin to move into the scrotum.	Si el bebé es varón, los testículos se mueven dentro del escroto.
If the baby is a girl, the uterus and ovaries are present; a lifetime supply of eggs is present in the ovaries.	Si el bebé es hembra, el útero y los ovarios están formados; una dotación de óvulos para toda la vida ya está presente en los ovarios.
The baby is now 12 inches long and weighs about 1 ½ pounds.	El bebé ahora mide doce pulgadas de largo y pesa una libra y media.

Third Trimester / Tercer trimestre

At 32 weeks the baby's bones are completely formed.	A las treinta y dos semanas, los huesos del bebé están totalmente formados.
The baby's kicks and movements are strong.	Las patadas y los movimientos del bebé son fuertes.
The eyes open and close and the baby is able to sense changes in light.	Los ojos se abren y cierran, y el bebé puede sentir los cambios de luz.
The baby begins to store vital minerals such as iron and calcium.	El bebé empieza a acumular minerales vitales, como el hierro y el calcio.

(continued / continuado)

(continued / continuado)

The baby is gaining weight quickly and now weighs about 4½ pounds and is 15 to 17 inches long.	El bebé sube de peso rápidamente, y ahora pesa cuatro libras y media, y mide entre quince y diecisiete pulgadas de largo.
At 36 weeks the baby is growing and has less space to move so the mother feels more frequent and stronger movement by the baby.	A las treinta y seis semanas, el bebé sigue creciendo y tiene menos espacio para moverse así que la madre siente el movimiento del bebé de manera más frecuente y más fuerte.
The baby is about 16- to 19-inches long and weighs about 6½ pounds.	El bebé mide entre dieciséis y diecinueve pulgadas de largo, y pesa aproximadamente seis libras y media.
At the end of week 37, the baby is full term.	Al final de la semana treinta y siete, el desarrollo del bebé está completo.
The baby's organs are ready to function on their own.	Los órganos del bebé pueden funcionar independientemente.
At birth the baby weighs 6 pounds to 9 pounds and is 19- to 21-inches long, but healthy babies can be smaller or larger!	Al momento de nacer, el bebé pesa entre seis y nueve libras, y mide entre diecinueve y veintiuna pulgadas de largo, ¡pero los bebés sanos pueden ser más grandes o más pequeños!

Maternal changes throughout pregnancy / Cambios durante el embarazo

The body of the woman who is pregnant undergoes many changes over the 40 weeks of pregnancy. The nurse often has the opportunity to talk to the woman about her body as it progresses through pregnancy and to explain what she can expect. The woman who can understand and expect these alterations will also be more aware of any negative changes, which may prompt her to seek help sooner. The following table lists facts about what a woman's body undergoes throughout her pregnancy written from the nurse to the newly pregnant woman.

AUDIO 8.9

First Trimester / Primer Trimestre

You can feel more fatigued.	Ud. puede sentirse más fatigada.
The breasts can become swollen and sore.	Puede sentir los pechos hinchados y adoloridos.
You may have cravings for certain foods or certain foods smell or taste bad to you.	Puede tener antojos por ciertas comidas o ciertas comidas pueden oler mal o tener un mal sabor.
You may have changes in your mood; be happy and then be sad.	Puede tener cambios de humor; estar feliz y luego estar triste.
You may feel the need to urinate more often.	Puede sentir necesidad de orinar más frecuentemente.

(continued / continuado)

(continued / continuado)

You may have heartburn.	Puede tener acidez.
These symptoms will reduce after the first 3 months of your pregnancy.	Estos síntomas aminoran después de los tres meses de embarazo.
Some women do not have any of these symptoms.	Algunas mujeres no tienen ninguno de estos síntomas.
Each pregnancy is different for every woman.	Cada embarazo es diferente para cada mujer.
You need to change some of your routines to help with these symptoms.	Podría tener que cambiar algunas de sus rutinas para ayudarle a sobrellevar los síntomas.
Eat smaller meals, eat more frequently, go to bed earlier.	Coma porciones pequeñas, coma más frecuentemente y váyase a la cama más temprano.

Second Trimester / Segundo Trimestre

Symptoms like nausea and fatigue go away.	Los síntomas como náusea y fatiga desaparecen.
You may have backaches or pain in the groin or thighs.	Puede tener dolor de espalda o dolor en la ingle o en los muslos.
You may notice patches of darker skin over your cheeks, forehead, and nose.	Puede notar manchas de piel más oscura sobre las mejillas, la frente o la nariz.
The abdomen may feel itchy.	Puede tener picazón en el abdomen.
Ankles and feet may swell.	Se le pueden hinchar los tobillos y los pies.
If you have nausea, loss of appetite, vomiting, or yellow skin with the skin itching, see your doctor or nurse-midwife immediately.	Si tiene náusea, pérdida de apetito, vómitos o piel amarillenta con picazón, vea a su doctor/a o a su matrona inmediatamente.
If you have sudden swelling of the face, feet, or hands or gain a lot of weight quickly, call your doctor or nurse-midwife immediately.	Si de pronto se le hinchan la cara, los pies o manos, o si sube de peso rápidamente, llame a su doctor/a o a su matrona inmediatamente.

Third Trimester / Tercer Trimestre

The baby is getting bigger and this may cause you to have to urinate more often or feel short of breath.	El bebé está creciendo y esto puede causar que Ud. tenga que orinar más frecuentemente o se sienta que le falta la respiración.
Some women notice a watery milky-like discharge from the breasts.	Algunas mujeres notan una descarga lechosa de los pechos.

(continued / continuado)

(*continued / continuado*)

You may have trouble sleeping; pillows under the abdomen and under the legs can help.	Puede tener problemas para dormir; ponerse almohadas bajo el abdomen o debajo de las piernas puede ayudar.
Try to sleep on your left side.	Intente dormir del lado izquierdo.
You can feel tightening of the abdomen that feels like contractions. Early in the third trimester these can be "false contractions" but if there is a regular pattern to the contractions, go to the hospital.	Es posible que sienta cierta presión en el abdomen que podrían semejarse a las contracciones. A principios del tercer trimestre estas pueden ser "contracciones falsas" pero si hay una regularidad en el tipo de contracciones, vaya al hospital.

AUDIO 8.10

Suggestions to help alleviate some of the symptoms of pregnancy / Sugerencias para aliviar algunos de los síntomas del embarazo

Drink water throughout your pregnancy.	Tome agua durante el embarazo.
Do not drink a lot of caffeine drinks.	No tome muchas bebidas con cafeína.
Get extra rest.	Descanse más de lo acostumbrado.
Eat healthy.	Coma comida saludable.
If you feel hungry in between meals, snack on healthy foods, such as fresh vegetables.	Si le da hambre entre las comidas, coma cosas saludables, como verdura fresca.
Avoid salty or high-sodium foods.	Evite los alimentos salados o altos en sodio.
Tell your doctor or nurse-midwife about the symptoms you are having.	Dígale a su doctor/a o matrona los síntomas que tiene.
Do not take herbs or other medications for the symptoms of pregnancy without first asking your doctor or nurse-midwife.	No consuma hierbas u otras medicinas para los síntomas del embarazo sin consultarlo con su doctor o matrona.
Walking is a good form of exercise.	Caminar es un buen tipo de ejercicio.

BASICS OF CONCEPTION AND CONTRACEPTION / ASPECTOS BÁSICOS DE LA CONCEPCIÓN Y CONTRACONCEPCIÓN

When assessing the patient for contraception, a gynecological history is essential. This history needs to include the health history of the patient's relatives as well. This is followed by a complete physical exam and, according to the established guidelines and the patient's history, appropriate screening tests are conducted.

To assist the patient with her choice of contraceptive method, the practitioner begins with assessing the patient's knowledge of how pregnancy occurs. Next, the patient is introduced to an overview of the various contraceptive options which then, by bridging her history and physical examination, help the patient and health care provider to determine the best contraceptive options for the patient.

The complete gynecological history and conducting the gynecological physical examination are found in Chapter 8.

 A summary of the basics of conception / Resumen de los aspectos básicos de la concepción

The following is a suggested presentation for the health care provider to use to explain the basics of conception to a Spanish-speaking patient. The Spanish translation is presented after the English explanation. Note that the diagram of the uterus and ovaries can assist in the presentation to the patient.

> Health care provider (HCP): The diagram shows the female reproductive organs. Each labeled structure is essential for conception to occur. The signal for the ovary to release an egg comes from the brain. The signal transmits the information necessary for the ovary to mature an egg and, as the egg is maturing, other changes are occurring. The lining of the uterus changes and becomes thicker, which will provide the necessary environment for the baby to grow. Also at this time, the mucus from the cervix located at the entrance to the uterus becomes thin and watery so that the sperm can reach the egg.

> As the egg matures, it leaves the ovary and travels through the fallopian tube where the sperm will meet the egg and a process called *fertilization* occurs. The fertilized egg is now called an *ovum* and it continues to travel through the fallopian tube and implants in the lining of the uterus. If the egg is not fertilized, the thick lining of the uterus is shed by the body and is called the woman's *menses* or *period*.

> HCP: El diagrama muestra los órganos reproductivos femeninos. Cada una de las estructuras nombradas son esenciales para que ocurra la concepción. La señal para que el ovario libere el huevo, viene del cerebro. Esta señal transmite la información necesaria para que el ovario madure el huevo y mientras el ovario madura el huevo, ocurren otros cambios. El revestimiento del útero cambia y se engruesa, lo cual va a proveer el ambiente necesario para que el bebé crezca. Al mismo tiempo, la mucosidad del cuello uterino ubicado a la entrada del útero se adelgaza y se vuelve acuoso para que el espermatozoide pueda llegar hasta el huevo. Al madurar, el huevo deja el ovario y viaja a través de las trompas de Falopio donde el espermatozoide se encuentra con el huevo y comienza el proceso llamado

fertilización. El huevo fertilizado ahora se llama "óvulo" y continúa viajando a través de las trompas de Falopio y se implanta en el revestimiento del útero. Si el huevo no es fertilizado, este grueso revestimiento uterino es despedido del cuerpo y se llama la menstruación o el período de la mujer.

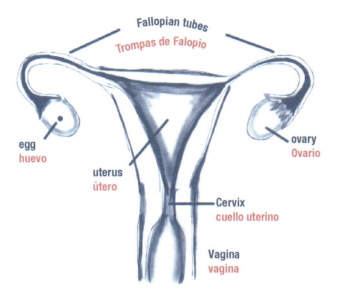

Fallopian tubes
Trompas de Falopio

egg
huevo

ovary
Ovario

uterus
útero

Cervix
cuello uterino

Vagina
vagina

Contraceptive options / Opciones de anticonceptivos

The following is a brief and basic discussion on some of the more popular methods of birth control. It is important to advise the woman that no method is 100% effective in preventing pregnancy. It is also important to advise the woman that the effectiveness of any method is improved with correct use by the woman and her partner.

HCP: The following is a brief overview of some of the forms of birth control. Please know that no method is 100 percent effective in preventing pregnancy, but the effectiveness of the method is improved with correct use.	HCP: Lo siguiente es un breve resumen de algunas formas de control de natalidad. Por favor, tenga en cuenta de que no hay un método que sea ciento por ciento efectivo en prevenir el embarazo, pero la eficiencia del método mejora si se usa correctamente.

Condom	El condón
The condom is a device that can prevent pregnancy and sexually transmitted infection. The condom needs to be put on the erect penis prior to any sexual encounter. The condom must be removed after intercourse before the male erection resolves.	El condón es un dispositivo que puede prevenir el embarazo y también las infecciones transmitidas sexualmente. El condón debe ponerse en el pene erecto antes de tener relación sexual. El condón debe sacarse después del coito antes de que la erección masculina termine.

Spermicides	Espermaticida
There are a variety of products, such as films, creams, jellies and foams, that contain a spermicide and are inserted into the female vagina before intercourse. These products must be used prior to each act of intercourse.	Hay una variedad de productos, como filmes, cremas, jaleas y espumas que contienen espermicidas y que se insertan en la vagina antes del coito. Estos productos tienen que usarse antes de cada relación sexual.

Birth control pill	La píldora anticonceptiva
There are a variety of contraceptive pills; some contain estrogen and progesterone and some contain only progesterone. The woman's history helps to determine which type is best. The hormones stop the woman from ovulating, which prevents her from becoming pregnant. The pills help the woman to also have periods that are lighter, shorter, and with fewer cramps. The pills are very effective in preventing pregnancy if the pills are taken correctly. The pill needs to be taken every day at about the same time. The effectiveness of the pill to prevent pregnancy begins after the woman is on the pill and taking it correctly for at least 2 weeks.	Hay una variedad de píldoras anticonceptivas; algunas contienen estrógenos y progesterona y otras contienen solamente progesterona. El historial de la mujer ayuda a determinar qué tipo es mejor. Las hormonas impiden que la mujer ovule, lo cual previene que quede embarazada. Las píldoras ayudan a que la mujer tenga períodos más ligeros, cortos y con menos dolores menstruales. Las píldoras son muy efectivas en impedir el embarazo si se toman correctamente. Se necesita tomar la píldora diariamente más o menos a la misma hora del día. La eficacia de la píldora para prevenir el embarazo comienza después de que la mujer esté tomando la píldora y que la tome correctamente por dos semanas.

Ring	El anillo
The vaginal ring is a device that is made of a soft pliable material in the shape of a ring. This device is inserted into the vagina by the woman and remains in place for 3 weeks. At the conclusion of the 3 weeks, the woman removes and discards the ring. Sometime during the following week, the woman will have a menses that is usually shorter, lighter, and with less cramping then her usual menses. Seven days from the removal of the ring, the woman places a new ring into the vagina. The ring contains estrogen and progesterone, which act similarly to the pill in that they prevent ovulation. The ring is effective after the first week of use and its effectiveness continues as long as the woman continues to use this method correctly.	El anillo vaginal es un dispositivo hecho de un material blando y moldeable en la forma de un anillo. El anillo se inserta en la vagina de la mujer y se deja allí por tres semanas. Al terminar las tres semanas, la mujer debe remover el anillo y tirarlo. En algún momento durante la siguiente semana, la mujer tendrá una menstruación corta, escasa, y con menos cólicos menstruales de los que usualmente tiene. Siete días después de haberse sacado el anillo, la mujer se pone un nuevo anillo en la vagina. El anillo contiene estrógeno y progesterona, lo que actúa de manera similar a la de la píldora en prevenir la ovulación. El anillo es efectivo después de una semana de uso y su eficacia se mantiene siempre y cuando la mujer continúe usando este método correctamente.

Progestin-only injection

This injection of the hormone progestin is given to the woman every 12 weeks. The hormone stops the woman from ovulating. The woman's menstrual cycles may become irregular or she may stop having periods, which is a normal effect of this method of contraception. The effectiveness of this method begins 2 weeks after the first injection.

Inyección de progestina

La inyección anticonceptiva de la hormona progestina se le pone a la mujer cada doce semanas. La hormona impide que la mujer ovule. Los ciclos menstruales de la mujer pueden volverse irregulares o la mujer puede dejar de menstruar, lo que cual es un efecto normal de este método de contracepción. La eficacia de este método comienza dos semanas después de la primera inyección.

Implant

There is a device that is placed under the skin on the inside of the upper arm. It is about the size of a matchstick and contains the hormone progesterone. It is effective for three years. It works to prevent pregnancy by preventing the release of an egg from the ovary as well as changing the cervical mucus making it more difficult for the sperm to pass through the cervix. Upon removal, a new implant can be placed in the same area of the original one. Depending upon when in the menstrual cycle it is inserted will depend on how long the woman will need to use additional contraception as the condom.

Implante anticonceptivo

Hay un dispositivo que se coloca debajo de la piel en la parte superior e interior del brazo. Es de un tamaño aproximado al de un fósforo y contiene hormona progesterona. Es efectivo por el espacio de tres años. Previene el embarazo al impedir la liberación del huevo del ovario como también al cambiar la mucosidad cervical, lo que hace que el espermatozoide tenga dificultad para pasar a través del cuello uterino. Al sacarlo, se puede colocar un nuevo implante en la misma área donde estaba el primero. Según en qué momento del ciclo menstrual se lo haya insertado va a depender de cuánto tiempo la mujer necesite para usar una forma anticonceptiva como el condón.

Intrauterine device

The intrauterine device (IUD) is a device placed inside the uterus. It prevents fertilization and implantation of a fertilized egg and also slows the transport of sperm. The IUD with the hormone progesterone is effective for 5 years. The IUD with copper is effective for 10 years. An additional form of contraception may be necessary for one week after insertion depending on the type of IUD and when during the woman's menstrual cycle the IUD is inserted.

Dispositivo intrauterino (DIU)

El DIU es un dispositivo que se coloca dentro del útero. Impide la fertilización y la implantación del huevo fertilizado y también retarda el desplazamiento del espermatozoide. El DIU con la hormona progesterona es efectivo por 5 años. El DIU con cobre es efectivo por 10 años. Una forma adicional de anticoncepción podría ser necesaria una semana después de que se haya colocado el dispositivo, dependiendo del tipo de DIU y también en qué momento del ciclo menstrual se insertó el DIU.

General Information	Información General
All methods of birth control may have side effects, which is why it is important that the woman talk with her health care provider so that the best method is chosen for the woman. It is also important that the woman return to her health care provider as instructed so that she be evaluated for any side effects, if there is a need to adjust dosage of the pill, or to change the type of method used.	Todos los métodos de control de natalidad pueden tener un efecto secundario, por lo cual es importante que la mujer hable con su doctor/a o matrona para que se utilice el mejor método para la mujer. También es importante que la mujer vuelva a ver a su doctor/a o matrona según se le haya indicado, para que la paciente pueda ser evaluada por si tiene algún efecto secundario, necesite ajustar las dosis de la píldora, o para cambiar el tipo de método.

Culture/Cultura: The word "guagua" is used instead of "baby" in the Andean Region. This word comes from Quechua (wawa), the indigenous language spoken by the Incas.

DIMINUTIVES AND RELATED EXPRESSIONS / LOS DIMINUTIVOS Y EXPRESIONES RELACIONADAS

A cultural aspect prevalent in many Spanish-speaking countries is the use of diminutives, words that are often shortened to indicate affection.

The following is a listing of a few diminutives/alternative words commonly used in Spanish:

A little bit	un poquito (from "un poco")
Arm	bracito (from "brazo")
Asleep (used with "estar")	dormidito/dormidita
Baby	bebé/bebito
Coffee	cafecito (from café)
Doggie	perrito
Hand	manito (from "mano")
Honey	amorcito
Kitty	gatito
Little brother/sister	hermanito/a
Little voice	vocecita (from "voz")
Slowly	despacito (from "despacio")
Tummy/belly	guata/guatita/panza/pancita

To form diminutives:

For words ending in a vowel, drop the vowel and add -ito or -ita:

abuela = abuelita (granny)

For words ending in -n or -r, add -cito/-cita:

corazón = corazoncito (sweetie)

For words ending in a consonant that is not "n" or "r," add –ito/-ita:

Miguel = Miguelito (Mikey)

READING: JONAS EDWARD SALK, PHYSICIAN AND VIROLOGIST / LECTURA: JONAS EDWARD SALK, MÉDICO Y VIRÓLOGO

Reading

Jonas Edward Salk (1914–1995, b. New York), physician and virologist, is known for his research as an American doctor and virologist recognized for discovering and developing the first effective vaccine against polio. At the beginning of the 1950s, polio was a terrible epidemic in the United States after the Second Word War, with almost 60,000 deaths occurring from the disease. In 1947, Salk was appointed to the School of Medicine at the University of Pittsburgh, and began a project to investigate the different types of polio that affect children. After testing the vaccine on almost 2 million children, on April 12, 1955, the vaccine was proclaimed successful. In 1960, Salk then founded the Salk Institute for Biological Studies in California, which still functions today as a center of investigation for medicine and science.

Lectura

Jonas Edward Salk, médico y virólogo (1914–1995, n. New York), es reconocido por su investigación como médico y virólogo estadounidense reconocido por descubrir y desarrollar la primera vacuna efectiva contra la poliomielitis (polio). Al principio de los años 1950, la polio es una epidemia terrible en los Estados Unidos después de la Segunda Guerra Mundial, con casi 60,000 muertos por la enfermedad. En 1947, Salk se integró a la Escuela de Medicina en la Universidad de Pittsburgh, y empezó un proyecto para investigar los diferentes tipos de polio que afectan a los niños. Después de probar la vacuna en casi dos millones de niños, el 12 de abril de 1955, la vacuna es declarada "exitosa." Salk después fundó, en 1960, el Instituto Salk para los Estudios Biológicos en California, el que todavía funciona hoy como un centro de investigación.

IDIOMATIC EXPRESSIONS / EXPRESIONES IDIOMÁTICAS

To cross one's fingers   English expression

Cruzar los dedos   Spanish expression

To cross the fingers   Literal translation

To burn the candle at both ends   English expression

Quemarse las pestañas   Spanish expression

To burn one's eyelashes   Literal translation

9

ASSESSMENT FOR THE ADVANCED HEALTH CARE PROVIDER

CONTENTS

Teaching the male testicular self-examination / Cómo enseñar un autoexamen testicular

Teaching the breast self-examination / Cómo enseñar el autoexamen de los pechos

Reading: Doctors Without Borders / Lectura: Medecins Sans Frontiers

Idiomatic expressions / Expresiones idiomáticas

SPECIFICS FOR THE ADVANCED HEALTH CARE PROVIDER / DETALLES ESPECÍFICOS PARA *ADVANCED HEALTH CARE PROVIDER*

This chapter introduces the language learner to specifics on conducting a thorough examination of the patient by the physician, nurse practitioner, nurse-midwife, and physician assistant. The vocabulary presented builds on vocabulary found in the initial chapters of this textbook. The sections that follow the vocabulary include information on obtaining an episodic health history followed by the complete health history. As the patient's exposure to violence must be addressed, the assessment for sexual, domestic, and intimate partner violence is included. Conducting the complete physical examination is detailed to include the male genital exam. A thorough guide is presented on obtaining gynecological histories for an initial woman's health examination and a history for a woman presenting with a vaginal infection. The items found in each of these histories also serve for assessing the woman for contraceptive needs. As a sensitive woman's examination is essential, the English with translation to Spanish of the measures used to obtain the woman's pelvic exam details will ensure the examiner demonstrates sensitivity to conducting this exam. Teaching the male testicular exam and the breast self-exam conclude the assessment portions of this chapter. The concluding reading provides an overview of Doctors Without Borders.

VOCABULARY FOR THE ADVANCED PRACTITIONER / VOCABULARIO PARA *ADVANCED PRACTITIONER*

Head and neck / Cabeza y cuello

Scalp	El cuero cabelludo
Eyebrow	La ceja
Eyelashes	Las pestañas
Eyelid	El párpado
Pupil	La pupila
Cornea	La córnea
Iris	El iris
Sclera	La esclerótica
Nostril	La fosa nasal
Nasal septum	El tabique nasal
Sinus	El seno nasal

Tooth	El diente
Molar	La muela
Throat	La garganta
Tonsils	Las amígdalas
Tongue	La lengua
Palate	El paladar
Thyroid gland	La glándula tiroides
Esophagus	El esófago
Trachea	La tráquea

Internal organs / Los órganos internos

AUDIO 9.2
www.springerpub.com/traverso

Lungs	Los pulmones
Stomach	El estómago
Large intestine	El intestino grueso
Colon	El colon
Liver	El hígado
Gall bladder	La vesícula
Kidneys	Los riñones
Uterus	El útero
Prostate	La próstata
Rectum	El recto
Heart	El corazón
Spleen	El bazo
Small intestine	El intestino delgado
Intestines	Los intestinos
Pancreas	El páncreas
Bladder	La vejiga
Appendix	El apéndice
Ovaries	Los ovarios
Testicles	Los testículos
Anus	El ano

www.springerpub.com/traverso
AUDIO 9.3

Bones / Huesos

Skull	El cráneo
Orbit	La órbita
Nasal bone	El hueso nasal
Maxilla	El hueso maxilar superior
Mandible	La mandíbula
Spine	La espina dorsal
Scapula	La escápula
Clavicle	La clavícula
Humerus	El húmero
Radius	El radio
Ulna	El cúbito
Carpals	Los carpianos
Phalanges	Las falanges
Ribs	Las costillas
Pelvis	La pelvis
Sacrum	El sacro
Coccyx	El cóccix
Femur	El fémur
Patella	La rótula
Fibula	El peroné
Tibia	La tibia
Ankle	El tobillo
Calcaneus	El calcáneo
Tarsals	Los tarsianos
Metartarsals	Los metatarsianos

www.springerpub.com/traverso
AUDIO 9.4

The circulatory system / El sistema circulatorio

Arteries	**Las arterias**
Carotid artery	la arteria carótida
Brachial artery	la arteria braquial

Axillary artery	la arteria axilar
Radial artery	la arteria radial
Aortic artery	la arteria aorta
Abdominal aortic artery	la arteria aorta abdominal
Renal artery	la arteria renal
Femoral artery	la arteria femoral
Subclavian artery	la arteria subclavia
Iliac artery	la arteria ilíaca
Popliteal artery	la arteria poplítea
Cephalic artery	la arteria cefálica
Tibial artery	la arteria tibial
Veins	**Las venas**
Subclavian vein	la vena subclavia
External jugular vein	la vena yugular externa
Axillary vein	la vena axilar
Saphenous vein	la vena safena
Cephalic vein	la vena cefálica
Brachial vein	la vena braquial
Inferior vena cava	la vena cava inferior
Iliac vein	la vena ilíaca
Femoral vein	la vena femoral
Popliteal vein	la vena poplítea
Tibial vein	la vena tibial

OBTAINING THE EPISODIC HEALTH HISTORY / GUÍA PARA OBTENER UNA HISTORIA CLÍNICA EPISÓDICA

To obtain the history of a present illness from the patient, the practitioner first must obtain information concerning the chief complaint and then the history of the present illness. Abdominal pain will be used in order to demonstrate obtaining the patient history in Spanish.

Chief complaint / Problema principal del paciente

Health Care Provider (*HCP*)

Patient (*PT*)   Juan is 19 years old / *Juan tiene 19 años.*

HCP: What health problem do you have today?

   ¿Qué problema de salud tiene hoy?

PT: I have pain in my abdomen.

   Tengo dolor en mi abdomen.

After the patient responds with the chief complaint, there are specific questions that are recommended for the health care provider to ask the patient in order to determine the nature of the patient's health issue, which forms the basis for the physical exam and supports the differential diagnosis and plan of care.

History of present illness / Historial de la enfermedad presente

HCP: Please tell me how long have you had the pain in your abdomen?

   Por favor dígame, ¿hace cuánto tiempo tiene dolor en el abdomen?

PT: Since yesterday.

   Desde ayer.

HCP: How did it begin; suddenly or slowly?

   ¿Cómo comenzó? ¿De repente o lentamente?

PT: Suddenly.

   De repente.

HCP: When did the pain begin?

   ¿Cuándo comenzó el dolor?

PT: The pain began in the evening.

   El dolor empezó en la tarde.

HCP: Point to where the pain is in your abdomen.

   Apunte dónde está el dolor en su abdomen.

PT: It is here. (Patient points to right lower quadrant.)

   Está aquí.

HCP: Describe the pain.

   Describa su dolor.

PT: The pain is sharp.

El dolor es fuerte.

HCP: Please describe the intensity of your pain where 1 is very little and 10 is very severe.

Por favor describa la intensidad de su dolor: uno es muy poco y diez es muy severo.

PT: My pain is a 9 now but sometimes it is a 10.

Mi dolor es un nueve ahora pero a veces es un diez.

HCP: Is the pain continuous?

¿El dolor es continuo?

PT: Yes, the pain is continuous.

Sí, el dolor es continuo.

HCP: Does the pain change when you move?

¿Cambia el dolor cuando se mueve?

PT: Yes, the pain is worse when I move or walk.

Sí, el dolor es peor cuando me muevo o camino.

HCP: Does anything make the pain better or worse?

¿Hay algo que mejore o empeore el dolor?

PT: The pain is less when I lie down, but the pain is always there. The pain is worse when I walk.

Tengo menos dolor cuando me acuesto, pero el dolor siempre está ahí. El dolor es peor cuando camino.

HCP: Are you taking any medication for the pain?

¿Está tomando medicina para el dolor?

PT: No, I am not taking any medication for the pain.

No, no estoy tomando ninguna medicina para el dolor.

HCP: Can you tell me anything else about how you are feeling?

¿Puede decirme algo más de cómo se siente?

PT: Yes, I feel nauseated and I have a fever. I feel like I am going to vomit. I cannot eat and I do not want to drink because I may vomit.

Sí, tengo náuseas y fiebre. Siento que voy a vomitar. No puedo comer ni quiero tomar nada porque puedo vomitar.

THE COMPLETE HEALTH HISTORY / HISTORIA COMPLETA LA SALUD

To obtain a complete health history of a patient with no specific health issues, the following format is recommended. It is assumed that the health care provider's comprehension of the Spanish language is basic, thus the history will be kept in a similar format yet will render sufficient information for the health care provider to conduct a thorough physical examination of the patient at the conclusion of the health history.

History of present illness / Historial de la enfermedad actual

All health histories should begin by first clarifying why the patient is present today and if there are any health issues.

Patient: Mr. Pérez is 32. / *El señor Pérez tiene 32 años.*

HCP: Hello, Mr. Pérez, my name is _____ and I am the family nurse practitioner. I understand that you are here for a physical to start work as an x-ray technician. Do you have any health problems today?

Hola Señor Pérez, mi nombre es _____ y soy el/la enfermero(a) calificado(a). Entiendo que usted está aquí para un examen físico antes de empezar a trabajar como radiólogo. ¿Tiene algún problema de salud hoy?

PT: Hello, you can call me David and I just need a physical for work. I do not have any health problems.

Hola, me puede llamar David y sólo necesito el examen físico para trabajar. No tengo ningún problema de salud.

Past medical history / Historia clínica pasada

HCP: OK, David, I need to ask you some questions about your health history first and then I am going to do your physical examination.

Está bien, David, necesito hacerle algunas preguntas sobre su historia clínica y luego le voy a hacer un examen físico.

PT: OK, thank you.

Está bien, gracias.

HCP: Do you have a history of heart murmurs, heart problems, high blood pressure, diabetes kidney problems, arthritis, or tuberculosis?

¿Tiene un historial médico de un soplo al corazón, problemas cardíacos, presión alta, diabetes, problemas renales, artritis o tuberculosis?

PR: No, I do not.

No, no tengo.

HCP: Do you have a history of pneumonia, measles, mumps, rubella, or chicken pox?

¿Tiene un historial médico de neumonia, sarampión, paperas, rubeola o varicela?

PT: No, I do not.

No, no tengo.

HCP: Do you have a history of any chronic health problems?

¿Tiene un historial médico de problemas crónicos de salud?

PT: No, I do not.

No, no tengo.

HCP: Were you ever in the hospital?

¿Alguna vez estuvo en el hospital?

PT: Yes, I had my tonsils removed as a child.

Sí, de niño me quitaron las amígdalas.

HCP: Did you ever have any accidents or injuries as, for example, broken bones or sutures?

¿Alguna vez tuvo algún accidente o lesiones como, por ejemplo, huesos rotos o suturas?

PT: Yes, I cut my arm last year on a broken window and had sutures.

Sí, me corté el brazo el año pasado en una ventana rota y me suturaron.

HCP: Do you have a history of any other injuries?

¿Tiene un historial médico de otras lesiones?

PT: No.

No.

HCP: Are you allergic to any medicines?

¿Es alérgico a alguna medicina?

PT: I am allergic to sulfa.

Soy alérgico a la sulfa.

HCP: What type of reaction do you have when you take sulfa?

¿Qué tipo de reacción tiene cuando toma sulfa?

PT: I get a rash and hives.

Me salen sarpullido y ronchas.

HCP: Are you allergic to foods?

¿Es alérgico a alguna comida?

PT: No, I am not allergic to any foods.

No, no soy alérgico a ninguna comida.

HCP: Do you have any seasonal allergies?

¿Tiene alergias estacionales?

PT: No, I do not have any seasonal allergies.

No, no tengo alergias estacionales.

HCP: Do you take any medications every day?

¿Toma algún medicamento diariamente?

PT: No.

No.

HCP: Do you take any over-the-counter medications, such as vitamins, laxatives, or herbs?

¿Toma algún medicamento sin receta médica, como vitaminas, laxantes o hierbas?

PT: No, I do not take any.

No, no tomo ninguno.

Personal and social history / Historial personal y social

HCP: I need to ask you about some types of habits.

Do you drink alcohol? If so, how much and how often?

Necesito preguntarle sobre algunos tipos de hábitos:

¿Usted bebe alcohol? Si lo hace, ¿cuánto bebe y con qué frecuencia?

PT: Yes, I drink two beers on Friday nights.

Sí, me bebo dos cervezas los viernes por la noche.

HCP: Do you smoke cigarettes?

¿Fuma cigarrillos?

PT: No, never.

No, jamás.

HCP: Do you use drugs?

¿Usa drogas?

PT: No, never.

No, nunca.

HCP: Do you drinks with caffeine, like coffee, tea, or soda pop?

¿Toma usted algo con cafeína como café, té, o soda?

PT: Yes, I drink one cup of coffee every morning.

Sí, me tomo una taza de café cada mañana.

HCP: Do you have any special diet or foods that you eat?

¿Sigue alguna dieta o tiene comida especial que usted prefiera comer?

PT: No.

No.

HCP: What type of exercise do you do?

¿Qué tipo de ejercicio hace usted?

PT: I run 5 miles every day!

¡Corro cinco millas todos los días!

Family history / Historial de la familia

HCP: I need to ask you about your family history.

Does anyone in your family have diabetes, high blood pressure, heart problems, cancer, kidney problems, or any other chronic health problems?

Necesito preguntarle sobre su historia familiar.

¿Alguien en su familia tiene diabetes, presión alta, problemas cardíacos, cáncer, problemas renales o algún otro problema crónico de salud?

PT: My father has high blood pressure.

Mi padre tiene presión alta.

Review of systems / Revisión de sistemas

HCP: I need to ask you some general questions about your health.

Necesito hacerle algunas preguntas generales sobre su salud.

HCP: Do you have a history of any skin problems, eczema or rashes?

¿Tiene usted un historial médico acerca de problemas de piel, eccema o sarpullido?

PT: No.

No.

HCP: Do you have a history of headaches, head trauma, or concussion?

¿Tiene un historial médico de dolores de cabeza, traumatismo cerebral, o conmoción cerebral?

PT: No.

No.

HCP: Do you have a history of vision problems? Do you wear glasses or contacts?

¿Tiene un historial médico de problemas de visión? ¿Usa usted anteojos o lentes de contacto?

PT: I wear contacts.

Uso lentes de contacto.

HCP: When did you have your eyes checked?

¿Cuándo le revisaron los ojos?

PT: In June of this year.

En junio de este año.

HCP: Do you have pain in your ears, hearing problems, dizziness, or ringing in your ears?

¿Tiene dolor en sus oídos, problemas auditivos, mareos o zumbidos en el oído?

PT: No.

No.

HCP: Do you have problems with sinus infections, nose bleeds, frequent colds, nasal trauma, or nasal polyps?

¿Tiene problemas de sinusitis, sangre de nariz, resfriados frecuentes, traumatismo nasal o pólipos nasales?

PT: No.

No.

HCP: Do you have painful gums or teeth, bleeding gums, sore tongue, hoarseness, or loss of taste?

¿Tiene dolor en las encías o en los dientes, sangrado de encías, dolor de lengua, ronquera o pérdida del gusto?

PT: No.

No.

HCP: Do you go to a dentist?

¿Visita usted al dentista?

PT: Yes, I go to the dentist every 6 months.

Sí, voy al dentista cada seis meses.

HCP: Do you have any pain in the neck or swollen glands?

¿Tiene algún dolor de cuello o ganglios linfáticos inflamados?

PT: Only when I have a sore throat.

Sólo cuando tengo dolor de garganta.

HCP: Do you have a sore throat now?

¿Tiene dolor de garganta ahora?

PT: No.

No.

HCP: How often do you get sore throats?

¿Con qué frecuencia tiene dolor de garganta?

PT: Maybe one or two times a year, usually in the winter.

Quizás una o dos veces al año, usualmente en el invierno.

HCP: Do you have a history of bleeding problems or anemia?

¿Tiene un historial médico de hemorragias o anemia?

PT: No.

No.

HCP: Do you have problems with wheezing, asthma, cough, being short of breath, coughing up blood, or history of bronchitis?

¿Tiene problemas de respiración con silbidos, asma, tos, falta de aliento, tos con sangre, o un historial médico de bronquitis?

PT: No.

No.

HCP: Do you have palpitations, or feel your heart beating too fast? Do you have pain in your chest or swelling in your feet?

¿Tiene palpitaciones o siente que su corazón late muy rápido? ¿Tiene dolor de pecho, o pies hinchados?

PT: No.

No.

HCP: Do you have leg cramps, varicose veins, or pain or heat in your legs?

¿Tiene calambres en las piernas, venas varicosas, dolor o calor en las piernas?

PT: No.

No.

HCP: Do you have problems with indigestion, constipation, difficulty swallowing foods, change in bowel habits, diarrhea, blood in the stool, pain in your abdomen, or pain after eating?

¿Tiene problemas de indigestión, estreñimiento, dificultad al tragar alimento, cambios en sus hábitos intestinales, diarrea, sangre en el excremento, dolor en el abdomen o dolor después de comer?

PT: I have heartburn after I eat very spicy foods.

Me da acidez estomacal después de comer comidas muy picantes.

HCP: Do you take medicine for this?

¿Toma medicina para esto?

PT: I take some antacid if the heartburn does not go away in an hour or two.

Tomo antiácido si la acidez no se va después de una o dos horas.

HCP: Does this happen frequently?

¿Esto le sucede frecuentemente?

PT: No, because I try not to eat very spicy foods.

No, porque intento no comer comidas muy picantes.

HCP: Do you have any pain when you urinate, have to urinate often, have to get up during the night to urinate, or have blood in the urine?

¿Tiene algún dolor cuando orina? ¿Tiene que orinar frecuentemente o tiene que levantarse por la noche para orinar o tiene sangre en la orina?

PT: No.

No.

HCP: Do you have a history of urinary infections or kidney infections?

¿Tiene un historial médico de infecciones urinarias o infecciones renales?

PT: No.

No.

HCP: I need to ask you some personal questions.

Are you sexually active, and, if so, are your partners male, female, or both?

Necesito hacerle algunas preguntas personales.

¿Tiene una relación sexual activa? De ser así, ¿sus parejas son hombres, mujeres o ambos?

PT: Yes, I have a girlfriend.

Sí, tengo una novia.

HCP: Do you have any pain with intercourse, discharge from the penis, testicular pain, or rashes?

¿Tiene dolor en las relaciones sexuales, descargas del pene, dolor testicular o erupciones?

PT: No.

No.

HCP: Do you have a history of any sexually transmitted infection?

¿Tiene un historial médico de alguna enfermedad de transmisión sexual?

PT: Yes, I had chlamydia 2 years ago.

Sí, tuve clamidia hace dos años.

HCP: Do you use anything to prevent from getting a sexually transmitted infection?

¿Utiliza algo para prevenir enfermedades de transmisión sexual?

PT: We sometimes use condoms.

A veces usamos condones.

HCP: Do you have a history of any muscle pain, pain or swelling in the joints?

¿Tiene un historial médico de dolores musculares, dolor o hinchazón en las articulaciones?

PT: No.

No.

HCP: Do you have a history of dizziness, seizures, loss of balance or coordination, or loss of consciousness?

¿Tiene un historial médico de mareos, convulsiones, pérdida de equilibrio o coordinación, o pérdida de conocimiento?

PT: No.

No.

HCP: Do you have a history of depression, anxiety, sleep problems, or memory problems?

¿Tiene una historia de depresión, ansiedad, problemas para dormir o de memoria?

PT: No.

No.

HCP: That completes the history; now I need to do your physical examination.

Eso completa la historia clínica, ahora necesito hacerle el examen físico.

Assessment for sexual, domestic, and intimate partner violence / Evaluación de violencia sexual, violencia doméstica, y violencia íntima por parte de la pareja

Although the aforementioned example is considered a thorough history, the area of sexual, domestic, and intimate partner violence should be included when conducting a complete health history and physical examination. This part of the history is presented separately as it needs to be integrated according to how the practitioner prefers to incorporate this questioning into the physical examination.

Note: Some of the following Spanish verb structures are in tenses not previously covered, but convey the desired meaning of the translation when conducting this type of history.

An option when assessing for sexual, domestic, and partner violence is to follow the RADAR mnemonic:

- **R**outinely screen every patient.
- **A**sk directly, kindly, and nonjudgmentally; listen attentively.
- **D**ocument your findings.
- **A**ssess the patient's safety.
- **R**eview options and provide referrals.

How do you begin? One suggestion is as follows:

"Violence is a problem for many women and men. I ask all my patients about it because it affects health and well-being."

La violencia es un problema para muchos hombres y mujeres. Les pregunto a todos mis pacientes sobre eso porque afecta la salud y el bienestar.

"I know that sexual violence and physical violence are common in the lives of many women, men, girls, and boys."

Yo sé que la violencia sexual y la violencia física son comunes en la vida de muchas mujeres, hombres, niñas y niños.

"Have you ever been touched in a way that made you feel uncomfortable?"

¿Alguna vez lo/la han tocado de una manera que lo/la ha hecho sentir incómodo/a?

"Have you ever been touched sexually against your will?"

¿Alguna vez lo/la han tocado sexualmente en contra de su voluntad?

"Have you ever been forced to have sex?"

¿Alguna vez lo/la han forzado a tener relaciones sexuales?

"Have you had experiences where there has been violence in your life?"

¿Ha tenido experiencias donde ha habido violencia en su vida?

"Has anyone close to you ever threatened or hurt you?"

¿Alguien cercano/a a usted alguna vez lo/la ha amenazado o lastimado?

"Has your partner (or anyone close to you) ever hit or tried to injure you?"

¿Su compañero/a (o alguien cercano/a a usted) alguna vez le ha pegado o intentado lastimarlo/a?

"Do you feel safe?"

¿Usted se siente seguro/a?

When a response of "yes" is received, the provider needs to chart the patient's responses using the patient's own words. The following are some possible responses from the health care provider to the patient.

"This is not your fault."

Esto no es su culpa.

"No one deserves to be treated this way."

Nadie merece ser tratado/a de esa manera.

"Do you want to talk about it?"

¿Usted quiere hablar sobre eso?

"I am concerned about your safety (and that of your children)."

Me preocupa su seguridad (y la de sus hijos).

"After listening to you, I want you to know that help is available for you."

Después de escucharlo/la, quiero que sepa que existe ayuda disponible para usted.

When the responses are "no" to the violence survey, the provider has indicated to the patient his or her willingness to discuss violence. This leaves future encounters open to the patient to discuss any violence concerns with the provider. If the patient experienced violence, the patient will choose when to disclose. The following is a recommendation for the health care provider when the responses are "no."

"If you ever want to talk about these issues in the future, I am available."

Si alguna vez quiere hablar de este problema en el futuro, estoy disponible.

Assessment of safety / Evaluación de seguridad

As the history of violence unfolds, the health care provider needs to include knowledge of any pattern and frequency of assaults, weapons, and drug and alcohol involvement in the assessment. Safety of children also must be addressed.

The health care provider needs to be aware of the multicultural support network available in the community. Having written information in the patient's language on referral sources is essential.

THE COMPLETE PHYSICAL EXAMINATION / EXAMEN FÍSICO COMPLETO

To conduct the physical examination, the practitioner must instruct the patient on what the exam entails as the exam moves from one body system to the next. The following is an example of conducting the physical exam on a Spanish-speaking patient by a health care provider who is knowledgeable in basic Spanish. The exam begins with taking the patient's vital signs.

Vital signs / Signos vitales

Taking blood pressure:

Hello Mr./Mrs._____, my name is _____.

I need to take your blood pressure.

Please give me your arm.

I need to place the cuff on the arm.

Please do not move the arm.

The cuff feels tight.

The blood pressure is 120 over 72.

That is good! Thank you!

Hola, Señor/ Señora _____, me llamo _____.

Necesito tomarle la presión.

Me da su brazo, por favor.

Necesito ponerle el brazalete en el brazo.

Por favor no mueva el brazo.

El brazalete le va a apretar.

La presión es ciento veinte con setenta y dos.

¡Está bien! Gracias!

Taking temperature and pulse:

Hello Mr./Mrs. _____, my name is _____.

I need to take your temperature and pulse.

I need you to place the thermometer under your tongue.

The temperature is 37°C (98.6°).

That is good.

I need to hold your wrist. I need to take your pulse.

Your pulse is good.

Thank you!

Hola, Señor/ Señora _____, me llamo _____.

Necesito tomarle la temperatura y el pulso.

Necesito ponerle el termómetro bajo la lengua.

La temperatura es treinta y siete grados Celsius (noventa y ocho punto seis grados).

¡Está bien!

Necesito sujetarle la muñeca. Necesito tomarle el pulso.

¡El pulso está bien!

¡Gracias!

Taking height and weight:

Hello Mr./Mrs. _____, my name is _____.

I need to take your weight and height.

Please stand on the scale.

Now please turn around on the scale. I need to take your height.

Your weight is 60 kg (132 lb.).

Your height is 1.7 m (66 in.).

That is good. Thank you.

Hola Señor/Señora _____, me llamo _____.

Necesito pesarlo/a y medirlo/a.

Por favor suba en la pesa.

Ahora, por favor gire. Necesito medirlo/a.

El peso es sesenta kilos (ciento treinta y dos libras).

La altura es un metro setenta (sesenta y seis pulgadas).

¡Está bien, gracias!

Head and neck examination / Examen de la cabeza y del cuello

HCP: For your physical exam, first I need to look at your eyes with this light, please follow my finger with your eyes, but do not move your head. Now look over my shoulder as I shine this light into your eyes.

Para su examen físico, primero necesito mirarle los ojos con esta luz, por favor siga mi dedo con sus ojos, pero no mueva la cabeza, ahora mire sobre mi hombro mientras yo alumbro sus ojos con esta luz.

HCP: I need to examine your ears. Please hold still as I look into your ears.

Necesito examinarle los oídos. Por favor no se mueva mientras le miro los oídos.

HCP: When I tap on your forehead or push above your cheeks, does that cause you any pain?

¿Le causa dolor cuando le toco la frente o le presiono arriba de las mejillas?

PT: No.

No.

HCP: Next, I need to shine a light into your nose and feel your nasal bone.

Ahora, necesito alumbrarle adentro de la nariz y tocarle el hueso nasal.

HCP: Please open your mouth and say, "AH."

Por favor, abra la boca y diga, "AH."

HCP: I need to feel your glands in your neck and I need you to swallow as I feel your thyroid gland.

Necesito palparle las glándulas en el cuello y necesito que trague mientras le siento la glándula tiroides.

Pulmonary system / Sistema pulmonar

HCP: With your mouth open, please take deep breaths as I move my stethoscope over your back.

Por favor respire hondo por la boca mientras muevo el estetoscopio por su espalda.

Cardiovascular system / Sistema cardiovascular

HCP: Please lie down. I am going to listen to your heart in several places on your chest. Please just breathe normally.

Por favor, acuéstese. Voy a escucharle el corazón en diferentes sitios de su pecho. Por favor, respire normalmente.

Breasts and lymph system / Pechos y sistema linfático

(The breast exam is included here as it is essential to assess the health changes in male and female breasts. Teaching the patient the self-breast exam is found later in this chapter.)

HCP: I need to examine your breasts. Place your hands on your waist and push in. Now, place your left hand behind your neck as I examine your left breast. You can put your arm down and now place your right hand behind your neck as I examine your right breast.

Necesito examinarle los pechos. Coloque las manos en su cintura y empuje hacia adentro. Ahora, coloque la mano izquierda detrás del cuello mientras yo le examino el pecho izquierdo. Baje su brazo y coloque la mano derecha detrás de su cuello mientras yo le examino el pecho derecho.

HCP: Please lie down so I can continue the breast exam. You can bend your knees up on the table so that you are more comfortable.

Por favor, acuéstese para continuar con el examen. Puede doblar sus rodillas encima de la mesa de exploración para que esté más cómodo/a.

HCP: Please place your hands behind your head. I need to examine your breast tissue.

Por favor, coloque las manos detrás de la cabeza. Necesito examinarle el tejido del pecho.

Abdomen / Abdomen

HCP: I need you to keep your abdomen soft as I first listen to your abdomen, now I need to tap on your abdomen. Now I need to feel your abdomen. Please take a deep breath as I examine you. And now take a deep breath as I examine the other side. Please tell me if this hurts you.

Necesito que mantenga el abdomen relajado, primero voy a escucharle el abdomen, ahora necesito darle golpecitos en el abdomen. Ahora necesito sentirle el abdomen. Por favor, respire hondo mientras lo/la examino. Y, ahora, respire hondo mientras le examino el otro lado. Por favor, dígame si esto le duele.

PT: No, I do not feel any pain.

No, no siento dolor.

HCP: Please sit up; I need to tap on your back over your kidneys.
Does that hurt you?

Por favor siéntese. Necesito darle golpecitos en la espalda sobre los riñones. ¿Esto le duele?

PT: No.

No.

Muscular skeletal system / Sistema músculo esquelético

HCP: I need to test the strength of your arms and legs. Do not let me pull your right arm down. Do not let me push your arm back. Put your arm out to your side and do not let me push your arm down. Now, I need to do this to the left arm.

Ahora necesito examinar la fuerza de sus brazos y piernas. No deje que le baje el brazo derecho, no deje que se lo empuje hacia arriba, extienda su brazo a un lado y no deje que se lo baje. Ahora necesito hacer lo mismo con el brazo izquierdo.

Squeeze my fingers with your hands.

Apriete mis dedos con sus manos.

HCP: Push your thighs against my hands; push your shins out against my hands; push your feet down against my hands. Now stand up and bend over and try to touch your toes.

Empuje sus muslos contra mis manos. Presione sus canillas hacia afuera contra mis manos. Presione sus pies contra mis manos. Ahora, levántese, dóblese hacia adelante e intente tocarse los dedos de los pies.

Neurological examination / Examen neurológico

HCP: I need to evaluate your nervous system with a couple of tests. This instrument feels sharp on one side and dull on the other. First close your eyes and tell me if this feels sharp or dull on either side of your face; now the same on your right and left hand and forearm, and on your feet and lower legs.

Necesito evaluarle el sistema nervioso con un par de exámenes. Este aparato tiene un lado punzante y el otro lado despuntado. Primero cierre los ojos y dígame si lo que siente es punzante o despuntado en cada lado de la cara. Ahora lo mismo en su mano derecha e izquierda en el antebrazo, en sus pies y la parte inferior de las piernas.

HCP: This is a tuning fork. I am going to place it behind your ear. Tell me if you feel it vibrating and when the vibration stops. Now, tell me if you can hear the vibration. Now, I am going to do the same thing to the other ear. Now, I am going to place the tuning fork on top of your head. Tell me where you feel the vibration.

Esto es un tenedor de sintonía. Voy a ponérselo detrás del oído. Dígame si puede sentir la vibración, y cuando deje de sentirla. Ahora, dígame si puede oír la vibración. Ahora, voy a hacer lo mismo con el otro oído. Ahora, voy a poner el tenedor de sintonía sobre la cabeza. Dígame dónde siente la vibración.

HCP: I need to test your reflexes with this reflex hammer. First, I need to test three areas on your right arm and then our left arm. Now I will test your knees and ankles.

Necesito medirle los reflejos con este martillo de reflejo. Primero necesito medirle en tres áreas en el brazo derecho y luego en el brazo izquierdo, ahora voy a medirle en las rodillas y en los tobillos.

HCP: Please stand and put your arms at your side, close your eyes, and keep your balance.

Por favor, párese y ponga los brazos a los lados, cierre los ojos y mantenga el equilibrio.

Genital examination in men / Examen genital de hombres

HCP: Now, I need to examine whether you have a hernia.

Ahora, necesito examinarle para ver si tiene una hernia.

HCP: Please stand up and hold the sheet in front of you. Turn your head to the left and cough, now turn your head to the right and cough.

Por favor párese y cúbrase con esta sábana. Gire su cabeza a la izquierda y tosa, ahora gire su cabeza a la derecha y tosa.

Note: The testicular exam is found in the section Teaching the Male Testicular Evaluation.

HCP: David, you are in very good health. Thank you and best of luck in your new job.

David, usted goza de muy buena salud. Muchas gracias y suerte con el nuevo trabajo.

PT: Thank you!

¡Gracias!

GUIDE TO THE PELVIC EXAMINATION / GUÍA PARA EL EXAMEN PÉLVICO

The nurse practitioner needs to obtain a gynecological history from the patient and then instruct the patient on how the pelvic examination is performed as this is the woman's first gynecological examination.

Gynecological history / Historial ginecológico

Patient: Carla is 22 years old. / *Carla tiene 22 años.*

HCP: Good afternoon Carla, I understand that you are here for an initial gynecological examination and you also have symptoms of a vaginal infection.

>*Buenas tardes Carla, entiendo que usted está aquí para su primer examen ginecológico y entiendo que también tiene síntomas de una infección vaginal.*

Carla: That is right.

>*Así es.*

HCP: First, I need to ask you some questions. How old were you when you started your menses?

>*Primero necesito hacerle algunas preguntas. ¿Cuántos años tenía cuando empezó a menstruar?*

Carla: I was 13 years old.

>*Tenía trece años.*

HCP: Tell me about your periods, is your flow light or heavy?

>*Cuénteme de sus períodos, ¿es un flujo escaso o abundante?*

Carla: They are light.

>*Es un flujo escaso.*

HCP: How many days do your periods last?

>*¿Cuántos días le dura el período?*

Carla: About 4 days.

>*Unos cuatro días.*

HCP: Do you have any cramps either before or during your period?

>*¿Tiene dolores antes o durante del período?*

Carla: Sometimes on the first day I have some cramps.

>*A veces tengo dolores menstruales en el primer día.*

HCP: Are you sexually active?

¿Usted tiene una relación sexual activa?

Carla: Yes.

Sí.

HCP: Are your partners male, female, or both?

¿Sus parejas son hombres, mujeres o ambos?

Carla: I have only had one boyfriend.

Sólo he tenido un novio.

HCP: What do you use to prevent pregnancy?

¿Qué hace para prevenir embarazos?

Carla: I use condoms all of the time!

¡Uso condones todo el tiempo!

HCP: Have you ever been pregnant?

¿Ha quedado embarazada alguna vez?

Carla: No.

No.

HCP: Does anyone in your family have a history of heart attacks, strokes, diabetes, breast or ovarian cancer, blood clots, or bleeding disorders?

¿Alguien en su familia tiene un historial médico de ataque al corazón, infarto cerebral, diabetes, cáncer de pecho o de ovario, coágulos sanguíneos o trastornos hemorrágicos?

Carla: No.

No.

HCP: Do you have a history of migraine headaches?

¿Tiene un historial médico de migrañas?

Carla: No.

No.

Obtaining the history of a patient with a vaginal infection / Cómo obtener el historial de una paciente con infección vaginal

HCP: Are you having any symptoms of a vaginal infection?

¿Tiene síntomas de infección vaginal?

PT: Yes.

Sí.

HCP: When did the symptoms begin?

¿Cuándo le empezaron los síntomas?

PT: One week ago.

Hace una semana.

HCP: What kind of symptoms are you having now?

¿Qué tipo de síntomas tiene ahora?

Carla: I have itching in the vaginal area.

Tengo comezón en el área vaginal.

HCP: Do you have any discharge?

¿Tiene alguna descarga?

Carla: Yes, it is thick and white.

Sí, es una descarga espesa y blanca.

HCP: Do you have any pain when you have intercourse?

¿Le duele cuando tiene relaciones sexuales?

Carla: No.

No.

HCP: Do you have any bleeding when you have intercourse?

¿Sangra cuando tiene relaciones sexuales?

Carla: No.

No.

HCP: Do you have any symptoms of a urinary tract infection, such as burning when you urinate?

¿Tiene usted algún síntoma de infección urinaria como, por ejemplo, dolor al orinar?

Carla: No.

No.

HCP: I am going to do your exam now. First I need to touch your neck to examine your thyroid.

La voy a examinar ahora. Primero necesito tocarle el cuello para examinarle la glándula tiroides.

(Please refer to the previous physical examination starting with the examination of the neck through to the abdominal exam.)

Conducting the pelvic examination / Cómo hacer un examen pélvico

HCP: Now I need you to slide down to the bottom of the examination table as you lie back and place your heels in the stirrups. I want you to focus on taking nice easy breaths and try not to hold your breath as this can cause you to tense your muscles.

Ahora necesito que usted se deslice al borde de la mesa de exploración, acostándose y colocando los talones en los estribos. Quiero que se concentre en respirar tranquilamente y sin contener la respiración ya que esto puede causar que se le tensen los músculos.

Carla: OK. Is this going to hurt?

OK. ¿Esto me va a doler?

HCP: No it does not hurt, you may feel some pressure, but if anything hurts, please tell me. I will tell you everything that I am doing as we proceed through your exam. Remember to take nice easy breaths.

No, no duele, pero sí puede sentir un poco de presión, pero si algo le duele por favor dígamelo. Yo le voy a decir todo lo que hago mientras hacemos el examen. Recuerde respirar tranquilamente.

Carla: OK.

OK.

HCP: Carla, first I am going to place my hand on the side of your leg. Now I am going to place my finger on this muscle (pelvic floor muscle) and I want you to relax that muscle. Next, I am going to place the speculum and I want you to take a nice deep breath in and then out. Carla, I am done with this part of the exam. Please stay as you are as I do the internal examination. As I place my hand on your abdomen I want you to relax this muscle (pelvic floor muscle). I am evaluating the size and shape of the uterus and if there is any pain please tell me. Now I am evaluating the ovaries. Carla, do you feel any pain?

Carla, primero voy a colocar mi mano a un lado de su pierna. Ahora voy a colocar un dedo en este músculo (pelvic floor muscle) y quiero que relaje ese músculo. Después, voy a poner el espéculo, y quiero que inhale profundamente y luego, que exhale. Carla, ya termino con esta parte del examen. Por favor, quédese donde está mientras le hago el examen interno. Mientras coloco mi mano sobre su abdomen, quiero que relaje este músculo (pelvic floor muscle). Ahora estoy evaluando el tamaño y forma de su útero y, si siente dolor, por favor dígamelo. Ahora estoy evaluando sus ovarios. Carla, ¿siente dolor?

Carla: No.

No.

HCP: Carla, the examination is done. Please, push yourself back up on the examination table and then sit up. You can get dressed and I need to look at the slides under the microscope to see if you have an infection. You did very well.

Carla, ya terminamos el examen. Por favor deslícese hacia la parte de atrás de la mesa de exploración y siéntese. Ahora se puede vestir, y necesito revisar las muestras bajo el microscopio para ver si hay infección. Usted estuvo muy bien.

Carla: Thank you.

Gracias.

HCP: Carla, you have a yeast infection. These are the prescriptions for the medications you need to take. One is a pill for the infection and one is a cream to help stop the itching. Please take the pill today. It can take the pill a couple of days to relieve the symptoms. You can apply the cream to the outside of the vaginal area two times per day. Do you have any questions?

Carla, tiene una infección de candida. Aquí están las recetas para las medicinas que necesita tomar. Una es una pastilla para la infección y la otra es una crema para ayudarla con la comezón. Por favor tómese la pastilla hoy. La pastilla puede tardar un par de días para aliviarle los síntomas. Puede aplicarse la crema por fuera del área vaginal dos veces al día. ¿Tiene alguna pregunta?

Carla: No, thank you.

No, gracias.

TEACHING THE MALE TESTICULAR SELF-EXAMINATION / CÓMO ENSEÑAR UN AUTOEXAMEN TESTICULAR

HCP: The best time to do the male testicular self-examination is after a shower or bath. It is best to examine one testicle at a time. First, hold the testicle between your thumb and index and middle fingers of both hands and gently but firmly roll the testicle. You need to feel the entire surface of the testicle. Repeat the same procedure with the other testicle. You are checking to feel that both testicles have no lumps, bumps, or swelling. Note that normally one testicle is slightly higher than the other testicle. This exam should be done monthly. If you feel that there is a difference, such as a lump on one testicle, you need to immediately tell your health care provider.

El mejor momento para auto-examinarse los testículos es después de la ducha o del baño. Es bueno examinarse un testículo a la vez. Primero, sujete un testículo entre el pulgar, el dedo índice y el dedo del medio de ambas manos y gentil pero firmemente haga girar el testículo. Necesita sentir toda la superficie del testículo. Repita el mismo procedimiento con el otro testículo. Revise que no haya bultos, hematomas ni inflamación. Note que normalmente un testículo está un poco más elevado que el otro testículo. Este examen se debe hacer una vez al mes. Si usted siente que hay alguna diferencia, como un bulto en un testículo, necesita contactar a su proveedor de salud inmediatamente.

TEACHING THE BREAST SELF-EXAMINATION / CÓMO ENSEÑAR EL AUTOEXAMEN DE LOS PECHOS

HCP: The breast self-examination has three parts. First, stand in front of a mirror with your hands first at your side, and then your hands behind your head, and then put your hands on your hips. In each position, observe that your breasts look the same in their size, shape, and contour and that there are no changes in the nipples.

El autoexamen de los pechos tiene tres partes. Primero, párese frente a un espejo primero con las manos a los lados, luego con ambas manos detrás de la cabeza, y después con las manos en las caderas. En cada posición, observe que sus pechos se vean de igual tamaño, forma y contorno y que no haya cambios en los pezones.

HCP: Next, examine your breasts while you are lying down. Place a pillow under the shoulder of the breast you are to examine. With the pads of your fingers begin at your underarm area and with small circles using light to medium pressure move your hand up and down all of the breast tissue until you reach the bone in the center of your chest (sternum). Once you are outside of the underarm area, move your fingers from the collarbone down to the bottom of your breast tissue. Then place the pillow under the other shoulder and repeat the same procedure.

Después, examine sus pechos mientras está acostada. Ponga una almohada debajo del hombro del lado del pecho que va a examinar. Con las yemas de los dedos empiece en el área de su axila y, haciendo pequeños círculos con una leve o mediana presión, mueva su mano de arriba hacia abajo por todo el tejido del seno hasta llegar al hueso en el centro del pecho (el esternón). Una vez que salga del área de la axila, mueva los dedos desde la clavícula hacia la parte baja del tejido del pecho. Luego ponga la almohada debajo del otro hombro y repita el procedimiento.

HCP: This exam of the breast tissues can also be done in the shower, placing the right arm behind the head and with the left hand using the same technique explained previously, examine the entire breast area. Repeat the same procedure for the left breast.

Este examen del tejido del pecho también se puede hacer en la ducha colocando el brazo derecho detrás de la cabeza y con la mano izquierda, usando la misma técnica que se acaba de explicar, examine toda el área del pecho. Repita el mismo procedimiento con el seno izquierdo.

HCP: Your breast tissue should feel the same each time you do this exam. For menstruating women, the best time to do this exam is during the week after the period. For women who no longer have periods, mark your calendar to do this exam the first of every month. If you find a change in one of your breasts that you have not felt before, you need to immediately tell your health care provider.

El tejido de su pecho debería sentirse de la misma manera cada vez que se haga el examen. Para las mujeres que tienen menstruaciones, el mejor momento es durante la semana después del período. Las mujeres que ya no tienen menstruaciones pueden marcar sus calendarios para realizarse este examen el primer día de cada mes. Si Ud. nota alguna diferencia en alguno de sus pechos que no haya sentido antes, necesita contactar inmediatamente a su proveedor de salud.

READING: DOCTORS WITHOUT BORDERS / LECTURA: MEDECINS SANS FRONTIERES

Reading

Doctors Without Borders, Medecins Sans Frontieres (MSF) was founded in 1971 with central offices located in Geneva, Switzerland. Since the early 1980s, these brave volunteers respond in "real time" to the urgent health needs of people worldwide. For example, a team can have the equivalent of two hospitals in supplies and staff ready to respond to a catastrophic event in less than 24 hours.

Facts about MSF

- Over 35,000 medical-related volunteers
- Present in over 70 countries
- Provides emergency medical care for those threatened in their attempts to obtain health care and in areas where epidemics, hunger, natural disasters, violence, war, and population displacement are prevalent.
- Primary principle: impartiality; MSF defines "impartiality" as the provision of services to those in major need with no preference to culture, location, or religious beliefs.
- Funding: 90% of support is received from donors.
- Population: Chosen by need not by political or economic pressure.
- All services are provided at no cost to the patients.

Overview of MSF functions in Latin America

- Present day
  - Honduras has major issues and is experiencing economic and social upheaval.
  - There are many victims of violence, including sexual violence.

- • MSF gives medical and psychological care to the victims.
  - • MSF provides health care to those fearful of retaliation for seeking care.
- • Present day
  - • In Bolivia there are many areas affected by the Chagas epidemic (a parasitic infection that can be fatal).
  - • MSF works with the people to identify those who are affected, evaluate for negative effects of this disease, and to educate on preventative measures.
- • Present day
  - • In Colombia, MSF provides care to the many who are battling the high prevalence of diseases and sexual violence.
  - • The MSF workers provide health care to the many who face barriers to obtaining essential health services.
- • 2013
  - • In Paraguay, MSF completed their work on the intervention into the Chagas epidemic.
  - • Their efforts were rewarded with support from the government and local communities to join in the treatment and prevention of this epidemic.
  - • MSF continues with support by providing updates on continued prevention and treatment strategies.
- • 2007
  - • MSF concluded work in the town of Guayaquil in Ecuador, which had the highest HIV incidence in Ecuador.
  - • Specialized centers for counseling, testing and treatment of HIV/AIDS were opened.
  - • MSF opened several maternity units to care for those with HIV/AIDS.
- • 2007
  - • A major earthquake in Peru left tens of thousands homeless.
  - • MSF arrived within 24 hours to the epicenter of the quake.
  - • These people who were hardest hit by the earthquake received prompt emergency relief.

Lectura

Doctores sin Fronteras/Medecins Sans Frontieres (MSF) se funda en 1971 con oficinas centrales en Ginebra, Suiza. Desde principios de los años 80 los valientes voluntarios de MSF responden en "tiempo real" a las necesidades urgentes de la gente alrededor del mundo. Por ejemplo, un grupo puede tener el equipo médico y personal equivalente a dos hospitales preparados para responder a un evento catastrófico en menos de 24 horas.

Datos sobre MSF

- Más de 35.000 voluntarios en el área de la medicina.

- Existe en más de 70 países.

- Su misión es ofrecer atención médica de emergencia para aquéllos que no pueden obtener el cuidado de salud por estar en zonas de peligro, y para los que están en regiones en donde predominan las epidemias, el hambre, los desastres naturales, la violencia, la guerra, y el desplazamiento de la población.

- Principio principal: la imparcialidad. MSF define la "imparcialidad" como proveer servicios a los que están en inminente necesidad, sin dar preferencia a la cultura, la ubicación, o a las creencias religiosas.

- Fondos: 90% son donaciones.

- Población: escogida por su necesidad, y no por razones políticas o económicas.

- Todos los servicios a los pacientes son gratis.

Descripción general de las funciones de MSF en Latinoamérica

- Hoy en día
    - Honduras tiene grandes problemas relacionados a la economía y disturbios sociales.
    - Hay muchas víctimas de violencia, incluso la violencia sexual.
    - MSF ofrece cuidado médico y psicológico a las víctimas.
    - Proveen atención médica a los que temen represalias por buscar este cuidado.

- Hoy en día
    - En Bolivia hay muchas zonas afectadas por la epidemia de Chagas (una infección parasítica que puede ser fatal).
    - MSF trabaja con la población afectada para identificar sus necesidades y para determinar los efectos negativos de la enfermedad, como también para educar sobre las medidas preventivas.

- Hoy en día
    - En Colombia, MSF les ofrece ayuda a los que luchan contra el prevalencia de enfermedades y la violencia sexual.
    - Los trabajadores MSF les ofrecen atención médica a los muchos que se enfrentan con barreras para obtener servicios básicos de salud.

- 2013

  - En Paraguay MSF concluyó su intervención en la epidemia Chagas.

  - Sus esfuerzos se recompensaron con apoyo de parte del gobierno y las comunidades locales, en un esfuerzo conjunto para tratar y prevenir la epidemia.

  - MSF sigue apoyando al actualizar medidas preventivas y estrategias de tratamiento.

- 2007

  - Concluyó su labor en Guayaquil (Ecuador), lugar con la mayor incidencia de VIH en Ecuador.

  - Se abrieron centros especializados para el apoyo psicológico, pruebas y tratamiento de VIH/ SIDA.

  - MSF abrió varios centros de maternidad para los que tienen VIH/ SIDA.

- 2007

  - Un terremoto en Perú dejó a decenas de miles de personas sin hogar.

  - MSF llegó en menos de 24 horas al epicentro del terremoto.

  - Las personas más afectadas por el terrremoto recibieron la ayuda de emergencia más rápido.

IDIOMATIC EXPRESSIONS / EXPRESIONES IDIOMÁTICAS

To lend a hand	English expression
Dar una mano	Spanish expression
To give a hand	Literal translation

To jump right in	English expression
Hincar el diente	Spanish expression
To sink the tooth	Literal translation

BEYOND LANGUAGE: TRANSCULTURAL ASSESSMENT OF THE SPANISH-SPEAKING PATIENT

CONTENTS

Reading: Madeleine Leininger, creator of transcultural nursing / Lectura: Madeleine Leininger, creadora de la enfermería transcultural

Idiomatic expressions / Expresiones Idiomáticas

THE ROLE OF TRANSCULTURAL NURSING AND THE CARE OF THE SPANISH-SPEAKING PATIENT / EL ROL DE LA ENFERMERÍA TRANSCULTURAL Y EL CUIDADO DEL PACIENTE HISPANOHABLANTE

The delivery of competent care to patients includes an awareness of the patient's culture, belief systems, and societal norms, which demonstrates sensitivity to these parameters. In the realm of the people living in Latin America, it is important to realize the diversity within and among these people. The focus of this chapter is to provide the reader with the tools to conduct a brief cultural assessment of a Spanish-speaking patient and to pictorially demonstrate the variations in culture by region.

Cultural sensitivity enables the practitioner to enhance the approach to the patient and lessen the possibility of being perceived as offensive or uncaring to the patient. To become culturally sensitive, the practitioner must conduct a brief cultural assessment. Although a more in-depth assessment may be considered essential, the practitioner's ability to speak and comprehend the patient's language may be a barrier in and of itself. Although all cultures may share similarities, it is the awareness of the differences that will lead to enhanced care of the patient. Avoiding assumptions in the initial meeting with the patient is key to establishing an ongoing dialogue and to allay any fears and concerns the patient holds.

BRIEF CULTURAL ASSESSMENT / BREVE EVALUACIÓN CULTURAL

AUDIO 10.1

Communication / Comunicación

The following represents a suggested dialogue to incorporate into the first meeting with the patient. *(Note that it is being assumed that the patient's major health care needs are being attended to and that the use of a translating device for a patient who does not speak English is in place in order to meet all the critical needs of the patient. It is recommended to keep the dialogue simple and immediately indicate to the patient the practitioner's Spanish-language ability.)*

Indicate the practitioner's Spanish-language ability. *(For the purpose of this text, the ability of the practitioner is at a novice level.)*

Health care provider (*HCP*)

Patient (*PT*; male from Honduras)

HCP: Hello, my name is _____.

Hola, mi nombre es _____.

HCP: What is your name?

¿Cuál es su nombre?

PT: My name is _____.

Me llamo _____.

HCP: Do you speak English?

¿Habla inglés?

PT: No, I only speak Spanish.

No, sólo hablo español.

HCP: I speak a little Spanish.

Yo hablo un poco de español.

HCP: How long have you been in the United States?

¿Hace cuánto tiempo que está en los Estados Unidos?

PT: I have been in the United States for 3 months.

Hace tres meses que estoy en los Estados Unidos.

HCP: What country are you from?

¿De qué país es usted?

PT: I am from Honduras.

Soy de Honduras.

HCP: Where is your family?

¿Dónde está su familia?

PT: My family is in Honduras. I am here to find work.

Mi familia está en Honduras. Yo estoy aquí para encontrar trabajo.

HCP: Are you married?

¿Está casado?

PT: Yes, I am married.

Sí, estoy casado.

HCP: Do you have children?

¿Tiene hijos?

PT: Yes, I have a son and a daughter.

Sí, tengo un hijo y una hija.

Response to touch / Reacción a ser tocado

A patient's response to touch is an important first step in the cultural-sensitivity assessment as well as is the patient's eye contact with the practitioner. To note how the patient responds to touch, observe how the patient reacts when informed that his or her pressure and other vital signs need to be taken.

Observing whether the patient maintains eye contact during the conversation with the practitioner traditionally has been used as part of the assessment. It is important to note that in some indigenous cultures in Latin America, direct eye contact with the practitioner is normally avoided.

HCP: As part of the physical examination, I need to take your blood pressure. This helps me to know how your heart is working when the blood circulates through your body.

Como parte del examen físico, necesito tomarle la presión. Esto me ayuda a saber cómo funciona su corazón cuando la sangre circula por su cuerpo.

HCP: Can I please have your arm in order to place the blood pressure cuff on your arm? The blood pressure cuff is going to be tight on your arm, but it will not hurt you.

¿Me puede dar su brazo para colocarle el tensiómetro? El tensiómetro le va a apretar el brazo pero no lo va a lastimar.

HCP: I need to take your temperature. I am going to place the thermometer under your tongue.

Necesito tomarle la temperatura. Voy a ponerle el termómetro debajo de la lengua.

HCP: I need to touch your wrist in order to take your pulse.

Necesito tocarle la muñeca para tomarle el pulso.

Biosociology / Bio-sociología

It is important to determine the health status of the patient by exploring this status within the context of the familial inheritance patterns. Ethnicity determination for a basic transcultural assessment would best be determined by asking the patient about his or her parental lineage and health-related concerns. To determine the ethnicity, the practitioner should ask the patient what other languages his or her parents and grandparents speak. With this information, the ethnicity of the patient can be determined.

The need to determine how the patient identifies according to race is not a tradition of the Latin American people. This is an American classification and, as such, unless there are U.S. forms that the patient needs to complete, race is not queried of the patient.

Patient (male from Bolivia)

HCP: Where are you from?

   ¿De dónde es usted?

PT: I am from Bolivia.

   Soy de Bolivia.

HCP: Where is your family from?

   ¿De dónde es su familia?

PT: They are from Bolivia.

   Son de Bolivia.

HCP: What languages do your parents and grandparents speak?

   ¿Qué lenguas hablan sus padres y sus abuelos?

PT: They speak Spanish and my grandparents speak a little Quechua.

   Hablan español y mis abuelos hablan un poco de quechua.

HCP: Does anyone in your family have any heart problems, cancer, diabetes, or bleeding problems?

   ¿Alguien en su familia tiene problemas cardíacos, cáncer, diabetes, o trastornos hemorrágicos?

PT: No, but my cousin died of Chagas disease.

   No, pero mi primo murió del mal de Chagas.

(For details of the Chagas epidemic, refer to the Culture Note at the end of this Brief Cultural Assessment.)

In any health care setting, inpatient or outpatient, knowing the patient's dietary preferences is essential. A brief dietary history is displayed in the following with attention to cultural preferences.

Nutrition / Nutrición

Patient (Female from Peru)

HCP: How often do you eat during the day?

   ¿Cuántas veces come al día?

PT: I eat three times a day.

   Como tres veces al día.

HCP: What do you normally eat for breakfast?

   ¿Qué desayuna normalmente?

PT: I eat sweet bread and coffee for breakfast.

Desayuno pan dulce y café.

HCP: What types of food do you eat for lunch?

¿Qué tipo de comida almuerza?

PT: Lunch is my main meal of the day and I usually eat it at 2 o'clock in the afternoon. I like to eat salad and soup with chicken, beans, and potatoes.

El almuerzo es mi comida principal del día y usualmente almuerzo a las dos de la tarde. Me gusta almorzar ensalada y sopa con pollo, frijoles y papas.

HCP: What types of food do you eat for dinner?

¿Qué tipo de comida cena?

PT: For dinner, I like to just eat eggs and rice or soup.

Para la cena, me gusta comer huevos con arroz o sopa.

HCP: What types of beverages do you drink during the day?

¿Qué tipo de bebidas toma durante el día?

PT: I like coffee and water.

Me gusta tomar café y agua.

HCP: Are there foods that you cannot eat?

¿Hay comidas que no puede comer?

PT: Shrimp.

Camarones.

HCP: Why can you not eat shrimp?

¿Por qué no puede comer camarones?

PT: Because I have hives when I eat shrimp.

Porque los camarones me dan urticaria.

HCP: Are there beverages that you cannot or do not drink?

¿Hay bebidas que no puede tomar o elige no tomar?

PT: No, but I do not like tea with sugar because it is too sweet. But I like to drink Inca Kola.

No, no me gusta el té con azúcar, porque es muy dulce. Pero me gusta beber Inca Kola.

(Inca Kola is a soft drink invented in Peru in 1935 that is high in sugar and caffeine.)

HCP: What are your favorite foods?

¿Cuál es su comida favorita?

PT: I like avocados and potatoes!

¡Me gustan las paltas y papas!

("Aguacates" is the name given for avocados by those living in the Northern part of Latin America; in the Southern Cone, avocados are called "paltas.")

Spirituality / Espiritualidad

Patient (Male from Venezuela)

Spirituality should not be taken for granted despite the patient's country of origin.

HCP: Do you have a religion?

> *¿Tiene una religión?*

PT: Yes, I am Catholic.

> *Sí, soy católico.*

(*HCP:* If the religion is unknown to the HCP, clarification should be pursued. Can you tell me about your religion? / *¿Me puede decir más sobre su religión?*)

HCP: Do you practice your religion?

> *¿Usted practica su religión?*

PT: Yes, my religion is very important to me.

> *Sí, mi religión es muy importante para mí.*

HCP: Do you want to have a priest come to see you?

> *¿Quiere que un sacerdote venga a verlo?*

PT: Does the priest speak Spanish?

> *¿El sacerdote habla español?*

HCP: Yes, there is a priest who speaks Spanish.

> *Sí, hay un sacerdote que habla español.*

Health care / Cuidado de la salud del paciente

Determining how the patient perceives health care is essential in order to formulate a plan of care. To do this it is important to assess the patient's past health care practices.

Patient (Male from Chile)

HCP: When you are sick, where do you go for help?

> *¿Cuándo usted está enfermo, dónde busca ayuda?*

PT: My mother knows about the benefits of herbs.

> *Mi madre sabe mucho de los beneficios de las hierbas.*

HCP: Is it OK for you to see a woman or man nurse/doctor?

¿Está bien que usted vea a un enfermero/doctor o a una enfermera/doctora?

PT: Yes, it is OK.

Sí, está bien.

HCP: Do you take any medicines?

¿Toma alguna medicina?

PT: No.

No

HCP: Do you take any herbs for your health?

¿Toma alguna hierba para la salud?

PT: Yes, I take propolis and verbena.

Sí, tomo propolio y hierba luisa.

HCP: Why do you take propolis and verbena?

¿Por qué toma propolio y hierba luisa?

(The information on propolis is in Chapter 5.)

PT: I take propolio when I am getting a cold and verbena for an upset stomach.

Tomo propolio cuando empiezo a resfriarme y hierba luisa para la molestia del estómago.

HCP: What do you do to be healthy?

¿Qué hace para mantenerse saludable?

PT: I work hard.

Trabajo mucho.

HCP: What kind of work do you do?

¿En qué trabaja?

PT: In Chile, I worked in construction.

En Chile trabajaba en construcción.

HCP: Do you have any physical disabilities?

¿Tiene alguna discapacidad física?

PT: No.

No.

Mental health / Salud mental

The United States is not the only country dealing with stigmas associated with mental illnesses. It is important to discover how the patient and those in the patient's culture respond to a patient who has a mental illness.

Patient (Female from Paraguay)

HCP: Did you ever have depression or anxiety?

　¿Alguna vez tuvo depresión o ansiedad?

PT: Yes, I had depression for a short time after I had my baby.

　Sí, tuve depresión por un tiempo después de tener mi bebé.

HCP: When was your baby born?

　¿Cuando nació su bebé?

PT: Two years ago.

　Hace dos años.

HCP: Did you need medicine?

　¿Necesitó tomar medicinas?

PT: No, I only felt depressed for a couple of weeks. I talked to my midwife and she and my husband helped me and I felt better.

　No, solamente me sentí deprimida por un par de semanas. Hablé con mi matrona y ella y mi esposo me ayudaron y me sentí mejor.

HCP: Did anyone in your family ever have depression?

　¿Alguien en su familia ha tenido depresión?

PT: No.

　No.

Occupation/Lifestyle / Ocupación/Estilo de vida

Past and present lifestyle are also important to determine, including work and leisure activities. For a female or male patient, it is first important to determine whether he or she is working outside of the home. Ability to work or the opportunity to work should not be assumed. If the patient is presently working, it is important to assess satisfaction with the work. If the patient is from another country, assessing past work experiences is essential. Satisfaction with the present lifestyle may or may not be a priority for your patient but may be important in the plan of care. It is important to determine satisfaction with present work conditions.

Patient (male from Chile)

HCP: Do you have a job here in the United States?

    ¿Tiene un trabajo aquí en los Estados Unidos?

PT: Yes. I work, but I am sick.

    Sí, trabajo, pero estoy enfermo.

HCP: What kind of work do you do?

    ¿Qué tipo de trabajo hace?

PT: I work in construction.

    Trabajo en construcción.

HCP: Do you like your work?

    ¿Le gusta su trabajo?

PT: Yes, I like my work.

    Sí, me gusta.

HCP: What kind of work experiences did you have in your country?

    ¿Qué tipo de experiencia laboral tenía en su país?

PT: I worked in construction for 10 years.

    Trabajé en construcción por diez años.

HCP: Do you like your job here?

    ¿Le gusta su trabajo aquí?

PT: Yes, the money I make supports my family.

    Sí, el dinero que gano mantiene a mi familia.

HCP: When you are not at work, what do you like to do?

    Cuando no está trabajando, ¿qué le gusta hacer?

PT: There is little time, but I like to play soccer with my children.

    Hay muy poco tiempo, pero me gusta jugar al fútbol con mis hijos.

HCP: Do you like living in the United States?

    ¿Le gusta vivir en los Estados Unidos?

PT: Yes, I like it a lot.

    Sí, me gusta mucho.

Education / Educación

Education varies in its priority among all people. It is important to gain an understanding of the patient's educational background as it aids in the continued assessment of the patient. This will vary with the age of the presenting patient. It should not be assumed that a child is in school any more than an adult has or has not achieved advanced education.

Patient (Male from Mexico)

HCP: What level of education do you have?

¿Qué nivel de educación tiene?

PT: I finished high school and began to work in the vineyards.

Terminé la secundaria y empecé a trabajar en viñedos.

HCP: Do your children go to school?

¿Van a la escuela sus hijos?

PT: They go to school but in the summer they work picking berries.

Van a la escuela pero en el verano recogen bayas.

Health risks / Riesgos para la salud

Health risks can vary from ingesting substances to activities such as not wearing helmets when riding a bike to unsafe occupational exposures. Patients from any culture may be hesitant to discuss their risks, making it the job of the practitioner to leave this topic open for the patient to return to when the patient feels that a strong foundation of trust has formed with his or her practitioner. The following are questions that can determine the health risks of the patient.

Do you smoke cigarettes?	¿Fuma usted cigarrillos?
If the response is "yes": How much do you smoke?	¿Cuánto fuma?
Does anyone in your home smoke cigarettes?	¿Alguien en su hogar fuma cigarrillos?
Do you take any drugs?	¿Usa alguna droga?
If the response is "yes": What kind of drugs do you take?	¿Qué tipo de drogas usa?
Do you drink alcohol?	¿Bebe alcohol?
If the response is "yes": How much alcohol do you drink a day?	¿Cuánto alcohol bebe al día?
When you ride in the car, do you wear a seatbelt?	¿Cuándo va en un carro, se pone el cinturón de seguridad?

Safety / Seguridad

AUDIO 10.11

Safety has many facets, but for a brief cultural-sensitivity assessment, only the major areas are addressed. The following are questions designed to assess the safety of the patient.

Do you feel safe at home?	¿Se siente seguro/a en su hogar?
Do you feel safe at work/school?	¿Se siente seguro/a en el trabajo/la escuela?
Do you feel safe where you live?	¿Se siente seguro/a donde vive?

This completes the brief cultural sensitivity assessment.

Culture/Cultura: **Chagas Disease.** Those living in impoverished areas as well as some of the rural areas of Latin America are battling a quiet but potentially deadly parasitic infection that causes chagas. This parasite lives and breeds in the mud and straw used to form the walls and roofs of houses primarily among the poorest population in this part of the world. The insects that cause this disease are called "triatomines" and, similar to the termite, they emerge at night to feed. The parasites transmit infection through unchecked blood transfusions, breastfeeding, and to the unborn through the infected mother. Rarely is this disease known to be transmitted through contaminated foods or drinking water.

During the acute stage of the infestation, the symptoms are similar to other minor illnesses and include myalgia, fatigue, vomiting, and fever. Over three fourths of those infected will go into remission with no negative sequelae. For those for whom the infection does not resolve, the infection becomes chronic. These individuals will go on to develop irreversible damage to the heart and gastrointestinal system. Also those in remission can be reinfested with the triatomines and may or may not go into remission.

Diagnosis of Chagas is difficult and expensive, requiring several blood tests to confirm the diagnosis. These essential tests also are in short supply in the vital areas where the disease is most rampant. Treatment must be instituted during the acute phase in order to prevent the irreversible damage that is done to the cardiovascular and gastrointestinal systems.

Doctors Without Borders is struggling to make strides against this illness by attempting to gain better diagnostic testing and treatment for Chagas. This volunteer organization is also working with the communities battling this infection by

(*continued / continuado*)

(continued / continuado)

setting up treatment programs as well as collaborating with the health ministries of countries, such as Bolivia, and inviting U.S. universities to launch a prevention and treatment program that will be integrated into the basic health care systems.

INTRODUCTION TO A VARIETY OF TRADITIONAL LATIN AMERICAN FOODS / INTRODUCCIÓN A UNA VARIEDAD DE COMIDAS LATINOAMERICANAS

Demonstrating the importance of becoming aware of the patient's culture shows respect for the patient and can bridge the road of trust between the health care provider and the patient. This further enables an integration of the patient's culture and beliefs into the delivery of health care, augmenting the patient's ability to attain a higher level of wellness. Although it is acknowledged that many countries in Latin America are battling high poverty rates, the focus of this discussion is on the inroads being made to support the positive growth of these countries. The following review enables the practitioner to acquire a basic cultural awareness of Spanish-speaking people according to regional origin. The purpose of the following overview of Latin America is to introduce the reader to this very diverse part of the world. For a more in-depth appreciation, the practitioner is referred to other external sources, including the World Health Organization, Latin America, and the Caribbean and Pan American Health Organization.

Vegetables and legumes / Verduras y legumbres

It is important for the health care provider to understand that even though Spanish is spoken everywhere, some items, especially foods, are called different names according to the region. In most of Latin America, beans are considered a staple food just as the potato is in the United States. Beans are called "frijoles" throughout Latin America, and in the Southern Cone they are also called "porotos." Corn is one of the main staples in Latin America. In the southern Cone, corn, usually referred to as "maíz," is called "choclo." Cucumbers are "pepinos," but in South America there is also a fruit called "pepino," which is sweet and originated in the Andean regions. It is considered to be an "ancient" fruit as it has been cultivated since the Inca civilization. The "pepino" fruit, named by a Spanish explorer, has a sweet taste similar to a melon or pear. The seeds are also edible. This fruit is low in calories, rich in antioxidants and fiber, and thought to promote healthy skin. Some vegetables and grains that originated in Latin America include tomatoes, corn, potatoes, avocadoes, a variety of peppers, and the cocoa grain from which chocolate is made. Peanuts are called "cacahuate" or "cacahuete" in Mexico and "maní" in the southern part of Latin America.

Meat and seafood / Carne y pescado

Meat and fish consumption varies throughout Latin American countries. Seafood is a favorite among those who live near the coast, especially in Chile, Peru, and Ecuador. There is a variety of seafood there not found in the U.S. market, such as sea urchins, cold-water fish that are a type of eel (congrio), and an assortment of shellfish and seaweed. In other parts of the world, beef may be considered a more expensive food choice, but beef is readily available to all in Latin America. Beef is also a major export of Argentina and Uruguay. Pork is preferred by those enjoying Caribbean cuisine.

AUDIO 10.13

Fruits and berries / Frutas y bayas

There are a variey of indigenous fruits throughout Latin America that are relatively unknown by those living in the United States. Níspero, mamey, and guanábana are examples of some of the many fruit varieties. The "cherimoya" or "chirimoya" is one of the favorite indigenous fruits in Latin America; it is semisweet and aromatic. Bananas and plantains are common fruit exports. The following are berries that are common to North and South America.

Blackberries	las moras
Blueberries	los arándanos
Cranberries	los arándanos agrios
Raspberries	las frambuesas
Strawberries	las fresas or las frutillas

AUDIO 10.14

Beverages / Bebidas

In the northern part of South and Central America beer is a preferred drink, whereas in the southern part of South America wine is preferred. In some areas people drink "chicha," which is made with fermented grapes, corn, or other grains. "Pisco" is a traditional brandy-like beverage found in Chile and Peru that is produced with a type of grape that grows in that area. Rum is distilled throughout the Caribbean. Tequila is a distilled beverage made from a cactus plant that grows in Mexico.

There are some typical nonalcoholic beverages, such as "yerba mate" (in the Southern Cone), which is prepared in a hollow gourd and drunk a metal straw. "Horchata" (Mexico and Central America) is made with rice, coconut, or seeds. In some areas of Central America they have "pinol" or "pinolillo," a sweet drink made with cornmeal and cacao. The "molinillo de madera" (pictured in the follwing) is used to blend and create the foam of the "pinol." There is also a variety of typical beverages made with sugar cane that are very popular in areas where sugar cane is grown. There are also many types of smoothies made with tropical fruits. Coffee is a favorite beverage throughout Latin America; it is grown in Colombia, Brazil, Costa Rica, Cuba, and many other tropical areas.

pocillos para salsas

molinillo de madera

Sauces / Salsas

AUDIO 10.15

Each region has its own type of salsa made with tomatoes, cilantro or parsley, and onion and served as an accompaniment to meats and fish: "salsa," "pico de gallo," "chimichurri," and "pebre." The origin of the word "ketchup" seems to be Chinese, and in Spanish the same word is used, "ketchup," and is pronounced as "ketchoop."

Typical desserts / Postres típicos

AUDIO 10.16

A popular dessert among many living in Spanish America is "tres leches"/three milks cake. This rich specialty is essentially a yellow cake infused with sweetened and evaporated milks and whipping cream and, after the saturation of this delicacy is complete, the cake is frosted with a fluffy white frosting. For the carbohydrate conscious, this cake weighs in at about 45 carbs per piece!

A traditional dessert made with milk, eggs, and sugar is "flan," a caramel custard. Another is "dulce de leche," a thick and creamy spread that results from slowly cooking milk and sugar. "Alfajores" are cookie sandwiches filled with "dulce de leche," and "arroz con leche" is a type of rice pudding made with milk and white rice.

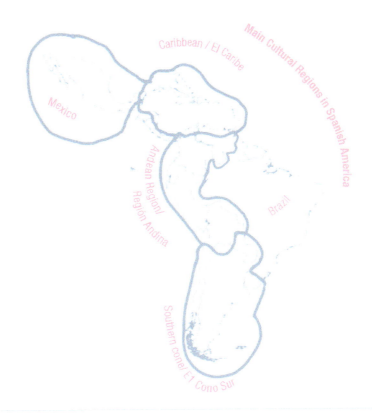

TRANSCULTURAL OVERVIEW OF THE MAIN CULTURAL REGIONS OF LATIN AMERICA / VISIÓN TRANSCULTURAL DE LAS PRINCIPALES REGIONES CULTURALES EN LATINO AMÉRICA

Mexico / México

Food preferences / Preferencias de comida

The people of Mexico demonstrate the Spanish influence in their diet and meal times. The diet consists of foods that are quite flavorful. Breakfast includes such food items as coffee with sweet breads, tropical fruits, or a plate of huevos rancheros, which are fried eggs with tomatoes, onions, and chili sauce atop a tortilla. Lunch is a time of socialization and is considered the main meal of the day; thus it is larger in sustenance and is taken in the midafternoon. Resembling the American-style dinner, the Mexican peoples' lunch is comprised of an appetizer, salad or soup, and the main dish, which includes rice and beans, warmed tortillas and a meat, seafood, or fowl. Dinner resembles more of an American lunch in that it is lighter and may be just tortillas or soup. Keeping with the Spanish influence, this meal is usually eaten later in the evening.

Predominant religion / Religión predominante

About three fourths of the Mexican population is Roman Catholic. The remaining primary religions include Protestant, Evangelical, and Jehovah's Witness.

Primary language / Lengua predominante

Although the primary language spoken in Mexico is Spanish, there are many indigenous languages. For example, Mayan languages are spoken in the Yucatan Peninsula and northern Belize; in the southwestern-central highlands of Mexico, Zapotec is spoken; and what was once called *Aztec*, Nahuatl is spoken by many of the people living in central Mexico.

Industry / Industria

In the 1980s, the Mexican government allowed more of the private sector to expand, which led to greater industrial progress in Mexico, but the controls continue to remain too restrictive for Mexico to reach its full economic potential. Despite the various economic setbacks observed in many South American countries over the past few decades, Mexican industry continues to grow and includes such products as food and beverages, textiles, iron, and steel. Agriculture, as observed in many industrial countries, has declined as a main force in the economy.

Economics / Economía

It is estimated that over 40% of the Mexican population lives below the national poverty line.

Caribbean / El Caribe

Food Preferences / Preferencias de comida

The combination of influences from Africa, the United States, Europe, East India, and China makes the cuisine of the Caribbean very unique. Ingredients common to most of the islands include rice, plantains, beans, cassava (tuberous root from a tropical tree), cilantro, bell peppers, chickpeas, black beans, tomatoes, sweet potatoes, coconut, and a variety of local meats or fish. A characteristic seasoning used is a green herb (culantro, thyme, or tarragon) and oil-based marinade that is unique to this region and is used in many foods, including curries, stews, and roasted meats.

 ### Predominant religion / Religión predominante

AUDIO 10.17

Although Christianity is the predominant religion, many different sects and cultural adaptations of Christianity are found throughout the islands. The influence of African religions is very important in the Caribbean. In the Afro-Caribbean, the practice of "santería" and "changó" are a mixture of African beliefs and traditions originally brought to the Americas by slaves, that are combined with Catholicism.

Primary language / Lengua predominante

The islands of Cuba, the Dominican Republic, and Puerto Rico comprise the islands of the Caribbean that are part of Spanish America and the Caribbean. Spanish is the primary language of these countries; however, English is the official language of Puerto Rico.

Industry / Industria

Tourism is the major industry of these islands.

Economics / Economía

The individual economies of the islands are open to free trade. The export business is beginning to show trends in growth. Crops are still grown for domestic use. Many islands note that tourism provides 70% of the jobs and accounts for over 70% of the gross domestic product (GDP).

Andean region / Región Andina

Food preferences / Preferencias de comida

The food of the people of the Andean region is quite diverse because of the Andes Mountains, which divide the area and provide a variety of climate differences and topography. Here, quinoa is considered a staple. A creamy potato soup called "ajiaco" that is served with chicken, potatoes, corn, rice, and capers is popular among those living in the higher elevation. A breakfast tradition is a soup made of milk, egg, bread, onions, and water called "changua." Peanut and potato soup is also a favorite in this region. In some parts of the Andean region, the people prefer extremely hot-spicy food. An example is empanadas salteñas, which includes meat, vegetables, and potatoes mixed with a variety of spices.

Predominant religion / Religión predominante

Different than other regions of South America, the Roman Catholic religion is not the majority religion in the Andean region. Catholicism blended with indigenous religions from the Andes with the arrival of the Spanish conquistadors in the 1500s. The Mexican tradition of celebrating the Day of the Dead, November 1, is also a tradition celebrated by the people of the Andean region. The people travel to the cemeteries where they honor their deceased relatives with food, music, and what the lost loved ones enjoyed when alive. Recently, the Protestant religions have gained a strong foothold in the Andes.

Primary language / Lengua predominante

Spanish is the official language in the Andean region, with Quechua and Aymara spoken by many. Of interest is the fact that Quechua and Aymara are primarily spoken languages among the indigenous people and, because of the lack of written material in these languages, it is difficult to continue the spread of these languages. Because of the presence of these languages among the people, a crossover exists between the languages with words from each incorporated into daily speech.

Industry / Industria

Manufacturing, agriculture, and mining are the main industrial sources of this region. As in other parts of the world, mining is taking its toll on the natural environment. The production of textiles is very prominent in this region, including wool from alpacas and vicuñas. Similar to the wool of the llama, the vicuñas' wool is much softer, warmer, and more expensive.

Economics / Economía

Marketing of a wide variety of crops heavy in tubers and other crops that are quite laborious to produce poses a significant challenge to the agricultural industry. As the modern world looks to foods that are excellent in nutritional value, foods such as quinoa are being sought after from these countries.

Southern Cone / El Cono Sur
Food preferences / Preferencias de comida

"Mate," as mentioned previously, is a favorite caffeine-rich drink among the people of the Southern Cone. Mate is made from dried leaves of yerba mate, which are steamed in hot water and sipped through a metal straw that filters out the leaves. It often is served during family and other social gatherings.

As mentioned, beef is a main staple of most of the people of Argentina, Uruguay, and Paraguay. In Chile, because there is a longer coastal area, people tend to eat more fish and seafood. Three to four meals a day are the norm with the main meal served sometime in the early afternoon. The other meals are usually lighter as with breakfast, which consists of toast and coffee or tea. Similar to the U.S. barbeque, "parrillada" are types of food prepared in a brick

outdoor oven and are very popular. One of the typical foods in the Southern Cone is "empanadas," a fried or baked stuffed pastry filled with meat, seafood, or vegetables.

Because of the Italian influence in this region, Italian cuisine is very popular, such as pizza, spaghetti, and "pascualina," which is similar to a spinach quiche.

Predominant religion / Religión predominante

The majority of the people of the Southern Cone are Roman Catholic. Other religions practiced by the people of this region include Judaism, Islam, Lutheran, Buddhism, Eastern Orthodox, and Anglican.

Primary language / Lengua predominante

Spanish is spoken by the majority of people living in the Southern Cone, and English is spoken in the Falkland Islands/Islas Malvinas. Demonstrating the heavy immigration of the Italian people into this area in the latter part of the 19th to 20th centuries, Rioplantense Spanish is spoken in Argentina and Uruguay. All the countries of the Southern Cone have a very distinctive pattern of "voseo," vocabulary, and pronunciation. As seen in the other parts of South America, the languages of the Southern Cone also include some native groups such as Mapuche, also known as Mapudungun, which is heard in southern Argentina and Chile, and Guarani, which is the language spoken in the northeastern part of Argentina and Paraguay. Part of the extreme northern area of Argentina and Chile is considered part of the Andean region, where Quechua is also spoken.

Industry / Industria

In Chile, copper mining and the export of copper continue to be growing industries. The growth in industrial corporations, including hydroelectric dams, biofuel productions, and other modern-day industries is evolving into controversy over natural land conservation and traditions, affecting the Argentinean "gauchos" (equivalent to the American cowboy) found throughout these regions. These are prosperous countries that are facing similar decisions about the proper use of the land for growth while preserving the tradition and protecting the habitats of these regions. Soy production, wine and fruit production, and exportation of cattle to other countries are growing industries.

Economics / Economía

The people of the Southern Cone are considered to be among those with the highest standard of living in all of Latin America. It is considered to be the most prosperous of all of the regions in South America.

READING: MADELEINE LEININGER, CREATOR OF TRANSCULTURAL NURSING / LECTURA: MADELEINE LEININGER, CREADORA DE LA ENFERMERÍA TRANSCULTURAL

Reading

Madeleine Leininger (1925–2012, b. Nebraska, United States), creator of transcultural nursing initially studied nursing and later received a master's degree in science from the Catholic University of America. Her interest in anthropology was made concrete when she earned a doctoral degree in anthropology from the University of Washington in Seattle. For Madeleine, to know the culture of the person was very important in order to be able to help and to maintain the health of the people. When health care workers know about the culture of the individuals they are attending, they establish a more confident relationship. With the globalization of the last few years, health care professionals are in contact with people from all different parts of the world, so it is very important to know about cultural diversity. At times, these people have a different way of seeing the world and they have different cultural traditions than we do. Diet is another characteristic of a specific culture. Religion or the beliefs of the people influence the way they live. It is also important to know about the geographical region of a person because this relates to the possible endemic illnesses of a region, such as Lyme disease in certain states of the United States, or dengue fever in tropical zones of Latin America. When we know about certain aspects of a culture, we avoid the stereotypes that are offensive to people in general.

Lectura

Madeleine Leininger, creadora de la enfermería transcultural (1925–2012, n. Nebraska, Estados Unidos): Madeleine Leininger primero estudió enfermería, después recibió su Maestría en Ciencias de la Universidad Católica de América y finalmente su interés por la antropología se concretizó cuando obtuvo su título de doctorado en antropología en la Universidad de Washington en Seattle. Para Madeleine, conocer la cultura de una persona era muy importante para ayudar y mantener la salud de las personas. Cuando los trabajadores de la salud tienen conocimiento de la cultura de una persona que atiende, se establece una relación de más confianza. Con la globalización de los últimos años, los profesionales de la salud están en contacto con personas de diferentes partes del mundo y por eso es muy importante conocer la diversidad cultural. Estas personas a veces tienen una manera diferente de ver la vida y por eso tienen tradiciones diferentes a las de nuestra cultura. La dieta también es característica de una determinada cultura. La religión o las creencias de las personas influye en la forma en que viven. También es importante conocer la región geográfica de una persona, porque esto se relaciona con las posibles enfermedades endémicas de una región, como la enfermedad de Lyme en algunos estados de Estados Unidos, o el dengue en zonas tropicales de Latinoamérica. Cuando conocemos aspectos de una cultura evitamos los estereotipos que son ofensivos para las personas en general.

IDIOMATIC EXPRESSIONS / EXPRESIONES IDIOMÁTICAS

A sight for sore eyes	English expression
Dichosos los ojos	Spanish equivalent
Ecstatic eyes	Literal translation

Talking up a storm	English expression
Habla hasta por los codos	Spanish equivalent
To talk even through the elbows	Literal translation

SECTION III

REVIEW EXERCISES

SUMMARY REVIEW EXERCISES

CONTENTS

Conversational spanish: "putting it all together" / Expresión oral en español: "juntando todas las piezas"

Review activities Chapter 1 / Actividades de repaso Capítulo 1

Review activities Chapter 2 / Actividades de repaso Capítulo 2

Review activities Chapter 3 / Actividades de repaso Capítulo 3

Review activities Chapter 4 / Actividades de repaso Capítulo 4

Review activities Chapter 5 / Actividades de repaso Capítulo 5

Review activities Chapter 6 / Actividades de repaso Capítulo 6

Reading: Eloisa Díaz, first woman to graduate from medical school in Chile and in Latin America / Lectura: Eloísa Díaz, la primera mujer graduada de la escuela de medicina en Chile y en Latinoamérica

Idiomatic expressions / Expresiones idiomáticas

CONVERSATIONAL SPANISH: "PUTTING IT ALL TOGETHER" / EXPRESIÓN ORAL EN ESPAÑOL: "JUNTANDO TODAS LAS PIEZAS"

This chapter contains practice exercises that relate specifically to the sections found within chapters 1 to 6. Answers to these review exercises, along with answers to the summary exercises located at the end of each chapter (1–6), are located in Chapter 12.

REVIEW ACTIVITIES CHAPTER 1 / ACTIVIDADES DE REPASO CAPÍTULO 1

Practice 1 / Práctica 1

Carlota and Fernando asked you to make reservations for their hotel in Montevideo, Uruguay. The receptionist cannot hear you well and she asks you to spell ("deletrear") their names. For example:

1. "Carlota" would be: **Ce-a-ere-ele-o-te-a**
2.
3.
4.

Carlota Godoy

Fernando Patiño

Activity 1 / Actividad 1

Using vocabulary on greetings, address the following individuals.

1. A child
2. Two patients
3. A gentleman
4. A patient at 9 a.m.
5. A group of individuals at 1 p.m.
6. A patient who does not speak English

7.   A patient's family member whose name you do not know

8.   Tell your patient Fernanda you will see her tomorrow

9.   Carlitos, 5 years old

10. A patient at 11:30 p.m.

Practice 2 / Práctica 2

Make the singular nouns plural and the plural nouns singular.

E.g., The ambulance: *La ambulancia*	The ambulances: *Las ambulancias*
The tendons: *Los tendones*	The tendon: *El tendon*

1. Name (El nombre)
2. Women (Las mujeres)
3. Female patient (La paciente)
4. Pencils (Los lápices)
5. Female doctor (La doctora)
6. Men (Los hombres)
7. Address (La dirección)
8. Communities (Las comunidades)
9. Last name (El apellido)
10. Hospitals (Los hospitales)

Practice 3 / Práctica 3

In column 1, what pronouns are used to directly address someone? In column 2, what pronouns are used to refer to someone?

COLUMN 1	COLUMN 2
E.g., Two women = Uds.	Two women = ellas
1. Humberto, 10 years old = _____	Humberto, 10 years old = _____
2. Roberta, a patient = _____	Roberta, a patient = _____
3. Mr. and Mrs. Sánchez = _____	Mr. and Mrs. Sánchez = _____
4. Three girls = _____	Three girls = _____
5. Pedro, 2 years old = _____	Pedro, 2 years old = _____

Practice 4 / Práctica 4

Determine whether to use "ser" or "estar," and circle the correct verb.

1. "Where is my father?"   Ser/Estar
2. "Where you are from?"   Ser/Estar
3. "Why are you sad?"   Ser/Estar
4. "What time is it?"   Ser/Estar
5. "How are you?"   Ser/Estar
6. "Who is he?"   Ser/Estar

REVIEW ACTIVITIES CHAPTER 2 / ACTIVIDADES DE REPASO CAPÍTULO 2

Dialogue 1 / Diálogo 1

la cabeza
el hombro
la espalda
el brazo
la cintura
los glúteos
el codo
la mano
la pierna
la pierna
los dedos de la mano
la rodilla
la pantorrilla
el tobillo
el pie

> This is Mr. Rodríguez. He is at the hospital because he has pain in various parts of his body. He is your patient and he needs your help. Complete the dialogue between you and Mr. Rodríguez using the vocabulary and structures already learned.

Dialogue with Mr. Rodríguez/Diálogo con el Sr. Rodríguez
Nurse: Hello, Mr. Rodríguez. I am your nurse. How are you?
Enfermera: _____, Sr. Rodríguez. _____ la enfermera. ¿_____?
Mr. Rodríguez: Hello. I have a lot of pain.
Sr. Rodríguez: Hola. _____ mucho dolor.

(continued / continuado)

(continued / continuado)

Dialogue with Mr. Rodríguez/Diálogo con el Sr. Rodríguez

Nurse: Where do you have pain, Mr. Rodríguez?
Enfermera: ¿_____ tiene dolor, Sr. Rodríguez?
Mr. Rodríguez: I have pain in my back and my left leg.
Sr. Rodríguez: Tengo _____ en mi _____ y mi pierna
                    _____

Nurse: What kind of a pain is it?
Enfermera: ¿_____ tipo de dolor es?
Mr. Rodríguez: I have a radiating pain in my back down to my right leg.
Sr. Rodríguez: Tengo _____ en mi _____ a la pierna
                    _____.

Nurse: What kind of pain do you have in your left leg?
Enfermera: ¿_____ tipo de dolor _____ en la pierna
                    _____?
Mr. Rodíguez: My left leg hurts a lot. It is a sharp pain.
Sr. Rodríguez: Mi pierna izquierda _____ mucho. Es un dolor
                    _____.

Activity 1 / Actividad 1

Carlos fell off his bike and the nurse is asking him questions about his injuries. Translate the following to Spanish.

Nurse: Where does it hurt you?
Carlos: I have pain when I move.
Nurse: Does your head hurt you?
Carlos: No, but it hurts when I open my mouth.
Nurse: Does it hurt when you breathe?
Carlos: No, but it hurts when you press on my chest with the stethoscope.
Nurse: Are you able to move your arms and legs?
Carlos: It hurts when I move my left leg.
Nurse: Does it hurt when I press on your knee?
Carlos: No, it hurts when you touch my ankle.
Nurse: Are you able to bend ("doblar") your toes?
Carlos: Yes, but it hurts when I bend my toes.
Nurse: Put the ice bag on your jaw. I have to put the elastic bandage on your ankle.
            You need to have an x-ray.

REVIEW ACTIVITIES CHAPTER 3 / ACTIVIDADES DE REPASO CAPÍTULO 3

Practice 1 / Práctica 1

Indicate a response to the following scenarios.

1. Ask your patient if he or she needs water.
2. Tell your patient that you need to take his or her temperature.
3. Ask the relative of your patient what the patient (he or she) needs.
4. Tell your patient that you need to take his or her blood pressure.
5. Tell your patient you need to listen to his or her heart.
6. Tell your patient you need to operate on him or her.
7. Tell your patient you need to touch his or her arm/leg/back.
8. Tell your patient you need to look at his or her eyes/throat.

Practice 2 / Práctica 2

Translate the following scenarios.

1. Ask your patient if he or she speaks English.
2. Tell your patient you need to speak with his or her family.
3. Tell your patient you need to speak about the medicine.
4. Ask your patient whether he or she needs to speak with the doctor.
5. Ask your patient whether he or she needs to speak about the operation.

Practice 3 / Práctica 3

Translate the following scenarios.

1. Ask your patient whether he or she wants something to drink; answer that you want water.
2. Ask your patient whether he or she wants to speak with the doctor; answer that you do not want to speak with the doctor.*
3. Ask your patient what he wants; answer that you want to eat now.

---

*Remember to use the word "no" twice: For example, ¿Hablas inglés? *No, no* hablo inglés.

4. Ask your patient whether he or she wants to drink something; answer that you want to sleep.

5. Tell your patient that you want to take his or her blood pressure; answer yes, that it is fine.

Practice 4 / Práctica 4

Translate the following scenarios.

1. Ask your patient how he or she feels.   ¿Cómo se siente (Ud.)?

   Answer that you feel anxious.   Me siento ansioso/a.

2. Ask your patient what he or she prefers to eat. ¿Qué prefiere (Ud.) comer?

   Answer that you prefer to eat soup (la sopa).   (Yo) Prefiero tomar la sopa.

3. Ask a relative of the patient whether the patient feels depressed or nervous.

   Answer that the patient feels angry and sad.

4. Ask your patient how he or she feels.

   Reply that you feel generally unwell and want pills for nausea.

5. Ask the patient whether she wants to take a bath.

   Reply that you do want to take a bath.

Practice 5 / Práctica 5

Ask and answer the following using "poder." The first one has been done for you.

1. Can you take a deep breath?	¿Puede respirar hondo?
Yes, I can take a deep breath.	Sí puedo, respirar hondo.
2. Can you move over to the stretcher?	Yes, I can move over to the stretcher.
3. Can you raise and lower your arms?	I can raise and lower my right arm, but I cannot raise and lower my left arm.
4. Can you sit down?	No, I cannot sit down because (porque) my back hurts.
5. Can you stand up and close your eyes?	No, I cannot stand up and close my eyes because I am dizzy.
6. Can you swallow?	I can swallow but (pero) my throat hurts when (cuando) I swallow.
7. Can you read the letters?	Yes, I can read the letters (letras).
8. Can you walk?	No, I cannot walk.

Dialogue / Diálogo # 1a

Señora Pérez is 8 months pregnant and is brought to the emergency department by the ambulance following a car accident. Read the following information and create a dialogue.

1. Ask Señora Pérez whether she has any pain and tell her that you need to take her vital signs.

2. She tells you that her head hurts and she has contractions.

3. You ask her whether her neck hurts her.

4. She tells you no, but that the contractions are strong and they are painful. She asks you whether you know where her husband is.

5. You tell her that her husband is in the waiting room and that the doctor and nurse-midwife are here now.

1. Nurse/Enfermero:

2. Mrs. Pérez/Señora Pérez:

3. Nurse/Enfermero:

4. Mrs. Pérez/Señora Pérez:

5. Nurse/Enfermero:

Dialogue / Diálogo # 1b

The police are talking to a person who witnessed the accident. Fill in the blanks with the correct Spanish phrase and form of "saber."

1. ¿ _____ del accidente? What do you (Ud.) know about the accident?

2. _____ que el accidente acaba de ocurrir en la calle Almagro. I know that the accident has just occurred on Almagro Street.

3. _____ si que la mujer está bien? Do you know whether the woman is okay?

4. _____ la mujer está embarazada. I know that the woman is pregnant.

5. _____ dónde vive la mujer? Do you know where the woman lives?

6. Los paramédicos _____ cómo contactar al esposo. The paramedics know how to contact the husband.

Dialogue / Diálogo # 1c

Señor Pérez was contacted by the paramedics and arrives at the hospital. He is speaking with the receptionist. Translate the following questions to Spanish using "saber" and vocabulary.

1. Hola, mi nombre es Señor Pérez. ¿_____?
   (Do you know where my wife is?)

2. Hola, señor. _____. (I know that she is in the emergency room.)

3. ¿_____? (Does the midwife know that my wife is here?)

4. Sí*. _____. (The doctor and midwife know that your wife is here.)

5. ¿_____? (Do you know whether I can see my wife?)

6. _____. (I do not know whether you can see your wife, but I can call the nurse.)

Dialogue / Diálogo # 2

The wives (Alicia and Paulina) of two men who are having open-heart surgery are talking to each other in the waiting room. Translate their conversation using the correct forms of "conocer" and vocabulary from the unit.

Alicia: Hola. ¿Yo te conozco?
Paulina: Creo que no nos conocemos.
Alicia: Soy Alicia, mucho gusto. ¿Cómo te llamas?
Paulina: Mi nombre es Paulina.
Alicia: ¿Tu esposo también tiene una operación a corazón abierto?
Paulina: Sí, mi esposo Pedro. El Doctor Ramírez va a operar a mi esposo Pedro. ¿Conoces al doctor Ramírez?
Alicia: Sí, mi esposo y yo lo (him) conocemos porque es el doctor de mi esposo.
Paulina: ¡Qué coincidencia! Creo que tu esposo conoce a mi esposo.
Alicia: Sí. Tú no eres de esta ciudad (city), ¿verdad?

---

* "Sí" with an accent "yes," "Si" without an accent "if."

Paulina:	No, pero conozco un poco de la ciudad. ¿Conoces algún restaurante vegetariano? Porque mi esposo va a estar a dieta después de la operación.
Alicia:	Sí, conozco un buen restaurante vegetariano que está cerca del (near) hospital.
Paulina:	¡Muy bien! Tenemos que esperar muchas horas en la sala de espera. Conozco un buen libro de comidas bajas en colesterol.
Alicia:	Pues (Well), yo no conozco la comida vegetariana, pero necesito información sobre qué va a poder comer Gerardo, mi esposo, después de la operación. ¿Conoces el programa de televisión de la chef Isabel? Ella prepara comidas muy sanas (healthy).
Paulina:	Sí, conozco el programa.
Alicia:	Es un gusto conocerte. ¡Ahora, nuestros esposos tienen que conocerse (each other)!

Practice 6 / Práctica 6

Translate the following sentences choosing the correct verb (saber/conocer) and using the correct conjugation form.

1. Do you know who is in the waiting room?

2. Does the patient know that her mother (su madre) is here (aquí)?

3. Are they familiar with the city?

4. Does the nurse know whether Dr. Sánchez is in the emergency department (sala de emergencia)?

5. Do you (*pl*) know when they open the cafetería (la cafetería)?

6. Are you familiar with the new protocol (el nuevo protocolo)?

7. Do you know how to speak Spanish?

8. Do you (*inf*) know her mother (su madre)?

9. Does the family know whether they are going home?

10. Do you (*F*) know that I eat vegetables (las verduras)?

11. Does the nurse know that (ese) patient?

12. Are you familiar with the cafeteria?

REVIEW ACTIVITIES CHAPTER 4 / ACTIVIDADES DE REPASO CAPÍTULO 4

Activity 1 / Actividad 1

Test your knowledge of numbers by writing (as words) and saying out loud at least three of the numbers depicted in each of the following drawings.

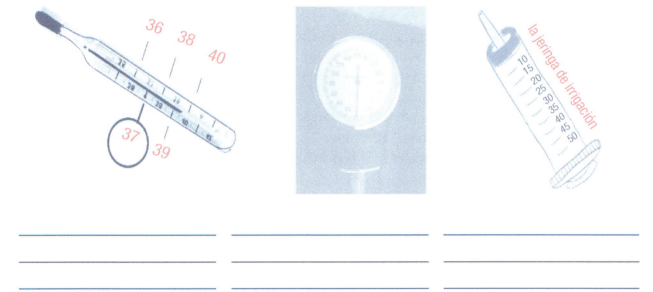

_____   _____   _____

_____   _____   _____

_____   _____   _____

Activity 2 / Actividad 2

Write out the following times that you see portrayed on the digital clocks in Spanish.

1. 2:40 p.m.	2. 12:15 a.m.	3. 3:17 a.m.	4. 7:43 a.m.
5. 1:18 a.m.	6. 4:25 p.m.	7. 10:57 p.m.	8. 9:36 p.m.

1. _____

2. _____

3. _____

4. _____

5. _____

6. _____

7. _____

8. _____

Practice 1 / Práctica 1

Diego is talking with his mother (Dora) and the admissions clerk (Cindy) in the admitting office of the hospital as they complete admission forms for Diego. Translate the following scenario.

Dora: Today is Tuesday, what is the date?
Cindy: Today is Wednesday, September 23.
Dora: Yes, today is Wednesday, it is not Tuesday! It is the first day of fall!
Cindy: When is your birthday, Diego?
Diego: My birthday is August 15th.
Dora: What year?
Diego: 2000.

Activity 3 / Actividad 3

The patient is waking up from a concussion. In order to assess the patient's orientation to time, place, and person, the nurse asks the following questions. Translate the following conversation.

Nurse: Hello. I am Yolanda, the nurse. How are you?
Rodrigo: (18 years old): I am OK.
Nurse: What is your name?
Rodrigo: Rodrigo Pastenes.
Nurse: I need to ask you some questions. Where are you?
Rodrigo: I am in the hospital.
Nurse: What day is today?
Rodrigo: Is today Tuesday?
Nurse: Yes, today is Tuesday. When is your birthday?
Rodrigo: December 24th.
Nurse: It is winter in December.
Rodrigo: Yes, but it is summer in Uruguay!

Practice 2 / Práctica 2

You have a 20-year-old female patient who presents to your office. Translate the following situation to Spanish.

Health Care Provider *(HCP)*/Patient *(PT)*

HCP:	Hello, my name is _____.
PT:	Hello, my name is Rosario Martínez.
HCP:	How old are you?
PT:	I am 20 years old. My birthday is February 2nd.
HCP:	What symptoms do you have?
PT:	I have pain when I urinate.
HCP:	Can you describe (describir) the pain please?
PT:	I have a burning pain when I urinate.
HCP:	Is there blood in the urine?
PT:	Yes, my urine is red.
HCP:	Do you have pain in your back?
PT:	No, I do not have pain in my back.
HCP:	Do you have a fever?
PT:	No, I do not have a fever.
HCP:	How much water do you drink?
PT:	I drink a little water but I drink lots of coffee.
HCP:	I need a urine specimen and I need to examine you.
PT:	Okay, thank you.

Activity 4 / Actividad 4

Read the following scenario and create the dialogue between María and the nurse in Spanish.

> *María is scheduled to have an operation later today. She was told she was not allowed to eat before the operation so she drank water. The operation is postponed.*
>
> María asks the nurse what time her operation is.
>
> The nurse responds that her operation is in 1 hour, at 2 p.m.
>
> María asks if she can drink a little water.
>
> The nurse responds that she cannot drink any water because she is not able to eat and is not able to drink for 10 hours before (antes de) the operation.
>
> María says that she has just drunk water.

The nurse responds that she needs to speak with the doctor.

María asks whether she can have her operation.

After speaking with the doctor, the nurse responds that the operation is not at 2 p.m. today but it is for 7 a.m. tomorrow. The nurse tells María that she is not able to eat or drink after eating today at 5:30.

REVIEW ACTIVITIES CHAPTER 5 / ACTIVIDADES DE REPASO CAPÍTULO 5

Activity 1 / Actividad 1: Hugo's family / La familia de Hugo

Respond to the questions that follow in Spanish using this diagram.

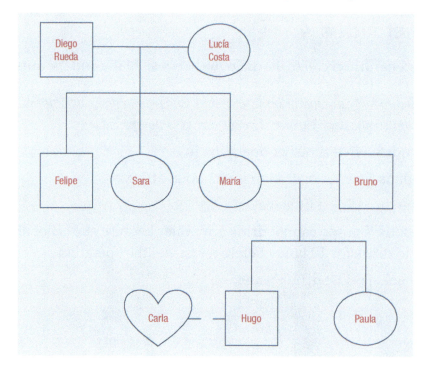

1. Who is the father?	¿Quién es el padre?
2. Who is María?	¿Quién es María?
3. Is Paula Sara's sister?	¿Es Paula la hermana de Sara?
4. Who is Felipe?	¿Quién es Felipe?
5. Who is Hugo's aunt?	¿Quién es la tía de Hugo?
6. What is the grandfather's name?	¿Cuál es el nombre del abuelo?
7. Who is the grandmother?	¿Quién es la abuela?
8. What is the name of Hugo's girlfriend?	¿Cómo se llama la novia de Hugo?

Practice 1 / Práctica 1

Translate the following dialogue into Spanish.

Where is your godmother? She is with my cousin. How old is your cousin? She is 12 years old. How many brothers and sisters does she have? She has one brother and one sister. Where are they? They are at their house. Are they going to come to my clinic? Yes, they are going to your clinic because they have a sore throat.

Practice 2 / Práctica 2

Refer to the drawings on the next page to express what you like and do not like for each meal.

For example,   Me gusta la cerveza: I like beer.

Breakfast:
_____

Lunch:
_____

Dinner:
_____

Snack:
_____

un huevo

el pan

el pollo

la fruta

la verdura

la leche

el pescado

la cerveza

el té

Situation 1 / Situación # 1

The grandfather is being discharged from the hospital after a diabetic crisis. The dietitian is talking with the patient and family about the grandfather's new diet. She first asks about what the family usually eats. Translate the following scenario.

Sr. Nicolás Torres	Grandfather
Olinda	Grandmother
Julieta	Daughter
Dietista	Dietician
Pablito	Grandson (Julieta's son)

Dietista:	Hello, I want to speak with Mr. Torres about (sobre) his diet. What do you and your family like to eat for (para) breakfast?
Olinda:	For breakfast, we eat toast and tea.
Sr. Torres:	I like a lot of jelly on my toast and two cups of strong coffee (café cargado) with milk.
Julieta:	Papá, you do not have to have jelly on your toast.
Dietista:	Mr. Torres, do you like decaffeinated coffee with skim milk?
Sr. Torres:	No, I do not drink decaffeinated coffee.
Julieta:	For lunch, we like to eat salad with shrimp and avocado, and soup.
Sr. Torres:	Before lunch, I like to drink an aperitif, pisco. I do not like soup and salad. I like steak with fried potatoes and fried onions (bistec a lo pobre), tres leches cake (tres leches), and two glasses of wine.
Pablito:	Grandfather, I like tres leches cake a lot.
Julieta:	Oh, papá and Pablito, you need to eat better (mejor).
Sr. Torres:	For dinner, we like tortillas with hamburger and beans with cheese.
Olinda:	Oh, Nicolás, we do not like hamburgers and beans at night, but that is what you like to eat.
Sr. Torres:	After dinner, for a digestive liqueur, I like a glass or two of aged wine (oporto) with a cigar (un cigarro).
Dietista:	Mr. Torres, you need help (ayuda) with your diet.

Practice 3 / Práctica 3

Ask and respond to the following exchanges between a HCP and a patient using Spanish.

HCP:	Are you hungry?
PT:	No, I am not hungry because I am nauseated.
HCP:	Do you like nuts?

PT:	Yes, I like nuts but my brother has an allergy to nuts.
HCP:	Is your mother able to order her breakfast?
PT:	Yes, she has just ordered her breakfast.
HCP:	How long have you been fasting?
PT:	It has been 8 hours.
HCP:	Does orange juice make you feel bad?
PT:	Yes, orange juice makes me feel bad in the morning.
HCP:	What food do you want to order for breakfast?
PT:	I want to order ham, eggs, and toast for breakfast.
PT:	Am I able to have coffee or tea with the diet?
HCP:	You can have coffee or tea with the diet.
HCP:	Do you like chicken or turkey?
PT:	I like chicken and turkey.
PT:	Am I able to order the food before noon?
HCP:	No, you have to order the food before 10 a.m.
HCP:	How many beers do you drink in a week?
PT:	I never drink any beer.

Practice 4 / Práctica 4

React to the following statements from your patient first in English, then in Spanish.
For example   Tengo mucho dolor: How much does it hurt?   ¿Cuánto le duele?

Tengo hambre.

¿Tiene jalea?

Tengo sed.

¿Puedo beber café?

Necesito una cuchara,
por favor.

¿Puedo comer fruta?

Necesito un poco de hielo,
por favor.

¿Por qué no puedo beber
agua?

¿A qué hora puedo pedir la
comida?

¿Puedo comer mayonesa?

el niño come en la cama porque está enfermo

¡No me gustan los huevos!

Yo no bebo leche, tengo alergia a la lactosa.

Quiero una tostada con mantequilla.

Me duele la cabeza porque no me dan café.

¡Ay! La comida está fría.

¿Por qué no puedo comer sal?

¿Hay flan en el hospital?

¡Necesito beber algo con cafeína!

El jugo de manzana es muy dulce, me hace mal.

Me gusta el queso, ¿puedo comer un poco?

Practice 5 / Práctica 5

Your patient presents to have blood work done. Translate the following scenario.

HCP:	Hello, Marta. Please sit down.
Marta:	Do I sit here?
HCP:	Yes, sit here please. I need to take a sample of your blood.
Marta:	Can I lie down? I get dizzy when I have a blood test.
HCP:	Yes, lie down. Roll up your sleeve. I need to put this around your arm and now make a fist. Do not move your arm please.

REVIEW ACTIVITIES CHAPTER 6 / ACTIVIDADES DE REPASO CAPÍTULO 6

Practice 1 / Práctica 1

The patient relates the following history; translate Rodrigo's history into Spanish.

Rodrigo states: "Last year I had a cough for 2 weeks and after tennis class, I had an asthma attack. I used my inhaler (inhalador). The next day I had another asthma attack and I had to go to the hospital. I had a chest x-ray and a blood test and I took some medicine. Yesterday I had a cough and I was short of breath. I used my inhaler and I took medicine. Last night I began to have problems with my breathing. This occurred after midnight. I feel the same now. Do I have to go to the hospital?"

Dialogue / Diálogo 1

La Señora Artaza brings her 3-year-old daughter to the clinic for her well-child checkup. The following is the interaction between the nurse and la Señora Artaza. Translate the following dialogue to Spanish.

Enfermera:	Good morning, Señora Artaza. What is your child's name?
La Señora Artaza:	My child's name is Alicia.
Enfermera:	How old is Alicia?
La Señora Artaza:	Alicia is 3 years old.
Enfermera:	Do you give vitamins to Alicia?
La Señora Artaza:	Yes, I give vitamins to Alicia.
Enfermera:	Does Alicia have allergies?
La Señora Artaza:	I am not able to give milk to Alicia because she has an allergy to milk.
Enfermera:	Did Alicia have problems with her vaccines?
La Señora Artaza:	No, she did not, but are you going to give her a vaccine today?
Enfermera:	I need to look at her chart to see whether she needs a vaccine. No, she does not need vaccines today.
La Señora Artaza:	Alicia, if you are a good girl, the nurse is going to give you a sticker.
Enfermera:	I need to weigh Alicia and take her temperature.
Alicia:	I am a good girl! Can you give me my sticker?

Activity 1 / Actividad 1

Using demonstrative adjectives and adverbs of location, translate the following scenarios into Spanish.

1. I need to take **this** prescription to **that** pharmacy *over there* by my house. Where is the doctor who prescribed **this** medication to me? He is with **those** doctors *there* at **that** hospital.

2. **These** pills are difficult to (para) swallow. I need to talk to **that** doctor now.

3. The baby in **that** waiting room *over there* is crying. Where is his mother? His mother is in **that** gift shop by the waiting room. Where is the father of **that** baby? He is with **those** three children in **that** restaurant. Where is **that** restaurant? It is *over there*.

4. *Here* is the x-ray of **that** patient.

5. *There* is the nurse who is going to give me **those** drops.

Practice 2 / Práctica 2

Translate the following questions and answers from English to Spanish.

1. Do you have any pain?

   No, I do not have any pain. No, I do not have any.

2. Did you have any problems with the medication?

   Yes, I had some problems with the medication.

3. Did anyone in your family have breast cancer (cáncer de seno)?

   No, nobody in my family had breast cancer.

4. Did you ever have shingles?

   Yes, I had shingles last year.

5. Do you like either steak or chicken?

   I like neither steak nor chicken.

6. Do you always drink strong coffee?

   I drink strong coffee sometimes.

7. Do you ever exercise?

   No, I never exercise.

8. Do you want to ask anything?

   No, I do not want to ask anything.

Practice 3 / Práctica 3

Translate the following to Spanish using "por" or "para."

1. It is necessary to fast for 8 hours.
2. You have to take the medication in order to feel better.
3. The nurse has to call the doctor in order to obtain [obtener] the prescriptions.
4. She is here on behalf of her mother.
5. The surgery is for tomorrow.
6. The toys are for the baby.
7. Thank you, María, for your help.
8. Melinda works for the surgeons.
9. I am going to go to the hospital for tests.
10. The doctor is going to do a procedure in order to help you.

Activity 2 / Actividad 2

Circle the correct preposition and explain why "por" or "para" is used, referring to the acronyms in Chapter 6 for help.

For example Trabajo (para/por) el hospital: para: I work for the hospital. (Employment)

(**1.Por / para**) ser tan joven, Inés es una enfermera muy preparada. Va a ir (**2. por / para**) San Francisco (**3.por / para**) visitar un hospital especializado en oncología. Va a estar en California (**4.por / para**) tres semanas (**5.por / para**) hablar con el Dr. Arellano. Antes de ir al hospital, Inés quiere pasar (**6. por / para**) la tienda de regalos (**7.por / para**) comprar algo (**8.por / para**) su hermana pequeña.

1.

2.

3.

4.

5.

6.

7.

8.

Practice 4 / Práctica 4

Form the following statements using the subjunctive.

1. It is important that you fast before (antes de) the test.

2. The doctor does not want you to do exercise for 4 weeks.

3. It is necessary that you take the medicine now.

4. It is important that you lower your cholesterol.

5. It is urgent that we call the ambulance.

6. The doctor does not want you to drink alcohol anymore (más).

7. I hope that you do not need surgery.

8. The doctor does not want you to do a lot (mucho) for a week.

9. We hope that your family is able to come.

10. I want you to try "propolio."

Activity 3 / Actividad 3

Mercedes is in the gift shop and looks at several greeting cards to give to her friend Ximena. Translate the following sentences from English to Spanish.

1. Do you know when you are coming home? I hope it is soon (pronto)!
2. We hope that you feel better soon!
3. In order to go home, you have to eat your Jell-O!
4. All (Todo lo que) I want is for you to be healthy.
5. I know a little bird (un pajarito) who has just told me that you are sick!
6. I wish you good luck (I hope that you have good luck) with your new baby.
7. It is urgent that you come home soon; I want you to play golf (golf) with me (conmigo) again (otra vez).
8. I hope that the birth of your child comes with many blessings (bendiciones).
9. I hope that you can still (todavía) eat chocolate.
10. I want you to know that I am here if you need me.

READING: ELOISA DÍAZ, FIRST WOMAN TO GRADUATE FROM MEDICAL SCHOOL IN CHILE AND IN LATIN AMERICA / LECTURA: ELOÍSA DÍAZ, LA PRIMERA MUJER GRADUADA DE LA ESCUELA DE MEDICINA EN CHILE Y EN LATINOAMÉRICA

Reading

Eloísa Díaz (1866–1950, b. Santiago, Chile) was the first woman to graduate from medical school in Chile and in Latin America. In 1881, when Eloísa Díaz was only 15 years old, she began her study of medicine at the University of Chile and she graduated in 1887. During her life she dedicated herself to women's studies. She also studied and concerned herself with children's health and the importance of vaccinations, student nutrition, and health care among people without resources.

Lectura

Eloísa Díaz fue la primera mujer graduada de la escuela de medicina en Chile y en Latinoamérica (1866–1950, n. Santiago, Chile): En 1881, cuando Eloísa tenía solamente 15 años comenzó los estudios de medicina en la Universidad de Chile y se graduó en 1887.

Durante su vida se dedicó a estudios de la mujer. También estudió y se preocupó por la salud de los niños y la importancia de las vacunas, la nutrición de los estudiantes y por el cuidado de la salud entre las personas sin recursos.

IDIOMATIC EXPRESSIONS / EXPRESIONES IDIOMÁTICAS

To sleep on it   English expression
Consultarlo con la almohada   Spanish expression
To consult with the pillow   Literal translation

Can't make heads or tails of it   English expression
No tiene ni pies ni cabeza   Spanish expression
It has neither feet nor a head   Literal translation

ANSWERS TO REVIEW ACTIVITIES AND CHAPTER SUMMARY EXERCISES

CONTENTS

Answers to Chapter 1 review activities and summary exercise / Respuestas a las actividades de repaso del Capítulo 1 y al ejercicio a modo de resumen

Answers to Chapter 2 review activities and summary exercise / Respuestas a las actividades de repaso del Capítulo 2 y al ejercicio a modo de resumen

Answers to Chapter 3 review activities and summary exercise / Respuestas a las actividades de repaso del Capítulo 3 y al ejercicio a modo de resumen

Answers to Chapter 4 review activities and summary exercise / Respuestas a las actividades de repaso del Capítulo 4 y al ejercicio a modo de resumen

Answers to Chapter 5 review activities and summary exercise / Respuestas a las actividades de repaso del Capítulo 5 y al ejercicio a modo de resumen

Answers to Chapter 6 review activities and summary exercise / Respuestas a las actividades de repaso del Capítulo 6 y al ejercicio a modo de resumen

ANSWERS TO CHAPTER 1 REVIEW ACTIVITIES AND SUMMARY EXERCISE / RESPUESTAS A LAS ACTIVIDADES DE REPASO DEL CAPÍTULO 1 Y AL EJERCICIO A MODO DE RESUMEN

Practice 1 / Práctica 1

1. Carlota   ce-a-ere-ele-o-t-a
2. Godoy   ge-o-de-o-i griega
3. Fernando   efe-e-ere-ene-a-ene-de-o
4. Patiño   pe-a-te-i-eñe-o

Activity 1 / Actividad 1

Answers will vary. Possible answers may include the following:

1. Hola, ¿cómo estás?
2. Hola, ¿cómo están Uds.?
3. Hola, señor.
4. Buenos días.
5. Buenas tardes.
6. Habla inglés o español?
7. ¿Cómo se llama Ud.?
8. Hasta mañana.
9. Hola Carlitos, ¿cómo estás?
10. Buenas noches.

Practice 2 / Práctica 2

1. Los nombres
2. La mujer
3. Las pacientes
4. El lápiz
5. Las doctoras
6. El hombre

7. Las direcciones

8. La comunidad

9. Los apellidos

10. El hospital

Practice 3 / Práctica 3

1. tú	él
2. usted	ella
3. ustedes	ellos
4. ustedes or vosotras	ellas
5. tú	él

Practice 4 / Práctica 4

1. Estar (location)

2. Ser (origin)

3. Estar (emotion)

4. Ser (time)

5. Estar (health)

6. Ser (identification)

SUMMARY EXERCISE / EJERCICIO A MODO DE RESUMEN

1. ¡Hola!

2. ¡Buenas noches!

3. ¿Está enfermo / enferma?

4. ¿De dónde es Ud.?

5. ¿Cuántos años tiene Ud.?

6. ¿Quién es su doctor?

7. ¿Cómo deletrea su apellido?

8. ¿Quién está con Ud.?

9. ¿Por qué está preocupado / a?

10. ¿Cuánto pesa?

ANSWERS TO CHAPTER 2 REVIEW ACTIVITIES AND SUMMARY EXERCISE / RESPUESTAS A LAS ACTIVIDADES DE REPASO DEL CAPÍTULO 2 Y AL EJERCICIO A MODO DE RESUMEN

Dialogue 1 / Diálogo 1

Hola, Sr. Rodríguez. Soy la enfermera. ¿Cómo está?

Hola. Tengo mucho dolor.

¿Dónde tiene dolor, Sr. Rodríguez?

Tengo dolor en mi espalda y mi pierna izquierda.

¿Qué tipo de dolor es?

Tengo un dolor en mi espalda que se irradia a la pierna derecha.

¿Qué tipo de dolor tiene en la pierna izquierda?

Mi pierna izquierda me duele mucho. Es un dolor punzante.

Activity 1 / Actividad 1

Nurse:	¿Dónde le duele?
Carlos:	Tengo dolor cuando me muevo.
Nurse:	¿Le duele la cabeza?
Carlos:	No, pero me duele cuando abro la boca.
Nurse:	¿Le duele cuando respira?
Carlos:	No, pero me duele cuando presiona mi espalda con el estetoscopio.
Nurse:	¿Puede mover sus brazos y piernas?
Carlos:	Me duele cuando me muevo la pierna izquierda.
Nurse:	¿Le duele cuando presiono su rodilla?
Carlos:	No, pero me duele cuando toca mi tobillo.
Nurse:	¿Puede doblar los dedos de los pies?
Carlos:	Sí, pero me duele cuando doblo los dedos de los pies.
Nurse:	Ponga la bolsa de hielo en su mandíbula. Voy a poner la venda elástica en su tobillo. Necesita tener una radiografía.

SUMMARY EXERCISE / EJERCICIO A MODO DE RESUMEN

Answers will vary. Possible answers may include the following:

4. ¿Cuánto te duele?

5. ¿Cuándo te duele?

6. ¿Te duele cuando respiras?

ANSWERS TO CHAPTER 3 REVIEW ACTIVITIES AND SUMMARY EXERCISE / RESPUESTAS A LAS ACTIVIDADES DE REPASO DEL CAPÍTULO 3 Y AL EJERCICIO A MODO DE RESUMEN

Practice 1 / Práctica 1

1. ¿Necesita agua?
2. Necesito tomarle la temperatura.
3. ¿Qué necesita él / ella?
4. Necesito tomarle la presión.
5. Necesito escucharle el corazón.
6. Necesito operarle.
7. Necesito tocarle…el brazo / la pierna / la espalda.
8. Necesito mirarle…los ojos / la garganta.

Practice 2 / Práctica 2

1. ¿Habla inglés?
2. Necesito hablar con la familia.
3. Necesito hablar de la medicina.
4. ¿Necesita Ud. hablar con el doctor / la doctora?
5. ¿Necesita Ud. hablar de la operación?

Practice 3 / Práctica 3

1. ¿Quiere beber algo?
   Sí, quiero agua.
2. ¿Quiere hablar con el doctor / la doctora?
   No, no quiero hablar con el doctor / la doctora.
3. ¿Qué quiere?
   Quiero comer ahora.
4. ¿Quiere beber algo?
   No, quiero dormir.
5. Quiero tomarle la presión.
   Sí, está bien.

Practice 4 / Práctica 4

1. ¿Cómo se siente Ud.?

    Me siento ansioso / a

2. ¿Qué prefiere Ud. comer?

    Prefiero tomar la sopa.

3. ¿Se siente deprimido / a o nervioso / a?

    Él se siente enojado y triste. OR Ella se siente enojada y triste.

4. ¿Cómo se siente?

    Me siento descompuesto / a. Quiero pastillas para la náusea.

5. ¿Quiere bañarse?

    Sí, quiero bañarme.

Practice 5 / Práctica 5

1. ¿Puede respirar profundo?

    Sí, puedo respirar profundo.

2. ¿Puede moverse a la camilla?

    Sí, puedo moverme a la camilla.

3. ¿Puede subir y bajar los brazos?

    Puedo subir y bajar el brazo derecho, pero no puedo subir y bajar el brazo izquierdo.

4. ¿Puede sentarse?

    No, no puedo sentarme porque me duele la espalda.

5. ¿Puede pararse y cerrar los ojos?

    No, no puedo pararme y cerrar los ojos porque estoy mareado / a.

6. ¿Puede tragar?

    Puedo tragar pero me duele la garganta cuando trago.

7. ¿Puede leer las letras?

    Sí, puedo leer las letras.

8. ¿Puede caminar?

    No, no puedo caminar.

Dialogue 1a / Diálogo 1a

1. Nurse / Enfermero: ¿Tiene dolor? Necesito tomarle los signos vitales.
2. Mrs. Pérez / Señora Pérez: Me duele la cabeza y tengo contracciones.

3. Nurse / Enfermero: ¿Le duele el cuello?

4. Mrs. Pérez / Señora Pérez: No, pero las contracciones son fuertes y me duelen. ¿Sabe dónde está mi esposo?

5. Nurse / Enfermero: Su esposo está en la sala de espera, y el doctor y la partera están aquí ahora.

Dialogue 1b / Diálogo 1b

1. ¿Qué sabe

2. Sé que

3. ¿Sabe

4. Sé que

5. ¿Sabe dónde

6. saben

Dialogue 1c / Diálogo 1c

1. ¿Sabe dónde está mi esposa?

2. Sé que ella está en la sala de emergencias.

3. ¿Sabe la partera que mi esposa está aquí?

4. Sí, el doctor / la doctora y la partera saben que su esposa está aquí.

5. ¿Sabe si puedo ver a mi esposa?

6. No sé si puede ver a su esposa, pero puedo llamar a la enfermera.

Dialogue 2 / Diálogo 2

Alicia: Hello. Do I know you?

Paulina: I believe that we do not know each other.

Alicia: I am Alicia, nice to meet you. What is your name?

Paulina: My name is Paulina.

Alicia: Is your husband also having open-heart surgery?

Paulina: Yes, my husband Pedro. Doctor Ramírez is going to operate on my husband Pedro. Do you know Doctor Ramírez?

Alicia: Yes, my husband and I know him because he is the doctor of my husband.

Paulina: What a coincidence! I believe that your husband knows my husband.

Alicia: Yes. You are not from the city, right?

Paulina: No, but I know a little about the city. Do you know a vegetarian restaurant? Because my husband is going to be on a diet after the operation.

Alicia: Yes, I know a good vegetarian restaurant that is near the hospital.

Paulina:	Very good! We have to wait many hours in the waiting room. I know a good book about foods low in cholesterol.
Alicia:	Well, I am not familiar with vegetarian food, but I need information about what Gerardo, my husband, will be able to eat after the operation. Are you familiar with the television program of Chef Isabel? She prepares very healthy foods.
Paulina:	Yes, I am familiar with the program.
Alicia:	It is a pleasure to meet you. Now, our husbands have to meet each other!

Practice 6 / Práctica 6

1. ¿Sabe quién está en la sala de espera?
2. ¿El / La paciente sabe que su madre está aquí?
3. ¿Conocen ellos la ciudad?
4. ¿Sabe el enfermero / la enfermera si el doctor Sánchez está en la sala de emergencia?
5. ¿Saben Uds. cuándo abren la cafetería?
6. ¿Conoce el nuevo protocolo?
7. ¿Sabe hablar español?
8. ¿Conoces a su madre?
9. ¿Sabe la familia si ellos se van a casa?
10. ¿Sabe usted que yo como verduras?
11. ¿Conoce el enfermero / la enfermera a ese paciente?
12. ¿Conoce la cafetería?

SUMMARY EXERCISE / EJERCICIO A MODO DE RESUMEN

Héctor:	Hola, padre. ¿Cómo estás?
Pablo:	Bien, hijo. ¿Conoces a la señora Vásquez? Es mi dietista.
Héctor:	No, no la conozco a ella. ¿Sabes ahora lo que necesitas comer?
Pablo:	Sí. ¿Podemos ir al supermercado?
Héctor:	Sí. ¿Dónde está?
Pablo:	¿Conoces la calle Peach?
Héctor:	Sí.

ANSWERS TO CHAPTER 4 REVIEW ACTIVITIES AND SUMMARY EXERCISE / RESPUESTAS A LAS ACTIVIDADES DE REPASO DEL CAPÍTULO 4 Y AL EJERCICIO A MODO DE RESUMEN

Activity 1 / Actividad 1

Answers will vary. Possible answers may include the following:

First picture (thermometer)

36	treinta y seis
37	treinta y siete
38	treinta y ocho
39	treinta y nueve
40	cuarenta

Second picture (blood pressure cuff)

20	veinte
40	cuarenta
60	sesenta
80	ochenta
100	cien
120	ciento veinte
140	ciento cuarenta
160	ciento sesenta
180	ciento ochenta
200	doscientos
220	doscientos veinte
240	doscientos cuarenta
260	doscientos sesenta
280	doscientos ochenta
300	trescientos

Third picture (syringe)

10	diez
15	quince

20	veinte
25	veinticinco
30	treinta
35	treinta y cinco
40	cuarenta
45	cuarenta y cinco
50	cincuenta

Activity 2 / Actividad 2

1. Son las dos y cuarenta. / Son las tres menos veinte de la tarde.
2. Son las doce y cuarto. / Son las doce y quince de la mañana.
3. Son las tres y diecisiete de la mañana.
4. Son las siete y cuarenta y tres. / Son las ocho menos diecisiete de la mañana.
5. Es la una y dieciocho de la mañana.
6. Son las cuatro y veinticinco de la tarde.
7. Son las diez y cincuenta y siete. / Son las once menos tres de la noche.
8. Son las nueve y treinta y seis. / Son las diez menos veinticuatro de la noche.

Practice 1 / Práctica 1

Dora: Hoy es martes. ¿Cuál es la fecha?
Cindy: Hoy es miércoles, el veintitrés de septiembre.
Dora: Sí, hoy es miércoles, no es martes. ¡Es el primer día del otoño!
Cindy: ¿Cuándo es su cumpleaños, Diego?
Diego: Mi cumpleaños es el quince de agosto.
Dora: ¿Qué año?
Diego: Dos mil.

Activity 3 / Actividad 3

Nurse: Hola. Soy Yolanda, la enfermera. ¿Cómo está?
Rodrigo: Estoy bien.
Nurse: ¿Cómo se llama?
Rodrigo: Rodrigo Pastenes.
Nurse: Necesito hacerle algunas preguntas. ¿Dónde está?
Rodrigo: Estoy en el hospital.

Nurse:	¿Qué día es hoy?
Rodrigo:	¿Hoy es martes?
Nurse:	Sí, hoy es martes. ¿Cuándo es su cumpleaños?
Rodrigo:	El veinticuatro de diciembre.
Nurse:	Es invierno en diciembre.
Rodrigo:	Sí, ¡pero es verano en Uruguay!

Practice 2 / Práctica 2

HCP:	Hola, mi nombre es_____.
PT:	Hola, mi nombre es Rosario Martínez.
HCP:	¿Cuántos años tiene?
PT:	Tengo veinte años. Mi cumpleaños es el dos de febrero.
HCP:	¿Qué síntomas tiene?
PT:	Me duele cuando orino.
HCP:	¿Puede describir el dolor por favor?
PT:	Tengo un dolor quemante cuando orino.
HCP:	¿Hay sangre en la orina?
PT:	Sí, la orina es roja.
HCP:	¿Tiene dolor en la espalda?
PT:	No, no tengo dolor en la espalda.
HCP:	¿Tiene fiebre?
PT:	No, no tengo fiebre.
HCP:	¿Cuánta agua bebe?
PT:	Bebo un poco de agua pero bebo mucho café.
HCP:	Necesito una muestra de orina y necesito examinarla.
PT:	Bien, gracias.

Activity 4 / Actividad 4

María:	¿A qué hora es la operación?
Enfermera:	La operación es en una hora, a las dos de la tarde.
María:	¿Puedo beber un poco de agua?
Enfermera:	No, no puede beber agua porque no puede comer ni beber diez horas antes de la operación.
María:	Acabo de beber agua.
Enfermera:	Necesito hablar con el doctor / la doctora.
María:	¿Puedo tener la operación?
Enfermera:	No, la operación no es a las dos de la tarde hoy. Es mañana a las siete de la mañana. No puede comer ni beber después de cenar hoy a las cinco y media.

SUMMARY EXERCISE / EJERCICIO A MODO DE RESUMEN

Dora:	Hoy es martes, y, ¿cuál es la fecha?
Cindy:	Hoy es miércoles, el veintitrés de septiembre.
Dora:	Sí, hoy es miércoles, ¡no es martes! ¡Es el primer día del otoño!
Cindy:	¿Cuándo es tu cumpleaños, Diego?
Diego:	Mi cumpleaños es el quince de agosto.
Dora:	¡Vas a tener quince años!
Cindy:	¿Por qué estás aquí?
Diego:	Hace un mes que me duele la garganta y ahora el doctor necesita sacarme las amígdalas.
Cindy:	Acabo de hablar con el enfermero / la enfermera y la operación es mañana.

ANSWERS TO CHAPTER 5 REVIEW ACTIVITIES AND SUMMARY EXERCISE / RESPUESTAS A LAS ACTIVIDADES DE REPASO DEL CAPÍTULO 5 Y AL EJERCICIO A MODO DE RESUMEN

Activity 1 / Actividad 1

1. El padre de Hugo es Bruno.
2. María es la madre de Hugo.
3. No, Paula no es la hermana de Sara. Es su sobrina.
4. Felipe es el tío de Hugo.
5. Sara es la tía de Hugo.
6. El abuelo es Diego Rueda.
7. La abuela es Lucía Costa.
8. La novia de Hugo se llama Carla.

Practice 1 / Práctica 1

¿Dónde está su madrina? Está con mi prima. ¿Cuántos años tiene su prima? Ella tiene doce años. ¿Cuántos hermanos tiene ella? Ella tiene un hermano y una hermana. ¿Dónde están ellos? Ellos están en su casa. ¿Ellos van a venir a mi clínica? Sí, ellos van a su clínica porque les duele la garganta.

Practice 2 / Práctica 2

Answers will vary. Possible answers may include the following:

Breakfast: Me gustan los huevos. No me gusta la leche.
Lunch: Me gustan el pollo y la fruta. No me gusta la cerveza.
Dinner: Me gustan el pescado y la verdura. No me gusta el huevo.
Snack: Me gusta la leche. No me gusta el pescado.

Situacion 1 / Situación 1

Dietista: Hola, quiero hablar con el señor Torres sobre su dieta. A Ud. y a su familia, ¿qué les gusta para el desayuno?

Olinda: Para el desayuno, comemos tostadas y té.

Sr. Torres: Me gusta mucha mermelada en las tostadas y dos tazas de café cargado con leche.

Julieta: Papá, no tienes que poner mermelada en las tostadas.

Dietista: Señor Torres, ¿le gusta el café descafeinado con leche sin grasa?

Sr. Torres: No, no tomo el café descafeinado.

Julieta: Para el almuerzo, nos gusta comer ensalada con camarones y palta, y sopa.

Sr. Torres: Antes del almuerzo, me gusta tomar un aperitivo, pisco. No me gusta la sopa ni la ensalada. Me gusta el bistec a lo pobre, tres leches, y dos vasos de vino.

Pablito: Abuelo, me gusta tres leches mucho.

Julieta: Ay, papá y Pablito, necesitan comer mejor.

Sr. Torres: Para la cena, nos gustan las tortillas con una hamburguesa y frijoles con queso.

Olinda: Ay, Nicolás, no nos gustan las hamburguesas y frijoles en la noche, pero es lo que te gusta comer.

Sr. Torres: Después de la cena, para un bajativo, me gusta(n) un vaso o dos de oporto con un cigarro.

Dietista: Señor Torres, necesita ayuda con su dieta.

Practice 3 / Práctica 3

HCP: ¿Tiene hambre?
PT: No, no tengo hambre porque tengo náuseas.
HCP: ¿Le gustan las nueces?
PT: Sí, me gustan las nueces pero mi hermano tiene alergia a las nueces.
HCP: ¿Su madre puede pedir el desayuno?
PT: Sí, ella acaba de pedir el desayuno.
HCP: ¿Hace cuánto tiempo que ayuna?
PT: Hace ocho horas.
HCP: ¿El jugo de naranja le hace mal?
PT: Sí, el jugo de naranja me hace mal en la mañana.

HCP:	¿Qué comida quiere pedir para el desayuno?
PT:	Quiero pedir jamón, huevos, y tostadas para el desayuno.
PT:	¿Puedo beber café o té con la dieta?
HCP:	Puede beber café o té con la dieta.
HCP:	¿Le gusta el pollo o el pavo?
PT:	Me gustan el pollo y el pavo.
PT:	¿Puedo pedir la comida antes del mediodía?
HCP:	No, tiene que pedir la comida antes de las diez de la mañana.
HCP:	¿Cuántas cervezas bebe en una semana?
PT:	Nunca bebo cerveza.

Practice 4 / Práctica 4

Answers will vary. Possible answers may include the following:

What do you want to eat?	¿Qué quiere comer?
Yes, we have Jell-O.	Sí, tenemos jalea.
Do you want a glass of water?	¿Quiere un vaso de agua?
You may drink decaffeinated coffee.	Puede beber el café descafeinado.
Here is the spoon.	Aquí está la cuchara.
Yes. Do you want an apple or a banana?	Sí. ¿Quiere una manzana o una banana?
Do you want ice chips?	¿Quiere hielo picado?
Because you are going to have an operation.	Porque va a tener una operación.
You may order the food after 10 a.m.	Puede pedir la comida después de las diez de la mañana.
No, mayonnaise is bad for the diet.	No, la mayonesa es mala para la dieta.
Do you prefer bacon?	¿Prefiere el tocino?
We have lactose-free milk.	Tenemos la leche sin lactosa.
You may have toast, but you may not have butter.	Puede comer tostadas, pero no puede poner mantequilla.
The dietician is going to speak with you.	El / la dietista va a hablar con Ud.
I can bring another tray of food.	Puedo traer otra bandeja con comida.
Salt is bad for the diet.	La sal es mala para la dieta.
Yes, we have flan.	Sí, tenemos flan.
You may have one cup of coffee.	Puede beber una taza de café.
Do you want orange juice?	¿Quiere el jugo de naranja?
You may have one slice of cheese.	Puede comer una tajada de queso.

Practice 5 / Práctica 5

HCP:	Hola, Marta. Siéntese por favor.
Marta:	¿Me siento aquí?
HCP:	Sí, siéntese aquí por favor. Necesito tomar una muestra de su sangre.
Marta:	¿Puedo acostarme? Me mareo cuando tengo una prueba de sangre.
HCP:	Sí, acuéstese. Arremánguese la manga. Necesito poner esto en su brazo, y, ahora, empuñe la mano. No mueva el brazo por favor.

SUMMARY EXERCISE / EJERCICIO A MODO DE RESUMEN

Dietician:	¿Qué le gusta desayunar?
Mr. Cortés:	Me gustan tres huevos, dos pedazos de tocino, tres pedazos de salchicha, tostadas y café con leche y dos cucharadas de azúcar.
Dietician:	Señor Cortés, necesita comer más frutas y vegetales.
Mrs. Cortés:	Y agregar fibra a la dieta.
Mr. Cortés:	Bien, para el desayuno, quiero cereal con fibra, una banana, y café con leche.
Dietician:	Muy bien, ¿qué quiere para el almuerzo?
Mr. Cortés:	Quiero comer dos hamburguesas con queso y pan, papas fritas con ketchoop y una soda con helado para postre.
Mrs. Cortés:	Tienes que escuchar a la dietista.
Dietician:	Señor Cortés, ¿quiere comer una ensalada con atún y pepinos para almuerzo, y agua para beber?
Mr. Cortés:	Sí, me gusta la ensalada con atún pero, ¿puedo tener aderezo con la ensalada?
Dietician:	Sí, señor Cortés, puede poner vinagre y aceite con la ensalada. ¿Qué quiere comer para la cena?
Mr. Cortés:	¡Quiero un bistec grande, una papa con mucha mantequilla, frijoles con queso, y flan!
Dietician:	Señor Cortés, ¿le gustan las verduras?
Mr. Cortés:	Sí, ¡me gustan las verduras con mantequilla!
Mrs. Cortés:	Coma verduras, pero no con mantequilla.
Mr. Cortés:	Sí, quiero un bistec pequeño con una papa, zanahorias sin mantequilla, y dos cervezas.
Mrs. Cortés:	La cerveza es mala para la dieta.
Mr. Cortés:	Bien, quiero tomar agua con la cena.
Dietician:	¿Quiere una merienda?
Mr. Cortés:	Quiero tres leches, gracias.
Mrs. Cortés:	Tienes que escuchar a la dietista. Comes demasiado azúcar.
Dietician:	Para una merienda, coma una manzana o naranja o tres tazas de palomitas sin mantequilla y sal.
Mr. Cortés:	¡Gracias!
Dietician:	¡Gracias Señor Cortés!

ANSWERS TO CHAPTER 6 REVIEW ACTIVITIES AND SUMMARY EXERCISE / RESPUESTAS A LAS ACTIVIDADES DE REPASO DEL CAPÍTULO 6 Y AL EJERCICIO A MODO DE RESUMEN

Practice 1 / Práctica 1

El año pasado, tuve una tos por dos semanas y después de la clase de tenis, tuve un ataque de asma. Usé mi inhalador. El próximo día, tuve otro ataque de asma y tuve que ir al hospital. Tuve una radiografía del pecho, y una prueba de sangre, y tomé la medicina. Ayer tuve tos y falta de aire. Usé mi inhalador y tomé medicina. Anoche empecé a tener problemas con mi respiración. Esto ocurrió después de la medianoche. Me siento igual ahora. ¿Tengo que ir al hospital?

Dialogue 1 / Diálogo 1

Enfermera: Buenos días, señora Artaza. ¿Cómo se llama su hija?

La Señora Artaza: Mi hija se llama Alicia.

Enfermera: ¿Cuántos años tiene Alicia?

La Señora Artaza: Alicia tiene tres años.

Enfermera: ¿Le da vitaminas a Alicia?

La Señora Artaza: Sí, le doy vitaminas a Alicia.

Enfermera: ¿Alicia tiene alergias?

La Señora Artaza: No puedo darle leche a Alicia porque tiene alergia a la lactosa.

Enfermera: ¿Tuvo Alicia problemas con las vacunas?

La Señora Artaza: No, pero, ¿le va a poner una vacuna hoy?

Enfermera: Necesito mirarle el historial para ver si necesita una vacuna. No, ella no necesita vacunas hoy.

La Señora Artaza: Alicia, si eres buena chica, la enfermera te va a dar una calcomanía.

Enfermera: Necesito pesar a Alicia y tomarle la temperatura.

Alicia: ¡Soy una buena chica! ¿Me puede dar la calcomanía?

Activity 1 / Actividad 1

1. Necesito tomar **esta** receta a **aquella** farmacia *allí* cerca de mi casa. ¿Dónde está el doctor que me receta **esta** medicina? Él está con **esos** doctores *ahí* en **ese** hospital.

2. **Estas** pastillas son difíciles de tragar. Necesito hablar con **ese** doctor ahora.

3. El bebé en **aquella** sala de espera *allí* está llorando. ¿Dónde está su madre? Su madre está en **esa** tienda de regalos cerca de la sala de espera. ¿Dónde está el padre de **aquel** bebé? Está con **aquellos** tres niños en **aquel** restaurante. ¿Dónde está **aquel** restaurante? Está *allí*.

4. *Aquí* está la radiografía de **ese** paciente.

5. *Ahí* está el enfermero que me va a dar **esas** gotas.

Practice 2 / Práctica 2

1. ¿Tiene algún dolor?

   No, no tengo ningún dolor. / No, no tengo ninguno.

2. ¿Tuvo algunos problemas con la medicina?

   Sí, tuve algunos problemas con la medicina.

3. ¿Alguien en su familia tuvo cáncer de seno?

   No, nadie en mi familia tuvo cáncer de seno.

4. ¿Jamás tuvo herpes zóster?

   Sí, tuve herpes zóster el año pasado.

5. ¿Le gusta el bistec o el pollo?

   No me gusta ni el bistec ni el pollo.

6. ¿Siempre bebe café cargado?

   Bebo café cargado a veces.

7. ¿Jamás hace ejercicio?

   No, nunca hago ejercicio.

8. ¿Quiere preguntar algo?

   No, no quiero preguntar nada.

Practice 3 / Práctica 3

1. Es necesario ayunar por ocho horas.

2. Tiene que tomar la medicina para sentirse mejor.

3. La enfermera tiene que llamar al doctor para obtener las recetas.

4. Ella está aquí por su madre. ("Por" is used as "on behalf of").

5. La operación es para mañana.

6. Los juguetes son para el bebé.

7. Gracias, María, por su ayuda.

8. Melinda trabaja para los cirujanos.

9. Voy a ir al hospital por pruebas.

10. La doctora va a hacerle una intervención para ayudarle.

Activity 2 / Actividad 2

1. para (comparison)
2. para (destination)
3. para (in order to)
4. por (duration)
5. para (in order to)
6. por (through / by)
7. para (in order to)
8. para (recipient)

Practice 4 / Práctica 4

1. Es importante que ayune antes del examen.
2. El doctor no quiere que haga ejercicios por cuatro semanas.
3. Es necesario que tome la medicina ahora.
4. Es importante que baje su colesterol.
5. Es urgente que llamemos a la ambulancia.
6. La doctora no quiere que beba más alcohol.
7. Espero que no necesite una operación.
8. El doctor no quiere que haga mucho por una semana.
9. Esperamos que su familia pueda venir.
10. Quiero que pruebe el "Propolio."

Activity 3 / Actividad 3

1. ¿Sabes cuando regresas a casa? ¡Espero que sea pronto!
2. ¡Esperamos que se sienta mejor pronto!
3. Para ir a casa, ¡tiene que comer la jalea!
4. Todo lo que quiero que es que esté sano / a.
5. Conozco a un pajarito que me acaba de decir que Ud. está enfermo / a.
6. Espero que tenga buena suerte con su nuevo bebé.
7. Es urgente que regrese a casa pronto. ¡Quiero que juegue al golf conmigo otra vez!
8. Espero que el nacimiento de su hijo le traiga muchas bendiciones.

9.   Espero que todavía pueda comer chocolate.

10.   Quiero que sepa que estoy aquí si me necesita.

SUMMARY EXERCISE / EJERCICIO A MODO DE RESUMEN

HCP: Javiera, ¿alguien en su familia tiene una historia de cáncer de seno?
Javiera: Sí, mi abuela y mi tía.
HCP: ¿Del lado de la madre o del lado del padre?
Javiera: Mi abuela paterna y su hermana tuvieron cáncer de seno.
HCP: ¿Están vivas su abuela y tía?
Javiera: Sí, las dos están vivas.
HCP: ¿Alguien en su familia tiene una historia de migrañas (or jaquecas)?
Javiera: No, nadie en mi familia tiene migrañas, pero yo tengo migrañas.
HCP: ¿Tiene una migraña con aura?
Javiera: Sí.
HCP: ¿Cuándo tiene migrañas?
Javiera: Tengo migrañas antes de la regla.
HCP: ¿Alguien en su familia tiene un trastorno hemorrágico?
Javiera: Sí, tengo el factor V Leiden.
HCP: Voy a recetarle la píldora anticonceptiva con progesterona sin estrógeno.

ENGLISH–SPANISH INDEX

SPANISH–ENGLISH INDEX